The Regulation of Emotion

The Regulation of Emotion

Edited by

Pierre Philippot
University of Louvain at Louvain-la-Neuve, Belgium

Robert S. Feldman
University of Massachusetts at Amherst

LEA
LAWRENCE ERLBAUM ASSOCIATES, PUBLISHERS
2004 Mahwah, New Jersey London

Camera ready copy for this volume was prepared by the editors.

Copyright © 2004 by Lawrence Erlbaum Associates, Inc.
All rights reserved. No part of this book may be reproduced in any form, by photostat, microform, retrieval system, or any other means, without the prior written permission of the publisher.

Lawrence Erlbaum Associates, Inc. Publishers
10 Industrial Avenue
Mahwah, New Jersey 07430-2262

Cover design by Kathryn Houghtaling Lacey

Library of Congress Cataloging-in-Publication Data

The regulation of emotion / edited by Pierre Philippot, Robert S. Feldman.

p. cm.

ISBN 0-8058-4201-2 (alk. paper)

1. Emotions. 2. Self-control. 3. Emotions.—Social aspects. I. Philippot, Pierre, 1960– . II. Feldman, Robert S. (Robert Stephen), 1947.

BF531.R45 2003

152.4—dc22 2003064371
cip

Books published by Lawrence Erlbaum Associates are printed on acid-free paper, and their bindings are chosen for strength and durability.

Printed in the United States of America
10 9 8 7 6 5 4 3 2 1

Contents

List of Contributors

Céline Baeyens, *University of Louvain, Louvain-la-Neuve, Belgium*
Roy F. Baumeister, *Case Western University*
Antoine Bechara, *University of Iowa*
Emily A. Butler, *Stanford University*
Susan D. Calkins, *University of North Carolina at Greensville*
Belinda Campos, *University of California, Berkeley*
Céline Douilliez, *University of Louvain, Louvain-la-Neuve, Belgium*
Nancy Eisenberg, *Arizona State University*
Catharine Evers, *University of Amsterdam, The Netherlands*
Robert S. Feldman, *University of Massachusetts*
Agneta Fisher, *University of Amsterdam, The Netherlands*
Benjamin Francast, *University of Louvain, Louvain-la-Neuve, Belgium*
James J. Gross, *Stanford University*
Robin B. Howse, *University of North Carolina at Greensville*
Daniel Hrubes, *College of Mount Saint Vincent*
Mayumi Karasawa, *Tokyo Women's University, Japan*
Dacher Keltner, *University of California, Berkeley*
Shinobu Kitayama, *Kyoto University, Japan*
Ann M. Kring, *University of California, Berkeley*
Antony S. R. Manstead, *University of Cambridge, England*
Batja Mesquita, *Wake Forest University*
Frédéric Nils, *University of Louvain, Louvain-la-Neuve, Belgium*
Cornelia Anna Pauls, *University of Marburg, Germany*
Pierre Philippot, *University of Louvain, Louvain-la-Neuve, Belgium*
Bernard Rimé, *University of Louvain, Louvain-la-Neuve, Belgium*
Michelle N. Shiota, *University of California, Berkeley*
Cynthia L. Smith, *Arizona State University*
Tracy L. Spinrad, *Arizona State University*
Gerhard Stemmler, *University of Marburg, Germany*
Dianne M. Tice, *Case Western University*
Monique Timmers, *University of Amsterdam, The Netherlands*
James Tyler, *University of Massachusetts*
Guido Valk, *University of Amsterdam, The Netherlands*
Kelly H. Werner, *University of California, Berkeley*
Emmanuelle Zech, *University of Louvain, Louvain-la-Neuve, Belgium*
Liqing Zhang, Case Western University

Preface

The ability to regulate emotion may be one of the most pervasive challenges by which human beings are confronted. From birth to death, from the most mundane daily activities to the most existential questions, we are inhabited by desires, wishes, aspirations—the very material of emotion—that we need to regulate. Emotions and their regulation are thus central to human life.

In the field of psychology, the concept of emotion regulation can be found in many different domains. Emotion regulation has been related to the field of well-being (Diener, 1984) and to the capacity to experience positive, or negative, affects (Lykken & Tellegen, 1996). Similarly, the concept of emotion regulation constitutes the basis on which the ubiquitous concept of coping has been developed (Lazarus, 1991). Emotion regulation is also a key component of emotional intelligence (Mayer, Caruso, & Salovey, 1999).

The concept of emotion regulation also holds an important position in developmental psychology. Not only does the socialization of emotions, and hence their regulation, constitute a sizable part of education, but emotion regulation also plays an important role in the development and maintenance of motivation. Indeed, emotions are largely determined by the goals pursued by the individual (Carver & Scheier, 1990). Successful attainment of these goals relies on the ability to regulate emotion and consequent action plans and tendencies toward the goal. Ultimately, the goals selected by individuals, and the strategies selected to attain these goals, are central to their identities (Conway & Pleydell-Pearce, 2000).

Emotion regulation has also been proposed as a central concept within the field of clinical psychology. Since the publication of Barlow's (1988) landmark volume, which put forward the notion that anxiety was essentially a problem of emotion—especially fear—regulation, the concept of emotion regulation has been applied to many areas of psychopathology. In the field of psychotherapy, new interventions, targeting emotion acknowledgement and regulation, have been designed (Greenberg & Paivio, 1997).

In sum, the study of emotion regulation is scattered across many different domains of psychology, mirroring the ubiquity of the phenomenon in human life. Furthermore, it is clear that emotional regulation, both in terms of the management and control of emotional experience and the expression of emotion, is an important aspect of everyday functioning, and that failures to adequately regulate emotions have negative consequences both at the intraindividual and interindividual levels.

The main goal of this volume is to present, in an integrated framework, the newest, most contemporary perspectives on emotion regulation. The book includes empirically-grounded work and theories that are central to our understanding of the processes that constitute emotion regulation and their consequences.

The volume has several secondary aims, as well. One is to highlight several newer subareas in the domain of emotion regulation that we believe hold much promise, such as the relation between psychopathology and emotion regulation. The book also presents data and theory that have applied value that may be useful for people working in such fields as communication, psychotherapy, and counseling. Finally, the volume gathers contributions across a variety of subfields and includes authors working not just in North America but in other areas of the world.

To help achieve these goals, the volume has been organized to begin with the presentation of the most molecular aspects of emotion regulation and to end with the most molar ones. It comprises four sections, each integrating different lines of research from related domains. The first section is devoted to basic processes in emotion regulation, such as neurological, physiological, or cognitive processes; the second section examines the interplays between emotion regulation and individual regulation; the third section presents work on individual differences and developmental processes in emotion regulation; and the final section examines the social functions and constraints of emotion regulation.

Specifically, the first section of the volume introduces the basic processes at work in emotion regulation. At the neurological level, Antoine Bechara discusses the brain structures that are operating in the generation of emotion and in its regulation. He presents a model based on the somatic marker hypothesis and its related evidences. This model provides a systems-level neuroanatomical and cognitive framework for decision making and its influence by emotion. Bechara defends the notion that decision-making defects are the result of defective engagement of emotion related signals ("somatic markers").

Next, at the physiological level, Gerhard Stemmler examines the century-old—and still unresolved—question of the specificity of peripheral body responses in emotion and of their regulation. He proposes a functional view, suggesting that emotions have distinct goals and need differentiated somatovisceral activations for the sake of behavior preparation to attain these goals. This hypothesis is corroborated by a meta-analysis demonstrating a considerable degree of somatovisceral differentiation between fear and anger. Stemmler then examines the different determinants of this somatovisceral activation and their regulation.

Finally, Pierre Philippot and colleagues consider the cognitive processes at work in emotion regulation. They present a multilevel cognitive model, partly inspired by the models of Leventhal (1984) and Teasdale and Barnard (1993). The implications of this model for emotion regulation are developed and a research program designed to test these implications is presented. They propose the counterintuitive hypothesis that focusing and specifying emotional information results in decreasing emotional arousal at the subjective and physiological levels.

Moving from basic processes to individual organization, the second section of the book examines the interplay between self-presentation and emotion regulation. This notion is considered from three different perspectives. Dianne Tice, Roy Baumeister, and Liqing Zang analyse how positive and negative emotions play a role in the regulation of self-esteem. They propose that people frequently sabotage their long-term self-regulatory goals to make themselves feel better in the short term. Their model proposes that when people's capacity to engage in self-regulation is depleted, positive emotional experiences help to recharge the system. In their perspective, positive emotional states can strengthen the self's capacity for regulating itself in a variety of ways. Daniel Hrubes, Robert Feldman, and James Tyler discuss the role of lying in emotion regulation in everyday life. They argue that deception is routinely used to regulate emotions, and that what they call emotion-focused deception permits people to control their own emotions and the emotions of others. Finally, Shinobu Kitayama and his collaborators examine intercultural differences, mostly between Asian and Western culture, in self-presentation and emotion regulation. They show that whereas socially disengaging emotions such as pride and anger are strongly afforded and reinforced in North America, socially-engaging emotions such as friendly feelings and shame are strongly promoted and reinforced in Japan. These evidences are interpreted in a framework distinguishing personal and collective regulatory strategies.

The third section of the book is devoted to individual and developmental differences in the regulation of emotion. The first two chapters of this section focus on developmental aspects, offering two complementary accounts. Susan Calkins and Robin Howse present the relation between emotional reactivity and emotion regulation in children. They propose that emotion regulation is one dimension of a multileveled self-regulatory system that governs children's behavior. These levels include physiological, attentional, emotional, cognitive, and interpersonal domains of functioning. Within this framework, they present data from longitudinal studies on childhood internalizing and externalizing disorders. Nancy

Eisenberg and collaborators focus on socialization and how emotion regulation is important in this respect.

The two other chapters of this section take a very different perspective. Anna Pauls examines how different individual styles in emotion regulation bare consequences at the physiological level and how they have health consequences. In a framework integrating situational constraints, emotion, and personality, she examines whether some emotion regulation strategies are really better than others with respect to their physiological effects, given the diversity of situations people are confronted with and the kind of emotion to be regulated. Finally, Ann Kring and Kelly Werner examine individual differences in emotion regulation from the extreme end of the continuum: psychopathology. Based on James Gross's (1998) model, they explore how different deficits in specific aspects of emotion regulation can lead to psychological dysfunction and psychopathology.

In the fourth and last section of the book, social factors are related to emotion regulation. This section is opened by Agneta Fischer and Antony Manstead, who review the social motives and norms, both in personal relations and in work relations, underlying emotion regulation. They conclude that general emotion norms concerning what to feel and how to express these feelings are waning. Instead, more personal norms, and especially motives that are related to the expected effects of one's emotional expressions, have gained in importance. Emily Butler and James Gross examine the consequences of suppressing the expression of emotion because of social constraints. They consider consequences at the cognitive, interpersonal, and health levels. They report evidence that individuals who suppress emotion expression also report relatively unhappy and socially conflicted lives. However, the impact of suppression is not always negative, especially when one includes not only the regulators but their social partners as well. They conclude that the regulatory demands of integrating the emotional needs of the individual with those of the community are not going to be met by any single emotion regulation strategy.

In the next chapter, Emmanuelle Zech, Bernard Rimé, and Frédéric Nils develop the concept of social sharing. After an emotional experience, most people tell about it to some others. The authors first examine the possibility that such social sharing plays a role in the regulation of emotion at an individual level, helping the person who has experienced the emotion to "recover" from it. Counterintuitively, their research shows that this is not the case. Rather, social sharing seems to serve social functions such as integration and social binding. Finally, on a positive touch, Michelle Shiota, Belinda Campos, and Dacher Keltner present a framework for understanding the social functions of positive emotion, associating specific positive emotions with particular types of relationships and particular regulatory tasks.

As these chapters so richly indicate, emotion regulation is a multidimensional concept that cuts across a variety of fields and perspectives. We hope that this collection of chapters, taken collectively, will advance our understanding of the phenomenon of emotion regulation and leading to new research and theories that may in turn lead to progress in the broader field of emotions, and—even more broadly—to individual and social behavior.

ACKNOWLEDGMENTS

This volume results from a long-standing collaboration between the two coeditors, a collaboration that has benefited from an ongoing exchange program between the University of Massachusetts and the University of Louvain at Louvain-la-Neuve. Initially funded by the U.S. Information Agency, the exchange program has been subsequently supported for over a decade by the Catholic University of Louvain and the University of Massachusetts. We are particularly grateful to Dean Guillaume Wunsch of the Catholic University of Louvain and Deans Glenn Gordon and Janet Rifkin of the University of Massachusetts for their support of this project. In addition, the FNRS (National Sciences Foundation) of Belgium provided indirect support for the book.

—*Pierre Philippot*
—*Robert S. Feldman*

REFERENCES

Barlow, D. H. (1988). *Anxiety and its disorders: The nature and treatment of anxiety and panic*. New York: Guilford.

Carver C. S., & Scheier M. F. (1990). Origins and functions of positive and negative affect: A control–process view. *Psychological Review.*

Conway M. A., & Pleydell–Pearce C. W. (2000). The construction of autobiographical memories in the self-memory system. *Psychological Review, 107,* 261–288.

Diener, E. (1984). Subjective well-being. *Psychological Bulletin, 95,* 542–575.

Frijda, N. H. (1986). *The emotions*. Cambridge, England: Cambridge University Press.

Greenberg, L. S., & Paivio, S. C. (1997). *Working with emotions in psychotherapy*. New York: Guilford.

Gross J.J. (1998). Antecedent- and response-focused emotion regulation: Divergent consequences for experience, expression, and physiology. *Journal of Personality and Social Psychology, 74,* 224–237.

Lazarus, R. S. (1991). Progress on a cognitive–motivational–relational theory of emotion. *American Psychologist, 46,* 819–834.

Leventhal, H. (1984). A perceptual-motor theory of emotion. In L. Berkowitz (Ed.), *Advances in experimental social psychology* (Vol. 17, pp. 117–182). New York: Academic.

Lykken, D., & Tellegen, A. (1996). Happiness is a stochastic phenomenon. *Psychological-Science, 7*, 186–189.

Mayer, J. D., Caruso, D. R., & Salovey, P. (1999). Emotional intelligence meets traditional standards for an intelligence. *Intelligence, 27*, 267–298.

Scherer, K. R. (Ed.). (1989). *Facets of emotion*. Hillsdale, NJ: Lawrence Erlbaum Associates, Inc.

Teasdale, J. D., & Barnard, P. J. (1993). *Affect, cognition and change: Re-modelling depressive thought*. Hove, England: Lawrence Erlbaum Associates, Inc.

I

Basic Psychological and Cognitive Processes in the Regulation of Emotion

1

A Neural View of the Regulation of Complex Cognitive Functions by Emotion

Antoine Bechara
Department of Neurology
University of Iowa

The somatic marker hypothesis provides a systems-level neuroanatomical and cognitive framework for decision making and its influence by emotion. The hypothesis posits that decision-making defects in the personal and social realms are the result of defective engagement of emotion related signals ("somatic markers") that normally operate, covertly or overtly, to facilitate the process of making advantageous choices. We review studies that have investigated the anatomical, physiological, and cognitive characteristics of a neural system presumed to underlie somatic marker activation and decision making. The VM prefrontal cortex represents one critical structure in this neural system. However, other regions including the amygdala and the somatosensory cortices (SII, SI, and insula) also compromise somatic state activation and decision making, suggesting that these several regions are part of a neural system involved in the emotional regulation of decision making. Although the reviewed studies support the view that emotions (somatic states) are beneficial to the process of decision making, there is a popular notion that emotions actually interfere with decision making and hinder good judgment. We present a hypothesis that helps reconcile these seemingly opposing views by describing the conditions under which decisions are helped or disrupted by emotion. Abnormal decision making and emotion regulation as encountered in neurological and psychiatric patient populations are extraordinarily costly in terms of individual human suffering and in financial terms. Elucidation of the neural mechanisms of how emotion regulate cognitive functions such as decision making is thus likely to have important practical consequences, in addition to its obvious value in advancing fundamental knowledge in neuroscience.

One of the first and most famous cases of the so-called "frontal lobe syndrome" was the patient Phineas Gage, described by Harlow (Harlow, 1848, 1868). Phineas Gage was a railroad construction worker, and survived an explosion that blasted an iron tamping bar through the front of his head. Before the accident, Gage was a man of normal intelligence, energetic and persistent in executing his plans of operation. He was responsible, sociable, and popular among peers and friends. After the accident, his medical recovery was remarkable. He survived the accident with normal intelligence, memory, speech, sensation, and movement. However, his behavior changed completely. He became irresponsible, untrustworthy, and impatient of restraint or advice when it conflicted with his desires.

Using modern neuroimaging techniques, Damasio and colleagues have reconstituted the accident by relying on measurements taken from Gage's skull (A. R. Damasio, 1994). The key finding of this neuroimaging study was that the most likely placement of Gage's lesion included the VM region of the prefrontal cortex, bilaterally. The ventromedial sector includes both the gyrus rectus and mesial half of the orbital gyri, as well as the inferior half of the medial prefrontal surface, from its most caudal aspect to its most rostral in the frontal pole. Mesial sectors of areas 10 and 11, areas 12, 13, and 25, and subgenual sectors of areas 24 and 32 of Brodmann are included in this sector, as is the white matter subjacent to all of these areas (see Fig. 1.1; see also pp. 24–25 of H. Damasio, 1995).

The case of Phineas Gage paved the way for the notion that the frontal lobes were linked to social conduct, judgement, decision making, and personality. A number of instances similar to the case of Phineas Gage have since appeared in the literature (Ackerly & Benton, 1948; Brickner, 1932; Welt, 1888). Interestingly, all these cases received little attention for many years. The revival of interest in various aspects of the "frontal lobe syndrome" was triggered in part by the patient described by Eslinger and Damasio (Eslinger & A. R. Damasio, 1985), a modern counterpart to Phineas Gage.

Over the years, we have studied numerous patients with this type of lesion. Such patients with damage to the VM prefrontal cortex develop severe impairments in personal and social decision making, in spite of otherwise largely preserved intellectual abilities. These patients had normal intelligence and creativity

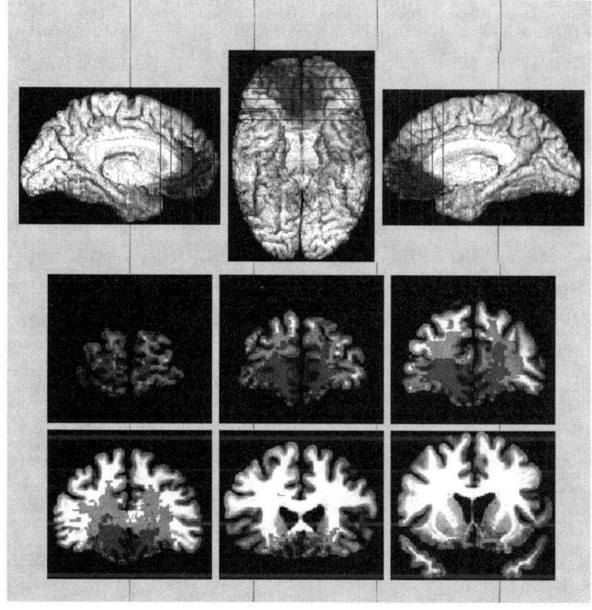

Fig. 1.1. Overlap of lesions in a group of ventro medial patients. The red color indicates an overlap of four or more patients. From Bechara, Damasio, & Damasio, 2000.

before their brain damage. After the damage, they began to have difficulties planning their workday and future, and difficulties in choosing friends, partners, and activities. The actions they elect to pursue often lead to losses of diverse order, for example, financial losses, losses in social standing, and losses of family and friends. The choices they make are no longer advantageous, and are remarkably different from the kinds of choices they were known to make in the premorbid period. These patients often decide against their best interests. They are unable to learn from previous mistakes as reflected by repeated engagement in decisions that lead to negative consequences. In striking contrast to this real-life decision-making impairment, problem-solving abilities in laboratory settings remain largely normal. As noted, the patients have normal intellect, as measured by a variety of conventional neuropsychological tests (Bechara, H. Damasio, Tranel, & Anderson, 1998; A. R. Damasio, Tranel, & H. Damasio, 1990; Eslinger & A. R. Damasio, 1985).

This particular class of patients presents a puzzling defect. It is difficult to explain their disturbance in terms of defects in knowledge pertinent to the situation, general intellectual compromise, defects in language comprehension or expression, or in working memory, or attention (Anderson, Bechara, H. Damasio, Tranel, & A. R. Damasio, 1999; Anderson, H. Damasio, Jones, & Tranel, 1991; Bechara et al., 1998; Saver & A. R. Damasio, 1991). For many years, the condition of these patients has posed a double challenge. First, although the decision-making impairment is obvious in the real life of these patients, there had been no laboratory probe to detect and measure this impairment. Second, there had been no satisfactory account of the neural and cognitive mechanisms underlying the impairment. Although these VM patients were intact on standard neuropsychological tests, the patients did have a compromised ability to express emotion and to experience feelings in appropriate situations. In other words, despite normal intellect, there were abnormalities in emotion and feeling, along with the abnormalities in decision making. Based on these observations, the Somatic Marker Hypothesis (A. R. Damasio, 1994; A. R. Damasio, Tranel, & H. Damasio, 1991) was proposed.

THE SOMATIC MARKER HYPOTHESIS

The hypothesis specifies a number of structures and operations required for the normal operation of decision making. The emotional changes are designated under the umbrella term "somatic state." This is because (a) emotion induces changes in the physiological state of the body, and (b) the results of emotion are represented primarily in the brain, in the form of transient changes in the pattern of activity in the somatosensory structures. The term *somatic*, therefore, refers to internal milieu, visceral, and musculoskeletal components of the soma. In brief, the hypothesis posits that the VM cortices contain convergence zones, which hold a record of temporal conjunctions of activity in varied neural units (i.e., sensory cortices and limbic structures) hailing from both external and internal stimuli. Thus, when parts of certain exteroceptive–interoceptive conjunctions are reprocessed consciously or unconsciously, their activation is signaled to VM cortices, which in turn activate somatic effectors in amygdala, hypothalamus, and brainstem nuclei. This latter activity is an attempt to reconstitute the kind of somatic state that belonged to the conjunction. Two chains of physiologic events are possible at this point (see Fig. 1.2):

1. In one chain, an appropriate emotional (somatic) state is actually reenacted in the body proper, and signals from its activation are then relayed back to subcortical and cortical processing structures, especially in the somatosensory (SII and SI) and insular cortices. This anatomical system is described as the "body loop" because it engages the body. The enacted somatic state can then act consciously or nonconsciously on the neural processes that enable the person to do, or to avoid doing, a certain action.

2. After emotions have been expressed and experienced at least once, one can form representations of these emotional experiences in the somatosensory and insular cortices. Therefore, after emotions are learnt, one possible chain

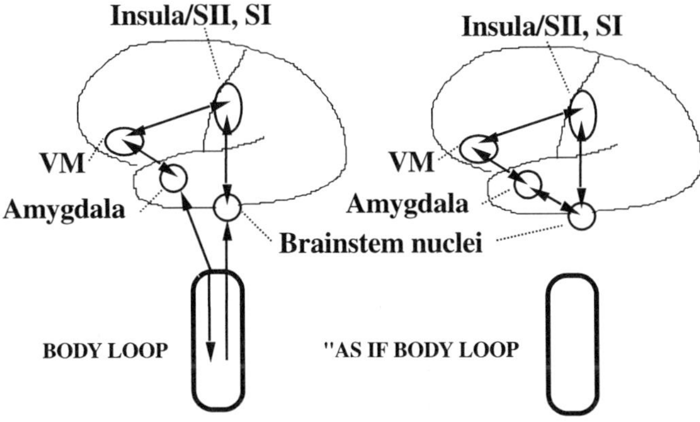

Fig. 1.2. Simple diagrams illustrating the "body loop" and "as if loop" chain of physiologic events. In both "body loop" and "as if loop" panels, the brain is represented by the top black perimeter and the body by the bottom one.

of physiologic events is to bypass the body altogether, activate the insular and somatosensory cortices directly, and create a fainter image of an emotional body state than if the emotion were actually expressed in the body. This anatomical system is described as the "as if body loop" because the somatic state is not reenacted in the body. In other words, although somatic signals are based on structures representing the body and its states, from the brain stem and hypothalamus to the cerebral cortex, the "somatic" signals do not need to originate in the body in every instance. Somatic states can in fact be generated intracerebrally, that is, "as if body loop." Thus, the neural system mediating the activation of somatic states involves several neural regions. The VM cortex is one critical region. However, there are other critical components in this neural network. The amygdala, hypothalamus, brainstem nuclei, peripheral nervous system, somatosensory cortices (SII, SI, insula), anterior cingulate, and basal ganglia are all components of this neural network (A. R. Damasio, 1994; A. R. Damasio, 1995; A. R. Damasio, 1996). The somatic marker hypothesis is based on the following main assumptions:

1. Human reasoning and decision making depend on many levels of neural operation, some of which are conscious and overtly cognitive, and some of which are not. Conscious, overtly cognitive operations depend on sensory

"images" constructed from activity in early sensory cortices. The term "image" here is not restricted to the visual modality, but it includes any form of representations that can be held in working memory.

2. Cognitive operations, regardless of the content, depend on support processes such as attention, working memory, and emotion.

3. Reasoning and decision making depend on the availability of knowledge about situations, actors, options for action, and outcomes. Such knowledge is stored in "dispositional" form throughout higher order cortices and some subcortical nuclei (the term dispositional is synonymous with implicit and nontopographically organized. Dispositional knowledge can be made explicit in the form of (a) motor responses of varied types and complexity (some combinations of which are part of emotions), and of (b) images. The results of motor responses, including those that are not generated consciously, can be represented in images.

4. Knowledge can be classified as follows: (a) innate and acquired knowledge concerning bioregulatory processes and body states and actions, including those which are made explicit as emotions; (b) knowledge about entities, facts (e.g., relations, rules), actions and action-complexes (stories), which are usually made explicit as images; (c) knowledge about the linkages between (a) and (b) items, as reflected in individual experience; (d) and knowledge resulting from the categorizations of items in (a), (b), and (c).

An emotion is defined as a collection of changes in body and brain states triggered by a dedicated brain system that responds to the content of one's perceptions, actual or recalled, relative to a particular entity or event. The responses toward the body proper are enacted in a body (somatic) state. This involves physiological modifications, from changes in internal milieu (e.g., heart rate, smooth muscle contraction, skin conductance, endocrine release) to changes perceptible to an external observer (e.g., skin color, body posture, facial expression, specific behaviors such as freezing, flight and fight, courting, parenting, and so on). The responses aimed at the brain lead to (a) the release of certain neurotransmitters in the telencephalon (e.g., dopamine, serotonin, noreadrenaline), (b) a filtering of signals from the body to somato-sensory regions at the level of the spinal cord and brainstem, and (c) "as-if-body loop" responses. The ensemble of all these enacted responses in the body proper and in the brain constitutes emotion. The signals generated by these changes toward the brain itself produce changes that are mostly perceptible to the individual in whom they were enacted and provide the essential ingredients for what is ultimately perceived as a feeling (A. R. Damasio, 1999). Thus, we will use the term *somatic* to refer to the collection of enacted responses in the body proper and in the brain.

Testing the Somatic Marker Hypothesis

The initial observations leading to the Somatic Marker Hypothesis were that despite normal intellect, VM patients showed abnormalities in emotion and feeling, along with the abnormalities in decision making.

Abnormalities in Emotion and Feeling after VM Damage. Several studies have shown that VM patients do show abnormalities in processing emotion:

A. VM patients generate weak somatic responses to emotionally charged stimuli. In an early study by Damasio and colleagues (A. R. Damasio et al., 1990), VM patients were shown two types of visual stimuli: (a) target stimuli, including pictures of emotionally charged stimuli such as mutilations and nudes; and (b) nontarget stimuli, including pictures of emotionally neutral stimuli such as farm scenes and abstract patterns. During the viewing of these pictures, the skin conductance response (SCR), a highly sensitive index of autonomic responding, was recorded (see Fig. 1.3).
When viewing the target and nontarget stimuli, normal control participants displayed large-amplitude SCRs to the target pictures, and little or no response to the nontargets. By contrast, the VM patients generated almost no response to the target pictures, and completely failed to show the standard target and nontarget SCR difference, despite the fact that their ability to gen-

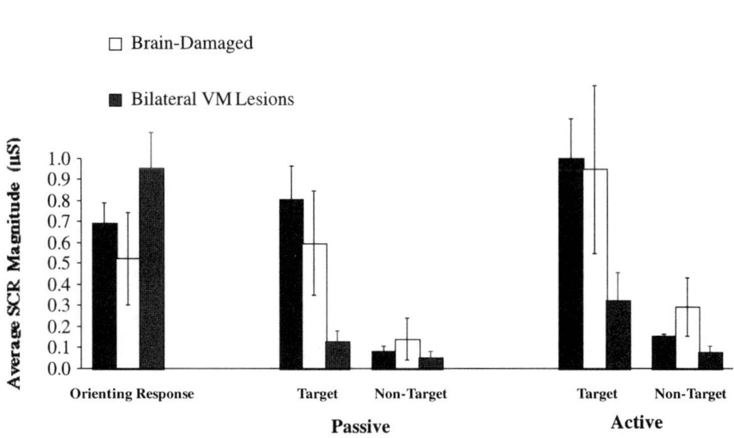

Fig. 1.3. Skin conductanced response (SCR) magnitudes to irienting stimuli, neurtral pictures, and emotionally charged pictures in normal controls, brain-damaged controls, and ventromedial (VM) prefrontal patients. In the VM group, the SCR magnitude for the emotionally charged pictures is abnormal. Note that when similar pictures were viewed actively (i.e., patients had to describe the content), the SCR magnitude from VM patients was increased (Damasio, Tranel, & Damasio, 1990).

erate SCRs to basic physical stimuli was intact. In subsequent studies, this finding was extended to other neural regions involved in somatic state activation, namely the amygdala and right insular and somatosensory (SII, SI) cortices (Tranel & H. Damasio, 1994). Patients with right hemisphere lesions were defective as VM patients, but amygdala patients were not. Amygdala damage attenuated, but it did not completely block the generation of SCRs to emotionally charged pictures (Tranel & H. Damasio, 1994).

B. VM patients generate weak somatic responses from internally generated images of emotional situations. We expanded our investigations using different paradigms for evoking emotional states, namely from the internal generation of images related to emotional situations, that is, "emotional imagery." We predicted that VM participants would have a reduced ability to experience emotions when they recall specific emotional situations from their personal life. We used a procedure where the participant is asked to think about a situation in his or her life in which he or she felt each of the following emotions: happiness, sadness, fear, and anger. After a brief description of each memory is obtained, the participant is then put to a physiological test. The participant is asked to image and reexperience each emotional experience, while his or her SCR and heart rate are monitored. As a control condition, the participant is asked to recall and imagine a nonemotional set of events. At the conclusion of the task, emotional as well as neutral, each participant is asked to rate how much emotion he or she felt (on a scale of 0 to 4). Using this emotional imagery procedure, we tested patients with bilateral VM lesions (see Fig. 1.4). It is clear that they were able to retrieve previous happy, sad, anger, and fear experiences, that is, they were able to recall emotion-laden events that occurred before their brain lesion (such as weddings, funerals, car accidents, and family disputes). However, they had difficulties reexperiencing the emotion of these situations as reflected by low physiological activity and low subjective rating of feeling the emotion, especially marked in the case of sadness (Tranel, Bechara, H. Damasio, & A. R. Damasio, 1998). This suggests that damage to the VM cortex weakens the ability to reexperience an emotion from the recall of an appropriate emotional event.

We extended our preliminary exploration to other regions of the somatic marker network, namely the amygdala and the right insular and SII, SI cortices (H. Damasio, Bechara, Tranel, & A. R. Damasio, 1997; Tranel et al., 1998). Findings indicate that right hemisphere individuals are comparable to VM individuals in that they can retrieve the memory of the emotional event, but they have difficulties in reexperiencing the emotion of these situations as reflected by low physiological activity and low subjective rating for the feeling of the emotion. Amygdala individuals, on the other hand, are not as defective in this domain. Their expression and feeling of the emotional state is somewhat attenuated, but not blocked.

C. Patients with bilateral VM damage are not emotionless. In other experiments, we showed that VM patients can increase the magnitude of their somatic states in response to emotional stimuli if they verbalize the content of the stimuli (A. R. Damasio et al., 1990). They can also evoke stronger responses to anger from recall of personal experiences (see Fig. 1.4). These observations are consistent with old observations of Butter and colleagues (Butter, Mishkin, & Mirsky, 1968; Butter, Mishkin, & Rosvold, 1963; Butter & Snyder, 1972) in monkeys with orbital lesions. The orbital lesions produced a clear reduction in the aggressive behavior of these monkeys, but the reduction was situational. In other words, the animals could still demonstrate aggression when brought back to the colony where they had been dominant, suggesting that the capacity to display aggression had not been eliminated in these monkeys, and that the lesions did not produce a consistent state of "bluntness of affect."

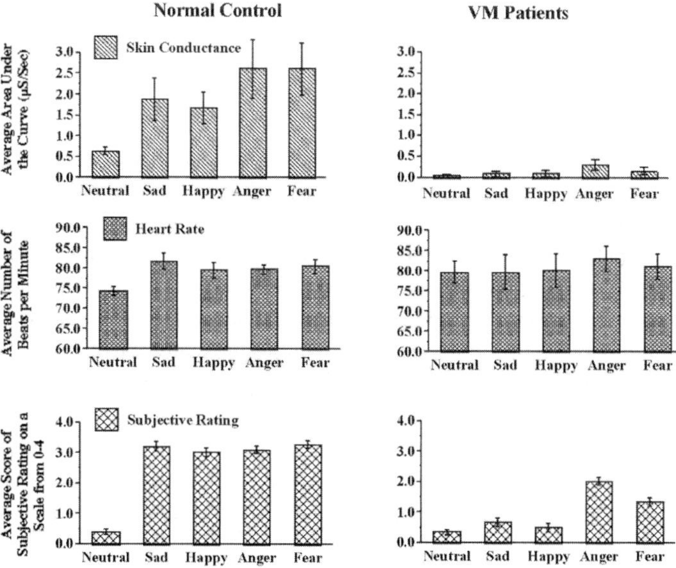

Fig 1.4. Skin conductance response (SCR), heart rate, and subjective rating of the feeling associated with the imagery of a personal emotional event experienced by individual normal control participants versus ventro medial (VM) prefrontal patients. In the VM group, the SCRs generated during the imagery procedure were abnormally low, the changes in heart rate were not significant, and the subjective ratings of feeling the target emotion were low, in spite of having a vivid memory and recall of the imagined personal emotional event.

Furthermore, in fear conditioning paradigms, we showed that VM patients could acquire the SCR conditioning with an aversive loud noise (Bechara, H. Damasio, A. R. Damasio, & Lee, 1999). We note that not all VM patients were able to acquire conditioned SCRs. The reason why some VM patients did not acquire emotional conditioning seems to depend on whether the anterior cingulate (especially area 25) or the basal forebrain was involved in the lesion. This suggestion is preliminary and we are still investigating this issue. The sparing of emotional conditioning by VM lesions is consistent with conditioning studies in animals that show that the VM cortex is not necessary for acquiring fear conditioning (Morgan & LeDoux, 1995). This is in contrast to the amygdala, which appears essential for coupling a stimulus with an emotional state induced by a primary aversive unconditioned stimulus such as an electric shock (Davis, 1992a, 1992b; Kim & Davis, 1993; Kim, Rison, & Fanselow, 1993; LeDoux, 1993a, 1993b, 1996). This also applies to learning the association between stimuli and the value of a particular reward (Malkova, Gaffan, & Murray, 1997). Human studies have also shown that lesions of the amygdala impair emotional conditioning with an aversive loud sound (Vechara et al.,. 1995; LaBar, LeDoux, Spencer, & Phelps, 1995), and functional neuroimaging studies have shown that the amygdala is activated during such conditioning tasks (LaBar, Gatenby, Gore, LeDoux, & Phelps, 1998).

Summary. Damage to the VM cortex weakens the ability of patients to generate somatic responses to emotionally charged stimuli. The damage also weakens the ability of VM patients to reexperience an emotion from the recall of an appropriate emotional event. However, the VM patients are not emotionless and are capable of generating somatic states in certain situations. The conditions under which VM patients can or cannot generate somatic states depend on the nature of the stimulus that induces the emotion. Based on the studies presented earlier as well as more recent studies, we have introduced the term *primary inducers* to include stimuli that unconditionally, or through learning (e.g., conditioning and semantic knowledge), can produce somatic states that are positive or negative . Encountering a fear object (e.g., a snake), or a stimulus predictive of a snake, or semantic information such as the announcement "you have won or lost a large sum of money," are all examples of primary inducers. Somatic responses to primary inducers seem to be blocked mostly by amygdala damage. On the other hand, *secondary inducers* are entities generated by the recall of a personal or hypothetical emotional event, or perceiving a primary inducer that generates "thoughts" and "memories" about the inducer; all of which, when they are brought to memory, induce a somatic state. The memory of encountering a snake or losing a large sum of money, imagining the encounter of a snake or loss of a large sum of money, are all examples of secondary inducers. We find that the VM cortex is a critical substrate in the neural system necessary for the triggering of somatic states from secondary inducers.

We note that primary and secondary inducer processing cannot be easily separated in an intact normal brain. The separation can only be brought to light in brain-damaged patients. For instance, when hearing or looking at a primary inducer, this may immediately bring to mind "thoughts," "imagination," "knowledge," or "empathy" pertaining to the primary inducer, all of which can now serve as secondary inducers. For example, our experiments indicate that the emotionally charged pictures in the earlier experiment possess very little primary inducer properties. However, looking at these pictures evokes "thoughts," "imagination," "knowledge," or "empathy" related to the emotional situation depicted in the picture, a form of secondary inducers. Accordingly, we found that amygdala damage interferes only a little bit with the generation of somatic states from looking at these emotional pictures. In contrast, VM damage significantly interferes with the generation of somatic states from viewing these pictures. In essence, the aforementioned can be illustrated in the following real-life example, which we have not actually tested in VM patients, but it serves to make the point clear: VM patients will, for instance, experience fear if a rattlesnake is unexpectedly thrown into their lap (primary inducer). However, such patients will not experience fear if they were told to watch out when they enter their office because behind the desk a rattlesnake is hiding (i.e., a secondary inducer).

Impaired Decision Making Linked to Abnormal Activation of Somatic States. For many years, the condition of VM patients has posed a challenge. Although the decision-making impairment is obvious in the real-world behavior life of these patients, there has been no effective laboratory probe to detect and measure this impairment. The development of the "gambling task," has enabled us to detect these patients' elusive impairment in the laboratory, measure it, and investigate its possible causes (Bechara, A. R. Damasio, H. Damasio, & Anderson, 1994). Why was the gambling task successful in detecting the decision making impairment in VM patients, and why is it important for the study of the neurology of decision making? Perhaps this is because the gambling task mimics real-life decisions so closely. The task is carried out in real time and it resembles real-world contingencies. It factors reward and punishment (i.e., winning and losing money) in such a way that it creates a conflict between an immediate, luring reward and a delayed, probabilistic punishment. Therefore, the task engages the individual in a quest to make advantageous choices. As in real-life choices, the task offers choices that may be risky, and there is no obvious explanation of how, when, or what to choose. Each choice is full of uncertainty because a precise calculation or prediction of the outcome of a given choice is not possible. The way that one can do well on this task is to follow one's "hunches" and "gut feelings."

A. The gambling task. This task has been described in detail elsewhere (Bechara et al., 1994; B echara, Tranel, & H. Damasio, 2000). Briefly, the task consists of four decks of cards named A, B, C, and D. The goal in the task is to maximize profit on a loan of play money. Participants are required to make a series of 100 card selections. However, they are not told ahead of time how many card selections they are going to make. Participants can select one card at a time from any deck they choose, and they are free to switch from any deck to another at any time, and as often as they wish. However, the participant's decision to select from one deck versus another is largely influenced by various schedules of immediate reward and future punishment. These schedules are preprogrammed and known to the examiner, but not to the participant. The reward and punishment schedules are set in such a way so that every time the participant selects a card from deck A or deck B, he or she receives $100. Every time the participant selects deck C or deck D, he or she receives $50. However, in each of the four decks, participants encounter unpredictable punishments (money loss). The punishment is set to be higher in the high paying decks A and B, and lower in the low paying decks C and D. If 10 cards were picked from deck A or deck B over the course of trials, one earns $1,000. However, in those 10 card picks, one to five unpredictable punishments are encountered, bringing a total cost of $1,250. On the other hand, every 10 cards from deck C or D earn only $500, but only cost $250 in punishment. In essence, decks A and B are disadvantageous because they cost more in the long run; that is, one loses $250 every 10 cards. Decks C and D are advantageous because they result in an overall gain in the end; that is, one wins $250 every 10 cards. We note that since this original task, we have devised a new computerized version of the task with slightly different schedules of reward and punishment. However, the basic principles of the task remain the same.

We investigated the performance of a large sample of normal controls with different demographic characteristics, and a large sample of VM patients on the gambling task. Normal participants avoided the bad decks (A and B) and preferred the good decks (C and D). By contrast, VM patients did not avoid (i.e., they preferred) the bad decks (A and B). From these results we suggested that the VM patients' performance profile is comparable to their real-life inability to decide advantageously (Bechara et al., 1994; Bechara, Tranel, et al., 2000).

The more pertinent evidence in support of the somatic marker hypothesis and the reactivation of somatic signals related to prior experience is the failure to generate somatic signals when pondering decisions. This evidence comes from a study where we added a physiological measure to the gambling task. The goal was to assess somatic state activation while participants were making decisions during the gambling task. We studied normal participants and VM patients. We had them perform the gambling task while we recorded their SCRs (Bechara, Tranel, H. Damasio, & A. R. Damasio, 1996).

Both normal individuals and VM patients generated SCRs after they had picked the card and were told that they won or lost money. The most important difference, however, was that normal individuals, as they became experienced with the task, began to generate SCRs prior to the selection of any cards, that is, during the time when they were pondering from which deck to choose. These anticipatory SCRs were more pronounced before picking a card from the risky decks A and B, when compared to the safe decks C and D. The VM patients entirely failed to generate SCRs before picking a card, and they also failed to avoid the bad decks and choose advantageously (see Fig. 1.5). These results provide strong support for the somatic marker hypothesis notion regarding the reactivation of signals related to previous individual contingencies. They suggest that decision making is guided by emotional signaling (or somatic states) that are generated in anticipation of future events.

B. Biases need not be conscious. In follow-up investigations, we showed that somatic signals generated in anticipation of future outcomes do not need to

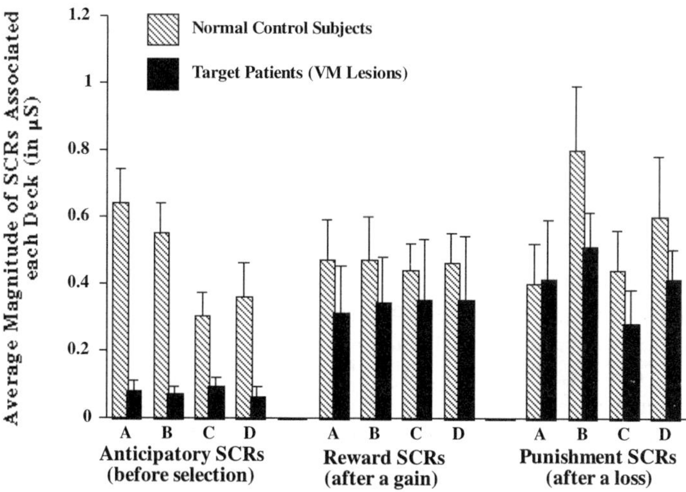

Fig. 1.5. Means ± s.e.m. Of the magnitudes of anticipatory, reward, and punishment skin conductance responses generated by normal controls and target patients (verntral medial lesions) averaged across all cards sedlected from a given deck.

be perceived consciously. We carried out an experiment similar to the one mentioned earlier, where we tested normal individuals and VM patients on the gambling task, while recording their SCRs. However, once the individual had picked 10 cards from the decks, we stopped the game briefly, and asked him or her to declare whatever he or she knew about what was going on in the game (Bechara, H. Damasio, Tranel, & A. R. Damasio, 1997). From the answers to the questions, we were able to distinguish four periods of performance as participants went from the first to the last trial in the task. The first was a "prepunishment" period, when participants sampled the decks, before they had yet encountered any punishment. The second was a "prehunch" period, when participants began to encounter punishment, but still had no clue about what was going on in the game. The third was a "hunch" period, when participants began to express a hunch about which decks were riskier, but they were not certain. The fourth was a "conceptual" period, when participants knew very well that there were good and bad decks, and which decks were good and bad.

When we examined the anticipatory SCRs from each period, we found that, in the normal individuals, there was no significant activity during the prepunishment period. There was a substantial rise in anticipatory responses during the prehunch period, that is, before any conscious knowledge developed. This SCR activity was sustained for the remaining periods. When we examined the behavior during each period, we found that there was a preference for the high paying decks (A and B) during the prepunishment period. Furthermore, there was a hint of a shift in the pattern of card selection, away from the bad decks, even in the prehunch period. This shift in preference for the good decks became more pronounced during the hunch and conceptual periods. The VM patients, on the other hand, never reported a hunch about which of the decks were good or bad. Furthermore, they never developed anticipatory SCRs, and they continued to choose more cards from decks A and B relative to C and D. Also, although 30% of controls did not reach the conceptual period, they still performed advantageously. Although 50% of VM patients did reach the conceptual period, they still performed disadvantageously (Bechara et al, 1997).

These results show that VM patients continue to choose disadvantageously in the gambling task, even after realizing the consequences of their action. This suggests that these anticipatory SCRs are an index of activated unconscious biases derived from prior experiences with reward and punishment. These biases help deter the normal individual from pursuing a course of action that is disadvantageous in the future. This occurs even before the individual becomes aware of the goodness or badness of the choice he or she is about to make. Without these biases, the knowledge of what is right and what is wrong may still become available. However, by itself, this knowledge may not be sufficient to ensure advantageous behavior. Therefore, although the VM patient may become fully aware of what is right and what is wrong, he or she fails to act accordingly. Thus the individual may "say" the right thing, but he or she "does" the wrong thing.

C. Characterization of the decision making deficit associated with VM damage. In other experiments, we have characterized the decision-making deficit in VM patients even further: First, we showed that decision making and working memory are distinct operations of the prefrontal cortex and are mediated by distinct anatomical substrates (Bechara etg al., 1998). We used delay task procedures (delayed response and delayed nonmatching to sample) to measure working memory, and the gambling task to measure decision making. The study revealed that working memory was not dependent on the intactness of decision making, that is, participants can have normal working memory in the presence or absence of deficits in decision making. Some VM patients who were severely impaired in decision making (i.e., abnormal in the gambling task) had superior working memory (i.e., normal in the delay tasks). On the other hand, decision making seems to be influenced by the intactness or impairment of working memory, that is, decision making is worse in the presence of abnormal working memory. Participants with right dorsolateral (DL) frontal lesions and severe working memory impairments showed low normal results in the gambling task (Bechara et al., 1998).
In another study, we showed that the mechanism by which emotion improves memory, as revealed by Cahill and others , is different from the mechanism through which emotion biases decisions. We found that at least as far as the amygdala is concerned, the mechanisms through which emotion modulates memory and decision making seem inseparable. However, at the level of the VM cortex, the two mechanisms are separable in that VM patients showed better memory for pictures with emotional content that was similar to that of normal controls (Bechara, H. Damasio, & A. R. Damasio, 2000).
We also considered three possibilities that may account for the behavior of VM patients. The first was hypersensitivity to reward, where the prospect of a large immediate gain outweighs any prospect of future loss. The second was insensitivity to punishment, where the prospect of a large loss cannot override any prospect of gain. The third was insensitivity to future consequences, positive or negative, so that the participant is oblivious to the future and is guided by immediate prospects (Bechara, Tranel et al., 2000). Using variant versions of the gambling task, in combination with physiological measures, the results were inconsistent with the hypersensitivity to reward and insensitivity to punishment explanations. A parsimonious explanation was that in most VM patients, the decision making impairment is due to insensitivity to future consequences, whatever they may be. The patient appears oblivious to the future and guided predominantly by immediate prospects.

In a separate experiment, we asked whether increasing the delayed punishment in the disadvantageous decks of the original task, or decreasing the delayed reward in the disadvantageous decks of a variant gambling task, would shift the behavior of VM participants away from the disadvantageous decks. We also asked whether, in the event there was a behavioral shift, the behavioral improvement is associated with an increase in anticipatory SCRs. We devised a computer version of the original gambling task where the frequency or magnitude of delayed punishment increased progressively in the disadvantageous decks. In another computer version of a variant version of the gambling task, we decreased the frequency or magnitude of delayed reward in the disadvantageous decks. In the variant version of the gambling task, we reversed the order of reward and punishment, so that the advantageous decks yielded high immediate punishment but even higher future reward. The disadvantageous decks yielded low immediate punishment but even lower future reward. In this variant task, we progressively decreased the magnitude or frequency of reward in the disadvantageous decks. We tested controls and VM patients with the two versions of the gambling task. Both manipulations failed to shift the behavior of VM patients away from the disadvantageous decks (see Fig. 1-6).

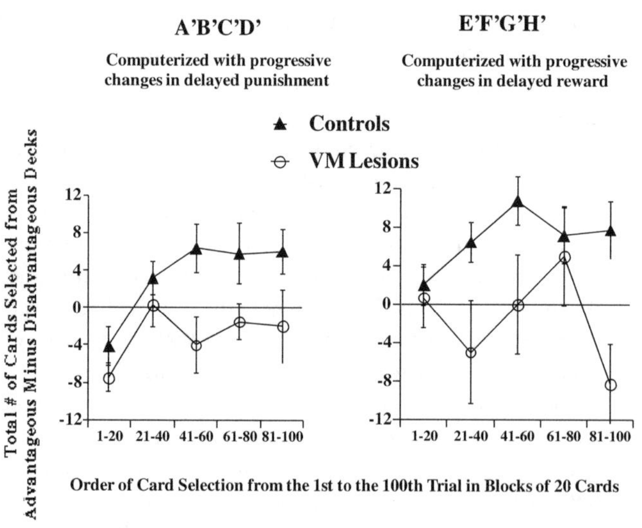

Fig. 1.6. Net scores, (C' + D')–(A' + B') or (E' + G')–(F' + H'), of cards selected by each group across different blocks expressed as mean ± s.c.m. Positive net scores reflect advantageous performance whereas negative net scores reflect disadvantageous performance. From Bechara, Tranel, & Damasio, 2000.

The reward and punishment SCRs of controls and VM patients in these computer gambling tasks were not significantly different, suggesting that VM patients are insensitive to future consequences, positive or negative, and are primarily guided by immediate prospects. This "myopia for the future" in VM patients persists in the face of severe adverse consequences, that is, rising future punishment, or declining future reward (Bechara, Trenel et al., 2000) .

As a further characterization of the decision making impairment in relation to the VM cortex, we asked whether the decision making deficit associated with VM damage is produced by right or left lesions. Unfortunately, this question is difficult to address with lesion studies, because of the rarity of individuals with unilateral damage on the medial and orbital side of the VM cortex. However, from these rare cases, it appears that the decision making deficit observed in real life and in the laboratory is most pronounced after right, as opposed to left, VM lesions (Manes et al., 2002; Tranel, Bechara, & Denburg, 2002). The findings are consistent with those from a case study of an individual with right orbitofrontal lesion (Angrilli, Palomba, Cantagallo, Maietti, & Stegagno, 1999). They are also consistent with studies showing that performances on decision making tasks, including the gambling task and "betting task" (Rogers, Everitt et al., 1999; Rogers, Owen et al., 1999), were predominantly impaired by right orbitofrontal, as opposed to left orbitofrontal, lesions (Manes et al., 2002; Tranel et al., 2002). These findings are also supported by functional neuroimaging studies showing increased activation of right orbitofrontal cortices in normal individuals performing tasks of decision making (Rahman, Sahakian, Rudolph, Rogers, & Robbins, 2001; Rogers, Owen et al., 1999).

Finally, we tested the effects of early versus adult onset of VM damage on decision making and moral judgment (Anderson et al., 1999). Individuals who acquired VM prefrontal lobe damage during childhood are relatively rare. However, evidence from two young adults who acquired focal damage to the prefrontal cortex in early childhood, prior to 16 months of age, revealed very important facts. The individuals with early-onset VM lesions superficially resemble adult-onset individuals in terms of disrupted social behavior, which contrasts with normal basic cognitive abilities. These individuals show insensitivity to future consequences, and their behavior is guided by immediate consequences, both in the social world and on the gambling task. The ability to generate somatic signals in anticipation of future outcomes (anticipatory SCRs) was also defective. However, a closer analysis revealed several distinctive features. First, the inadequate social behaviors are present throughout development and into adulthood, that is, there was no recovery of function such as happens with language when the left hemisphere is damaged at an early age. Second, these behavioral defects are more severe in early-onset individuals relative to adult-onset. Third, the inadequate emotional responses are also more severe. Finally, the early-onset individuals cannot retrieve socially relevant knowledge at factual level as adult-onset individuals do (Anderson et al., 1999).

D. Roles of other neural structures of the somatic marker network in decision making. We tested the roles of two other structures hypothesized to be components of the somatic marker network in decision making, namely, the amygdala, and somatosensory and insular cortices. Central autonomic structures, such as the amygdala, can activate somatic responses in the viscera, vascular bed, endocrine system, and nonspecific neurotransmitter systems. Furthermore, the amygdala plays an important role in emotion as demonstrated repeatedly in various lesion and functional neuroimaging studies (Davidson & Irwin, 1999). Therefore, we tested the hypothesis that the amygdala plays a role in decision making. Using the gambling task as a tool for measuring decision making, we found that amygdala patients, like VM patients, perform poorly on the gambling task (Bechara et al., 1999). When examining the anticipatory SCRs of amygdala patients, the amygdala patients were similar to the VM patients in that they also failed to generate anticipatory SCRs before the selection of a card. However, we found a difference between VM and amygdala patients. When participants were given feedback such as "you won or lost a certain amount of money," the VM patients were able to generate somatic states in response to this feedback, whereas the amygdala patients failed to do so. We note that in the VM patients, this emotional reaction to feedback was somewhat weaker in comparison to normal controls (Bechara et al., 1999), but not abolished, thus consistent with the finding of compromised somatic reactions to emotional target pictures. VM and amygdala patients were similar in that they failed to generate anticipatory SCRs in anticipation of future outcomes, and they chose disadvantageously in the gambling task.

Finally, we also studied a group of patients with lesions in the right somatosensory and insular cortices. We monitored the SCR activity of these patients during their performance of the gambling task. As in the case of the VM and amygdala patients, the right somatosensory and insular (but not left) patients performed poorly on the gambling task. These studies are still in progress and detailed accounts of the findings have not been published.

Summary. The VM patients' performance profile in the gambling task is comparable to their real-life inability to decide advantageously. Most important, the results provide strong support for the notion that decision making is guided by emotional signaling (or somatic states) generated in anticipation of future events. These results are consistent with the specific defect in emotional processing related to damage in the VM cortex, that is, inability to generate somatic states from secondary inducers. We have shown that these patients do generate somatic responses to reward and punishment when it actually happens (primary inducer). However, when the reward or punishment is in the future, that is, the patient has to "anticipate" or "imagine" the consequence of a given action (secondary inducer), the VM patients fail to respond. This failure to generate somatic responses in anticipation of an outcome deprives the patient of an important signal that guides behavior in the advantageous direction.

Decision making and working memory are distinct operations of the prefrontal cortex and are mediated by distinct anatomical substrates. Working memory is not dependent on the intactness of decision making, that is, participants can have normal working memory in the presence or absence of deficits in decision making. On the other hand, decision making seems to be influenced by the intactness or impairment of working memory, that is, decision making is worse in the presence of abnormal working memory. Although emotion (somatic states) plays a role in both decision making and working memory, the evidence indicates that the mechanism by which emotion improves memory is separable from the mechanism through which emotion biases decisions.

Decision making is a complex process that relies on weighing the value of reward against punishment. Although various abnormal mechanisms of processing somatic states may contribute to defective decision making, a parsimonious explanation of the nature of the decision making deficit in VM patients is that in most patients, the decision making impairment is due to insensitivity to future consequences, whatever they may be. The patient appears oblivious to the future and guided predominantly by immediate prospects. This "myopia for the future" in VM patients persists in the face of severe adverse consequences, that is, rising future punishment, or declining future reward.

With respect to brain asymmetry, it appears that the decision making deficit observed in real life and in the laboratory is most pronounced after right, as opposed to left, VM lesions. With respect to early versus late onset damage, patients with early-onset VM lesions superficially resemble adult-onset patients in terms of disrupted social behavior, which contrasts with normal basic cognitive abilities. However, in many respects, the deficit acquired in childhood results in more severe behavioral defects than when the impairment is acquired in adulthood. Most remarkable is that, for instance, in the language domain, there is an impressive recovery of function when the damage is acquired early on. This is not the case with regard to moral and social behavior, that is, there is no recovery of function.

A Neural System for Somatic State Activation and Emotion Regulation

As alluded to earlier, somatic states can be induced from (a) "primary inducers," and (b) "secondary inducers." Briefly, primary inducers are stimuli that are evolutionarily and largely innately set as pleasurable or aversive, and automatically and involuntarily elicit a somatic response. Secondary inducers are entities that have become associated by learning with the primary inducers, and that can be presented as an image generated by recall, that elicit a somatic response:

1. The amygdala is a trigger structure for somatic states from a primary inducer. It couples the features of primary inducers, which can be processed subliminally (e.g., via the thalamus) or explicitly (e.g., via early sensory and high order association cortices), with the somatic state associated with the inducer. This somatic state is evoked via effector structures such as the hypothalamus, basal forebrain, ventral striatum, periacqueductal gray (PAG), and other brainstem nuclei. Thus, the induction of somatic states from primary inducers requires the integrity of primary and high order association cortices or thalamus, of effector structures, and of the amygdala, which serves as a convergence–divergence zone that couples inducer and effector (A. R. Damasio, 1995).

2. Once somatic states from primary inducers are activated, signals from these somatic states are relayed to the brain. Representations of these signals can remain covert at the level of the brainstem, or can reach the insular/SII, SI cortices and posterior cingulate cortices and be perceived as a feeling (Verthier, Starkstein, & Leiguarda, 1988; A. R. Damasio, 1994; A. R. Damasio, 1999; A. R. Damasio et al., 2000; Maddock, 1999).

3. When we process a secondary inducer, that is, recall an event associated with a feeling, we may reenact the somatic state characteristic of the feeling. The normal acquisition of secondary inducers requires the integrity of the amygdala. When the amygdala is damaged, primary inducers cannot induce somatic states, and secondary inducers cannot be acquired. Provided that secondary inducers were developed normally, the induction of somatic states from secondary inducers is dependent on cortical circuitry in which the VM cortex is a critical substrate. The VM cortex is a trigger structure for somatic states from secondary inducers. It serves as a convergence–divergence zone, which links (a) a certain category of event based on memory records in high order association cortices to (b) the effector structures that induce the somatic responses, and to (c) the substrates of feeling in, for example, the insula/SII, SI cortices. In some instances, the VM cortex couples knowledge of secondary inducer events to covert response effectors at the level of the basal forebrain or brainstem. The anticipatory SCRs acquired during the prehunch period of the gambling task are an example of this instance (Bedchara et al., 1997).

4. Once somatic states induced by primary or secondary inducers are enacted in the body by the "body loop," or in somatosensory structures via the "as-if-body loop," they participate in two functions: (a) providing a substrate for feeling the emotional state, as explained earlier; and (b) biasing the decision to select a response (see Fig. 1.7). The neural structures pro-

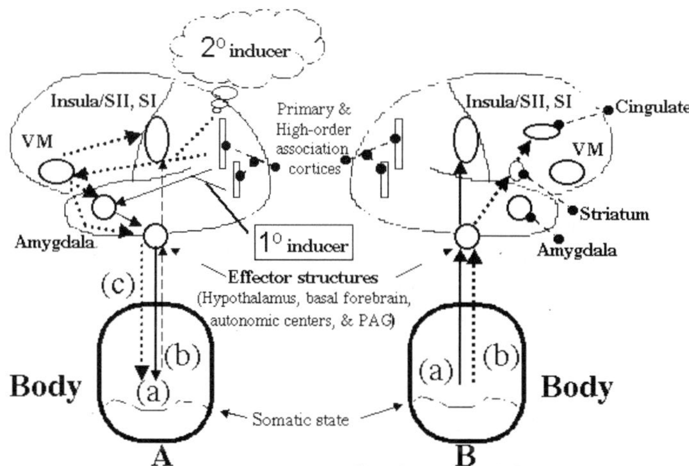

(a) A 1° inducer induces a somatic state (solid line).
(b) Somatic state signals generate representations in brainstem and insular/SII, SI cortex, which can be perceived as a feeling (dashed line).
(c) Images associated with the 1° inducer can now induce a somatic state, i.e., a 2° inducer (dotted line).

Somatic state signals from 1° or 2° inducer are relayed back to the brain. These somatic signals participate in two operations:
(a) feeling the emotional state (solid line).
(b) biasing the decision to select a response (dotted line).

Fig. 1.7. A schematic model of somatic state activation and decision making. From Bechara et al., 2001.

cessing the "feeling" and "biasing effect" associated with somatic states are the following:

A. Evidence suggests that there may be two variant forms of feelings subserved by partially separate neural sectors. The insular/SII, SI cortices are necessary although they may not be sufficient for feelings of an emotion to occur (A. R. Damasio, 1999). However, the anterior cingulate appears related to feelings that are associated with an action. The neural mechanisms of pain provide a good example: the conscious feeling of the intensity of pain seems dependent on insular and surrounding somatosensory cortices, whereas the feeling of a desire and drive to avoid the pain, which probably corresponds to the image representation of likely but not yet realized action, is more dependent on substrates in the anterior cingulate (Berthier ete al., 1988; Rainville, Duncan, Price, Carrier, & Bushnell, 1997). There is support for this notion from the study of the alleviation of thirst (Denton, Shade, Zamarippa, Egan, Blair–West, McKinley, & Fox, 1999; Denton, Shade, Samarippa, Egan, Blair–West, McKinley, Lancaster et al., 1999) as well as studies of drug craving (Childress eet al., 1999) . Thus, in the gambling task experiments, we speculate that the somatic states associated with winning and losing money may remain nonconscious, or they may become conscious in the form of good and bad feelings at the level of the insular/SII, SI cortex. During the pondering of a decision, the feeling of a somatic state may remain nonconscious, or it may become conscious in the form of a "gut feeling" or a feeling of a desire to choose or avoid a particular deck.

B. Besides feeling, somatic states will influence behavior (approach or withdrawal) by modulating activity in motor structures in the brainstem, cortex, or both. The modulating (biasing) effect of somatic states on behavior may occur unconsciously (i.e., act without any feeling and knowledge) or may occur consciously (i.e., in the presence of a gut feeling or a desire to act in a certain way and full knowledge of the contingencies). Evidence suggests that the striatum, especially the dorsal striatum, is a critical site where somatic states can bias decision making and response selection nonconsciously. The supracallosal sector of the anterior cingulate and the adjacent supplementary motor area (SMA) is a critical site where somatic states can bias decision making and response selection consciously.

Human studies also suggest that the action selection function of the dorsal striatum system is covert. On a task called "the weather forecast task," normal and amnesic individuals implicitly learned to make correct choices without awareness of the complex rules governing performance of the task (Knowlton, Mangels, & Squire, 1996; Knowlton & Squire, 1993). The behavioral guidance that occurred without awareness of the rules of the task was absent in individuals with Parkinson's disease (PD), and they did poorly on this task (Knowlton et al., 1996; Knowlton & Squire, 1993) . However, as soon as PD individuals acquired an explicit knowledge of the rules governing the task, they began to improve their performance, that is, behavioral guidance under the control of explicit knowledge was not impaired (Knowlton et al., 1996). In contrast, patients whose brain damage involves both medial temporal lobes, a portion of the orbital prefrontal cortex and the anterior cingulate, but spare the striatum and basal ganglia completely, demonstrated covert, but not overt, learning of affective valences (Tranel & A. R. Damasio, 1993). These results suggest that the striatum is both necessary (Knowlton et al., 1996) and sufficient (Tranel & A. R. Damasio, 1993) to modify behavior through the influence of secondary inducers at a covert (implicit) level.

There is evidence to suggest that the supracallosal sector of the anterior cingulate plays a role in response selection at a conscious level. For example, performance on target detection tasks and the Stroop interference task is associated with activity in the anterior cingulate (Pardo, Pardo, Janer, & Raichle, 1990; Posner & Petersen, 1990: Posner, Petersen, Fox, & Raichle, 1988) . Another study (Frith, Friston, Liddle, & Frackowiak, 1991) compared willed acts requiring explicit deliberate choice to automatic and routine acts and detected a significant increase in activity in the supracallosal anterior cingulate during the willed acts. Another (Petit ete al.,

1993) study showed that the anterior cingulate region was activated during response selections associated with self-paced voluntary horizontal saccadic eye movements. These results suggest that the supracallosal anterior cingulate is involved in response selection when a wide range of novel choices is required, and when the response selection is carried at a conscious or explicit level.

CONCLUSION

The somatic marker hypothesis provides a systems-level neuroanatomical and cognitive framework for decision making and its influence by emotion. The key idea of this hypothesis is that decision making is a process which is influenced by marker signals that arise in bioregulatory processes, including those that express themselves in emotions and feelings. This influence can occur at multiple levels of operation, some of which occur consciously, and some of which occur nonconsciously. The VM prefrontal cortex represents one critical structure in this neural system subserving decision making. However, decision making depends on large-scale systems that include other cortical and subcortical components, that is, the amygdala, the somatosensory and insular cortices, and the peripheral nervous system.

Although the somatic marker view argues that emotions are an important factor in the process of decision making, there is a popular notion that "emotions cloud the mind and interfere with good judgment," and that "wise decisions and judgments come only from cool heads." How can we reconcile these seemingly conflicting views? When do moods and emotions help the process of making advantageous decisions or disrupt it?

We are addressing this issue using a theoretical model that explains when emotions are helpful or disruptive to decision making. An emotion (e.g., fear or anxiety) may be evoked when contemplating a decision associated with a possible punishment. In this instance, we describe the emotion as an integral part of the decision-making task. The evidence we have presented shows that the triggering of a somatic state from a previous experience with punishment plays a critical role in guiding decisions in the advantageous direction. On the other hand, the emotion may be unrelated to the decision-making task, that is, it either existed before the decision-making task, or it was triggered during the decision-making task through unrelated means.

Our model is based on the hypothesis that emotions evoked by conditions that are unrelated to the contents of a particular decision making task will have a negative impact on the process of making advantageous choices. By contrast, emotions evoked by conditions that are an integral part of a particular decision making task are beneficial to the process of making advantageous choices. More specific, in the gambling task, when the participant ponders from which deck to choose, one thought may trigger a positive somatic state related to reward, and another may trigger a negative response related to punishment. Depending on the relative strengths of the negative versus the positive states, the result is a net overall somatic state that is either positive or negative. Somatic states induced from the thoughts of gains or losses during the gambling task are integral to the decision making task, and therefore they help bias behavior toward advantageous choices. The effectiveness of the emotion (somatic state) integral to the decision making process depends on the strength of the unrelated emotion that exists in the background. We envision several conditions under which somatic states (integral to the decision task) can be altered by emotions in the background (i.e., somatic states that are unrelated to the decision-task):

1. A neutral or weak emotion in the background. When a neutral or weak emotional state exists in the background, the triggering of a somatic state from pondering a decision that can lead to punishment, for example, should be effective in overriding the existing state and inducing changes onits own. In this case, the signal (triggered somatic state) to noise (background emotion) ratio is high, that is, the somatic state triggered by events related to the decision making task should be effective in inducing changes in the body state. This in turn will provide feedback signals to the brain, which bias behavior in the advantageous direction (see Fig. 1.8A).

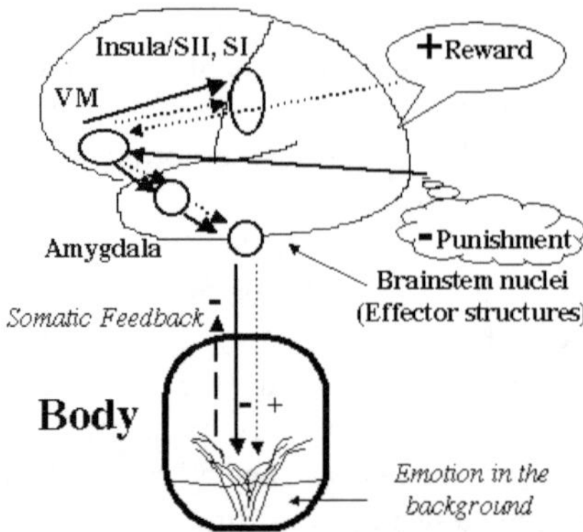

A.

• Background emotion is weak.
• Somatic states from thoughts of punishment (solid line) are stronger than those from reward (dotted line).
• When (+) and (-) somatic states impinge on the emotional state in the background, the signal to noise ratio is high (big splash).
• The result is a strong somatic feedback to the brain.

Fig. 1.8A. A schematic model of somatic state activation and decision making in a hypothetical condition in which (s) the somatic state of the thought of punishment is greater than that or reward, and (b) the background emotion is neurtal or week.

2. The triggered somatic state by the decision making task is incongruous with a strong emotion in the background. When a strong emotional state exists in the background, for example, anger, the triggering of a somatic state from pondering a decision that can lead to punishment, an emotion that is different from anger, becomes ineffective in overriding the existing state and inducing changes on its own. For example, if a person is very angry (background emotion) and engages in a driving activity where decisions about whether to drive at a very high speed must be made, the emotion related to the consequences of high speed driving (e.g., fear of an accident), which is integral to the decision task at hand, becomes ineffective in overriding the anger emotion in the background. In this case, the signal to noise ratio is too low. This creates a situation like the VM patients, where anticipatory somatic responses that signal the potential danger of high speed are no longer effective in guiding behavior (see Fig. 1.8B).

3. The triggered somatic state by the decision making task is congruous with a strong emotion in the background. When a strong state of pain, for example, exists in the background, the triggering of a somatic state from pondering a decision that can lead to pain, a state that is congruous with the pain state in the background, will be exaggerated. For example, if a person is in pain

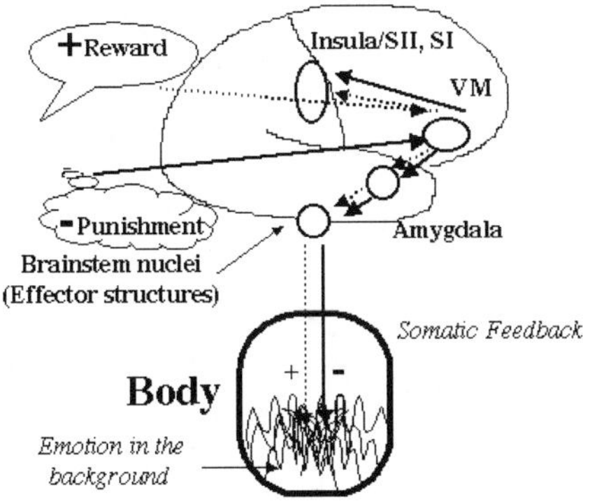

B.
- Background emotion is strong and incongruous.
- Somatic states from thoughts of punishment (solid line) and from reward (dotted line) are the same as in A.
- When (+) and (-) somatic states impinge on the emotional state in the background, the signal to noise ratio is low (no splash).
- The result is an absent somatic feedback to the brain.

Fig. 1.8B. A schematic model of somatic state activationand decision making in a hypothetical condition in which (a) the somatic stae of the thought of punishment is greater than that of reward, and (b) the background emition is strong and incongruous.

(background emotion) and engages in a decision of how much pain medicine one should buy, the thought of having pain if not enough pain medicine were available would trigger a somatic state related to pain. In this case, the somatic feedback signal will be exaggerated, and the decision will involve overanticipation of the degree of pain in the future and overestimation of the amount of pain medicine that needs to be purchased (see Fig. 1.8C). Indeed, the work of George Loewenstein supports this prediction, in that conditions in which, for example, a person is too hungry and goes to a grocery store, the decision of how much food to buy to avoid hunger is altered by the hunger state itself, so that the person is likely to overestimate the amount of food needed.

In conclusion, this theoretical model is only in its preliminary stage of development, and studies are currently conducted to test various aspects of this model. Regardless of the validity of this particular model, the main point is that there is strong neurological evidence in support of the view that the influence of emotions on cognition is sometimes helpful and sometimes disruptive. Attempts to explore the conditions and neurobiological mechanisms of emotion regulation that have either positive or negative influence on cognition are very significant and important from both clinical and neuroscientific perspectives.

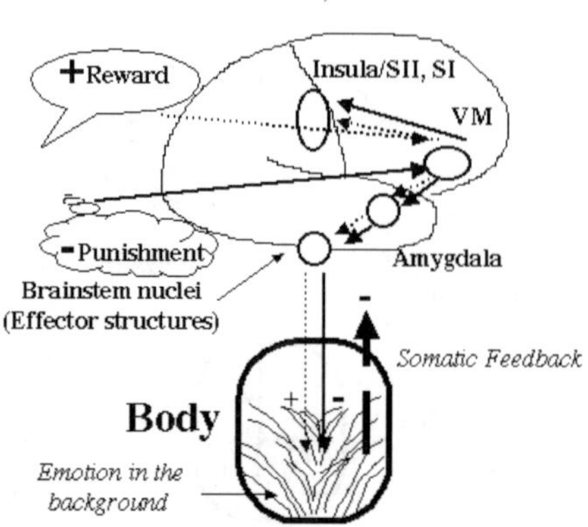

C.
• Background emotion is strong and congruous.
• Somatic states from thoughts of punishment (solid line) and from reward (dotted line) are the same as in A.
• When (+) and (-) somatic states impinge on the emotional state in the background, the signal is in sink with the noise (I.e., it creates a strong splash).
• The result is an exaggerated somatic feedback to the brain.

Fig. 1.8C. A schematic model of somatic state activation and decision making in a hypothetical condition in which (a) the somatic state of the thought of punishment is greater than that of reward, and (b) the background emotion is strong and congruous with the triggered somatic states.

REFERENCES

Ackerly, S. S., & Benton, A. L. (1948). Report of a case of bilateral frontal lobe defect. *Proceedings of the Association for Research in Nervous and Mental Disease, USA, 27*, 479–504.

Anderson, S. W., Bechara, A., Damasio, H., Tranel, D., & Damasio, A. R. (1999). Impairment of social and moral behavior related to early damage in the human prefrontal cortex. *Nature Neuroscience, 2*, 1032–1037.

Anderson, S. W., Damasio, H., Jones, R. D., & Tranel, D. (1991). Wisconsin card sorting test performance as a measure of frontal lobe damage. *Journal of Clinical and Experimental Neuropsychology, 3*, 909–922.

Angrilli, A., Palomba, D., Cantagallo, A., Maietti, A., & Stegagno, L. (1999). Emotional impairment after right orbitofrontal lesion in a patient without cognitive deficits. *NeuroReport, 10*, 1741–1746.

Bechara, A. (2003). Risky business: Emotion, decision-making and addiction. *Journal of Gambling Studies.*

Bechara, A., Damasio, A. R., Damasio, H., & Anderson, S. W. (1994). Insensitivity to future consequences following damage to human prefrontal cortex. *Cognition, 50*, 7–15.

Bechara, A., Damasio, H., & Damasio, A. R. (2000). Emotion, decision-making, and the orbitofrontal cortex. *Cerebral Cortex, 10*, 295–307.

Bechara, A., Damasio, H., Damasio, A. R., & Lee, G. P. (1999). Different contributions of the human amygdala and ventromedial prefrontal cortex to decision-making. *The Journal of Neuroscience, 19*, 5473–5481.

Bechara, A., Damasio, H., Tranel, D., & Anderson, S. W. (1998). Dissociation of working memory from decision making within the human prefrontal cortex. *The Journal of Neuroscience, 18*, 428–437.

Bechara, A., Damasio, H., Tranel, D., & Damasio, A. R. (1997). Deciding advantageously before knowing the advantageous strategy. *Science, 275*, 1293–1295.

Bechara, A., Tranel, D., & Damasio, H. (2000). Characterization of the decision-making impairment of patients with bilateral lesions of the ventromedial prefrontal cortex. *Brain, 123*, 2189–2202.

Bechara, A., Tranel, D., Damasio, H., Adolphs, R., Rockland, C., & Damasio, A. R. (1995). Double dissociation of conditioning and declarative knowledge relative to the amygdala and hippocampus in humans. *Science, 269*, 1115–1118.

Bechara, A., Tranel, D., Damasio, H., & Damasio, A. R. (1996). Failure to respond autonomically to anticipated future outcomes following damage to prefrontal cortex. *Cerebral Cortex, 6*, 215–225.

Berthier, M., Starkstein, S., & Leiguarda, R. (1988). Asymbolia for pain—A sensory-limbic disconnection syndrome. *Annals of Neurology, 24*, 41-49.

Brickner, R. M. (1932). An interpretation of frontal lobe function based upon the study of a case of partial bilateral frontal lobectomy. Localization of function in the cerebral cortex. *Proceedings of the Association for Research in Nervous and Mental Disease, USA, 13*, 259–351.

Butter, C. M., Mishkin, M., & Mirsky, A. F. (1968). Emotional responses toward humans in monkeys with selective frontal lesions. *Physiology and Behavior, 3*, 213–215.

Butter, C. M., Mishkin, M., & Rosvold, H. E. (1963). Conditioning and extinction of a food-rewarded response after selective ablations of frontal cortex in rhesus monkeys. *Experimental Neurology, 7*, 65–75.

Butter, C. M., & Snyder, D. R. (1972). Alternations in aversive and aggressive behaviors following orbital frontal lesions in rhesus monkeys. *Acta Neurobiological Experiments, 32*, 525–565.

Cahill, L., Babinsky, R., Markowitsch, H. J., & McGaugh, J. L. (1995). The amygdala and emotional memory. *Nature, 377*, 295–296.

Childress, A. R., Mozley, P. D., McElgin, W., Fitzgerald, J., Reivich, M., & O'Brien, C. P. (1999). Limbic activation during cue-induced cocaine craving. *American Journal of Psychiatry, 156*, 11–18.

Damasio, A. R. (1994). *Descartes' error: Emotion, reason, and the human brain*. New York: Putnam.

Damasio, A. R. (1995). Toward a neurobiology of emotion and feeling: operational concepts and hypotheses. *The Neuroscientist, 1*, 19–25.

Damasio, A. R. (1996). The somatic marker hypothesis and the possible functions of the prefrontal cortex. *Philosophical Transactions of the Royal Society of London (Biology), 351*, 1413–1420.

Damasio, A. R. (1999). *The feeling of what happens: Body and emotion in the making of consciousness*. New York: Harcourt Brace.

Damasio, A. R., Grabowski, T. G., Bechara, A., Damasio, H., Ponto, L. L. B., Parvizi, J., et al. (2000). Subcortical and cortical brain activity during the feeling of self-generated emotions. *Nature Neuroscience, 3*, 1049–1056.

Damasio, A. R., Tranel, D., & Damasio, H. (1990). Individuals with sociopathic behavior caused by frontal damage fail to respond autonomically to social stimuli. *Behavioral Brain Research, 41*, 81–94.

Damasio, H. (1995). *Human brain anatomy in computerized images*. New York: Oxford University Press.

Damasio, H., Bechara, A., Tranel, D., & Damasio, A. R. (1997). Double dissociation of emotional conditioning and emotional imagery relative to the amygdala and right somatosensory cortex. *Society For Neuroscience Abstracts, 23*, 1318.

Davidson, R. J., & Irwin, W. (1999). The functional neuroanatomy of emotion and affective style. *Trends in Cognitive Sciences, 3*, 11–21.

Davis, M. (1992a). The role of the amygdala in conditioned fear. In J. P. Aggleton (Ed.), *The amygdala: Neurobiological aspects of emotion, memory, and mental dysfunction* (pp. 451–473). New York: Wiley–Liss.

Davis, M. (1992b). The role of the amygdala in fear and anxiety. *Annual Review of Neuroscience 15*, 353–375.

Denton, D., Shade, R., Zamarippa, F., Egan, G., Blair–West, J., McKinley, M., et al. (1999). Correlation of regional cerebral blood flow and change of plasma sodium concentration during genesis and satiation of thirst. *Proceedings of the National Academy of Sciences, USA, 96*, 2532–2537.

Denton, D., Shade, R., Zamarippa, F., Egan, G., Blair–West, J., McKinley, M., et al. (1999). Neuroimaging of genesis and satiation of thirst and an interoceptor-driven theory of origins of primary consciousness. *Proceedings of the National Academy of Sciences, USA, 96*, 5304–5309.

Eslinger, P. J., & Damasio, A. R. (1985). Severe disturbance of higher cognition after bilateral frontal lobe ablation: Patient EVR. *Neurology, 35*, 1731–1741.

Frith, C. D., Friston, K., Liddle, P. F., & Frackowiak, R. S. J. (1991). Willed action and the prefrontal cortex in man—A study with PET. *Proceedings of the Royal Society of London Series B—Biological Sciences, 244*, 241–246.

Harlow, J. M. (1848). Passage of an iron bar through the head. *Boston Medical and Surgical Journal, 39*, 389–393.

Harlow, J. M. (1868). Recovery from the passage of an iron bar through the head. *Publications of the Massachusetts Medical Society, 2*, 327–347.

Kim, J. J., Rison, R. A., & Fanselow, M. S. (1993). Effects of amygdala, hippocampus, and periaqueductal gray lesions on short and long term contextual fear. *Behavioral Neuroscience, 107*, 1093–1098.

Kim, M., & Davis, M. (1993). Lack of a temporal gradient of retrograde amnesia in rats with amygdala lesions assessed with the fear-potentiated startle paradigm. *Behavioral Neuroscience, 107*, 1088–1092.

Knowlton, B. J., Mangels, J. A., & Squire, L. R. (1996). A neostriatal habit learning system in humans. *Science, 273*, 1399–1402.

Knowlton, B. J., & Squire, L. R. (1993). The learning of categories: Parallel brain systems for item memory and category knowledge. *Science, 262*, 1747–1749.

LaBar, K. S., Gatenby, J. C., Gore, J. C., LeDoux, J. E., & Phelps, E. A. (1998). Human amygdala activation during conditioned fear acquisition and extinction: A mixed-trial fMRI study. *Neuron, 20*, 937–945.

LaBar, K. S., LeDoux, J. E., Spencer, D. D., & Phelps, E. A. (1995). Impaired fear conditioning following unilateral temporal lobectomy in humans. *Journal of Neuroscience, 15*, 6846–6855.

LeDoux, J. E. (1993a). Emotional memory systems in the brain. *Behavioral Brain Research, 58*, 69–79.

LeDoux, J. E. (1993b). Emotional memory: In search of systems and synapses. *Annals of the New York Academy of Sciences, 702*, 149–157.

LeDoux, J. E. (1996). *The Emotional Brain: The mysterious underpinnings of emotional life.* New York: Simon&Schuster.

Loewenstein, G. F., Weber, E. U., Hsee, C. K., & Welch, N. (2001). Risk as feelings. *Psychological Bulletin, 127*, 267–286.

Maddock, R. J. (1999). The retrosplenial cortex and emotion: New insights from functional neuroimaging of the human brain. *Trends in Neurosciences, 22*, 310–320.

Malkova, L., Gaffan, D., & Murray, E. A. (1997). Excitotoxic lesions of the amygdala fail to produce impairment in visual learning for auditory secondary reinforcement but interfere with reinforcer devaluation effects in rhesus monkeys. *Journal of Neuroscience, 17*, 6011–6020.

Manes, F., Sahakian, B., Clark, L., Rogers, R., Antoun, N., Aitken, M., et al. (2002). Decision-making processes following damage to the prefrontal cortex. *Brain, 125*, 624–639.

Morgan, M. A., & LeDoux, J. E. (1995). Differential contribution of dorsal and ventral medial prefrontal cortex to the acquisition and extinction of conditioned fear in rats. *Behavioral Neuroscience, 109*, 681–688.

Pardo, J. V., Pardo, P. J., Janer, K. W., & Raichle, M. E. (1990). The anterior cingulate cortex mediates processing selection in the stroop attentional conflict paradigm. *Proceedings of the National Academy of Sciences, USA, 87*(1), 256–259.

Petit, L., Orssaud, C., Tzourio, N., Salamon, G., Mazoyer, B., & Berthoz, A. (1993). Pet study of voluntary saccadic eye-movements in humans—Basal ganglia-thalamocortical system and cingulate cortex involvement. *Journal of Neurophysiology, 69*, 1009–1016.

Posner, M. I., & Petersen, S. E. (1990). The attention system of the human brain. *Annual Review of Neuroscience, 13*, 25–42.

Posner, M. I., Petersen, S. E., Fox, P. T., & Raichle, M. E. (1988). Localization of cognitive operations in the human-brain. *Science, 240*, 1627–1631.

Rahman, S., Sahakian, B. J., Rudolph, N. C., Rogers, R. D., & Robbins, T. W. (2001). Decision making and neuropsychiatry. *Trends in Cognitive Sciences, 6*, 271–277.

Rainville, P., Duncan, G. H., Price, D. D., Carrier, B., & Bushnell, M. C. (1997). Pain affect encoded in human anterior cingulate but not somatosensory cortex. *Science, 277, 968–971.*

Rogers, R. D., Everitt, B. J., Baldacchino, A., Blackshaw, A. J., Swainson, R., Wynne, K., et al. (1999). Dissociable deficits in the decision-making cognition of chronic amphetamine abusers, opiate abusers, patients with focal damage to prefrontal cortex, and tryptophan-depleted normal volunteers: Evidence for monoaminergic mechanisms. *Neuropsychopharmacology, 20*, 322–339.

Rogers, R. D., Owen, A. M., Middleton, H. C., Williams, E. J., Pickard, J. D., Sahakian, B. J., et al. (1999). Choosing between small, likely rewards and large, unlikely rewards activates inferior and orbital prefrontal cortex. *Journal of Neuroscience, 20*, 9029–9038.

Saver, J. L., & Damasio, A. R. (1991). Preserved access and processing of social knowledge in a patient with acquired sociopathy due to ventromedial frontal damage. *Neuropsychologia, 29*, 1241–1249.

Tranel, D., Bechara, A., Damasio, H., & Damasio, A. R. (1998). Neural correlates of emotional imagery. *International Journal of Psychophysiology, 30*, 107.

Tranel, D., Bechara, A., & Denburg, N. L. (2002). Asymmetric functional roles of right and left ventromedial prefrontal cortices in social conduct, decision-making, and emotional processing. *Cortex, 38,* 589–612.

Tranel, D., & Damasio, A. R. (1993). The covert learning of affective valence does not require structures in hippocampal system or amygdala. *Journal of Cognitive Neuroscience, 5*, 79–88.

Tranel, D., & Damasio, H. (1994). Neuroanatomical correlates of electrodermal skin conductance responses. *Psychophysiology, 31*, 427–438.

Welt, L. (1888). Uber Charaktervaranderungen des Menschen infoldge von Lasionen des Stirnhirns. *Deutsch Archive der Klinishchen Medizin, 42*, 339–390.

2

Physiological Processes During Emotion

Gerhard Stemmler
University of Marburg

This chapter discusses physiological processes during emotion with special emphasis on the controversial issue of emotion specificity. A functional view suggests that emotions have distinct goals and need differentiated somatovisceral activations for the sake of body protection and behavior preparation. The autonomic nervous systems support the necessary precise and fine-tuned regulations. The brain orchestrates coordinated autonomic regulation patterns. It is shown that psychophysiological recordings are able to reveal such differentiated regulation patterns which can be described in the state-space of physiological responses. Such "physiological maps" show both stability and change along expected trajectories. A meta-analysis of the available research literature demonstrates a considerable degree of somatovisceral fear versus anger specificity. It is argued that unspecific but overlapping emotion responses should not be disregarded when describing physiological signatures of emotion. Finally, it is pointed out that emotion physiologies combine at least three different components: the nonemotional context, specific somatovisceral adaptations or "emotion signatures," and the effects of demands necessitated by the momentary situation in the pursuit of an emotion goal.

Physiological processes allow, subserve, and accompany all gross and subtle contents and expressions of life, from behaving to emoting and to thinking. The widespread autonomic and somatomotor responses during emotions are an obvious clue that emotions possess organismic and behavioral functions. But which functions do emotions serve?

FUNCTIONS OF EMOTIONS

The evolutionary account of emotion is a helpful starting point for our discussion of the functions of emotions (Nesse, 1990). Animals encounter in their lives recurring problems and opportunities. Some of these problems are not easily solved, neither do they have only negligible consequences if the animal fails to solve them: They are critical for survival and reproduction, and they press for adaptational solutions. Emotions evolved as solutions to such perennial problems and opportunities. Different kinds of problems and opportunities made necessary different adaptive behaviors. Eventually, this link between specific problems and opportunities and specific adaptive behaviors established a small set of separate emotion systems. These emotion systems "can be seen as *time-tested solutions to timeless problems and challenges*" (Levenson, 2003, emphasis by author).

In distinction to reflexes which are activated by specific, adequate stimuli, one and the same emotion can be elicited by physically very different stimuli, circumstances, and even thoughts (Izard, 1993). These different routes to emotion activation share however a common meaning. For example, we get angry when betrayed by a cashier, when criticized for being lazy when in fact we gave our best, when carelessly hurt by a shopping cart while lining up at the cash register, or when we recall such episodes. Thus, emotion systems are activated by specific, adequate meaning structures. Or, to borrow from Allport (1937), emotion systems make diverse situations with similar meaning structures functionally equivalent.

On a high level of abstraction, then, emotions function to secure survival and procreation of oneself or of one's kin. Different emotions serve these goals in that they solve different adaptational problems and opportunities. The function of disgust is rejection; of anger, destruction; of fear, protection; of sadness, reintegration; of joy, reproduction (Plutchik, 1980). The goal of most (negative) emotions is to "maintain a relatively steady (or 'normal') state in the face of interpersonal challenges" (Plutchik, 1997, p. 20), for example, to reinstate one's dominance, or even more specific, to win a fight. Emotions provide the cognitive and bodily means to accomplish these goals.

On a lower level of abstraction, emotions in general have at least three functions (see also the statements of various authors in Ekman & Davidson, 1994). The first function is to allocate perceptual, cognitive, and bodily resources to accomplish an emotion's goals. This function includes preparation of the body for prototypical behaviors (e.g., approach, withdrawal, attack, defense). The second function is to communicate to others one's emotional state (e.g., through posture, facial expression, skin coloration, prosody in speech). This communication provides others with information about one's likely behavioral intentions and gives them some extra time to adapt accordingly before one's behavioral actions are actually launched. The third function is to enhance intraorganismic communication and protect the body from adverse consequences of injury or disease (e.g., through cardiovascular reflexes or increased immunological activity). Intraorganismic communication includes the tuning of otherwise only loosely coupled brain, somatomotor, and autonomic nervous systems (Gellhorn, 1970) and also reafferences from the organs to the brain. Such reafferences were a key element of William James's theory of emotion (James, 1884); they gained new attention in Damasio's Somatic Marker Hypothesis (Damasio, 1994; see Bechara, this volume), according to which somatic consequences of life events are marked and reproduced in similar circumstances allowing individuals to make more parsimonious and better decisions.

AUTONOMIC PHYSIOLOGY OF EMOTION REGULATION

Physiological processes are intricately involved in the implementation of the functions of emotions. Yet more interesting than this general assertion is the question, whether individual emotions have different underlying physiologies. If researchers could demonstrate the existence of different physiologies underlying at least some emotional states, one could trace the physiological demarcation lines between different emotions and find answers to such perennial questions as "How many emotions are there?", "Which biological functions do individual emotions have?" and "What is the relation among emotion physiology, feelings, and behavior?"

If researchers could not demonstrate the existence of different emotion physiologies, one could seriously challenge categorical models of emotion and resort instead to a dimensional model, for example, with the dimensions activation and valence. It should be kept in mind, however, that if different emotion physiologies cannot be shown reliably, there may be either methodological problems in detecting them or they are truly nonexistent. Methodological problems of physiological emotion specificity research have been treated in detail elsewhere (Davidson, 1994; Levenson, 2003; Stemmler, 1992b, 2003) and will be summarized later in this chapter. However, continuing arguments insist that the autonomic nervous system is unable to show "particular" activations, but instead produces rather "diffuse" excitations of target organs (Cannon, 1927, p. 109) in the service of "housekeeping functions [such as] energy metabolism, tissue repair, and the like" (Gray, 1994, p. 243). Another argument holds that instead of reflecting the arousal of a particular emotion, autonomic and somatomotor activity would indicate the demands of an action disposition, action tendency, or action proper (Davidson, 1993, 1994; Frijda, 1986; Lang, Bradley, & Cuthbert, 1990), which can be very similar in different emotional states and thus make it difficult if not impossible to find different autonomic emotion physiologies. We now turn to a discussion of these arguments.

Is the Autonomic Nervous System Unable to Show "Particular" Activations?

As indicated earlier, research on autonomic emotion specificity to these days is confronted with Cannon's (1927) principal argument that the sympathetic nervous system mediates a largely undifferentiated, "diffuse" innervation of its target organs abolishing in principle any chances for a manifestation of emotion specific physiologies. Recent evidence from research into the physiology of the autonomic nervous system is, however, at variance with this position (see reviews by Jänig, 2003; Jänig & Häbler, 2000). In the following paragraphs, we present a brief sketch of these authors' outline.

The Autonomic Nervous System. Since Langley (1921), the autonomic nervous system is subdivided into the sympathetic (SNS), the parasympathetic (PNS), and the enteric nervous systems. The distinction between the SNS and the PNS is based on neuroanatomical features of the central nervous system's autonomic outflow to the target tissues (thoracolumbar and craniosacral outflow, respectively). Target tissues of the SNS are (a) the smooth musculature of blood vessels, erector pili muscles, pupil, lung, and evacuative organs; (b) the heart; (c) sweat, salivary, and digestive glands; and (d) adipose tissue, liver cells, the pineal gland, and lymphatic tissues. In addition, the SNS innervates preganglionically the adrenal medulla, which secretes adrenaline and noradrenaline into the blood for circulation throughout the body. Target tissues of the PNS are (a) pacemaker cells and the atria of the heart, (b) exocrine glands of the head, (c) intraocular smooth muscles, (d) the smooth muscles and glands of the airways, (e) the smooth muscles and glands of the gastrointestinal tract, (f) the pelvic organs, and (g) epithelia and mucosa throughout the body, as well as some intracranial, uterine, and facial blood vessels, which, however, do not contribute to the regulation of the blood pressure.

Most target tissues respond to only one of the autonomic nervous systems, only a few respond to both the SNS and the PNS as, for example, the pacemaker cells and the atria of the heart. A reciprocal effect of the SNS and the PNS ("antagonism") is rare (Koizumi, Terui, & Kollai, 1983). In vivo and under physiological conditions the systems work either synergistically or under separate functional or temporal conditions. A systematic differentiation of autonomic regulatory states has been presented by Berntson, Cacioppo, and Quigley (1991).

The Final Autonomic Pathway. The autonomic nervous systems are constituted by sets of preganglionic and postganglionic neurons. They are the pathways along which central nervous system messages travel to their target tissues. In analogy to the "final common motor path," Jänig (1988) spoke of these pathways as "final autonomic pathways." These pathways are functionally isolated from one another and permit a specific central autonomic control of autonomic targets (Jänig & McLachlan, 1992). This central control can be modified along the way within the autonomic ganglia and within the target organ. As a consequence, the regulation of body functions by the autonomic nervous systems is precise and highly efficient in that they integrate control from the central nervous system, from afferent pathways contributing information about the functioning of other organs, and from the state of the target tissue itself. Jänig (2003) concluded that the ideas (a) of the sympathetic nervous system functioning in an "all-or-none" fashion and (b) of a simple functional antagonistic organization between sympathetic and parasympathetic nervous system are untenable.

Spinal and Supraspinal Control of Autonomic Pathways. The spinal cord contains many autonomic reflex circuits. These circuits connect preganglionic efferent neurons via putative interneurons with spinal afferent inputs. The activity in some autonomic pathways depends predominantly on spinal reflexes (e.g., autonomic tone in muscular, visceral, and renal vasoconstrictor neurons); in others, more on supraspinal control (e.g., hypothalamic thermoregulatory input on cutaneous vasoconstrictor neurons). In sum, the spinal autonomic mechanisms function as integrative controls of the autonomic target organs.

Supraspinal centers in the lower brain stem perform the homeostatic regulation of the cardiovascular system, the respiratory system, and the gastrointestinal tract, for example, the homeostatic regulation of the arterial blood pressure through arterial baroreceptor reflexes. Supraspinal centers in the upper brain stem, hypothalamus, and limbic system produce distinct response patterns, which combine somatomotor, autonomic, and hormonal adjustments. These adjustments serve to coordinate body functions across different response systems under various challenges encountered by an organism. The distinct response patterns are elicited by the forebrain; at least those that mediate defensive behaviors and autonomic adjustments are probably generated by the midbrain periaqueductal gray in combination with the hypothalamus (Bandler, Keay, Floyd, & Price, 2000; Floyd, Price, Ferry, Keay, & Bandler, 2001). Different columns of the periaqueductal gray mediate separate emotion behaviors under threat and pain and allow for fast neuronal adjustments that are critical for survival:

- Confrontational defense (active coping); characterized by hypertension, tachycardia, decrease of blood flow through limb muscles, and an increase, through the face.
- Flight (active coping); characterized by hypertension, tachycardia, increase of blood flow through limb muscles, and a decrease, through the face.
- Quiescence (passive coping); characterized by hypotension and bradycardia.

Folkow (2000) defined six supraspinally integrated response patterns with specific activity patterns of cardiovascular targets:

1. Defense reaction—increase in mean arterial blood pressure and in cardiac output, which is directed toward the skeletal muscles, the heart, and the brain. Blood flow to gastrointestinal tract, kidneys, and skin is diminished.

2. Vigilance or orienting reaction—increase in mean arterial blood pressure, slight bradycardia, decrease in cardiac output, vasoconstriction in most blood vessels.

3. Defeat reaction—increase in mean arterial blood pressure, slight bradycardia, and increase in total peripheral resistance through sympathetic vasoconstriction. In addition, the adrenal cortex secrets glucocorticoid hormones with marked metabolic and immune-suppressive consequences (see Selye's stress response, Selye, 1979).

4. Playing dead reaction—strong decrease in mean arterial blood pressure, heart rate, and cardiac output. The blood flow at all arterial sites is elevated through a loss of tone in the vasoconstrictor systems.

5. Feeding reaction—mean arterial blood pressure, heart rate, and cardiac output are elevated. Blood flow is redirected from skeletal muscles to the gastrointestinal tract.

6. Diving response—strong decrease in heart rate and cardiac output. A strong increase in various vasoconstrictor systems effectively redistributes blood from skeletal muscles, skin, kidney, and the gastrointestinal tract to the heart and the brain.

The principle point of this brief review of the physiology of the autonomous nervous systems is that the organism displays specific and integrated responses which are represented in the brain. Insofar as the emotions represent psychobiological states which have the functions (a) to allocate perceptual, cognitive, and bodily resources to accomplish an emotion's goals; (b) to communicate to others one's emotional state; and (c) to enhance intraorganismic communication and protect the body from adverse consequences of injury or disease, all or at least some emotions require and make use of autonomic nervous systems that function in a specific and differentiated way.

"Physiological Maps:" Demonstrating "Particular" Activations

The physiology of the autonomous systems strongly suggests that its target organs are distinctly regulated during different states of the organism. This expectation should be verifiable in psychophysiological data sets, which are based on multichannel physiological recordings during different conditions and thus allow an assessment of situational response specificity. Situational response specificity denotes the concept that situations exert a unique influence on physiological profiles across most or all individuals (Engel, 1960; Fahrenberg, 1986; Foerster, 1985; Foerster, Schneider, & Walschburger, 1983; Oken et al., 1966). Descriptively, situational response specificity can be made visible on the physiological response surface, where situations are points in a multidimensional state-space. Each point represents the average physiological profile across the sample of participants. To capture both situational "uniqueness" (i.e., maximizing differences among situations) and "consistency" (i.e., minimizing differences between individuals within situations), the discriminant analysis of physiological profiles has been recommended as an appropriate analysis tool (Stemmler, 1988, 1992a). The discriminant functions in such analyses are the components of situational response specificity encountered in a particular study.

To illustrate, Stemmler (1989) described a study on the psychophysiological differentiation of fear, anger, and happiness with 42 participants, 52 situations, and 34 physiological variables. Situations and physiological variables are described in Table 2.1. In the number task, participants had to detect two visually presented target digits in auditorily delivered five-digit numbers. The "fear induction" consisted of a confusing instruction, followed by a "radio play" with a dramatic recitation of parts of E. A. Poe's, "The Fall of the House of Usher," dubbed with sections of Prokofiev's second symphony, and ended with an unanticipated sudden darkness in the experimental room. The "anger induction" was couched in the task of solving five-letter anagrams, presented as an intelligence test. After 15 solvable anagrams, participants were asked to speak louder to compensate for an alleged breakdown of the intercom. After each of the next anagrams, the second of them unsolvable, the experimenter aggressively insisted that the participant should speak louder. The last eight anagrams were a combination of solvable and unsolvable ones. The "happiness induction" reassured the participants of their success and announced an extra monetary bonus. In the speech tasks, participants were asked to recall and speak about a frightening, an annoying, or an interesting and exciting life episode. These speech tasks were presented in randomized order after the fear, the anger, and the happiness inductions. After the speeches the participants were asked to imagine their stories vividly.

Fig. 2.1(a & b) shows the "physiological maps" on the response surface of the first three discriminant functions, which explain 64% of the total discriminative variance. It is readily apparent that the situations evoked a considerable degree of specificity in the physiological response patterns.

Function 1 discriminates among phases with speech activity (D1–D3), the anger induction phases (A1–A7), and phases with speech preparation (B1–B3) on the one hand, and prestimulus phases (P1–P7), poststimulus phases (Q1–Q4),

TABLE 2.1

Situations and Physiological Variables

Situations								
#	*Label*	*Situation*	*#*	*Label*	*Situation*	*#*	*Label*	*Situation*
		System Check	19	N2	Task 2			Instruction for
1	P1	Prestimulus 1	20	Q2	Poststimulus 2	37	M2	Imagination 2
2	I1	Instruction 1			**Anger Induction**			**Number Task 3**
3	W1	Waiting 1	21	P4	Prestimulus 4	38	P5	Prestimulus 5
4	W2	Waiting 2	22	I5	Instruction 5	39	N3	Task 3
		Number Task 1	23	A1	Anagrams 1–15	40	Q3	Poststimulus 3
5	I2	Instruction 2	24	A2	1st Interrupt			**Happiness**
6	N1	Task 1	25	A3	Anagram 16			**Induction**
7	Q1	Poststimulus1	26	A4	2nd Interrupt	41	P6	Prestimulus 6
		Fear Induction	27	A5	Anagram 17	42	I8	Instruction 8
8	P2	Prestimulus 1	28	A6	3rd Interrupt	43	W5	Waiting Happy 1
9	I3	Instruction 3	29	A7	Anagrams 17–25	44	W6	Waiting Happy 2
10	F1	Radio Play	30	I6	Instruction 6			**Speech Task 3**
11	F2	Darkness	31	W3	Waiting Angry 3	45	I9	Instruction 9
12	F3	Lights on	32	W4	Waiting Angry 4	46	B3	Before Speech 3
		Speech Task 1			**Speech Task 2**	47	D3	During Speech 3
13	I4	Instruction 4	33	I7	Instruction 7	48	T3	After Speech 3
14	B1	Before Speech 1	34	B2	Before Speech 2			Instruction for
15	D1	During Speech 1	35	D2	During Speech 2	49	M3	Imagination 3
16	T1	After Speech 1	36	T2	After Speech 2			**Number Task 4**
		Instruction for				50	P7	Prestimulus 7
17	M1	Imagination 1				51	N4	Task 4
		Number Task 2				52	Q4	Poststimulus 4
18	P3	Prestimulus 3						

TABLE 2.1 (cont.)

Physiological Variables					
#	*Variable*	#	*Variable*	#	*Variable*
1	EMGT extensor digitorum	13	SCL Finger	25	Skin Temperature Forehead
2	EMGT trapezious	14	SCL Forehead	26	EEG P3-Cz 6–7.5 Hz
3	EMGT orbicularis oculi	15	Heart Period	27	EEG P3-Cz 7.5–9 Hz
4	EMGT frontalis	16	PVA Finger	28	EEG P3-Cz 9–10.5 Hz
5	EGMP extensor digitorum	17	BV Finger	29	EEG P3-Cz 10.5–12 Hz
6	EMGP trapezious	18	PVA Forehead	30	EEG P3-Cz 12–15 Hz
7	EMGP orbicularis oculi	19	BV Forehead	31	EEG P3-Cz 15–18 Hz
8	EMGP frontalis	20	Pulse Transit Time	32	EEG Pe-Cz 18–21 Hz
9	Movement finger	21	Respiration Period	33	EEG P3-Cz 21–24 Hz
10	Movement forehead	22	EOG horizontal	34	EEG P3-Cz 24–44.5 Hz
11	Movement body	23	Number of Eyeblinks		
12	SCR Finger	24	Skin Temperature Finger		

Note. EMGT = Electromyogram Tonic (Sustained) Activity. EMGP = Electromyogram Phasic Activity. SCR = Skin Conductance Response. SCL = Skin Conductance Level. PVA = Pulse Volume Amplitude. BV = Blood Volume. EOG = Electrooculogram. EEG = Electroencephalogram.

most instruction phases (I1–I5, I9), waiting phases (W1–W6), and the number tasks (N1–N4) on the other hand. Thus, Function 1 seems to reflect a dimension of behavioral activity. This interpretation is supported by the loadings of the physiological variables on Function 1: Most somatomotor variables have high correlations with Function 1, as have skin conductance responses, shortened heart period, the forehead pulse volume amplitude, and alpha frequency reductions in the electroencephalogram.

Function 2 discriminates phases without from phases with anticipatory threat, such as the instruction periods (I1–I5, I7, I9), and the phases of speech preparation (B1–B3), as well as the fear induction phases (F1–F3), the first two number tasks (N1, N2), and the instructions for the first two imagery phases (M1, M2). Confirming the interpretation of this function as anticipatory threat is the observation that with repeated exposure to the same anticipatory situations, scores on Function 2 continuously become smaller, as notable, for example, in the speech preparation

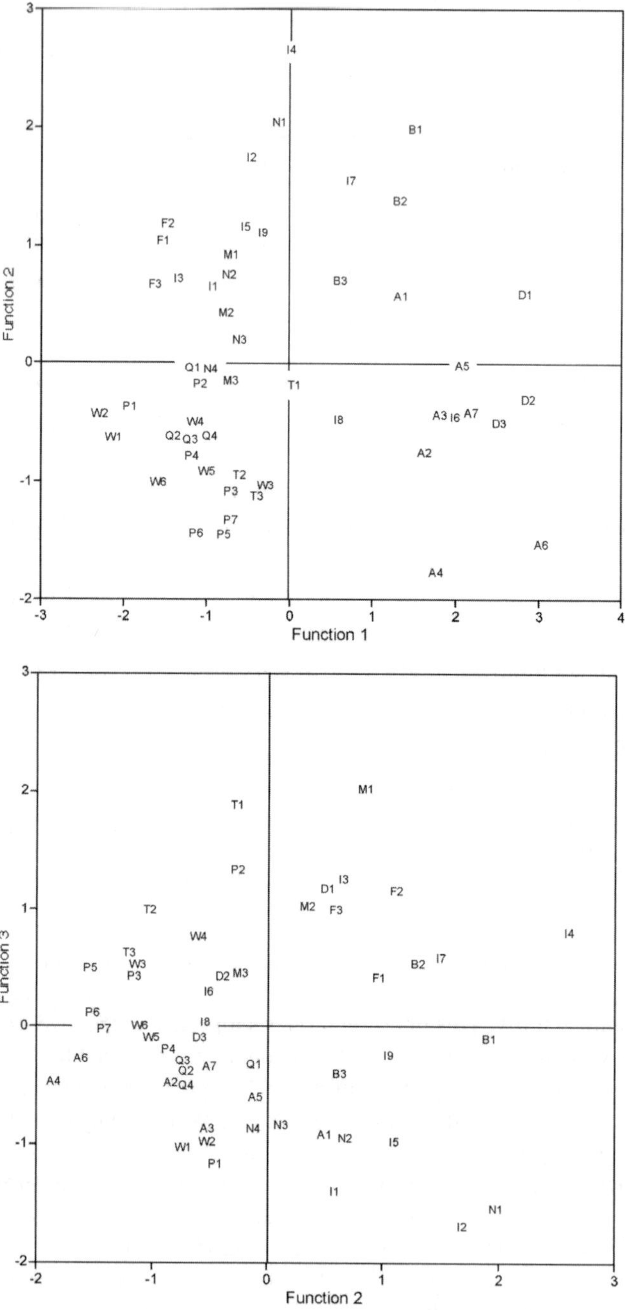

Fig. 2.1A and 2.1B. Physiological maps of 52 situations on the basis of 34 physiological variables and 42 participants (Stemmler, 1989). Labels are explained in Table 2.1. Upper panel—Discriminant Functions 1 and 2. Lower panel—Discriminant Functions 2 and 3.

phases (B1–B3). This interpretation is also supported by the physiological variables with high loadings on Function 2: The number of skin conductance responses, shortened heart period, reduced pulse transit time, finger vasoconstriction, slower breathing, and reduced electroencephalographic activity in the beta bands (15–24 Hz).

High values on Function 3 are seen for phases that presumably have self-relevance. These are situations that gave participants the opportunity to become confronted with personally relevant thoughts: during the first two speech tasks (D1, D2) and also after the speech tasks (T1–T3), when participants could ruminate about their story for a while; during the fear induction (I3, F1–F3) and after the anger induction (I6, W3, W4) extending into speech task 2 (I7, B2); during the instructions for imagery (M1–M3); and during some prestimulus phases. Physiological variables with high loadings on Function 3 were skin conductance level at the forehead ("emotional" sweating?), sustained trapezious muscle activity (tension in the shoulder), and lowered sustained frontalis muscle activity.

The plane of Function 2 and Function 3 (Fig. 2. 1, Panel b) is particularly interesting, because these functions have been given tentative psychological interpretations, "anticipatory threat" and "self-relevance," respectively. Following these interpretations, phases in the upper right quadrant should be characterized by a higher anticipatory threat and a higher self-relevance potential. This characterization applies to the instructions for the first two imagination tasks, instruction for and speech period of speech task 1, instruction for and before speech task 2, and the fear induction phases. Higher anticipatory threat and lower self-relevance (lower right quadrant) would be attributed to the three number tasks and the anagram task before the anger induction. Lower anticipatory threat and higher self-relevance (upper left quadrant) would describe the phases after the speech tasks and after the anger induction. Finally, lower anticipatory threat and lower self-relevance (lower left quadrant) would characterize waiting periods, the anger induction phases, and poststimulus phases. Clearly, the psychological attributes used in this paragraph are quite speculative and could be easily substituted by other terms.

The point to be made here is a different one, however. First, empirical psychophysiological data, like the ones in the example just presented, clearly match the view of modern physiology, that the body responds to various challenges, including emotions, in a highly differentiated manner. Given appropriate data sets, the analysis of physiological profiles is able to capture this differentiation (Fahrenberg, 1987; Lacey, 1967; Stemmler & Fahrenberg, 1989) in what has been called here the physiological state-space, or short, "physiological maps." Concepts such as "sympathetic mass action" or of somatovisceral arousal predominantly reflecting an intensity aspect of the behavioral response (unidimensional arousal) clearly have outlived their usefulness. Second, the example has demonstrated that there is an appreciable stability of physiological response patterns, that is, similar locations in state-space, on repetition of the "same" situation, such as the number or speech tasks. Of course, replication of a situation in one and the same experiment is impossible. Familiarization, learning, anticipation, ennui—these and other factors change the perceptions, threat values, and performances participants have of even identical tasks when presented repeatedly. Close inspection of the physiological maps presented earlier reveals that profiles of repeated situations are dislocated in roughly the same direction in state-space. It has been shown earlier that this effect is a consequence of changes alone in profile levels, that is, not necessarily of changes in profile patterns (Stemmler, 1988, 1992a, 2003). Finally, the example also showed that physiological response patterns are not only the physiological concomitants of observable behavior but also indicators of biological adaptations that are accompanied by distinct psychological states.

The conclusion of this section is that the autonomic nervous system is able to show, or better, is built to exhibit, "particular" activations. Why then shouldn't it initiate specific activations under emotions, which have specific functions for human adaptation?

PHYSIOLOGICAL SPECIFICITY OF EMOTION

The first objection against somatovisceral emotion specificity, that is, that autonomic activity is largely undifferentiated, is no longer tenable as has been discussed in the previous section. But what about the second objection, that instead of reflecting the arousal of a particular emotion, autonomic and somatomotor activity would indicate the demands of an action disposition, action tendency, or action proper? For example, Lang, Bradley, and Cuthbert (1990) proposed "that such physiological specificity in emotion may be tactical. That is, although specific action dispositions may be implicit in the conception of particular emotions (e.g., avoidance behavior with fear states, inhibition with sadness), they are also heavily modified by the demands of any specific context of expression" (p. 388).

Does Autonomic Activity Serve Only "Emotion Tactics?"

This objection presents a serious challenge to the notion of somatovisceral emotion specificity. Indeed, once that behavior is initiated, the somatovisceral activity is in the service of this behavior and putative autonomic differences among emotions will be blurred. However, before behavior begins, specific action dispositions and protective reflexes might be detectable. It is perhaps because of this narrow time window open for the identification of action dispositions and protective reflexes that Ekman (1994, p.16) suggested that emotions last in the realm of only minutes and seconds. In principle, laboratory experiments are capable of locating this time window; they are also more or less immune against the argument that specific behaviors would gain dominance over somatovisceral activity, simply because behavioral options are typically not available for the hooked-up participant.

However, even in the narrow time window where action dispositions and protective reflexes might reign over somatovisceral activation, still other, nonemotional influences could exert an effect on somatovisceral activation: background and focal stimuli; social factors, for example, to be alone or with others during an emotion episode; perception, attention, thinking; ambient temperature; or posture. In the following, the term *context* will be used to denote this ensemble of nonemotional physical, behavioral, social, and psychological factors that influence somatovisceral activation during or shortly after an emotion induction. Because studies on the psychophysiology of emotion have used not only many different ways to induce an emotion but also markedly different contexts in which these inductions were embedded, the purportedly low consistency of these studies' results (Cacioppo, Klein, Berntson, & Hatfield, 1993) would not come unexpectedly.

Beyond the context, emotions might still influence somatovisceral activation. But their effects would certainly be confounded with context effects, rendering their separate identification difficult. The typical scientific answer to problems of confounded effects is threefold: First, build one or more models that might describe the nature of the confound. Second, derive from these models adequate research strategies. Third, use the appropriate statistical methods to disentangle the confounded effects. In the following, I discuss the first two points; the third one is covered more fully in Stemmler (2003).

Models that describe the nature of the emotion-context confound are rare. Stemmler (1984, 1992b, 2003) has suggested four models of physiological emotion specificity, which are based on different assumptions about this confound. Nonspecificity of emotion holds that physiological responses are not an integral part of emotions (Averill, 1980; Cannon, 1929; Ginsburg & Harrington, 1996; Mandler, 1980; Ortony & Turner, 1990; S. Schachter, 1975; Valins, 1970). Physiological responses during emotions are produced by the nonemotional characteristics of the context of emotion induction. Absolute emotion specificity assumes that even across different contexts, at least some emotions are accompanied by specific physiological patterns (Alexander, 1950; Ekman, 1984, 1994; Lange, 1922; Levenson, 1988, 1992, 2003). Prototypical-behavior specificity assumes that emotions evoke specific action tendencies. Physiological adaptations prepare the organism for these prototypical behaviors. Granted that emotions are linked to functionally distinct behaviors (Plutchik, 1980), physiological response patterns could show some degree of specificity (Davidson, 1994; Frijda, 1986; Lang et al., 1990; Levenson, 1994) but also overlap. Context-deviation specificity views emotion specificity as a conditional concept. An emotional "stimulus" is assumed to modify a preexisting context-bound physiological pattern. Thus, somatovisceral emotion and context effects are usually confounded. Emotion specificity can be demonstrated only after this confound has been pulled apart. Emotion specificity is found whenever there are systematic and specific deviations of the emotion-plus-context pattern of physiological reactivity from the context-alone pattern. This position is the basis of experimental work that tries to find control conditions that are as similar as possible to the emotion inductions, yet stripped of their emotional content (Nyklicek, Thayer, & van Doornen, 1997; Sinha & Parsons, 1996; Stemmler, Heldmann, Pauls, & Scherer, 2001).

Research strategies that derive from these models are based on the general considerations of discriminant and convergent validation strategies (Campbell & Fiske, 1959). In emotion research, at least three different forms of discriminant validity (DV) and three forms of convergent validity (CV) can be distinguished:

- DV 1 (situational response specificity). Are the physiological profiles of the nonemotional contexts used for the emotion inductions different? To study DV 1, control groups are needed that are not exposed to a specific emotional arousal but to exactly the same induction context as the treatment groups. For example, Stemmler et al. (2001), in a repeated measures design, used a real-life and a recall context for the induction of both fear and anger. The response profiles of these contexts differed within the control groups.

- DV 2 (necessary condition for physiological emotion specificity). Is the physiological profile of an emotion induction different from the profile of its context? In the aforementioned study (Stemmler et al., 2001), the physiological real-life fear, real-life anger, and anger recall profiles were significantly different between treatment and control groups, meeting with the exception of the fear recall condition the necessary condition for physiological emotion specificity.

- DV 3 (sufficient condition for physiological emotion specificity). Are the physiological profiles of separate emotions after controlling for their contexts (DV 1) different? Ax (1953), in his classic study, compared fear and anger in two different real-life contexts, but context effects remained confounded with putative emotion effects. Studies that use imagination of different emotion episodes can more easily claim the equivalence of contexts (e.g., Contrada, Hilton, & Glass, 1991; de Jong-Meyer, Hubert, Ostkamp Hovekamp, & Vennen, 1993; Fridlund, Schwartz, & Fowler, 1984; Grossberg & Wilson, 1968; Levenson, Carstensen, Friesen, & Ekman, 1991; Levenson, Ekman, & Friesen, 1990; Roberts & Weerts, 1982; Schwartz, Weinberger, & Singer, 1981; Sinha, Lovallo, & Parsons, 1992; Stemmler, 1989; Waldstein et al., 2000). The explicit controlling of context effects in the comparison of fear and anger profiles has been reported in the study of Stemmler et al. (2001). After controlling for context effects, real-life fear and anger inductions elicited specific physiological profiles.

- CV 1 (situational response nonspecificity). If different emotions are elicited in the same context (e.g., imagination, films, pictures), are these nonemotional contexts equal across emotions? For the lack of appropriate control groups, this assumption has rarely been put to a test. Stemmler et al. (2001) did not find physiological profile differences between fear and anger during recall; differences emerged, however, during real life.

- CV 2 (nonspecificity of emotion intensity). Do the physiological profiles after the induction of differently intense but otherwise identical emotions have equal profile shapes (profile shape is the characteristic configuration of a profile, and it is independent of a profile's scatter and level)? A variation of the intensity of emotions has been accomplished through different cognitive sets (Dandoy & Goldstein, 1990; Lazarus & Alfert, 1964; Lazarus, Opton, Nomikos, & Rankin, 1965; Steptoe & Vögele, 1986), differently intense stimuli (Cacioppo, Petty, Losch, & Kim, 1986), or through the imagination of differently strong emotion episodes (Roberts & Weerts, 1982).
- CV 3 (necessary condition for physiological emotion specificity). Are the physiological profiles of one and the same emotion, which however is induced in different contexts, equal after controlling for their contexts (DV 1)? The directed facial action task and imagination were used as contexts for the induction of the same emotion (e.g., Ekman, Levenson, & Friesen, 1983; Fridlund et al., 1984; Levenson et al., 1990); a real life induction and imagination (Lang, Levin, Miller, & Kozak, 1983; Stemmler, 1989; Stemmler et al., 2001); film, recall, and imagination (Waldstein et al., 2000). However, a comparison of physiological profiles of one and the same emotion with context effects controlled has rarely been done, because appropriate control groups were missing.

A rigorous application of these validation strategies has seldom been employed in the literature. The often-cited inconsistency in the literature on physiological emotion specificity (Cacioppo et al., 1993) could thus be due to less than optimal research strategies if the model of context-deviation specificity were more valid than the model of absolute specificity. But how strong are these inconsistencies after all?

A Meta-Analysis of Studies Comparing Somatovisceral Effects of Fear and Anger

This meta-analysis is restricted to the comparison of the two negatively valenced emotions of fear and anger. Reasons for this choice are as follows: (a) The data base for physiological fear–anger comparisons is larger than for any other emotion combination (Cacioppo et al., 1993); (b) perhaps more importantly, fear and anger have been induced in different contexts: in real life settings, during imagination, and with the directed facial action task—real life inductions have not been used for emotions other than fear, anger, or happiness (Cacioppo et al., 1993); and (c) should they exist, somatovisceral differences between fear and anger cannot be attributed to their common negative valence.

The current meta-analysis includes 15 studies, which report fear and anger contrasts in at least two somatovisceral responses. Somatovisceral variables with at least three occurrences across these studies were used as separate outcome variables in the meta-analysis. Table 2.2 summarizes information about these studies including as potential moderator variables the induction context (real life, imagination, or directed facial action), the design of the emotion effect (within-subjects, i.e., repeated emotion inductions within individuals, or between-subjects, i.e., only one emotion induction per individual), and the design of the control strategy used (within-subjects comparison of emotion inductions with a rest, prestimulus, or poststimulus period, within-subjects comparison with a control condition that controls for context effects, and between-subjects comparison of emotion inductions in a treatment group with an emotionally "flat", but otherwise identical condition in a control group). Table 2.2 also reports the kind of primary data available for calculation of effect sizes. Because effect sizes could not be calculated from the available information, two otherwise pertinent studies were not included (Boiten, 1996; Miller et al., 1987). The study by Chessick, Bassan, and Shattan (1966) was excluded because the anger induction involved a strong and uncontrolled context demand (forced drinking).

Some studies report multiple contexts of emotion induction within the same individuals, for example, directed facial action and relived emotions (Levenson et al., 1991), or real life and imagery (Stemmler, 1989; Stemmler et al., 2001). In these cases, only one data set was chosen to ensure independence of effect sizes (Rosenthal, 1994). Averaging across data sets within these studies was inappropriate here because these studies reported significant interactions of Variables × Data Sets. To accumulate more studies within the directed facial action and the real-life sets of studies, the relived (Levenson et al., 1991) and the imagery data sets (Stemmler, 1989; Stemmler et al., 2001) were not included in the meta-analysis.

As a measure of effect size, the point-biserial correlation *r* was chosen. By convention, an *r* of .10 denotes a "weak" effect; an *r* of .30, a "medium" effect; and an *r* of .50, a "large" effect (Cohen & Cohen, 1983). For each study, effect sizes were calculated for three contrasts: (a) Fear versus Control (necessary condition for fear specificity, see DV 2 earlier), (b) Anger versus Control (necessary condition for anger specificity), and (c) Fear versus Anger (sufficient condition for fear–anger specificity, see DV 3 earlier). The direction of effects was coded as positive, whenever the predictions in Table 2.3 were met; otherwise, effects were coded as negative. These predictions represented the author's expectation that fear is characterized by a strong cardiovascular, beta-adrenergic-like activation together with somatomotor inhibition, reduced finger and face temperature, and a strong increase of electrodermal activity; whereas anger is characterized by a medium-to-strong cardiovascular, mixed alpha-adrenergic and beta-adrenergic activation together with muscle tensioning, increased finger and face temperature,

TABLE 2.2

Studies on Physiological Responses in Fear and Anger Used in Meta-Analysis

Study	*N*	*Induction Context*	*Variables*	*Emotion Effect*	*Control Strategy*	*Effect Size Calculation*
1) Ax (1953)	43	RL	HR, SBP, DBP, TmpFi, TmpFa, SCR#, RSP, EMG frontalis	w-Ss	w-Ss(rest) prestimulus periods	by *M*, *SD*
2) Funkenstein, King, and Drolette (1954)	9, 21[c]	RL	HR, SBP, DBP	b-Ss	w-Ss(rest) initial rest period	by *M*, *SD*
3) J. Schachter (1957)	48	RL	SBP, DBP, TmpFi, TmpFa, RSP, EMG frontalis	w-Ss	w-Ss(rest) prestimulus periods	by *M*, *F*-value, adjusted[a] HR and SCR# excluded[b]
4) Adsett, Schottstaedt, and Wolf (1962)	5, 9[c]	RL	HR, SBP, DBP, SV, CO, TPR	b-Ss	w-Ss(rest) initial rest period	by *M*, *SD*
5) Schwartz, Weinberger, and Singer (1981)	32	IM	HR, SBP, DBP	w-Ss	w-Ss(ctxt) control imagery	by *M*, *F*-value, adjusted[a]
6) Roberts and Weerts (1982)	16	IM	HR, SBP, DBP	w-Ss	w-Ss(rest) prestimulus periods	by *M*, *SD*
7) Stemmler (1989)	42	RL	HR, TmpFi, TmpFa, SCR#, SCL, RSP, EMG extensor digitorum	w-Ss	w-Ss(rest) poststimulus periods of preceding number tasks	by *M*, *SD*

TABLE 2.2 (cont.)

Study	*N*	*Induction Context*	*Variables*	*Emotion Effect*	*Control Strategy*	*Effect Size Calculation*
9) Levenson, Cartensen, Friesen, and Ekman (1991)	20	DF	HR, TmpFi	w-Ss	w-Ss(ctxt) standard control face	by *M*, *SEM* from Figure 1
10) Levenson, Ekman, Heider, and Friesen (1992)	27	DF	HR, TmpFi, SCL, RSP	w-Ss	w-Ss(ctxt) standard control face	by *M*, *SEM*
11) Sinha,Lovallo, and Parsons (1992)	27	IM	HR, SBP, DBP, SV, CO, TPR	w-Ss	w-Ss(ctxt) neutral imagery	by *M*, *SD*
12) Uchiyama (1992)	6	RL	HR, SBP, DBP, SCR#, RSP	w-Ss	w-Ss(rest) initial rest period	by *M*, *SD*
13) Sinha and Parsons (1996)	27	IM	HR, SBP, DBP, TmpFi, SCL	w-Ss	w-Ss(ctxt) neutral imagery	by *M*, *SD*
14) Prkachin, Wil-liams-Avery, Zwaal, and Mills (1999)	31	IM	HR, SBP, DBP, SV, CO	w-Ss	w-Ss(ctxt) control imagery	by *M*, *SD*[d]
15) Stemmler, Heldmann, Pauls, and Scherer (2001)	79, 79[c]	RL	HR, SBP, DBP, SV, CO, TPR, TmpFi, TmpFa, SCR#, SCL, RSP, EMG extensor digitorum	b-Ss	w-Ss(rest) initial rest, b-Ss(ctxt) control group	by *M*, *SD*

TABLE 2.2 (cont.)

Notes: HR = Heart rate. SB = Systolic blood pressure. DBP = Diastolic blood pressure. SV = Stroke volume. CO = Cardiac output. TPR = Total peripheral resistance. TmpFi = Skin temperature finger. TmpFa = Skin temperature face. SCR# = Number of skin conductance responses. SCL = Skin conductance level. RSP = Respiration rate. EMG = Electromyogram. RL = Real life. IM = Imagination. DF = Directed facial action. W-Ss = Within-subjects emotion design. B-Ss = Between-subjects emotion design. W-Ss(rest) = Within-subjects control with rest, prestimulus, or poststimulus baseline. W-Ss(ctxt) = Within-subjects control of context. B-Ss(ctxt) = Between-subjects control of context with a control group exposed to identical but non-emotional context.

[a]Mean square errors were derived from treatment means and *F*-values and then used to calculate effect sizes. Mean square errors from repeated measures analyses of variance lead, however, to an inflation of effect size estimates, in the case of the correlation effect size *r*, by 1/sqrt(1 – *s*) with s = correlation between repeated conditions (Dunlap, Cortina, Vaslow, & Burke, 1996). To keep this study in the meta-analysis, s was assumed to be .70 and a corrected $r_c = r^*\text{sqrt}(1-s)$ was calculated. This nearly halved the original effect size estimate.

[b]HR was excluded because of heterogeneous variance across emotion conditions. SCR# was excluded because the reported *F*-value was unbelievably large leading to a miniscule mean square error.

[c]The first number gives the sample size in the fear, the second number, the sample size in the anger population.

[d]Data supplied by the author.

TABLE 2.3

Predictions of Effect Directions in Fear (F), Anger (A), and Control (C) Contrasts

Variable	*Fear vs. Control*	*Anger vs. Control*	*Fear vs. Anger*
CO	F>C	A>C	F>A
DBP	F>C	A>C	F<A
EMG	F<C	A>C	F<A
HR	F>C	A>C	F>A
RSP	F>C	A>C	F>A
SBP	F>C	A>C	F>A
SCL	F>C	A>C	F>A
SCR#	F>C	A>C	F>A
SV	F<C	A>C	F<A
TmpFa	F<C	A>C	F<A
TmpFi	F<C	A>C	F<A
TPR	F<C	A>C	F<A

Note. CO = Cardiac output. DBP = Diastolic blood pressure. EMG = Electromyogram. HR = Heart rate. RSP = Respiration rate. SBP = Systolic blood pressure. SCL = Skin conductance level. SCR# = Number of skin conductance responses. SV = Stroke volume. TmpFa = Skin temperature face. TmpFi = Skin temperature finger. TPR = Total peripheral resistance.

and a medium increase of electrodermal activity. Meta-analysis proceeded by converting *r*s to Fisher's *Z* and weighting them by the inverse of the variance of *Z*. Results are reported in terms of weighted mean *r*s, their two-tailed 95% confidence interval, and a chi-square statistic *Q* depicting heterogeneity of effect sizes across studies included in each weighted mean *r*.

Meta-Analysis on the Fear Versus Control Contrast. "Large" effects were observed for systolic blood pressure, heart rate, and number of skin conductance responses; "medium" effects for cardiac output, diastolic blood pressure, respiration rate, and finger temperature; and "small" effects for stroke volume and total peripheral resistance (Table 2.4). The direction of these effects was as predicted. Contrary to prediction was the finding of zero effects for skin conductance level, face temperature, and of a "small," negative effect for muscle tension, indicating an increase during fear compared to control conditions. Fig. 2.2 illustrates the pattern of effects just as the contrasts depict them (i.e., fear minus control, anger minus control, fear minus anger) disregarding the predicted direction of the contrasts.

TABLE 2.4

Results of Meta-Analysis by Physiological Variable and Emotion Contrast

		Fear vs. Control				Anger vs. Control				Fear vs. Anger			
Variable	*k*	*N*	WMR	95%–CI	*Q*	*N*	WMR	95%–CI	*Q*	*N*	WMR	95%–CI	*Q*
CO	4	142	.39**	.24–.53	13.36**	146	.21*	.04–.36	4.17	230	.20**	.07–.32	12.51**
DBP	11	322	.42**	.32–.51	43.74**	338	.62**	.54–.68	64.31**	431	.21**	.12–.30	34.11**
EMG	4	212	-.16*	-.29– -.02	63.59**	212	.46**	.34–.56	32.02**	291	.18**	.07–.29	25.43**
HR	14	426	.55**	.48–.62	71.20**	442	.57**	.50–.63	51.65**	535	.08	-.01–.16	19.42**
RSP	7	307	.40**	.30–.49	16.44*	307	.23**	.11–.33	17.51**	386	.20**	.10–.30	6.35
SBP	11	323	.64**	.57–.70	44.00**	339	.67**	.60–.73	56.35**	432	.03	-.07–.12	6.74
SCL	5	237	.06	-.07–.19	12.42*	237	.24**	.11–.36	2.33	316	-.09	-.20–.02	10.01*
SCR#	4	170	.50**	.37–.60	5.52	170	.47**	.34–.58	26.74**	249	.01	-.12–.13	23.63**
SV	4	142	.21*	.04–.36	9.96*	146	-.30**	-.45– -.14	7.89*	230	-.06	-.19–.07	3.20
TmpFa	4	212	.01	-.13–.14	52.16**	212	.32**	.19–.44	27.33**	291	.22**	.11–.33	34.47**
TmpFi	8	348	.32**	.22–.42	80.49**	348	-.16**	-.27– -.06	69.72**	427	.09	-.01–.18	8.47
TPR	3	111	.28**	.09–.45	2.28	115	.16	-.02–.34	11.45**	199	.21**	.07–.34	14.45**

Note: WMR is the weighted mean correlation effect size of *k* independent studies with a total of *N* participants. CI = Confidence interval around WMR. *Q* is a chi-square statistic with $df = k–1$ testing the null hypothesis that the *k* studies have homogeneous effect sizes. CO = Cardiac output. DBP = Diastolic blood pressure. EMG = Electromyogram. HR = Heart rate. RSP = Respiration rate. SBP = Systolic blood pressure. SCL = Skin conductance level. SCR# = Number of skin conductance responses. SV = Stroke volume. TmpFa = Skin temperature face. TmpFi = Skin temperature finger. TPR = Total peripheral resistance.

$*p < .05$.

$**p < .01$.

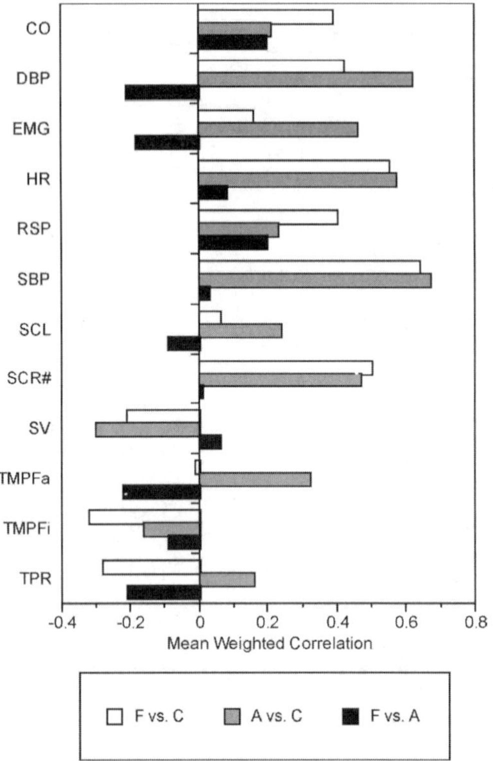

Fig. 2.2. Effect size display of meta-analysis of contrasts Fear (F) versus Control (C). Anger (A) versus Control, and Fear versus Anger. The direction of the effect sizes is based on the actual values of the contrasts, not on the expected directions of contrasts. CO = cardiac output; DBP = diastolic blood pressure; EMG = electromyogram; HR = heart rate; RSP = respiration rate; SBP = systolic blood pressure; SCL = skin conductance level; SCR# = number of skin conductance responses; SV = stroke volume; TmpFa = skin temperature face; TmpFi = skin temperature finger; TPR = total peripheral resistance.

Meta-Analysis on the Anger Versus Control Contrast. "Large" effects were noted for systolic and diastolic blood pressure and for heart rate; "medium" effects for number of skin conductance responses, somatomotor activity, and face temperature; "small" effects for cardiac output, skin conductance level, and respiration rate (Table 2.4). The effect of total peripheral resistance was only marginally significant ($p = .07$). Contrary to expectation, stroke volume as well as finger temperature were consistently smaller during anger than control. Again, Fig. 2.2 illustrates these effect sizes as explained earlier.

Meta-Analysis on the Fear Versus Anger Contrast. Differences between fear and anger responses had only "small" effect sizes. As predicted, cardiac output and respiration rate were larger during fear than anger; and diastolic blood pressure, muscle tension, face temperature, and total peripheral resistance were larger during anger than fear (Table 2.4, Fig. 2.2). Thus, there is consistent evidence that in 6 out of 12 variables studied, fear and anger exhibited differentially strong somatovisceral responses. Three variables—cardiac output, total peripheral resistance, and respiration rate—showed both the necessary (fear vs. control) and the sufficient conditions (fear vs. anger) for fear specificity. Three variables—diastolic blood pressure, somatomotor activity, and face temperature—showed both the necessary (anger vs. control) and the sufficient conditions (fear vs. anger) for anger specificity. This is quite a different picture than painted by critics of the specificity position or summarized by Cacioppo et al. (1993).

It is interesting to note, however, that specificity of emotion response is not seen in heart rate, systolic blood pressure, number of skin conductance responses, or finger temperature. Thus, we can observe both a marked degree of specificity and a considerable degree of overlap in somatovisceral fear and anger responses. It remains to be noted that for many variables, the Q statistic is significant. This indicates that the studies integrated in one mean weighted correlation do not exhibit homogeneous effect sizes. We now turn to the question of whether the moderator variables specified in Table 2.2 capture some of this variance. The analysis of moderator variables was restricted to data sets with at least 10 studies. This criterion left only the heart rate and the diastolic and systolic blood pressure data sets.

Moderator "Emotion Induction Context." In heart rate, there were virtually no differences among the induction contexts of imagination, real life, and directed facial action with respect to the effect sizes of the emotion versus control contrasts (Table 2.5). Differences among contexts were, however, notable in the fear versus anger contrast: Fear had a larger average effect size than anger in the real-life context. In diastolic blood pressure, the real-life context elicited a larger average fear versus control effect size than imagination; the reverse was true for the fear versus anger contrast, where the imagination context made the average effect size larger than the real-life context. Systolic blood pressure's effect sizes were not influenced by the emotion induction context. In conclusion, diastolic blood pressure in particular seems to be sensitive to the emotion induction context; the fear versus anger contrast is more accentuated during imagination.

Moderator "Design of Emotion Effect." In heart rate, fear versus control and fear vresus anger contrasts had larger average effect sizes in studies using a between-subjects emotion design than in studies with a within-subjects design (Table 2.6). Conversely, diastolic blood pressure exhibited larger average effect sizes for the anger versus control and the fear versus anger contrasts in the within-subjects design of the emotion effect. Systolic blood pressure's effect sizes were once again not influenced by the moderator. In sum, heart rate and diastolic blood pressure seem to profit differently from the design of the emotion effect. The fear versus anger contrast for heart rate is stronger in between-subjects designs, but for diastolic blood pressure, it is stronger in within-subjects designs.

TABLE 2.5

Meta-Analysis Results Qualified by Emotion Induction Context

		Imagination				*Real Life*				*Directed Facial Action*			
Emotion Contrast	Q_b	*k*	WMR	95%–CI	Q_w	*k*	WMR	95%–CI	Q_w	*k*	WMR	95%–CI	Q_w
							Heart Rate						
Fear vs. Control	4.52	5	.58**	.45–.69	15.25**	6	.60**	.50–.69	49.84**	3	.41**	.24–.56	1.59
Anger vs. Control	.08	5	.58**	.45–.69	11.51**	6	.56**	.46–.65	37.57**	3	.56**	.42–.68	2.50
Fear vs. Anger	6.60*	5	-.02	-.20–.16	.07	6	.18**	.06–.29	11.38*	3	-.09	-.27–.11	1.36
							Diastolic Blood Pressure						
Fear vs. Control	9.35**	5	.22*	.04–.38	.40	6	.53**	.41–.63	33.99**				
Anger vs. Control	.34	5	.64**	.52–.74	19.18**	6	.60**	.50–.68	44.80**				
Fear vs. Anger	13.90**	5	.47**	.31–.59	14.85**	6	.09	-.02–.21	5.36				
							Systolic Blood Pressure						
Fear vs. Control	.57	5	.61**	.48–.71	18.48**	6	.66**	.57–.74	24.95**				
Anger vs. Control	2.06	5	.61**	.48–.71	15.46**	6	.70**	.62–.77	38.83**				
Fear vs. Anger	.54	5	-.03	-.21–.15	.37	6	.05	-.06–.17	5.83				

Note: Q_b is a chi-square statistic with $df = 1$ (diastolic and systolic blood pressure) or 2 (heart rate) or testing the null hypothesis of no differences in the weighted mean correlation effect size (WMR) across emotion induction contexts; Q_w tests for the homogeneity of the effect sizes of the *k* studies within emotion induction contexts, $df = k - 1$. CI = Confidence interval.

$^*p < .05$.

$^{**}p < .01$.

TABLE 2.6

Meta-Analysis Results Qualified by Design of Emotion Effect

		Between-Subjects Design				*Within-Subjects Design*			
Emotion Contrast	Q_b	*k*	WMR	95%–CI	Q_w	*k*	WMR	95%–CI	Q_w
		Heart Rate							
Fear vs. Control	4.91*	3	.68**	.55–.78	1.14	11	.51**	.42–.59	65.15**
Anger vs. Control	.36	3	.53**	.38–.66	.38	11	.58**	.50–.65	50.90**
Fear vs. Anger	10.80**	3	.25**	.12–.38	3.06	11	-.04	-.15–.07	5.56
		Diastolic Blood Pressure							
Fear vs. Control	2.76	3	.28**	.08–.46	1.32	8	.47**	.35–.57	39.90**
Anger vs. Control	6.84**	3	.47**	.30–.60	17.71**	8	.68**	.59–.74	39.76**
Fear vs. Anger	7.90**	3	.07	-.07–.21	3.88	8	.34**	.21–.45	22.32**
		Systolic Blood Pressure							
Fear vs. Control	.69	3	.59**	.43–.71	8.71*	8	.66**	.57–.73	34.59**
Anger vs. Control	.15	3	.65**	.52–.75	11.05**	8	.68**	.60–.74	45.14**
Fear vs. Anger	.00	3	.03	-.11–.17	5.23	8	.02	-.11–.16	1.51

Note: Q_b is a chi-square statistic with *df* = 1 for testing the null hypothesis of no differences in the weighted mean correlation effect size (WMR) across designs of emotion effect; Q_w tests for the homogeneity of the effect sizes of the *k* studies within designs of emotion effect, *df* = *k* – 1. CI = Confidence interval.

*$p < .05$.

**$p < .01$.

Moderator "Design of Control Strategy." Average effect sizes in diastolic blood pressure were influenced by the design of the control strategy (Table 2.7). Studies using a within-subjects control with rest evidenced larger fear versus control effects than studies using context control. Conversely, context control yielded larger average fear versus anger effect sizes than the control by a rest period. In systolic blood pressure, the average effect size of the anger versus control contrast was larger in studies employing the control by a rest period than context control. In heart rate, no moderator effects were observed. These results demonstrate that in comparison with the control by a rest period, context control tends to reduce some emotion effects but enhances the fear versus anger effect in diastolic blood pressure. This is exactly what has been expected under the notion of context-deviation specificity and underscores the importance of context control for guarding against unwarranted influences of the context of emotion induction itself.

In sum, the meta-analysis of studies comparing somatovisceral effects of fear and anger revealed a notable degree of specificity. Thus, not only is the peripheral nervous system equipped for a precise and specific neuronal regulation of its target organs and not only do psychophysiological recordings show the existence of situation-specific patterns ("physiological maps"), but it is also the case that in accordance with a functional view, emotions allocate specific bodily resources to help achieve their goals. Now we turn to the question of whether physiological emotion profiles can inform us about just what are these goals.

The Challenge of Unspecific Responses: Of Overlap, Mechanisms, and Context Confounds

Earlier it was stated that the meta-analysis unveiled a considerable degree of somatovisceral fear and anger specificity, but at the same time showed a marked overlap of "unspecific" fear and anger responses. Unspecific responses are those that exhibit significant weighted mean effect sizes of the fear versus control or the anger versus control contrasts without significant differences between fear and anger. Overlapping unspecific responses were observed for heart rate, systolic blood pressure, number of skin conductance responses, and finger temperature. It could well be that these variables are a genuine part of the physiologies of fear and anger, for example, because both of them mobilize for action. Thus, to completely understand the physiological "signature" of an emotion and its functional meaning, both specific responses and overlapping unspecific responses must be considered.

Somatovisceral emotion specificity has often been discussed on the level of individual variables like heart rate or blood pressure. Alternatively, emotion specificity could as well be studied on the level of mechanisms: Emotions might be specifically linked to different brain or neurohormonal mechanisms, which contribute to the unique organismic adaptation during an emotion. However, in a particular autonomic variable, different combinations of these mechanisms might

TABLE 2.7

Meta-Analysis Results Qualified by Design of Control Strategy

Emotion Contrast	Q_b	*Within-Subjects Control with Rest*				*Within-Subjects Control of Context*			
		k	WMR	95%–CI	Q_w	*k*	WMR	95%–CI	Q_w
		Heart Rate							
Fear vs. Control	1.27	6	.58**	.44–.70	50.30**	7	.49**	.38–.58	16.67*
Anger vs. Control	.15	6	.59**	.46–.70	38.78**	7	.56**	.46–.70	12.69*
Fear vs. Anger	2.78	6	.13	-.04–.29	11.41*	7	–.05	-.19–.08	1.64
		Diastolic Blood Pressure							
Fear vs. Control	16.76**	6	.66**	.53–.75	22.75**	4	.22*	.03–.39	.40
Anger vs. Control	2.02	6	.74**	.65–.81	24.57**	4	.64**	.51–.74	19.17**
Fear vs. Anger	4.80*	6	.23**	.06–.38	2.78	4	.47**	.31–.61	14.75**
		Systolic Blood Pressure							
Fear vs. Control	3.73	6	.74**	.64–.81	18.68**	4	.60**	.46–.70	18.21**
Anger vs. Control	7.97**	6	.78**	.70–.84	28.79**	4	.59**	.45–.70	14.75**
Fear vs. Anger	.58	6	.09	-.08–.25	5.90	4	–.01	-.20–.18	.06

produce the same response under fear and anger, making the responses unspecific (Berntson, Cacioppo, & Quigley, 1994; Berntson, Cacioppo, Quigley, & Fabro, 1994; Stemmler, 1991, 1993).

One example for a mechanism-based model of emotion specificity is the adrenaline–noradrenaline hypothesis of fear and anger proposed by Funkenstein (Funkenstein, 1955, 1956; Funkenstein, King, & Drolette, 1954). According to this proposal, the autonomic signature of fear corresponds to the effects of adrenaline, and that of anger, to the mixed effects of noradrenaline and adrenaline (see also Breggin, 1964; Wagner, 1989). The effects of adrenaline include reductions in finger temperature (redistribution of blood from the periphery to skeletal muscles) and increases in heart rate, systolic blood pressure, stroke volume, cardiac output, number of skin conductance responses, and respiration rate. The effects of noradrenaline include increases in systolic and diastolic blood pressure, number of skin conductance responses, and in total peripheral resistance, which via baroreceptor-linked increased cardiac vagal tonus reduces heart rate (Chessick et al., 1966; Löllgen, Meuret, Just, & Wiemers, 1985; Wenger et al., 1960).

Two variables that should show the difference between the autonomic effects of adrenaline and a mixture of noradrenaline plus adrenaline are diastolic blood pressure and total peripheral resistance, both of which should be larger under the influence of noradrenaline, that is, under anger. This expected effect indeed corresponds to the results of the meta-analysis (see Fig. 2.2). The observed overlap of unspecific responses during fear and anger in systolic blood pressure and in number of skin conductance responses would also be predicted by the Funkenstein (1955) hypothesis.

However, the increase of diastolic blood pressure under fear is inconsistent with the adrenaline hypothesis of fear. It has been shown in the moderator analyses (Table 2.5) that the real life context of the fear induction produced significantly larger effect sizes in diastolic blood pressure than the imagination context. Thus, part of this inconsistency of the observed diastolic blood pressure response under fear with the adrenaline hypothesis of fear is clearly due to the cardiovascular demands of the induction context.

Another inconsistency of observed and expected outcomes under the Funkenstein (1955) hypothesis are the heart rate and cardiac output increases as well as the finger temperature decrease under anger. With respect to heart rate, none of the moderator analyses offered a clue as to why anger elicited a heart rate response as large as during fear. This inconsistency could only be explained by assuming that the anger inductions led to an overtly strong adrenaline response as part of the suggested noradrenaline plus adrenaline excretion pattern under anger. Thus, the Funkenstein hypothesis is able to explain only part of the picture displayed in Fig. 2.2.

Another mechanism-based model of emotion specificity could refer to major receptor types in the autonomic nervous system. For example, alpha-adrenergic, beta-adrenergic, and cholinergic cardiovascular tonus might be described as distal mechanisms and diastolic blood pressure as a proximal variable. Blockade studies suggested that diastolic blood pressure rises both with alpha-adrenergic tone (Nelson, Silke, Hussain, Verma, & Taylor, 1984) and with loss of vagal tone (Knoebel, McHenry, Phillips, & Widlansky, 1974; Levine & Leenen, 1989; Martin et al., 1974). In contrast, diastolic blood pressure is not controlled by beta-adrenergic tone under resting conditions (Silke, Nelson, Ahuja, Okoli, & Taylor, 1983). Thus, diastolic blood pressure will rise both during an alpha-adrenergic state and during a state of vagal withdrawal. The unspecific increases of diastolic blood pressure in the real-life inductions of both fear and anger (Table 2.5) could have been produced by different mechanisms: an alpha-adrenergic state in the case of anger and a state of vagal withdrawal in the case of fear. But why were diastolic blood pressure responses specific during imagination?

The action of different mechanisms during emotions is obviously not the complete picture. As has been posited in the context-deviation model of emotion specificity, the somatovisceral effects of emotions are necessarily confounded with the prevailing context effects. Conceivably, a particular context may render an emotion response unspecific that in a different context is specific. In the case of diastolic blood pressure discussed earlier (Table 2.5), the fear versus anger weighted mean r (WMR) during imagination was approaching a "large" effect (WMR = .46), whereas during real life, it was not different from zero (WMR = .09). The data show that this discrepancy in effect size was a consequence of the significantly different fear versus control effect sizes during imagination (WMR = .22) and real life (WMR = .53). In contrast, under imagination and real life the effect sizes of anger versus control were practically equal (WMR = .63 and .60, respectively). It appears then that the real-life fear context had a unique influence on the fear versus control effect size rendering the fear versus anger effect unspecific.

To conclude, overlap in the physiological fear and anger profiles could represent common mechanisms such as to be expected under the Funkenstein (1955) hypothesis or under an autonomic receptor-based view of organ regulation. In addition, the context of emotion induction exerts a marked influence on whether overlap exists. All responses, unspecific or specific, need consideration when the functional meaning of the emotion physiologies are to be explored.

A Component Model of Somatovisceral Response Organization in Emotion

It has been argued that the identification of emotion-specific somato-visceral patterns is hampered by the fact that more than one influence may impinge on various target organs of the somatic and autonomic nervous systems. As explicitly recognized by the context-deviation model of emotion specificity, such multiple influences necessarily impair the signal-to-noise ratio for the identification of physiological "emotion signatures." Two influences have been discussed thus far: effects of the nonemotional context and effects of an emotion proper. A recently proposed "component model of somatovisceral emotion specificity" (Stemmler et al., 2001) suggests an additional source of influence on somatovisceral activations:

1. The first component is characterized by the nonemotional context of emotion induction, such as posture, ambient temperature, ongoing motor activity, or demands by cognitive processes, which are not in the service of an emotion.

2. The second component reflects specific somatovisceral adaptations, which have two prominent functions: the protection of the organism through autonomic reflexes and the preparation of the organism for prototypical behaviors. These somatovisceral emotion signatures are recognizable only during a rather short temporal window after the arousal of an emotion and before actual behavior has started.

3. The third component embraces effects of organismic, behavioral, and mental demands, which are necessitated by the momentary situation in the pursuit of an emotion goal, for example, running toward a safe place. Thus, when an organism enters an emotional state, this component allows for a flexible organization of bodily resources given the momentary situational circumstances. For example, where an opportunity for "fight or flight" arises, the defense reflex is likely to be activated, because it prepares an organism "to cope with an emergency and specifically to perform the extreme muscular exertion of flight or attack" (Hilton, 1982, p. 159). Depending on the context as it is physically laid out and as the individual perceives and understands it, responses elicited by this third component may produce a marked overlap of physiological responses across emotions.

What could be the functional value of somatovisceral signatures of fear and anger? To begin with anger, this emotion is in its basic sense a neurobehavioral system, which motivates an individual to avoid failure through the goal of removing an obstacle and gaining superiority. Plutchik (1980) called the prototypical adaptation pattern of anger "destruction." Attack is a common behavioral response which requires a strong activation of sympathetic systems for its support. Yet I propose that the core signature of anger is a circulatory response to enable sustained muscular strength in addition to a preactivation of alpha-motoneurons. Isometric exercise is an analog of the kind of somatovisceral changes to expect. At the core of the response to isometric exercise is a rise in diastolic blood pressure and in peripheral resistance, which function in opposition to the reduced effective perfusion pressures in the regions of intense muscle contraction (Buell, Alpert, & McCrory, 1986; Shanks, 1984). This pattern is seen already in anticipation of handgrip tasks (Mäntysaari, Antila, & Peltonen, 1988).

Fear in its basic sense is a neurobehavioral system, which motivates an individual to avoid failure through the goal of escaping threat. Plutchik (1980) called its prototypical adaptation pattern "protection." Although flight is a common behavioral response if opportunities for escape exist, fear also tends to obstruct escape by making us tremble, think inefficiently, or even faint. I propose that the somatovisceral core signature of fear is not the support of an action tendency but a protective circulatory response in anticipation of life threatening severe blood loss. Hemorrhage is the likely outcome of a predator's attack and once it happens, hypovolemic shock develops (Larsen, 1996): The sympathetic nervous systems are strongly activated with increased heart rate, myocardial contractility, and respiration rate. The blood distribution is "centralized" to ensure blood supply to the heart and the brain. Centralization is accomplished through a strong alpha-adrenergically mediated vasoconstriction of renal, muscular, splanchnical, and dermal arterial and postcapillar venous blood vessels. This blood redistribution is recognizable as paleness of the face and coldness of the hands. I propose that the somatovisceral signature of fear is a very mild form of the hypovolemic shock syndrome, with a variably strong alpha-adrenergic response contribution depending on fear intensity. Thus, from this account, a decreased muscle blood flow as well as diastolic blood pressure and total peripheral resistance increases are expected during strong fear.

SUMMARY

In this chapter I have tried to argue that emotion physiologies, at least in some emotions, are distinct. The principal arguments were that

- emotions have distinct goals and need differentiated somatovisceral activations for body protection or behavior preparation.
- the anatomy and physiology of the autonomic nervous systems are built to allow fine-tuned regulations: Specific autonomic responses are possible, and they are necessary. The brain orchestrates coordinated autonomic regulation patterns.
- differentiated regulation patterns can be described in the state-space of physiological responses. Such "physiological maps" show both stability and change along expected trajectories.
- despite many methodological inconsistencies, a meta-analysis of the available research literature demonstrates a considerable degree of somatovisceral fear versus anger specificity. I have argued that unspecific but overlapping emotion responses should not be disregarded when describing physiological signatures of emotion. A considerable influence of the context of emotion induction was found.

- emotion physiologies combine at least three different components: the nonemotional context, specific somatovisceral adaptations or "emotion signatures," and the effects of demands necessitated by the momentary situation in the pursuit of an emotion goal.

Many questions remain to be answered. But there is enough solid ground to build on, as I hope this chapter has shown.

REFERENCES

Adsett, C. A., Schottstaedt, W. W., & Wolf, S. G. (1962). Changes in coronary blood flow and other hemodynamic indicators induced by stressful interviews. *Psychosomatic Medicine, 24*, 331–336.

Alexander, F. (1950). *Psychosomatic Medicine: Its principles and applications*. New York: Norton.

Allport, G. W. (1937). *Personality: A psychological interpretation*. New York: Holt.

Averill, J. R. (1980). A constructivist view of emotion. In R. Plutchik & H. Kellerman (Eds.), *Emotion. Theory, research, and experience* (Vol. 1, pp. 305–339). New York: Academic.

Ax, A. F. (1953). The physiological differentiation between fear and anger in humans. *Psychosomatic Medicine, 15*, 433–442.

Bandler, R., Keay, K. A., Floyd, N., & Price, J. (2000). Central circuits mediating patterned autonomic activity during active vs. passive emotional coping. *Brain Research Bulletin, 53*, 95–104.

Berntson, G. G., Cacioppo, J. T., & Quigley, K. S. (1991). Autonomic determinism: The modes of autonomic control, the doctrine of autonomic space, and the laws of autonomic constraint. *Psychological Review, 98*, 459–487.

Berntson, G. G., Cacioppo, J. T., & Quigley, K. S. (1994). Autonomic cardiac control. I. Estimation and validation from pharmacological blockades. *Psychophysiology, 31*, 572–585.

Berntson, G. G., Cacioppo, J. T., Quigley, K. S., & Fabro, V. T. (1994). Autonomic space and psychophysiological response. *Psychophysiology, 31*, 44–61.

Boiten, F. (1996). Autonomic response patterns during voluntary facial action. *Psychophysiology, 33*, 123–131.

Breggin, P. R. (1964). The psychophysiology of anxiety. *Journal of Nervous and Mental Disease, 139*, 558–568.

Buell, J. C., Alpert, B. S., & McCrory, W. W. (1986). Physical stressors as elicitors of cardiovascular reactivity. In K. A. Matthews, S. M. Weiss, T. Detre, T. M. Dembrowski, B. Falkner, S. B. Manuck, & R. B. Williams (Eds.), *Handbook of stress, reactivity, and cardiovascular disease* (pp. 127–144). New York: Wiley.

Cacioppo, J. T., Klein, D. J., Berntson, G. G., & Hatfield, E. (1993). The psychophysiology of emotion. In M. Lewis & J. M. Haviland (Eds.), *Handbook of emotions* (pp. 119–142). New York: Guilford.

Cacioppo, J. T., Petty, R. E., Losch, M. E., & Kim, H. S. (1986). Electromyographic activity over facial muscle regions can differentiate the valence and intensity of affective reactions. *Journal of Personality and Social Psychology, 50*, 260–268.

Campbell, D. T., & Fiske, D. W. (1959). Convergent and discriminant validation by the multitrait–multimethod matrix. *Psychological Bulletin, 56*, 81–105.
Cannon, W. B. (1927). The James-Lange theory of emotions: A critical examination and an alternative theory. *American Journal of Psychology, 39*, 106–124.
Cannon, W. B. (1929). *Bodily changes in pain, hunger, fear and rage*. New York: Appleton–Century–Crofts.
Chessick, R. D., Bassan, M., & Shattan, S. (1966). A comparison of the effect of infused catecholamines and certain affect states. *American Journal of Psychiatry, 123*, 156–165.
Cohen, J., & Cohen, P. (1983). *Applied multiple regression/correlation analysis for the behavioral sciences* (2nd ed.). Hillsdale, NJ: Lawrence Erlbaum Associates, Inc.
Contrada, R. J., Hilton, W. F. J., & Glass, D. C. (1991). Effects of emotional imagery on physiological and facial responses in Type A and Type B individuals. *Journal of Psychosomatic Research, 35*, 391–397.
Damasio, A. R. (1994). *Descartes' error. Emotion, reason, and the human brain*. New York: Avon Books.
Dandoy, A. C., & Goldstein, A. G. (1990). The use of cognitive appraisal to reduce stress reactions: A replication. *Journal of Social Behavior and Personality, 5*, 275–285.
Davidson, R. J. (1993). Parsing affective space: Perspectives from neuropsychology and psychophysiology. *Neuropsychology, 7*, 464–475.
Davidson, R. J. (1994). Complexities in the search for emotion-specific physiology. In P. Ekman & R. J. Davidson (Eds.), *The nature of emotion: Fundamental questions* (pp. 237–242). New York: Oxford University Press.
de Jong-Meyer, R., Hubert, W., Ostkamp Hovekamp, G., & Vennen, J. (1993). Bodily sensations, facial EMG, and autonomic changes in the course of prolonged emotional imagery. *Journal of Psychophysiology, 7*, 34–45.
Dunlap, W. P., Cortina, J. M., Vaslow, J. B., & Burke, M. J. (1996). Meta-analysis of experiments with matched groups or repeated measures designs. *Psychological Methods, 1*, 170–177.
Ekman, P. (1984). Expression and the nature of emotion. In K. R. Scherer & P. Ekman (Eds.), *Approaches to emotion: A book of readings* (pp. 319–343). Hillsdale, NJ: Lawrence Erlbaum Associates, Inc.
Ekman, P. (1994). All emotions are basic. In P. Ekman & R. J. Davidson (Eds.), *The nature of emotion: Fundamental questions* (pp. 15–19). New York: Oxford University Press.
Ekman, P., & Davidson, R. J. (Eds.). (1994). *The nature of emotion: Fundamental questions*. New York: Oxford University Press.
Ekman, P., Levenson, R. W., & Friesen, W. V. (1983). Autonomic nervous system activity distinguishes among emotions. *Science, 221*, 1208–1210.
Engel, B. T. (1960). Stimulus-response and individual-response specificity. *Archives of General Psychiatry, 2*, 305–313.
Fahrenberg, J. (1986). Psychophysiological individuality: A pattern analytic approach to personality research and psychosomatic medicine. *Advances in Behaviour Research and Therapy, 8*, 43–100.
Fahrenberg, J. (1987). Theory in psychophysiology: The multi-component analysis of psychophysiological reactivity. *Journal of Psychophysiology, 1*, 9–11.
Floyd, N. S., Price, J. L., Ferry, A. T., Keay, K. A., & Bandler, R. (2001). Orbitomedial prefrontal cortical projections to hypothalamus in the rat. *Journal of Comparative Neurology, 432*, 307–328.

Foerster, F. (1985). Psychophysiological response specificities: A replication over a 12-month period. *Biological Psychology, 21*, 169–182.

Foerster, F., Schneider, H.-J., & Walschburger, P. (1983). The differentiation of individual-specific, stimulus-specific, and motivation-specific response patterns in activation processes: An inquiry investigating their stability and possible importance in psychophysiology. *Biological Psychology, 17*, 1–26.

Folkow, B. (2000). Perspectives on the integrative functions of the 'sympatho-adrenomedullary system.' *Autonomic Neuroscience, 83*(3), 101–115.

Fridlund, A. J., Schwartz, G. E., & Fowler, S. C. (1984). Pattern recognition of self-reported emotional state from multiple-site facial EMG activity during affective imagery. *Psychophysiology, 21*, 622–637.

Frijda, N. (1986). *The emotions*. Cambridge, England: Cambridge University Press.

Funkenstein, D. H. (1955). The physiology of fear and anger. *Scientific American, 192*, 74–80.

Funkenstein, D. H. (1956). Nor-epinephrine-like and epinephrine-like substances in relation to human behavior. *Journal of Nervous and Mental Disease, 124*, 58–68.

Funkenstein, D. H., King, S. H., & Drolette, M. (1954). The direction of anger during a laboratory stress-inducing situation. *Psychosomatic Medicine, 16*, 404–413.

Gellhorn, E. (1970). The emotions and the ergotropic and trophotropic systems. *Psychologische Forschung, 34*, 48–94.

Ginsburg, G. P., & Harrington, M. E. (1996). Bodily states and context in situated lines of action. In R. Harré & W. G. Parrott (Eds.), *Emotions* (pp. 229–258). London: Sage.

Gray, J. A. (1994). Three fundamental emotion systems. In P. Ekman & R. J. Davidson (Eds.), *The nature of emotion: Fundamental questions* (pp. 243–247). New York: Oxford University Press.

Grossberg, J. M., & Wilson, H. K. (1968). Physiological changes accompanying the visualization of fearful and neutral situations. *Journal of Personality and Social Psychology, 10*, 124–133.

Hilton, S. M. (1982). The defence-arousal system and its relevance for circulatory and respiratory control. *Journal of Experimental Biology, 100*, 159–174.

Izard, C. E. (1993). Four systems for emotion activation: Cognitive and noncognitive processes. *Psychological Review, 100*, 68–90.

James, W. (1884). What is emotion? *Mind, 19*, 188–205.

Jänig, W. (1988). The function of the autonomic system as interface between body and environment. Old and new concepts: W. B. Cannon and W. R. Hess revisited. In D. Hellhammer, I. Florin, & H. Weiner (Eds.), *Neurobiological approaches to human disease* (pp. 143–173). Toronto, Canada: Huber.

Jänig, W. (2003). The autonomic nervous system and its co-ordination by the brain. In R. J. Davidson, H. H. Goldsmith, & K. R. Scherer (Eds.), *Handbook of affective science* (pp. 135–186). New York: Oxford University Press.

Jänig, W., & Häbler, H.-J. (2000). Specificity in the organization of the autonomic nervous system: A basis for precise neural regulation of homeostatic and protective body functions. *Progress in Brain Research, 122*, 273–287.

Jänig, W., & McLachlan, E. M. (1992). Specialized functional pathways are the building blocks of the autonomic nervous system. *Journal of the Autonomic Nervous System, 41*, 3–14.

Knoebel, S. B., McHenry, P. L., Phillips, J. F., & Widlansky, S. (1974). Atropine-induced cardioacceleration and myocardial blood flow in subjects with and without coronary artery disease. *American Journal of Cardiology, 33*, 327–332.

Koizumi, K., Terui, N., & Kollai, M. (1983). Neural control of the heart: Significance of double innervation re-examined. *Journal of the Autonomic Nervous System, 7*, 279–294.

Lacey, J. I. (1967). Somatic response patterning and stress: Some revisions of activation theory. In M. H. Appley & R. Trumbull (Eds.), *Psychological stress* (pp. 14–37). New York: Appleton-Century-Crofts.

Lang, P. J., Bradley, M. M., & Cuthbert, B. N. (1990). Emotion, attention, and the startle reflex. *Psychological Review, 97*, 377–395.

Lang, P. J., Levin, D. N., Miller, G. A., & Kozak, M. J. (1983). Fear behavior, fear imagery, and the psychophysiology of emotion: The problem of affective response integration. *Journal of Abnormal Psychology, 92*, 276–306.

Lange, C. (1922). *The emotions* (I. A. Haupt, Trans.). Baltimore: Williams & Wilkins. (Original work published 1885)

Langley, J. N. (1921). *The autonomic nervous system. Part I.* Cambridge, England: Heffer.

Larsen, P. (1996). *Anästhesie* [Anesthesia]. München, Germany: Urban & Schwarzenberg.

Lazarus, R. S., & Alfert, E. (1964). Short-circuiting of threat by experimentally altering cognitive appraisal. *Journal of Abnormal and Social Psychology, 69*, 195–205.

Lazarus, R. S., Opton, E. M. J., Nomikos, M. S., & Rankin, N. O. (1965). The principle of short-circuiting of threat: further evidence. *Journal of Personality, 33*, 622–635.

Levenson, R. W. (1988). Emotion and the autonomic nervous system: a prospectus for research on autonomic specificity. In H. L. Wagner (Ed.), *Social psychophysiology and emotion: theory and clinical applications* (pp. 17–42). Chichester, England: Wiley.

Levenson, R. W. (1992). Autonomic nervous system differences among emotions. *Psychological Science, 3*, 23–27.

Levenson, R. W. (1994). The search for autonomic specificity. In P. Ekman & R. J. Davidson (Eds.), *The nature of emotion: Fundamental questions* (pp. 252–257). New York: Oxford University Press.

Levenson, R. W. (2003). Autonomic specificity and emotion. In R. J. Davidson, H. H. Goldsmith, & K. R. Scherer (Eds.), *Handbook of affective science* (pp. 212–224). New York: Oxford University Press.

Levenson, R. W., Carstensen, L. L., Friesen, W. V., & Ekman, P. (1991). Emotion, physiology, and expression in old age. *Psychology and Aging, 6*, 28–35.

Levenson, R. W., Ekman, P., & Friesen, W. V. (1990). Voluntary facial action generates emotion-specific autonomic nervous system activity. *Psychophysiology, 27*, 363–384.

Levenson, R. W., Ekman, P., Heider, K., & Friesen, W. V. (1992). Emotion and autonomic nervous system activity in the Minangkabau of West Sumatra. *Journal of Personality and Social Psychology, 62*, 972–988.

Levine, M. A., & Leenen, F. H. (1989). Role of beta 1-receptors and vagal tone in cardiac inotropic and chronotropic responses to a beta 2-agonist in humans. *Circulation, 79*, 107–115.

Löllgen, H., Meuret, G., Just, H., & Wiemers, K. (1985). Sympathikomimetika in der Notfall- und Intensivmedizin[Sympathicomimetics in emerging and intensive care medicine]. *Deutsches Ärzteblatt, 82*, 1951–1955.

Mandler, G. (1980). The generation of emotion: A psychological theory. In R. Plutchik & H. Kellerman (Eds.), *Emotion. Theory, research, and experience* (Vol. 1, pp. 219–243). New York: Academic.

Mäntysaari, M. J., Antila, K. J., & Peltonen, T. E. (1988). Circulatory effects of anticipation in a light isometric handgrip test. *Psychophysiology, 25*, 179–184.

Martin, C. E., Shaver, J. A., Leon, D. F., Thompson, M. E., Reddy, P. S., & Leonard, J. J. (1974). Autonomic mechanisms in hemodynamic responses to isometric exercise. *Journal of Clinical Investigation, 54*, 104–115.

Miller, G. A., Levin, D. N., Kozak, M. J., Cook, E. W., McLean, A., & Lang, P. J. (1987). Individual differences in imagery and the psychophysiology of emotion. *Cognition and Emotion, 1*, 367–390.

Nelson, G. I., Silke, B., Hussain, M., Verma, S. P., & Taylor, S. H. (1984). Rest and exercise hemodynamic effects of sequential alpha-1- adrenoceptor (trimazosin) and beta-adrenoceptor (propranolol) antagonism in essential hypertension. *American Heart Journal, 108*, 124–131.

Nesse, R. M. (1990). Evolutionary explanations of emotions. *Human Nature, 1*, 261–289.

Nyklicek, I., Thayer, J. F., & van Doornen, L. J. P. (1997). Cardiorespiratory differentiation of musically-induced emotions. *Journal of Psychophysiology, 11*, 304–321.

Oken, D., Heath, H., Shipman, W., Goldstein, I. B., Grinker, R. R., & Fish, J. (1966). The specificity of response to stressful stimuli. *Archives of General Psychiatry, 15*, 624–634.

Ortony, A., & Turner, T. J. (1990). What's basic about basic emotions? *Psychological Review, 97*, 315–331.

Plutchik, R. (1980). *Emotion—A psychoevolutionary synthesis*. New York: Harper & Row.

Plutchik, R. (1997). The circumplex as a general model of the structure of emotions and personality. In R. Plutchik & H. R. Conte (Eds.), *Circumplex models of personality and emotion* (pp. 17–45). Washington, DC: American Psychological Association.

Prkachin, K. M., Williams-Avery, R. M., Zwaal, C., & Mills, D. E. (1999). Cardiovascular changes during induced emotion: An application of Lang's theory of emotional imagery. *Journal of Psychosomatic Research, 47*, 255–267.

Roberts, R. J., & Weerts, T. C. (1982). Cardiovascular responding during anger and fear imagery. *Psychological Reports, 50*, 219–230.

Rosenthal, R. (1994). Parametric measures of effect size. In H. Cooper & L. V. Hedges (Eds.), *The handbook of research synthesis* (pp. 231–244). New York: Russell Sage Foundation.

Schachter, J. (1957). Pain, fear, and anger in hypertensives and normotensives. *Psychosomatic Medicine, 19*, 17–29.

Schachter, S. (1975). Cognition and peripheralist—centralist controversies in motivation and emotion. In M. S. Gazzaniga & C. Blakemore (Eds.), *Handbook of psychobiology* (pp. 529–564). New York: Academic.

Schwartz, G. E., Weinberger, D. A., & Singer, J. A. (1981). Cardiovascular differentiation of happiness, sadness, anger, and fear following imagery and exercise. *Psychosomatic Medicine, 43*, 343–364.

Selye, H. (1979). The stress concept and some of its implications. In V. Hamilton & D. M. Warburton (Eds.), *Human stress and cognition: An information processing approach* (pp. 11–32). New York: Wiley.

Shanks, R. G. (1984). The physiological role of alpha- and beta-adrenoceptors in the regional circulation. In W. Kobinger & R. P. Ahlquist (Eds.), *Alpha and beta adrenoceptors and the cardiovascular system* (pp. 109–123). Princeton, NJ: Excerpta Medica.

Silke, B., Nelson, G. I., Ahuja, R. C., Okoli, R. C., & Taylor, S. H. (1983). Comparative haemodynamic dose-response effects of intravenous propranolol and pindolol in patients with coronary heart disease. *European Journal of Clinical Pharmacology, 25*, 157–165.

Sinha, R., Lovallo, W. R., & Parsons, O. A. (1992). Cardiovascular differentiation of emotions. *Psychosomatic Medicine, 54*, 422–435.

Sinha, R., & Parsons, O. A. (1996). Multivariate response patterning of fear and anger. *Cognition and Emotion, 10*, 173–198.

Stemmler, G. (1984). *Psychophysiologische Emotionsmuster* [Psychophysiological patterns of emotions]. Frankfurt, Germany: Lang.

Stemmler, G. (1988). Effects of profile elevation, scatter, and shape on discriminant analysis results. *Educational and Psychological Measurement, 48*, 853–871.

Stemmler, G. (1989). The autonomic differentiation of emotions revisited: Convergent and discriminant validation. *Psychophysiology, 26*, 617–632.

Stemmler, G. (1991). Cardiovascular activation components: Their estimation and use for task characterizations. *Psychophysiology, 28*, S 52.

Stemmler, G. (1992a). *Differential psychophysiology: Persons in situations*. New York: Springer.

Stemmler, G. (1992b). The vagueness of specificity: Models of peripheral physiological emotion specificity in emotion theories and their experimental discriminability. *Journal of Psychophysiology, 6*, 17–28.

Stemmler, G. (1993). Receptor antagonists as tools for structural measurement in psychophysiology. *Neuropsychobiology, 28*, 47–53.

Stemmler, G. (2003). Methodological considerations in the psychophysiological study of emotion. In R. J. Davidson, H. H. Goldsmith, & K. R. Scherer (Eds.), *Handbook of affective science* (pp. 225–255). New York: Oxford University Press.

Stemmler, G., & Fahrenberg, J. (1989). Psychophysiological assessment: Conceptual, psychometric, and statistical issues. In G. Turpin (Ed.), *Handbook of clinical psychophysiology* (pp. 71–104). Chichester, England: Wiley.

Stemmler, G., Heldmann, M., Pauls, C. A., & Scherer, T. (2001). Constraints for emotion specificity in fear and anger: The context counts. *Psychophysiology, 38*, 275–291.

Steptoe, A., & Vögele, C. (1986). Are stress responses influenced by cognitive appraisal? An experimental comparison of coping strategies. *British Journal of Psychology, 77*, 243–255.

Uchiyama, I. (1992). Differentiation of fear, anger, and joy. *Perceptual and Motor Skills, 74*, 663–667.

Valins, S. (1970). The perception and labeling of bodily changes as determinants of emotional behavior. In P. Black (Ed.), *Physiological correlates of emotion* (pp. 229–243). New York: Academic.

Wagner, H. (1989). The peripheral physiological differentiation of emotions. In H. Wagner & A. Manstead (Eds.), *Handbook of social psychophysiology* (pp. 77–98). Chichester, England: Wiley.

Waldstein, S. R., Kop, W. J., Schmidt, L. A., Haufler, A. J., Krantz, D. S., & Fox, N. A. (2000). Frontal electrocortical and cardiovascular reactivity during happiness and anger. *Biological Psychology, 55*, 3–23.

Wenger, M. A., Clemens, T. L., Darsie, M. L., Engel, B. T., Estess, F. M., & Sonnenschein, R. R. (1960). Autonomic response patterns during intravenous infusion of epinephrine and nor-epinephrine. *Psychosomatic Medicine, 22*, 294–307.

3

Cognitive Regulation of Emotion: Application to Clinical Disorders

Pierre Philippot, Céline Baeyens,
Céline Douilliez, and Benjamin Francart
University of Louvain, Belgium

This chapter investigates how multilevel models of emotion contribute to our understanding of the cognitive mechanisms that regulate emotion. A theoretical framework, attempting to synthesize different multilevel cognitive models of emotion, is presented. This framework distinguishes between different types of processes and structures and shows how emotion and its regulation entail a complex interacting system, including automatic and controlled processes that converge in certain cases and diverge in other cases. The model also demonstrates how all important domains of cognition are recruited by emotion and its regulation: perception, attention, memory, decision making, and consciousness. Then, cognitive processes leading to emotion regulation are considered within that framework. Finally, empirical evidence for such processes is reviewed with a special focus on attention, autobiographical memory, and consciousness.

Common sense and folk theories of psychology often pit cognition against emotion. The former would reflect high level processes related to intelligence and voluntary decision making; the latter would be akin to low level processes, such as instincts, operating automatically and beyond one's volition. In the past, this dichotomy has also been emphasized in scientific psychology and raised a debate that culminated with the controversy between Zajonc (1984), who promoted a strict distinction between cognition and emotion that was summarized in his aphorism "preference needs no inference," and Lazarus (1984), who defended the notion that no emotion can arise without a cognitive appraisal attributing an emotional meaning to a situation. Since then, most researchers agree that this debate is more an issue of semantic controversy over the definition of *cognition* than a real theoretical issue (Leventhal & Scherer, 1987). There is now a strong consensus that emotion is elicited, supported, and regulated by a variety of cognitive processes, many of which are implicit and automatic in nature (Öhman, 1999).

Schematically, cognitive processes take place at the input and output levels in emotional phenomena. At the input level, situations, whether external or internal stimuli, are appraised as either emotionally significant or emotionally insignificant. This appraisal process is cognitive in nature and relies on a range of cognitive processes operating at various levels of automaticity, voluntariness, and complexity (Leventhal & Scherer, 1987; Smith & Kirby, 2000). At the output level, emotional states prime or facilitate specific cognitive modes. For instance, Christianson (1992) has shown that negative emotion biases attention toward the focal aspects of the situation that are emotionally relevant. Such focal attention might feed back in continuous appraisal, biasing the evaluation of the situation toward the activated emotion (McNally, 1995). Thus, from a regulation perspective, emotion might be modulated at different stages through cognitive processes: through appraisal that gives emotional meaning to a situation (Butler and Gross, this volume) and through the cognitive processing mode that is elicited by the emotional state.

In this chapter, we explore the different cognitive processes that might operate in emotion regulation. We first present a cognitive model of emotion that will serve as theoretical framework articulating different cognitive regulation processes. Then, we turn to specific aspects of the cognitive regulation of emotion, examining successively attentional aspects, memory processes, consciousness, and awareness of emotional experience. We conclude by integrating these different aspects, examining their clinical implications, and suggesting future directions for research.

MULTILEVEL COGNITIVE MODELS OF EMOTION

Traditionally, cognitive models of emotion have focused on the central question of how emotional meaning is ascribed to a situation. Such research has identified a series of dimensions, such as novelty, valence, goal congruence, or potency, along which a situation is evaluated to yield emotional meaning and which accounts for the nature of emotional feelings and responses (e.g., Roseman, Antoniou, & Jose, 1996; Scherer, 2001). Recently, that approach has been criticized for its excessive "cognitivism" (Scherer, 2001), for being descriptive rather than explicative, and for not integrating the knowledge cognitive sciences have accumulated on basic processes such as attention or memory (Philippot & Schaefer, 2001). Consequently, an alternative to classic cognitive models of emotion, pioneered by Leventhal (1984), has recently gained interest: multilevel modeling of emotion (Philippot & Schaefer, 2001; Power & Dalgleish, 1997; Smith & Kirby, 2000; Teasdale & Barnard, 1993). This approach is based on the premises that emotional information can be processed on at least two distinct levels and that the outputs of these levels lead to different emotional consequences. The type of emotional memory activated and the type of processes operating are central to multilevel models. These cognitive models are also remarkably consistent with recent neurological evidence, such as that presented by Bechara (this volume). These characteristics suggest that multilevel models are excellent candidates for understanding how emotion is cognitively regulated.

Observing important convergences among the different multilevel models proposed in the literature (Leventhal, 1984; Power & Dalgleish, 1997; Smith & Kirby, 2000; Teasdale & Barnard, 1993), we have recently attempted an integration of these models: the dual memory model of emotion. The development of this model was driven by our ambition to provide a theoretical framework both for our experimental research on the cognitive regulation of emotion (Philippot & Schaefer, 2001) and for our clinical practice with emotional disorders (Philippot, Deplus, Schaefer, Baeyens, & Falise, 2001). In the next sections, we present this model.

The basic characteristic of the dual memory model architecture is the distinction between the types of memory—the structure—involved in the elicitation and regulation of emotion and the processes operating on these structures. At the structural level, two types of memory systems are postulated, a "schematic" system and a "propositional" system. These two types represent a distinction common to all multilevel models. The schematic system refers to an implicit memory that conveys the immediate emotional meaning of a situation for a given individual. The propositional system pertains to declarative, conceptual knowledge about emotion. The schematic and the propositional system receive their input from different systems—the sensory and the object recognition systems, respectively—and in turn feed into different output systems (e.g., the body response system). The structures postulated in the dual memory model are illustrated in Fig. 3.1. At the process level, different types of processes operating on these structures are postulated. They differ in terms of automaticity and voluntariness and of consciousness. Before specifying these processes, we detail the structural level, following the natural flow of information.

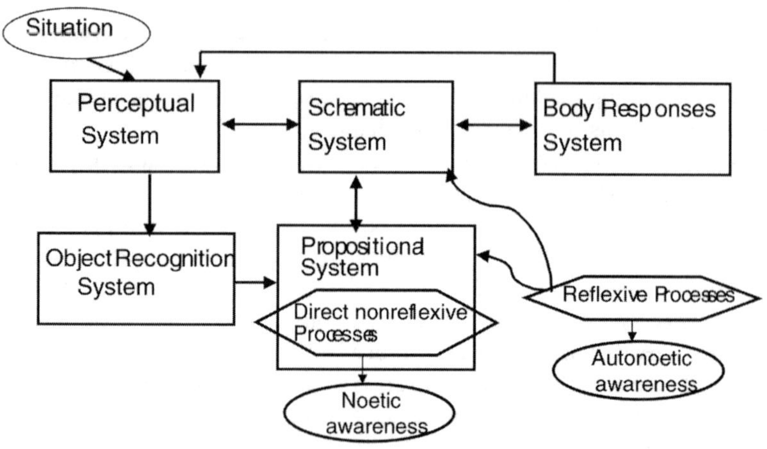

Fig. 3.1. Architecture of the Dual Memory Model of Emotion

The Structures Involved in the Dual Memory Model

The Perceptual System. Raw sensory input from each perceptual modality is automatically integrated and analyzed to extract basic perceptual features. For example, features of shape, movement pattern, and depth are extracted from raw visual input. There are different systems for different sensory modalities. These structures are innate and develop early in ontogeny, and they have an innate output to the body response system. That is, certain patterns of perceptual stimulation, automatically identified at the perceptual system level, automatically trigger specific body responses. For instance, a sudden loud noise, which has the perceptual feature of unanticipated stimulation, automatically triggers a startle response.

The Body Response System. Body responses in emotion are organized to support logistically certain types of interactions between the organism and its environment (see the development of this idea in Pauls and in Stemmler, this volume). The concept of action tendency has been proposed by Frijda (1986) to account for this notion. These body responses encompass facial expression, body postures and movements, as well as the whole range of visceral responses (see Stemmler, this volume, for an in-depth analysis of this topic). A set of such prepared body responses is innate, and organizes the first emotional responses in ontogeny with the aim of fostering the survival of individuals, their social integration, and their affective and intellectual development. Frijda (1986) has proposed eight innate action tendencies in the human species: approach, inhibition, play, dominance, submission, aggression, rejection, and panic. Each of these action tendencies is supported by a specific body state.

The body response system can be activated directly by outputs from the perceptual system. Early in ontogeny, this automatic and innate connection between perceptual and body responses systems constitutes the first manifestations of emotion. For instance, an infant's perception of loss of support will automatically trigger the panic body response system. Such innate responses can still be observed in adulthood, such as in the example of startle mentioned earlier. Innate body responses constitute the building blocks of later, more elaborate—yet still automatic—responses.

Automatic links between the perceptual and the body response systems correspond to the concept of primary emotion proposed by Damasio (1994; see also Bechara, this volume) and to the concept of sensory-motor level proposed by Leventhal (1984).

The Schematic System. The schematic system (or implicational subsystem, following Barnard & Teasdale, 1991; or associative processing, according to Smith & Kirby, 2000) is based on schemata: A schema is an abstract and implicit representation which integrates sensory, perceptual, and semantic information typical of a given category of emotional experiences, on the one hand, and their relation to the activation of specific body response systems, on the other hand. All authors do not agree on the specific nature of schemata: Some see them as associative representations, whereas others view them as analogical or metaphoric representations. Following the germinal work of Leventhal (1984), we propose that schemata can be conceptualized as the records of the individual's emotional classical conditioning. When perceptual elements are repeatedly activated at the same time as innate connections between perceptual features and body responses, they become integrated in an abstract representation that encodes high order reoccurrences between the activation of perceptual—and, later in ontogeny, semantic—elements and body responses. For example, touch and odor features of the mother's breast are perceptual features that automatically trigger an approach body response in the newborn. Repeated associations between experiences of activation of these basic innate features and the approach response, together with new features, such as auditory features of the mother's voice or the smell of her perfume, will become integrated in a schema.

Several authors endorse the assumption that each schema carries an implicit meaning which can be conceived of as a holistic theme (e.g.,the notion of core relational theme proposed by Lazarus, 1991). For example, the theme of "hopelessness-lost" is hypothesized to underlie the schema of "sadness." Some have proposed that the implicit holistic meanings carried by the schemata are best expressed in metaphors or in poetry (Teasdale & Barnard, 1993).

In sum, schemata are built automatically by abstracting communalities in the similar experiences lived by an individual. Direct experience is the only means wherebyinformation can enter into a schema. The schema, as a representation, is not available to consciousness. However, its content can be inferred based upon the changes it induces in feelings and body state.

The Object Recognition System. Once basic perceptual features have been identified by the perceptual system, they can feed into another cognitive system that allows their identification as an "object." For instance, a specific visual pattern of lines and of a square surface can be identified as a chair; a pattern of noise can be recognize as a bird song or as a word. The cognitive ability to identify a stability in perceptual information and to recognize objects develops very early in infancy (Lindsay & Norman, 1977). It allows for the construction of discrete mental representations, the concepts that are the building blocks of the propositional system.

The Propositional System. The propositional system consists of declarative knowledge about emotion. Representation units of this system are discrete concepts about the different elements of emotional situations. These concepts are linked with one another through specific relations that obey the laws of semantic propositional logic. In contrast to the schematic system, the meaning stored in the propositional system is thus specific and has a "truth validity" (i.e., a meaning statement can be declared true or false). For instance, the knowledge that A should feel anger against B if B prevents A's pursuit of an important goal and B acts intentionally, can be declared true, whereas the statement that A should feel sadness when receiving a pleasant present can be declared false. Knowledge at the propositional level can be activated willfully and consciously. It constitutes the basis for conscious identification of emotion, for verbal communication about emotion, and for willful problem solving and coping in emotional situations. Any source of information that can be translated into propositional networks of concepts can be incorporated in the propositional representational system. Thus, it can be augmented through conversation, readings, and the like. The capacity of this representational system is potentially unlimited.

Processes Operating on the Schematic and Propositional Systems

As mentioned in the preceding section, different types of processes can operate on the information contained in the schematic and propositional systems. These processes differ in terms of automaticity and voluntariness, in terms of consciousness, and in terms of the output they produce.

Automatic Processes and Conscious Processes. At the schematic level, processes are automatic and unconscious. The activation of any facet of a schema has the potential to activate the whole representation. An important aspect of these automatic processes is that activation is bidirectional. Indeed, as these representations are associative in nature, information can flow in one direction as well as in the other. For instance, a schema can activate one or more specific body response systems. Conversely, the activation of a response system can trigger a related schema. At the neurological level, this circular activation has been described as an "as if" loop in the brain, in which central body makers can reactivate a "primary" emotion representation (Bechara, this volume; Damasio, 1994). Thus, the activation of a body state can feed back positively in the activation of a schema in two ways: first, centrally, by the direct association between schemata and body response systems; and secondly, peripherally, via the production of actual body responses that feed into the schema via the perceptual system. A large literature has demonstrated that the activation of a specific body state activates the other facets of the corresponding emotion responses, be it via the face (Matsumoto, 1987), the posture (Stepper & Strack, 1993), or respiration (Philippot, Chapelle, & Blairy, 2002).

Similarly, although perceptual indexes from the perceptual system automatically activate the related schema, the activation of a schema will automatically influence the activity of the perceptual system by lowering the perceptual threshold for indexes congruent with the schema. There is some evidence of this phenomenon in the clinical literature. For instance, trait social anxiety, which can be conceptualized as the chronic activation of a social fear schema, is characterized by a lowered perceptual threshold for threatening face, a very relevant stimulus for the social fear schema (Mogg & Bradley, in press; see the next sections for a further development of this point).

At the propositional level, different types of processes can be activated. Some processes are automatic and unconscious. For instance, some concepts can be activated at an unconscious level and influence subsequent processing of information, as in priming effects. However, information at the propositional level can also be made conscious; propositions—i.e., networks of concepts and their relations—can be sufficiently activated to be transferred into working memory and made conscious. We can thus deliberately activate our knowledge about emotion, identify and label our emotional states, talk about them, and make decisions about how to behave. Indeed, these are the main functions attributed by most multilevel theorists to the conscious processes operating in the propositional system.

Reflexive Processes. However, there is another class of processes that operates on both the schematic and the propositional representations and that enables reflexive consciousness of emotional experience. Two types of consciousness, producing different phenomenological experiences and mental phenomena (such as memory experiences), have been proposed: noetic and autonoetic consciousness (Tulving, 1985; Wheeler, Stuss, & Tulving, 1997). In a state of noetic awareness,[1] individuals experience the direct consciousness of being aware of things, of knowing them. For example, we can know that once, we have been angry against X, but without being able to remember or to reevoke the specific experience of it. In the state of autonoetic awareness, individuals are experiencing a reflexive type of consciousness: They know they are or have been the subjects of a specific experience. We can remember and reactivate the experience of that anger episode against X. These qualities of consciousness apply to past as well as to future or present events. For instance, awaiting a thesis defense, "Alex" can not only know that he is anxious (noetic awareness) given his jittery state, pounding heart, and apprehensive ruminations, but he can also realize that he is the subject of a specific emotional experience and consciously experience himself as being anxious, or, in other words, feel himself as experiencing anxiety (autonoetic awareness).

The capacity for autonoetic consciousness, and the processes that underlie that capacity, allow for several mental phenomena that might be uniquely human and that would thus characterize human emotions and their regulation. First, autonoetic consciousness allows the mind to travel in time. As demonstrated by Wheeler et al. (1997), this capacity is necessary to remember past specific personal experiences, as well as to envision hypothetical future personal experiences. For instance, brain-damaged patients who have lost the capacity for autonoetic consciousness not only cannot remember past personal experience, but, correlatively, they cannot envision future ones (see Wheeler et al., 1997, for a review of this question). This capacity to travel in time would be uniquely human, as suggested by a recent meta-analysis of the animal literature (William, 2002).

Autonoetic consciousness also allows for the capacity to produce voluntarily and immediately an emotional experience via mental imagery. Clinical evidence supporting this notion has been gathered in our laboratory. In a profoundly amnesiac individual, "A. C.," we have demonstrated that this absence of autonoetic capacities was associated with the inability to recollect any past personal experience or to envision future personal experience but was also associated with the inability to produce any emotion via mental imagery (Chapelle, Philippot, & Vanderlinden, 1996). However, as compared to controls, A. C. evidenced perfectly normal emotional reactions in immediate emotional situations. For instance, when exposed to emotional film clips or slides, his expressive, physiological, and subjective responses were well within the normal range. A. C. had also perfectly preserved his emotional knowledge at the propositional level, holding, for instance, the same expectations than controls about the elicitors and responses that are most typical of given emotions.

These two types of phenomenological experience—on the one hand simply "knowing" that oneself is anxious, and on the other hand, being self-reflexively aware that oneself is experiencing anxiety—require different processing of emotional information. In the present theoretical framework, the state of noetic awareness requires only the conscious activation of propositional information. In contrast, the state of autonoetic awareness implies the strategic combination of both schematic and propositional information. This statement is based on a notion presented by Conway and Pleydell–Pearce (2000), who suggested that voluntary activation of personally and emotionally relevant memories (or predictions about future experiences) implies the combination of two sources of information: one pertaining to "event-specific knowledge"—in the present framework, to a specific propositional network of concepts describing the event in its factual specificity—and the other pertaining to the emotional implications of the event—in the present framework, to a schema. According to Conway and Pleydell–Pearce, human autobiographical memory would have confronted a dilemma in its evolution. On the one hand, the capacity to reevoke past experiences and their emotional impact yields obvious adaptive advantages (see Bechara, this volume). On the other hand, if each time one reevoked an emotional memory, the (potentially strong) emotional state that one initially experienced was reactivated, the whole cognitive system could be disrupted by the emotional arousal and would start to disfunction. Conway and Pleydell–Pearce have proposed that to protect itself against such catastrophic functioning, human autobiographical memory would have evolved two systems, one containing factual, event-specific knowledge, and the other containing emotional traces. The similarity between these notions and the notions of propositional and schematic systems is striking. Conway and Pleydell–Pearce have further proposed that the process of building event-specific knowledge has the capacity to inhibit emotional traces.

Along these lines, we propose that the processes leading to a state of autonoetic awareness of emotion need to activate information contained in the propositional networks—because this is the material on which they can operate consciously—and that they also need to access information contained in the schemata because the affective tone of the information is required for autonoetic awareness and because of the many affordances it offers to human cognitive functioning. However, the schema has the propensity to generate positive feedback loops perpetuating and even enhancing its activation, and, consequently, to disrupt high level cognitive processes, as suggested by Conway and Pleydell–Pearce (2000). In the dual memory framework, this disruption could occur in at least three ways: by generating supraoptimal physiological arousal (the Yerkes–Dodson law, 1908), by biasing attention toward perceptual features congruent with the schema, and by automatically activating schema-connected concepts in the propositional network.

To protect themselves against such disruption, autonoetic consciousness processes should have the capacity to regulate the activation of the schema to obtain only the schematic information needed, without risking potential disturbances for high level cognitive processes. This implies a strategic, finely-tuned regulation. One possibility is that this regulation operates on the loops that positively feed into the schema, perhaps by redirecting attention toward elements (perceptual indexes or concepts in propositional networks) that are congruent with the strategic aim but not with the schema. These processes might also have an inhibitory effect on the body response system. We have explored some of these different possibilities in a research program that will be described in the following sections.

In sum, many aspects of the capacity of autonoetic consciousness suggest that the processes underlying this capacity are central to the voluntary regulation of emotion. First, autonoetic consciousness relies on the integration of schematic and propositional information. Processes leading to autonoetic awareness thus have the capacity to activate and to regulate both schemata and propositional networks. Specifically, it is postulated that such processes have the capacity to inhibit the overactivation of emotional schemata. Second, autonoetic consciousness allows for the recollection of specific past experiences. This capacity offers to individuals large, detailed, and very particularized data banks of what happened to them in the past and how best to decide their present course of action, given that rich knowledge. Third, autonoetic consciousness yields the possibility of immediate generation of a mental and emotional representation of how one would feel in a future hypothetical situation. This information has been demonstrated to be central for personal decision making in many life situations (Bechara, this volume; Damasio, 1994). Finally, autonoetic consciousness plays a central role in the definition of the self and of how it is regulated. Indeed, the self is constituted from the memory of one's past experiences and goals and of one's future goals, all mental constructions for which autonoetic consciousness is central (Conway & Pleydell–Pearce, 2000).

The Regulation of Emotion in the Dual Memory Model

From this perspective, the core of emotional activation rests in the schema. This cognitive structure provides the organism with wholly-prepared, immediate response modes to challenging situations in the environment. This capacity yields important adaptive capacities (see Stemmler, this volume). However, this fast, powerful, and automatic response system, as a result of these very characteristics, also has the potential to prevent or disrupt slower, more cognitively elaborated responses. This becomes problematic when such thoughtful responses provide a better alternative than automatic ones, or when conflicts arise between the two response modes. From this perspective, the question of emotion regulation becomes a question of modulating the activation of the schema. This question can be divided into two more specific subquestions: How can the schema be inhibited when more thoughtful types of response would better serve the individual's adaptation or well-being, and how can the self-perpetuating activation of the schema via the many feedback loops be controlled?

In the framework of the dual memory model, schema activation can be regulated by three means: the regulation of peripheral feedback, the redirection of attention, and the elaboration of emotional information. We will examine each of these means in the following sections.

The Regulation of the Peripheral Feedback. There is ample empirical evidence that modulating one's body state alters one's emotional state. In the emotion literature, the facial feedback effect—the fact that altering one's facial expression produces the corresponding emotional state—has received much attention. A wealth of studies has documented that manipulating facial expression influences feeling state (Laird, 1984; Manstead, 1988; Matsumoto, 1987; McIntosh, 1996). The impact of facial muscle manipulation has been extended to studies of physiological changes, such as heart rate or skin temperature (Hess, Kappas, McHugo, Lanzetta, & Kleck, 1992; Kappas, 1989; Levenson, 1992; Levenson, Carstensen, Friesen, & Ekman, 1991; Levenson, Ekman, & Friesen, 1990). Further, Stepper and Strack (1993) have documented that manipulating posture also has an impact on subjective feeling states and influences subsequent judgment of valenced material, extending previous findings from Duclos et al. (1989) showing that posture affects mood. Finally, studies from our laboratory have demonstrated that manipulating breathing patterns has a strong impact on feeling state (Philippot, Chapelle, & Blairy, 2002) and that this effect can occur outside of awareness of the process (Philippot & Dallavalle, 1998).

At the clinical level, controlled breathing and muscle relaxation are known to be powerful means to alleviate intense negative emotions such as anxiety or anger. For instance, it has been demonstrated that hyperventilation (i.e., breathing faster than required by an organism's needs), which can be associated with tense situations, plays a pivotal function in rapid and automatic onset of extreme fears in certain anxious conditions, such as panic attack (Beck & Scott, 1988; Huey & West, 1983). Feedback loops among the activation of a fear schema, the production of bodily sensations, and their positive feedback on the schema have been documented in clinical samples (Ehlers, Margraf, & Roth, 1988; Kenardy, Oei, & Evans, 1990). In these conditions, breathing retraining is a central component of the therapeutic intervention (Barlow, 2002). Similarly, after the pioneering works of Jacobson (1957) and Wolpe (1961), muscle relaxation is a key component of the regulation of emotional arousal in psychotherapeutic intervention.

In sum, there is ample evidence that altering body state induced by the activation of an emotional schema has an impact on the course of emotion. As this chapter is focused on the cognitive regulation of emotion, we won't develop this point further and refer the reader to Pauls's chapter in this volume.

The Redirection of Attention. As presented in the preceding sections, once activated, a schema lowers the perceptual threshold for elements that are congruent with it. Thus, perceptual elements, as well as conceptual ones, linked to a schema will be primed by the activation of the schema. This results in preconscious and automatic attentive biases for perceptual and conceptual elements that are congruent with the schema. Positive feedback loops are thus created, reinforcing the activation of the schema. For instance, when afraid, we would more readily perceive frightening stimuli than neutral or positive ones. The clinical literature has documented such attentive biases for words (concepts) and for images, such as expressive faces. This literature will be reviewed in a subsequent section.

These perceptual priming and attentive biases are postulated to be instantiated automatically. Thus, there is the possibility that these automatic processes might be overridden by a willful attentional focus on elements that are incongruent with the schema. This rationale constitutes one of the bases of cognitive therapy. Indeed, the main principle of this approach is to identify the irrational thinking underlying dysfunctional attitudes, feelings, and behaviors and to help the individual to engage in more rational thinking (Beck, Rush, Shaw, & Emery, 1979). Irrational thinking is most often supported by biased attention to negative elements that reinforce it (Beck & Clark, 1997). Therefore, one important therapeutic approach involves training people to redirect their attention toward elements that are incongruent with their negative interpretation to develop a more balanced and objective view of the situation.

The dual memory model also postulates that schema activation might be maintained by positive feedback loops between the schema and elements of the propositional system that are automatically associated with the schema. Indeed, specific conceptual representations in the propositional system might be recurrently activated during the arousal of a schema. For example, individuals suffering from panic disorder might repeatedly interpret their panics as heart attacks. Thus, the concepts of "heart," "heart attack," "cardiologist," and the like are systematically activated during the arousal of their panic schema. These re-occurrences generate an association between the panic schema and these concepts. Eventually, simply activating the concept of heart, as when seeing the drawing of a heart on a Valentine card, will automatically trigger the panic schema. The latter will in turn activate its related concepts, including "heart." A positive and automatic feedback is thereby created, maintaining and even enhancing the activation of the schema. Such a phenomenon has also been described in depression, in which depressive thinking maintains the activation of a depressogenic schema (Nolen–Hoeksema, 1996), a notion labeled "cognitive interlock" (Teasdale & Barnard, 1993).

The positive feedback loop between a schema and propositional elements is supposed to result from automatic processes: specifically, the activation of associations originating in the repetitive contingent activation of the schema and these propositional elements. Yet, as presented in a preceding section, propositional elements can be strategically activated and inhibited by willful processes that are directed by an intention and not by a schema. This opens the possibility of modulating the feedback loops between schema and propositional elements, either by inhibiting these propositional elements or by activating elements that are incongruent.

This process, however, might not be as straightforward as it first appears. Indeed, schema activation and feedback operate automatically, relying on fast processes requiring few cognitive resources but having a great impact in terms of attentional focus, concept priming, and physiological arousal. In contrast, the voluntary processes that might modulate the feedback loop between schema and propositional elements are slower, require more cognitive resources (as they involve much inhibition), and are likely to be disrupted by the high level of physiological arousal generated by the schema. For instance, awaiting a difficult exam, a student painfully experiences the activation of his or her anxiety schema and of the arousal state it generates. Ideas and images of failure are likely to intrude automatically into his or her consciousness and to nourish his or her anxiety (via the positive feedback loop between schema and propositional elements). The student might attempt to distract himself or herself from these negative thoughts, for instance, by trying to focus on reviewing class material or by chatting with other students. However, he or she might not be very successful in this strategy, as ideas and images primed by the anxiety schema are likely to intrude regularly into his or her consciousness. For instance, reviewing material might make him or her more conscious of the difficulty of the class and of the possibility of failure, thereby reactivating schema feedback. Similarly, conversation with friends is likely to address the exam and their fears.

In sum, several feedback loops in which the direction of attention toward schema-associated elements at the perceptual or at the propositional levels are likely to maintain schematic activation and the resulting emotional arousal.

The Elaboration of Emotional Information. An alternative to the redirection of attention toward elements that are not associated with the schema would be to focus willfully on anxiogenic images and thoughts. The student waiting anxiously for his or her exam would try to specify what is really at stake in the situation and what are the objective dangers. Indeed, according to cognitive therapists, such a willful and confrontational approach (as opposed to avoidance) of anxiogenic thinking is likely to disrupt irrational thinking that maintains the activation of the anxious schema and to help the individual to focus on all aspects of the situation, rather than focusing only on the negative aspects (Clark, 1999). From a different perspective, and based on neurological evidence, we have proposed that such willful elaboration of emotional information using executive processing has a functional inhibitory action on automatic processes that activate the schema and its feedback loops (Schaefer & Philippot, 2002).

According to these considerations, it appears that applying willful cognitive strategies to prevent schema feedback is not a simple endeavor and that we know little about how these processes might operate. The hypotheses mentioned in this paragraph will be further developed and linked to research findings in a subsequent section.

Conclusion. From the perspective of the dual memory model, the regulation of emotion is mostly a question of modulation of the schema to facilitate the individual's adaptation and and meet his or her needs. This regulation can be achieved indirectly by acting on the feedback loops that maintain and enhance schema activation. These feedback loops may be peripheral, as in the modulation of body state generated by the schema. They can also be central, as when they pertain to attention redirection or controlled elaboration of emotional information. In conclusion, the dual memory model provides a useful theoretical framework for the exploration of the many cognitive processes regulating emotion. Yet, these speculations require an empirical validation. The concluding section of this chapter presents empirical evidence pertaining to these issues.

EMPIRICAL EVIDENCE REGARDING COGNITIVE REGULATION OF EMOTION

Many areas of research, in clinical, social, and cognitive psychology, as well as in neuropsychology, are pertinent to the regulation hypotheses developed in the preceding section. The most directly relevant areas concern attentional processes in emotion, more specifically attentional biases in emotional state, on the one hand, and the elaboration of emotional information (e.g., remembering past emotional experiences or imagining future emotional consequences of a hypothetical situation), on the other hand. We review these research domains in the following paragraphs with a particular focus on the work conducted in our laboratory.

Attention Biases

In the preceding section, we developed the notion that schema activation automatically lowers the perceptual threshold for perceptual elements associated with the schema. We suggested that this process should result in an attentional bias for schema-relevant stimuli. Indeed, a wealth of studies has evidenced an attentional bias in the processing of threatening stimuli by anxious individuals. Such biases have been documented for different anxiety disorders such as generalized anxiety disorder (Bradley, Mogg, White, Groom, & de Bono, 1999; Mac Leod, Mathews, & Tata, 1986; Mogg, Mathews, & Eysenck, 1992; Mogg, Mathews, & Weinman, 1989), panic disorder (Ehlers, Margraf, Davies, & Roth, 1988; McNally, Rieman, & Kim, 1990; McNally, Riemann, Louro, Lukach, & Kim, 1992), spider phobia (Lavy, van den Hout, & Arntz, 1993; Watts, Mc Kenna, Sharrock, & Trezise, 1986) and social phobia (Amir, Foa, & Coles, 1998; Gilboa–Schechtman, Foa, & Amir, 1999; Mattia, Heimberg, & Hope,1993).

However, the nature of these attentional biases are the object of a controversy. Indeed, some predict that anxious individuals focus on schema-congruent information, thereby sustaining its activation (Beck, Emery, & Greenberg, 1985). For instance, socially anxious individuals would more quickly perceive that a conversation partner is frowning than would nonanxious individuals. The overactive schema would also increase the likelihood that ambiguous information would be interpreted as threatening. For instance, a neutral face might be perceived as hostile by a socially anxious individual. However, some researchers predict that anxious individuals will avoid any information linked to the schema. For instance, actively avoiding social stimuli, (e.g., faces) constitutes a form of cognitive escape from anxiety-provoking situations for social phobics (e.g., avoiding looking at others' faces makes conversation less likely; Clark & Wells, 1995).

We have proposed that, in actuality, both focusing and avoidance processes would be present, but at a different times. According to this view, anxious individuals would show an initial hypervigilance for threat-relevant stimuli. This hypervigilance would be the consequence of automatic processes, and it could be observed without conscious perception of threat-relevant information (Mogg & Bradley, 1999). However, at further and less automatic stages of information processing, people would actively turn away from threatening information to escape the discomfort associated with it. Thus, this model postulates a dynamic shift of attention allocation from initial threat hypervigilance to later threat avoidance. For instance, while speaking to other people, socially anxious individuals would have their attention automatically attracted to frowns more readily than would nonanxious individuals. Because of this perception bias, socially anxious individuals are likely to automatically overactivate a state of social anxiety. However, as soon as a frown was detected, they would turn their attention away from it—and, more generally, from others' faces—to avoid the threatening stimulus and the discomfort associated with it. Unfortunately, in doing so, they are likely to maintain their anxiety: Not only are they likely to behave socially inappropriately, but they will also be unable to determine whether the frowns were a sign of actual social threat or, for instance, simply a sign of perplexity.

We tested this hypothesis in an experiment using the dot prime paradigm (Mogg, Philippot, & Bradley, 2003). Social phobics and matched controls were exposed to pairs of facial expressions presented on a computer monitor. Each pair comprised a neutral face with either a friendly or threatening face. After facial stimulus offset, a single probe, consisting of an arrow pointing either up or down, was presented in the location of one of the faces. Participants were asked to press as quickly and as accurately as possible the key corresponding to the arrow (up or down). The rationale is that participants' reaction time is faster if they are looking at the face location on which the probe appears. It can thus be deduced from reaction times, whether participants were looking at the neutral or at the emotional face. Further, to observe if the focus of attention changed over time, the stimulus duration was manipulated (either 500 msec or 1250 msec). It was predicted, and observed, that social phobics initially focus their attention on the threatening face, but that this attentional bias rapidly disappears. In contrast, nonphobics showed the opposite pattern. Although no initial bias for threatening faces was observed, further in the process, nonphobics strategically focused their attention on the threatening face. Similar results, using a different paradigm (homograph paradigm) were reported by Amir, Foa, and Coles (1998). They fit nicely our prediction of an automatic lowering of perceptual threshold resulting from schema activation, followed by a protective voluntary attempt to redirect attention away from the threatening stimulus.

However, an important alternative hypothesis has been proposed in the literature: The attentional bias could be determined by an evaluative bias. For instance, Mogg and Bradley (1998) proposed a cognitive-motivational view relying on two different systems: the Valence Evaluation System that assesses the stimulus threat value and the Goal Engagement System that orients allocation of attention as a function of the output of the former system. If a stimulus in the environment is evaluated as threatening, the Goal Engagement System interrupts ongoing activities and orients attention toward the threat. This model postulates that anxious individuals overevaluate the threat value of environmental stimuli. This notion is widely accepted by clinicians (e.g., Beck, Emery, & Greenberg, 1985) but, curiously, has been submitted to very little empirical investigation.

In a study by Merckelbach, Van Hout, Van den Hout, and Mersch (1989), social phobics and controls had to evaluate angry, neutral, and joyful faces with respect to their pleasantness. Contrary to the cognitive-motivational model's prediction, no differences were observed between the two populations. We recently replicated this intriguing result (Douilliez & Philippot, 2003): Socially anxious and control participants were asked to evaluate the threatening value of fearful, joyful, and neutral faces. In addition, we extended the study with other types of stimuli: words and pictures, of which we manipulated valence (positive, negative, and neutral) and social relevance (socially relevant and not socially relevant). Our rationale was that faces are potent innate stimuli (Öhman & Soares, 1993), and, as such, the processing of faces should not be influenced by social anxiety. In contrast, words and scenes depicted in the pictures require an interpretation and can therefore be affected by experience, including social anxiety.

As predicted, replicating Merkelbach et al. (1989), no differences between anxious individuals and controls were observed for the evaluation of faces. In contrast, anxious individuals evaluated negative pictures and words as more threatening, compared to evaluations by normal controls. Thus, the notion that attentive biases in anxiety are necessarily supported by an evaluative bias cannot be sustained.

In conclusion, initial attentive biases toward threatening stimuli in anxiety disorders are supported by a wealth of empirical studies. We propose that these biases are generated by an enhanced activation of the anxiogenic schema. Attentive biases maintain schema activation and prevent people from voluntarily processing threatening information in depth. This process is likely to constitute one mechanism underlying the maintenance of emotion disorders (Clark, 1999). Further research must specify attentive bias with respect to valence and relevance for individual's preoccupations, and thereby test the existence of explicit and implicit evaluative biases and examine the relation between these two types of biases.

ELABORATION OF EMOTIONAL INFORMATION AND REGULATION OF EMOTIONAL EXPERIENCE

The way people think about their emotions (or, in other words, how they elaborate emotion information), is very likely to influence their ability to regulate emotional experience. Recent research suggests that one important dimension in this respect is the level of specificity at which emotional information is processed. Indeed, clinical evidence indicates that processing emotional information at an overgeneral level is associated with problems in emotion regulation. For instance, Williams (1996; Williams, Stiles, & Shapiro, 1999) has shown that depression and possibly Post-Traumatic Stress Disorder are associated with an overgeneral retrieval mode for memories of personal emotional experiences, whatever the emotional tone of the memory. Depressed individuals have difficulties accessing specific personal memories, that is, discrete personal episodes with a precise and circumscribed location in time and space (e.g., "I was afraid last Saturday afternoon when I was attacked by a big dog while I was jogging on Pleasant Street"). Rather, they report overgeneral memories, that is, personal episodes that are extended in time or repetitive, with no precise location in space or time (e.g., "I am afraid when I am attacked by dogs while I am jogging"). The development of a specific retrieval mode for autobiographical memory is associated with a lower risk for relapse into depression and effective relapse prevention treatments (Williams, Teasdale, Segal, & Soulsby, 2000).

This specificity deficit for personal memories has also been recently observed in schizophrenia (Riutort, Cuervo, Danion, Peretti, & Salamé, 2002).), a result replicated in our laboratory for emotional memories (Neumann, Philippot, & Danion, 2002). In this latter study, schizophrenic patients and controls completed two tasks. In the first task, participants were shown a series of neutral, positive, or negative pictures from the International Affect Picture System (IAPS; Lang, Bradley, & Cuthbert, 1999). The next day, they were exposed to the same pictures, mixed with new "distractor" pictures. Participants were asked to identify which pictures had been shown the day before. They could give a "remember" answer—meaning that they specifically remembered having seen that picture and that their recall was accompanied by autonoetic awareness —or a "know" answer, indicating that they knew the picture was in the previous set but had no specific memory of it, reflecting a recall marked by noetic awareness. In this episodic memory recall test, schizophrenic patients reported more "know" answers than "remember" ones, whereas control participants displayed the opposite pattern. This deficit had already been established by Danion and collaborators for nonemotional material (Danion, Rizzo, & Bruant, 1999). In a second task, participants were asked to recall and describe personal memories of emotional experiences. Their descriptions were coded for specificity according to Williams's (1996) criteria. The second day, they were presented with personal memories and distractors and asked to recall which memories they reported the first day. Schizophrenic patients' memories for personal emotional experiences were more general than controls' memories. In addition, overgeneral memories produced more "know" answers during the second recall by schizophrenic patients than by controls. This pattern of results suggests that both deficits—the autonoetic consciousness one and the memory specificity one—might be related to a unique functional deficit in reflexive processes that are necessary both for the reconstruction of specific memories and for autonoetic consciousness.

Another line of research also suggests a relation between generality in emotional information processing and deficits in emotional regulation. Studying mental rumination in anxiety, Borkovec (Borkovec & Inz, 1990; Borkovec, Ray, & Stöber, 1998) has shown that such recurrent thinking patterns were characterized by their overgenerality: In a state of anxious apprehension, people tend to think of possible threats in an unspecific, abstract way.

Williams and his collaborators (1999) explained the phenomenon of overgeneral memory as a protective mechanism from acute emotions associated with specific memories. Similarly, Borkovec (Borkovec, Ray, & Stöber, 1998) has proposed that the lack of specificity in mental rumination results from an avoidance of specific threatening information. By remaining at a general—and therefore more abstract—level of information, individuals attempt to avoid the reactivation of acute and painful emotions felt in specific personal experiences.

This interpretation is based on the notion that specifying emotional information would make this information more vivid and would increase associated feelings. However, according to multilevel models of emotion and to the dual memory model in particular, the opposite prediction could be formulated: Voluntarily focusing on emotional information and willfully elaborating it as specifically as possible should decrease schematic activation and, as a consequence, the intensity of emotional arousal and feelings. Indeed, willfully elaborating emotional information necessarily implies executive processing. As presented in the first section of this chapter, the activation of such processes strategically orients attention toward elements that may not be related to the schema (interruption of feedback loops to the schema). Further, and most importantly, executive processes might entail the inhibition of schematic activation. This latter notion is congruent with the proposal of Conway and Pleydell–Pearce (2000) that elaborating specific personal information implies the inhibition of intense autonoetic feeling states that would otherwise disrupt elaborated cognitive processing. This notion is also in accordance with the clinical observation that, in exposure therapy, people can learn to regulate anxiety only if they focus their attention on the emotional information that they usually avoid and if they attempt to attend to it as specifically as possible (Foa & McNally, 1996).

Thus, understanding why people with emotional disorders tend to process emotional material at an overgeneral level—and how this characteristic might play a role in the etiology of their emotional disregulation—necessitates addressing several key questions. First, do people hold a naïve theory that focusing on personal emotional cognition increases emotional intensity? Second, does overgeneral processing of emotional information induce more intense emotional states than does specific processing? Third, does voluntarily specifying painful emotional material decrease or increase discomfort? Our underlying hypothesis was that people indeed believe that focusing on emotion will increase its intensity (Question 1). Therefore, when confronted with painful spontaneous thoughts—either about a personal memory or about predictions related to possible future negative situations—people would not invest any effort in elaborating them; rather, they would attempt to avoid them, resulting in the overgenerality bias we have observed. However, in actuality, overgeneral processing would favor schema activation (Question 2). If this is indeed the case, constraining people to focus on painful personal cognitions and to elaborate them should result in a decrease in painful feelings (Question 3). We recently investigated these hypotheses in our laboratory.

In the first experiment (Philippot, Burgos, Verhasselt, & Baeyens, 2002), participants were asked to imagine themselves thinking as specifically as possible about a past personal positive experience and about a negative one. They then had to predict how their emotional intensity would evolve over time during this task. Outpatients suffering from anxiety disorders were compared to healthy matched controls. Results showed that both groups of participants hold a naïve theory that thinking specifically about an emotional experience intensifies the emotional feelings during the first minutes and maintains this intensity thereafter at a high level. This general pattern is observed for positive as well as for negative emotions. Interestingly, control participants anticipated less intense feelings when thinking about a negative as compared to a positive experience. This suggests a "protective" inhibition of negative emotion. In comparison, anxious patients anticipated a higher emotional intensity for negative events, suggesting that they did not believe they could modulate the aversive arousal resulting from the processing of negative personal experience. It is therefore likely that anxious individuals avoid the specification of negative emotional information more than do nonanxious individuals.

Is people's naïve theory correct? In other words, does specifying emotional information increase emotional feelings? To answer this question, we conducted several series of experiments, using different methods, in which we examined how emotional intensity was influenced by the induction of an overgeneral versus specific mode of processing emotional information. In the first series of experiments (Philippot, Schaefer, & Herbette, 2003), we used Williams's (1996) distinction between overgeneral and specific autobiographical memories to prime an overgeneral or a specific mode of processing autobiographical information. In a first experimental session, participants were invited to report personal memories related to particular emotions. In the second experimental session, before undergoing an emotion induction procedure, participants were primed with two of these memories. According to the experimental condition, participants were primed for 60 sec with either overgeneral or specific memories. In a control condition, participants spent 60 sec finding synonyms and antonyms of common neutral words. In the first study, emotion induction consisted of reliving a recent negative experience through a mental imagery procedure (Vrana, Cuthbert, & Lang, 1986). Results showed that participants clearly reported more intense emotion when primed with overgeneral memories than when primed with specific memories or when they completed the control task. The second study replicated these results with a different method of emotion induction (exposing participants to film excerpts) and different types of emotion: joy, anger, fear, and sadness. All emotion conditions displayed the same pattern of results, although it was statistically significant only for joy and anger. Overall, the results of these two studies suggest that people's naïve theory is incorrect. In contrast, these results support the prediction of the dual memory model: Priming a general mode of processing emotional information resulted in more intense emotions during subsequent emotional situations than did priming a specific mode of processing.

One could object that emotional memories were primed at a specific or a general level before emotion induction. Participants were not explicitly instructed to process information at a general or a specific level during emotion induction. This procedure was chosen to ensure perfectly similar and comparable emotion induction conditions and to avoid biases due to different instructions during emotion induction. However, this conservative choice produces the limitation that one does not know whether the effect observed is due to the priming procedure itself or to the mode of information processing that has been primed and applied during the subsequent emotion induction procedure. To overcome this limitation, another study was designed (Schaefer, Collette, et al., 2003). In that study, participants were trained to generate emotional mental imagery (Vrana et al., 1986). In addition, during imagery trials, participants had to repeat sentences reflecting a particular way of appraising the scenario and to imagine that these sentences were their own thoughts occurring during the situation being imagined. The overgeneral or specific mode of processing was manipulated using one of two sets of sentences. For the overgeneral mode, metaphoric sentences reflecting a holistic way of appraising the situation were used (e.g., "Everything collapses around me."). For the specific mode, explicit, analytical questions about specific emotional elements of the scenario were used ("Is this situation important for me?"). This procedure was used with scenarios of joy, anger, tenderness, sadness, and a neutral state. Heart rate and brain activity (recorded via a Siemens CTI 951 R 16/31 PET scanner) were recorded during baseline and imagery trials. Participants reported the intensity of their feeling state after each trial. The results of this study clearly show that for all emotions, participants reported more intense feelings for the overgeneral condition than for the specific one. These subjective reports were corroborated by heart rate differences. Finally, brain activity clearly differentiated the two modes of processing: Specifically, the over-general mode of processing was associated with increased activity in the ventromedial prefrontal cortex, whereas the specific mode was associated with activation of the dorsolateral prefrontal cortex. These results were replicated in another study that did not use brain activity recording (Schaefer & Philippot, 2002).

Overall, these results support our counterintuitive hypothesis: Processing emotional information at a general level results in more intense emotional feelings and arousal than does elaborating it at a specific level. This has been demonstrated using procedures that prime one processing mode or the other before emotion induction as well as in a procedure that constrains it during emotion induction. However, in none of the experimental situations reported until now were the participants attempting to rein in a negative emotional state. Rather, they were either trying to produce an emotional state (during mental imagery trials) or, at best, trying not to regulate their emotion (when exposed to film excerpts). As most emotional disorders are characterized by a failure to keep negative emotions in check, one may wonder how well our results generalize to clinically relevant situations.

To address this question, we conducted another study (Philippot, Burgos, et al., 2002) in which participants (students) were placed in a state of anxious apprehension: They were expecting to have to give an oral presentation and to be evaluated based on their presentation. Before the presentation was to take place, participants were told that they would have to perform a mental training task to help them diminish their anxiety. According to the condition to which they were assigned, participants performed one of three tasks: a specific thinking task, a general thinking task, and a control task. In all three tasks, participants listened to a 10-min audiotape that asked them questions to which they were instructed to answer mentally. In the specific thinking task, participants had to answer a series of questions requiring them to specify in progressively greater and greater detail their worries about the speech. In the general thinking task, participants likewise had to answer a series of questions about their worries, but this time the questions addressed general impressions and meanings evoked by the situation. The control task was actually a distraction task: Participants had to find antonyms of a series of nonemotional words. Participants reported the intensity of their anxiety before and after the manipulation. Results showed that anxiety and fear diminished very significantly in the specific thinking condition, $F(9, 50) = 5.90, p < .000, \eta^2 = .52$, whereas these feelings tended to increase in the general thinking condition and to remain stable in the control condition. These results suggest that the conclusions of the preceding studies can be applied to the regulation of negative emotions in clinically significant situations.

In sum, the empirical evidence gathered in our laboratory support our counterintuitive hypothesis. Voluntarily focusing on and specifying personal emotional information induces less emotional arousal than does thinking about the same information at a general level. However, people believe just the opposite. Thus, in an attempt to protect themselves from acute painful feelings, they are likely to think at a very general level about their negative emotional experiences. Negative mental ruminations perfectly illustrate this tendency. Unfortunately, such overgeneral processing of emotional information favors the activation of the corresponding emotional schema or, at the least, such overgeneral processing does not counteract the schema. The negative emotional schema is thereby likely to become chronically activated. For instance, anxiously ruminating about a future exam will maintain the activation of the anxiety schema. On the other hand, specifying emotional information will produce at least two positive outcomes. First, our results demonstrate that such voluntary specific elaboration will inhibit the activation of the schema. Second, accessing specific, concrete, and differentiated information about an emotional situation provides the necessary basis for strategic problem solving that can facilitate discovery of more functional ways to deal with the situation. Coming back to our anxious student example, attempting to specify what is actually feared—and what exactly constitutes the anxiety reaction—should diminish the activation of the anxiety schema and, hence, the anxiety arousal and feelings. In addition, knowing what is feared and what constitutes his or her immediate reaction will help the student find more appropriate ways to deal with his or her anxious apprehension of the exam.

CONCLUSIONS AND FUTURE DIRECTIONS

In this chapter, we have investigated how multilevel models of emotion contribute to our understanding of the cognitive mechanisms that regulate emotion. A dimension that is central to the cognitive perspective, but that is often overlooked in the emotion tradition, is the distinction between automatic and controlled processes. We have shown that emotion and its regulation entail a complex interacting system that includes automatic and controlled processes that converge in certain cases and diverge in other cases. These processes vary with respect to consciousness and intent. We have also attempted to demonstrate that all important domains of cognition are recruited by emotion and its regulation: perception, attention, memory, decision making, and consciousness. The dual memory model we propose is an attempt to synthesize previous multilevel models of emotion and to provide a theoretical framework for emotion, articulating the different emotion-relevant domains of cognition and their different types of processes.

As we have seen, the dual memory model generates many testable hypotheses, some of which are counterintuitive, such as the notion that specifying emotional information lowers emotional intensity. Many of these hypotheses await further investigation. For instance, the notion that executive processes have an inhibitory effect on emotional arousal needs to be tested against the hypothesis of Gross (Butler & Gross, this volume; see also Kring & Werner, this volume) that reappraisal has a major influence on emotional arousal. Indeed, in our experiments (e.g., Philippot, Burgos, et al. 2002), when participants had to specify and make explicit their apprehension, their anxiety was reduced. It could be that the process of specification induced a reappraisal of the situation, although our instructions were designed to prevent this possibility. Still, a direct test, weighing the effects of specification of anxious apprehension with reappraisal of the situation against those of specification of apprehension without reappraisal, is needed.

Finally, the clinical implications of the model are similarly numerous. Indeed, it suggests new types of interventions for disorders of emotion regulation. These new types of interventions include the redirection of attention, the specification of sensitive autobiographical memories or of catastrophizing predictions, and the enhancement of autonoetic awareness of present experience. It is interesting to observe that new forms of treatments specifically target these facets. For instance,

Segal, Williams, and Teasdale (2002) have recently validated a new approach to preventing depression relapse that is primarily based on attention redirection and the development of autonoetic awareness of present experience. Similary, Schauer, Roth and Elbert (2002) have proposed a short treatment for trauma victims that is based on the specification of autobiographical memories.

Clearly, cognitive regulation of emotion opens a vast field where fundamental research and clinical applications potentially cross-pollinate each other. We hope that this chapter will bring its modest contribution to that thrilling scientific adventure.

REFERENCES

Amir, N., Foa, E. B., & Coles, M. E. (1998). Automatic activation and strategic avoidance of threat-relevant information in social phobia. *Journal of Abnormal Psychology, 107*, 285–290.

Barlow, D. H. (2002). *Anxiety and its disorders: The nature and treatment of anxiety and panic* (2nd ed.). New York: Guilford.

Barnard P. J., & Teasdale J. D. (1991). Interacting cognitive subsystems: a systemic approach to cognitive–affective interaction and change. *Cognition and Emotion, 5*, 1–39.

Beck, A. T., & Clark, D. A. (1997). An information processing model of anxiety: Automatic and strategic processes. *Behavior Research and Therapy, 35*, 49–58.

Beck, A. T., Emery, G., & Greenberg, R. L. (1985). Cognitive structures and anxiogenic rules. In A. T., Beck, G., Emery & R. L. Greenberg (Eds), *Anxiety disorders and phobias* (pp. 54–66). New York: Basic books.

Beck, A. T., Rush, A. J., Shaw, B. F., & Emery, G. D. (1979). *Cognitive therapy of depression: A treatment manual.* New York: Guilford.

Beck, J. G., & Scott, S. K. (1988). Physiological and symptom responses to hyperventilation: A comparison of frequent and infrequent panickers. *Journal of Psychopathology and Behavioral Assessment, 10*, 117–127.

Borkovec, T. D., & Inz, J. (1990). The nature of worry in generalized anxiety disorder: A predominance of thought activity. *Behavior Research and Therapy, 28*, 153–158.

Borkovec, T. D., Ray, W. J., & Stöber, J. (1998). Worry: A cognitive phenomenon intimately linked to affective, physiological, and interpersonal behavioral processes. *Cognitive Therapy and Research, 22*, 561–576.

Bradley, B., Mogg, K., White, J., Groom, C., & de Bono, J. (1999). Attentional bias for emotional faces in generalized anxiety disorder. *British Journal of Clinical Psychology, 38*, 267–278.

Chapelle, G., Philippot, P., & Vanderlinden, M. (1996). Amnesia and emotion: A case study. *Brain and Cognition, 30*, 338–340.

Christianson, S. A. (1992). Emotional stress and eyewitness memory: A critical review. *Psychological Bulletin, 112*, 284–309.

Clark, D. M. (1999). Anxiety disorders: Why do they persist and how to treat them. *Behavior Research and Therapy, 37*, 5–27.

Clark, D. M., & Wells, A. (1995). A cognitive model of social phobia. In R. Heimberg, M. Liebowitz, D.A. Hope, & F.R. Schneier (Eds.), *Social phobia: Diagnosis, assessment and treatment* (pp. 69–93). New York: Guilford Press.

Conway M. A., & Pleydell–Pearce C. W. (2000). The construction of autobiographical memories in the self-memory system. *Psychological Review, 107*, 261–288.

Damasio, A. R. (1994) *Descartes' error: Emotion, reason and the human brain*. New York: Putnam.

Danion, J-M., Rizzo, L., Bruant, A. (1999). Functionnal mechanisms underlying impaired recognition memory and conscious awareness in patients with schizophrenia. *General Archives of Psychiatry, 56*, 639–648.

Duclos, S. D., Laird, J. D., Schneider, E., Sexter, M., Stern, L., & VanLighten, O. (1989). Emotion-specific effects of facial expressions and postures on emotional experience. *Journal of Personality and Social Psychology, 57*, 100–108.

Douilliez, C., & Philippot, P. (2003). Biais dans l'évaluation volontaire de stimuli verbaux et non-verbaux: Effet de l'anxiété sociale [Bias in voluntary evaluation of verbal and non-verbal stimuli: Effect of social anxiety]. *Revue Francophone de Clinique Comportementale et Cognitive, 8*, 12–18.

Ehlers, A., Margraf, J., & Roth, W. T. (1988). Selective information processing, interoception, and panic attacks. In I. Hand & H. V. Wittchen (Eds.), *Panic and phobia 2. Treatment and variables affecting course and outcome*. Berlin, Germany: Springer Verlag.

Ehlers, A., Margraf, J., Davies, S. & Roth, W. T. (1988). Selective processing of threat cues in subjects with panic attack. *Cognition and Emotion, 2*, 201–219.

Foa, E. B., & McNally, R. J. (1996). Mechanisms of change in exposure therapy. In R. M. Rapee (Ed.). *Current controversies in the anxiety disorders* (pp. 329–343). New York: Guilford.

Frijda, N. H. (1986). *The emotions*. Cambridge, England: Cambridge University Press.

Gilboa-Schechtman, E., Foa, E. B & Amir, N. (1999). Attentional biases for facial expressions in social phobia:The face-in-the-crowd paradigm. *Cognition and Emotion, 13*, 305–318.

Hess, U., Kappas, A., McHugo, G. J., Lanzetta, J. T., & Kleck, R. E. (1992). The facilitative effect of facial expression on the self-generation of emotion. *International Journal of Psychophysiology, 12*, 251–265.

Huey, S. R., & West, S. G. (1983). Hyperventilation: Its relation to symptom experience and to anxiety. *Journal of Abnormal Psychology, 92*, 422–432.

Jacobson, E. (1957). *You must relax*. New York: McGraw-Hill.

Kappas, A. (1989). Control of emotion. Unpublished doctoral dissertation, Dartmouth College, Hanover, New Hampshire.

Kenardy J., Oei T. P. S., & Evans L. (1990). Hyperventilation and panic attacks. *Australian and New Zealand Journal of Psychiatry, 15*, 25–39.

Laird, J. (1984). The real role of facial response in the experience of emotion: A reply to Tourangeau and Ellsworth, and others. *Journal of Personality and Social Psychology, 47*, 909–917.

Lang, P. J., Bradley, M. M., & Cuthbert, B. N. (1999). *International Affective Picture System (IAPS): Technical manual and affective ratings*. Gainsville, FL: The Center for Research in Psychophysiology.

Lavy, E., van den Hout M.& Arntz, A. (1993). Attentional bias and spider phobia: Conceptual and clinical issues. *Behavior Research and Therapy, 31*, 17–24.

Lazarus, R. S. (1984). On the primacy of cognition. *American Psychologist, 39*, 123–129.

Lazarus, R. S. (1991). Progress on a cognitive-motivational-relational theory of emotion. *American Psychologist, 46*, 819–834.

Levenson, R. W. (1992). Autonomic nervous system differences among emotions. *Psychological Science, 3*, 23–27.

Levenson, R. W., Carstensen, L. L., Friesen, W. V., & Ekman, P. (1991). Emotion, physiology, and expression in old age. *Psychology and Aging, 6*, 28–35.

Levenson, R. W., Ekman, P., & Friesen, W. V. (1990). Voluntary facial action generates emotion-specific autonomic nervous system activity. *Psychophysiology, 27*, 363–384.

Leventhal, H. (1984). A perceptual-motor theory of emotion. In L. Berkowitz (Ed.), *Advances in Experimental Social Psychology* (vol. 17, pp. 117–182). New York: Academic.

Leventhal, H., & Scherer, K. (1987). The relationship of emotion to cognition: A functional approach to a semantic controversy. *Cognition and Emotion, 1*, 3–28.

Lindsay, P. H., & Norman, D. A. (1977). *Human information processing: An introduction to psychology* (2nd ed.). New York: Academic.

Mac Leod, C., Mathews, A., & Tata, P. (1986). Attentional bias in emotional disorders. *Journal of Abnormal Psychology, 95*, 15–20.

Manstead, A. S. R. (1988). The role of facial movement in emotion. In H. L. Wagner (Ed.), *Social psychophysiology and emotion: Theory and clinical application*. Chicheseter, England: Wiley.

Matsumoto, D. (1987). The role of facial responses in the experience of emotion: More methodological problems and a meta-analysis. *Journal of Personality and Social Psychology, 52*, 769–774.

Mattia, J. I., Heimberg, R. G., & Hope, D. A. (1993). The revised Stroop color-naming task in socials phobics. *Behavior Research and Therapy, 31*, 305–313.

McIntosh, D. N. (1996). Facial feedback hypotheses: Evidence, implications, and directions. *Motivation and Emotion, 20*, 121–147.

McNally, R. J. (1995). Automaticity and the anxiety disorders. *Behavior Research and Therapy, 33*, 747–754.

McNally, R. J., Riemann, B. C., Louro, C. E., Lukach, B. M & Kim, E. (1992). Cognitive processing of emotional information in panic disorder. *Behavior Research and Therapy, 30*, 143–149.

McNally, R. J., Riemann, B. C., & Kim, E. (1990). Selective processing of threat cues in panic disorder. *Behavior Research and Therapy, 28*, 407–412.

Merckelbach, H., Van Hout, W., Van den Hout, M. A., & Mersch, P. P. (1989). Psychophysiological and subjective reactions of social phobics and normals to facial stimuli. *Behavior Research and Therapy, 27*, 289–294.

Mogg, K., & Bradley, B. V. P. (1998). A cognitive-motivational analysis of anxiety. *Behavior Research and Therapy, 36*, 809–848.

Mogg, K., & Bradley, B. P. (1999). Orienting attention to threatening facial expressions presented under conditions of restricted awareness. *Cognition and Emotion, 13*, 713–740.

Mogg, K., & Bradley, B. (2003). Selective processing of non-verbal information in anxiety: Attentional biases for threat. In P. Philippot, E. J. Coats, & R. S. Feldman (Eds.), *Nonverbal behavior in clinical settings* (pp. 127–144). New York: Oxford University Press.

Mogg, K., Mathews, A., & Eysenck, M.(1992).Attentional bias to threat in clinical anxiety states. *Cognition and Emotion, 6*, 149–159.

Mogg, K., Mathews, A.& Weinman, J. (1989). Selective processing of threat cues in anxiety states: A replication. *Behavior Research and Therapy, 27*, 317–323.

Mogg, K, Philippot, P., & Bradley B. (in press). Selective attention to angry faces in a clinical sample with social phobia. *Journal of Abnormal Psychology.*

Neumann, A., Philippot, P., & Danion, J. M. (2002). Memory deficits for emotional information in schizophrenia. Manuscript in preparation.

Nolen-Hoeksema, S. (1996). Chewing the cud and other ruminations. In R. S. Wyer (Ed.), Ruminative thoughts. *Advances in social cognition, 9*, 135–145. Mahwah, NJ: Lawrence Erlbaum Associates.

Öhman, A. (1999). Distinguishing unconscious from conscious emotional processes: Methodological considerations and theoretical implications. In T. Dalgleish & M. J. Power (Eds.), *Handbook of cognition and emotion* (pp. 321–352). Chichester, England: Wiley.

Öhman, A., & Soares, J. J. F. (1993). On the automatic nature of phobic fear: Conditioned electrodermal responses to masked fear-relevant stimuli. *Journal of Abnormal Psychology, 102*, 121–132.

Philippot, P., Burgos, A. I., Verhasselt, S., & Baeyens, C. (2002). Specifying emotional information: Modulation of emotional intensity via executive processes. In J. M. Fernandez–Dols (Ed.). *Proceedings of the XIIth conference of the International Society for Research on Emotion* (pp. 34–35). Cuenca, Spain: ISRE.

Philippot, P., Chapelle, C., & Blairy, S. (2002). Respiratory feedback in the generation of emotion. *Cognition & Emotion, 16,* 605–627.

Philippot, P., & Dallavalle, C. (1998, August). Respiratory feedback influences affective judgment. In A. Fischer & N. Frijda (Ed.). *Proceedings of the Xth conference of the International Society for Research on Emotion* (p. 87). Amsterdam, The Netherlands: International Society for Research on Emotion.

Philippot, P., & Schaefer, A. (2001). Emotion and memory. In T. J. Mayne and G. A. Bonano (Eds.), *Emotion: Current issues and future directions* (pp. 82–122). New York: Guilford.

Power, M., & Dagleish, T. (1997). Cognition and emotion: From order to disorder. Hove, England: Lawrence Erlbaum Associates

Roseman, I. J., Antoniou, A. A., & Jose, P. E. (1996). Appraisal determinants of emotions: Constructing a more accurate and comprehensive theory. *Cognition and Emotion, 10*, 241–277.

Riutort, M., Cuervo, C., Danion, J. M., Peretti, C. S., & Salamé, P. (2002). Reduced level of specific autobiographical memories in schizophrenia. Manuscript submitted for publication.

Schaefer, A., Collette, F., Philippot, P., Van der Linden, M., Laureys, S., Delfiore, G., et al., (2003). Neural correlates of hot and cold emotions: A multilevel approach to the functional anatomy of emotion. *Neuroimage, 18,* 938–949.

Schaefer, A., & Philippot, P. (2002). Multilevel processing during emotional imagery. Manuscript in preparation.

Schauer, M., Roth, W. T., Elbert, T. (2002) A narrative exposure treatment as intervention in a refugee camp: A case report. *Behavioural and Cognitive Psychotherapy, 30*, 211–215

Scherer, K. R. (2001). Appraisal considered as a process of multilevel sequential checking. In K. R. Scherer, A. Schorr, & T. Johnstone (Eds.), *Appraisal processes in emotion: Theory, methods, research* (pp. 92–120). New York: Oxford University Press.

Segal, Z. V., Williams, J. M. G., & Teasdale, J. D. (2002). *Mindfulness-based cognitive therapy for depression: A new approach to preventing relapse*. New York: Guilford Press.

Smith, C. A., & Kirby, L. D. (2000). Consequences requires antecedents: Towards a process model of emotion elicitation. In J. D. Forgas (Ed.), *Feeling and thinking: The role of affect in social cognition* (pp. 83–106). New York: Cambridge University Press.

Stepper, S., & Strack, F. (1993). Proprioceptive determinants of affective and nonaffective feelings. *Journal of Personality and Social Psychology, 64*, 211–220.

Teasdale, J. D., & Barnard P. J. (1993). *Affect, cognition and change: Re-modelling depressive thought.* Hove, UK: Lawrence Erlbaum Associates, Inc.

Tulving, E. (1985). Memory and consciousness. *Canadian Psychologist, 25*, 1–12.

Vrana, S. R., Cuthbert, B. N., Lang, P. J. (1986). Fear imagery and text processing. *Psychophysiology, 23*, 247–253.

Watts, F. N., Mc Kenna, F. P., Sharrock, R., & Trezise, L. (1986). Colour-naming of phobia-related words. *British Journal of Clinical Psychology, 77*, 97–108.

Wheeler, M. A., Stuss, D. A. T., & Tulving, E. (1997). Toward a theory of episodic memory: The frontal lobes and autonoetic consciousness. *Psychological Bulletin, 121*, 331–354.

William, R. A. (2002). Are animals stuck in time? *Psychological Bulletin, 128*, 473–489.

Williams, J. M. G. (1996). Depression and the specificity of autobiographical memory. In D. C. Rubin (Ed.), *Remembering our past: Studies in autobiographical memories* (pp. 244–270). Cambridge, England: Cambridge University Press.

Williams, J. M. G., Stiles, W. B., & Shapiro, D. A. (1999). Cognitive mechanisms in the avoidance of painful and dangerous thoughts: Elaborating the assimilation model. *Cognitive Therapy and Research, 23*, 285–306.

Williams, J. M. G., Teasdale, J. D., Segal, Z. V., & Soulsby, J. (2000). Mindful meditation reduces overgeneral autobiographical memory in depressed patient. *Journal of Abnormal Psychology, 109*, 150–155

Wolpe, J. (1961). The systematic desensitization treatment of neuroses. *Journal of Nervous and Mental Disease, 132*, 189–203.

Yerkes, R. M., & Dodson, J. D. (1908). The relation of strength of stimulus to rapidity of habit formation. *Journal of Comparative Neurological Psychology, 18*, 459–482.

Zajonc, R. B. (1984). On the primacy of affect. *American Psychologist, 39*, 117–123.

NOTES

[1]As commonly accepted in the literature, consciousness refers to capacities and processes, whereas awareness refers to a state resulting from the activation of these capacities and processes (Wheeler, et al., 1997).

II

Social and Motivational Aspects of Emotional Regulation

4

Hiding Feelings in Social Contexts: Out of Sight Is Not Out of Mind

Emily A. Butler and James J. Gross
Stanford University

"When genuine passion moves you, say what you've got to say, and say it hot."
—D. H. Lawrence (1924/1964)

"The constancy of the wise is nothing else but the knack of concealing their passion."
—Duc De La Rochefoucauld (trans.1665–1678/1706)

Western attitudes concerning emotion expression are notoriously ambivalent. This ambivalence reveals itself in the plethora of vigorously defended but contradictory opinions in philosophical and literary texts as to whether emotions should be freely expressed or carefully checked. On the one hand, as in Lawrence's quote, we are admonished to freely and directly express the emotions we have. On the other hand, as in Rochefoucauld's quote, we are told that it is wise to conceal the emotions we have.

The importance of this issue is underscored by contemporary research implicating emotion expression and inhibition in such diverse domains as the development of intimacy (Hornstein & Truesdell, 1988), marital satisfaction, and divorce (Gottman & Levenson, 1992), social support , decisions regarding employee hiring and promotion (Tiedens, 1002), prosocial behavior, social competence, and aggression (Halberstadt, Crisp, & Eaton, 1999), relapse of schizophrenia (Greenley, 1986), cancer onset and progression (Gross, 1989), and a wide range of other general psychological and physical health outcomes (see, for example, Kennedy–Moore & Watson, 2001; Pennebaker, 1993; Petrie, Booth, & Pennebaker, 19998). Unfortunately, although this diverse research clearly points to the importance of emotion expression and inhibition, it too is contradictory with regards to whether we should freely express or routinely inhibit our emotions (Kennedy–Moore & Watson, 2001).

Empirical research that specifically contrasts emotion expression and inhibition is of recent vintage (Gross & Levenson, 1993). The relative paucity of research makes it difficult to judge the empirical standing of competing claims about whether emotions should be expressed or suppressed. Compounding this difficulty is the fact that researchers have focused on the effects that inhibiting emotions have for the suppressing individual himself or herself, without considering the effects on social partners (Butler, Egloff, et al., 2003). Given that much of emotion expression takes place in social interactions, and that many of our goals are inherently social in nature, a complete analysis of the relative merits of emotion expression versus suppression needs to take such social consequences into account (see Fischer, Manstead, Evers, Timmers, & Valk, this volume).

In this chapter, we first locate expressive suppression—defined as the inhibition of ongoing emotion-expressive behavior—within a model of emotion regulation and review empirical evidence regarding its consequences for the regulator himself or herself. We then extend our analysis by considering expressive suppression in the context of social interaction and examine its social consequences, by which we mean its impact on the regulator's social partners and on the relationship between the two of them. Next, we turn to evidence suggesting that in some contexts, suppression fulfills important social functions, thereby benefiting the regulator, the social partner, or their relationship. On the basis of these findings, we argue that longstanding cultural ambivalence about emotion expression may be warranted. In many contexts, expressive suppression appears to be a fairly costly form of emotion regulation, but in some of these contexts, the outcome may well be worth that cost. In light of this analysis, we suggest that the critical question becomes not whether it is generally better to express or inhibit emotion, but when, where, and with whom it is advantageous to suppress rather than express one's emotions.

A PROCESS MODEL OF EMOTION REGULATION

In considering the relative merits of expressing versus inhibiting emotion, much depends on just how that emotion inhibition is achieved (Gross & John, 2002). To set the stage for a consideration of the one form of emotion inhibition that is our focus in this chapter—namely expressive suppression—it is useful to first consider the broader domain of emotion regulation.

Emotion regulation is a research domain characterized by exceptionally flexible boundaries (Thompson, 1994). This fact means that there are marked differences across researchers and theorists about what is actually included under this rubric (see, for example, Campos, Campos, & Barrett, 1989; Cole, Zahn–Waxler, Fox, Usher, & Welsh, 1996; Eisenberg, Fabes, Guthrie, & Reiser, 2000; Thompson, 1994). Our own research has been guided by a definition that considers emotion regulation to refer to the processes by which we influence which emotions we have, when we have them, and how we experience and express these emotions (Gross, 1998b). The processes involved may be conscious or unconscious, they may target negative or positive emotions, and they may serve to dampen, sustain, enhance, or replace a given emotion.

To organize the potentially limitless number of emotion regulatory strategies, we have developed a process model of emotion regulation that shows how specific strategies can be differentiated along the timeline of the unfolding emotional response (Gross, 1998b, 1999, 2001). Our model is founded on a conception of the emotion-generative process that can be found in many current theories of emotion (see, for example, Arnold, 1960; Buck, 1985; Ekman, Friesen, & Ellsworth, 1972; Frijda, 1986; Izard, 1977; Lazarus, 1991; Levenson, 1994; Scherer, 1984). This conception posits that an emotion begins with an evaluation of emotion cues which, if attended to and evaluated in emotional terms, can trigger a coordinated set of experiential, behavioral, and physiological response tendencies. The fundamental claim of our model is that emotion regulation strategies differ in when they have their primary impact on the emotion-generative process.

Within this framework we can locate two broad categories of emotion regulation: antecedent focused and response focused. Antecedent-focused strategies refer to things we do before the emotion response tendencies have become fully activated and have changed our behavior and peripheral physiological responding. An example of antecedent-focused emotion regulation is seeing a job interview as an opportunity to learn more about the company, rather than as a pass–fail test of life-defining proportions. In contrast, response–focused strategies refer to things we do once an emotion is already underway, after the response tendencies have been generated. Expressive suppression is one form of response-focused regulation and entails the conscious inhibition of expressive behavior while an individual is emotionally aroused. An example of expressive suppression is trying one's best not to let one's anxiety show during an important social interaction such as a placement interview.

THE PERSONAL CONSEQUENCES OF EXPRESSIVE SUPPRESSION

Our focus here is on expressive suppression. The question that we address is what consequences this form of response-focused emotion regulation has relative to emotion expression. In this analysis, our starting point is the proposition that expressive suppression involves more than a simple lack of emotion expression. Expressive suppression involves a conscious regulatory effort that specifically targets expressive behavior. Given its focus, we might expect that suppression would dramatically reduce the regulator's behavioral signs of emotion. In contrast, because expressive suppression does not alter attention to, or the appraisal of, the emotion eliciting event, we would not expect commensurate changes to subjective experience. Suppression's differential effects on behavior versus experience might lead to an incongruence between behavioral and experiential responses that could be experienced by the regulator, and potentially seen by others, as reflecting inauthenticity (Sheldon, Ryan, Rawsthorne, & Ilardi, 1997). Because suppression is an active form of self-regulation, we might further expect that the ongoing work of monitoring and inhibiting expressive impulses would lead to increases in cognitive load as well as heightened physiological responding.

When considering these predictions, a distinction can be made between questions about the short-term, acute effects of a single act of suppression and the long-term, cumulative effects of chronic suppression. From a short-term perspective, the question is whether there are discernible consequences, as our model would suggest there should be, of even a single instance of suppression. From a longer-term perspective, some people use suppression on a regular basis as a preferred form of emotion regulation (Gross & John, 2002). Do these individuals show cumulative outcomes in accord with the short-term costs? The first question calls for evidence based on laboratory studies in which emotion regulation was directly manipulated, whereas the second question is best addressed by evidence based on individual differences in the frequency of suppression. In general, we expect the acute and long-term effects to mirror each other, and so in the following sections we combine experimental and individual difference evidences concerning the consequences of expressive suppression in the domains of behavior, emotion experience, authenticity, cognitive functioning, and physiological responding.

Expressive Behavior

By early adulthood, individuals are quite adept at inhibiting the outward signs of emotion (see Manstead, 1991). In experimental work, participants told to suppress their expressive behavior show fewer facial expressions of both positive and negative emotion (a) while viewing powerful emotionally evocative slides or films (Gross, 1998a; Gross & Levenson, 1993, 1997; Richards & Gross, 1999, 2000); (b) while in the presence of, but not interacting with, several peers who they have just met (Friedman & Miller–Herringer, 1991; Harris, 2001); and (c) while having a conversation about an upsetting topic with someone they had just met (Butler, Egloff, et al., 2003). It is important to emphasize, however, that adults' suppression efforts are by no means perfect. Thus, when participants were shown a disgusting amputation film, those who were asked to suppress did show less disgust behavior than did the nonsuppression group, however, they still showed significantly more disgust than they did during a neutral film (Gross & Levenson, 1993). Sometimes, failures of suppression are evident not just in signs of leakage, but also in signs of nontarget emotions. In two studies (Friedman & Miller-Herringer, 1991; Gross & Levenson, 1997), while suppressing positive emotions, participants showed more sad behavior than did a nonsuppression group, suggesting that in their efforts to control their smiles they may have inadvertently overdone it, pulling down the corners of their mouths so far that they actually looked sad. Thus, everyday attempts at suppression appear to result in a range of behavioral changes, including a complete lack of emotional expression, partial emotional expression leaking through the suppression attempt, and facial control efforts that may be interpreted by observers in emotional terms.

These experimental findings speak to the ability of adults to suppress their emotions on command in a standardized laboratory context. What are the behavioral consequences of frequently using expressive suppression in everyday life? Gross and John (2002) addressed this question using the suppression scale of the Emotion Regulation Questionnaire (ERQ). This scale assesses how frequently an individual engages in expressive suppression. Peer-reports showed that participants who reported frequent use of suppression were seen as being generally less expressive than individuals who did not suppress.

Emotion Experience

Experimental evidence suggests that expressive suppression does not reduce, and may even increase, negative emotional experiences such as disgust, anger, sadness, and embarrassment (Gross, 1998a; Gross & Levenson, 1993, 1997; Harris, 2001; Richards & Gross, 1999, 2000). Interestingly, the effects of expressive suppression on emotion experience appear to vary according to the valence of the emotion that is being suppressed. For positive emotions, the experimental literature suggests that suppression may actually reduce emotion experience (Butler, Egloff, et al., 2003; Gross & Levenson, 1997; McCanne & Anderson, 1987; Strack, Martin, & Stepper, 1988). In keeping with the experimental findings, individual difference studies show that individuals who frequently engage in expressive suppression generally report increased levels of negative experience and decreased levels of positive experience (Gross & John, 2002).

It is not clear why the experiential effects of expressive suppression vary by valence. One possibility is that individuals are more accustomed to suppressing negative than positive emotions, and are thus more accustomed to discounting their expressions when making judgments about what they feel in negative than in positive emotion-eliciting contexts. Another possibility is that the suppression of emotion-expressive behavior in itself has a negative impact on emotional states, thus decreasing positive emotional states.

Authenticity

Both experimental and individual data suggest that suppression is accompanied by a sense of inauthenticity and alienation. Gross and John (2002) found that self-reported suppression was strongly related to Masking, a measure of the tendency to hide one's true inner feelings, attitudes, and beliefs because of concerns about self-presentation and social acceptance. Similarly, in an experimental study in which we directly manipulated suppression in the context of conversations between peers (Butler, Egloff, et al., 2003; Study 2) those individuals who had been asked to suppress their emotions during the conversation reported feeling nongenuine and inauthentic. A particularly interesting finding was that they also thought that their nonsuppressing, normally expressive partners were similarly inauthentic, suggesting a sense of alienation not only from self but from their social partners as well.

Cognitive Functioning

Turning to the cognitive consequences of suppression, in a series of slide and film viewing studies, suppression has been found to reduce memory for social information (e.g., names of individuals in the slides) presented during the period in which participants were regulating their emotions (Richards & Gross, 1999, 2000). Similarly, suppressing emotion during a conflict conversation with a romantic partner led to reduced memory for what was said during the conversation (Richards, Butler, & Gross, in press). These findings suggest that suppression increases cognitive load, which becomes particularly relevant when we consider suppression in a social context. If suppression is cognitively costly then it might be expected to distract the regulator from the interaction, impairing his or her ability to carry out the behaviors necessary to sustain a conversation. This hypothesis was clearly supported by our studies of suppression during conversations (Butler, Egloff, et al., 2003): In two experiments, those individuals who were asked to suppress their emotions reported significantly higher levels of distraction from the conversation and produced fewer appropriately contingent responses to their partners.

Physiological Responding

In the physiological domain, findings have been mixed. Although occasional studies have found either no differences between expressive suppression and spontaneous responding (Bush, Barr, McHugo, & Lanzetta, 1989), or even decreases in physiological activation associated with suppression (Zuckerman, Klorman,

Larrance, & Spiegel, 1981), the more typical finding is that suppression is accompanied by increased sympathetic and cardiovascular responding (for an early review, see Manstead, 1991; for recent experimental results, see Gross, 1998a; Gross & Levenson, 1993, 1997; Harris, 2001; Richards & Gross, 1999, 2000). Thus, although the bulk of the evidence points towards a physiological cost of expressive suppression (as compared with expression), important questions remain regarding the boundary conditions and moderating factors.

THE SOCIAL CONSEQUENCES OF EXPRESSIVE SUPPRESSION

Our analysis of the personal consequences of expressive suppression began with the premise that expressive suppression is not simply the absence of emotion behavior. We argued that suppression is instead an actively generated and maintained state, whose creation should have clear consequences for the regulator across multiple response domains. We believe that a similar claim can be made in the context of an analysis of social consequences. Contemporary theory and research on face-to-face communication posit that the lack of an expected behavior is not simply an absence—it is registered and interpreted by observers as a meaningful act in it's own right (Bilmes, 1988; Brown & Levinson, 1987). With specific reference to a lack of emotion expression Barthes (1977/1978) has written the following:

> To hide a passion totally (or even to hide, more simply, its excess) is inconceivable: not because the human subject is too weak, but because passion is in essence made to be seen: the hiding must be seen: I want you to know that I am hiding something from you. ...I want you to know that I don't want to show my feelings: that is the message I address to the other. (p. 196)

In support of this claim, experimental evidence shows that if the expressive signs of an expected emotion are not apparent, even children will infer that the person is inhibiting expression and will search for a cause of that inhibition (Rotenberg & Eisenberg, 1997).

What social consequences would we expect to follow from the suppressor's (often unintentional) message? Perhaps, "I am withholding my emotions from you." Because authenticity is valued in close relationships, and deception or withholding the self are detrimental to intimacy (DePaulo & Kashy, 1998; Kashy & DePaulo, 1996), we expect that in many circumstances, the suppressor's lack of expressivity will result in reduced interpersonal connection as indexed by decreases in rapport (feelings of closeness and connection), affiliation, and relationship satisfaction.

Another prediction regarding the social consequences of suppression arises from a consideration of interpersonal coordination, which is a fundamental aspect of face-to-face interaction (Clark, 1996). If there is a complete lack of coordination then all communication is impossible. Simply imagine trying to have a conversation with someone who speaks at the same time that you are speaking and is silent when you are. Such an extremely uncoordinated dyad would dissolve into two isolated individuals. Many authors have emphasized that responsiveness—the provision of appropriately contingent responses—is the minimal requirement for coordination among individuals (Berg & Derlega, 1987; Cappella, 1997; Davis, 1982; Davis & Perkowitz, 1979; Laurenceau, Barrett, & Peitromonaco, 1998; Reis & Shaver, 1988). Thus, because expressive suppression distracts the regulator from the conversation and decreases responsive behavior (Butler, Egloff, et al., 2003), it should disrupt interpersonal coordination and the smooth flow of interaction. Such conversations would be unpredictable, awkward, and difficult to engage in, which would produce a fairly stressful encounter (Tomaka, Blascovich, Kelsey, & Leitten, 1993). As such, we might expect to see physiological signs of stress in both the regulator and his or her partner.

In the following sections, we consider evidence relevant to our hypotheses that expressive suppression should (a) diminish interpersonal connection, and (b) enhance physiological stress responses in both the regulator and his or her social partner.

Interpersonal Connection

Indirect evidence that suppression reduces interpersonal connection comes from the study of the salutary social effects of emotion expression. Specifically, appropriate emotion expression has been shown to have a number of positive interpersonal consequences. For example, expressivity is considered to be a component of social skill (Riggio, 1986; Riggio & Friedman, 1982), the social sharing of emotions is a very common response following an emotional episode (Rime, Mesquita, Philippot, & Boca, 1991), positive emotion expression has been linked with the development of affiliation and rapport (Bernieri, Gillis, Davis, & Grahe, 1996; Harker & Keltner, 2001; Tickle–Degnan & Rosenthal, 1990), and the self-disclosure of emotions appears to be central to both initial attraction and the development of intimacy (Berg & Derlega, 1987; Collins & Miller, 1994; Hornstein & Truesdell, 1988; Laurenceau et al., 1998).

Direct evidence of the acute, detrimental relational consequences of suppression comes from our studies of suppression during conversations (Butler, Egloff, et al., 2003). In two studies we asked unacquainted pairs of women to watch an upsetting film, and then discuss their reactions. Unbeknownst to the other, one member of each dyad had been asked to either suppress or interact naturally with her conversation partner. The partners of the suppressors reported significantly reduced levels of rapport and were less willing to form a friendship as compared to the natural interaction group.

Turning to cumulative outcomes, one line of evidence comes from research on marital interaction. In this context, researchers have investigated "stonewalling," which includes expressive suppression under its rubric. Stonewalling "... involves controlling and suppressing verbal behavior, emotional expressive behavior, and listener backchannel behaviors such as head nods and eye contact" (Gottman & Levenson, 1988, p. 189). Within the context of marital interaction, stonewalling has been associated with reduced marital satisfaction in both partners (Gottman & Levenson, 1988; Levenson, Carstensen, & Gottman, 1994). In addition, it has typically been found that men in unhappy marriages are more withdrawing in the face of conflict than are men in more satisfying marriages (Gottman & Levenson, 1988; Levenson & Gottman, 1985) and relationships in which the man does not reciprocate his wife's negative emotions are more likely to decline in satisfaction than are more expressive relationships (Levenson & Gottman, 1985).

Individual difference data from college students using the ERQ (Gross & John, 2002) also suggest that the chronic use of suppression in daily life is accompanied by interpersonal distance and potential isolation. Individuals who reported frequently using suppression were unlikely to share either their negative or positive emotions with others, were uncomfortable with closeness and sharing, and reported very low levels of social support. In addition, their peers and roommates also reported reduced relationship closeness, suggesting that the suppressors' responses reflected actual relationship qualities, rather than a negative reporting bias. Taken together with the experimental evidence, it appears that inhibiting emotion expression is an effective way of avoiding interpersonal connection whether or not the regulator intends to pursue that goal.

Physiological Responding

Several experimental studies of social support are relevant to the hypothesis that suppression increases physiological stress responding, not only in the regulator, but in his or her partner as well (Christenfeld et al., 1997; Glynn, Christenfeld, & Gerin, 1999; Lepore, 1995; Lepore, Allen, & Evans, 1993). In these studies, participants gave a speech to a confederate who enacted either "supportive" or "nonsupportive behavior." Supportive behavior included high levels of positive emotion expression and responsiveness. In the nonsupportive condition, the confederates did not smile or express other emotions, and were unresponsive. Participants' stress responses were indexed by cardiovascular responding as well as self-report. Although the researchers' focus was on the stress-reducing capacity of supportive behavior, we would additionally predict that the nonsupportive behavior would be particularly stressful. Indeed, the cardiovascular results for women provide consistent support across these studies. The women who had an unsupportive confederate experienced larger blood pressure increases to the speech task than did women who were alone or with a supportive confederate.

Direct evidence that expressive suppression produces physiological stress responses in both the regulator and his or her social partner was obtained in our studies of suppression during conversation (Butler, Egloff, et al., 2003). Across two studies, the partners of suppressors showed the largest blood pressure increases as compared to all other participants in the experiments. Suppression thus appears to not only exacerbate the suppressors' own physiological responding in response to an emotionally taxing conversation, but also increases the cardiovascular responding of their interaction partners as well.

THE HEALTH CONSEQUENCES OF EXPRESSIVE SUPPRESSION

When we consider the previous findings—that suppression is associated with increased negative experience, self-alienation, negative relationship outcomes, and increased physiological reactivity in both the regulator and his or her social partner—we might expect an association between suppression and poor cumulative psychological and physical health outcomes. In the following sections we consider these hypotheses.

Psychological Health

No one can entirely escape negative emotional events. The evidence that we have reviewed, however, suggests that if an individual chronically responds to these events with expressive suppression, then the negative experience is likely to be exacerbated. Given the centrality of negative experience to many forms of psychopathology, it seems possible that this magnification of negative emotion could directly contribute to prolonging and intensifying episodes of such disorders as depression and anxiety. Although the data on individual differences in the use of suppression support this conclusion—individuals who reported frequent suppression also reported increased depressive symptoms (Gross & John, 2002)—it is also possible that the causal link is the other way around, or that a third variable was responsible for both outcomes. Such alternate explanations do not apply to laboratory studies in which the use of suppression was manipulated, however, and so our understanding of the acute effects of suppression can help to guide our interpretation of cumulative outcomes. In this case, the laboratory studies clearly show that suppression does not reduce, and may even increase, negative emotion experience (Butler, Egloff, et al., 2003), supporting the hypothesis that chronic suppression may foster emotional disorder.

Physical Health

Turning to physical health, a large literature documents the physiological and health benefits of self-disclosure, including improved immune functioning and reduced visits to medical health facilities (see, for example, Pennebaker, 1989,

1993; Pennebaker, Hughes, & O'Heeron, 1987). These benefits are typically assumed to arise due to reduced suppression, which is theorized to involve physiological effort. Thus, reducing suppression is expected to reduce wear-and-tear on the body with accompanying positive health effects. Indeed, there is evidence that unnecessary cardiovascular activation in excess of metabolic demand contributes to the development of coronary heart disease (Krantz & Manuck, 1984). In both our own studies and those of others (Gross, 1998a; Gross & Levenson, 1993, 1997; Harris, 2001; Richards & Gross, 1999, 2000), we have seen direct evidence of such increased physiological strain accompanying suppression. Furthermore, in two studies, suppression led to increased cardiovascular responding in the social partners of suppressors as well (Butler, Egloff, et al., 2003). If suppression was engaged in frequently over the course of decades within the context of a long-term relationship, it might exact a toll on the physical health of both partners (Krantz & Manuck, 1984).

Research on HIV pathogenesis supports the notion that inhibitory forms of emotion regulation are linked with increased autonomic reactivity, which in turn increases viral illnesses (Cole, Kemeny, Fahey, Zack, & Naliboff, 2002). Specifically, Cole and his colleagues investigated HIV-infected individuals and considered the links between social inhibition (which includes reduced emotional expressiveness and a heightened sensitivity to others), autonomic reactivity to a series of lab tasks, and disease outcomes. They found that social inhibition was strongly associated with increased sympathetic nervous system activity and, furthermore, that this increased autonomic reactivity mediated their poorer health outcomes.

In addition to such direct effects on health, an indirect route by which expressive suppression could impact both psychological and physical health is by limiting access to social support. We have seen that suppression is a powerful tool for increasing social distance. As such, the chronic use of suppression may limit access to new relationships and hinder the maintenance and growth of existing ones. In addition, suppressing emotional displays of distress would reduce the likelihood that the regulator's social partners would become aware of the need to provide assistance resulting in the suppressor more often facing problems alone. Social isolation has been linked with psychological problems ranging from loneliness to suicide, and has been repeatedly associated with both physical morbidity and mortality (Cohen & Thomas, 1985; House, Landis, & Umberson, 1988; Seeman, 2001; Uchino, Cacioppo, & Kiekolt–Glaser, 1996). Although there is debate as to the precise mechanism by which social support fosters health, one of the mechanisms may be the reduction of psychological and physiological stress responses (Christenfeld et al., 1997; Cohen & Thomas, 1985; Glynn et al., 1999; Lepore, 1995; Lepore et al., 1993; Uchino et al., 1996). Regardless, the fact that social support enhances well-being is uncontested. Thus, if the chronic use of suppression increases social isolation and weakens social bonds, we would expect suppression to lead to adverse health consequences for the regulator.

We must also consider the long-term partner of a chronic suppressor. Suppression would not only inhibit the receipt of social support but the giving of it as well, especially emotional and esteem support which involve the free display of caring and affection. This would mean that both members of the dyad might pay a price for one partners' suppression. This analysis, together with the fact that men generally engage in expressive suppression more frequently than do women (Gross & John, 2002), suggests that long-term relationships with men might have fewer health benefits than long-term relationships with women. Findings from studies of the health benefits of relationships show just this predicted asymmetric benefit. For example, married men—as compared to single men—report higher life satisfaction and lower rates of mental health problems. The reverse is true for women. Similarly, bereaved men show a lower survival rate than still-married men whereas bereavement does not predict women's health (for a review, see Levenson, Carstensen, & Gottman, 1993). It appears that having a relationship with a woman is associated with better health, whereas having a relationship with a man confers no such benefits (Levenson, Carstensen, & Gottman, 1993).

DOES EXPRESSIVE SUPPRESSION HAVE ANY BENEFITS?

So far, the evidence we have presented favors the "express" side of the age-old debate over whether emotions should be expressed or inhibited. The experimental and survey data we have reviewed have demonstrated that—in some contexts at least—expressive suppression (a) increases negative emotion experience while reducing positive experience, (b) leads the regulator to feel alienated from both the self and the social partner, (c) distracts the regulator from ongoing social interactions leading to less responsive conversational behavior and reduced memory for what was said during the interaction (d) results in reduced feelings of rapport and affiliation in the regulators' partners, (e) is associated with reduced relationship satisfaction and closeness, and finally, (f) increases physiological stress responding in both the regulator and the social partner.

So why have social commentators so often argued that expressive suppression is essential for social harmony (Elias, 1978)? We believe the answer to this lies in the fact that expressing emotions can have a wide range of repercussions in the world, both good and bad, and so impeding these expressions can also have diverse effects. In addition, the full scope of suppression can only be appreciated when we look beyond the individual to consider the larger social group. Although suppressing emotion may entail costs, in many situations it also fulfills important functions, such as avoiding the negative effects of unregulated expression, and modulating the regulator's behavior to fit smoothly within socially dictated social norms, or to accommodate the relationship goals and intentions of the partner. In such contexts, the costs of suppression may be reduced, or at least compensated by the desirable outcomes.

Avoiding Negative Consequences of Expression

Expressions of extremely intense negative emotions that are directed toward children, friends, or other social partners are likely foremost in the minds of commentators who espouse the benefits of expressive suppression. Such unregulated expression can clearly have disruptive effects on interpersonal relations and on the recipient. For example, exchanges involving high levels of such expressions have been shown to predict divorce (Gottman & Levenson, 1992; Levenson & Gottman, 1985), expressing anger at another person can escalate the conflict by making them angry too (Tavris, 1984), repeated expressions of negative emotion by family members of remitted schizophrenics predicts the patients' relapse (Greenley, 1986), and expressing anger freely is associated with increased aggressive behavior (Bushman, Baumeister, & Phillips, 2001). In the case of strong negative emotions directed at one's partner, expressive suppression may help to avert an interpersonal escalation of negative emotion, or the debasement of the recipient, and thus may help to pave the way for more constructive responses. As Fischer et al. (this volume) argued, one powerful impetus for engaging in emotion regulation (e.g., inhibiting hurtful emotional outbursts) is avoiding negative social consequences. One relevant behavioral sequence that has been studied is called "accommodation" (Rusbult, Verette, Whitney, Slovik, & Lipkus, 1991). Accommodation refers to "... an individual's willingness, when a partner has engaged in a potentially destructive behavior, to (a) inhibit tendencies to react destructively in turn and (b) instead to engage in constructive reactions" (Rusbult et al., 1991, p. 53). Not surprisingly, accommodation predicts relationship satisfaction. It is worth noting that accommodation likely involves a large dose of suppression, since "inhibiting a tendency to react destructively" would often include suppressing negative emotions.

Excessive expressions of distress have also been argued to result in negative psychological and social outcomes (Kennedy–Moore & Watson, 2001). For example, rumination includes repetitive rehearsing of the distress and has been shown to intensify and prolong the negative emotions (Nolen–Hoeksema, 1991). In addition, individuals who engage in rumination report receiving less social support, possibly because others find their ruminative expressions aversive (Nolen–Hoeksema & Davis, 1999). Likewise, constant expressions of negative emotions are often seen as complaining, which can lead others to avoid the expresser (Kowalski & Erikson, 1997). In these cases, and others like them, more modulated expression, such as could be achieved by some degree of expressive suppression, might help to elicit positive responses from the regulator's social network.

Excessive expressions of both anger and distress appear to have little redeeming value and so suppression in these cases is very likely to be beneficial. In contrast, in some situations expressing an emotion is neither entirely good nor bad, but rather involves a trade-off between mutually exclusive costs and benefits. Mild expressions of anger provide one context in which this tradeoff function can be seen.

Anger is interesting because it appears to be one of the few emotions for which suppression can actually foster affiliation—people like someone more if he or she refrains from displaying anger (Tiedens, 2001). On the other hand, expressing moderate levels of justified anger leads to being perceived as competent and others are more likely to grant the expresser power and authority (Tiedens, 2001). This appears to be particularly true if the person expressing anger is male (Coats & Feldman, 1996). Thus, anger is a prototypical case in which a person must choose between a social benefit—increased status—and a social cost—potentially reduced affiliation. In such cases, suppression is inherently neither beneficial nor detrimental, but rather depends on the goals of the regulator.

Adhering to Social Norms

Social norms make interactions more predictable, thereby facilitating the smooth flow of communication and reducing interpersonal friction. Another benefit of suppression, therefore, may be to modulate an individual's expressive behavior to fit into these socially dictated guidelines (Timmers, Fischer, & Manstead, 1998; see also, Fischer et al., this volume). For example, Fischer et al. (this volume) reviewed extensive evidence from workplace settings that impression management goals guide many efforts at emotion regulation. Another set of norms that has been empirically studied revolves around the distinction between exchange and communal relationships (Berg & Clark, 1986; Clark & Taraban, 1991). In exchange relationships, individuals engage in a tit-for-tat kind of interaction, such as exchanging goods or services. Parties to such an interaction do not expect to be responsible for each other's welfare or to be burdened by the other person's emotional upsets. Empirical work has demonstrated that in such relationships, people generally prefer reduced levels of emotion expression, particularly negative emotions. As a result, some degree of suppression would be normative and should help to preserve smooth interaction among members of an exchange relationship (Clark & Taraban, 1991).

Similarly, although expressing positive emotions is often socially beneficial (Frank, Ekman, & Friesen, 1993; Harker & Keltner, 2001; Tickle–Degnan & Rosenthal, 1990), there are some situations in which suppressing positive emotion could benefit one's social partners. For example, if you have out-performed someone in a competitive context, then freely expressing your joy at beating them is unlikely to endear you to that person. In situations such as these, cultural display rules call for the suppression of positive emotion (Ekman et al., 1972). This sort of situation was studied by Friedman and Miller–Herringer (1991). Participants solved difficult logic problems either alone, or with two confederates posing as fellow participants. They then received positive feedback on their performance which told them that they had performed in the top 10% of college students. Their emotional expressions in response to this feedback was recorded. The results clearly showed that the participants spontaneously suppressed their expressions of happiness when they were in the social situation. Unfortunately, no measures were taken of the social consequences of this suppression. It is an appealing hypothesis, but we do not know if the people who engaged in the normative suppression of positive emotion were better liked.

Just as adhering to social norms can be beneficial, so violating those norms can be disruptive. Thus, if an individual fails to suppress emotion in a situation where the social norm would dictate it, we would expect to see negative ramifications. Research on social support suggests one such situation. As reviewed in a previous section of this chapter, the typical finding from this research is that low expressivity by a confederate results in increased stress-related cardiovascular responding in participants who must give a speech to that confederate (Christenfeld et al., 1997; Glynn et al., 1999; Lepore, 1995; Lepore et al., 1993). What we did not mention there is that this result may depend on the sex of the confederate. In one study that investigated sex differences, an inexpressive male confederate elicited smaller blood pressure increases than did a more expressive male (Glynn et al., 1999). One explanation of this finding is that stereotypical gender roles encourage less emotional expressivity in men than in women (Gross & John, 1995; Fischer et al., this volume; Riggio & Friedman, 1982) and so the normative case would be for a man to demonstrate reduced levels of emotion expression. The finding that men report engaging in expressive suppression more often than do women is in accord with these normative dictates (Gross & John, 2002). Thus, in certain cultural contexts at least, an inexpressive, suppressing man may be reassuring whereas a suppressing woman may be disconcerting.

Adapting to the Goals and Intentions of the Partner

The outcome of any act of emotion expression, or expressive suppression, depends to a large degree on how it interacts with the intentions and goals of the partner. For example, if one person has no interest in affiliating or furthering a relationship, then an intimate sharing of emotions by the other may represent unwanted friendly overtures and actually be experienced as aversive. We would expect that in these situations, a person would prefer to interact with someone more restrained in emotional expression. Our study of suppression during conversations between w omen (Butler, Egloff, et al., 2003; Study 2) provided evidence in support of this hypothesis. When participants arrived at the lab, they were briefly introduced to, and then separated from, their partner for the experiment. Prior to further interaction, they reported on how much they wanted to get to know their partner. This provided a state-dependent measure of their interest in affiliating with that specific partner in that specific situation. Results showed that individuals who initially reported high interest in getting to know the partner were particularly frustrated when that partner suppressed his or her emotions. In contrast, participants who reported a preference for maintaining their interpersonal distance were satisfied with a suppressing partner, and by some measures actually preferred interacting with a suppressor than with an expressive individual (Butler, Horowitz, & Gross, 2002).

A related issue is that, although the benefits of self-disclosure are well documented (Berg & Derlega, 1987; Collins & Miller, 1994; Hornstein & Truesdell, 1988; Laurenceau et al., 1998; Pennebaker, 1989, 1993; Pennebaker et al., 1987), they generally depend on a positive, supportive response from the recipient. As such, expressing emotions freely is a risky business and a clear function of suppression in some contexts is to protect the self from such emotions as rejection, vulnerability, and embarrassment (Kennedy–Moore & Watson, 2001). For example, expressing positive emotions is generally seen as affiliative and if reciprocated can foster positive relationships (Fredrickson, 1998; Fridlund, 1994; Harker & Keltner, 2001). If, however, the recipient spurns the affiliative gesture, the instigator is likely to feel rejected or embarrassed at best. The finding that suppression is positively correlated with masking (hiding true feelings due to concerns about self-presentation and social acceptance; Gross & John, 2002) suggests that this risk is salient for individuals who chronically suppress their emotions. As another example, expressing fear and sadness is generally perceived as a sign of vulnerability and incompetence (Tiedens, 2001; Timmers et al., 1998). Although such expressions can elicit compassion and support (Kennedy–Moore & Watson, 2001), a hostile partner could use such an opportunity to attack or dominate the expresser.

Finally, in the case of expressing intense anger at a social partner, we have seen that this is typically detrimental, escalating conflict or demeaning the recipient. Nevertheless, if we consider the intentions of the partner, we see that in some cases expressing anger at them is justified and perhaps desirable. If the other person is actually doing or intending something that would have undesired consequences for the self, then negative emotions are a protective response, and expressing them may avert negative self-relevant outcomes. In contrast, if we have simply misinterpreted our partner's intentions, then our negative emotions at them would be misplaced and expressing them is likely to generate unnecessary conflict. Thus, in the warranted case, suppression could be self-protective, whereas in the unwarranted case, a lack of suppression could damage a desirable relationship.

DIRECTIONS FOR FUTURE RESEARCH

Our analysis suggests that Western culture's longstanding ambivalence regarding whether to express or to inhibit emotion expressions may be well founded. We have seen that expressive suppression can entail numerous personal and social costs, including increased negative experience, self-alienation, poor cognitive functioning, reduced affiliation and rapport, and increased cardiovascular responding in both the regulator and the social partner. At the same time, it is apparent that if the act of suppression is contextually sensitive, it may serve desirable personal and interpersonal functions. Unfortunately, the evidence for this is largely tangential and circumstantial, because research on emotion regulation has focused on the individual in a fairly limited range of social situations. As a result, it is far from clear what mediating mechanisms generate the costs or which moderators determine how to minimize costs and maximize benefits. In the following, we consider three questions that are important for understanding the pragmatic effects of suppression within a social context: (a) What constitutes optimal suppression? (b) what role does ambivalence play? and (c) what processes underlie the social outcomes of suppression?

What Constitutes Optimal Suppression?

It is not yet clear whether suppression always entails costs or whether in some situations it is entirely beneficial. In the former case, optimal self-regulation would entail a cost–benefit analysis and suppression should only be invoked when expression would be detrimental and other less expensive forms of regulation are not available. If, on the other hand, there are situations in which suppression is cost-free and bestows benefits, then an additional regulatory challenge is recognizing those situations and employing suppression accordingly.

Either way, flexibility appears to be crucial for optimal emotion regulation. In fact, it seems plausible that the many negative outcomes that have been associated with the frequent use of suppression as a preferred regulation strategy arise due to inflexibility. If a person were to indiscriminately employ suppression across all contexts, he or she may occasionally gain some benefits, but would also maximize the costs of suppressing in inappropriate contexts. Longitudinal studies in which both the frequency and the flexibility of suppression were tracked could help to address this issue, along with the question of whether frequent suppression independently predicts negative outcomes, or whether some underlying personality characteristic is responsible for both.

Given the likely importance of regulatory flexibility it will also be important to conduct research distinguishing the relative merits of other forms of emotion regulation. For example, experimental and survey data suggest that cognitive reappraisal, which entails altering the way one thinks about a stimulus to alter one's emotional responding to it, does not entail the same costs as does suppression (Butler, Egloff, et al., 2003; Gross, 1998a, 2002; Gross & John, 2002; Richards & Gross, 1998). Further research investigating a range of theoretically derived forms of emotion regulation within clearly specified social contexts could help to elucidate the parameters that determine the ideal match between emotion regulation strategies and contextual demands.

Finally, any definition of "optimal" must take into account not only the individual but his or her social partners as well. In some cases, there may exist forms of emotion regulation by which both the regulator and the community benefit, but often there may need to be some trade-off. Understanding this balance will clearly demand studying emotion regulation within social contexts.

The Role of Ambivalence

Ironically, the very ambivalence regarding suppression that is culturally so widespread may itself play a role in generating the many costs that we have seen accompanying suppression. An interesting possibility is that, at the level of the individual, it is ambivalently motivated acts of suppression that are problematic, and nonambivalent ones may not entail such costs.

An example of ambivalent suppression would be hiding our annoyance while talking to a boring coworker because that person is more powerful and we are afraid of retaliation. In this case, we are torn between the motive to get out of the conversation and the fear of being fired. On the other hand, we may suppress our emotions because a countervening motivation is significantly stronger than the impulse to express. For example we may choose not to laugh when a friend makes an embarrassing error. In this case, we are not ambivalent in our suppression attempt—there was little or nothing to be gained by the expression and we can be proud of our successful attempt which has benefited our friend. One hypothesis is that ambivalent suppression necessarily entails personal and social costs, but that with nonambivalent suppression the costs are not inevitable.

This idea has been suggested before (Pennebaker, 1985) and evidence from correlational research demonstrates that ambivalence regarding emotion expression is indeed associated with many of the same costs that we have seen accompanying suppression, including psychological distress and physical health symptoms (King & Emmons, 1990), social deficits in skills such as decoding the emotion expressions of others (King, 1998), and high negative emotion experience, depression, and psychosomatic complaints (Emmons & King, 1988). It is unknown, however, how these results relate to suppression and whether nonambivalent suppression efforts would be less costly than ambivalent ones.

Social Processes

It is clear that we can no longer think about expression and suppression in black-and-white terms. The question under debate thus must evolve from "Should we routinely express or suppress our emotions?" to "When, where, and with whom is it optimal to express or suppress emotion expression?" This shift calls for increased research attention to such factors as social roles, norms, and cultural differences. It also demands a better understanding of interpersonal dynamics and relationship contexts. For example, we have seen that the match between one person's suppressive behavior and his or her partner's interpersonal intentions and wishes can alter whether the suppression has positive or negative interpersonal consequences. Unfortunately very little is known about such processes, in part due to the fact that most research on emotion regulation has focused on the individual in social isolation.

A related research question is the nature of the mechanisms underlying the social consequences of suppression. How does one person's attempts to conceal his or her feelings impact the social partner and the relationship? We have touched on various possibilities, including authenticity and disrupted communication. In our studies of suppression during conversation, we focused on the potential impact of disruptions to interpersonal coordination and tested the hypothesis that the regulators' distraction from the conversation, and hence reduced conversational responsiveness, would mediate their partners' reduced rapport and affiliation, and their increased cardiovascular responding. Although suppressors were indeed distracted and unresponsive, and this did mediate rapport, it did not mediate affiliation or impact the partners' physiological responses (Butler, Egloff, et al., 2003). Thus, the exact behavioral interface linking one person's attempts at emotion suppression to his or her partner's outcomes is yet to be discovered.

Another process that may underlie suppression's impact on interpersonal outcomes is the disruption of empathic, or shared emotional experience. When one person expresses an emotion about something, either positive or negative, an interpersonal feedback loop often develops based on the processes of mimicry and contagion (Kappas, 1991). Experimental evidence has shown that merely perceiving a behavior is adequate to induce mimicry of that behavior (Chartrand & Bargh, 1999). In addition, Neumann and Strack (2000) have shown that merely perceiving an emotional cue is adequate to induce a congruent mood state. Thus, if one person expresses an emotion, their partner often begins to both mimic the first person's expressive behavior and to experience a congruent emotion. If either person were to suppress emotion expression, such an emotional feedback-loop would be impeded, potentially disrupting the sense of interpersonal connection that such a shared emotional state could induce.

Finally, an intriguing process by which suppression might contribute to cumulative social outcomes is through memory, which is the basis for a shared perception of a relationship. A couple's level of agreement about the narrative of their relationship has been associated with marital satisfaction (Veroff, Sutherland, Chadiha, & Ortega, 1993). Such agreement would require mutually shared memories of past conversations and important shared social interactions. As we have seen, there is ample evidence that expressive suppression results in reduced memory for information that was present at the time of the suppression effort (Richards et al., in press; Richards & Gross, 1999, 2000). Such memory decrements associated with suppression could result in social partners' holding very different memories of critical interactions, and that could result in increasing antagonism and eroding relationship satisfaction.

CONCLUDING COMMENT

Experimental studies show that suppressing emotion entails a host of personal and social costs. In addition, survey research demonstrates that individuals who frequently (and perhaps inflexibly) suppress emotion expression also report relatively unhappy and socially conflicted lives. Although suppression can keep an emotion out of sight, it cannot keep it out of mind, either for the regulator or for his or her social partners. It also cannot prevent that emotion from having an impact on the world, because the act of suppression itself has consequences. Nevertheless, as we extend our consideration of the effects of suppression to a wider range of social situations, and redefine "beneficial" to include not only the regulator but his or her social partners as well, we see that these impacts are not always negative. Clearly the regulatory demands of integrating the emotional needs of the individual with those of the community are not going to be met by any single emotion regulation strategy. Future research faces the challenge of specifying the conditions that determine whether a given act of suppression is likely to be more or less harmful than other potential regulatory strategies, and which strategy in which situation is likely to reap what rewards for which person or group of people. Such research could help to elucidate the ways in which emotional and social processes interact either to enhance or diminish personal and social well-being and health.

AUTHOR NOTE

Preparation of this chapter was supported by Grant MH53859 from the National Institute of Mental Health. Correspondence should be addressed to James Gross, Department of Psychology, Stanford University, Stanford, CA 94305–2130. E-mail may be sent to james@psych.stanford.edu

REFERENCES

Arnold, M. (1960). *Emotion and personality*. New York: Columbia University Press.

Barthes, R. (1978). *A lover's discourse: Fragments.* (R. Howard, Trans.). New York: Hill and Wang. (Original work published 1977)

Berg, J. H., & Clark, M. S. (1986). Differences in social exchange between intimate and other relationships: Gradually evolving or quickly apparent? In V. J. Derlega & B. A. Winstead (Eds.), *Friendship and social interaction* (pp. 101–128). New York: Springer–Verlag.

Berg, J. H., & Derlega, V. J. (1987). *Responsiveness and self-disclosure*. New York: Plenum.

Bernieri, F. J., Gillis, J. S., Davis, J. M., & Grahe, J. E. (1996). Dyad rapport and the accuracy of its judgement across situations: A lens model analysis. *Journal of Personality & Social Psychology, 71*, 110–129.

Bilmes, J. (1988). The concept of preference in conversation analysis. *Language Sociology, 17*, 161–181.

Brown, P., & Levinson, S. (1987). *Politeness: Some universals in language usage*. Cambridge, England: Cambridge University Press.

Buck, R. (1985). Prime theory: An integrated view of motivation and emotion. *Psychological Review, 92*, 389–413.

Bush, L. K., Barr, C. L., McHugo, G. J., & Lanzetta, J. T. (1989). The effects of facial control and facial mimicry on subjective reactions to comedy routines. *Motivation and Emotion, 13*, 31–52.

Bushman, B. J., Baumeister, R. F., & Phillips, C. M. (2001). Do people aggress to improve their mood? Catharsis beliefs, affect regulation opportunity, and aggressive responding. *Journal of Personality and Social Psychology, 81*, 17–32.

Butler, E. A., Egloff, B., Wilhelm, F. H., Smith, N. C., Erickson, E. A., & Gross, J. J. (2003). The social consequences of expressive suppression. *Emotion, 3*(1), 48–67..

Butler, E. A., Horowitz, L., & Gross, J. J. (2002, May). Who is frustrated and who is satisfied by an inexpressive social partner? Paper presented at the Society for Interpersonal Theory and Research, Toronto, Canada.

Campos, J. J., Campos, R. G., & Barrett, K. C. (1989). Emergent themes in the study of emotional development and emotion regulation. *Developmental Psychology, 25*, 394–402.

Cappella, J. N. (1997). Behavioral and judged coordination in adult informal social interactions: Vocal and kinesic indicators. *Journal of Personality and Social Psychology, 72*, 119–131.

Chartrand, T. L., & Bargh, J. A. (1999). The chameleon effect: The perception–behavior link and social interaction. *Journal of Personality and Social Psychology, 76*, 893–910.

Christenfeld, N., Gerin, W., Linder, W., Sanders, M., Mathur, J., Deich, J. D., et al. (1997). Social support effects on cardiovascular reactivity: Is a stranger as effective as a friend? *Psychosomatic Medicine, 59*, 388–398.

Clark, H. H. (1996). *Using language*. Cambridge, England: Cambridge University Press.

Clark, M. S., & Taraban, C. (1991). Reactions to and willingness to express emotion in communal and exchange relationships. *Journal of Experimental Social Psychology, 27*, 324–336.

Coats, E. J., & Feldman, R. S. (1996). Gender differences in nonverbal correlates of social status. *Personality and Social Psychology Bulletin, 22*, 1014–1022.

Cohen, S., & Thomas, A. W. (1985). Stress, social support, and the buffering hypothesis. *Psychological Bulletin, 98*, 310–357.

Cole, P. M., Zahn–Waxler, C., Fox, N. A., Usher, B. A., & Welsh, J. D. (1996). Individual differences in emotion regulation and behavior problems in preschool children. *Journal of Abnormal Psychology, 105*, 518–529.

Cole, S. W., Kemeny, M. E., Fahey, J. L., Zack, J. A., & Naliboff, B. D. (2002). Psychological risk factors for HIV pathogenesis: Mediation by the autonomic nervous system. Manuscript submitted for publication.

Collins, N. L., & Miller, L. C. (1994). Self-disclosure and liking: A meta-analytic review. *Psychological Bulletin, 116*, 457–475.

Davis, D. (1982). Determinants of responsiveness in dyadic interactions. In W. Ickes & E. G. Knowles (Eds.), *Personality, roles and social behavior* (pp. 85–140). New York: Springer–Verlag.

Davis, D., & Perkowitz, W. T. (1979). Consequences of responsiveness in dyadic interaction: Effects of probablity of response and proportion of content-related responses on interpersonal attraction. *Journal of Personality and Social Psychology, 37*, 534–550.

DePaulo, B. M., & Kashy, D. A. (1998). Everyday lies in close and casual relationships. *Journal of Personality and Social Psychology, 74*, 63–79.

Duc De La Rochefoucauld, F. (1706). *Moral Maxims and Reflections, no. 21*. New York: F.A. Stokes Co. (Original work published during 1665–1678)

Eisenberg, N., Fabes, R. A., Guthrie, I. K., & Reiser, M. (2000). Dispositional emotionality and regulation: Their role in predicting quality of social functioning. *Journal of Personality and Social Psychology, 78*, 136–157.

Ekman, P., Friesen, W. V., & Ellsworth, P. (1972). *Emotion in the human face: Guidelines for research and an integration of findings*. New York: Pergamon.

Elias, N. (1978). *The civilizing process: The history of manners*. New York: Urizon Books.

Emmons, R. A., & King, L. A. (1988). Conflict among personal strivings: Immediate and long-term implications for psychological and physical well-being. *Journal of Personality and Social Psychology, 54*, 1040–1048.

Frank, M. G., Ekman, P., & Friesen, W. V. (1993). Behavioral markers and recognizability of the smile of enjoyment. *Journal of Personality and Social Psychology, 64*, 83–93.

Fredrickson, B. L. (1998). What good are positive emotions? *Review of General Psychology, 2*, 300–319.

Fridlund, A. J. (1994). *Human facial expression: An evolutionary view.* San Diego, CA: Academic.

Friedman, H. S., & Miller–Herringer. (1991). Nonverbal display of emotion in public and in private: Self-monitoring, personality, and expressive cues. *Journal of Personality and Social Psychology, 61*, 766–775.

Frijda, N. H. (1986). *The emotions*. Cambridge, England: Cambridge University Press.

Glynn, L. M., Christenfeld, N., & Gerin, W. (1999). Gender, social support, and cardiovascular responses to stress. *Psychosomatic Medicine, 61*, 234–242.

Gottman, J. M., & Levenson, R. W. (1988). The social psychophysiology of marriage. In P. Noller & M. A. Fitzpatrick (Eds.), *Perspectives on marital interaction*. (pp. 182–200). Clevedon, England: Multilingual Matters.

Gottman, J., M., & Levenson, R. W. (1992). Marital processes predictive of later dissolution: Behavior, physiology, and health. *Journal of Personality and Social Psychology, 63*, 221–233.

Greenley, J. R. (1986). Social control and expressed emotion. *The Journal of Nervous and Mental Disease, 174*, 24–30.

Gross, J. J. (1989). Emotional expression in cancer onset and progression. *Social Science Medicine, 28*, 1239–1248.

Gross, J. J. (1998a). Antecedent- and response- focused emotion regulation: Divergent consequences for experience, expression, and physiology. *Journal of Personality and Social Psychology, 74*, 224–237.

Gross, J. J. (1998b). The emerging field of emotion regulation: An integrative review. *Review of General Psychology, 2*, 271–299.

Gross, J. J. (1999). Emotion and emotion regulation. In L. A. Pervin & O. P. John (Eds.), *Handbook of personality: Theory and research* (2nd ed., pp. 525–552). New York: Guilford.

Gross, J. J. (2001). Emotion regulation in adulthood: Timing is everything. *Current Directions in Psychological Science, 10*, 214–219.

Gross, J. J. (2002). Emotion regulation: Affective, cognitive, and social consequences. *Psychophysiology, 39*, 281–291.

Gross, J. J., & John, O. P. (1995). Facets of emotional expressivity: Three self-report factors and their correlates. *Personality and Individual Differences, 19*, 555–568.

Gross, J. J., & John, O. P. (2002). Individual differences in two emotion regulation processes: Implications for affect, relationships, and well-being. Manuscript submitted for publication.

Gross, J. J., & Levenson, R. W. (1993). Emotional suppression: Physiology, self-report, and expressive behavior. *Journal of Personality and Social Psychology, 64*, 970–986.

Gross, J. J., & Levenson, R. W. (1997). Hiding feelings: The acute effects of inhibiting negative and positive emotion. *Journal of Abnormal Psychology, 106*, 95–103.

Halberstadt, A. G., Crisp, V. W., & Eaton, K. L. (1999). Family expressiveness: A retrospective and new directions for research. In P. Philippot, R. S. Feldman, & E. J. Coats (Eds.), *Studies in emotion and social interaction.* (pp. 109–155). Cambridge, England: Cambridge University Press.

Harker, L., & Keltner, D. (2001). Expressions of positive emotion in women's college yearbook pictures and their relationship to personality and life outcomes across adulthood. *Journal of Personality and Social Psychology, 80*, 112–124.

Harris, C. R. (2001). Cardiovascular responses of embarrassment and effects of emotional suppression in a social setting. *Journal of Personality and Social Psychology, 81*, 886–897.

Hornstein, G. A., & Truesdell, S. E. (1988). Development of intimate conversation in close relationships. *Journal of Social and Clinical Psychology, 7*, 49–64.

House, J. S., Landis, K. R., & Umberson, D. (1988). Social relationships and health. *Science, 241*, 540–545.

Izard, C. E. (1977). *Human emotions*. New York: Plenum.

Kappas, A. (1991). The illusion of the neutral observer: On the communication of emotion. *Cahiers de Linguistique Francaise, 12*, 153–168.

Kashy, D. A., & DePaulo, B. M. (1996). Who lies? *Journal of Personality and Social Psychology, 70*, 1037–1051.

Kennedy–Moore, E., & Watson, J. C. (2001). How and when does emotional expression help? *Review of General Psychology, 5*, 187–212.

King, L. A. (1998). Ambivalence over emotional expression and reading emotions in situations and faces. *Journal of Personality and Social Psychology, 74*, 753–762.

King, L. A., & Emmons, R. A. (1990). Conflict over emotional expression: Psychological and physical correlates. *Journal of Personality and Social Psychology, 58*, 864–877.

Kowalski, R. M., & Erikson, J. R. (1997). Complaining: What's all the fuss about? In R. Kowalski (Ed.), *Aversive interpersonal behaviors* (pp. 91–110). New York: Plenum.

Krantz, D. S., & Manuck, S. B. (1984). Acute psychophysiological reactivity and risk of cardiovascular disease: A review and methodologic critique. *Psychological Bulletin, 96*, 435–464.

Laurenceau, J., Barrett, L. F., & Peitromonaco, P. R. (1998). Intimacy as an interpersonal process: The importance of self-disclosure and partner disclosure, and perceived partner responsiveness in interpersonal exchanges. *Journal of Personality and Social Psychology, 74*, 1238–1251.

Lawrence, D. H. (1964). *Studies in classic American literature*. London: Heinemann. (Original work published 1924)

Lazarus, R. S. (1991). *Emotion and adaptation*. Oxford, England: Oxford University Press.

Lepore, S. J. (1995). Cynicism, social support, and cardiovascular reactivity. *Health Psychology, 14*, 210–216.

Lepore, S. J., Allen, K. A. M., & Evans, G. W. (1993). Social support lowers cardiovascular reactivity to an accute stressor. *Psychosomatic Medicine, 55*, 518–524.

Levenson, R. W. (1994). Human emotions: A functional view. In P. Ekman & R. J. Davidson (Eds.), *The nature of emotion: Fundamental questions* (pp. 123–126). New York: Oxford University Press.

Levenson, R. W., Carstensen, L. L., & Gottman, J. M. (1993). Long-term marriage: Age, gender, and satisfaction. *Psychology and Aging, 8*, 301–313.

Levenson, R. W., Carstensen, L. L., & Gottman, J. M. (1994). The influence of age and gender on affect, physiology, and their interrelations: A study of long-term marriages. *Journal of Personality and Social Psychology, 67*, 56–68.

Levenson, R. W., & Gottman, J. M. (1985). Physiological and affective predictors of change in relationship satisfaction. *Journal of Personality and Social Psychology, 49*, 85–94.

Manstead, A. S. (1991). Expressiveness as an individual difference. In R. S. Feldman & B. Rime (Eds.), *Fundamentals of nonverbal behavior* (pp. 285–328). New York: Cambridge University Press.

McCanne, T. R., & Anderson, J. A. (1987). Emotional responding following experimental manipulation of facial electromyographic activity. *Journal of Personality and Social Psychology, 52*, 759–768.

Neumann, R., & Strack, F. (2000). "Mood contagion": The automatic transfer of mood between persons. *Journal of Personality and Social Psychology, 79*, 211–223.

Nolen-Hoeksema, S. (1991). Responses to depression and their effects on the duration of depressive episodes. *Journal of Abnormal Psychology, 100*, 569–582.

Nolen-Hoeksema, S., & Davis, C. G. (1999). "Thanks for sharing that": Ruminators and their social support networks. *Journal of Personality and Social Psychology, 77*, 801–814.

Pennebaker, J. W. (1985). Traumatic experience and psychosomatic disease: Exploring the roles of behavioural inhibition, obsession, and confiding. *Canadian Psychology, 26*, 82–95.

Pennebaker, J. W. (1989). Confession, inhibition, and disease. *Advances in Experimental Social Psychology, 22*, 211–244.

Pennebaker, J. W. (1993). Putting stress into words: Health, linguistic, and therapeutic implications. B*ehavioral Research Therapy, 31*, 539–548.

Pennebaker, J. W., Hughes, C. F., & O'Heeron, R. C. (1987). The psychophysiology of confession: Linking inhibitory and psychosomatic processes. J*ournal of Personality and Social Psychology, 52*, 781–793.

Petrie, K. J., Booth, R. J., & Pennebaker, J. W. (1998). The immunological effects of thought suppression. *Journal of Personality and Social Psychology, 75*, 1264–1272.

Reis, H. T., & Shaver, P. (1988). Intimacy as an interpersonal process. In S. W. Duck (Ed.), *Handbook of personal relationships* (pp. 367–389). Chichester, England: Wiley.

Richards, J. M., Butler, E. A., & Gross, J. J. (in press). Emotion regulation in romantic relationships: The cognitive consequences of concealing feelings. To appear in *Journal of Social and Personal Relationships*.

Richards, J. M., & Gross, J. J. (1998, July). Emotion regulation and memory: The divergent consequences of reappraisal and suppression. Paper presented at the American Psychological Association, San Francisco.

Richards, J. M., & Gross, J. J. (1999). Composure at any cost? The cognitive consequences of emotion suppression. *Personality and Social Psychology Bulletin, 25*, 1033–1044.

Richards, J. M., & Gross, J. J. (2000). Emotion regulation and memory: The cognitive costs of keeping one's cool. *Journal of Personality and Social Psychology, 79*, 410–424.

Riggio, R. E. (1986). Assessment of basic social skills. *Journal of Personality and Social Psychology, 51*, 649–660.

Riggio, R. E., & Friedman, H. S. (1982). Impression formation: The role of expressive behavior. *Journal of Personality and Social Psychology, 50*, 421–427.

Rime, B., Mesquita, B., Philippot, P., & Boca, S. (1991). Beyond the emotional event: Six studies on the social sharing of emotion. *Cognition & Emotion, 5*, 435–465.

Rotenberg, K. J., & Eisenberg, N. (1997). Developmental differences in the undersanding of and reaction to others' inhibition of emotional expression. *Developmental Psychology, 33*, 526–537.

Rusbult, C. E., Verette, J., Whitney, G. A., Slovik, L. F., & Lipkus, I. (1991). Accomodation processes in close relationships: Theory and preliminary empirical evidence. *Journal of Personality and Social Psychology, 60*, 53–78.

Scherer, K. R. (1984). On the nature and function of emotion: A component process approach. In K. R. Scherer & P. Ekman (Eds.), *Approaches to emotion* (pp. 293–317). Hillsdale, NJ: Lawrence Erlbaum Associates, Inc.

Seeman, T. (2001). How do others get under our skin? In C. D. Ryff & B. H. Singer (Eds.), *Emotion, social relationships, and health*. (pp. 189–210). New York: Oxford University Press.

Sheldon, K. M., Ryan, R. M., Rawsthorne, L. J., & Ilardi, B. (1997). Trait self and true self: Cross-role variation in the Big-Five personality traits and its relation with psychological authenticity and subjective well-being. *Journal of Personality and Social Psychology, 73*, 1380–1393.

Strack, F., Martin, L. L., & Stepper, S. (1988). Inhibiting and facilitating conditions of the human smile: A nonobtrusive test of the facial feedback hypothesis. *Journal of Personality and Social Psychology, 54*, 768–777.

Tavris, C. (1984). On the wisdom of counting to ten: Personal and social dangers of anger expression. *Review of Personality & Social Psychology, 5*, 170–191.

Thompson, R. A. (1994). Emotion regulation: A theme in search of definition. *Monographs of the Society for Research in Child Development, 59*(2-3) 25–52, 250–283.

Tickle–Degnan, L., & Rosenthal, R. (1990). The nature of rapport and its nonverbal correlates. *Psychological Inquiry, 1*, 285–293.

Tiedens, L. Z. (2001). Anger and advancement versus sadness and subjugation: The effect of negative emotion expressions on social status conferral. *Journal of Personality and Social Psychology, 80*, 86–94.

Timmers, M., Fischer, A. H., & Manstead, A. S. (1998). Gender differences in motives for regulating emotions. *Personality and Social Psychology Bulletin, 24*, 974–985.

Tomaka, J., Blascovich, J., Kelsey, R. M., & Leitten, C. L. (1993). Subjective, physiological, and behavioral effects of threat and challenge appraisal. *Journal of Personality and Social Psychology, 65*, 248–260.

Trobst, K. K., Collins, R. L., & Embree, J. M. (1994). The role of emotion in social support provision: Gender, empathy and expressions of distress. *Journal of Social and Personal Relationships, 11*, 45–62.

Uchino, B., Cacioppo, J. T., & Kiekolt–Glaser, J. K. (1996). The relationship between social support and physiological processes: A review with emphasis in underlying mechanisms and implications for health. *Psychological Bulletin, 119*, 488–531.

Veroff, J., Sutherland, L., Chadiha, L., & Ortega, R. M. (1993). Newlyweds tell their stories: A narrative method for assessing marital experiences. *Journal of Social and Personal Relationships, 10*, 437–457.

Zuckerman, M., Klorman, R., Larrance, D. T., & Spiegel, N. H. (1981). Facial, autonomic, and subjective components of emotion: The facial feedback hypothesis versus the externalizer–internalizer distinction. *Journal of Personality and Social Psychology, 41*, 929–944.

5

Positive Emotion and the Regulation of Interpersonal Relationships

Michelle N. Shiota, Belinda Campos, and Dacher Keltner
University of California, Berkeley

Matthew J. Hertenstein
DePauw University

Emotions serve a wide range of important social functions, including the regulation of interpersonal relationships. Positive emotions, although understudied, are particularly critical to the formation and maintenance of social bonds. This chapter presents a framework for understanding the social functions of positive emotion, associating specific positive emotions with particular types of relationships and particular regulatory tasks. Evidence for the importance of positive emotion experience and expression in regulating interpersonal relationships is reviewed according to this framework, and implications for future research on the social functions of positive emotion are discussed.

Although emotion theorists disagree about many things, most agree on the premise that emotions are functional (Ekman, 1992; Lazarus, 1991; Shweder, 2000; Tomkins, 1984; Tooby & Cosmides, 1990). From one perspective, emotions serve intrapersonal functions including the regulation of memory, perception, attention, and a number of physiological processes (Ekman, 1992; Levenson, 1999; Tooby & Cosmides, 1990). In the past decade, however, the social functions of emotion within relationships have received increasing attention (Averill, 1980; Barrett & Campos, 1987; Keltner & Haidt, 1999; Keltner & Kring, 1998; Lutz & White, 1986). Humans are social creatures by nature, for whom group living is a key survival strategy (de Waal, 1996). Humans depend on social connections for survival across the life course, performing tasks such as generating, collecting, and sharing resources, detecting and responding to threats, and raising offspring in groups (Ainsworth, 1989; Caporael & Brewer, 1995; de Waal, 1996). Extended dyadic and group interaction presents specific opportunities and problems that must be resolved for social units to succeed (Krebs & Davies, 1993; Trivers, 1971). Emotions play a critical role in the negotiation of this social terrain.

Positive emotions, in particular, serve important interpersonal functions. For instance, it is claimed that some positive emotions, such as love for attachment figures, evolved specifically to facilitate social bonding (Bowlby, 1979; Buck, 1999; Panksepp, 1998). Several positive emotions, such as sympathy and desire, involve social targets by definition (Buck, 1999; Eisenberg et al., 1989; Panksepp, 1998). In this chapter we discuss the functions of several positive emotions—joy, love, desire, compassion, gratitude, pride, amusement, awe, and interest—from a social functional perspective. Earlier analyses of these emotions have emphasized intrapersonal functions, such as "undoing" the effects of negative emotions on the autonomic nervous system (Fredrickson, Mancuso, Branigan, & Tugade, 2000) and the broadening of immediately salient thought–action repertoires to facilitate responses to opportunities (Fredrickson, 2001). We build on these theories by describing the functions of several positive emotions at another level of analysis—that of interpersonal relationships.

In this chapter we present a new social functional perspective on positive emotion that differentiates among specific emotions, relationship tasks, and relationship types. We begin by describing three processes through which emotional experience and display help to shape social interactions. We then describe three fundamental tasks relationships face: the identification of relationship partners, the development and maintenance of relationship structure, and the coordination of successful collective action. Next we present examples of ways in which specific positive emotions might facilitate performance of these tasks in the context of four types of relationships: parent–child dyads, romantic dyads, friendships, and small groups. In concluding, we discuss particular challenges and questions that emotion researchers working from a social functional perspective must address in future research.

HOW EMOTIONS SHAPE SOCIAL INTERACTION

Emotional experience and expression help to shape social interactions through three processes: by providing information, by evoking emotional responses in others, and by providing incentives for others' behavior (see also Keltner and Kring, 1998). First, emotional experience and expression are sources of information about the social world—the informative function. Emotion displays convey information about the sender's current emotions, behavioral intentions, and perceptions of his or her relationship with the target (Ekman, 1993; Fridlund, 1992; Keltner, 1995). Emotion displays convey information about the environment external to the relationship as well, allowing individuals to coordinate their responses to outside opportunities or threats (e.g., Klinnert et al., 1984; Sorce, Emde, Campos, & Klinnert, 1985). Emotion experience also provides information about the state of a particular social relationship, allowing people to decide quickly how to behave toward an interaction partner. For instance, the experience of embarrassment and shame is related to perceptions of diminished social status relative to others in an interaction (e.g., Tangney, Miller, Flicker, & Barlow, 1996). Emotional experiences can influence the perception of a particular relationship even when the emotion elicitor is external to the relationship (e.g., Keltner, Ellsworth, & Edwards, 1993). In providing information about social relationships, emotional experience—an intrapersonal phenomenon—promotes behavior with social consequences.

Second, emotion displays have evocative functions in the context of social interactions, eliciting complimentary or matching emotions from relationship partners (Eibl–Eibesfeldt, 1989; Keltner & Kring, 1998). For example, photographed facial displays of anger tend to enhance fear conditioning in observers, even when the photographs are not consciously perceived (Esteves, Dimberg, & Ohman, 1994; Ohman & Dimberg, 1978). Several studies have also shown that expressions of distress evoke compassion or sympathy in observers (e.g., Batson & Shaw, 1991; Eisenberg et al., 1989). Empathy, or the actual experience of another's emotion, may also contribute to processes such as moral regulation and altruistic helping (Batson & Shaw, 1991; Hoffman, 1984). We expect that both of these phenomena help to coordinate successful social exchange.

Third, emotion displays provide incentives for desired social behavior (Keltner & Kring, 1998). Displays of positive emotion are often used by parents to reward desired behaviors in children, thus increasing the probability of those behaviors in the future (e.g., Tronick, 1989). Laughter from interaction partners also rewards desirable social behavior in adults (Owren & Bachorowski, 2001). Thus, emotion displays can have long-term consequences for relationships, as shared norms for behavior are developed and communicated.

Through these three processes emotions have significant impact on interpersonal relationships. In the section that follows, we describe three tasks, fundamental to interpersonal relationships, to which these processes provide partial solutions. Later in the chapter we discuss some of the ways in which particular positive emotions aid in the completion of particular relationship tasks, in the context of particular types of relationships, via the processes outlined earlier.

FUNDAMENTAL TASKS FOR SOCIAL RELATIONSHIPS

Understanding the functional role that positive emotions play in social interaction requires identifying the major tasks encountered during the course of social relationships. Keltner and Haidt (1999) have described a social functional approach to emotion that differentiates among various levels of social analysis (e.g., dyads vs. small groups vs. cultures). We expand on that approach by identifying general categories of tasks, fundamental to relationships but unfolding differently in different kinds of relationships. Positive emotions, in turn, meet these tasks in different ways. Three tasks are common to all relationships: the identification of relationship partners, the development and maintenance of a particular intrarelationship style, and preparation for and enactment of collective agency.

Identifying Relationship Partners

A potential relationship begins when one individual becomes aware of the other for the first time (Berscheid & Graziano, 1979; Levinger, 1974). Beyond that, one must determine how much energy, and of what kind, to invest in that person. The determinants and implications of this "allocation of resources" decision vary across relationship types, depending on the goals for the relationship, the biological and social fixedness of the relationship, and the extent to which the relationship is exclusive. This variability is important because, as we shall see, the factors indicating a promising relationship partner are linked to the elicitors of particular emotions that facilitate a particular type of bonding.

At one extreme, parent–child relationships are biologically fixed and relatively exclusive, and the goal is the survival of the child. Successful parent–child relationships require unique recognition of one's caregivers or offspring—a necessity when rapid decisions about whom to call for or protect must be made in the face of danger or want. Because human childhood is so long compared to other mammalian species, extended needs for protection, nurturance, and education translate into tremendous parental investment in each child (Hrdy, 1999). Failure to identify one's offspring leads at best to wasted energy (from a reproductive standpoint), and at worst to the loss of offspring if one chooses the "wrong" child to protect from threat. From the child's perspective, vigilance in keeping one's parents in close range is necessary to ensure that someone motivated to offer this level of protection and care is always available (Bowlby, 1979). Evidence from several mammalian species suggests that "decisions" about who is one's parent or child are correspondingly based on a few triggers that evoke rapid, intense emotional bonding, such as childbirth, nursing, and early physical contact for parents and contingency of care for infants (Bowlby, 1979; Hrdy, 1999).

A wider range of factors should predict investment in less fixed relationships, such as romantic dyads and friendships. In the domain of romantic relationships, our attention must be guided toward promising reproductive partners. Information as to whether a given person is likely to produce healthy offspring and to prove an effective and committed parent can come from many features, however, and our weighting of that information will depend on whether we are seeking a short-term sexual encounter or a long-term, exclusive mate (Buss, 1989; Cunningham, Roberts, Barbee, Druen, & Wu, 1995; Gross & Crofton, 1977; Langlois & Roggman, 1990; Sadalla, Kenrick, & Vershure, 1987).

Friendships are on the low end of the exclusivity spectrum, and as a result a greater number of "chance" or superficial factors appear in the selection process. Friend selection is driven by proximity, familiarity, similarity, and physical attractiveness, as well as more complex processes such as self-disclosure, emotion matching, and empathy (Brockner & Swap, 1976; Hatfield, Cacioppo, & Rapson, 1992; Provine, 2000; Reis & Shaver, 1988; Segal, 1974).

At the group level, it is necessary to distinguish one's ingroup from the outgroup for the purposes of coalition forming and resource distribution. The bulk of empirical research in this area has emphasized the role of cognitive factors such as stereotypes and differential perceptions of within-group variability in group identification (Ostrom & Sedikides, 1992). New studies provide evidence, however, that automatic processes contributing to prejudice involve particular emotional responses, such as fear (Phelps et al., 2000). People also consistently respond to emotional threats by derogating outgroups and reaffirming ingroup values (Greenberg et al., 1990).

Emotion display and experience are among the processes that contribute to the identification of relationship partners. In particular, positive emotions serve informative functions relevant to this relationship task. The experience of positive emotion can indicate that a current interaction partner deserves a high level of resource investment based on a close genetic relationship or signs that the relationship will be profitable. In addition, displays of positive emotion by a potential relationship partner advertise his emotional and interpersonal traits, and thus provide useful information about that person as a relationship partner. We discuss specific examples of these processes later. Although other factors also contribute to partner identification, such as formal roles (e.g., teacher–student or coworker), emotions are one important proximal mechanism by which this task is completed.

Developing, Negotiating, and Maintaining Key Relationships

For a relationship to succeed, the relevant individuals must negotiate and agree on rules of interaction, such as communication styles, expected behaviors, and roles. During this process, emergent properties of the relationship itself are developed—qualities not of the individuals, but reflecting interdependence of their behavior in each other's presence (Kelley et al., 1983). Relationship development of this kind rarely involves deliberate, conscious negotiation. On the contrary, subtle exchanges of emotion—often unintentional or uncontrolled—lead to behavioral coordination. For example, emotion expression helps to establish what behaviors are desired by others, as well as which are inappropriate, by using positive or negative displays as a reward or punishment (Keltner & Kring, 1998). For example, a parent might smile when a child pets a dog gently, thus reinforcing the behavior, and might frown or express fear when the child pulls the dog's tail. In this way positive emotion displays serve important incentive functions.

Social partners must also establish roles for each person in the relationship. In groups, for example, negotiation of the status hierarchy is a necessary and ongoing process (Ohman, 1986), required to organize the distribution of labor and resources among members (de Waal, 1986, 1988). Individuals must also keep track of their obligations to others—a key to human reciprocal altruism (de Waal, 1996; McCullough et al., 2001). Finally, long-term romantic partners and friends benefit from emotion displays that reaffirm mutual commitment to the relationship (Gonzaga, Keltner, Londahl, & Smith, 2001). Several of these social processes involve informative functions of emotion display, in that displays of emotion communicate perceptions of and intentions regarding the relationship to the relationship partner(s).

To the extent that a particular aspect of relationship development is common to multiple relationship types, the same emotion may be involved in this task across parent–child dyads, romantic pairs, friendships, and so on. For instance, affirmation of commitment to the relationship is a key feature of all three; thus, expression of the emotion "compassion," a signal of commitment, should facilitate relationship development in each relationship type. Some tasks are more specific to relationship type, however, such that a given positive emotion will only be relevant in that context. For example, status hierarchies are more prominent features of small groups than of friendship pairs (Fiske, 1992), so we would expect expressions of pride and embarrassment to be more central to relationship negotiation in the context of small groups. Such expression might even be problematic in the context of an egalitarian friendship, unless conditions make "shared pride" appropriate.

Collective Agency

The importance of social interaction to human survival lies not only in the care we provide for each other, but also in the enhanced ability of dyads and groups to act successfully on the outside world. Humans typically raise children, pursue resources, and respond to threats in groups rather than alone (Ainsworth, 1989; Caporael & Brewer, 1995; DeWaal, 1996). For this reason, social units must coordinate the performance of activities external to the relationship—a process we call "collective agency." At this "systemic" level of analysis the dyad or group prepares to interact as a unit with the larger social or physical world. This involves reaching a shared understanding of the nature of the situation ("Is that large mammal prey or threat? Is it strong or weak?"), agreeing on the proper course of action ("Do we attack with spears, try to trap it, or run away?"), and commitment to supporting others in the group ("If you attack, I won't run").

Collective agency begins in infancy, and continues throughout life. Around the last quarter of the first year of life, infants begin to engage in two-person communication about third events in the world—an ability known as *secondary intersubjectivity* (Butterworth & Jarrett, 1991; Cohn & Tronick, 1987; Tomasello & Farrar, 1986; Trevarthen, 1993). The development of secondary intersubjectivity is a critical milestone, as it expands the life of the infant and facilitates exploration and learning. This new ability allows parents and offspring to communicate with each other about the nature of and proper response to novel objects and situations. At this point, collective agency largely involves parents "teaching" infants how to interpret and react to the world (although infants teach parents as well, as any parent knows). In later relationships characterized by more equal power distribution, such as friendships and marriages, collective agency evolves from this top-down process to more mutual "discussion" of situations and exploration of possible responses. Dyad and group members send each other cues about the presence of opportunities and threats in the local environment (Seyfarth & Cheney, 1990), and reach decisions about collective action (Turner, Pratkanis, Probasco, & Leve, 1992) in part by expressing emotion and monitoring the emotional displays of others.

Unfortunately, social processes at the systemic level of analysis, such as collective agency, have generally received less empirical attention than the individual- or dyad-level processes occurring during relationship formation or relationship development—the other two fundamental relationship tasks we have identified (Berscheid & Reis, 1998). As a result, little empirical evidence is available regarding the role of positive emotion in collective agency in the context of some relationships, such as long-term romantic couples. By contrast, more evidence supports the role of positive emotion in the collective agency of parent–child dyads and friends. In the remainder of the chapter, collective agency will only be discussed when earlier research has specifically examined the role of positive emotion in this process.

Summary and Discussion

Coordinating successful relationships involves a number of tasks, which we have grouped into three categories: identifying relationship partners, developing and maintaining the relationship, and collective agency. Emotions contribute to the performance of these relationship tasks in a number of ways. Emotions promote communication between relationship partners of needs, expectations, and intentions via facial expressions and other behavioral channels (Ekman & Friesen, 1971). Positive emotional displays, in particular, serve a number of important functions during communication: they indicate that the partner should continue interaction, they regulate the other's emotional state, and they help to coordinate communication between partners. We now describe some specific roles played by each of the positive emotions in the three relationship tasks across several kinds of relationships.

FUNDAMENTAL TASKS AND POSITIVE EMOTION: FOUR RELATIONSHIP MODELS

The particular form taken by each of the three relationship tasks—identifying relationship partners, developing and maintaining the relationship, and collective agency—depends on the type of relationship in question. We expect that different processes will be involved in the identification and development of parent–child relationships, romantic and mating relationships, friendships, and group interactions, as well as in collective agency by each of these social units (Fiske, 1992; Keltner & Haidt, 1999). As a result, the particular positive emotions involved in any given task will vary according to the type of relationship. In this section we examine ways in which the three tasks described earlier play out in the context of these four relationship types, and explore the roles of positive emotions within each relationship.

Parent–Offspring Relationships

Identifying Parents and Offspring. The roles of positive emotion in identifying parents and offspring, developing the parent–child relationship, and parent–child collective agency, are summarized in Table 5.1. Early in life, infants must figure out who are their primary caregivers. Considering their perceptual limitations, infants begin to differentiate between the mother and other adults surprisingly soon after birth on the basis of facial characteristics, scent, and voice (DeCasper & Fifer, 1980; Pascalis, de Schonen, Morton, Deruelle, & Fabre–Grenet, 1995). Once infants learn to crawl, and face the trade-off between exploring the world and risking separation from protective parents, the ability to recognize when parents are "out of range" and summon them quickly depends on distinguishing them from other adults. By the second half of the first year of life, infants specifically and intentionally direct their emotional displays toward parents and other frequent caregivers whose behavior seems to be contingent on their own—at this point, the infant has formed an *attachment* to the caregiver (Sroufe, 1996).

Emotion is an integral part of the attachment process (Bowlby, 1969; Sroufe, 1996). Parent and child each use displays of emotion to regulate the other's behavior. Although the negative side of attachment-related affect or "social panic" receives the bulk of empirical attention, the positive emotion we call "love" is prominent as well (Panksepp, 1998). The English word "love" is used in the con-

TABLE 5.1

Positive Emotions Contributing to Completion of Parent-Child Relationship Tasks

Fundamental Task	*Emotion*	*Social Process*	*Emotion Function*
Identify parents	Love	Attachment	Informative (experience)—Parents are those in whose presence one experiences intense love.
Identify offspring	Compassion	Bonding	Informative (experience)—Offspring are those toward whom one experiences intense compassion.
Develop relationship	Joy	Social smiling	Evocative—Duchenne smile elicits parent's attention.
	Joy	Social learning	Incentive—Parental joy rewards desired behavior.
Collective agency	Joy	Social referencing	Informative (display)—Parental expression of joy signals safety of novel situation and promotes exploratory behavior by infant.
	Joy	Affect Sharing	Evocative—Infant displays of joy in response to an experience; elicit attempts by parents to repeat exposure to that experience.
	Interest, joy	Joint attention	Evocative—Parental displays direct child's attention to an object, thus facilitating learning.

text of a wide range of feelings, but we follow a number of theorists in distinguishing among three fundamental love-related emotions, which we have labeled *love*, *compassion*, and *desire* (Bowlby, 1979; Panksepp, 1998; Shaver, Morgan, & Wu, 1996; Sternberg, 1988). Although all three share the common functional element of proximity maintenance, each also has distinct components (Ainsworth, 1989). Following Bowlby (1979), we define love as the positive emotion experienced during closeness or reunion with an attachment figure. Love differs from compassion and desire in that it involves feelings of security, dependence, and comfort derived from proximity to the target (Ainsworth, 1989; Gonzaga et al., 2001). Thus, the experience of intense love serves an informative function to the infant, identifying parents or other primary caregivers and highlighting their proximity. Once attachment has been established, infants rely on parents to act as a secure base during exploration of the larger world, as well as a safe haven during unfamiliar or dangerous situations.

Whereas attachment refers to the emotional tie of the infant to the caregiver, the term *bonding* typically refers to the caregiver's affective tie to the infant (Klaus & Kennell, 1976; Sroufe, 1996). We have used the label compassion to denote the emotion that evolved along with increasing periods of infant dependence to seal parents' commitment to the needs of their offspring (Klaus & Kennell, 1982; Shaver er al., 1996). Compassion facilitates nurturing, care giving behavior toward those who are small, weak, or in distress. In the mother–infant relationship, bonding may be related to the release of oxytocin and prolactin during childbirth and nursing (Panksepp, 1998), as well as skin-to-skin touch during the first few hours of the infant's life (Klaus & Kennell, 1976), and thus provides a potent cue to the identity of offspring. In this way, compassion serves an important informative function for the parent. Compassion is typically elicited in response to displays of distress (e.g., crying) by the infant, and more generally by apparent weakness and helplessness (Keltner & Haidt, 2001). In our own research leading to the development of the Dispositional Positive Affect Scale (DPAS; a 75-item self-report measure of trait levels of 11 positive affects), we found that statements such as "I often notice people who need help" and "It's important to take care of people who are vulnerable" correlate substantially with statements such as "I am a very compassionate person" (Shiota, Keltner, & John, 2003). People with high scores on the Compassion scale of the DPAS are more likely than others to report that their favorite activities include tutoring and playing with children (Shiota, 2003). Infants are demanding, labor-intensive creatures; without the compassionate affective bond that typically occurs between caregivers and their infants, the latter can easily become the victims of neglect and abuse rather than love and care (Hrdy, 1999).

Developing and Maintaining the Parent–Offspring Relationship. Positive emotional displays play a central role in the infant–caregiver communication system . As the first social relationship in an infant's life, the parent–child unit acts as a "training ground" for future interactions. In this unit, children learn some of the fundamentals of social exchange, such as reciprocity and turn-taking (Tronick, 1989). The infant–caregiver communication system is dynamic and bidirectional. Parent and child shape and are shaped by each other's evocative emotional displays.

For instance, the infant's *social smile*–which develops by about 10 weeks of life—is one of the most powerful social regulatory tools that the infant possesses. These smiles involve a brightening and crinkling of the eyes with the corners of the mouth in a full "grin", a display linked to the experience of "joy" or "happiness" (Ekman et al., 1987). The breadth of effects of the social smile has led theorists to call it the "most significant aspect of social development to occur in the first half-year of life". One major effect of the social smile is to elicit frequent positive interaction with and assistance from others (Bower, 1977). Thus, the infant's expression of positive affect serves both evocative and incentive social functions, as it motivates the parent to engage in and continue moment-to-moment interaction.

Evidence demonstrating the regulatory effect of smiling comes from children with Down's syndrome, whose social smiling is impoverished. In one study, parents of these children reported that their infants were not as "rewarding" as other infants because they did not return their smiles as intensely (Emde, Katz, & Thorpe, 1978). Some parents indicated that they lacked an incentive to interact with their children when they received no smiling behaviors during their interactions.

Until now we have emphasized the crucial role that positive emotional displays play in infant–caregiver communication. However, positive emotion expression continues to play an important role throughout childhood. Parental expression of emotion is a key part of the *social learning* process (Bandura, 1986; Campos, Campos, & Barrett, 1989; Tronick, 1989). Parents' expressions of joy when their children attain a goal or standard of conduct not only increase the frequency of the desired actions by rewarding behavior—an incentive function (Tronick, 1989), but also generate and facilitate the development of self-esteem in children (Saarni, Mumme, & Campos, 1998). As discussed in detail by Eisenberg, Spinrad, and Smith in this volume, the behaviors rewarded by parents often themselves involve children's regulation of emotion displays. This process is especially helpful because many of the behaviors parents wish to reward—such as concentration on some task or restraint of an undesirable behavior—involve self-regulation and, as Tice, Baumeister, and Zhang Case (this volume) noted in their contribution to this volume, the positive affect experienced by the child in response to the parent's display may help to "recharge" the child's self-regulatory batteries.

Collective Agency: Social Referencing, Affect Sharing, and Joint Attention. Infants become capable of two-person communication toward the end of the first year of life, a process referred to earlier as secondary intersubjectivity . Once infants are able to communicate with others about objects, people, and situations, their emotional world both expands and deepens . Researchers have investigated a number of phenomena that involve secondary intersubjectivity including social referencing, affect sharing, and joint attention . Positive emotions are centrally involved in these phenomena, all of which allow parents to help their children explore, learn about, and successfully navigate an expanding world.

A developmental milestone occurs when infants begin to attend to others for information on how to feel about and respond to an unfamiliar event in the environment, a process known as *social referencing* . When a novel person or object is encountered, smiling and other positive affect displays by the parent prompt the infant to view the situation with comfort and interest . In essence, a parent's positive vocal and facial displays of joy are the "everything's ok" signal, indicating that a novel stimulus may be safely approached—an informative function (Walden

& Baxter, 1989). This process allows infants to explore new people (including potential caregivers) and objects such as toys and tools, and to take advantage of potential resources and learning opportunities. In this way, parent and infant collaborate in shaping the infant's interaction with the larger world.

A phenomenon known as *affect sharing* is also involved in the collective agency of parent and infant. Affect sharing is the complement of social referencing; whereas the infant "socially references" by seeking out information from a caregiver about an event, the infant "affect shares" by displaying her own emotional reaction to the caregiver . When children express joy on encountering novel and exciting objects or events, parents are encouraged to place similar events in their environment in the future. In this way, children use positive affect display to let parents know what will help them to develop and learn.

Shared interest about events in the environment also plays an important role in infant–caregiver collective agency. By the end of the first year of life, infants are capable of jointly attending to objects toward which caregivers direct their gaze or point (Butterworth & Jarrett, 1991). During episodes of *joint attention*, parents use displays of interest and joy to direct children's attention (Cohn & Tronick, 1987). This provides a context in which children can readily learn new information about the world. For example, parents are most likely to teach their children new vocabulary while the referent is the subject of joint attention (Tomasello & Farrar, 1986). Thus, the emotional communication between parent and child stimulates and facilitates the child's overall education.

Summary. Love and compassion are critically involved in the attachment and bonding processes by which infants claim parents' protection and nurturance. The development of the parent–offspring relationship involves exchanges of joy as children reward parents' investment of time and attention, and parents reward desired behavior in children. Social referencing, affect sharing, and joint attention all tie the expression of positive emotion to children's learning processes, as parents communicate reactions to and information about novel objects and events, and children let parents know what experiences provide ideal stimulation. This, in turn, prepares children to deal effectively with their ever-expanding world. In general, positive emotions play key roles as parents help their offspring to survive the vulnerable years of infancy, and to grow and develop agency throughout childhood.

Romantic Relationships: Mating and Reproduction

Identifying Reproductive Partners. The roles of positive emotion in mate selection and in the development and maintenance of the romantic bond are summarized in Table 5.2. Enhanced reproductive success depends on the selection of a mating partner (Buss, 1989), and positive emotion critically assists this process by providing the *attraction* that motivates individuals to form these relationships. The

TABLE 5.2

Positive Emotions Contributing to Completion of Relationship Tasks in Romantic Couples

Fundamental Task	*Emotion*	*Social Process*	*Emotion Function*
Identify partner	Desire	Attraction	Informative (experince)—Desire experienced in the presence of a person with strong reproductive potential.
	Compassion	Mate selection	Informative (display)—Displayed compassion signals high potential as a long-term partner and parent.
	Joy	Mate selection	Informative (display)—Duchenne smiles signal high affiliativeness, competence, emotional stability.
Develop relationship	Desire	Flirting	Evocative—Display of desire evokes comparable displays in potential partner, coordinating early stages of relationship development.
	Love	Attachment	Informative (experience)—Felt love indicates that a relationship partner is trustworthy and can be depended on.
	Compassion	Commitment	Informative (display)—Displays of compassion signal willingness to forego individual self-interest for the benefit of the relationship.
	Joy	Self-expansion	Informative (experience)—felt joy in the context of a novel experience with partner indicates continued growth of relationship and merging of expanded selves.

experience of desire signals to the individual that a particular person may be a promising reproductive partner (Buss, 1989; Buss & Schmidt, 1993). Some theorists have also proposed that the experience of desire can motivate an individual to engage in actions that promote the formation of a new reproductive bond, to the possible detriment of other relationships (Abu–Lughod, 1986).

Although many determinants of sexual attractiveness are idiosyncratic (Morse & Gruzen, 1976), some qualities are near-universally considered attractive (Cunningham et al., 1995). In women, a waist-to-hip circumference ratio of .80 (Singh, 1993) and baby-faced features (Cunningham, 1986) are considered attractive in most societies. In men, faces and behaviors suggesting maturity and dominance are appealing (Sadalla et al., 1987). In both sexes, physical symmetry predicts attractiveness, as well as high levels of agreeableness (Gross & Crofton, 1977; Langlois & Roggman, 1990). Some have argued that these qualities may indicate genetic strength, reproductive health, or high parenting ability (Buss, 1989; but see Hrdy, 1999, for a challenge to this interpretation).

In addition to emotion experienced by "choosers," emotion displayed by "targets" helps drive *mate selection*. Both men and women report that kindness, or displayed compassion, is one of the most important qualities they seek when looking for a long-term mate (Buss & Barnes, 1986). Displayed compassion thus serves an informative function by signaling capacity for long-term commitment to a romantic partner and offspring. Display of joy through a Duchenne smile is also widely considered attractive, possibly because of the correlation between these positive emotion displays and affiliativeness, competence, and emotional stability (Harker & Keltner, 2001).

"Flirting" and Maintaining the Bond between Mates. Desire also plays important evocative functions in coordinating the early stages of sexual relationship development. In all sexually reproducing species, mating is preceded by a more or less elaborate courtship ritual, in which behavioral cues communicate increasing mutual interest (Eibl-Eibesfeldt, 1989). Human behaviors associated with this *flirting* include neck displays and sidelong glances by women, status displays by men, and lip licks and puckers by both sexes (Gonzaga et al., 2001). Under the right circumstances, these displays may lead to mating.

Because human childhood is relatively long by mammalian standards, however, reproduction involves much more than mating, gestation, and delivery. Human offspring are most likely to survive to their own reproductive years if they are raised for many years by more than one caregiver (Alexander & Noonan, 1979; Hrdy, 1999). An emotional bond between parents that outlives the initial feelings of desire and facilitates long-term commitment to the relationship will benefit the child (Gonzaga, 2002; Hrdy, 1999). Love and compassion, discussed earlier in the context of the parent–child relationship, also contribute to pair bonding in romantic couples. In fact, the primary theoretical approach to adult romantic relationships involves application of the *attachment* construct (Hazan & Shaver, 1987, 1994). Many of the behaviors children exhibit toward attachment figures are also displayed by lovers, including hugging, wrestling, proximity maintenance, and separation anxiety (Shaver et al., 1996). Self-reported levels of love have been positively associated with higher levels of reported trust in a relationship (Wieselquist, Rusbult, Foster, &

Agnew, 1999). Thus, felt love serves an informative function, indicating that the romantic partner can be depended on in times of need.

Research with romantic couples has shown that displays of affection serve another informative function by signaling relationship *commitment* and willingness to forgo individual self-interest for the benefit of the relationship (Gonzaga et al., 2001; Van Lange et al., 1997). The self-reported momentary experience of romantic love—which includes both love and compassion as defined here—has been associated with nonverbal displays of "affiliative cues" such as Duchenne smiles, forward leans, and head nods (Gonzaga et al., 2001). These cues occur outside of the sexual context, during discussions of difficult topics, and predict couples' use of conflict-reducing, commitment enhancing approaches during the conversation. In turn, romantic partners who report feeling more committed toward each other also report greater willingness to sacrifice self-interest to benefit their partners (Van Lange et al., 1997). Thus, the display of compassion signals to the partner one's ongoing commitment to the relationship.

Finally, some researchers have suggested that the mutual experience of joy, in the context of a shared novel experience, can help sustain commitment to romantic bonds (Aron, Norman, Aron, McKenna, & Heyman, 2000). According to the *Self-Expansion* model, one motive for becoming close to others is the continued expansion of the self through new information and experiences (Aron et al., 2000). In several studies, romantic couples who shared "exciting" novel activities reported greater relationship satisfaction and less boredom with the relationship than couples who engaged in mundane activities (Aron et al., 2000). The experience of joy in these situations may be informative of continued personal growth in the context of the relationship, making ongoing commitment to the relationship beneficial. Converging evidence suggests that romantic partners' feeling and display of several positive emotions help to enhance and sustain the bonds between mates.

Summary. Perceptions of joy and compassion, as well as the experience of desire, provide information about others as promising reproductive partners or mates. Displays of desire also contribute to romantic relationship formation, as "flirting" helps to coordinate the initial stages of interaction and signals mutual interest. Later in romantic relationships, love and compassion signal increased reliance on, and commitment to, the romantic partner, and joy signals growth of the relationship itself. In these ways, several positive emotions contribute to the formation of a stable, long-term relationship that facilitates maximal investment by both parents in their common offspring.

Peers and Friendships

Identifying Friends. Human dependence on social units for survival extends beyond the bonds of family to include important relationships with genetically unrelated peers. Reciprocal altruism—a basis of friendship—is an important feature of human sociality (Trivers, 1971). The subjective importance of friendships derives from qualities of emotional support and encouragement in the relationship, as well as material support (Hartup & Stevens, 1997). Friendships with peers develop early in life and become increasingly important sources of emotional support during development (Ainsworth, 1989). The roles of positive emotion in the identification of friends, the development of friendships, and collective agency by friends are summarized in Table 5.3.

How are trustworthy, loyal friends identified? Several predictors of one's attractiveness as a friend involve the informative functions of positive affect. For example, people who *smile* more often and more intensely tend to be thought of as better potential friends (Harker & Keltner, 2001; LaFrance & Hecht, 1995; Otta, Abrosio, & Hoshino, 1996; Reis et al., 1990). This is probably due to the correla-

TABLE 5.3

Positive Emotions Contributing to Completion of Relationship Tasks in Friendship

Fundamental Task	*Emotion*	*Social Process*	*Emotion Function*
Identify friend	Joy	Smiling	Informative (display)—Duchenne smiling associated with desirable traits such as affiliativeness, emotional stability.
	Love	Mere Exposure	Informative (experience)—Repeated exposure triggers early attachment processes.
Develop relationship	Love	Attachment	Informative (experience)—Felt love indicates that a relationship partner is trustworthy and can be depended on.
	Compassion	Commitment	Informative (display)—Displays of compassion signal willingness to forego individual self-interest for the benefit of the relationship.
	Gratitude	Reciprocity	Informative (experience)—Indicates that a relationship merits investment and reciprocal prosocial behavior.
			Incentive—Rewards another's prosocial behaviors from which one benefits.
Collective agency	Amusement	Social support	Informative (display)—Mutual laughter in novel or threatening situation is assurance of social support.

tion between Duchenne smiling and desirable personality traits such as competence and emotional stability—in one study, the intensity of Duchenne smiles in college yearbook photographs predicted a number of personality traits and life outcomes decades later, including affiliativeness, neuroticism, and marriage (Harker & Keltner, 2001). We also prefer people who are familiar over people who are less familiar, even when we are not aware of the previous exposure (Bornstein & D'Agostino, 1992; Zajonc, 1968). This "Mere Exposure Effect" (Zajonc, 1968) may involve very early activity in the love or "attachment" system. This suggests that the initial development of trust and security in a relationship can be based simply on a person's consistent presence in the environment.

Developing and Maintaining Friendships. Friendships, like romantic relationships, involve bonds of mutual support and sharing (Ainsworth, 1989). Love and intimacy and compassion play similar informative roles in both relationship types—signaling commitment to the relationship and motivating attachment, or reliance on the partner for support. Several studies have examined the interplay between love-related displays and compassion displays among adult peers. The display of "affiliation cues" previously related to romantic love has also been found to predict self-reported willingness to support friends during a conversation (Gonzaga et al., 2001). Adult facial displays of compassion include oblique brows and "concerned" gaze, and predict overt helping behavior in potential friends (Eisenberg et al., 1989). Thus, emotional behaviors that probably evolved to guide parent–child bonding have also proved relevant and functional in the domain of friendships and other reciprocal adult relationships.

Love and intimacy and compassion govern the exchange of support and caregiving in the moment of need. In long-term relationships within a social group, however, obligation must also be tracked over time (Trivers, 1971). This may be especially true when particular "gifts" are too great or unusual to be "repaid" immediately, such as a substantial loan or long-term caregiving during an illness or emotional crisis. To meet these demands, friendships may rely more heavily on emotional displays that reinforce and promote *reciprocity* over long periods of time. Gratitude is likely to serve this purpose through both incentive and informative functions (McCullough et al., 2001). First, experience of gratitude informs the grateful party that a given relationship is valuable, and motivates him to return the behavior in kind, leading to reciprocity. McCullough and colleagues (2001) have found that individuals scoring high on dispositional gratitude are more likely than low scorers to engage in prosocial activities, such as doing favors for others and volunteering time. Second, the display of gratitude rewards another's supportive behavior, and confirms the recipient's commitment to the relationship although actual reciprocation has not yet taken place —an expression that "I have not forgotten what you did for me."

Collective Agency. Friendships enhance the ability of relationship members to marshal strengths and resources in the service of common goals. Individuals often report forming friendships based on shared experiences, such as being on the same sports team or starting a family at the same time (Hartup & Stevens, 1997). Friends then help each other in these contexts, to win soccer matches or to share successful parenting strategies. The reciprocity and goal-directedness of this type of bond may lead to enhanced perceptions of how much support the friendship provides. For example, McGuire and McGuire (1985) found that women reported receiving more child-care assistance from other women friends, although objective measures showed that family and romantic partners provided more consistent assistance. Although this sense of working toward mutual goals may reflect perceptions that are less than objectively accurate, it is clear that friendships are an important part of people's day-to-day interaction.

One important benefit of friendships is the enhanced ability of two people to deal with novel or threatening situations. There is some evidence that friendships with a strong love or attachment component are especially likely to form in dangerous situations in which members must be able to rely on each other, like wartime service (Ainsworth, 1989; Weiss, 1982). Indeed, the review by Zech, Rimé and Nils, in this volume, highlights the extent to which intense, emotion-eliciting experiences are likely to be shared with others, opening the door for emotional processing and more practical forms of support. Even in less intensely threatening situations, friends use positive emotion displays to inform themselves and each other of *social support*. In one study, an experimenter approached pairs of people in public places and asked them to participate in a study—a novel situation (Provine, 2000). A typical response was for the participants to make eye contact with each other—but not with the experimenter—and then to laugh in amusement, thereby establishing a united front. People do tend to laugh in tense or threatening situations, and given that laughter is an almost exclusively social phenomenon, shared laughter may serve to reassure relationship partners of mutual social support (Keltner & Bonnano, 1997; Provine, 2000). This tendency is so strong that some researchers have defined friends as "those you laugh with" (Provine, 2000). In this way, friendship dyads are able to take risks one person might not attempt alone.

Summary. Many qualities of a "good friend" can be predicted by one's smile, a display of joy. In addition, we tend to be drawn emotionally toward people who are around often, suggesting that early stages of love and attachment may be based on "mere exposure" to another person. Love and compassion become increasingly characteristic of friendships as trust in and commitment to the friend increases. As the friendship extends over time and is marked by the kinds of commitment gestures that are not rapidly repaid, gratitude reminds the recipient of the obligation and communicates to the giver that the gesture is valued and the implicit debt acknowledged. When friends encounter novel or even threatening situations, shared laughter and amusement help to reaffirm mutual support and defuse tension. These processes all allow the development of reciprocal altruism—the commitment to mutual support outside of, but similar to, kinship.

Group Relationships

The roles of positive emotion in ingroup identification, the development of group structure, and collective agency by small groups, are summarized in Table 5.4. Positive emotions serve instrumental functions in the process of group identification, although research has traditionally emphasized outgroup derogation and neg-

TABLE 5.4

Positive Emotions Contributing to Completion of Group Relationship Tasks

Fundamental Task	*Emotion*	*Social Process*	*Emotion Function*
Identify ingroup	Amusement	Collective laughter	Evocative/Informative (display)—Those who laugh when you do constitute a support network.
		Teasing	Informative (display)—When an outgroup member is teased, those who laught are clearly part of the ingroup.
			Evocative—Tends to elicit embarrassment, an attempt to show deference to the group.
	Awe	Cultural events	Informative (own experience and others' display)—Others who experience awe when we do are working with the same social units of meaning, or worldviews.
Develop relationship	Pride	Dominance	Informative (display)—Advertises a socially valued success, leading to increased status within the group.
	Awe	Leadership	Informative (experience)—Awe experienced in response to another's achievements associates them with greatness, leadership.
	Amusement	Groupthink	Informative (display)—Can signal group's rejection of dissenter.
			Incentive—Process may lead to self-suppression of dissent and increased motivation to maintain group cohesion.

ative emotions such as fear and anger (Greenberg et al., 1990; Phelps et al., 2000). Just as laughter and amusement mark the presence of individual friends, *collective laughter* in response to one's own laughter can help to identify a support network within a particular situation (Provine, 2000). Amused laughter and humor in the context of *teasing* can also be used to emphasize distance between laughing ingroup members and outgroup tease targets (Keltner, Young, Heerey, Oemig, & Monarch, 1998). This process serves an informative function, in which laughers demonstrate their allegiance to the teaser and thus the ingroup. Teasing also serves evocative functions. People often respond to a tease with embarrassment, which communicates a desire to appease the group and acknowledgment of the group's standards and norms (Keltner, 1995).

Awe—experienced during the formation or revision of cognitive schemas to cope with a challenging stimulus (Keltner & Haidt, in press; Shiota et al., 2003)—is also likely to contribute to the identification of group members. Because schemas are fundamentally social units of meaning (Shweder, 1990), people who are part of a common group culture will tend to experience awe in response to the same events. For example, collective awe may often be experienced in the context of *cultural events* such as the Olympics, political conventions, and holiday celebrations. In this way, collective awe may reinforce group identity (Heise & O'Brien, 1993).

Negotiating and Maintaining the Social Structure of a Group. Within a group of several people, the structure of relationships must be negotiated on a continual basis as members age, develop new skills, and make or break alliances, and as hierarchies change (de Waal, 1996; Ohman, 1986). In all human societies, the social structure includes some form of status hierarchy which helps guide the distribution of labor and resources (de Waal, 1986, 1988; Fiske, 1992). The role of negative emotions such as anger and fear in status negotiations has been documented in other literature (Anderson, John, Keltner, & Kring, 2001; Keltner et al., 1998), but positive emotion displays play important informative roles as well. Display of pride signals to the group that one has just succeeded at a valued endeavor, and that one's status within the group should rise (Gilbert, 2001). The result is increased *dominance* within the group, which carries a wide range of social and material benefits (Hrdy, 1999). People who experience frequent and intense pride (as measured via the Pride scale of our DPAS) are more likely to have been promoted or to have won an award and less likely to have been fired within the last 6 months than people scoring low on dispositional pride (Shiota et al., 2003). Awe also plays a role in the negotiation and maintenance of status hierarchies. Awe is often experienced in response to a remarkable achievement that tests the limits of human ability, and is generally associated with greatness (Keltner & Haidt, in press; Weber, 1957). As a result, group members endow those who perform awe-inspiring acts with increased social status or formal or informal *leadership*. The elicitation of awe (through artistic performances, apparent command over natural events, or spectacles such as fireworks) can also be used to justify the positions of group leaders (Keltner & Haidt, in press).

Positive affect displays are also involved in the day-to-day coordination of group interaction. For instance, humor or amusement may be used to inform group members whose opinion differs from that of the majority that their status within the group is at risk. This might result in greater overall group cohesion, but likely contributes to the phenomenon known as *groupthink* (Janis, 1982). For example, this process was observed when President Johnson once responded to assistant Bill Moyers's arrival at a meeting regarding the Vietnam War by saying, "Well, here comes Mr. Stop-the-Bombing." Ridicule such as this serves incentive functions as well, motivating the targeted individual to confirm his or her investment in the group, often by suppressing dissent. As noted by Hrubes, Feldman, and Tyler, in this volume, people often conceal their true opinions on a subject to preserve their own good mood, in this case by avoiding the humiliation of group derision. Although studies of group decision-making have tended to emphasize poor outcomes associated with groupthink in complex situations, emotion processes that intensify group cohesion may contribute to efficient, rapid decision making and collective action in more prototypical situations.

Summary. Amusement and awe both assist in the identification of ingroup members and the distinction and exclusion of the outgroup. Exchanges of amusement also help to maintain group cohesion. Expressions of pride contribute to the negotiation of the status hierarchy within the group, and necessary and never-ending process. Elicitation of awe provides an alternative to physical aggression as a way to justify leadership positions, thereby reducing costs of status negotiation to the group. Overall, positive emotion experience and expression assist in the difficult task of defining group structure—who is in the group, and how group members should relate to each other.

SUMMARY, CONCLUSIONS, AND FUTURE PROSPECTS

Emotion theorists from a wide range of theoretical and methodological traditions agree that emotions are functional. However, the functions of emotion cross multiple levels of analysis. Most theories of emotion emphasize intrapersonal function—the regulation of physiology, perception, cognition, and memory. Theories of the negative emotions fall largely into this domain. Earlier theories of positive emotion have also emphasized intrapersonal functions such as the "undoing" of the autonomic effects of negative affect and the "broadening and building" of individual thought and action repertoires (Fredrickson, 2001; Fredrickson et al., 2000). Although these functions of emotion are of strong theoretical importance, emotions clearly serve important social functions as well. This is especially true for the positive emotions, which typically occur in the context of social interaction and in response to social elicitors.

The framework we have proposed in this chapter leads to a number of predictions about the roles of positive emotion in relationships. First, we hypothesize that certain positive emotions will be functional in the context of some relationships, but not others. Display of pride, for instance, may be functional in the context of small group interactions where status negotiation is necessary to establish group structure, but may be dysfunctional or threatening when expressed in the context of an egalitarian relationship, such as a romantic relationship. Similarly, desire promotes the formation of romantic relationships, but would be dysfunctional or inappropriate in family and friend relationships. We might also predict that the expression of gratitude is more important in the development and maintenance of friendships than in family or romantic relationships, where the expectation of certain kinds of care precludes the need for expressions of gratitude (Essock-Vitale * McGuire, 1985).

Second, we expect that within the context of a given relationship, positive emotions might be experienced or displayed more often at certain stages or periods than at others. For example, desire is typically felt most strongly by romantic partners early on in the relationship; as the relationship grows and develops, feelings of love and commitment should better predict relationship stability than desire. Similarly, experience and expression of joy should be most commonly observed during reunion of friends or lovers, and somewhat less often during the course of an actual interaction.

The social functional approach to positive emotion we have developed in this chapter raises two key questions, the answers to which will help direct and clarify future emotion research. One question stems from the impact emotion expression has on social interaction. The second involves the range of stimuli that can be said to elicit a given emotion, and of experiences that can justifiably be included in that emotion category.

First, what communication channels are used most often in the expression of positive emotion? Most research on emotion expression has emphasized facial display, and the Duchenne smile has been associated globally with positive emotion (Ekman et al., 1987). The face is an important medium for communication of negative emotion, because the target of the emotion is typically at some distance from the person experiencing the emotion. In positive affect, however, the two may be closer, making the use of other channels more feasible. Preliminary research suggests that other channels such as whole-body behavior, voice, and touch may be more critical to differentiating among the positive emotions (e.g., Hertenstein, 2002; Scherer, 1986). Studies of the channels listed earlier may succeed in identifying distinct markers of different positive emotions, where studies of the face have run into barriers. Some of our research is exploring the ways in which touch between parents and children can communicate specific positive emotions (e.g., Hertenstein, 2002). We also continue to examine the possibility that some positive emotions are, in fact, marked by specific facial displays other than the Duchenne smile.

Second, what range of experiences will elicit each of the positive emotions? Because we have emphasized an evolutionary approach to emotion in this account, our theories of emotion function (and thus the situations in which emotions are likely to occur) have focused on prototypical, relatively universal elicitors. It is likely, however, that the increasing cognitive complexity that accompanied human evolution has led to a broader range of circumstances that can trigger a given emotion. For instance, although disgust originally evolved as a reaction to rotten or unhealthy foods, humans have generalized the appraisal "contaminated" to other elicitors, including peoples' behavior (Rozin, Haidt, & McCauley, 2000). As a result, we can be "disgusted" by another's social or sexual behavior. Processes like this may be crucial for positive emotions, in which the "stimulus" is typically social. For instance, to what degree and under what circumstances can roles prototypically observed in one kind of relationship—and the emotions that go with them—generalize to other types of relationships? Much of our own current research examines the distinct features of various kinds of relationships and the circumstances in which these boundaries are crossed—when does a friend become, emotionally, a member of the family, and what are the consequences?

We have proposed a framework for understanding the roles played by positive emotions in the context of several types of relationships, and the different tasks associated with those relationships. Embedded within this framework are predictions about the distinctive importance of particular emotions in the context of some relationships (but not others), and in particular aspects of the relationship (but not others). A social functional approach to emotion is particularly well served by the study of positive emotion, and this focus involves a number of new theoretical, methodological, and empirical questions to be addressed by future researchers.

REFERENCES

Abu–Lughod, L. (1986). *Veiled Sentiments*. Berkeley: University of California Press.

Adamson, L. B. (1996). *Communication development during infancy.* Boulder, CO: Westview.

Ainsworth, M. D. A. (1989). Attachments beyond infancy. *American Psychologist, 44*, 709–716.

Alexander, R. D., & Noonan, K. M. (1979). Concealment of ovulation, parental care, and human social evolution. In N. A. Chagnon & W. Irons (Eds.), *Evolutionary biology and social behavior* (pp. 436–453). North Sciutate, MA: Duxbury.

Anderson, C., John, O. P., Keltner, D., & Kring, A. M. (2001). Who attains social status?: Effects of personality and physical attractiveness in social groups. *Journal of Personality and Social Psychology, 72*, 1373–1395.

Aron, A., Norman, C. C., Aron, E. N., McKenna, C., & Heyman, R. E. (2000). Couples' shared participation in novel and arousing activities and experienced relationship quality. *Journal of Personality and Social Psychology, 78*, 273–284.

Averill, J. R. (1980). A constructionist view of emotion. In R. Plutchik & H. Kellerman (Eds.), *Emotion: Theory, research, and experience* (pp. 305–339). New York: Academic.

Bandura, A. (1986). *Social foundations of thought and action: A social cognitive theory.* Englewood Cliffs, NJ: Prentice Hall.

Barrett, K. C., & Campos, J. J. (1987). Perspectives on emotional development II: A functionalist approach to emotions. In J. D. Osofsky (Ed.), *Handbook of infant development* (2nd ed., pp. 558–578). New York: Wiley.

Batson, C. D., & Shaw, L. L. (1991). Evidence for altruism; Toward a pluralism of prosocial motives. *Psychological Inquiry, 2*(2), 107–122.

Berscheid, E., & Graziano, W. (1979). The initiation of social relationships and interpersonal attraction. In R. L. Burgess & T. L. Huston, (Eds.), *Social exchange in developing relationships* (pp. 31–60). New York: Academic.

Berscheid, E., & Reis, H. T. (1998). Attraction and close relationships. In D.T. Gilbert, S.T. Fiske, & G. Lindzey (Eds.), *Handbook of social psychology,* 4th edition (Vol. 2, pp. 193–281). New York: McGraw-Hill.

Bornstein, R. F., & D'Agostino, P. R. (1992). Stimulus recognition and the mere exposure effect. *Journal of Personality and Social Psychology, 63*, 545–552.

Bower, T. G. (1977). *A primer of infant development.* San Francisco: Freeman.

Bowlby, J. (1969). *Attachment and loss, vol. 1, attachment.* New York: Basic Books.

Bowlby, J. (1979). *The making and breaking of affectional bonds.* New York: Routledge.

Brockner, J. & Swap, W. C. (1976). Effects of repeated exposure and attitudinal similarity on self disclosure and interpersonal attraction. *Journal of Personality and Social Psychology, 33*, 531–540.

Buck, R. (1999). The biological affects: A typology. *Psychological Review, 106*, 301–336.

Buss, D. M. (1989). Sex differences in human mate preferences: Evolutionary hypotheses tested in 37 countries. *Behavioral and Brain Sciences, 12*, 1–49.

Buss, D. M. & Barnes, M. F. (1986). Preferences in human mate selection. *Journal of Personality and Social Psychology, 50*, 559–570.

Buss, D. M., & Schmidt, D. P. (1993). Sexual strategies theory: An evolutionary perspective on human mating. *Psychological Review, 100*, 204–232.

Butterworth, G., & Jarrett, N. (1991). What minds have in common is space: Spatial mechanisms serving joint visual attention in infancy. *British Journal of Developmental Psychology, 9*, 55–72.

Campos, J. J., Campos, R. G., & Barrett, K. C. (1989). Emergent themes in the study of of emotional development and emotion regulation. *Developmental Psychology, 25*, 394–402.

Campos, J. J., & Stenberg, C. (1981). Perception, appraisal, and emotion: The onset of social referencing. In M. E. Lamb & L. R. Sherrod (Eds.), *Infant social cognition: Empirical and theoretical considerations*. Hillsdale, NJ: Lawrence Erlbaum Associates, Inc.

Caporael, L. R., & Brewer, M. B. (1995). Hierarchical evolutionary theory: There is an alternative, and it's not creationism. *Psychological Inquiry, 6*, 31–34.

Cohn, J. F., & Tronick, E. Z. (1987). Mother infant face-to-face interaction: The sequence of dyadic states at 3, 6, and 9 months. *Developmental Psychology, 23*, 68–77.

Conrad, R. (1995). Infant affect sharing and its relation to maternal availability. Unpublished doctoral dissertation, University of California, Berkeley, Berkeley.

Cunningham, M. R. (1986). Measuring the physical in physical attractiveness: Quasi-experiments on the sociobiology of female facial beauty. *Journal of Personality and Social Psychology, 50*, 925–935.

Cunningham, M. R., Roberts, A. R., Barbee, A. P., Druen, P. B., & Wu, C. (1995). "Their ideas of beauty are, on the whole, the same as ours": Consistency and variability in the cross-cultural perception of female physical attracíveness. *Journal of Personality and Social Psychology, 68*, 261–279.

DeCasper, A. J., & Fifer, W. P. (1980). Of human bonding: Newborns prefer their mothers' voices. *Science, 280*, 1174–1176.

de Waal, F. B. M. (1986). The integration of dominance and social bonding in primates. *Quarterly Review of Biology, 61*, 459–479.

de Waal, F. B. M. (1988). The reconciled hierarchy. In M. R. A. Chance (Ed.), *Social Fabrics of the Mind* (pp. 105–136). Hillsdale, NJ: Lawrence Erlbaum Associates, Inc.

de Waal, F. B. M. (1996). *Good natured.* Cambridge, MA: Harvard University Press.

Eibl-Eibesfeldt, I. (1989). *Human ethology.* New York: de Gruyter.

Eisenberg, N., Fabes, R. A., Miller, P. A., Fultz, J., Shell, R., Mathy, R. M., & Reno, R. R. (1989). Relation of sympathy and distress to prosocial behavior: A multi-method study. *Journal of Personality and Social Psychology, 57*, 55–66.

Ekman, P. (1992). An argument for basic emotions. *Cognition and Emotion, 6*, 169–200.

Ekman, P. (1993). Facial expression and emotion. *American Psychologist, 48*, 384–392.

Ekman, P. and Friesen, W. V. (1971). Constants across cultures in the face and emotion. *Journal of Personality and Social Psychology, 17*, 124–129.

Ekman, P., Friesen, W. V., O'Sullivan, M., Chan, A., Diacoyanni-Tarlatzis, I., Heider, K., Krause, R., LeCompte, W. A., Pitcairn, R., Ricci-Bitti, P. E., Scherer, K., Tomita, M., & Tzavaras, A. (1987). Universals and cultural differences in the judgments of facial expressions of emotion. *Journal of Personality and Social Psychology, 53*, 712–717.

Emde, R. N., Katz, E. L., & Thorpe, J. K. (1978). Emotional expression in infancy. II. Early deviations in Down's syndrome. In M. Lewis & L. Rosenblum (Eds.), *The development of affect* (pp. 351–360). New York: Plenum.

Essock-Vitale, S. M., & McGuire, M. T. (1985). Women's lives viewed from an evolutionary perspective: II. Patterns of helping. *Ethology & Sociobiology, 6*(3), 155–173.

Esteves, F., Dimberg, U., & Ohman, A. (1994). Automatically elicited fear: Conditioned skin responses to masked facial expressions. *Cognition and Emotion, 8*, 393–413.

Fiske, A. P. (1992). Four elementary forms of sociality: Framework for a unified theory of social relations. *Psychological Review, 99*, 689–723.

Fredrickson, B. L. (2001). The role of positive emotion in psychology: The broaden-and-build theory of positive emotions. *American Psychologist, 56*, 218–226.

Fredrickson, B. L., Mancuso, R. A., Branigan, C., & Tugade, M. M. (2000). The undoing effect of positive emotions. *Motivation and Emotion, 24*, 237–258.

Fridlund, A. J. (1992). The behavioral ecology and sociality of human faces. *Review of Personality and Social Psychology, 13*, 90–121.

Gilbert, P. (2001). Evolution and social anxiety: The role of attraction, social competition, and social hierarchies. *Psychiatric Clinics of North America, 24*, 723–751.

Gonzaga, G. C. (2002). *Distinctions between sexual desire and love in narrative report, nonverbal experssion, and physiology.* Unpublished doctoral dissertation. University of California, Berkeley.

Gonzaga, G. C., Keltner, D., Londahl, E. A., & Smith, M. D. (2001). Love and the commitment problem in romantic relationships and friendship. *Journal of Personality and Social Psychology, 81*, 247–262.

Greenberg, J., Pyszcynski, T., Solomon, S., Rosenblatt, A., Veeder, M., Kirkland, S., et al. (1990). Evidence for terror management theory II: The effects of mortality salience on reactions to those who threaten or bolster the cultural worldview. *Journal of Personality and Social Psychology, 58*, 308–318.

Gross, A. E., & Crofton, C. (1977). What is good is beautiful. Sociometry, 40, 85–90.

Harker, L. A., & Keltner, D. (2001). Expressions of positive emotion in women's college yearbook pictures and their relationship to personality and life outcomes across adulthood. *Journal of Personality and Social Psychology, 80*, 112–124.

Hartup, W. W., & Stevens, N. (1997). Friendships and adaptation in the life course. *Psychological Bulletin, 121*, 355–370.

Hatfield, E., Cacioppo, J. T., & Rapson, R. L. (1992). Primitive emotional contagion. In M. S. Clark (Ed.), *Emotion and social behavior: Review of personality and social psychology,4*, 151–177. Newbury Park, CA: Sage.

Hazan, C., & Shaver, P. R. (1987). Romantic love conceptualized as an attachment process. *Journal of Personality and Social Psychology, 52*, 511–524.

Hazan, C., & Shaver, P. R. (1994). Attachment as an organizational framework for research on close relationships. *Psychological Inquiry, 5*, 1–22.

Heise, D. R., & O'Brien, J. (1993). Emotion expression in groups. In M. Lewis & J. M. Haviland (Eds.), *Handbook of Emotions* (pp. 489–498). New York: Guilford.

Hertenstein, M. J. (2002). Touch: Its communicative functions in infancy. *Human Development, 45*,70–94.

Hoffman, M. L. (1984). Interaction of affect and cognition in empathy. In C. Izard, J. Kagan, & R. Zajonc (Eds.), *Emotions, cognition, and behavior* (pp. 103–131). New York: Cambridge University Press.

Hrdy, S. B. (1999). *Mother nature: Maternal instincts and how they shape the human species*. New York: Ballantine.

Janis, I.L. (1982). *Groupthink: Psychological studies of policy decisions and fiascoes* (2nd ed.). Boston: Houghton Mifflin.

Kelley, H. H., Berscheid, E., Christensen, A., Harvey, J. H., Huston, T. L., Levinger, et al. (1983). *Close relationships*. New York: Freeman.

Keltner, D. (1995). The signs of appeasement: Evidence for the distinct displays of embarrassment, amusement, and shame. *Journal of Personality and Social Psychology, 68*, 441–454.

Keltner, D., & Bonnano, G. A. (1997). A study of laughter and dissociation: Distinct correlates of laughter and smiling during bereavement. *Journal of Personality and Social Psychology, 73*, 687–702.

Keltner, D., Ellsworth, P. C., & Edwards, K. (1993). Beyond simple pessimism: Effects of sadness and anger on social perception. *Journal of Personality and Social Psychology, 64*, 740–752.

Keltner, D., & Haidt, J. (2003). Approaching awe, a moral, aesthetic, and spiritual emotion. *Cognition and Emotion, 17*(2), 297–314.

Keltner, D., & Haidt, J. (2001). Social functions of emotions. In T. Mayne & G. Bonanno (Eds.), *Emotions: Current issues and future directions* (pp. 192–213). New York: Guilford.

Keltner, D., & Haidt, J. (1999). Social functions of emotions at four levels of analysis. *Cognition and Emotion, 13*, 505–521.

Keltner, D., & Kring, A. M. (1998). Emotion, social function, and psychopathology. *Review of General Psychology, 2*, 320–342.

Keltner, D., Young, R. C., Heerey, E., Oemig, C., & Monarch, N. D. (1998). Teasing in hierarchical and intimate relations. *Journal of Personality and Social Psychology, 75*, 1231–1247.

Klaus, M., & Kennell, J. (1976). *Maternal–infant bonding.* St. Louis: Mosby.

Klaus, M. H., & Kennell, J. H. (1982). *Bonding: The beginnings of parent–infant attachment.* New York: Mosby.

Klinnert, M. D. (1984). The regulation of infant behavior by maternal facial expression. *Infant Behavior & Development, 7*, 447–465.

Krebs, J. R.,& Davies, N. B. (1993). *An Introduction to behavioural ecology.* Oxford, UK: Blackwell.

LaFrance, M., & Hecht, M. A. (1995). Why smiles generate leniency. *Personality and Social Psychology Bulletin, 21*, 207–214.

Langlois, J. H., & Roggman, L. A. (1990). Attractive faces are only average. *Psychological Science, 1*, 115–121.

Lazarus, R. S. (1991). *Emotion and adaptation.* New York: Oxford University Press.

Levenson, R. W. (1999). The intrapersonal functions of emotion. *Cognition and Emotion, 13*, 481–504.

Levinger, G. (1974). A three-level approach to attraction: Toward an understanding of pair relatedness. In T. L. Huston (Ed.), *Foundations of Interpersonal Attraction* (pp. 99–120). New York: Academic.

Lewis, M., Sullivan, M., Stanger, C., & Weiss, M. (1989). Self development and self-conscious emotions. *Child Development, 60*, 146–156.

Lutz, C. A., & White, G. (1986). The anthropology of emotion. *Annual Review of Anthropology, 15*, 405–436.

McCullough, M. C., Kilpatrick, S. D., Emmons, R. A., & Larson, D. B. (2001). Is gratitude a moral affect? *Psychological Bulletin, 127*, 249–266.

Morse, S. J., & Gruzen, J. (1976). The eye of the beholder: A neglected variable in the study of physical attractiveness. *Journal of Psychology, 44*, 209–225.

Ohman, A. (1986). Face the beast and fear the face: Animal and social fears as prototypes for evolutionary analysis of emotions. *Psychophysiology, 23*, 123–145.

Ohman, A., & Dimberg, U. (1978). Facial expressions as conditioned stimuli for electrodermal responses: A case of "preparedness?" *Journal of Personality and Social Psychology, 36*, 1251–1258.

Ostrom, T. M., & Sedikides, C. (1992). Out-group homogeneity effects in natural and minimal groups. *Psychological Bulletin, 112*, 536–552.

Otta, E., Abrosio, F. F. E., & Hoshino, R. L. (1996). Reading a smiling face: Messages conveyed by various forms of smiling. *Perceptual and Motor Skills, 82*, 1111–1121.

Owren, M. J., & Bachorowski, J. (2001). The evolution of emotional experience: A "selfish-gene" account of smiling and laughter in early hominids and humans. In T. J. Mayne

& G. A. Bonanno (Eds.), *Emotions: Current issues and future directions* (pp. 152–191). New York: Guilford.

Panksepp, J. (1998). *Affective neuroscience: The foundations of human and animal emotions.* New York: Oxford University Press.

Pascalis, O., de Schonen, S., Morton, J., Deruelle, C., & Fabre–Grenet, M. (1995). Mother's face recognition by neonates: A replication and extension. *Infant Behavior and Development, 18*, 79–85.

Phelps, E. A., O'Connor, K. J., Cunningham, W. A., Funayama, E. S., Gatenby, J. C., Gore, J. C., et al. (2000). Performance in indirect measures of race evaluation predicts amygdala activation. *Journal of Cognitive Neuroscience, 12*, 729–738.

Provine, R. R. (2000). *Laughter: A scientific investigation.* New York: Viking Putnam.

Reis, H. T., & Shaver, P. (1988). Intimacy as an interpersonal process. In S. W. Duck (Ed.), *Handbook of personal relationships* (pp. 367–389). Chichester, England: Wiley.

Reis, H. T., Wilson, I. M., Monestere, C., Bernstein, S., Clark, K., Seidl, E., Franco, M., Gioioso, E., Freeman, L., & Radoane, K. (1990). What is smiling is beautiful and good. *European Journal of Social Psychology, 20*, 259–267.

Rozin, P., Haidt, J., & McCauley, C. R. (2000). Disgust. In M. Lewis & J. M. Haviland (Eds.), *Handbook of emotions* (2nd ed., pp. 637–653). New York: Guilford.

Saarni, C., Mumme, D. L., & Campos, J. J. (1998). Emotional development: Action, communication, and understanding. In W. Damon (Ed.), *Handbook of child psychology: Social, emotional, and personality development* (pp. 237–310). New York: Wiley.

Sadalla, E. K., Kenrick, D. T., & Vershure, B. (1987). Dominance and heterosexual attraction. *Journal of Personality and Social Psychology, 52*, 730–738.

Scherer, K. R. (1986). Vocal affect expression: A review and a model for future research. *Psychological Bulletin, 99*, 143–165.

Schweder, R. (1990). Cultural psychology: What is it? In J. Stigler, R. Shweder, & G. Herdt (Eds.), *Cultural psychology: The Chicago symposia on culture and human development* (pp. 1–43). New York: Cambridge University Press.

Segal, M. W. (1974). Alphabet and attraction: An unobtrusive measure of the effect of propinquity in a field setting. *Journal of Personality and Social Psychology, 30*, 654–657.

Seyfarth, R. M., & Cheney, D. L. (1990). *How monkeys see the world.* Chicago: University of Chicago Press.

Shaver, P. R., Morgan, H. J., & Wu, S. (1996). Is love a "basic" emotion? *Personal Relationships, 3*, 81–96.

Shiota, M. N. (2003). *A discrete emotion approach to dispositional positive affect.* Unpublished doctoral dissertation, University of California, Berkeley.

Shiota, M. N., Keltner, D., & John, O. P. (2003). The Differential Positive Affect Scale: Development and validation. Manuscript in preparation.

Singh, D. (1993). Adaptive significance of female physical attractiveness: Role of waist to hip ratio. *Journal of Personality and Social Psychology, 65*, 293–307.

Sorce, J. F., Emde, R. N., Campos, J. J., & Klinnert, M. D. (1985). Maternal emotional signaling: Its effects on the visual cliff behavior of 1-year-olds. *Developmental Psychology, 21*, 195–200.

Sroufe, L. A. (1996). *Emotional development: The organization of emotional life in the early years.* New York: Cambridge University Press.

Sternberg, R. J. (1988). Triangulating love. In R. J. Sternberg & M. L. Barnes (Eds.), *The Psychology of Love* (pp. 119–138). New Haven, CT: Yale University Press.

Tangney, J. P., Miller, R. S., Flicker, L., & Barlow, D. H. (1996). Are shame, guilt, and embarrassment distinct emotions? *Journal of Personality and Social Psychology, 70*, 1256–1269.

Tomasello, M., & Farrar, M. J. (1986). Joint attention and early language. *Child Development, 57*, 1454–1463.

Tomkins, S. S. (1984). Affect theory. In K. Scherer & P. Ekman (Eds.), *Approaches to emotion* (pp. 163–195). Hillsdale, NJ: Lawrence Erlbaum Associates, Inc..

Tooby, J., & Cosmides, L. (1990). The past explains the present: Emotional adaptations and the structure of ancestral environments. *Ethology and Sociobiology, 11*, 375–424.

Trevarthen, C. (1993). The self born in intersubjectivity: The psychology of an infant communicating. In E. Ulric Neisser (Ed.), *The perceived self: Ecological and interpersonal sources of self-knowledge. Emory symposia in cognition, 5* (pp. 121–173). New York: Cambridge University Press.

Trivers, R. L. (1971). The evolution of reciprocal altruism. *Quarterly Review of Biology, 46*, 35–57.

Tronick, E. Z. (1989). Emotions and emotional communication in infants. *American Psychologist, 44*, 112–119.

Turner, M. E., Pratkanis, A. R., Probasco, P., & Leve, C. (1992). Threat cohesion and group effectiveness: Testing a social identity maintenance perspective on groupthink. *Journal of Personality and Social Psychology, 63*, 781–796.

Van Lange, P. A. M., Rusbult, C. E., Drigotas, S. M., Arriaga, X. B., Witcher, B. S., & Cox, C. L. (1997). Willingness to sacrifice in close relationships. *Journal of Personality and Social Psychology, 72*, 1373–1395.

Walden, T. A., & Baxter, A. (1989). The effect of context and age on social referencing. *Child Development, 60*, 1511–1518.

Weber, M. (1957). *The theory of social and economic organization*. New York: Free Press.

Weiss, R. S. (1982). Attachment in adult life. In C. M. Parkes & J. S. Hinde (Eds.), *The place of attachment in human behavior* (pp. 171–184). New York: Basic Books.

Wieselquist, J., Rusbult, C. E., Foster, C. A., & Agnew, C. R. (1999). Commitment, pro-relationship behavior, and trust in close relationships. *Journal of Personality and Social Psychology, 77*, 942–966.

Witherington, D. C., Campos, J. J., & Hertenstein, M. J. (2001). Principles of emotion and its development in infancy. In A. Fogel & G. Bremner (Eds.), *Blackwell handbook of infant development* (pp. 427–464). London: Blackwell.

Wolf, P. H. (1987). *The development of behavioral states and the expression of emotions in early infancy: New proposals for investigation.* Chicago: Chicago University Press.

Zajonc, R. B. (1968). Attitudinal effects of mere exposure. *Journal of Personality and Social Psychology Monograph Supplement, 9*, 1–27.

6

Social Sharing of Emotion, Emotional Recovery, and Interpersonal Aspects

Emmanuelle Zech, Bernard Rimé, and Frédéric Nils
University of Louvain, Belgium

Social sharing of emotion is a very common long-term consequence of emotional experiences. Despite the fact that it reactivates the emotions associated with the experience, people are prone to talk about the negative events they face. So, why do people share their emotions? From an intrapersonal perspective, a widespread belief exists that verbalizing an emotion alleviates the impact of an emotional event. The purpose of our research was to examine whether verbalization of emotions effectively contributed to the recovery from the emotion. We reviewed the correlative and experimental studies that were conducted to test this hypothesis. They consistently failed to support the view that *mere talking* about an emotional memory can lower its emotional load. Nevertheless, participants generally reported that they perceived the sharing process as beneficial. The question then remains as to why people share their emotions and report it is a beneficial process, if it does not bring emotional recovery. To answer this question, we shifted perspective and studied the interpersonal factors implied in the social sharing process. In the chapter, we suggest that the effects of social sharing depend on the social context in which they occur. We first consider types of sharing partners that are commonly chosen both as a function of age and according to the type of emotional situation experienced. Then, the types of helpful responses from sharing partners are examined. Finally, recent studies on the effects of specific sharing partner's reactions on affiliation and cognitive benefits are presented. In the conclusion of this chapter, implications of the research on social sharing for the field of emotion regulation are considered.

Our life is rarely devoid of emotional experiences for a very long time. Emotions are elicited as a function of the significance or appraisal of a specific antecedent event to the experiencing person. Emotion theorists usually consider that emotions consist of three additional components: physiological changes, expressive behaviors or reactions, and subjective or experiential changes (Arnold, 1960; Ekman, 1984, 1992; Frijda, 1986; Izard, 1977; Lang, 1983; Leventhal, 1984; Ortony, Clore, & Collins, 1988; Roseman, 1984; Scherer, 1984). Since the classic writings of Walter Cannon (1929), emotions are rightly conceived as emergency reactions taking place in the framework of homeostasis. Energy-consuming physiological responses that are central to an emotional state cannot last long. Emotional responses are thus usually considered to last a few seconds or minutes and to be regulated immediately (Frijda, Mesquita, Sonnemans, & Van Goozen, 1991). Thus, emotions generally appear as short-lived phenomena, essentially consisting of brief and temporally well-circumscribed disruptions affecting the course of the person's life. An emotion would immediately be concluded by a self-control, or self-restoration, procedure (e.g., Carver & Scheier, 1990; Frijda, 1986).

Now, consider the following questions. In the hours and days following an emotional experience, how often would it come back to the person's mind? How many thoughts—whether spontaneous or deliberate—does he or she have for what happened, for the feelings he or she had, or for elements of this specific experience? And how often did he or she talk about it, in what delay after the episode, and to whom? To how many people did he or she tell what happened? Quite generally, when such questions are answered, it becomes obvious that emotions do not really stop with the emotional circumstances and that they imply long-lasting regulatory processes.

In this chapter, we focus our attention on one long-lasting regulatory process called social sharing of emotion. We first review the empirical evidence regarding its frequency and characteristics. One of these characteristics is that social sharing of emotion reactivates the initial components of the emotional experience. The question is then addressed as to why people share their emotions with others? The following part of this chapter focuses on the intrapersonal recovery effect of emotional verbalization. Both common sense and scientific literature hold the assumption that sharing an emotional episode should serve a cathartic or venting function by bringing emotional relief. The research addressing this hypothesis is reviewed. Next, it is proposed that social sharing is not per se beneficial, but that it could be beneficial depending on emotional experiences and sharing goals, characteristics of the sharing partners, as well as their reactions. We thus extend our analysis by considering emotional sharing in the context of social interaction, and examine the types of sharing partners chosen as well as their responses. Next, we turn to evidence suggesting that depending on the type of partner and his or her reactions, social sharing of emotion has interpersonal and cognitive–affective beneficial effects. On the basis of these findings, we argue that social sharing may have beneficial effects because it fulfills the two fundamental needs of affiliation and social consensus.

EMOTION REGULATION AND LONG-TERM COMPONENTS OF EMOTIONS

It has long been known that traumatic experiences are generally followed by recurrent trauma-related thoughts and by an urge to talk about the experience. Over a decade ago, we hypothesized that not only trauma, but every emotional experience had long-lasting intrapersonal and interpersonal consequences (Rimé, 1989; for a discussion, see Philippot & Rimé, 1998). Numerous studies using diverse designs were then conducted to test this hypothesis. They led to the conclusion that, in an overwhelming manner, people ruminate about their emotional episodes and share their emotions with other people. They do so recurrently in the following days and weeks, or even months. More intense emotional experiences are ruminated and socially shared more often and for a longer time than less intense experiences (Rimé, Finkenauer, Luminet, Zech, & Philippot, 1998; Rimé, Mesquita, Philippot, & Boca, 1991; Rimé, Noël, & Philippot, 1991; Rimé, Philippot, Boca, Mesquita, 1992).

Our social psychology perspective then led us to develop a particular interest in the "social sharing of emotion" and for the potential role played by these processes in coping with or regulating emotion. Under this label, we examined a process that takes place during the hours, days, and even weeks and months following an emotional episode. It involves the evocation of an emotion in a socially shared language to some addressee by the person who experienced it. Very generally, this person will talk with others about the event's emotional circumstances and his or her feelings and reactions to it. In particular cases, the addressee is only present at the symbolic level, as is the case when people write letters or diaries.

The basic evidence in support of the view that very generally (i.e., in 89% to 100%), emotion is followed by the social sharing of emotion were reviewed elsewhere (Rimé, Mesquita et al., 1991; Rimé, Noël et al., 1991; Rimé et al., 1992, 1998) and can be summarized as follows:

1. The need people have to share their emotional experiences with others does not depend on a person's level of education. Social sharing of emotion is

equally shown whether the persons hold a university degree, or whether their education was limited to elementary school:

2. Social sharing is observed with approximately equal importance in regions as diverse as Asia, North America, and Europe:

3. The type of basic emotion felt in the episode is not a critical factor with regard to the need to talk about it. Episodes which involve fear, anger, or sadness are reported to others as often as episodes which involve happiness or love. However, emotional episodes involving shame and guilt tend to be verbalized at a somewhat lesser degree:

4. Social sharing is started in the majority of cases very early after the emotion—usually on the day it happened. It most often extends over the following days and weeks—or even months when the episode involved a highly intense emotion:

5. Social sharing is typically a repetitive phenomenon, as the majority of emotions are shared repeatedly, and with a variety of intimate persons (e.g., parents, spouse or partner, friends, siblings):

6. The exposure to the narrative of an emotional experience of another person leads the receiver to socially share this narrative with other people (secondary social sharing).

THE PARADOX OF THE SOCIAL SHARING OF EMOTION

An important feature of this process of talking about one's past emotional experience is the fact that it elicits the reactivation of the shared emotion. When the memory of an emotional episode is accessed, the components of the associated emotional responses (i.e., physiological, expressive, experiential) are also activated (e.g., Bower, 1981: Lang, 1983; Leventhal, 1984). Pennebaker (e.g., 1993a) showed that writing about one's past emotional experiences had an impact on autonomic responses and on mood state. That this is elicited also during a social sharing situation was confirmed in a study wherein participants had first to describe a past emotional experience in a detailed manner (Rimé, Noël et al., 1991). Immediately after, these participants had to complete a form with items examining what they had experienced when reaccessing the emotional memory. A majority of participants reported the experience of mental images of the emotional event, as well as accompanying subjective feelings and bodily sensations. This suggested that sharing an emotion elicits an emotion in the individual. Participants' affective reactions to the study-induced emotional evocation were assessed by a further question: "To what extent was completing this questionnaire a pleasant or painful experience for you?" The type of primary emotion involved markedly influenced the answers. Not surprisingly, reporting an experience of joy was rated as more pleasant than reporting an emotion of sadness, fear, or anger. However, more surprising was the fact that reporting fear, sadness, or anger was rated as painful or extremely painful only by a minority of the participants. Notwithstanding the reactivation of vivid images, feelings, and bodily sensations of a negative emotional experience, the sharing did not appear as aversive as one might have expected. Before terminating the study, a final question was addressed to the participants: "If you were asked now, would you be ready to complete a similar questionnaire on another past emotional event of the same kind: yes or no?" The answers were observed to be exactly the same whether the emotion shared previously was positively valenced (joy) or negatively valenced (fear, sadness, or anger). Overall 93.7% of the participants gave a positive answer.

Thus, these data suggest the paradoxical character of social sharing situations. On the one hand, social sharing reactivates the various components of the emotion which, in the case of negative emotion, should be experienced as aversive. On the other hand, sharing an emotion, whether positive or negative, is a situation to which people are inclined to expose themselves quite willingly. If people are so eager to engage in a social process in which they will experience negative affect, then they should be driven to do so by some powerful incentive. What could be the rewards they find?

THE UBIQUITOUS CATHARTIC VIEW OF EMOTIONAL EXPRESSION

When the question arises of the motives driving people to the verbal expression and social sharing of their emotions, the first consideration which comes to mind in our Western culture regards the *intrapersonal* aspects of the question. We immediately concentrate on the assumption that this process serves some "cathartic function." We presume that the person who experienced an emotion made use of talking as a discharge process which should eliminate the load of the emotional experience. We thus predominantly see talking about emotional experiences as a regulatory process which is initiated early after the emotional experience.

That this is the case is illustrated by the frequent allegation by laypersons that "talking about emotions makes you feel good," or that "talking about one's emotions brings relief." On this basis, the person who has just gone through a painful emotional experience is often recommended to "talk it out" or "to get it out off his or her chest." Such admonishments are meant to induce the person in telling the story and in expressing the related thoughts and feelings. Common sense thus seems to assume that verbalizing an emotional memory can transform it and that after verbalization, this memory would lose a significant part of its emotional load.

One of our studies clearly confirmed this. We found that 89% of respondents in a large sample of laypersons (N = 1,024) endorsed the view that talking about an emotional experience brings relief (Zech, 2000). Virtually no one refuted this view. Common sense actually holds firmly to the assumption that the mere talking about an emotional experience is conducive to emotional relief and emotional recovery. If this layperson belief could be supported by empirical data confirming that verbalizing an emotion brings "emotional recovery" or "emotional relief," then the paradox mentioned above earlier would become clear. People would tolerate reexperiencing because of this final benefit in terms of well-being.

This line of reasoning would probably be left unquestioned by most psychologists. Indeed, we all share the laypersons view. Our discipline exposes us to abundant theoretical information which is, at least at first sight, relatively consistent with the laypersons belief. Indeed, most of the psychotherapy schools consider that expressing emotion is a critical tool to psychotherapeutic change. In addition to this consistent theoretical support of the beneficial effects of emotional expression, reviews of the psychotherapy outcome literature often conclude that high levels of client experiencing in therapy sessions counted among the variables related to a good outcome (e.g., L. S. Greenberg & Malcolm, 2002; Klein, Mathieu–Coughlan, & Kiesler, 1986; Orlinsky & Howard, 1986; Pos, Greenberg, Goldman, & Korman, 2002). Thus, psychotherapy theories, emotional expression, and psychotherapy outcomes are seen as linked in many regards. The processes behind these links are probably much more complex than what a simple ventilation hypothesis would propose. Nevertheless, considering this framework, it is very tempting for psychologists to endorse, as lay people do, a general a priori according to which expressing and verbalizing emotion would help to recover from the emotional experience.

The ventilation, or cathartic, a priori view of the effects of expression or verbalizing an emotion can be explained as follows. When people recall an emotional experience, the emotional intensity of the felt emotion generally decreases as a function of the time elapsed since the original episode happened. This represents the natural recovery from the emotion. According to a ventilation or cathartic view, socially sharing an emotional experience is predicted to accelerate this process and thus, to bend the slope of the recovery process at the moment the sharing was completed. It should be stressed that strictly speaking, with the exception of the expression of emotions, the ventilation view makes no proposition regarding the way in which the sharing process should be achieved, or regarding the way the sharing partner should react or behave. In its essence, the ventilation view attributes the expected relief effects to the mere verbalizing of the emotional experience.

It is remarkable that despite the popularity of the topic and despite the place taken by the sharing of emotions in everyday life, empirical research on this question was virtually absent from the literature throughout the 20th century. In the last 10 years, we conducted a large number of investigations—both in naturalistic conditions and in the laboratory environment—aimed at assessing how far the social sharing of emotion actually had the predicted impact on people's degree of emotional recovery from the shared episode.

IS SOCIAL SHARING OF EMOTION CONDUCIVE TO EMOTIONAL RECOVERY?

Spontaneous Social Sharing and Emotional Recovery

We examined this question in many of our questionnaire studies of social sharing. The research design generally involved assessing (a) the initial intensity of the emotion elicited by the episode, (b) the extent of sharing that developed after, and (c) the intensity of the emotion elicited when the memory of the episode was activated later. We tested the hypothesis that there is a positive correlation between the amount of social sharing after the emotional event and the degree of emotional recovery—or the difference between (a) and (c). The latter variable was called the "recovery index" and thus represented the difference between the initial and the residual intensity of the emotion elicited by the target event. This correlational hypothesis was first considered in one of the autobiographic recall investigations conducted by Rimé, Mesquita, et al. (1991: Study 6). Unexpectedly, neither the amount of social sharing nor the delay of social sharing were found to be related to emotional recovery. After this first study, we conducted innumerable studies using questionnaires and autobiographic recall to examine either some specific aspect of the sharing process, or some specific respondent variables such as age, education, culture, personality differences, and so forth (for a review, see Rimé et al., 1998). In all of them, we systematically assessed the correlation between the extent of sharing and the recovery index, and quite generally, the observed coefficient failed to be significant. In studies using the diary design (Rimé, Philippot et al., 1994; Study 3), recovery was assessed by the difference between the impact each daily event had when it occurred and its residual impact as rated several weeks later, at follow-up. Again no significant relation was observed between this recovery index and extent of social sharing manifested when the event happened. In the studies which used a follow-up design, the extent of social sharing naturally developed by participants was generally assessed in the days following the emotional event, and the degree of recovery was usually checked later on several occasions (e.g., after 1 week, after 2 weeks, and so on). They generally failed to confirm the existence of a significant positive correlation between the two sets of variables, and in some cases, a negative correlation was observed (e.g., Zech, 1994). Our studies comparing secret and shared emotions offered another opportunity to test the common sense view (Finkenauer & Rimé, 1998b). However, in the two different studies we conducted, when shared and secret emotional episodes were compared for the intensity of the emotion these episodes still elicited in respondents, no significant difference occurred (Finkenauer & Rimé, 1998a). Paradoxically, as compared to shared emotions, emotional memories which were never shared were found no more or less emotionally arousing when reaccessed at the time of the investigation.

In conclusion, the layperson's view was in no manner supported by these data. To our surprise, our studies never supported the prediction that sharing an emotion would reduce the emotional load. Our data were perfectly consistent in this regard. In sum, our correlational findings overwhelmingly suggested that verbalizing an emotional experience does not contribute to emotional recovery as such. Yet, it might be premature to conclude from these generally negative data that social sharing of emotion has no effect on emotional recovery. From studies conducted on the health effects of a procedure in which participants are instructed to write extensively about past emotional traumas, Pennebaker and colleagues suggested that qualitative aspects of expression should be considered (for a review, see Lepore & Smyth, 2002; Pennebaker, 1989). Thus, in a study by Pennebaker and Beall (1986), writing about factual aspects of an emotional episode did not affect health variables, whereas writing about factual and feeling aspects did. Emphasising the feeling dimension might thus be critical for social sharing to have some impact. However, assessing qualitative aspects of spontaneous social sharing in survey research raises difficulties. In general, respondents do not seem to be able to precisely determine what they were talking about, or which aspect—fact or feeling—they had emphasised in a previous social sharing. To illustrate, items assessing respectively to what extent "facts" and "feelings" were shared usually yield high correlations, suggesting that they did not really tap distinct elements. Therefore, subsequent studies were conducted using the experimental induction of social sharing of emotion.

Experimental Induction of Sharing and Emotional Recovery

Experiments comparing several forms of sharing were thus conducted to assess how far qualitative distinctions have consequences for emotional recovery (Zech, 1999, 2000). Rimé, Zech, Finkenauer, Luminet, and Dozier (1996) had 127 psychology students interview one person each about a recent negative emotion. Four types of sharing were created by emphasising, respectively, (a) factual aspects, (b) feelings and emotions, and (c) meanings elicited by the event. In the fourth condition, no specific emphasis was adopted. The emotional impact of the event was assessed on seven indexes before the sharing situation and again 1week after. Dependent variables included a good deal of indexes likely to reflect the current subjective experience of the respondent relative to the target emotional episode (e.g., emotional intensity of the memory, intensity of bodily sensations when thinking about the event, intensity of action tendencies when thinking about the event, challenged basic beliefs, extent of episode-related mental rumination, need to socially share, etc.). No effect of sharing type was found for these indexes, and it was not found for extent of sharing in the following week.

Zech and Rimé (2002, Study 1) attempted a replication in a more controlled laboratory study. Interviews with three conditions of sharing were conducted by the same person. In two of them, participants talked about the most upsetting event of their lives for 20 min, with a focus on felt emotions in one and with a focus on facts in the other. In a control condition, they talked about a trivial topic. Dependent variables were collected before sharing, immediately after, at a 1-week follow-up, and at a 2-months follow-up. No significant effects of type of sharing were found. However, at the final follow-up, participants in the felt emotions condition rated the sharing as more meaningful, more interesting, and higher in overall subjective impact than participants in the other two conditions.

In a third study, 278 psychology students each had to interview two volunteers about a recent unrecovered negative event (Zech & Rimé, 2002: Study 2). Before manipulation, all participants had to rate how much this memory still affected them. Four conditions were conducted: (a) the verbalisation of the emotional event whose emotional impact has been rated in the questionnaire (Target emotion), (b) the verbalisation of another emotional episode (Other emotion), (c) the verbalisation of trivial topics (Trivial), and (d) no verbalization at all (No verbalization control). For one of the two volunteers, student interviewers had to conduct an interview on the Target emotion. For the other volunteer, the student interviewers were randomly assigned to one of three other conditions (Other emotion vs. Trivial vs. No verbalization). Detailed instructions had to be followed by interviewers in conducting each of the experimental conditions. At the end of the 30-min interview, participants were rated by interviewers on how much they had overtly expressed feelings. In addition to emotional recovery variables, dependent variables also included the perceived subjective benefits brought by the verbalization. For example, participants were asked whether the experiment had been meaningful for them, whether it was relieving for them, whether it had clarified their view of the event, whether they were comforted by others, and whether it had helped them. Follow-up ratings of emotional impact and subjective benefits of the experiment were collected at a follow-up session conducted 3 days later. Results of this study again confirmed that verbalization of emotion does not alleviate the emotional impact of unrecovered events. Indeed, participants reported a similar decrease of emotional impact in each condition. However, participants who talked about emotional topics with the experimenter (in the Target and Other emotion conditions) reported significantly more subjective benefits of having participated in the study. Compared to participants in the two control conditions (Trivial and No sharing controls), participants in the felt emotions conditions consistently rated the sharing as more beneficial to them in general (e.g., it was useful), as more emotion-relieving (e.g., made them feel good), more cognitively helpful (e.g., it helped in putting order in themselves), and as more socially beneficial (e.g., they experienced comforting behaviors from the part of the recipient).

These studies using a social sharing induction procedure thus led to contrasting observations. On the one hand, no changes were found in the degree of emotional recovery of the emotional memory, which suggested that sharing emotional experiences failed to alleviate the load of the emotional memory. However, participants who shared their emotions openly reported that the experience was ultimately beneficial compared to the controls. Thus, whereas objective benefits failed to be evidenced, subjective—or alleged— benefits clearly showed up from our procedure.

Recovered or Unrecovered Events

Faced repeatedly with these unexpected negative findings regarding effects of sharing on emotional recovery, we wondered whether the notion of emotional recovery on which our studies relied made sense at all. Rimé, Hayward, and Pennebaker (1996) addressed this question. Students were instructed to recall one emotional experience they "had recovered from" and one they "had not recovered from." For each, they rated initial and residual emotional impact, as well as initial and residual sharing. The data showed that the two types of episodes had initially elicited a comparable emotional impact. Consistent with all of our previous studies, they also failed to differ in initial sharing. Both were shared to a very large extent in the days and weeks after they occurred. However, confirming that the notion of "recovery" makes sense, the two types of episodes differed markedly in their residual emotional impact and thus yielded marked differences in the recovery index. This index was indeed much lower for nonrecovered emotional memories than for recovered emotional memories. Moreover, episodes not recovered elicited much more residual sharing than recovered ones. We could therefore conclude that the notion of emotional recovery really makes sense. Emotional memories that people selected as "unrecovered" evidenced a stronger impact on subjective feelings and on social behavior than was the case for emotional memories that people selected as "recovered." And the two types of episodes were socially shared a comparable number of times at origin.

Unrecovered Events and Need to Share

In eight different studies we conducted, participants rated the emotional intensity felt when remembering a recent emotional event ("residual emotional intensity") and the extent to which they (a) still felt the need to talk about it, and (b) still talked about it ("residual social sharing"). The delay between the target emotional event and follow-up assessments varied from a week (Rimé, Zech, et al., 1996) to several months (e.g., Luminet, Zech, Rimé, & Wagner, 2000), or even several years (e.g., Rimé, Finkenauer, & Sangsue, 1994). Correlations were computed between residual emotional intensity and residual sharing for each data set. Across all studies, we found that the higher the residual emotional intensity, the higher the residual social sharing (for a review, see Rimé et al., 1998). This confirmed that unrecovered emotional memories do surface more in sharing behaviors than recovered ones.

How can we interpret this relation? On the one hand, talking about an emotional memory can reactivate event-related emotional feelings. On the other hand, residual event-related feelings elicit residual sharing. Does this mean that people who have failed to recover from an emotion keep talking about it without limits? Examining the size of the correlations revealed that in six of our eight studies, residual emotional intensity was linked more closely to the need for sharing than to actual residual sharing. In short, when people fail to recover from an emotional episode, they feel the need to talk about it and they actually do so to some extent. Certain social constraints (Pennebaker, 1993b) are likely to moderate the relation between residual emotionality and actual residual sharing. However, such constraints will at the very least leave intact a person's need to share. In other words, as long as an emotional memory elicits actual emotional feelings, the person can be expected to feel the need to talk about it.

Conclusion

People who experience an emotion feel compelled to talk about it and to share it, preferably with their intimates. They do it quite willingly, despite of the fact that the sharing process reactivates the negative aspects of the emotional experience. A very widespread belief exists according to which sharing an emotion should bring emotional relief. Yet, both correlative and experimental studies, which were conducted to test the validity of this belief, consistently failed to support this view. It does not seem that *mere talking* about an emotional memory has a significant impact on the emotional load associated with this memory. Nevertheless, people who share their emotions generally express the feeling that the process is beneficial. Additionally, whereas sharing was not found to have an impact on recovery, data were supportive of the opposite conclusion. Lack of recovery was markedly associated with the perpetuation of sharing, and even more markedly with the perpetuation of the need to share.

The abundance of the null findings finally led us to accept that despite stereotypes, socially sharing an emotion does not bring emotional relief as such. The data collected so far strongly suggest that the mere social sharing of an emotion is unable to change the emotional memory. After all, it does make sense with regard to adaptation. An emotional memory carries important information with respect to future situations. If we had the potential to alter the emotion-arousing capacities of such memories by mere talking about them, such equipment would deprive us of vital fruits of our experience (Rimé, 1999).

HOW DO WE FARE WITH REGARD TO THE LITERATURE?

As was mentioned earlier, the 20th century was empirically silent most of the time with regard to the question of emotional ventilation and its effects. During the last two decades however, an important scientific interest has emerged regarding the relation existing between the disclosure of emotion on the one hand, and well-being and health on the other hand. This interest was stimulated by the experimental work undertaken by James Pennebaker and his colleagues on the effects of disclosure of traumatic events. In the so-called "writing paradigm" (e.g., Pennebaker & Beall, 1986; Pennebaker, Colder, & Sharp, 1990; Pennebaker, Kiecolt–Glaser, & Glaser, 1988), participants are assigned to write about past stressful or traumatic events in their lives for 15 to 30 min during sessions held on several consecutive days. They are compared with participants instructed to write about trivial topics. Writing is generally done in the laboratory with no feedback given. A critical part of the procedure is that experimental participants are encouraged to really let go and explore their deepest thoughts and feelings about their experiences. The main outcome measures in these studies consist of the assessment of participants' health indexes in the weeks following their participation. The basic finding was that when compared to participants in the trivial topic condition, those who wrote about their trauma showed less frequent illness-related visits to the health center and fewer self-reported illness symptoms (e.g., Pennebaker & Beall, 1986). Various studies extended these positive findings to other health outcomes, including improved immune functions indexes such as antibody responses to the Epstein–Barr virus (Esterling, Antoni, Fletcher, Margulies, & Schneiderman, 1994). Although repetitive writing sessions are usually designed in these studies, a single 30-min writing session on real or imagery traumas was sufficient to produce a reduction of long-term number of illness visits to the health center and of self-reported symptoms (M. A. Greenberg, Wortman, & Stone, 1996). A large number of writing studies have now been conducted. Reviewers of these studies generally concluded that "opening up" and expressing stress-related thoughts and feelings was associated with improved physical and mental health (Esterling, L'Abate, Murray, & Pennebaker, 1999; Littrell, 1998; Pennebaker, 1993a, 1997; Smyth, 1998).

The findings issued from these writing studies are often understood as supporting the view that "putting emotion into words" is conducive to emotional recovery and emotional relief. However, whereas the design of these studies allows one to conclude that there are some positive effects of "putting emotion into words" on health indexes, it does not address the process through which such effects are achieved. This process might involve factors totally alien to a ventilation effect. For instance, it might be that putting emotions into words in a solitary session stimulates the need to be with others and to share one's emotions with them. The resulting increase in received social support could thus account for health improvements. In sum, the writing design does not address the empirical question raised by the commonsense belief. It does not test whether putting a specific emotional episode into words ends up in some emotional relief and in some sizeable alleviation of the person's memory of this episode.

Whereas laboratory studies addressing this verbalization-recovery question are scarce, recently developed clinical research conducted on the effects of Critical Incident Stress Debriefing (CISD) or Psychological Debriefing (PD) provides data which are much relevant in this regard. CISD is a group intervention technique developed for implementation immediately after a potentially traumatizing event to prevent the development of a posttraumatic stress disorder (PTSD) among exposed individuals (see Dyregrov, 1997; Mitchell & Everly, 1995; for overviews). In PD or CISD, participants each describe what happened from their perspective, then express their prominent thoughts concerning the event, and they communicate "what was the worst thing for them in this situation." The technique thus clearly involves "putting emotions into words," or "talking it out." The use of this technique has been growing so rapidly in the last decade that a concern about its real beneficial effects on PTSD symptomatology (i.e., intrusion, avoidance, and hypervigilence) has emerged (Deahl, 2000; Raphael, Meldrum, & McFarlane, 1995; Rose & Bisson, 1998). Several studies that have assessed the effects of CISD or PD failed to find significant results (e.g., Deahl, Gillham, Thomas, Searle, & Srinivasan, 1994; Griffiths & Watts, 1992; Kenardy et al., 1996). A recent review of existing randomized controlled studies on the effects of PD interventions following trauma indicated that out of six studies, two found positive outcomes on indexes of psychopathology (PTSD), two demonstrated no difference on outcomes, and two showed some negative outcomes in the intervention group as compared to nonintervention groups (Rose & Bisson, 1998). A recent meta-analysis conducted with very strict selection criteria concluded that "Despite the intuitive appeal of the technique, our results show that CISD has no efficacy in reducing symptoms of post-traumatic stress disorder and other trauma-related symptoms, and in fact suggest that it has a detrimental effect" (Van Emmerik, Kamphuis, Hulsbosch, & Emmelkamp, 2002, p. 769). However, a variety of studies also indicated that a vast majority of victims or professionals involved in traumatic situations reported that psychological debriefings were useful and beneficial (e.g., Arendt & Elklit, 2001; Robinson & Mitchell, 1993).

Altogether, the reviewed data suggests that despite lay people's unanimous view, the effects of "putting emotions into words" are anything but a simple matter. Studies conducted with the writing paradigm showed that putting emotion into words in solitary sessions is related to improvements in health condition. These results are often taken as evidence that putting emotion into words brings emotional recovery. However, debriefing studies failed to evidence a "talking-recovery effect." Indeed, debriefing procedures did not consistently result in a significant alleviation of the emotional impact of the eliciting event (such as uncontrolled intrusive thoughts, avoidance of event-related cues, general emotional arousal, etc.). Such negative results are at odds with any simple cathartic or ventilation view of the effects of verbalizing emotions. On the other hand, debriefing procedures generally evidenced a "talking-relief effect." It showed that people who talked out their emotional experience report global, nonspecific feelings of relief or of personal benefits that they attribute to the expression situation. Such an effect is consistent with abundant evidence from social sharing studies that people are generally quite eager to talk about their emotional experiences and to share them with those around them (e.g., Rimé et al., 1998).

INTERPERSONAL ASPECTS OF SOCIAL SHARING

If the social sharing that spontaneously develops after emotional exposure does not affect the recovery process, why does it accompany emotional experiences almost systematically? Should it be concluded that the urge to share generally elicited by an emotion is a useless manifestation and that it should not be considered as an emotion regulation process? Alternative potential effects of socially sharing an emotion are currently under investigation in our laboratory. They may involve important health, cognitive, and social functions (see Rimé et al., 1998). In the following, we want to focus on one of these lines of research that specifically deals with interpersonal aspects of social sharing of emotion. Because social sharing is a fundamental interpersonal process, its study should involve the examination of the interpersonal context in which it occurs. In addition, perceived and objective benefits of social sharing might go beyond the intrapersonal sphere and extend to interpersonal effects.

Research conducted on related areas such as self-disclosure, social support, and affiliation can shed some light on why people may want to share their emotions, with whom, and on the effects of the partner's reactions.. A recent model proposed that self-disclosure—that is, personal information verbally communicated to another person—should only occur if it is a good strategy to achieve goals such as self-clarification, social validation, or relationship development (Omarzu, 2000). In addition, it also proposed that self-disclosure should only occur if there is an appropriate target for self-disclosure. Complementing these hypotheses, Horowitz and colleagues (2001) proposed that an appropriate target is someone who is able to satisfy the distressed person's goal, that is, getting either emotional or esteem support. As a consequence, social support provided to a sharer would be most effective in reducing his or her distress if the listener's reactions match the sharer's goal.

Research on the effects of self-disclosure, however, showed that, without concerns about who the partner is, or how he or she reacts, people who engage in intimate disclosures tend to be liked more than people who disclose less. In addition, it has also been shown that disclosure causes people to like their listeners (for a review, see Collins & Miller, 1994). In fact, self-disclosure has been conceived as a key component of the development of intimate relationships (Reis & Patrick,

1996). Although contradictory findings have been found (e.g., Stroebe, Stroebe, Abakoumkin, & Schut, 1996), social support research has also indicated that supportive social networks tend to reduce distress in individuals under stress, whereas unsupportive or critical social networks can actually increase distress (e.g., Lepore, 1992; Major, Zubek, Cooper, Cozzarelli, & Richards, 1997; Manne, Taylor, Dougherty, & Kemeny, 1997).

Helpful and unhelpful reactions provided by listeners have already been described in the disclosure and social support literature (e.g., Dakof, & Taylor, 1990; Kelly & McKillop, 1996; Lehman, Ellard, & Wortman, 1986; Lepore, Ragan, & Jones, 2000; Pennebaker & Harber, 1993; Reis & Shaver, 1988). Partners are perceived as more helpful when they display empathy, understanding, validation, and care (Reis & Shaver, 1988). Other types of helpful behaviors have been observed such as giving advice or new information, telling a similar experience, and reassessing the situation (Goldsmith, McDermott, & Alexander, 2000; Horowitz et al., 2001).

Within the context of social sharing of emotion, perceived benefits of social sharing could thus be linked to the reinforcement of affective bonds that would result from emotional sharing. If a sharer chose appropriate partners, and if partners respond supportively, social sharing could thus have lasting affective consequences for the sharer, but also for the relationship between the sharer and the listener. Reis and Patrick (1996) proposed that affective bonds consist of two dimensions: one called attachment (i.e., partners feel safe and close), the other called intimacy (i.e., partners share personal common knowledge). In this sense, sharing emotions may help to maintain close relationships, and develop new ones, but also increase social consensus between people and thus help social integration.

In the following, we present new data on sharing partners, on their responses, and when these are considered to be helpful or not for the sharer. Experimental studies manipulating the listener's reactions as well as the group belongingness of the listener (whether intimate or stranger) are also presented. These studies examined the potential effects of social sharing of emotion on feelings of closeness or attachment to the listener, feelings of loneliness, and basic beliefs.

Who Are the Sharing Partners?

People may not share their emotions without concern for the identity and qualities of the sharing partner. Because they are immediately available, the more likely sharing partners should be those present in the immediate surroundings of the person, that is, intimates. But, among those that are available, potential sharers may in fact search for a specific partner who has the abilities to answer the sharer's specific needs at a moment (see also Horowitz et al., 2001). For example, children may have different types of intimates, such as their parents, siblings, or peers. As compared to siblings or peers, their parents could be considered as more relevant for sharing their emotions because they represent the most important figures that can fulfill their needs. During adolescence, however, peers and friends become an increasing reference for the adolescent's evolving behavior and thoughts. They might also become the main sharing partners. Later on, at adulthood, romantic relationships could take up this role. To examine this hypothesis, we examined whether, as types of intimates and needs may evolve over age periods, types of sharing partners chosen would change over development and adulthood.

In one study, participants were school children, aged 6 and 8 years (Rimé, Dozier, Vandenplas, & Declercq, 1996). Each child was told either a high or a low emotion narrative. Immediately after, the child was brought to a playroom where two peers were playing. For 15 minutes, social sharing was monitored. Sharing occurred infrequently with no difference between emotion conditions or between age groups. This observation suggested either that children at this age range do not yet share their emotions, or that peers do not represent appropriate sharing partners for them. Further data argued in favor of the latter explanation. Parents, who were blind to the experimental conditions, rated their child's behavior during the evening following the narrative session. These ratings revealed that 42% of the children who heard the low emotion narrative and 71% of the children who heard the high emotion narrative had shared the narrative with their parents. The latter rate is consistent with diary data from adults showing that some 60% of emotional experiences are shared during the day they occurred. As with adults, social sharing tended to be more repetitive among children who heard the high emotion narrative. However, it did not seem that children shared with partners other than parents.

A second study was conducted with boys aged 8 to 12 who attended a scout camp and took part in a frightening and exciting game during the night (Rimé et al., 1996). After the game, children rated their game-related emotionality on a 20-degree "emotion thermometer." The data suggested that a moderate intensity emotion was induced. The boys went back home on the next day. Three days later, parents rated their child's sharing since the camp. The ratings showed that children shared the night game in 97% of the cases. Six days after the game, parents again rated their child's sharing. Sharing rates amounted to 39%, thus showing a sharp decline over time. Children's self-reports 1 week after the game revealed that sharing had occurred for 87% of the sample. Parents clearly emerged as the privileged sharing partners in this age group—mother in 93% and father in 89%. Siblings served as recipients in 48% of the cases, best friends in 33%, peers in 37%, and grandparents in only 5%.

In a third recent study conducted with 12- to 17-year-old participants (Rimé, Charlet, & Nils, 2002), over 600 students were asked to recall an emotional episode in their recent past which was related to one of four basic emotions: fear, anger, sadness, or joy. They were then asked to report the extent to which they had shared it with 13 different categories of people. Results revealed that, regardless of the emotional valence or type of emotion experienced, the family and especially parents remained the main sharing partners of emotional experiences in this age group. However, as age cohorts got older, friends, including girl and boy friends and female best friends became increasingly important. Other people were rarely mentioned as sharing partners.

In a fourth study (Rimé, Finkenauer, & Sevrin, 1995), older adults (60 to 75 years of age) and elderly adults (76 to 94 years of age) were compared to a group of younger adults (25 to 40 years of age). Participants completed a questionnaire on the most emotional event of the day for five successive evenings. Among adults and elderly people, the profile of preferred sharing partners was very similar. From adulthood on, spouses and companions became the main sharing partners (over 75%), then the family (over 30%) and friends (about 20%) were preferred. As previously mentioned, other categories of people, such as strangers or professionals, were rarely used (less than in 5% of the cases).

In sum, in line with our hypothesis, types of sharing partners of one's emotional experiences change over age cohorts. Childhood is characterized by a choice in attachment figures or parents. Over age, new attachment figures are chosen. During adolescence, girlfriends and boyfriends and female best friends become increasingly important. At adulthood and among elderly people, spouses and companions become the main sharing partners. These results suggest that from childhood to old age, people who experience emotional situations share them not only with those who are available in their immediate surroundings but with those with whom they share the most intimate or close relationships.

In addition to the category of intimates that were chosen to socially share an emotional experience, a recent study investigated the age and gender of sharing partners of young adults (Zech, Christophe, Herbette, & Stroebe, 2002). Social science students (54.5% girls) were asked to recall a negative emotional episode that they had shared with at least one person. The description of the person with whom they had primarily shared their emotions revealed that they had shared them in the majority of the cases with people older than themselves (66%) rather than with younger people (13%). Sharing partners were on average 30.73 years old (*SD* = 13.42) and no partner was younger than 18 years old. Independently of the participant's own gender, they also had shared with more female (61%) than male sharing partners.

In addition to these results, recent investigation on social sharing after professional rather than personal emotional situations added some interesting nuances to the aforementioned pattern. One study was conducted on 133 nurses who were asked about their sharing partners when they experienced an emotional situation at work, for example, when they were confronted with an upsetting situation regarding their patient (Laurens, Herbette, & Rimé, 2000). In this case, professionals such as their own colleagues, physicians, or a psychologist became their primary partners of social sharing. Their spouse or partner, friends or family, were chosen to a lesser extent. In another study, 79 police officers, medical and psychosocial aid personnel who arrived after a train crash involving eight deaths in Belgium, shared their emotions and feelings about the catastrophe primarily with their spouseor companion (61%) but for 39% of them, their primary sharing partners were their colleagues and work team (Zech, Ucros, Rimé, & DeSoir, 2002).

Altogether, these studies suggest that, depending on the emotional situation, people primarily share their emotions with different partners and not only with intimates, as was suggested by the initial research. After professional situations, colleagues were privileged, whereas after personal situations, partners such as older people and women were preferred. Depending on the situation, people may thus choose partners who can provide an answer to their specific need. In professional situations, colleagues and other professionals could be seen as more knowledgeable about ways to cope with emotions related to work. Alternatively, the choice of evolving attachment figures over the age cohorts suggests that sharers of personal situations may select people who will provide them with empathy and emotional support. Women who were also preferred after personal situations could be selected because of their known interest and receptivity to emotional expression. In sum, these results suggest that people share their emotions with partners that can meet their needs either to receive interest, relevant information, or emotional support and empathy.

What Are the Helpful Reactions of the Listener?

In addition to the aforementioned pattern, we also investigated the possible helpful behaviors or reactions provided by a listener. In natural settings, a specific dynamic takes place between the speaker and the listener. A typical response of the listener is the expression of interest in the emotional story (Christophe & Rimé, 1997). Another response of the listener is empathy. The more emotional a story is, the more the listener will experience emotion. As a consequence of empathy, it is likely that the listener will express support. A fourth response is distance reduction. Indeed, Christophe and Rimé (1997) also observed that when intense emotions are shared, listeners reduce their use of verbal mediators in their responses. As a substitute, they display nonverbal comforting behaviors like hugging, kissing, or touching. This suggests that sharing an intense emotional experience may decrease the physical distance between two people.

These results were consistent with one study in which participants were asked to recall a social sharing interaction that they had found either helpful, or unhelpful (Zech, Christophe, et al., 2002). To examine whether the perceived (un)helpfulness of the interaction was related to particular behaviors that the listener had shown (or not) during the interaction, participants were asked to rate the extent to which their listener had shown various behaviors (drawn from Christophe & Rimé, 1997) Results revealed that the listener had provided more attention and understanding, informational support (e.g., advice, reappraisal), reciprocity or empathy-type behaviors (e.g., sharing of own experiences, felt the same emotions), and attachment or attraction-type behaviors (e.g., came physically closer, consoled, made them feel safe and secure) in the helpful interaction condition as compared to the unhelpful interaction.

In sum, these results are consistent with data on the types of preferred sharing partners. They are also in line with the hypothesis that some partners would behave in ways that would match the sharer's particular needs in personal emotional situations. Within the context of intimate relationships, showing interest, sharing new information and knowledge, and providing empathy or support to the sharer, are reported as being helpful responses. These behaviors should certainly have consequences. But, what are these effects? In the following, we present new research that addressed this question.

What Are the Helpful Effects of Such Helpful Interactions?

Helpful effects of the partner's behavior may be numerous and could be found at both intrapersonal and interpersonal levels. From an intrapersonal perspective, they could facilitate the cognitive–emotional processing of the emotional episode (Lepore et al., 2000). From an interpersonal perspective, these behaviors could lead to the development or reinforcement of the relationship. In one recall study previously mentioned (Zech, Christophe, et al., 2002), participants who had recalled a helpful versus unhelpful interaction were asked whether they had perceived changes in the way they viewed their emotional episode and their relationship with the listener. Results revealed that participants in the helpful interaction condition reported that the interaction had changed their view about their emotional experience in a positive way, whereas there was no change in opinion among sharers of the unhelpful interaction. Similarly, the former reported to have changed their opinion about their listener in a positive way, whereas the latter reported a slight negative influence. Results also revealed that, since the interaction, sharers felt more attached and had exchanged more information. This suggested that a helpful interaction had long-lasting subjective interpersonal consequences between the sharer and the listener. This was further confirmed by an item assessing whether the sharer–listener relationship was likely to continue: Sharers in the helpful interaction evaluated that this was more likely than in the unhelpful interaction.

Because these data may have been subject to a reconstruction bias, the potential effects of a helpful interaction were then further investigated in two experiments where the listener's responses were manipulated. In a first study (Nils, 2002), these two types of behaviors were manipulated in comparison to a control condition. Eighty-five psychology students were asked to come to the laboratory with a good friend. On arrival, the friend watched an emotion inducing film. During that time, the experimenter explained to the student that his or her friend was watching an emotional film and that his or her task was thereafter to interact with him or her. They were randomly assigned to one out of three instructions conditions: (a) providing empathy, understanding, and validation to their friend's emotional reactions to the film; (b) reappraising and minimizing their friend's emotional reactions to the film; or (c) no sharing at all. In the two sharing conditions, the 5 to 10 min of conversation were monitored (to check for conformity to instructions). The friend (sharer) then rated the extent to which he or she felt affectively close to the listener, his or her feelings of loneliness, and his or her views about a just world. Results revealed that participants who received empathetic responses felt affectively closer to their listener and less lonely than participants in the reappraisal and minimization condition. There was also a tendency for those in the empathetic condition to believe more in a just world as compared to participants who were only exposed to the film. Thus, in a sharing situation with an intimate, it seems that empathetic and supportive behaviors of the listener led to more positive effects for the relationship (affective closeness) between the intimates. Consistently, these behaviors were also related to a decrease of loneliness. Finally, they led to partially restore a basic belief that was shattered by the film. This effect could be explained by a feeling of consensus or agreement during the interaction between intimate partners about the challenging information involved in the film.

In a second experiment (Nils & Rimé,2001), we specifically tested whether agreement or disagreement with the sharer's viewpoint and feelings led to the same effects. The same procedure was used but this time, the sharing partner also varied: Friends were either kept as they arrived (intimate partner), or switched with another student-friend couple, leading to a sharing situation with a stranger. A new set of instructions was given, similar to those used in Lepore et al. (2000), to test the effects of the listener's supportive versus unsupportive responses to the social sharing. One-hundred thirty-one student-confederates were randomly assigned to reply to the sharer (a) showing agreement with the sharer's reactions (e.g., nodded, maintained mutual eye contact, and smiled approvingly while listening to the sharer; agreed with several thoughts and feelings), (b) showing disagreement with the sharer's reactions (e.g., maintained a neutral countenance, avoided eye contact while listening to the sharer, and disagreed with several thoughts and feelings), or (c) showing no reaction (asking only predetermined questions). The same dependent variables were assessed. As could be expected, feelings of closeness to the listener were rated as more intense between intimate partners as compared to strangers. Sharers in the intimate partners condition also felt less lonely as compared to sharers in the strangers condition. In the case of intimate partners, results also indicated that when the listener reacted with disagreement, the sharer reported a decrease of perceived affective closeness with him or her as compared to the agreement sharing condition. Consistently, they also reported feeling more lonely than in the agreement condition. Consistent with previous results, there was again a tendency for sharers to believe more in a just world when their intimate had reacted with agreement as compared to when he or she had reacted with disagreement. In the case of strangers, when a stranger reacted with agreement to the sharer's emotional reactions, the sharer reported an increase in perceived affective closeness with his or her listener as compared to either the disagreement or no reaction conditions. Type of sharing with a stranger had no effect on loneliness or on beliefs in a just world.

Thus, it seems that, when social sharing is perceived as helpful, it is associated with more salient affective bonds among participants of the interaction. The increase of perceived closeness with a stranger who agrees with the sharer's emotional reactions may contribute to the development of new relationships. In support of our hypothesis, social sharing can have lasting affiliative consequences for the relationship between the sharer and the listener, but also for cognitive–affective dimensions related to the impact of the emotional experience.

Emotions are known to challenge the beliefs that people hold to preserve a sense of coherence, predictability, and control over themselves and the world (Janoff–Bulman, 1992; Parkes, 1972; Tait & Silver, 1989). Hence, emotions elicit a mental "working through" process aimed either at the restoration of beliefs or at finding meaning in the event (e.g., Silver & Wortman, 1980; Tait & Silver, 1989). When intimate listeners react in agreement with the sharer's reactions or when they react with empathy, social sharing was found to play some role in restoring the belief in a just world. Social sharing may thus help complete the cognitive processes elicited by the emotion. In our current studies, we are investigating the extent to which social sharing can also contribute to reinstating a person's sense of coherence and predictability, as well as a sense of control and mastery.

These preliminary results should be confirmed by future experimental research. As Horowitz et al. (2001) have noted, the sharing partner's reactions should be helpful only if they match the needs of the sharing person. Future studies will thus investigate both personal and professional emotional situations where needs for getting emotional support or relevant information and reactions may differ. In addition, it will be important to check whether the beneficial effects found in the lab after the induction of emotions by a film would still be found after more intense and long-lasting emotional situations. Finally, the investigation of other specific types of listener reactions should be pursued (e.g., providing informational support) as well as their interaction with the manipulation of the characteristics of the listener (e.g., from ingroup vs. outgroup members, male or female listener).

CONCLUSIONS

To sum up, the research described in this chapter was consistently faced with three sets of facts. First, there is overabundant evidence that people who experience an emotion want to talk about it and want to socially share this experience despite the emotional reactivation that is aroused in the process. Second, our studies systematically failed to provide evidence that sharing an emotional experience accelerates emotional recovery. Social sharing would thus not per se be an emotion regulation process. Third, in the course of these studies, we very consistently observed that after having shared an emotion, participants expressed positive feelings and subjective benefits. This set of facts raises a number of questions. Why do people want to share their emotions? Why do they have positive feelings after having shared their emotions?

In this chapter, we proposed that the beneficial effects of social sharing would in fact depend on the characteristics of the sharing partners and on their reactions. The reviewed evidence suggested that one does not share with any available person but that sharing partners were chosen according to the relevant information they could provide about coping with emotions, or according to the warmth and emotional support that they would provide to the sharer. If the listener reacts a certain way, such as with interest and understanding, gives informational support, shows reciprocity-type, and attachment or attraction-type of behaviors, social sharing may well provide help in meeting two fundamental human needs: affiliation and social consensus. We have shown that agreement as well as empathy with the listener led to more affective closeness, to a partial restoration of a belief in a just world, and to a decrease of loneliness. Still, it is not known why this would be so. To be able to answer this question, we need to reconsider what is going on exactly in an emotional experience.

We know that emotion arises from rapid and automatic meaning analyses of supervening events (e.g., Frijda, 1986; Scherer, 1984). For example, if meanings such as "danger," "no control," and "no escape" are elicited in a situation in which one is faced, a variety of emergency reactions will develop in one's body and one will experience fear. There is, however, a second wave of meanings in emotion of which people are generally unaware. Situation-specific meanings such as "danger," "no control," and "no escape" spread to broader meanings such as "the world is unsafe," "I am vulnerable and helpless," and "life is unfair." Meanings of this kind affect how one views the world and how one views oneself. In other words, they pervade one's symbolic universe. What is meant by symbolic universe? In current life, people live and behave under a subjective canopy of apparent order and meaning—a symbolic universe. Because of this, they can face the world and manage it relatively peacefully. Because of this, they can act as if it was normal that they stand here on this planet, somewhere between the Milky Way and eternity. Emotional events often have the power to undermine this delicate architecture. They challenge the canopy. Traumatic situations have been shown to be particularly deleterious in this regard (Epstein, 1987; Janoff–Bulman, 1992; Parkes, 1972). But any emotion has an impact on this symbolic architecture because emotion precisely develops at its fissures—or where things go unpredicted, unexpected, out-of-control, and so forth. By making fissures apparent, emotion makes people feel the weakness of the construction. This is probably the source of this obscure need for cognitive clarification, for understanding, for finding meaning, abundantly reported by people who recently went through some important emotional episode.

Then, why do people also feel the need to be with others and to talk with others after an emotion? It should be stressed that the symbolic universe is anything but a solitary construction. No one could make sense of the world alone. Sociologists showed that people enter a culturally-shaped subjective universe early in life (Berger & Luckmann, 1967). The attachment process is the basic tool through which the construction is instilled in the young human being. All along the development process, in everyday interactions, parents transmit to their child the view of the world that is shared in their culture. Later on, the construction is kept alive, strong and valid by the social consensus in which everyone takes part minute after minute throughout their life as members of our community. Consequently, a crack in this symbolic universe not only opens a breach in their meanings that will elicit cognitive needs, but it also has the effect of making people feel insecure and lonely, eliciting a very strong urge to re-immerse themselves in the social consensus. These are probably the reasons why, after a personal emotion, people feel the need to be with their intimates and to share the emotion with them. Their intimates are those who keep the attachment process alive for them, providing them with social support and security. They are those with whom people share the social consensus, providing them with a coherent subjective universe. Other categories of people could also become relevant after specific emotional circumstances. It is likely that they become relevant sharing partners because they would then be the holders of the social consensus.

Theories on emotion regulation propose that emotional reactions can be enhanced or decreased according to the degree of pleasure or displeasure of the consequences of these responses. Regulation can affect all the emotion components, that is, appraisal, experiential, behavioral, and physiological responses (Butler & Gross, this volume; Gross, 1999, 2001). For example, the appraisal of an event may be modified by selective attention and cognitive activities. Should social sharing of emotion be considered as an emotion-regulation strategy? The evidence reviewed in this chapter indicated that being with people who provide social consensus and sharing the emotional experience with them will probably not alter the memory of the emotion and bring emotional relief. This chapter argued that beneficial effects of social sharing depend on the partner's characteristics and reactions rather than on the extent of emotion expression alone. Partner's reactions will be helpful to the extent that they match the sharer's goal for sharing. In some cases, sharers may require partners just to listen, understand, and show support. A corresponding response can then result in enhancing people's affiliative bonds. Changing and regulating the emotional reactions just by receiving support seems less likely. However, if partners, in addition to listening and understanding, provide information that would actually allow a reappraisal of the sharer's experience or a meaning construction—much like what can be done in therapy—this could then allow some emotion regulation to take place. Future studies are of course needed to address these hypotheses.

REFERENCES

Arendt, M., & Elklit, A. (2001). Effectiveness of psychological debriefing. *Acta Psychiatrica Scandinavia, 104,* 423–437.

Arnold, M. B. (1960). *Emotion and personality* (Vols. 1 and 2). New York: Columbia University Press.

Berger, P. L., & Luckmann, T. (1967). *Social construction of reality.* Garden City, NY: Doubleday.

Bower, G.H. (1981). Mood and memory. *American Psychologist, 36,* 129–148.

Cannon, W. B. (1929). *Bodily changes in pain, hunger, fear and rage, on account of recent researches into the function of emotional excitement* (2nd ed.). New York: Appleton-Century-Crofts.

Carver, C. S., & Scheier, M. F. (1990). Origins and functions of positive and negative affect: A control-process view. *Psychological Review, 97,* 19–35.

Christophe, V., & Rimé, B. (1997). Exposure to the social sharing of emotion: Emotional impact, listener responses and secondary social sharing. *European Journal of Social Psychology, 27,* 37–54.

Collins, N. L., & Miller, L. C. (1994). Self-disclosure and liking: A meta-analytic review. *Psychological Bulletin, 116,* 457–475.

Dakof, G. A., & Taylor, S. E. (1990). Victims' perceptions of social support: What is helpful from whom? *Journal of Personality and Social Psychology, 58*, 80–89.

Deahl, M. P. (2000). Psychological debriefing: Controversy and challenge. *Australian and New Zealand Journal of Psychiatry, 34,* 929–939.

Deahl, M. P., Gillham, A. B., Thomas, J., Searle, M. M., & Srinivasan, M. (1994). Psychological sequelae following the Gulf War. Factors associated with subsequent morbidity and the effectiveness of psychological debriefing. *British Journal of Psychiatry, 165,* 60–65.

Dyregrov, A. (1997). The process in psychological debriefings. *Journal of Traumatic Stress, 10,* 589–605.

Ekman, P. (1984). Expression and the nature of emotion. In K. S. Scherer & P. Ekman (Eds.), *Approaches to emotion* (pp. 319–344). Hillsdale, NJ: Lawrence Erlbaum Associates, Inc.

Ekman, P. (1992). An argument for basic emotions. *Cognition and Emotion, 6*, 169–200.

Epstein, S. (1987). Implications of cognitive self-theory for psychopathology and psychotherapy. In N. Cheshire & H. Thomae (Eds.), *Self, symptoms, and psychotherapy* (pp. 43–58). New York: Wiley.

Esterling, B. A., Antoni, M. H., Fletcher, M. A., Margulies, S., & Schneiderman, N. (1994). Emotional disclosure through writing or speaking modulates latent Epstein–Barr Virus antibody titers. *Journal of Consulting and Clinical Psychology, 62,* 130–140.

Esterling, B. A., L'Abate, B. A., Murray, E. J., & Pennebaker, J. W. (1999). Empirical foundations for writing in prevention and psychotherapy: Mental and physical health outcomes. *Clinical Psychology Review, 19,* 79–96.

Finkenauer, C., & Rimé, B. (1998a). Socially shared emotional experiences vs. emotional experiences kept secret: Differential characteristics and consequences. *Journal of Social and Clinical Psychology, 17,* 295–318.

Finkenauer, C., & Rimé, B. (1998b). Keeping emotional memories secret: Health and subjective well-being when emotions are not shared. Journal of Health Psychology, 3, 47–58.

Frijda, N. H. (1986). *The emotions.* New York: Cambridge University Press.

Frijda, N. H., Mesquita, B., Sonnemans, J., & Van Goozen, S. (1991). The duration of affective phenomena or emotions, sentiments and passions. In K. T. Strongman (Ed.), *International review of studies on emotion* (pp. 187–225). Chichester, England: Wiley.

Goldsmith, D. J., McDermott, V. M., & Alexander, S. C. (2000). Helpful, supportive and sensitive: Measuring the evaluation of enacted social support in personal relationships. *Journal of Social and Personal Relationships, 17*, 369–391.

Greenberg, L. S., & Malcolm, W. (2002). Resolving unfinished business: Relating process to outcome. *Journal of Consulting and Clinical Psychology, 70,* 406–416.

Greenberg, M. A., Wortman, C. B., & Stone, A. A. (1996). Emotional expression and physical health: Revising traumatic memories or fostering self-regulation? *Journal of Personality and Social Psychology, 71,* 588–602.

Griffiths, J., & Watts, R. (1992). *The Kempsey and Grafton bus crashes: The aftermath.* East Lismore, NSW: Instructional Design Solutions, University of New England.

Gross, J. J. (1999). Emotion and emotion regulation. In L. A. Pervin & O. P. John (Eds.), *Handbook of personality: Theory and research* (2nd ed., pp. 525–552). New York: Guilford.

Gross, J. J. (2001). Emotion regulation in adulthood: Timing is everything. *Current Directions in Psychological Science, 10,* 214–219.

Horowitz, L. M., Krasnoperova, E. N., Tatar, D. G., Hansen, M. B., Person, E. A., Galvin, K. L., et al. (2001). The way to console may depend on the goal: Experimental studies of social support. *Journal of Experimental Social Psychology, 37,* 49–61.

Izard, C. E. (1977). *Human emotions.* New York: Plenum.

Janoff-Bulman, R. (1992). *Shattered assumptions: Towards a new psychology of trauma.* New York: Free Press.

Kelly, A. E., & McKillop, K. J. (1996). Consequences of revealing personal secrets. *Psychological Bulletin, 120,* 450–465.

Kenardy, J., Webster, R. A., Lewin, T. J., Carr, V. J., Hazell, P. L., & Carter, G. L. (1996). Stress debriefing and patterns of recovery following a natural disaster. *Journal of Traumatic Stress, 9,* 37–49.

Klein, M. H., Mathieu–Coughlan, P., & Kiesler, D. J. (1986). The experiencing scales. In L. S. Greenberg & W. M. Pinsof (Eds.), *The psychotherapeutic process: A research handbook* (pp. 21–71). New York: Guilford.

Lang, P. J. (1983). Cognition in emotion: Concept and action. In C. E. Izard, J. Kagan, & R. B. Zajonc (Eds.), *Emotion, cognition, and behavior* (pp. 192–226). New York: Cambridge University Press.

Laurens, F., Herbette, G., & Rimé, B.(2000). *Le partage social des épisodes émotionnels vécus en milieu hospitalier par le personnel infirmier* [Social sharing of emotion among nurses working in the hospital]. Unpublished manuscript, University of Louvain, Belgium.

Lehman, D. R., Ellard, J. H., & Wortman, C. B. (1986). Social support for bereaved: Recipients' and providers' perspectives on what is helpful. *Journal of Consulting and Clinical Psychology, 5,* 338–346.

Lepore, S. J. (1992). Social conflict, social support, and psychological distress: Evidence of cross-domain buffering effects. *Journal of Personality and Social Psychology, 63,* 857–867.

Lepore, S. J., Ragan, J. D., & Jones, S. (2000). Talking facilitates cognitive-emotional processes of adaptation to an acute stressor. *Journal of Personality and Social Psychology, 78*, 499–509.

Lepore, S. J., & Smyth, J. M. (2002). *The writing cure.* Washington, DC: American Psychological Association.

Leventhal, H. (1984). A perceptual-motor theory of emotion. In L. Berkowitz (Ed.), *Advances in experimental social psychology* (Vol. 17, pp. 117–182). New York: Academic.

Littrell, J. (1998). Is the reexperience of painful emotion therapeutic? *Clinical Psychology Review, 18,* 71–102.

Luminet, O., Zech, E., Rimé, B., & Wagner, H. (2000) Predicting cognitive and social consequences of emotional episodes: The contribution of emotional intensity, the Five Factor Model and alexithymia. Journal of Research in Personality, 34, 471–497.

Major, B., Zubek, J. M., Cooper, M. L., Cozzarelli, C., & Richards, C. (1997). Mixed messages: Implications of social conflict and social support within close relationships for adjustment to a stressful event. *Journal of Personality and Social Psychology, 72,* 1349–1363.

Manne, S. L., Taylor, K. L., Dougherty, J., & Kemeny, N. (1997). Supportive and negative responses in the partner relationship: Their association with psychological adjustment among individuals with cancer. *Journal of Behavioral Medicine, 20,* 101–125.

Mitchell, J. T., & Everly, G. S. (1995). Critical incident stress debriefing (CISD) and the prevention of work-related traumatic stress among high risk occupational groups. In G. S. Everly & J. M. Lating (Eds.), *Psychotraumatology. Key papers and core concepts in post-traumatic stress* (pp. 267–280). New York: Plenum.

Nils, F. (2002, April). *Symbolic universes, social integration and social sharing of emotions.* Oral presentation presented at the meeting of the Consortium of European Research on Emotion, Paris.

Nils, F. & Rimé, B. (2001, June). *L'efficacité du partage social en fonction des caractéristiques de son destinataire* [The efficacy of social sharing of emotion in function of the characteristics of its partner]. Poster presented at the Conference on Emotion, Interaction & Développement: Rencontre Internationale, Grenoble, France.

Omarzu, J. (2000). A disclosure decision model: Determining how and when individuals will self-disclose. *Personality and Social Psychology Review, 4,* 174–185

Orlinsky, D. E., & Howard, K. I. (1986). The psychological interior of psychotherapy: Explorations with the Therapy Session Reports. In L. S. Greenberg & W. M. Pinsof (Eds.), *The psychotherapeutic process: A research handbook* (pp. 477–501). New York: Guilford.

Ortony, A., Clore, G., & Collins, A. (1988). *The cognitive structure of emotions*. Cambridge, England: Cambridge University Press.

Parkes, C. M. (1972). *Bereavement: Studies of grief in adult life.* London: Tavistock.

Pennebaker, J. W. (1989).Confession, inhibition, and disease. In L. Berkowitz (Ed.), *Advances in experimental social psychology* (Vol. 22, pp. 211–44). New York: Academic.

Pennebaker, J. W. (1993a). Putting stress into words: Health, linguistic, and therapeutic implications. *Behaviour Research and Therapy, 31,* 539–548

Pennebaker, J. W. (1993b). Mechanisms of social constraint. In D. M. Wegner & J. W. Pennebaker (Eds.), *Handbook of mental control* (pp. 200–219). Englewood Cliffs, NJ: Prentice Hall.

Pennebaker, J. W. (1997). Writing about emotional experiences as a therapeutic process. *Psychological Science, 8*, 162–166.

Pennebaker, J. W., & Beall, S. (1986). Confronting a traumatic event: Toward an understanding of inhibition and disease. *Journal of Abnormal Psychology, 95,* 274–81.

Pennebaker, J. W., Colder, M., & Sharp, L. K. (1990). Accelerating the coping process. *Journal of Personality and Social Psychology, 58,* 528–537.

Pennebaker, J. W., & Harber, K. D. (1993). A social stage model of collective coping: The Loma Prieta earthquake and the Persian Gulf war. *Journal of Social Issues, 49*(4), 125–145.

Pennebaker, J. W., Kiecolt–Glaser, J. K., & Glaser, R. (1988). Disclosure of traumas and immune function: Health implications for psychotherapy. *Journal of Consulting and Clinical Psychology, 56,* 239–245.

Philippot, P., & Rimé, B. (1998). Social and cognitive processing in emotion: A heuristic for psychopathology. In W. F. Flack & J. D. Laird (Eds.), *Emotions and psychopathology: Theory and research* (pp. 114–129). Oxford, England: Oxford University Press.

Pos, A. E., Greenberg, L. S., Goldman, R., & Korman, L. (2002). *Emotional processing during experiential treatment of depression.* Manuscript submitted for publication. York University, Toronto, Ontario, Canada.

Raphael, B., Meldrum, L., & McFarlane, A. C. (1995). Does debriefing after psychological trauma work? *British Medical Journal, 310,* 1479–1480.

Reis, H. T., & Patrick, B. C. (1996). Attachment and intimacy: Component processes. In E. T. Higgins & A. W. Kruglanski (Eds.), *Social psychology: Handbook of basic principles* (pp. 523–563). New York: Guilford.

Reis, H. T., & Shaver, P. (1988). Intimacy as an interpersonal process. In S. Duck (Ed.). *Handbook of personal relationships* (pp. 367–389). Chichester, England: Wiley.

Rimé, B. (1989). Le partage social des émotions [The social sharing of emotions]. In B. Rimé & K. R. Scherer (Eds.), *Les émotions* (pp. 271–303). Neufchâtel et Paris: Delachaux et Niestlé.

Rimé, B. (1999). Expressing emotion, physical health, and emotional relief: A cognitive–social perspective. *Advances in Mind–Body Medicine, 15,* 175–179.

Rimé, B., Charlet, V., & Nils, F. (2002). *Social sharing of emotion in adolescents and college students: Preferred partners and their evolution across age groups.* Manuscript in preparation, University of Louvain, Belgium.

Rimé, B., Dozier, S., Vandenplas, C. & Declercq, M. (1996). Social sharing of emotion in children. In N. Frijda (Ed.), *ISRE 96. Proceedings of the IXth Conference of the International Society for Research in Emotion* (pp. 161–163). Toronto, Ontario, Canada: ISRE.

Rimé, B., Finkenauer, C., Luminet, O., Zech, E., & Philippot, P. (1998). Social sharing of emotion: New evidence and new questions. In W. Stroebe and M. Hewstone (Eds.), *European review of social psychology* (Vol. 9, pp. 225–258). Chichester, England: Wiley.

Rimé, B., Finkenauer, C., & Sangsue, J. (1994). How do you feel now? A retrospective investigation on the adjustment to positive and negative emotional events. Unpublished manuscript, University of Louvain, Belgium.

Rimé, B., Finkenauer, C., & Sevrin, F. (1995). *Les émotions dans la vie quotidienne des perosonnes âgées: Impact, gestion, mémorisation, et réevocation* [Emotions in everyday life of the elderly: Impact, coping, memory and reactivation]. Unpublished manuscript, University of Louvain, Belgium.

Rimé, B., Hayward, M. S., & Pennebaker, J. W. (1996). [Characteristics of recovered vs. unrecovered emotional experiences]. Unpublished raw data.

Rimé, B., Mesquita, B., Philippot, P., & Boca, S. (1991). Beyond the emotional event: Six studies on the social sharing of emotion. *Cognition and Emotion, 5,* 435–65.

Rimé, B., Noël, M. P., & Philippot, P. (1991). Episode émotionnel, réminiscences mentales et réminiscences sociales [Emotional episodes, mental remembrances and social remembrances]. *Cahiers Internationaux de Psychologie Sociale, 11,* 93–104.

Rimé, B., Philippot, P., Boca, S., & Mesquita, B. (1992). Long-lasting cognitive and social consequences of emotion: Social sharing and rumination. In W. Stroebe & M. Hewstone (Eds.), *European review of social psychology* (Vol. 3, pp. 225–258). Chichester, England: Wiley.

Rimé, B., Philippot, P., Finkenauer, C., Legast, S., Moorkens, P., & Tornqvist, J. (1994). *Mental rumination and social sharing in current life emotion.* Unpublished manuscript, University of Louvain, Belgium.

Rimé, B., Zech, E., Finkenauer, C., Luminet, O., & Dozier, S. (1996, July). *Different modalities of sharing emotions and their impact on emotional recovery.* Poster session presented at the 11th General Meeting of the European Association for Experimental Social Psychology, Gmunden, Austria.

Robinson, R. C., & Mitchell, J. T. (1993). Evaluation of psychological debriefings. *Journal of Traumatic Stress, 6,* 367–382.

Rose, S., & Bisson, J. (1998). Brief early psychological interventions following trauma: A systematic review of the literature. *Journal of Traumatic Stress, 11,* 697–710.

Roseman, I. J. (1984). Cognitive determinants of emotion: A structural theory. *Review of personality and Social Psychology, 5,* 11–36.

Scherer, K. R. (1984). Emotion as a multicomponent process: A model and some cross-cultural data. In P. Shaver (Ed.), *Review of personality and social psychology* (Vol. 5, pp. 37–63). Beverly Hills, CA: Sage.

Silver, R. L., & Wortman, C. B. (1980). Coping with undesirable life events. In J. Garber & M. E. P. Seligman (Eds.), *Human helplessness: Theory and applications* (pp. 279–340). New York: Academic Press.

Smyth, J. M. (1998). Written emotional expression: Effect sizes, outcome types, and moderating variables. *Journal of Consulting and Clinical Psychology, 66,* 174–184.

Stroebe, W., Stroebe, M., Abakoumkin, G., & Schut, H. (1996). The role of loneliness and social support in adjustment to loss: A test of attachment versus stress theory. *Journal of Personality and Social Psychology, 70,* 1241–1249.

Tait, R., & Silver, R. C. (1989). Coming to term with major negative life events. In J. S. Uleman & J. A. Bargh (Eds.), *Unintended thought* (pp. 351–382). New York: Guilford .

Van Emmerik, A. A., Kamphuis, J. H., Hulsbosch, A. M., & Emmelkamp, P. M. (2002). Single session debriefing after psychological trauma: A meta-analysis. *The Lancet, 360,* 766–771.

Zech, E. (1994). *La gestion du deuil et la gestion des émotions* [Coping with grief and coping with emotions]. Unpublished master's thesis, University of Louvain, Belgium.

Zech, E. (1999). Is it really helpful to verbalise one's emotions? *Gedrag en Gezondheid, 27,* 42–47.

Zech, E. (2000). *The effects of the communication of emotional experiences.* Unpublished doctoral dissertation, University of Louvain, Belgium.

Zech, E., Christophe, V., Herbette, G., & Stroebe, M. (2002). *Social sharing of emotion: Perceptions of helpful interactions.* Manuscript in preparation, University of Louvain, Belgium.

Zech, E., & Rimé, B. (2002). *Is talking about an upsetting experience helpful? Effects on emotional recovery and perceived benefits.* Manuscript submitted for publication, University of Louvain, Belgium.

Zech, E., Ucros, C., Rimé, B., & DeSoir, E. (2002). [The emotional impact of the Pécrot train crash among federal police service personnel]. Unpublished raw data.

AUTHOR NOTE

Emmanuelle Zech, Bernard Rimé, and Frédéric Nils, Department of Psychology, University of Louvain, Belgium.

Research reported in this chapter was supported by grants FRFC 8.4510.94 and 2.4546.97 from the Belgian National Fund for Scientific Research. Emmanuelle Zech is postdoctoral researcher at the Belgian National Fund for Scientific Research and NATO research fellow.

We thank the editors and Sarah Hayden for their helpful comments on an earlier version of this chapter.

Correspondence should be addressed to Emmanuelle Zech, University of Louvain, Department of Psychology, Place du Cardinal Mercier, 10, B–1348 Louvain-la-Neuve, Belgium, or by e-mail to Emmanuelle.Zech@psp.ucl.ac.be

7

Motives and Norms Underlying Emotion Regulation

Agneta H. Fischer
University of Amsterdam

Antony S.R. Manstead
University of Cambridge

Catharine Evers, Monique Timmers, and Guido Valk
University of Amsterdam

This chapter focuses on why individuals regulate their emotions. Moreover, we focus on regulation motives that are elicited in a social context. First of all, we review research on emotion norms, both in personal relations and in work relations. It is concluded that general emotion norms concerning what to feel and how to express these feelings are waning. Instead, more personal norms, and especially motives that are related to the expected effects of one's emotional expressions, have gained in importance. Our own studies on emotion norms and motives for regulation also show less adherence to general norms and greater importance of social goals at a microlevel.

> "I will not:
> Allow in-tray to rage out of control.
> Get annoyed with mum, Una Alconbury, or Perpetua.
> Get upset over men, but instead be poised and cool ice-queen.
> Bitch about anyone behind their backs,
> but be positive about everyone."
>
> — Helen Fielding, from *Bridget Jones's Diary* (p. 2)

These are just a few examples of the good intentions concerning our emotional behavior that Bridget Jones and many of the rest of us make. Emotions are continuously subjected to regulation in daily life. We suppress our anger if we understand that our colleague only made a mistake, we exaggerate our enthusiasm when we know that this will help our child to perform better, we hide our envy, because we know this is a detestable emotion, and we don't try to stop our tears when watching a tearjerker, because we enjoy being engulfed in sentimentality. Emotion regulation refers to those processes by which "individuals influence which emotions they have, when they have them, and how they experience and express these emotions" (Gross, 1999, p. 557). In other words, individuals do something with their emotions. They like them or hate them, they judge them as appropriate or inappropriate, or as effective or ineffective, and they adjust them accordingly.

Emotion regulation can take place at different phases of the emotion process (Frijda, 1986). We may try to change our appraisals of the situation, or to avoid or approach the emotional situation itself (antecedent-focused emotion regulation), and we may also try to control or modify our emotional responses (response-focused emotion regulation; Gross, 1998[a]).

This chapter focuses neither on how individuals regulate their emotions, nor on the effectiveness of such regulation, but rather on the question of why they regulate their emotions. Moreover, we focus on regulation motives that are elicited in a social context. Why would one want to change or modify what one actually feels, or what one tends to express? One obvious answer to this question is because people want to feel good and therefore try to avoid negative states. However, feeling good is generally not something that occurs independently of others. We suppress, modify, enhance or change our emotions, especially because of the presumed effects they have on others, or on our relations with others. The need for adjustment of our emotions thus lies largely in the need to live a good social life. Being too frightened, or too angry, or too sad is a problem not so much for our biological system, but rather for our social system. It is not surprising therefore that appropriate emotion regulation is seen as a core ingredient of an emotionally intelligent person (see also Feldman Barrett & Gross, 2001; Salovey, Hsee, & Mayer, 1993; Salovey & Mayer, 1990). Individuals who do not respond emotionally in an adequate manner may survive physically, but will become social outcasts.

Emotion regulation may be studied in different ways. One way is indirect, by investigating its cognitive and affective consequences (e.g., Richards & Gross,

1999, 2000). From these consequences we may infer some motives for emotion regulation. However, the effects of emotion regulation do not necessarily inform us why individuals try to regulate their emotions. If, for example, the suppression of negative emotion leads to enhanced memory, we could possibly infer that better cognitive functioning is a motive for emotion regulation, but this is unlikely to be the motive that instigated the regulation of negative emotions. Persons who regulate negative emotions may have had other motives, such as the expectation that their negative state would make others worry, or would result in a negative evaluation by others. In other words, the motives for engaging in emotion regulation cannot be simply inferred from their consequences.

To summarize, in this chapter we focus on the question of why individuals regulate their emotions. We start with some theoretical points about what is required for emotion regulation to occur. We then review research on emotion norms and emotion knowledge, which we regard as the most important source of one's motivation to regulate emotions in intimate and public settings.

EMOTIONAL AWARENESS, EMOTION KNOWLEDGE, AND MOTIVES FOR EMOTION REGULATION

Not all changes in emotional responses are the result of emotion regulation. They may occur as a result of changes in the situation, for example when one's fear diminishes as the barking dog moves away. We do not define such emotional changes as the result of regulation processes because they do not involve any attempt to influence one's emotions. For emotion regulation to be said to occur, there are two prerequisites. The first is a degree of awareness or monitoring of one's own emotional state (see Lane, 2000). There are various levels at which one may become conscious of one's emotion. At the most conscious level, this awareness is similar to what some authors have called a metamood experience (Mayer & Gaschke, 1988; Scheier & Carver, 1982), namely a reflective experience that leads individuals to think about their emotion. At a more preconscious level, however, there may be a rapid evaluation of the emotional response, leading to emotion regulation. Thus, at some level of consciousness, one must know what emotional state one is in, what one's emotional responses are, or what the outcomes of one's emotions will be, to be able to evaluate one's emotion and to modulate the emotion process (Frijda, 1986).

The second prerequisite for emotion regulation to occur is that one should register a discrepancy between what one wants to feel or express and the actual emotional response, or between what one wants to accomplish and what is actually accomplished, or between what one thinks is adequate and what one actually does (Frijda, 1986; see also Jansz & Timmers, 2002, for a similar argument). In other words, emotion regulation can be seen as the product of one's emotional awareness of a discrepancy between one's actual emotions and expected emotional outcomes and some representation of the ideal or appropriate emotions in that specific context.

Does the prerequisite of emotion awareness in emotion regulation imply that regulation always is a conscious process? This obviously is not the case (e.g., Gross, 1998[b], 1999). Emotion regulation can occur largely automatically, once we have had similar experiences with the outcomes or effects of our emotional response. For example, we may have learned that hitting others while in a rage has bad effects, or that laughing out loud when someone is hurt creates a negative impression. In such situations, one may not be completely aware of the undesirable outcome, and may automatically engage in the suppression of one's emotion or emotion expression. Nevertheless, emotion regulation would not have occurred if an evaluation of the emotional outcome had not taken place, rapid and automatic although it may have been.

To become aware of one's emotions, and to recognize, judge, or evaluate one's emotional state, we obviously need to have a representation of which emotion we are experiencing, and how it affects us or others. In short, we make use of emotion knowledge about specific emotions and emotional situations. There is abundant evidence that individuals have and use such knowledge about the prototypical course of at least the most frequently occurring emotions (Fehr & Russell, 1984; Russell, Fernández-Dols, Manstead, & Wellenkamp, 1995; Shaver, Schwartz, Kirson, & O'Connor, 1987). This emotion knowledge, whether implicit or explicit, is the source of our emotional awareness and of the judgement of our emotions. Moreover, it should provide information about how to redirect our emotions to decrease the discrepancy. This idea is supported by the results of a study by Feldman Barrett, Gross, Christensen, and Benvenuto (2001) who found that the better individuals were able to differentiate between negative emotional states, the more frequent were their attempts to regulate these emotions. These findings suggest that the more one knows about emotions, the more one is aware of possible discrepancies, and the more one is inclined to adjust one's emotions. In short, emotion knowledge forms the cognitive and most likely also the motivational base for emotion regulation.

The question, then, is what are the types of discrepancy that elicit motives to regulate one's emotions? We first distinguish motives at the intraindividual level. One principle that has been mentioned in relation to mood regulation, or more generally with respect to self-control, is that people are motivated to feel good (Larsen, 2000; Tice & Bratslavsky, 2000). This "hedonistic principle" may also apply to emotion regulation, suggesting that individuals are motivated to create or maintain positive emotional states, and thus will suppress any negative emotional state. Although this often seems to be the case, it raises the issue of whether we suppress all tendencies to express negative emotions. It does not require much fantasy to imagine that there are situations in which individuals are not particularly motivated to suppress their tears, or to hold down their anger, but rather feel relieved by their crying or satisfied with their outbursts of rage. In other words, in addition to a hedonic principle, we can identify a "cathartic" principle that reflects individuals' pleasure in venting their feelings, especially if the feelings are negative. Although the hedonistic and cathartic motives predict different attempts to regulate negative emotions, they share the feature that individuals go about regulating their emotions to feel better.

One obvious criticism of these principles is that emotion regulation is not merely an individual endeavor, but generally occurs in a social setting. Individuals take into account the (expected) reactions of others on their own emotions, as a result of which they engage in emotion regulation (Erber & Erber, 2000; Erber, Wegner, & Therriault, 1996; Manstead & Fischer, 2000). Thus, individuals not only seek to maximize positive emotions in general, but pursue interpersonal goals in social interactions, and use their emotions to serve these goals. In this chapter we focus on motives at the interindividual level. Averill (1982) was one of the first investigators to make a careful consideration of individuals' motives for becoming emotional. His study showed that both cathartic principles and social goals shaped subjects' anger expression. In response to a question about why they would become angry, respondents in Averill's study provided the following motives (in order of occurrence): to assert authority or independence or to improve one's image, to take revenge, to bring about a change in the behavior of the other, to strengthen the relation with the instigator, to get even for past wrongs, to let off steam over miscellaneous frustrations, to express general dislike, to get the other to do something for you, to break off a relation, and to get out of doing something for the instigator.

Categorizing these motives, and also taking account of the results of studies on other emotions, we can distinguish three different types of motives at the interpersonal level. The first is "impression management," implying that individuals regulate their emotions to avoid being evaluated unfavorably, because of the potential inappropriateness of their emotions (see also Erber & Erber, 2000). The second type is a "prosocial motive," implying that individuals are motivated not to hurt and offend others, but rather to please or protect others (see also Zaalberg, Manstead, & Fischer, in press). The third type of motive we distinguish is a motive to "influence" the behavior of others. By expressing their emotions, individuals pursue emotivational goals (Roseman, Wiest, & Swartz, 1994), such as wanting to please another, wanting to hurt the other, wanting to get something done by the other, wanting to get rid of the other, and so on (see also De Rivera & Grinkis, 1986).

All the aforementioned motives are elicited in response to an experienced discrepancy between one's actual emotional reaction and the appropriate or desirable emotional reaction. Which motive is elicited and in which direction one's emotions are regulated, however, depends on the type of discrepancy one experiences. The discrepancy between one's actual emotions and how one should emotionally respond according to prevailing emotion norms has been one of the most frequently studied topics in psychological and sociological research on emotion during the past decades. This discrepancy is particularly likely to stimulate an impression management motive, which would prevent negative evaluation as a result of inappropriate emotional behavior. Following we review some of this research on emotion norms.

Emotion Norms and Emotion Management in Personal Relations

We regulate our emotions in all kinds of different settings, and especially in the context of intimate relations, as was apparent in the quotation at the start of this chapter. This emotion regulation is driven by emotion rules about what and how one should feel toward intimate others. There are, for example, norms and rules about how we should adequately react to insults, unfair treatment, loss, achievements, disobedience, and so on. Moreover, these norms are not only situation dependent (e.g., "one should hide one's disappointment when receiving a disappointing present"), but also change over time, and vary with culture, or with one's role in the situation (see Fischer & Manstead, 2000).

In the course of the 20th century, a general lack of interest in emotions in many Western countries seems to have been replaced by an emphasis on the importance, nature, and functionality of individuals' emotions. This is illustrated by the changing norms for parenthood during recent centuries, as depicted by Stearns and Stearns (1986) in their emotional history of anger from the premodern period to the 20th century in the United States. Premodern Western society did not have clear codes for anger control and people were not very much concerned with anger. Anger was considered normal, and even functional, because it served a key function in regulating social relations. Thus, moralists in the 17th century were more concerned with preventing the excessive violence associated with anger outbursts than with controlling the emotion itself. As a consequence, parents in the 17th century were taught how anger could find outlets other than attacks on family members, but they were not instructed about general emotional control. Due to cultural, economic, and intellectual changes in American society, however, a new emotionology emerged at the end of the 19th century, with an emphasis on controlling anger, and making families free of anger. As well as a concern about angry children, quarreling spouses also received a great deal of attention, among other things because of rising divorce rates. This resulted in advice to parents to inhibit their own anger, and not to punish their children if they were angry but rather to search for the causes of their anger (Stearns & Stearns, 1986). This suggests a change from the application of expression rules to an orientation in which emotions themselves are dealt with more seriously.

This shifting focus from emotional adjustment to emotional understanding can be regarded as part of a larger social cultural development in the late 20th century, especially in the United States, but also in other Western countries, which has been labeled "the age of 'narcissism" (Lasch, 1979) or "the tyranny of intimacy" (Sennett, 1978), and which can be characterized by an increasing "emotionalization." This not only means that emotions are more frequently displayed in a variety of social settings, but also that social interactions are not seen as meaningful or real if we do not know what each other feels. Thus, the desire to reveal our feelings to others has become increasingly important in any communication. "Masses of people are concerned with their single life histories and particular emotions as never before" (Sennett, 1978, p. 5). This emotionalization is also reflected in the rise of television programs in which the display of emotions is the central goal. Whereas tears used to be taboo, they are increasingly shed in public, on television, in newspapers, magazines, or on sports fields. Moreover, the question of how to deal with one's emotions became a component of educational training programs, for example in medical or sport settings, or in management training programs (e.g., Wouters, 1990), and has culminated in the broadly disseminated idea of emotional intelligence (Goleman, 1995). These developments suggest that norms with regard to the display of emotions in personal relations have become less rigid. In other words, we do not regulate our emotions because we have to, but rather because we want to show our true selves and our genuine feelings.

This importance attached to the "real" nature of emotions rather than on the more artificial display of emotions is typical of Western countries, and not a universal phenomenon. Suh, Diener, Oishi, and Triandis (1998) illustrated this by showing that individuals' emotions are especially likely to have a major impact on judgments of general life satisfaction in individualistic cultures. In collectivist cultures, however, emotions were no more important as determinants of life satisfaction judgments than cultural norms regarding satisfaction with life, suggesting that one's "genuine" or "authentic" feelings play a less important role in these cultures. Because of differences between cultures with respect to the relation between self and social context (Triandis, 1995), and because of culture-specific emotionologies, we can expect cultural differences in whether, when, and how emotions should be displayed (see also Matsumoto, Takeuchi, Andayani, Kouznetsova, & Krupp, 1998). For example, although anger is generally seen as a potentially dangerous emotion, the display of anger is strongly discouraged in some groups or societies, such as the Utku Inuit (Briggs, 1970), whereas it is openly discussed and expressed, preferably in socially arranged meetings, in other societies, for example on the island of Santa Isabel (White, 1990). In still other cultures, for example in honor cultures, anger expression is seen as a legitimate way of restoring one's honor (Fischer & Rodriguez Mosquera, 2001; Cohen & Nisbett, 1994, 1997).

Culture-specific emotion norms can also be inferred from the distinction between "socially engaged" and "socially disengaged" emotions (Kitayama, Markus, & Matsumoto, 1995). In collectivistic cultures, the norm to maintain harmony within one's ingroup should elicit the norm of suppressing those emotions that create tensions or distance between people, such as anger, contempt, annoyance, or pride. On the other hand, there is a norm to display emotions that show one's interdependence with others, such as shame, guilt, friendly feelings, or feelings of respect. In individualistic cultures, the opposite pattern can be found. Westerners are reluctant to show emotions, such as shame, that display their faults or weaknesses, and therefore place a taboo on these emotions. Emotions that emphasize one's independence, assertiveness, or uniqueness, on the other hand, are encouraged.

These culture-specific social orientations have been shown to have an impact on the relation between the experience of specific emotions and judgments of one's general well-being (Kitayama, Markus, & Kurokawa, 2000). The correlation between ratings of general well-being and the experience of positive socially engaging emotions was higher among Japanese respondents than among Americans. By contrast, the Americans' self-reports of general well-being were more strongly correlated with positive socially disengaging emotions, like calmness, elation, relaxed feelings, and happiness.

One of our own studies (Fischer, Manstead, & Rodriguez Mosquera, 1999) also supports the importance of the dimension of social engagement–disengagement, especially in relation to shame and pride. We investigated emotion prototypes, including the normative beliefs individuals held regarding anger, shame, and pride, in two cultures. We predicted that norms concerning these emotions would vary between honor cultures and individualistic cultures because of the different social implications these emotions are assumed to have in those cultures. The findings were consistent with these predictions. Respondents from an honor culture more often reported social disapproval in relation to pride, and stated more often that the expression of pride should be restricted, as compared with respondents from a more individualistic culture. Further, respondents from an honor culture more often mentioned positive beliefs about shame, in the sense that shame shows that your are willing to admit and repair faults that you have made. No differences in normative beliefs were found with respect to anger. Respondents from the two cultures believe equally strongly that the expression of anger should be restricted, and held relatively more negative (e.g., "anger is a dangerous emotion," "anger is irrational") than positive beliefs about anger.

In sum, there are cultural differences in emotion norms, reflecting the different social implications of specific emotion expressions in different cultures.

Emotion Norms and Impression Management at Work

Some norms have been studied particularly in relation to emotion management at work (see, e.g., Fineman, 1997, 2000; Hochschild, 1983; Thoits, in press; Wouters, 1990). These include display rules (Ekman & Friesen, 1969), applying to the expression of emotions, and feeling rules (Hochschild, 1983), applying to the experience of emotions. The general conclusion drawn from research on emotional labor is that the successful performance of specific professional tasks requires the display of some emotions and the suppression of others. Individuals in service industries, including supermarket clerks, sale managers, and flight attendants, are all explicitly trained to suppress negative emotions and to display smiles, even if they don't feel very happy in the presence of demanding and grumpy clients or passengers (Hochschild, 1983; Parkinson, 1991; Thoits, in press). Moreover, these professionals are told that their smiles should look genuine to have the desired effects. This has led Hochschild to conclude that many professionals in the service industries engage in "deep acting," a type of emotion management that operates at the feeling level as well as at the expressive level.

Although the display of positive emotions is particularly evident in the service industries, there are also professions in which employees are trained to engage in a reverse pattern of emotion management. Prison guards, bill collectors, or police officers, for example, are taught to "act angry" in situations where their clients refuse to cooperate. Negative emotions other than anger, however, are generally supposed to be suppressed at work. There is a dominant emotional norm in most professions, at least in Western cultures, that imposes coolness, toughness, or rationality at work. Soldiers, firemen, or policemen, for example, are trained not to feel afraid, and that if they do feel fear that they should hide it; construction workers who have to work on tall buildings also receive informal pressure never to show any fear, and never to lose control; and medical students learn that it is important to maintain a stance of affective neutrality toward their patients (Thoits, in press).

This norm also applies to most white-collar jobs. Management, for example, has been represented as a set of skills including decisiveness, analytic competence, rationality, and ambition, and excluding any emotion (e.g., Schein, Muelller, Lituchi, & Liu, 1996). Emotions are assumed to interfere with successful leadership, because they hinder rational decisions and communicate weakness. We investigated this tension between emotions and leadership in a study of organizational culture in the Netherlands (Fischer, Rodriguez Mosquera, & Rojahn, 2000). We asked senior managers in a variety of large companies which emotions they thought would be appropriate for successful leadership. Positive emotions (enthusiasm, joy, empathy) received the highest score, followed at some distance by anger and annoyance. The lowest ratings were assigned to shame, uncertainty, and concern, emotions that were considered completely inappropriate for a good leader. In other words, within this group of senior managers a similar coolness and toughness norm is found, with the display of positive emotions regarded as desirable, and the display of "powerless" emotions as taboo.

We can conclude that several studies on emotion management at work have shown that there exist strong emotion norms in many different professions, requiring employees to adjust their emotions, generally in the expectation that there will be negative sanctions for failing to comply (not being promoted, being fired, etc.). However, this emphasis on strict regulation seems recently to have diminished. A number of studies have demonstrated that mere adjustment to emotion norms in work contexts, without paying attention to what employees actually feel and how they deal with these feelings, has positive consequences (e.g., Fineman, 2000).

Particular attention has been paid to issues such as "emotional dissonance" and authenticity (e.g., Abraham, 1998; Richman, 1988). Various studies have shown that employees do not feel motivated to regulate their emotions in the required direction if these required expressions clash with their actual feelings, or if they feel they are no longer being authentic (e.g., Ashforth & Tomiuk, 2000; Jansz & Timmers, 2002). The feelings of unease, dissonance, or tension, created by such requirements can result in job dissatisfaction and increased employee turnover. Ashfort and Tomiuk (2000), for example, interviewed a variety of service agents, asking them whether they felt authentic, and what made them feel that way. Interestingly, most respondents claimed that although they indeed had to "act" in their role as service agent, they also believed that they were still being themselves. However, this was not the case when they had to display negative emotions (being tough, acting like a sheriff), because the interviewees distanced themselves from this role identity. Thus, the paradox of authenticity can be explained in terms of identity. When one can identify with one's role, then being true to the display rules associated with the role means being true to oneself, even if one is not currently feeling the emotions that one is displaying. A similar point is made by Jansz and Timmers (2002), who argued that emotional dissonance is particularly felt when the emotions that are displayed are at odds with one's identity.

In other words, these studies suggest that if emotion regulation were to go beyond what individuals consider to be an accepted part of their role-identity, the social costs may become larger than the social benefits. Thus, it is likely that individuals sometimes experience and express emotions that break the strict boundaries of what a company considers to be appropriate emotional behavior. Mumby and Putnam (1992) have investigated a similar phenomenon, which they called *bounded emotionality*. This refers to the expression of a broader range of emotions than is usually admitted in traditional organizations. Bounded emotionality also sets constraints on emotional expressions, however, in the sense that individuals should attempt to function effectively in interpersonal relationships and to improve the understanding of their own and others' work-related feelings. This would also strengthen one's feelings of being authentic.

These studies suggest that there is a switch in emphasis from a focus on adjustment to emotional display and feeling rules to a focus on emotional awareness and understanding. One of the factors that has probably accelerated this change is the introduction and rapid popularization of the notion of emotional intelligence (Goleman, 1995; Salovey & Mayer, 1990). Emotional intelligence provides a new set of norms for managers, and there is a rapidly expanding market of management and organizational consultants who specialize in these issues (Fineman, 2000). The core ingredient of emotional intelligence and of stimulating emotionally intelligence in the workplace is that individuals should understand their own and others' emotions, know the effects of emotions on themselves and others, and regulate them accordingly. This implies that prescriptive rules that need be followed to execute one's job properly have become less salient.

However, this does not mean that emotion norms are no longer operative, or that employees are allowed to express any feeling that comes up. Rather, the dissemination of the concept of "emotional intelligence" in organizations seems to have set a new norm of sincerity and sensitivity, meaning that one should be aware of one's feelings and one should express one's emotions in a restricted and controlled way, taking the feelings of others into account. This may imply, however, that a general coolness and toughness norm whereby one should not express emotions at work, has become less prominent, and less informative as a general guideline for one's behavior. Instead, individuals are required to think about the impact, consequences, and goals of their own emotional behavior to be able to foresee effects of their emotions on their social interactions.

Gender Differences in Current Emotion Norms

It has often been assumed that there are distinct emotion norms for men and women and that this could account for sex differences in emotion expression (e.g., Brody & Hall, 1993; Fischer, 1993; Kring & Gordon, 1998; Shields, 1987). Some evidence for the existence of such gender-specific norms may be based on stereotypes about rational men and emotional women (e.g., Shields, 1987). Shields and Koster (1989), for example, found that the emotions of mothers and fathers were evaluated quite differently in childrearing manuals from 1915 to 1980 in the United States. They observed a consistent and relatively stable pattern whereby mothers were told to control their emotions, because of the danger of being too emotional or out of control, whereas fathers were advised to be more emotionally expressive to their children, given their inclination to be more distant and objective toward their children. Other evidence about sex-specific norms may be derived from different social sanctions that men or women expect when deviating from gender-appropriate emotional behavior. For example, Graham, Gentry, and Green (1981) found that the expression of positive emotion is more prescribed for women than for men, in that women expected more negative social sanctions if they failed to express positive emotions. This seems to be especially the case when these positive emotions are about others. Stoppard and Gunn Gruchy (1993), for example, found that women expected more negative consequences for themselves than did men if they failed to express positive emotions directed toward others. By contrast, men expected positive consequences when expressing positive emotions, regardless of whether these emotions were self- or other-oriented.

Sex-specific norms are assumed to vary across emotions, as a consequence of the relation of the emotion to male and female roles and identities. Relationship-enhancing (positive, socially engaging emotions) and powerless emotions (sadness, disappointment, shame, or guilt) are assumed to be compatible with the traditional feminine identity and should therefore be more encouraged or permitted in women than in men. For men, the expression of these emotions is more likely to be interpreted as a sign of weakness and out of keeping with their masculine identity; men should therefore be much more restricted in their display of these emotions. By contrast, the display of emotions that reflect power, or the potential to hurt others, as is the case with anger, annoyance, rage, or contempt (e.g., Eagly & Steffen, 1986) is more in keeping with the traditional male identity than with the female identity, with corresponding implications for sex-specific emotion norms. Emotion norms relating to powerful emotions should be more restrictive for women than for men, whereas emotion norms with respect to powerless and positive emotions should be more restrictive for men than for women.

An alternative line of reasoning would hold that sex differences in emotion norms (both feeling rules and display rules) should be slowly dissolving as the result of the increasing emotionalization of Western culture (see also Labott, Martin, Eason, & Berkey, 1991). In particular, the fact that men display their emotions in public more frequently than used to be the case should result in greater tolerance of emotional behavior in men.

To investigate whether current emotion norms still differentiate between men and women, we (Timmers, Fischer, & Manstead, 2003) conducted a series of studies in which we systematically varied the sex-stereotypicality of the norm and the sex of target to whom the norm was applied (e.g., "men should not cry" vs. "women should not cry"). Respondents were asked to judge a range of statements expressing normative views with respect to stereotypically male or female emotions. In addition, we investigated the prescriptive nature of the statements, by distinguishing between highly prescriptive (e.g., "men should not cry") and more descriptive statements that reflect knowledge of the stereotypically emotional behavior of men and women (e.g., "men are more aggressive than women").

In the first study we found that all respondents (who were students) endorsed the descriptive statements more strongly than the prescriptive statements, with men endorsing more strongly than women to the prescriptive. Turning to the contents of these norms and beliefs, respondents endorsed the beliefs that women generally have more powerless emotions than do men (see Fig. 7.1), implying that they cry more, and express more disappointment and anxiety than do men. Re-

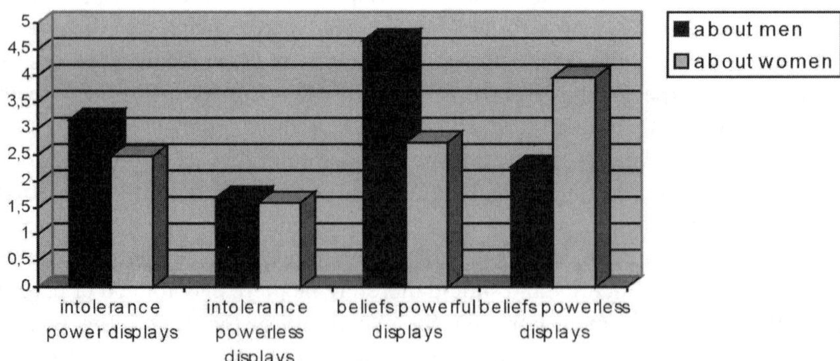

Fig 7.1. Mean endorsement scores for prescriptive (intolerance of power[less] displays) and descriptive items (beliefs) concerning powerful and powerless emomtions in relation to a generalized male or female other.

spondents also reported more negative attitudes toward women displaying their emotions in general. Men, on the other hand, were assumed to display more powerful emotions than women (see Fig. 7.1), implying that they express their anger more directly and show their pride more overtly than do women. Fewer sex differences were found with respect to prescriptive items or emotion norms, although displays of anger or aggression were less tolerated in men. This finding should not be interpreted as a greater tolerance of aggression in women, but rather as reflecting the use of different anchors when imposing norms. Because men are expected to behave more aggressively, there is a stronger norm for them to inhibit this aggression. In contrast with the assumption that there would be greater intolerance of male displays of powerless emotions, no differences were found with respect to norms concerning these emotions. According to these findings, the ideal of the unemotional man is a thing of the past: Men are permitted to show their sadness, fear, or disappointment as much as women.

In a second study, we used a similar but shortened questionnaire to replicate these results in respondents drawn from a different population, namely a less highly educated group with lower socioeconomic status. The pattern of results was replicated, but anticipated differences between the student respondents used in Study 1 and the less highly-educated group used in this study were not found. The central question of the third study was the extent to which emotion norms would be seen as applying equally to oneself as to others. We argued that in the current period of changing emotion norms in Western society, individuals may be well aware of what the norms are, and what they should believe, without necessarily internalizing these norms or using them as a framework for judging and modifying their own emotions. The questionnaire used was the same as that used in Study 2, but the protagonist in the items was "I" rather than "Men" or "Women". The results again showed that prescriptive items, or emotion norms, were less endorsed than were descriptive statements, or beliefs (see Fig. 7.2). Moreover, no differences were found with respect to the prescriptions male and female respondents applied to their own emotions (see Fig. 7.2). However, there were differences in self-stereotypes. Women agreed more with stereotypically feminine statements ("my emotions are dysfunctional at work;" "I do not show much masculine emotions or emotional preferences") than with other statements, whereas men believed the stereotypically masculine and feminine stereotypes to be equally applicable to themselves (see Fig. 7.2).

Comparing the extent of agreement with general norms and agreement with norms applicable to one's own emotions, we can conclude that respondents agreed with statements more when they expressed norms applying to themselves than when they expressed norms applying to generalized others. Although there is no direct evidence that individuals actually use these norms as a source for emotion regulation, the results strongly suggest that this is the case.

In sum, we can conclude from this study that general norms with respect to the emotional behavior of women and men are not especially marked and are rather

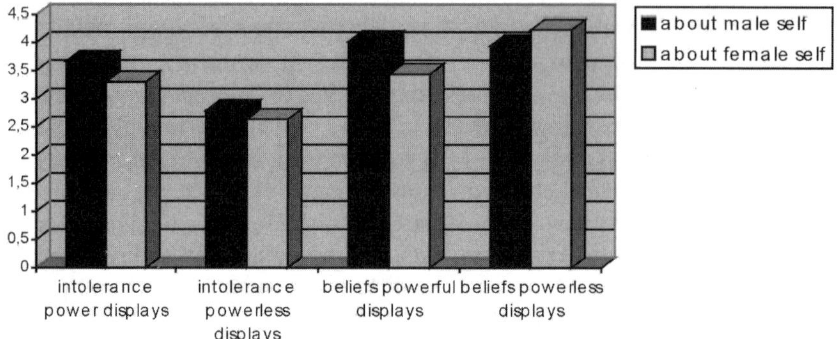

Fig 7.2. Mean endorsement scores for prescriptive items (intolerance) and descriptive items (beliefs) concerning powerful and powerless emotions in relation to oneself.

gender-neutral. An exception was the norm that one should inhibit one's aggressive tendencies, which was found to be more applicable to men than to women, probably due to the higher likelihood that men will aggress. With respect to stereotypical beliefs, it is clear that women are still seen as the more emotional sex, and that they are expected to express powerless emotions more than are men. Interestingly, the fact that women are seen as the more emotional sex does not imply that they are also generally permitted to show more emotions, as is sometimes suggested. On the contrary, negative attitudes toward emotional women are stronger than negative attitudes toward men, apparently because the expression of powerless emotions by men is seen as having an extra value. It makes men suitable for female roles, without making them unsuitable for male roles.

One explanation for the more negative attitudes and stronger norms with respect to women's emotions may well be due to one specific emotional expression, namely women's greater inclination to cry. Crying is generally considered to be the ultimate sign of powerlessness and weakness, whether or not an event justifies one's crying. Does the tolerance for male expression of powerless emotions extend to this ultimate display of powerlessness?

Gendered Crying Norms

Everyday observation strongly suggests that boys are still confronted with more rigid norms regarding crying than are girls. This is to some extent supported by empirical studies. Crester, Lombardo, Lombardo, and Mathis (1982), for example, found that respondents were less accepting of crying by men than by women. Cornelius (1982) also found that women's crying resulted in more positive consequences than did the crying of men. However, Labott et al.,'s (1991) study of social reactions to crying showed that men who cried were liked more than women who cried. They suggested that gender role expectations regarding crying may have changed in the years leading up to their study, in the sense that both men and women now found it more appropriate for men to weep than they had done in previous times.

To investigate current crying norms, we devised a questionnaire in which respondents were asked to read various vignettes in which a male or female protagonist was described as crying (Valk, Fischer, & Manstead, 2002). We then asked respondents to judge the appropriateness of the protagonist's crying in different social contexts: alone, in the company of a friend, or when more others were present. Female respondents generally judged the crying of the protagonist to be more appropriate than did men. The crying of a woman was generally more often approved of than was men's crying. However, this was not the case in extreme situations, such as the death of an intimate, where the sex of the protagonist was found to be unrelated to the perceived appropriateness of his or her crying. The social context also induced different norms with respect to crying: Crying was considered to be more inappropriate in public contexts than when the protagonist was alone or with a good friend.

This context-specificity of crying norms was replicated in another study (Fischer & Manstead, 1998), in which we found that it was mainly situations that were not very extreme in evoking emotions, and thus did not really "justify" tears, that elicited differences in the responses of men and women. In this study we asked the respondents the extent to which they found it appropriate to cry in situations of differing extremity. In the most extreme situations, such as the death of an intimate and the breakup of a romance, men and women found it equally justified to cry. In somewhat less extreme situations, such as a burglary and a computer crash, on the other hand, women and men differed in the extent to which they believed that display rules were applicable, with women being more tolerant of crying than were men. However, this was not the case if one was unfairly treated by a superior, where both men and women found it appropriate to suppress their crying. This may reflect the fact that work situations still evoke norms that are strong enough to override gender differences—at least with respect to crying.

Overall, we can conclude from these studies that traditional norms still prevail in the case of crying. Women's crying is generally more approved of, and—in the event of less extreme eliciting situations—women are also more tolerant with respect to their own and others' crying. A possible explanation for Labott et al.'s (1991) finding that men are liked more when they cry is that the differential likelihood of men's and women's crying means that crying women are judged less sympathetically because their crying is seen as more exaggerated and less justified than the crying of men under similar circumstances.

Emotion Norms as Motives for Emotion Regulation

Studies on sex differences in crying consistently show that women cry more than men. Drawing on the studies of crying norms described earlier, it seems likely that these sex differences in crying are caused by different crying norms. Yet there is no direct evidence to support this conclusion. More general evidence for the differential role emotion norms play in the emotion regulation of men and women was provided by a study by Grossman and Wood (1993). They showed that when explicit instructions were given to men and women to enhance or attenuate their emotions for reasons of health, thereby manipulating expectations about emotional response, sex differences in self-reported intensity of emotional experience were not observed. In contrast, when no instructions were given concerning appropriate emotional responses, women reported more intense emotions to both negative and positive stimuli than did men. The researchers concluded that a general gender stereotypical norm whereby women are allowed to display their emotions to a greater extent than men can therefore account for the gender differences they found in the no-instruction condition.

To investigate the influence of crying norms on one's talking about crying, we (Fischer & Manstead, 1998) indirectly manipulated the general crying norm that one should not cry in public by creating two different social contexts: (a) an "alone" condition in which respondents were asked to complete a written questionnaire, alone in a room, and in which the anonymity of their answers was emphasized; and (b) a "social" condition in which a male or female interviewer posed the same questions as in the questionnaire, and the answers were openly tape-recorded. The questions concerned the probability of crying and the suppression of crying in general and in specific contexts.

As well as the expected difference that women said that they would cry more than men, we found that type of condition influenced participants' responses. General crying frequency was rated lower in the social condition, compared to the alone condition. Moreover, when respondents were asked to report the last time they cried, those in the social condition recalled this as longer ago than did those in the alone condition. We also found a difference between men's and women's reports as a function of whether the experimenter was a man or a woman, such that women reported that their most recent crying was longer ago when the experimenter was a man, whereas men reported that their most recent crying was longer ago when the experimenter was a woman. This suggests that the presence of the opposite sex may have enhanced the operation of an impression management motive. Apparently, one's likelihood of crying is judged by both sexes as not especially favorable for one's image. Respondents therefore adjusted their reports about crying, especially when confronted with someone on whom they want to make a good impression.

This interpretation is supported by the fact that, in response to the second part of the procedure, in which respondents had to read vignettes, a similar effect was found for reported inclination to cry in response to the breakup of a romantic relationship: Women reported crying less often when responding to a male experimenter, whereas men reported crying less often reported when responding to a female experimenter. The interactions were not found with respect to the other vignettes. Because the content of this vignette involves a situation in which the judgment of the opposite sex is likely to be important, it seems probable that an impression management motive is at work here.

Expected Social Implications of Emotion Expression

Emotions are not only regulated because individuals feel that their emotions should be in keeping with prevailing emotion norms, but also because of the expected consequences of emotional behavior. As Averill's (1982) study on anger motives suggested, individuals have some general knowledge about the implications of their emotion expressions. If these implications are not in line with what individuals want to achieve through their emotional behavior, they may regulate their emotions.

Indirect evidence for a discrepancy between expected social implications and desired emotional outcomes can be derived from a study on the regulation of jealousy (Zammuner & Fischer, 1995). Respondents were asked to imagine a prototypical jealousy situation in which one's partner is assumed to be flirting with someone else, and to indicate which emotions the protagonist in the story would feel in such a situation. They were then asked to imagine a hypothetical conversation between the protagonist and his or her partner about the incident. The results showed that most respondents (51.7%) indicated that they would feel jealousy and anger, followed by fear and concern (41.7%), surprise (39.8%), sadness (36.1%), insecurity (32.6%), and irritation (28.4%). There was also a discrepancy between emotions that were felt and emotions that were communicated to the partner. In particular, jealousy was communicated with lower intensity than it was felt, whereas surprise, sadness, and insecurity were communicated with a greater intensity than they were felt. Although we did not assess individuals' motives for regulating their emotions in the way they did, we can infer that respondents assumed that expressing jealousy, or for that matter anger and irritation, would not have had any beneficial effect on their partner's behavior. Expressing these emotions would imply that they blamed the partner, which would probably cause the partner to become angry or irritated. The expression of sadness, surprise, or concern on the other hand is likely to elicit empathy and sympathy in the partner, and is therefore more likely to result in reparatory behavior.

We also assume that men and women anticipate different reactions to their emotional behavior as a result of the general stereotype of women being the more emotional sex, and as a result of gender-specific roles. In keeping with a feminine, caring role, women are likely to be more prosocially motivated to protect and please others, whereas men should be more highly motivated to control and influence others, as the result of their more agentic role. Displaying anger suggests that one is in control, or at least that one is allowed to correct others, or to change the behavior of others. Anger expression may therefore reflect the goal of controlling others or influencing the behavior of others. Crying and other displays of powerless emotions, on the other hand, are expected to elicit comfort, support, or reparatory behavior from others. We assume that men suppress powerless emotions to improve their image or to establish or increase control over others, whereas women suppress powerful emotions because of prosocial motives.

In a vignette study (Timmers, Fischer, & Manstead, 1998), we presented respondents with different types of vignettes that had been selected via pretesting as eliciting powerful and powerless emotions. Respondents were asked what emotion they would express, and why they would downplay or enhance this expression. To make the different motives more salient, we manipulated the role of the other person present. This other person was either the person who caused the emotion, or a person who just happened to be present, and to whom one could vent one's emotions.

Men and women reported different motives with respect to the expression or suppression of their anger, fear, disappointment and sadness. Men more often reported a control motive for the expression of their anger, whereas women more often reported that the fact that they would receive support and sympathy was a major motive for expressing disappointment, and sadness. Women were also more likely to mention a cathartic motive with respect to all four emotions, suggesting that they were more likely than men to experience the expression of their emotions as a relief. This suggests that the expression of these emotions is associated with more positive feelings for women than for men. Men, on the other hand, still seem to be more concerned with control and with avoiding making an emotional impression.

We tested this assumption by asking respondents whether they expected that others would judge them as emotional when expressing these emotions. The results showed that men and women had different expectations. Following their anger expressions, women expected to be judged as more emotional if they expressed their anger directly, whereas men expected to be judged as more emotional if they expressed their anger indirectly (i.e., to a third person).

Following the expression of powerless emotions (i.e., disappointment), the sex of the target also affected participants' expectations that they would be judged as emotional. When a powerless emotion was expressed to a third person (object is not target), men assumed that they would be judged as more emotional by a woman, whereas for women the reverse pattern emerged (see Fig. 7.3). If the powerless emotion was directly expressed to the source of the emotion (object is target), however, the sex of the target only made a difference for male respondents. They expected to be judged as more emotional by a man than by a woman (see Fig. 7.3).

In the case of powerful emotions, the sex appropriateness of the expression affected expectations about negative evaluations. Women are not stereotypically expected to display anger, and it is therefore not surprising that they were found to expect to be evaluated as emotional if they did express their anger. Men, on the other hand, are stereotypically expected to express their anger directly, and they were found to expect to be evaluated as emotional if they expressed their anger

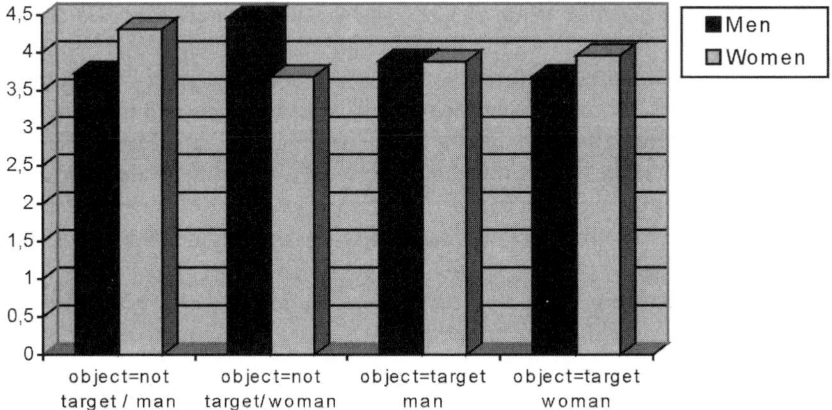

Fig 7.3. Means ratings by men and women of how emotional one expects to be judged by a male or female target, after expressing disappointment.

indirectly. Finally, we also found sex differences in relation to the suppression of anger and disappointment. Women were more likely than men to mention a prosocial motive for suppressing these emotions, especially when the target and object of their emotions were the same. This suggests that women are more concerned with the fact that they could hurt the other by directly expressing their anger or disappointment.

CONCLUSION

This chapter has focused on the question of why individuals regulate their emotions. A simple answer is that individuals become aware of a discrepancy between their actual or anticipated emotion and what they perceive to be the appropriate or ideal emotion, and therefore want to modify their emotional response. Awareness of this discrepancy is based on emotion knowledge, which is both normative and prototypical. There is evidence that individuals with more elaborate emotion knowledge—that is, those who are better able to differentiate between emotions—are more likely to regulate their emotions.

A key issue we addressed in this chapter is the extent to which emotion norms form the motivational basis of emotion regulation. In other words, do individuals regulate their emotions primarily to accommodate to perceived emotion norms? Although firm answers to such broad questions are hard to provide, it seems clear that emotion norms do play a role in emotion regulation: Individuals don't want to be seen as abnormal, to be laughed at, or to be socially excluded. Research on emotion norms in work and personal settings are consistent with this idea.

However, the importance of general emotion norms seems to be waning. Our review of studies on emotion norms suggests that emotion norms do exist, for example in various professions, but also that other norms, such as authenticity or prosociality, are important. Current social and cultural changes in Western countries tend to stress the importance of emotional awareness, emotional sensitivity, and understanding. This is apparent from the significance of topics such as "emotional dissonance," "emotional intelligence," and "bounded emotionality." Analyses of these phenomena suggest that simply adjusting one's emotional behavior to conform to general emotion norms is not sufficient, either individually or interpersonally.

Our own studies on emotion norms suggest that people believe that stringent norms about how one should behave emotionally are not regarded as applicable, either to men or women in general or to oneself. Even sex stereotypic emotion norms, like "women should not cry" or "men should be cool and not show any emotion" appear to have lost importance. This does not mean that gender has become completely irrelevant in relation to emotion and emotion expressions; however, it is not important in terms of general norms to which one should adhere.

Emotion knowledge, especially knowledge about the likely effects of expressing one's emotions, seems to be a more important source of emotion regulation. For example, men are still seen as expressing more powerful emotions (e.g., aggression) and women as expressing more powerless emotions (e.g., crying), and these expectations seem to be closely linked to motives for emotion regulation. More specifically, expecting to be negatively evaluated by another person (e.g., being regarded by them as an emotional person), especially someone of the opposite sex, leads individuals to engage in emotion regulation. Indeed, studies that have explored individuals' self-reported motives suggest that these anticipated consequences constitute the most important reasons for engaging in emotion regulation.

REFERENCES

Abraham, R. (1998). Emotional dissonance in organizations: Antecedents, consequences, and moderators. *Genetic, Social and General Psychology Monographs*, *124*, 229–246.

Ashforth, B. E., & Tomiuk, M. A. (2000). Emotional labour and authenticity: Views from service agents. In S. Fineman (Ed.), *Emotion in organizations* (pp. 184–203). London: Sage.

Averill, J. R. (1982). *Anger and aggression*. New York: Springer.

Brody, L. R., & Hall, J. A. (1993). Gender and emotion. In M. Lewis & J. M. Haviland (Eds.), *Handbook of emotions* (pp. 447–461). New York: Guilford.

Briggs, J. (1970). *Never in anger: Portrait of an Eskimo family*. Cambridge, MA: Harvard University Press.

Cohen, D., & Nisbett, R. E. (1994). Self-protection and the culture of honor: Explaining southern violence. *Personality and Social Psychology Bulletin, 20*, 551–567.

Cohen, D., & Nisbett, R. E. (1997). Field experiments examining the culture of honor: The role of institutions in perpetuating norms about violence. *Personality and Social Psychology Bulletin, 23*, 1188–1199.

Cornelius, R. R. (1982). Weeping as social interaction: The interpersonal logic of the moist eye. *Dissertation Abstracts International, 42*(X), 3491B–3492B.

Crester, G. A., Lombardo, W. K., Lombardo, B., & Mathis, S. (1982). Reactions to men and women who cry: A study of sex difference in perceived societal attitudes versus personal attitudes. *Perceptual and Motor Skills, 55*, 479–486.

De Rivera, J., & Grinkis, C. (1986). Emotions as social relationships. *Motivation and Emotion, 10*, 351–369.

Eagly, A. H., & Steffen, V. J. (1986). Gender and aggressive behaviour. A meta-analytic review of the social psychological literature. *Psychological Bulletin, 100*, 309–330.

Ekman, P., & Friesen, W. V. (1969). The repertoire of non-verbal behavior: Origins, usage, and coding. *Semiotica, 1*, 49–98.

Erber, R., & Erber, M. W. (2000). The self-regulation of moods: Second thoughts on the importance of happiness in everyday life. *Psychological Inquiry, 11*, 142–149.

Erber, R., Wegner, D., & Therriault, N. (1996). On being cool and collected: Mood regulation in anticipation of social interaction. *Journal of Personality and Social Psychology, 70*, 757–766.

Fehr, B. & Russell, J.A. (1984). Concept of emotion viewed from a prototype perspective. *Journal of Experimental Psychology: General, 113*, 464–486.

Feldman Barrett, L., & Gross, J. J. (2001). Emotional intelligence: A process model of emotion representation and regulation. In T. Mayne & G. Bonanno (Eds.), *Emotions: Current issues and future directions* (pp. 286–310). New York: Guilford.

Feldman Barrett, L., Gross, J. J., Christensen, T., & Benvenuto, M. (2001). Knowing what you're feeling and knowing what to do about it: Mapping the relation between emotion differentiation and emotion regulation. *Cognition and Emotion, 15*, 713–724.

Fineman, S. (1997). Emotion and management learning. *Management Learning, 28*, 13–25.

Fineman, S. (Ed.). (2000). *Emotion in organizations*. London: Sage.

Fischer, A. H. (1993). Sex differences in emotionality: Fact or stereotype? *Feminism and Psychology, 3*, 303–318.

Fischer, A. H., & Manstead, A. S. R. (1998). Gender, powerlessness, and crying. In A. H. Fischer (Ed.), *ISRE '98. Proceedings of the Xth Conference of the International Society for Research on Emotion* (pp. 95–98). Amsterdam: Faculty of Psychology.

Fischer, A. H., & Manstead, A. S. R. (2000). The relation between gender and emotion in different cultures. In A. H. Fischer (Ed.), *Gender and emotion: Social psychological perspectives* (pp. 71–94). Cambridge, England: Cambridge University Press.

Fischer, A. H., Manstead, A. S. R., & Rodriguez Mosquera, P. M. (1999). The role of honor-based versus individualistic values in conceptualizing pride, shame, and anger: Spanish and Dutch cultural prototypes. *Cognition and Emotion, 13*, 149–179.

Fischer, A. H., & Rodriguez Mosquera, P. M. (2001). What concerns men: Women or other men? A critical appraisal of the evolutionary theory of sex differences in aggression. *Psychology, Evolution, and Gender, 3*, 5–25.

Fischer, A. H., Rodriguez Mosquera, P. M., & Rojahn, K. (2000). *Masculiniteit met een feminien gezicht* [Masculinity with a feminine face]. Den Haag, The Netherlands: Elsevier.

Frijda, N. H. (1986). *The emotions*. Cambridge, England: Cambridge University Press.

Goleman, D. (1995). *Emotional intelligence. Why it can matter more than IQ*. New York: Bantam.

Graham, J. W., Gentry, K.W., & Green, J. (1981). The self-presentational nature of emotional expression: Some evidence. *Personality and Social Psychology Bulletin, 7*, 467–474.

Gross, J. J. (1998a). Antecedent- and response-focused emotion regulation: Divergent consequences for experience, expression, and physiology. *Journal of Personality and Social Psychology, 74*, 224–237.

Gross, J. J. (1998b). The emerging field of emotion regulation: An integrative review. *Review of General Psychology, 2*, 271–299.

Gross, J. J. (1999). Emotion regulation: Past, present, future. *Cognition and Emotion, 13*, 551–573.

Grossman, M., & Wood, W. (1993). Sex differences in the intensity of emotional experience: A social role interpretation. *Journal of Personality and Social Psychology, 65*, 1010–1022.

Hochschild, A. (1983). *The managed heart*. Berkeley: University of California Press.

Jansz, J. & Timmers, M.(2002). Emotional dissonance. *Theory and Psychology, 12*, 79–95.

Kitayama, S., Markus, H. R., & Kurokawa, M. (2000). Culture, emotion, and well-being: Good feelings in Japan and the United States. *Cognition and Emotion, 14*, 93–124.

Kitayama, S., Markus, H. R., & Matsumoto, H. (1995). Culture, self, and emotion: A cultural perspective on self-conscious emotions. In J. P. Tangney & K. W. Fischer (Eds.), *Self conscious emotions: The psychology of shame, guilt, embarrassment, and pride* (pp. 523–550). New York: Guilford.

Kring A. M., & Gordon, A. H. (1998). Sex differences in emotion: Expression, experience and physiology. *Journal of Personality and Social Psychology*, 74, 686–703.

Labott, S. M., Martin, R. B., Eason, P. S., & Berkey, E. Y. (1991). Social reactions to the expression of emotion. *Cognition and Emotion, 5*, 397–419.

Lane, R. (2000). Levels of emotional awareness: Neurological, psychological, and social perspectives. In R. Bar-On & J. D. A. Parker (Eds), *The handbook of emotional intelligence: Theory, development, assessment, and application at home, school, and in the workplace* (pp. 171–191). San Francisco: Jossey-Bass.

Larsen, R. L. (2000). Towards a science of mood regulation. *Psychological Inquiry, 11*, 129–142.

Lasch, C. (1979). *The culture of narcissism*. New York: Norton.

Mayer, J. D., & Gaschke, Y. N. (1988). The experience and meta-experience of mood. *Journal of Personality and Social Psychology, 55*, 102–111.

Manstead, A.S.R., & Fischer, A. H. (2000). Emotion regulation in full. *Psychological Inquiry, 11*, 188–191.

Matsumoto, D., Takeuchi, S., Andayani, S., Kouznetsova, N., & Krupp, D. (1998). The contribution of individualism vs. collectivism to cross-national differences in display rules. *Asian Journal of Social Psychology, 1*, 147–165.

Mumby, D. K., & Putnam, L. L. (1992). The politics of emotion: A feminist reading of bounded rationality. *Academy of Management Review, 17*, 465–485.

Parkinson, B. (1991). Emotional stylists: Strategies of expressive management among trainee hairdressers. *Cognition and Emotion, 5*, 419–434.

Richards, J., & Gross, J. J. (1999). Composure at any cost? The cognitive consequences of emotion suppression. *Personality and Social Psychology Bulletin, 25*, 1033–1044.

Richards, J., & Gross, J. J. (2000). Emotion regulation and memory: The cognitive costs of keeping one's cool. *Journal of Personality and Social Psychology, 79*, 410–424.

Richman, J. A. (1988). Deviance from sex-linked expressivity norms and psychological distress. *Social Forces, 63*, 208–215.

Roseman, I. J., Wiest, C., & Swartz, T. S. (1994). Phenomenology, behaviors, and goals differentiate discrete emotions. *Journal of Personality and Social Psychology, 67*, 206–221.

Russell, J. A., Fernández-Dols, J.M., Manstead, A. S. R., & Wellenkamp, J. (Eds.) (1995). *Everyday conceptions of emotion*. Dordrecht, The Netherlands: Kluwer.

Salovey, P., Hsee, C. K., & Mayer, D. (1993). Emotional intelligence and the self-regulation of affect. In D. M. Wegner & J. W. Pennebaker (Eds.), *Handbook of mental control* (pp. 258–277). Englewood Cliffs, NJ: Prentice Hall.

Salovey, P., & Mayer, D. (1990). Emotional intelligence. *Imagination, Cognition, and Personality, 9*, 185–211.

Shaver, P., Schwartz, J., Kirson, D., & O'Connor, C. (1987). Emotion knowledge: Further exploration of a prototype approach. *Journal of Personality and Social Psychology, 52*, 1061–1086.

Scheier, M. F., & Carver, C. S. (1982). Cognition, affect, and self-regulation. In M. S. Clark & S. T. Fiske (Eds.), *Affect and cognition: The 17th Annual Carnegie Symposium on Cognition* (pp. 157–183). Hillsdale, NJ: Lawrence Erlbaum Associates, Inc.

Schein, V. E., Mueller, R., Lituchy, T., & Liu, J. (1996). Think manager—think male: A global phenomenon? *Journal of Organizational Behavior, 17*, 33–41.

Sennett, R. (1978). *The fall of public man*. New York: Vintage Books.

Shields, S. A. (1987). Women, men, and the dilemma of emotion. In P. Shaver & C. Hendrick (Eds.), *Sex and gender* (pp. 229–250). Newbury Park, CA: Sage.

Shields, S. A., & Koster, B. A. (1989). Emotional stereotyping of parents in child rearing manuals, 1915–1980. *Social Psychological Quarterly, 52*, 44–55.

Stearns, C. Z., & Stearns, P. (1986). *Anger: The struggle for emotional control in America's history*. Chicago: University of Chicago Press.

Stoppard, J. M., & Gunn Gruchy, C. D. (1993). Gender, context and expression of positive emotion. *Personality and Social Psychology Bulletin, 19*, 143–150.

Suh E., Diener E., Oishi, S., & Triandis, H. C. (1998). The shifting basis of life satisfaction judgments across cultures: Emotions versus norms. *Journal of Personality and Social Psychology, 74*, 482–493.

Thoits, P. A. (in press). Emotion norms, emotion work, and social order. In A. S. R. Manstead, N. H. Frijda, & A. H. Fischer (Eds.), *Feelings and emotions: The Amsterdam symposium*. New York: Cambridge University Press.

Tice, D. M., & Bratslavsky, E. (2000). Giving in to feeling good: The place of emotion regulation in the context of general self-control. *Psychological Inquiry, 11*, 149–159.

Timmers, M., Fischer, A. H., & Manstead, A. S. R. (1998). Gender differences in motives for regulating emotions. *Personality and Social Psychology Bulletin, 24*, 974–985.

Timmers, M., Fischer, A. H., & Manstead, A. S. R. (2003). Ability versus vulnarability: Beliefs about men's and women's emotional behavior. *Cognition and Emotion, 17*, 41–63.

Triandis, H. (1995). *Individualism and collectivism*. Boulder, CO: Westview.

Valk, G., Fischer, A. H., & Manstead, A. S. R. (2002). *Display rules on crying* (Unpublished report). University of Amsterdam, Faculty of Psychology.

White, G. (1990). Moral discourse and the rhetoric of emotion. In C. A. Lutz & L. Abu-Loghod (Eds.), *Language and the politics of emotion* (pp. 45–68). Cambridge, England: Cambridge University Press.

Wouters, C. (1990). *Van minnen en sterven* [About loving and dying]. Amsterdam: Bert Bakker.

Zaalberg, R., Manstead, A. S. R. & Fischer, A. H. (In press). *Relations between emotions, display rules, social motives, and facial behavior.* Manuscript submitted for publication.

Zammuner, V., & Fischer, A. H. (1995). The social regulation of emotions in jealousy situations. *Journal of Cross-Cultural Psychology, 26*, 189–208.

III

Self-Presentation and Emotion Regulation

8

The Role of Emotion in Self-Regulation: Differing Roles of Positive and Negative Emotion

Dianne M. Tice, Roy F. Baumeister, and Liqing Zhang
Case Western Reserve University

Positive and negative emotions play very different roles in self-regulatory processes. The first part of the chapter discusses the role that negative emotions have in undermining self-regulatory tasks. Research is reviewed which indicates that people often undermine their own self-regulatory attempts in fields as diverse as dietary control, delay of gratification, and time management because affect regulation takes priority over other programs of self-regulation. People frequently sabotage their long term self-regulatory goals to make themselves feel better in the short term. The second half of the chapter focuses on one of the roles positive emotion plays in self-regulation. When people's capacity to engage in self-regulation is depleted, positive emotional experiences help to recharge the system. Positive emotional states can strengthen the self's capacity for regulating itself in a variety of ways.

Processes of self-regulation pervade many aspects of human functioning, and emotions are involved in many different ways. In this chapter we focus on two of them that have emerged in our research program. The first focuses on negative emotions. We show that concern over regulating negative emotions, especially in attempting to escape bad moods and emotions, often takes priority over other forms of self-regulation, often thereby impairing these other efforts. The second focuses on positive emotions. We suggest that positive emotion has special power to increase the self's capacity for all manner of self-regulation, especially when that capacity has been depleted through recent use.

We propose that positive emotions can facilitate self-regulation, whereas negative emotions can impair self-regulation. Although these basic effects may seem parallel, we suggest that the mechanisms differ. Negative emotions impair self-regulation through a priority shift, namely shifting self-regulatory attempts from long-term goals to short-term feeling states. Positive emotions have a restorative effect on self-regulation by returning the system to its predepleted state.

WHY NEGATIVE EMOTIONS IMPAIR SELF-REGULATION

Many observers have remarked that self-regulation is often impaired by emotional distress. That is, people may seem capable of regulating their behavior according to goals, standards, and other ideals when they feel good, but when they become upset these patterns of desirable behavior break down. Our own first survey of the many research literatures on self-regulation showed us this pattern over and over: In one sphere of self-regulation after another, emotional distress had been shown or at least repeatedly suggested as undermining effective control (Baumeister, Heatherton, & Tice, 1994).

But why does emotional distress impair self-regulation? Various authors had proposed multiple ideas, and in fact we suspected (and still do) that there is more than one correct answer. Perhaps when people are upset they cease to care about proper behavior. Perhaps emotion impairs people's ability to monitor their behavior. Perhaps it reduces awareness of personal goals or standards of social desirability.

Although we do not rule out the possibility that some of these pathways may explain the deleterious effects of distress on self-regulation, in this chapter we want to focus on a different one. The core of it is that regulating unpleasant emotional states is inherently opposed to many other forms of self-regulation, and when people become sufficiently upset they give priority to regulating affect. Put more simply, sometimes there is a basic conflict between keeping your diet and feeling better, and if you are very unhappy your first priority is to feel better, even if this means sacrificing your diet.

We call this the priority hypothesis: Affect regulation takes priority over other programs of self-regulation. It does not require any suggestion that emotional distress actually reduces one's capacity for self-regulation. Rather, all it means is that when affect regulation is in conflict with some other form of self-regulation, one or the other has to be given priority. By virtue of the power and immediacy of emotional distress, regulating the emotion often manages to gain top priority.

The conflict between affect regulation and other forms of self-regulation is rooted in the general patterns of what people regulate and why. In general, we understand self-regulation as a matter of overriding certain responses. Effective self-regulation may involve resisting temptation, controlling impulses, regulating thoughts, managing performance, and the like. Crucially, many forms of self-regulation involve overriding a wish to do something that promises to feel good. Self-regulation thus often has an ascetic turn to it.

Examples are not hard to find. Dieting is one of the most widespread forms of self-regulation, and in general dieting requires the person to resist the urge to eat appealing, tasty foods. Likewise, attempts to regulate one's alcohol or drug use involve resisting the temptations and pleasures that come with substance abuse. Cigarettes, too, offer the promise of immediate pleasure, and to quit smoking one has to forego these pleasures. Delay of gratification is another prototype of self-regulation, but successful delay of gratification requires the person to resist the temptations of immediate pleasure to pursue some greater good in the future.

Thus, self-regulation often doesn't feel good. It requires the person to renounce some offers of pleasure.

The renunciation of pleasure is what sets up the conflict with affect regulation. One general principle is that when people feel bad, they want to feel better. Pleasures and satisfactions hold the promise of feeling good and hence offer a cure for bad moods. But what happens when these pleasures are associated with behaviors that the person is seeking to regulate? Under such circumstances, the person is faced with a choice between maintaining the behavioral self-regulation (and therefore prolonging the emotional distress) versus pursuing good feelings (but undermining the behavioral self-regulation).

The core of the priority hypothesis is that in such conflicts, the emotional distress takes precedence. Yes, ideally the person wants to avoid overeating, or spending money, or indulging in substance abuse, but these goals are less pressing than the wish to feel better as soon as possible.

Empirical Studies

A series of research studies has sought to test the priority hypothesis. In each of these, we sought to show that people would undermine self-regulation to make themselves feel better. To do this, we had to accomplish two things in each study. First, we had to show that some form of behavioral self-regulation broke down when people were upset or in a bad mood. Second, we had to show that the effect of emotional distress depended on the person's efforts to make himself or herself feel better.

The first task was relatively easy to accomplish. All it required was manipulating the emotional state of research participants and then measuring their behavior.

If they engaged in behaviors that were less socially or personally desirable, we could safely conclude that somehow the emotional distress had interfered with normal, effective self-regulation.

The second task was considerably harder. As we said earlier, there are many possible ways that emotional distress could interfere with self-regulation, such as by undermining the willingness to self-regulate, making goals and standards less salient, or reducing the ability to monitor one's behavior. We needed a procedure that would confirm the priority shift and rule out these other possible explanations.

The procedure we used was borrowed from Manucia, Baumann, and Cialdini (1984). Their work was concerned with a similar issue, namely the effect of bad moods on helping. Previous studies had confirmed that people become more helpful when they feel bad, but disputes raged as to why the bad moods promoted helping. Manucia et al. (1984) sought to show that people help because they anticipate that helping will make them feel better. To test this hypothesis, they offered some research participants a "mood-freezing pill." That is, they gave research participants a pill that allegedly would render their current mood or emotional state impervious to change. Of course, there is no such pill, and in fact participants merely received a placebo. But the researchers were able to manipulate the participants' beliefs effectively. They pointed out that many drugs have side effects on moods and emotional states, such as making people feel less anxious (e.g., valium), or intensifying whatever emotional reaction one might have (e.g., cannabis). The researchers said that the pill they were giving would stabilize the pill-taker's emotional state, so that no change was possible for about an hour.

The crucial effect of the mood-freezing pill manipulation is that it renders affect regulation ostensibly impossible. There is no point in trying to feel better if you have taken a mood-freezing pill. The pill will prevent you from feeling better if you are upset. Manucia et al. (1984) showed that people who were put into a sad mood and given the mood-freezing pill failed to show the increase in helping that was normally associated with sad moods. Thus, they concluded that sadness leads to helping as a means of making oneself feel better. Sad people only help more when they have the prospect of feeling better as a result.

We used several variations on this procedure to examine how self-regulation breaks down in the context of emotional distress. In our first study (Tice, Bratslavsky, & Baumeister, 2001), we examined a familiar form of self-regulation: eating unhealthy snack foods. Many people have reported anecdotally that their efforts to maintain a diet or simply to eat healthy foods are sometimes undermined when they are upset. Could this be one manifestation of the priority hypothesis?

In this study, we induced emotional distress in research participants by having them engage in vivid imagery. Specifically, they were told to imagine a scene in which they accidentally caused the death of a child. Other participants imagined a positive or a neutral episode. After the emotional state had been manipulated, we had them take part in what they thought was marketing research designed to assess perceptions of various foods. These were all snack foods that students had previously rated as unhealthy and fattening (cookies and crackers). Each participant was given three bowls of these foods and asked to fill out a questionnaire to rate each one. This procedure has been used frequently to measure eating in a subtle way. The participant does not know that the point of the study is to count how much he or she eats, and people can rationalize eating a large quantity by telling themselves that they are simply trying to do a good job in the experiment. In reality, the questionnaires are of little interest to us, and the main dependent measure is how much food the person consumes.

Some participants went straight from the emotional distress manipulation to the marketing and eating task. Others were, however, given one additional instruction. They were told that research had shown that eating these foods would not alter their emotional state. The experimenter said that some people think that eating will make them feel better or otherwise alter their mood, but research had clearly shown these beliefs to be false. This was our mood-freezing manipulation. In effect, we said that eating the cookies won't cure your bad mood.

The results of this study confirmed that emotional distress normally leads to more eating of unhealthy snack foods—but not if the bad mood was frozen. In the control (changeable mood) condition, the people who felt bad ate more cookies and other snacks. However, in the mood freeze condition, people in the bad mood ate no more than in the neutral or good mood conditions.

The implication of this pattern of results is that bad moods lead to eating as a strategy for feeling better. When people thought they might feel better by eating the tasty, fattening snacks, they ate more of them. But if we removed the prospect of feeling better, bad moods failed to stimulate more eating. Thus, the priority hypothesis was confirmed.

We then turned to studying delay of gratification. The study of delay of gratification was one of the original empirical roots of self-regulation theory (see Mischel, 1974, 1996). In these studies, people are faced with a choice between getting a small reward now and a larger reward that comes after a delay. The situation is deliberately set up so that the rational, optimal strategy is to take the delayed reward. Indeed, we suspect that the human capacity for self-regulation evolved in substantial part because it enabled people to resist the temptation of immediate pleasure for the sake of larger, delayed rewards, which would be highly adaptive. Taking the smaller but more immediate reward is thus an important form of self-regulation failure.

Most research on delay of gratification has been done with children, because adults generally do not find it very difficult to achieve the brief delays that laboratory studies involve. To study these processes in adults, we borrowed a procedure that Knapp and Clark (1991) had developed. It involved playing a hypothetical resource management game. Specifically, participants could earn money by harvesting fish from a fish pond. They received a certain amount of (real) money for each pound of fish. The catch was that the fish would only reproduce themselves based on how many were left. Just as overfishing has depleted the fish stocks in many parts of the world, the player would end up losing money by taking too many fish too soon. Restraint was required to take only a limited amount of fish at each interval so that the pond would stay fully stocked. Taking too many fish too soon would reduce the amount of money that the participant could earn down the road.

We induced bad moods using the same procedure of imagining that one caused the death of a child. Other participants were left in a neutral mood. Then a mood-freezing manipulation was administered. This time, the experimenter burned scented candles in the room, which she presented as part of her research on aromatherapy. She told some participants that the candles would freeze their current mood state for about an hour. The rest were told that the candles would not affect their moods.

The results of the fishing game confirmed that delay of gratification can succumb to the priority shift. When participants believed their moods to be changeable, then bad moods caused people to take more immediate gratification. They harvested more fish right away and ended up winning less money than the people in neutral moods. However, in the mood-freeze condition, bad moods did not undermine delay of gratification.

This effect was moderated by trait scores on the Negative Mood Regulation (NMR) scale (Catanzaro & Mearns, 1990). Participants who habitually regulated their bad mood adapted their behavior more strongly in response to the mood-freeze manipulation than people who did not habitually regulate their moods. In other words, people who scored high on the NMR scale exhibited the affect priority shift we found in the experiment we just described: Under emotional distress, they showed an increased preference for immediate gratification (thus a decrement in impulse control), but freezing their mood eliminated this effect. People who scored low on the NMR presumably did not believe they can (or should) control their moods anyway, and so the distress and mood-freezing manipulations had less effect on them.

The implication is that people abandon their rational pattern of maximizing rewards by delaying gratification to feel better. People who are upset grab for the immediate reward, even if it is less than the delayed one. However, they only do so if they believe that taking the immediate rewards will make them feel better. The mood-freezing manipulation eliminated the prospect of feeling better, and it also eliminated the shift toward immediate gratification. The fact that this pattern was moderated by dispositional tendencies to engage in mood regulation is further proof that regulating mood is central to the entire pattern.

Our third and final study in this series focused on another set of behaviors that constitute a common challenge for self-regulation: procrastination. Procrastination can be regarded as a failure of time management. People accept that they should work toward a goal or deadline, but instead of starting in a timely fashion and making steady progress toward it, they put it off. Often they end up having to perform the task at the last minute, which can be highly stressful. A pair of longitudinal studies by Tice and Baumeister (1997) confirmed the destructive effects of procrastination. Procrastinators received lower grades than nonprocrastinators, and they also suffered considerably more stress as well as poorer health. Crucially, the health effects depended on the timing of measurement. Early in the semester, when procrastinators are putting off their assignments while others are getting to work on them, procrastinators actually reported better health and less stress than the others. However, at the end of the semester, when the deadlines were imminent, the procrastinators were more stressed and sicker. (And, in fact, the late increase in stress and illness more than offset the early gains, so that the net effect of procrastination was negative.) This fits a standard pattern of poor self-regulation and self-defeating behavior: Procrastination brings short-term gains but long-term costs.

We conducted a laboratory experiment to assess procrastination. Research participants were told that they were going to be given an important test involving difficult arithmetic problems. Because many people rely on calculators to do their math in everyday life, we stressed the desirability of practicing some multiplication and long division problems to prepare for the test. The experimenter said that she would leave the participant alone for 15 min to practice. However, she said, the participant did not actually have to practice for the entire 15 min. The experimenter invited the participant to feel free to spend part of the time doing other things. In fact, the laboratory was set up to include several items that could be used to "waste time" (as the experimenter put it) if the participant so desired, and indeed the experimenter said that although these items were for another study, she sometimes spent time with them if her research participants failed to show up for their appointments.

The nature of these distractor tasks constituted another independent variable. If emotional distress simply causes procrastination because it makes people not want to think about the test (for example), then people should procrastinate regardless of what might be the alternatives. In contrast, the priority hypothesis held that people fail to self-regulate because they are trying to feel better, and so only distracters that promise pleasure should tempt them. In one condition, the distracters were set up to be appealing and fun. The included a popular video game, popular magazines such as People, and challenging crossword puzzles. In the other condition, the distracters were unappealing and perhaps even boring. They included an out-of-date technical journal, and some word puzzles and games designed for very young children.

As in the preceding studies, we induced either a bad or a neutral mood by random assignment, and we also administered a mood-freezing manipulation to half the participants by using the aromatherapy candles as in the previous study (Study 2). Then we measured how much time each participant spent preparing for the test, as opposed to procrastinating.

The results confirmed the priority hypothesis once again. People who were in a bad mood procrastinated more than those in a neutral mood. But this only occurred (a) if the distracter tasks were fun, and (b) if they had not been given the mood-freezing manipulation. They did not procrastinate with the boring tasks, which suggests that bad moods made people seek out and prefer activities that offered pleasure. And they only procrastinated if they believed that their moods could change. This signifies that they procrastinated as a means of feeling better.

Converging evidence was obtained from another investigation that focused on anger and aggression (Bushman, Baumeister, & Phillips, 2001). These researchers noted that nearly all theorists and researchers assume that anger leads to aggression. That is, many studies have found that provoking people into an angry state leads to an increase in aggressive behavior. In fact, the link is so widely assumed that many studies of aggression include an anger provocation simply as a matter of course, even if they have no interest in anger—the anger is a kind of research tool that is employed because without anger, levels of aggression are often too low to permit the testing of any hypotheses.

But why does anger increase aggression? Some theorists propose that anger automatically activates various motor responses or other innately prepared fighting tendencies. In such views, anger evolved so as to cause animals to fight for what they need, especially if they have been attacked or threatened.

In contrast, the priority hypothesis holds that angry people aggress (at least in part) because they expect that aggressing will make them feel better. This sort of belief is supported by widespread exhortations to vent one's anger as a healthy, natural response.

Moreover, aggression may often involve a breakdown in self-regulation. As many writers have noted (e.g., Baumeister, 1997), people often feel angry or violent impulses but usually restrain them. The proximal cause of much violent, aggressive behavior is therefore a failure of these inner restraints and controls that normally keep behavior peaceful (see also Gottfredson & Hirschi, 1990).

Thus, angry aggression offered another test case for the priority hypothesis. People normally seek to restrain their aggressive impulses, but angry people might believe that aggressing would make them feel better.

A series of laboratory studies by Bushman et al. (2001) confirmed the priority hypothesis. In these studies, some participants were provoked into feeling angry, and some of these were given mood-freezing pills (just as in the original Manucia et al., 1984, procedure). Following this, participants had the opportunity to aggress against the person who had insulted them. The provocation came in the form of an insulting evaluation of an essay written by the participant. The aggressive retaliation was presented in the form of an ostensible reaction-time competition. At a signal, the participant and the confederate were supposed to respond as fast as they could, and whoever responded slower (the loser) would be punished with a blast of loud, aversive noise. We told participants that they could set the level and duration of noise for their opponent. Thus, in effect, each participant controlled a noise weapon that could be used to blast his or her opponent with aversive stimulation.

Another feature of these studies was concerned with the belief about whether venting is a good way to feel better. In different studies, this was either measured or manipulated (or both). The measurement approach consisted of asking people whether they believed that expressing their anger was a good way to make them feel better. The manipulation involved exposing people to a bogus news report that claimed that recent research findings showed that venting one's anger was either an effective way to feel better or was counterproductive and made people feel worse.

In these studies, anger sometimes led to higher aggression, but not always—consistent with the priority hypothesis. People who believed that venting was a good way to escape from anger were more likely to become aggressive than others, but only when they were angry. Crucially, the mood-freezing pill eliminated this effect. Thus, angry people may lash out at those who have provoked them, but they only do so if they believe that their moods are changeable. The implication is that aggression is itself often an affect regulation strategy. Take away the prospect of affect regulation (as the mood-freezing manipulation does), and anger no longer leads to increased aggression.

Conclusion

Taken together, these studies show that a broad range of behaviors are performed for the sake of regulating affect. Our studies included eating unhealthy and fattening snack foods, favoring immediate gratification over delayed but larger rewards, procrastinating, and aggressing. In each case, we showed that emotional distress by itself increased the undesirable pattern. In that sense, emotional distress undermined self-regulation. More important, we showed that these effects could be eliminated with mood-freezing manipulations. The implication is that emotional distress only leads to self-regulation failure when people believe their moods can change. That, in turn, indicates that these undesirable behaviors are done for the sake of affect regulation. It is only the prospect of repairing one's bad mood that causes sad people to eat more, pursue immediate gratification, and procrastinate. Likewise, it is only the prospect of repairing the bad mood that causes angry people to aggress. Emotional distress did not impair self-regulation when people believed that their moods would not change.

POSITIVE EMOTIONS RECHARGE THE DEPLETED SELF

We turn now to a different kind of emotion and a different kind of effect on self-regulation. Specifically, we shall suggest that positive emotional states can strengthen the self's capacity for regulating itself in a variety of ways.

To appreciate this effect, it is necessary first to provide some context. Some years ago we began to investigate how self-regulation in general operates. We noted several viable theories and set about testing them against each other

Our findings converged on the conclusion that self-regulation operates on the basis of a limited resource that operates like an energy or strength. In particular, any act of self-regulation appears to deplete the self's resource, thereby impairing subsequent attempts at self-regulation. This effect has been found to carry over between seemingly widely different spheres of self-control. Thus, in various studies, we had people engage in one act of self-regulation (such as controlling their emotions, suppressing unwanted thoughts, or resisting the temptation to eat chocolate) and then measured self-regulation in some very different sphere (such as physical stamina, stifling smiles while watching a funny video, or persisting on difficult and frustrating problems). In study after study, performance on the second task was impaired as a function of having performed the first one (see Baumeister, Bratslavsky, Muraven, & Tice, 1998; Muraven, Tice, & Baumeister, 1998).

We named this pattern ego depletion. It has two noteworthy features. First, the same resource appears to be used for many widely different spheres of self-control. (That is why, for example, the exercise of trying not to think about a white bear will cause the person subsequently to give up faster on a difficult puzzle.) Second, the resource appears to be quite limited, so that even brief laboratory tasks are sufficient to produce a discernible decrement in subsequent self-control.

Thus, the self operates on the basis of a limited resource, akin to energy or strength, that is used for a wide variety of tasks but is easily depleted. This raises the question of how the resource is replenished after it becomes depleted. After all, no one would suggest that the resource simply diminishes until it is gone, after which there is no more self-control. If that were true, young children would show the highest levels of self-control, and the older people became the poorer their self-control would be!

Undoubtedly one source of replenishment is sleep (and other forms of rest, possibly including meditation). A good night's sleep restores the self's powers. One sign of this is that most breakdowns in self-regulation occur late in the day rather than first thing in the morning: Hardly anyone gets up and immediately embarks on a drinking or eating binge, crime spree, or other indulgence (see Baumeister et al., 1994).

But what else? We hypothesized that positive emotions and moods might be able to replenish the self's resources and thereby restore its capacity for self-regulation.

To show this, we refined our research designs in a straightforward fashion. Already we had conducted many studies in which people performed two consecutive acts of (seemingly unrelated) self-control. The refinement involved introducing a manipulation of positive effect in between these two acts, for some participants. We sought to show that these manipulations of positive affect would eliminate the ego depletion effect. That is, without the positive emotion, we would replicate the usual pattern by which people who performed the first act of self-control would be impaired on the second one. But people who performed the first act of self-control and then received a dose of positive emotion should be able to perform better on the second self-control task.

Several studies confirmed that prediction. In the first one, depletion was manipulated by requiring some participants to form and then break a habit. (Specifically, the habit consisted of crossing out all instances of the letter "e" in a page of text; people then had to override this by crossing out only certain instances of "e.") Positive, negative, and neutral moods were then induced by having participants watch a brief film clip of a either a stand-up comedy routine, a scene about a young mother dying of cancer, or about communication among dolphins, respectively. Self-regulation was then measured in terms of performance on an anagram-solving task, on the assumption that solving anagrams requires the person to constantly form and then re-form combinations of letters so as to make a word.

The results of this study suggested the beneficial effects of positive moods for overcoming ego depletion. Depleted participants in neutral or sad moods performed worse on the anagram task than their counterparts who were not depleted. The happy mood eliminated the effects of depletion, however.

A second study used the same "e" manipulation of ego depletion and then induced happy or neutral moods with the same films. Then participants played a frustrating game for as long as they wished. Although past work has suggested that people in happy moods are reluctant to do anything that might damage their mood (Isen, Nygren, & Ashby , 1988; Nygren, Isen, & Taylor 1996), we did not find any effect of the happy versus neutral mood among nondepleted participants. Among depleted ones, however, the happy mood led to longer persistence, suggesting that it counteracted the effect of ego depletion. Put another way, the lowest persistence was shown among participants who were depleted and in a neutral mood.

In a third study, depletion was created by having people trying to suppress the thought of a white bear (see Wegner, Schneider, Carter, & White, 1987). Non-depleted participants simply listed their thoughts (as did those in the depletion condition) without trying to control them in any way. Next, mood was manipulated by giving half the participants in each condition a small gift consisting of a bag of candy (borrowed from Isen & Daubman, 1984). In the neutral mood condition, participants received only their credit for participating in the study. After this, ostensibly in a separate experiment, participants were encouraged to drink as much as they could of a bad-tasting beverage, consisting of unsweetened Kool-Aid powder mixed with vinegar and water. We assumed that it requires self-regulation to override one's dislike of the taste and make oneself drink more of it.

Measurement of amount of Kool-Aid consumed showed that the positive affect induction overcame the effects of depletion. In the neutral mood condition, depleted participants drank less than nondepleted ones, consistent with previous findings (Baumeister, Dale, & Tice, 2002). However, in the positive mood condition, the effect of depletion was entirely eliminated.

In another study, ego depletion was induced (in all participants) by first assigning them to forego eating for several hours prior to the experiment and then by requiring these food-deprived individuals to resist the temptation to eat tasty food. Specifically, they were seated within reach of a tray of freshly baked cookies and delicious chocolates but were instructed to eat unappetizing radishes instead. Next, mood was manipulated by having them watch either a Robin Williams comedy video (good mood condition) or an educational video about communication among dolphins (neutral mood condition). Last, self-control was measured in terms of how long people persisted at unsolvable geometric puzzles. We assumed that unsolvable puzzles create a feeling of frustration and discouragement so that people would want to desist, and so persistence requires self-control to override the impulse to quit. Consistent with the view that positive affect counteracts the effects of ego depletion, happy participants persisted significantly longer than neutral mood participants.

Taken together, these studies show that inducing a positive emotional state, such as with humorous stimuli, can counteract the effects of ego depletion; when people engage in self-regulation, they consume some limited resource. As long as this resource is depleted, the self's ability to regulate itself further is substantially reduced. Our findings suggest that a dose of positive emotion can help overcome this deficiency. It is as if positive emotion recharges the self's batteries, restoring it to something closer to full power and thereby facilitating its ability to control itself again.

These results have interest beyond the technicalities of self-regulation. Indeed, they suggest an important function for positive emotions. Many writers have remarked that the functions of positive emotion are less readily apparent than those of negative emotions, because the latter are seemingly associated with behavioral impulses. Positive emotions do not prompt overt behavior in ways that seem as direct and obvious as negative emotions. However, if positive emotions restore the self's ability to regulate itself, this would be highly adaptive and would indicate a very powerful and important way that these emotions could improve overall psychological functioning.

Our findings are highly compatible with those of Barbara Frederickson and her colleagues, who have also examined the function of positive emotions and have demonstrated that positive emotions can "undo" some of the harmful physiological effects caused by negative emotions (e.g., Frederickson and Levenson, 1998; Frederickson, Mancuso, Branigan, & Tugade, 2000). For instance, Frederickson & Levenson (1998) described two experiments showing that positive emotions sped recovery from the cardiovascular sequelae of negative emotions. In the first study, participants were shown a fear inducing filmstrip, and were then shown subsequent filmstrips that elicited either positive, neutral, or negative emotions. Participants who viewed the films that induced positive emotions showed the most rapid return to the prefilm levels of cardiovascular activation. In the second study, participants who smiled spontaneously during a sad filmstrip were quicker to return to their prefilm levels of cardiovascular activation than were participants who did not smile. Thus, Frederickson and her colleagues showed that one of the functions of positive emotions is to return the person to a neutral state, and undo the effects of negative emotions. This is highly consistent with our view that positive emotions return the self-regulatory system to its predepleted state.

CONCLUSION

The research we have described indicates that emotions can facilitate or impair self-regulation of behavior. We have suggested that positive, pleasant emotions can facilitate self-regulation, whereas negative, unpleasant emotions can impair self-regulation. Although these basic effects may seem parallel, in fact our work suggests that the mechanisms are quite different.

The impact of negative emotions depended on what we called a priority shift. That is, emotional distress impairs self-regulation because when people feel bad, they assign top priority to feeling better, and this priority causes them to disregard behavioral self-regulation. The everyday targets of self-regulation include a large number of behaviors that promise good feelings, such as eating fattening foods or abusing drugs and alcohol. Normally, people may be able to resist the promise of fleeting pleasure that these behaviors carry, but when people feel bad and want to feel better, they yield to these temptations and thereby abandon self-control.

The impact of positive emotions appears to be a restorative effect involving recharging the self's resources. We have shown that effective self-regulation often depends on an inner resource that operates like a strength or energy. After regulating one's own behavior, the individual's stock of this resource is typically depleted. Positive emotion appears to help replenish this resource, enabling people to function effectively again.

AUTHOR NOTE

Address correspondence to Dianne Tice, Dept. Of Psychology, Case Western Reserve University, 10900 Euclid Avenue, Cleveland, OH 44106–7123. E-mail: dxt2@po.cwru.edu, phone: (216) 368–3471. The preparation for this manuscript was supported by a grant from the National Institutes of Health MH–57039 and the Center for Advanced Study in the Behavioral Sciences.

REFERENCES

Baumeister, R. F. (1997). Esteem threat, self-regulatory breakdown, and emotional distress as factors in self-defeating behavior. *Review of General Psychology, 1*, 145–174.

Baumeister, R. F., Bratslavsky, E., Muraven, M., & Tice, D. M. (1998). Ego depletion: Is the active self a limited resource? *Journal of Personality and Social Psychology, 74*, 1252–1265.

Baumeister, R. F., Dale, K. L., & Tice, D. M. (2002). Replenishing the self: Effects of positive affect on performance and persistence following ego depletion. Manuscript in preparation.

Baumeister, R. F., Heatherton, T. F., & Tice, D. M. (1994). *Losing control: How and why people fail at self-regulation*. (San Diego, CA: Academic).

Bushman, B. J., Baumeister, R. F., & Phillips, C. M. (2001). Do people aggress to improve mood? Catharsis beliefs, affect regulation opportunity, and aggressive responding. *Journal of Personality and Social Psychology, 81*, 17–32.

Catanzaro, S. J., & Mearns, J. (1990). Measuring generalized expectancies for negative mood regulation: Initial scale development and implications. *Journal of Personality Assessment, 54*, 546–563.

Frederickson, B.L., & Levenson, R.W. (1998). Positive emotins speed recovery for the cardiovascular sequeleae of negative emotions. *Cognition and Emotion, 12*, 191–220.

Frederickson, B.L., Mancuso, R.A., Branigan, C., & Tugade, M.M. (2000). The undoing effect of positive emotions. *Motivation and Emotion, 24*, 237–258.

Gottfredson, M. R., & Hirschi, T. (1990). *A general theory of crime*. Stanford, CA: Stanford University Press.

Isen, A. M., & Daubman, K. A. (1984). The influence of affect on categorization. *Journal of Personality and Social Psychology, 47*, 1206–1217.

Isen, A. M., Nygren, T. E., & Ashby, F. G. (1988). Influence of positive affect on the subjective utility of gains and losses: It is just not worth the risk. *Journal of Personality and Social Psychology, 55*, 710–717.

Knapp, A., & Clark, M. S. (1991). Some detrimental effects of negative mood on individuals' ability to solve resource dilemmas. *Personality and Social Psychology Bulletin, 17*, 678–688.

Manucia, G. K., Baumann D. J., & Cialdini R. B. (1984). Mood influences on helping: Direct effects or side effects? *Journal of Personality and Social Psychology, 46*, 357–364.

Mischel, W. (1974). Processes in delay of gratification. In L. Berkowitz (Ed.), *Advances in experimental social psychology* (Vol. 7, pp. 249–292). San Diego, CA: Academic.

Mischel, W. (1996). From good intentions to willpower. In P. M. Gollwitzer & J. A. Bargh (Eds.), *The psychology of action: Linking cognition and motivation to behavior* (pp. 197–218). New York: Guilford.

Muraven, M., Tice, D. M., & Baumeister, R. F. (1998). Self-control as a limited resource: Regulatory depletion patterns. *Journal of Personality and Social Psychology, 74*, 774–789.

Nygren, T. E., Isen, A. M., & Taylor, P. J. (1996).The influence of positive affect on the decision rule in risk situations: Focus on outcome (and especially avoidance of loss) rather than probability. *Organizational Behavior and Human Decision Processes, 66*, 59–72.

Tice, D. M., & Baumeister, R. F. (1997). Longitudinal study of procrastination, performance, stress, and health: The costs and benefits of dawdling. *Psychological Science, 8*, 454–458.

Tice, D. M., Bratslavsky, E., & Baumeister, R. F. (2001). Emotional distress regulation takes precedence over impulse control: If you feel bad, Do it! *Journal of Personality and Social Psychology, 80*, 53–67.

Wegner, D. M., Schneider, D. J., Carter, S. R., & White, T. L. (1987). Paradoxical effects of thought suppression. *Journal of Personality and Social Psychology, 53*, 5–13.

9

Emotion-Focused Deception: The Role of Deception in the Regulation of Emotion

Daniel Hrubes
College of Mount Saint Vincent

Robert S. Feldman and James M. Tyler
University of Massachusetts, Amherst

"Why do people lie?"
—Kenny Loggins, *Why do People Lie* (1977)

Deception is a surprisingly typical part of social interactions. For example, some findings suggest that people tell lies in one of five of their social encounters, whereas other findings show that 60% of strangers lie to each other at least once during the course of a 10-minute encounter (DePaulo, Kashy, Kirkendol, Wyer, & Epstein, 1996; Feldman, Forrest, & Happ, 2002).

Despite memorable examples where people have lied to achieve material gains (such as the University of Notre Dame football coach who was forced to resign after it was discovered he lied about his athletic and academic qualifications on his resume), the most common reasons for lying are to achieve psychological gains (DePaulo et al., 1996). One important psychological gain for which people lie is to regulate emotions. Emotion regulation refers to how individuals affect their own emotions, such as when and what emotions they have as well as how they experience and express their emotions (Gross, 1998). Although the language of emotion suggests that emotions control individuals (Averill, 1980)—people "fall" in love, they are "gripped" with fear, or they are "overcome" with sorrow—the truth is that individuals are quite adept at controlling their emotions (Gross, 1998). They seek out situations that make them happy, leave others before becoming angry, try not to think about things that make them sad, and smile instead of cringe when they receive disappointing gifts.

In their efforts to regulate emotions, individuals employ myriad tactics. In this chapter we argue that one of the important tactics that people use to regulate emotions is deception. For example, a woman who has been asked out on a date may lie and say that she is busy to avoid spending time with someone she finds boring or annoying. Or a man who has lingered over drinks with a female coworker may lie to his wife to avoid a confrontation that might ruin his good mood. In both cases, deception is used to regulate emotions.

The idea that emotions and deception are linked is not new. Theorists agree that emotions play a central role in deception (Buller & Burgoon, 1998; Lewis & Saarni, 1993). Furthermore, DePaulo and her colleagues suggested that one of the many functions of everyday lying is the regulation of emotions (Depaulo et al., 1996). However, little empirical or theoretical attention has been directly aimed at exploring the relation between deception and emotion regulation.

The purpose of this chapter is to develop a theoretical framework for emotion-focused deception to identify different ways in which deception may be used to regulate emotions. We define emotion-focused deception as deception whose function, either in whole or in part, is to regulate the emotions experienced by the deceiver. First, we outline working definitions for deception and emotion. Second, we examine the role of deception in the regulation of emotions using a process model of emotional regulation (Gross, 1999). Third, we investigate possible applications of emotion-focused deception. Finally, we describe directions for future research.

DECEPTION

Deception, which can be defined as any act designed to deliberately create a false belief (Ekman, 1988; Miller & Stiff, 1996), can be achieved in several ways. Imagine that a teenage girl has buried her parents' car in a snow bank while driving home. She may deceive her parents about the accident by withholding relevant information such as the fact that she was intoxicated when the accident occurred. She may also deceive them by fabricating information such as if she falsely claims to have swerved out of the way of an oncoming car. A third way that she may deceive her parents is by distorting factual information. Distortions include exaggerations in which the true nature of facts or events is overstated, such as if she claims that she was driving in a blinding snowstorm during her accident when, in fact, it was only snowing lightly. Distortions also include understatements, in which the true nature of facts or events is minimized, such as if she admits to drinking prior to the accident but says she consumed only one beer when, in fact, she actually had several.

Generally speaking, deceptions can be communicated through two modes, or channels. People can deceive through the verbal channel by using language to create false beliefs. The teenage driver's description of a fictitious oncoming car is an instance of this mode of deception. People can also deceive through nonverbal channels, such as when someone feigns an expression of an emotion they are not really experiencing. If the teenage driver displayed facial expressions of shock and anger at being accused of drinking when, in fact, she was really experiencing fear, shame, or no emotion at all, she would have been deceiving through the nonverbal channel. Such nonverbal deception can also involve tone of voice, body posture, or hand gestures.

Finally, the target of deception can vary. Deceptive efforts can be aimed at others, or they may be aimed at oneself. Although the idea that individuals can deceive others is generally accepted, there is an ongoing debate regarding whether individuals can deceive themselves. In short, the debate revolves around a paradox that can be summed up in the question, "how can an individual know something and not know it at the same time?" (Lockard & Paulhus, 1988, p. 72). Various theorists have suggested ways of conceptualizing self-deception that resolve this paradox (e.g., Greenwald, 1988; Snyder, 1985). In this chapter we examine how some of these conceptualizations relate to the regulation of emotion.

In summary, deception can have a variety of forms and targets. Deception can be accomplished by withholding, fabricating, or distorting information. It can be achieved through words or through actions, and it can be used to create false beliefs in other people as well as in the deceiver. This variety in the forms and targets of deception increases the potential for deception to be used in a number of different processes related to the regulation of emotion.

EMOTION-FOCUSED DECEPTION

Theorists differ in their focus when dealing with emotions: some focus on "affective reactions," which include evaluation, preference, liking, and pleasure (e.g., Zajonc, 1980); whereas others focus on more complex emotions such as anger, sadness, and happiness (e.g., Ekman, 1992; Lazarus, 1991). In this chapter, the term emotion is used broadly. We examine theory and research that relates deception to affect and evaluation as well as to the more complex emotions such as happiness, sadness, jealousy, and shame. This allows us to explore more fully the characteristics of emotion-focused deception.

Gross (1998, 1999) has suggested five processes related to the generation of emotions that can be targeted by regulatory efforts. These include situation selection, situation modification, attention deployment, cognitive change, and response modulation. This theoretical approach provides an effective framework for examining the various roles that deception might play in the regulation of emotion.

Situation Selection

Situation selection refers to approaching or avoiding situations or people based on their potential to influence experienced emotions (Gross, 1999). Although deception may not be the most common tactic for selecting situations, it may still be used somewhat regularly. In the absence of alternatives, people might use deception to avoid or escape disagreeable situations. Most people can probably recall occasions when they have fabricated an excuse to avoid spending time with an annoying acquaintance or colleague. In fact, making up excuses to avoid or escape situations or people to maintain a good mood, or to prevent a bad mood, may be a relatively common type of emotion-focused deception.

There is empirical support for this idea. Using diary studies, DePaulo et al. (1996) and Lippard (1988) examined the types of deception used by individuals. DePaulo and her colleagues had 77 college students and 70 community residents record their deceptions over a 7-day period. Based on their classification system, lies told to avoid unpleasant situations were considered to be self-oriented lies told for personal advantage. Because their data presentation collapsed these lies into a category that included several other types of lies not relevant to situation selection, it is not possible to determine exactly how frequently these specific types of lies were told. However, it is clear that they were at least occasionally used (Kashy & DePaulo, 1996). More direct evidence of lying to avoid situations comes from Lippard, who had 75 college students record their deceptive behaviors over a 3-week period. Results indicated that approximately 7% of the deceptions these individuals told over the course of the 3 weeks were used to avoid or leave undesired social interactions (Lippard, 1988).

More recently, we asked a sample of 265 college undergraduates from two different schools to report how frequently they had engaged in 13 different emotion-focused deceptions. The students in this sample reported that the deceptions they used most frequently were deceptions that allowed them to avoid or escape situations that they did not enjoy, and over 99% of these students indicated that they had used this type of deception at least once (see Table 9.1). In other research targeted at assessing outcomes associated with deception, we asked students to rate which outcomes they believed were most likely to result from engaging in emotion-focused deception. Results revealed that ability to avoid unpleasant tasks

TABLE 9.1

Mean Frequency Ratings and Percent Reporting at Least One Occurrence of Emotion-Focused Deceptions (*N* = 265)

	Deceptive Behavior	*Mean frequency*	*Minimum One Occurrence (Percent)*
1.	I have made up excuses to avoid spending time in situations that I do not enjoy.	5.11 (1.67)	99.3
2.	I have said that I have done something that I really haven't to avoid embarrassment.	4.50 (1.83)	98.9
3.	I have exaggerated how I felt about something to make a situation more comfortable for me and the person I am with.	4.81 (1.85)	99.6
4.	I have told someone that I had positive feelings for him or her when I really didn't so that a situation would go more smoothly.	3.90 (2.03)	94.9
5.	I have deliberately not told somebody something to avoid an emotional "scene."	4.82 (2.14)	96.0
6.	I have gone along with what others wanted without telling them that I would prefer to do something else.	4.27 (2.09)	96.3
7.	I have intentionally avoided telling people about an embarrassing event.	3.63 (2.05)	93.0
8.	I have avoided telling someone something because I didn't want him or her to get mad at me.	4.22 (2.03)	95.6
9.	I have made up an excuse so that I could leave a situation that I was not enjoying (e.g., left a party early because you're not having fun but you told the host that you had to work early the next morning)..	4.95 (1.78)	97.4
10.	I have known that someone was lying to me but decided not to say anything because I didn't want to cause a scene or embarrass him or her.	4.25 (2.12)	97.1
11.	I have said that I agree with someone else's opinion although I don't because I wanted to keep the conversation friendly.	3.37 (2.07)	92.3
12.	I have laughted at a joke that I didn't think was funny to be polite.	4.23 (2.08)	95.2
13.	I have made up a story about something I did or somewhere I went because the truth was too embarassing to me.	2.98 (2.08)	87.9

Note. Ratings were made on 9-point scales with 0 = *never* and 8 = *frequently*. Standard deviations are in parentheses. Individuals reporting "1" through "8" were coded as having at least one occurrence of the indicated behavior.

and situations was among the outcomes most strongly associated with deception (Hrubes & Feldman, 2001). Taken together, these research findings suggest that deception is used to avoid or escape unpleasant situations. Thus, situation selection is one way that deception can be used to regulate emotion.

Situation Modification

Situation modification refers to attempts to change a situation to alter its emotional effects (Gross, 1998, 1999). Deception in the service of situation modification might involve attempts to change the nature of one's own emotions as well as the emotions of others. We examine three types of situation modification strategies: conformity, maintenance of positive self-views, and the manipulation of emotion in others.

Conformity. When individuals follow the norms, beliefs, or actions of others they are conforming. Of particular relevance to this analysis is when individuals conform despite the fact that doing so conflicts with their privately held thoughts or beliefs. In such cases, individuals are described as publicly complying with the group norms without privately accepting them. In some of these cases, they are being deceptive. They are attempting to convince the group that they agree with the group's actions when they actually do not. In these cases, individuals seek to modify the situation from one in which they are a group deviant to one in which they are a member of the group majority.

The desire to avoid deviating from the group can in part be attributed to the regulation of emotion. The consequences of deviation from a group include being disliked, rejected, and treated with hostility (Festinger, Schacter, & Back, 1950; Levine, 1980; Sampson & Brandon, 1964; Schacter, 1951). Such treatment can lead to negative emotional experiences (e.g., anxiety, shame, embarrassment, sadness, anger). For example, being ostracized during even minimal interaction experiences such as virtual game playing over the Internet can cause bad feelings and lead to subsequent conformity (Williams, Cheung, & Choi, 2000). Thus, conformity can be seen as a way to avoid the negative emotions that may be inflicted by the group in response to deviance. However, even without the threat of negative consequences directly imposed by the group, individuals may use conformity as a tactic for emotional regulation. For some, it may be anxiety-inducing to stand out or to be different from the group and these individuals may seek to avoid such negative experiences.

Asch (1952) conducted the classic study demonstrating conformity. In his well-known study, he had participants engage in a perception task in which they had to determine which of three lines matched a target line. Unbeknownst to the participants, all of the other members of the group they were participating with were accomplices of the experimenter trained to agree on clearly wrong answers in a predetermined number of the trials. Asch found that the participants in his study conformed with the group's erroneous judgments about 33% of the time, and that about 75% of his participants agreed with the group's erroneous judgments at least once. This was despite the fact that, as Asch put it, the judgments concerned "relations that possess considerable, and at times unquestionable, certainty" (Asch, 1952, p. 460). In other words, participants agreed with the group's judgments alhough they were clearly wrong.

In Asch's (1952) study, the participants who did not conform were not subjected to any form of negative consequence by other group members, yet in exit interviews these individuals reported feeling awkward and conspicuous. "Most subjects miss the feeling of belonging to the group. In addition, there is a frequent reference to the concern that they feel that they might appear strange and absurd to the majority" (Asch, 1952, p. 465). One of Asch's subjects stated, "I felt disturbed, puzzled, separated, like an outcast from the rest. Every time I disagreed I was beginning to wonder if I wasn't beginning to look funny" (Asch, 1952, p. 465). If failing to conform triggered such unpleasant feelings, it is understandable why the participants conformed as often as they did. Based on Asch's results and the results from numerous replications, it seems reasonable to assume that in some situations, avoiding these feelings would provide the motivation to go along with the group even if it meant being deceptive.

Obviously not all forms of conformity involve deception. In some instances, individuals conform because they come to genuinely agree with the group. In other cases, individuals conform begrudgingly. They go along with the group but they make it clear that they are doing so despite their personal misgivings. Neither of these two types of conformity involves deception. Deception occurs only when individuals privately hold views that conflict with the group's but publicly maintain the illusion that their agreement with the group is sincere.

This type of conformity has been demonstrated in numerous laboratory studies (see Bond & Smith, 1996, for a recent meta-analysis). However, one might argue that the judgments and decisions made in laboratory settings are inconsequential and do not match those in real-world settings. Thus, this type of conformity might not occur outside of the laboratory. If this is true, then this kind of emotion-focused deception should not be prevalent in real-world settings. However, in our survey, college students reported that they occasionally have gone along with what others in a group have wanted without telling the group that they would have preferred something else (see Table 9.1). This suggests that this kind of emotion-focused deception does occur in real-world settings.

Maintaining Positive Self-views. Another way that deception may be used to modify a situation in the service of emotional regulation is through impression management (DePaulo et al., 1996), not only in terms of other's impressions, but also in terms of self-evaluation maintenance. Impression management refers to efforts to create a specific view of oneself in others (Fiske & Taylor, 1991) whereas self-evaluation maintenance refers to efforts to maintain a positive self-view for one's own benefit (Tesser, 1988).

People are highly motivated to create and maintain positive views of themselves (Baumeister, 1982; Snyder, 1985; Tesser, 1988; Tesser & Collins, 1988) as well as positive impressions on others (Fiske & Taylor, 1991; Goffman, 1959; Schlenker, 1980). Theorists have suggested that the desire for positive self-evaluations and positive impressions may operate simultaneously and influence each other (Baumeister, 1997; Fiske & Taylor, 1991). Although the distinction between these self-appraisals and appraisals of the self by others is theoretically important, their relation to the use of emotion-focused deception is similar. Consequently, they will be dealt with simultaneously and referred to collectively as self-views.

Although lying is usually associated with negative consequences for self-views, in some situations people may overlook those consequences in favor of the more immediate self-enhancement that might be gained through deception. When faced with information that is threatening to their self-views, individuals might exaggerate their accomplishments, minimize their failures, or fabricate completely fictitious information that makes them appear more positive than they really are.

Information threatening to self-views may be gained through social comparison. In their quest to create positive evaluations of themselves, individuals often use social comparisons to gain information relevant to their self-views (Tesser, 1988). If these social comparisons result in threats to self-views, negative affect may result (Baumeister, 1997, 1993; Brickman & Bulman, 1977; Tesser & Collins, 1988; Wayment & Taylor, 1995). In an effort to regulate this negative affect, individuals might try to modify their relative standing by engaging in self-presentational strategies (Tesser, 1988). Goffman (1959) argued that individuals create impressions in a kind of performance and when they feel that their projected impressions are threatened they engage in "defensive practices."

Consistent with these ideas, threats to self-view have been found to trigger self-presentational strategies (Kashy & DePaulo, 1996; Wills, 1981). If the threats to self-views are serious enough, long-term self-regulation strategies are abandoned in the service of short-term strategies to escape the negative affect associated with the threats (Baumeister, 1997). Thus, in the face of strong threats to their self-view, individuals may abandon concerns about the long-term repercussions of deception in favor of using deception to regulate affect in the immediate situation (Tyler & Feldman, 2001).

Recent research supports the idea that deception can be employed as a defensive tactic to protect positive self-views. First, in a sample of college students given different goals to pursue while getting acquainted with another student in a laboratory setting, the use of deception was greatest for those motivated to create a positive self-view (Feldman, Forest, & Happ, 2002). Moreover, in a sample of college students writing accounts of hypothetical scenarios in which they caused a negative consequence, the use of deception in students' accounts increased as their blame for the event increased (Hodgins, Liebeskind, & Schwatz, 1996).

This suggests that these students were using deception to protect their self-views. Finally, in diary studies and our self-report study, individuals reported using deception in real settings to avoid embarrassment and disapproval (DePaulo et al, 1996; see Table 9.1).

Taken together, the findings from across several different research methodologies support the idea that people use deception to modify their self-views. When self-views are threatened, or when more positive self-views are desired, individuals may resort to the use of deception (Tyler & Feldman, 2001). In these cases, individuals are avoiding the negative affect associated with negative self-views by using deception. Thus, deception is used to modify the situation so that individuals appear more positive to themselves and to others.

Manipulating the Emotions of Others. A third way that deception may be used to modify a situation is through the manipulation of emotions felt by others. Sometimes this is can be done for material gain, as when in Shakespeare's *Othello*, Iago uses deception to manipulate Othello into a destructive jealousy. It is more likely, however, that the emotions of others are manipulated to influence the emotional tone of a situation. One of the goals of influencing the emotional tone of a situation is to regulate one's own emotional experiences, such as when information that will trigger anger in another is withheld to avoid feeling negative in response to becoming the target of that anger. In these cases, deception is being used to modify the emotional characteristics of a situation in the service of emotion regulation.

From this perspective, the deceptive self-presentational strategies described earlier may also be motivated by a desire to manipulate the emotions of others. Liking can be increased by presenting a more positive view to others. Because being liked leads to experiencing positive affect whereas being disliked leads to experiencing negative affect, creating a positive impression can be seen as an effort to regulate emotions through the manipulation of emotions in others. It should be noted, however, that although such self-enhancement strategies may initially increase liking, in the long run impressions of self-enhancers seem to deteriorate (Paulhus, 1998). This suggests that deceptive self-presentational strategies may be effective emotion regulation strategies in the short run, but may be detrimental to those efforts in the long run.

Another way that deception may be used to manipulate the emotions of others is by influencing their responses to negative outcomes or social transgressions. At least two deceptive strategies are possible when trying to influence others' responses to negative outcomes. The first strategy is to simply withhold the upsetting information. In this tactic, others are prevented from reacting to a negative consequence by deceiving them into believing that the consequence did not really happen. Returning to the earlier example involving the mishap with the snowbound family car, the daughter could have deceived her parents by not telling them about the accident at all and, instead, could have arranged a way to rescue the car without their knowledge.

Research findings indicate that this is what people sometimes do. In our survey of college students' use of deception, participants reported that one of the more frequently used deceptions was to withhold information from others to avoid an emotional "scene" or to prevent others from getting mad at them (see Table 9.1). In another survey of college students involved in romantic relationships, more than 41% of respondents reported deceiving their partners about being unfaithful (Shusterman & Saxe, 1990, described in Saxe, 1991). Although none of the data reported in this study indicated that the reason for using deception was to manipulate their partner's emotion, other research findings indicate that emotional responses to infidelity are quite strong (Buss, 1994). Therefore, it seems reasonable to assume that deceptions concerning infidelities may be used, at least in part, to manipulate a relationship partner's emotions. Further support for this idea can be found in another investigation of the deceptions used in romantic relationships. In this study, a sample of college students in romantic relationships responded to questions about the type, frequency, and effect of deception used in their relationships. Those who reported using deception indicated that they used it as a method to avoid conflicts with their romantic prtners (Peterson, 1996). Thus, using deception to prevent the discovery of some negative circumstance is one way that individuals may manipulate others' (and presumably ultimately their own) emotions.

The second way that deception may be used to manipulate the emotional response of others to negative outcomes is to influence the way that others react when they discover a particular undesirable outcome. In these instances, deceivers seek to deflect blame for the outcome away from themselves in an attempt to avoid becoming the target of anger. One way of accomplishing this is through the fabrication of excuses. Excuses have been defined as the "the conscious supplanting of one cause by another, with the goal of influencing others" (Weiner, Figueroa–Munoz, & Kakihara, 1991, p. 4).

Theoretically, excuses are most effective when they shift responsibility for a negative outcome entirely away from the person and onto a situational cause or another person (Snyder & Higgins, 1988). Therefore, if an excuse shifts the blame for a negative outcome away from the excuse-maker and onto someone else or onto an uncontrollable event, the excuse-maker may avoid becoming the target of anger. In the hypothetical auto incident described earlier, the daughter might have used this tactic to prevent her parents from becoming angry with her by claiming that circumstances out of her control, such as icy roads or heavy snowfall, caused the accident.

Weiner and his colleagues have argued that excuse giving should be considered an intentional strategy designed to shift the causal beliefs of excuse recipients and, consequently, to influence the emotions of excuse recipients (Graham, Weiner, & Benesh–Weiner, 1995). They conducted a series of studies investigating whether people strategically use excuses to mitigate the anger of others (Weiner, Amirkhan, Folkes, & Verette, 1987). In one of these studies, a sample of college students was asked to recall two recent occasions in which they had broken a social contract, one in which they had communicated the real reason for breaking the contract, and another in which they had communicated a false reason for breaking the contract. For the situations in which the communicated reasons were false, participants were also required to describe the real reasons for breaking the contract.

First, supporting the idea that deceptive excuse-making is commonplace, the findings showed that 72% of the participants were able to recall at least one recent time when they had used a deceptive excuse. Second, the findings revealed that if the real reason for breaking a contract indicated personal responsibility (e.g., "I did not want to go"), it was usually withheld and replaced with an excuse that was less likely to indicate personal responsibility (e.g., "my car broke down"). Finally, the findings indicated that participants rated their withheld reasons as more likely to cause anger than their communicated reasons. In sum, the results revealed that people used deception to avoid becoming the target of anger in others.

Consistent with these results, our study of outcomes associated with deception revealed that college students believe that "preventing others from becoming angry" is one of the outcomes most likely to result from using deception (Hrubes & Feldman, 2001). Furthermore, other results show that even young children understand that reasons for transgressions that increase their personal responsibility will cause anger to be directed at them and that they are, therefore, more likely to withhold these reasons (Weiner & Handel, 1985).

Taken together, these results support the idea that people seek to reduce the anger directed at them by others in response to transgressions through the use of excuses. Moreover, they suggest that if the real reason for the transgression is likely to cause anger, then people will fabricate a better excuse. This supports the idea that deception can be used to modify a situation by manipulating the emotions of others.

In summary, theory and research support the idea that individuals use deception to modify the situations in which they find themselves. One strategy is to withhold dissenting personal views and go along with the group, thereby shifting relative status from that of a deviant to that of a majority group member. Another strategy is to enhance self-views in hopes of affecting how others react. This strategy modifies how the deceiver is perceived in the situation. A third method is to directly manipulate the emotions of others to create a more positive situation. In all three cases, the situation is modified in to alter its emotional effects on the deceiver.

Attentional Deployment

Attentional deployment describes a variety of tactics used to move the focus of attention away from emotional aspects of a situation, as in distraction, or to focus attention on emotional aspects of a situation, as in rumination (Gross, 1998, 1999). The potential relationship of deception to these tactics is that some may involve forms of self-deception. For example, ideas or beliefs that trigger negative affect may be shifted out of awareness whereas more favorable thoughts or ideas are shifted into awareness. These effects have been described as self-deception (Whisner, 1989).

Whisner provides one approach to defining self-deception directly related to attentional deployment in the service of emotion regulation. He defines self-deception as the disavowal of responsibility for an emotion, or an emotion influencing thought or action by refusing to focus attention or by attempting to shift attention away (Whisner, 1989). Returning once again to our earlier example, after successfully deceiving her parents about her car accident, the teenage daughter may have believed that it was wrong to do so. This may have led her to feel guilt whenever she thought about the deception. To maintain a positive self-view, she would have been motivated to avoid feeling this guilt and to disavow responsibility for it. Therefore, every time thoughts about the deception occurred she may have shifted her attention away from them. If these attentional shifts caused thoughts about the deception to eventually stop occurring, she would have successfully eliminated her guilt through self-deception.

Research investigating coping strategies supports the idea that this type of self-deception may be employed in the regulation of emotion. When confronted with stressful events, one way that people respond is through avoidant coping mechanisms such as denial. Denial, which involves the refusal to accept the reality of a situation, implies "attempting to adhere to a worldview that is no longer valid" (Carver & Scheier, 1999, p. 570). In other words, denial involves self-deception. Findings indicate that denial is used most frequently by pessimists. For example, results from a study that assessed how college students adjusted to school revealed that pessimistic students were more likely to use avoidant coping than were optimistic students (Aspinwall & Taylor, 1992). Similarly, findings from a study designed to assess coping strategies among patients diagnosed with cancer indicated that pessimism was positively associated with denial (Carver et al., 1993). In these cases, pessimistic individuals sought to shift stress-inducing information or thoughts out of their awareness. Ironically, although pessimists may be using denial to regulate their negative affect in response to stressful events, the overall consequence of such avoidant coping styles seems to be a reduction in emotional well-being (Carver & Scheier, 1999). Thus, this form of emotion-focused deception may be effective at regulating short-term but not long-term emotion.

Denial is one example of self-deception in which one purposefully tries to affect attentional deployment to regulate emotions. However, some definitions of self-deception do not require conscious intent or even awareness of one's actions. According to Gilbert and Cooper (1985), conscious intent of attentional deployment is not necessary for an action to qualify as self-deception. Based on this definition, all forms of self-serving biases in which individuals focus on self-enhancing information and avoid self-damaging information can be included in our examination of emotion-focused deception (see Miller & Ross, 1975; Taylor & Brown, 1988; for reviews). Thus, self-serving deployment of attention is one way that deception may be used to regulate emotions. The prevalence of this type of emotion-focused deception depends on how self-deception is conceptualized. If conscious intent to divert attention is required, the frequency may be limited to situations that cause significant negative emotions. However, if conscious intent to divert attention is not required, this type of emotion-focused deception may be a regular part of daily life.

Cognitive Change

Cognitive perspectives on emotion indicate that there are a series of cognitive steps or appraisals that are necessary for individuals to respond emotionally to a situation or event (Scherer, 1988; Smith & Ellsworth, 1985). Cognitive change strategies of emotional regulation refer to tactics designed to modify these emotion-eliciting appraisals (Gross, 1998, 1999). Similar to attentional deployment strategies, the link between cognitive change tactics and deception is that some cognitive change tactics may involve self-deception.

One line of research relevant to this idea involves excuses. Unlike the excuses used to manipulate the emotions of others, these excuses are used by individuals to alter their responsibility for negative personal outcomes in an effort to directly control their own emotional states (Snyder & Higgins, 1988). In these instances, excuses are defined as "the motivated process of shifting causal attributions for negative personal outcomes from sources that are relatively more central to the person's sense of self to sources that are relatively less central, thereby resulting in perceived benefits to the person's image and sense of control" (Snyder & Higgins, 1988, p. 24). Typically, such excuses are employed to maintain self-image and avoid negative affect such as anxiety and depression. Investigations of these types of excuses have most often involved assessing responses to negative performance on ego-involving or achievement tasks such as exams.

A variety of different studies have demonstrated that making excuses such as emphasizing task difficulty or derogating the source of the information can effectively regulate emotions experienced in response to negative personal outcomes (see Snyder & Higgins, 1988, for a review). What is unclear is to what degree these excuses represent self-deception. Snyder has argued that self-deception is a regular part of excuse-making. In his conceptualization, the desire for excuse making is triggered by two conflicting beliefs: (a) I am a good person and (b) I am responsible for a bad outcome. These conflicting beliefs motivate the individual to reduce awareness of the second belief and increase awareness of the first, which constitutes self-deception (Snyder, 1985). In making excuses one can "reframe performance" so that bad personal outcomes seem less negative. Tactics for achieving this include such well documented effects as victim derogation and source derogation. One can also "transform responsibility" so that personal responsibility for the negative outcome is decreased (Snyder, 1985). This can be accomplished by emphasizing external factors such as task difficulty. Empirical support for these effects include studies in which participants are given false negative feedback on a task after which excuse-making is either facilitated or not. Results typically indicate that when participants are allowed to make an excuse such as derogating the source of the feedback or emphasizing task difficulty, their negative affect decreases (e.g., Burish & Houston, 1979)

In one interesting application of this paradigm, half of the participants given failure feedback were given a questionnaire that facilitated their ability to make excuses. While completing the questionnaire, these participants were attached to an instrument that was either described as a "lie detector" or a means of measuring physiological responses. Participants who believed that they were attached to a "lie detector" reported more negative affect than did participants in the control group. Participants who believed that they were attached to a physiology recording device reported less negative affect than did those in the control group (Mehlman & Snyder, 1985). Presumably, believing that the "lie detector" would expose deceptive excuses eliminated the benefit of those excuses. The presence of the "lie detector" heightened the participants' awareness of their own excuses, thus rendering them ineffective. This supports the idea that self-deception is involved when using these kinds of excuses.

Thus, cognitive change through self-deception seems to be one tactic people may use to regulate emotion. They may convince themselves that their performance was not really so bad, or they may convince themselves that their bad performance was not really their fault. In either case, self-deception serves to regulate emotions by altering cognitive appraisals.

Response Modulation

This strategy refers to altering physiological, experiential, or behavioral components of responding after emotional responses have been initiated (Gross, 1998, 1999). Facial expressions are considered by many emotion theorists to be one of the most central components of emotional responding (Darwin, 1872/1965; Ekman, 1993; Izard, 1971; Tomkins, 1962, 1963), and a great deal of research has explored deception in the form of repressing or falsifying facial expressions.

Ekman and Friesen (1969, 1975) described several ways in which emotional responses may be modified. These methods include minimization, which are attempts to decrease the intensity of a display so that it understates the experienced emotion; maximization, which are attempts to exaggerate a display so that it overstates the experienced emotion; masking, which are attempts to keep a "poker face" and show no indication of the experienced emotion; and substitution, which are attempts to display an expression for an emotion that is categorically different than the experienced emotion. Finally, one may display false emotions, which are attempts to display an emotion when none is felt (Ekman, 1993).

These modifications often occur in response to display rules or cultural norms prescribing what are appropriate and inappropriate emotional displays for specific situations (Ekman & Friesen, 1969). A good example of this is the forced smile that is displayed in response to a disappointing gift. The smile is substituted for the display of disappointment because a cultural display rule indicates that it would be inappropriate to display disappointment and risk hurting the gift giver's feelings. When the goal of modifying emotional expressions in these ways is to create false beliefs about what emotions are actually experienced, this constitutes deception.

Use of this form of emotion-focused deception begins at a young age. Children learn early that modifying their emotional expressions can help them gain rewards and avoid punishments, and they also learn that their emotional responses should be guided by display rules, (Saarni, 1993). Although the ability to control facial expressions is not fully developed in children, it improves as children grow older (Feldman, Jenkins, & Popoola, 1979). By adulthood, people become quite skilled at posing facial expressions of emotion (Zuckerman, Hall, DeFrank, & Rosenthal, 1976) and these skills are often employed in the service of self-presentational goals (DePaulo, 1992; DePaulo & Friedman, 1998). For example, our sample of college students reported that they have laughed at jokes that were not funny to be polite (see Table 9.1). In sum, theory and research suggests that the modulation of emotional expression occurs frequently and that even young children use this form of emotion-focused deception.

To sum up, it is clear that emotion-focused deception can affect every process involved in emotion regulation. Deception can play a part in situation selection, situation modification, attention allocation, cognitive change, and response modulation. The processes of situation selection, situation modification, and response modification are largely influenced through the deception of others whereas the processes of attention allocation and cognitive change involve tactics that are self-deceptive. Moreover, research findings suggest that deception may be one of the tactics that people regularly use to regulate their emotions. In that sense, the ideas outlined here are consistent with previous arguments stating that deception is a part of daily life and is often aimed at psychological rather than material rewards (DePaulo, et. al, 1996).

APPLICATIONS

Thus far our examination of how deception might be used to regulate emotions has been largely theoretical in nature. We have suggested various ways that deception might be used to regulate emotions and, where possible, described research supporting those ideas. We now turn to two applied areas where emotion-focused deception might be particularly germane: romantic relationships and the workplace.

Emotion-focused deception may be used at the beginning, middle, or end of romantic relationships. In the beginning, when evaluating potential romantic partners, individuals may use deception to select and modify situations. At this stage, individuals may use deceptions such as excuses to avoid spending time with people they don't find attractive. "I'd love to but I already have other plans" may be one effective method for dealing with requests for unwanted dates. Individuals may also use deception in an effort to manipulate the emotions of those they do find attractive. A study investigating deceptive mating acts and tactics concluded that men tend to feign commitment, sincerity, and resource acquisition ability when attempting to appeal to women. Women, on the other hand, tend to alter their appearance when attempting to appeal to men (Tooke & Camire, 1991). Thus, it appears that people do use deception when trying to influence the emotional responses of individuals to whom they are attracted.

There is evidence that deception continues once relationships have been established. Although diary studies indicate that people lie less frequently to those with whom they are close (DePaulo & Kashy, 1998), when people describe the most serious lies they have ever told, or that have been told to them, the lies described most frequently involved romantic partners (DePaulo, Ansfield, Kirkendol, & Boden, 1997, cited in Anderson, Ansfield, & DePaulo, 1999). These findings are supported by the prevalence of infidelity in most cultures (50%, Tavris & Sadd, 1975) and the fact that, in at least one sample, the most frequent lie told by college students to their romantic partner involved infidelity (Shusterman & Saxe, 1990, cited in Saxe, 1991). Given that infidelity is argued to be a universal cause of jealousy (Buss, 1994), it is reasonable to assume that lies about infidelity are told in part to avoid experiencing the negative affect associated with exposed infidelities.

Finally, emotion-focused deception may play a role in the ending of relationships. For most people, the breakup of a relationship is a stressful event. Because people tend to use more avoidant coping tactics if stress levels and depression become high enough (Mearns, 1991), they may turn to attempts at self-deception which affect attentional allocation and cognitive change (Carver & Scheier, 1999).

Another area where investigations of emotion-focused deception are emerging relates to the workplace. The regulation of emotions in the workplace has been termed "emotional labor" (Hochschild, 1983). Some researchers in this area are exploring how people manage their emotions to achieve success at work (Grandey, 2000). Of particular significance is the modification of emotional expression. Many occupations have display rules regarding what emotions workers can express to the public. These rules may require workers to exaggerate, mask, or substitute one expression for another (Ashforth & Humphrey, 1993; Hochschild, 1983). Anyone who has worked as a server in a restaurant knows the importance of displaying a smile and acting pleasant regardless of what emotion is really felt.

Other work roles have their own display rules. For example, some types of therapy may require practitioners to mask all emotional responses (Grandey, 2000). Whether it's a waitperson cheerfully delivering a meal to a hostile customer, or a therapist maintaining a "poker face" in response to shocking revelations from a client, these forms of response modulation constitute emotion-focused deception.

Deception may be used as a situation selection strategy in the workplace as well. Individuals who are physically healthy but who call in sick because they need a "mental health day" may be using deception to avoid a situation that they feel will trigger negative emotions. Similarly, individuals may feign illness to leave work in the service of avoiding negative emotions. In both examples, deception is used to avoid unpleasant situations.

A third area where emotion-focused deception is relevant to the workplace is in coping with situational characteristics such as work overload. Work overload can trigger negative emotional responses (e.g., Repetti, 1993). In an attempt to regulate these responses, individuals might use deception to shift their attention away from the negative aspects of the situation. This potentially involves situation modification through self-deception. In support of this idea, research indicates that one method for dealing with stress in the workplace is to use avoidant coping strategies (Beehr, Johnson, & Nieva, 1995; Keoske, Kirk, & Keoske, 1993). These avoidant coping strategies may include self-deceptive tactics such as denial (Carver, Scheirer, & Wientraub, 1989).

In sum, it appears that examining romantic relationships and workplace settings from the perspective of emotion-focused deception has the potential to further the understanding of how emotion and deception function in these settings. When attempting to establish romantic relationships, emotion-focused deception may be used to select and modify potential romantic situations. Once a relationship is established, it may be used to modify situations, and when relationships end, it may be used to divert attention or cause cognitive change. Similarly, emotion-focused deception may be used in the workplace to select and modify situations as well as to divert attention. These ideas suggest that examining emotion-focused deception in applied settings can help illuminate specific tactics that individuals use to control their emotional lives in real-world settings.

CONCLUSIONS AND FUTURE DIRECTIONS

Deception research has examined the prevalence and functions of deception from a variety of perspectives. Like DePaulo and her colleagues, we believe that some forms of deception are a part of everyday life (DePaulo et. al, 1996). We have argued that the emerging field of emotional regulation provides a theoretical framework from which some of the more commonplace types of deception may be explored and understood. By examining deception in terms of its role in the regulation of emotion, different types of deceptions can be organized together according to their function. We have defined deception that functions to regulate emotions as emotion-focused deception.

Emotion-focused deception is similar to that described by Depaulo (DePaulo et. al., 1996) as deception for psychic rewards. However, emotion-focused deception is a broader category in some respects. Its focus on the regulation of emotion leads to the inclusion of deceptions that fall outside of DePaulo's deceptions for psychic rewards. For example, DePaulo categorizes deception used to avoid unpleasant situations as deception for personal convenience rather than deception for psychic rewards (DePaulo et al., 1996). Because we believe that these lies are told to avoid experiencing negative emotion, we include them in the category of emotion-focused deception. Similarly, we include certain forms of self-deception in emotion-focused deception that are not described in DePaulo's deception for psychic rewards.

The idea that deception may be used to regulate emotions raises many empirical questions. One important question concerns the prevalence of these types of deception. Our research indicates that people use a variety of different emotion-focused deceptions at least occasionally (see Table 9.1). However, these findings relied on people's estimates of past behaviors. Diary studies would give a more accurate picture of the frequency with which these deceptions occur. Additionally, the relations among the different types of emotion-focused deception should be explored. Do those who use deception to avoid unpleasant situations also engage in self-deception to divert attention? It may be that people who use one type of emotion-focused deception are likely to use others.

Another important question involves the consequences of emotion-focused deception. More information is needed to understand the effects of emotion-focused deception on outcomes such as social functioning, work performance and satisfaction, and subjective well-being. Some data indicate that strategies such as suppression of emotional expression may have negative health consequences (Morris & Feldman, 1997), but more research is needed. In a related topic, the difference between short-term and long-term consequences of the use of emotion-focused deception should be examined. Although emotion-focused deception may lead to short-term positive consequences, the most obvious of which may be a decrease in negative emotion experienced in the immediate situation, the long-term consequences may be more negative. The findings that avoidant coping styles are associated with more negative emotional well-being support this idea (Carver & Scheier, 1999).

A third question regards the theoretical and empirical integrity of the category of emotion-focused deception. The question of concern is whether emotion-focused deception can be distinguished empirically from other categories of deception. If the various forms of deception outlined in this chapter do comprise a unique category, they should exhibit similar characteristics in terms of their antecedents (e.g., situations with potential for emotional consequences) as well as their associated motivations (e.g., desire to avoid negative affect). They should also be empirically distinguishable from other types of deception. In a related vein, investigations of beliefs about deception should address the question of whether individuals perceive emotion-focused deception differently than other types of deception. Perhaps the moral approbation associated with emotion-focused deception is less severe than that for other types of deception.

Two other important areas for future research involve developmental and individual difference questions. Research should investigate when and how children learn to use emotion-focused deception. Some evidence for the development of the use of deception already exists, but distinguishing between emotion-focused deception and other types of deception may shed light on how children come to their beliefs and actions regarding deception. Individual differences in the use of emotion-focused deception is another topic of importance. Findings indicate that when compared to optimists, pessimists are more likely to use self-deception to regulate emotion. Emotionality, Machiavellianism, self-monitoring, and public self-consciousness are just a few of the other individual difference variables that might also influence the use of emotion-focused deception.

This is an important time for research in deception. With the realization that deception is commonplace, understanding the types of deception that occur as well as the functions that those deceptions serve becomes a task of great theoretical and practical importance. The emerging field of emotional regulation suggests one important function that deception may serve. It also provides a theoretical framework for asking more refined questions about the role of deception in people's emotional lives. Thus, the integration of ideas from emotion regulation and deception in the investigation of emotion-focused deception offers an effective perspective for understanding the role of deception and emotion in people's everyday lives. In response to the song lyric "why do people lie?" quoted at the beginning of this chapter, it certainly appears that at least some of the time people lie to control their emotions.

REFERENCES

Anderson, D. E., Ansfield, M. E., & DePaulo, B. M. (1999). Deception in relationships. In P. Philippot, R. S., Feldman, & E. J. Coats (Eds.), *The social context of nonverbal behavior* (pp. 372–409). New York: Cambridge University Press.

Asch, S. E. (1952). *Social psychology*. Englewood Cliffs, NJ: Prentice Hall

Ashforth, B. E., & Humphrey, R. H. (1993). Emotional labor in service roles: The influence of identity. *Academy of Management Review, 18*, 88–115.

Aspinwall, L. G., & Taylor, S. E. (1992). Modeling cognitive adaptation: A longitudinal investigation of the impact of individual differences and coping on college adjustment and performance. *Journal of Personality and Social Psychology, 61*, 755–765.

Averill, J. R. (1980). The emotions. In E. Staub (Ed.), *Personality: Basic aspects and current research* (pp. 134–199). Englewood Cliffs, NJ: Prentice Hall.

Baumeister, R. F. (1982). A self-presentational view of social phenomena. *Psychological Bulletin, 91*, 3–26.

Baumeister, R. F. (1993). Understanding the inner nature of low self-esteem: Uncertain, fragile, protective, and conflicted. In R. Baumeister (Ed.), *Self-esteem: The puzzle of low self-regard* (pp. 201–218). New York: Plenum.

Baumiester, R. F. (1997). Esteem threat, self-regulatory breakdown, and emotional distress as factors in self-defeating behavior. *Review of General Psychology, 1*, 145–174.

Beehr, T. A., Johnson, L. B., & Nieva, R. (1995). Occupational stress: Coping of police and their spouses. *Journal of Organizational Behavior, 16*, 3–26.

Brickman, P., & Bulman, R. J. (1977). Pleasure and pain in social comparison. In J. M. Suls & R. L. Miller (Eds.), *Social comparison processes: Theoretical and empirical perspectives,* (pp. 149–186). Washington, DC: Hemisphere.

Buller, D. B., & Burgoon, J. K. (1998). Emotional expression in the deception process. In P. A. Anderson & L. K. Guerrero (Eds.) *Handbook of communication and emotion,* (pp. 381–402). San Diego, CA: Academic.

Burish, T. G., & Houston, K. B. (1979). Causal projection, similarity projection, and coping with threats to self-esteem. *Journal of Personality and Social Psychology, 47,* 57–70.

Buss, D. M. (1994). *The evolution of desire.* New York: Basic.

Carver, C. S., Pozo, C., Harris, S. D., Noriega, V., Scheier, M. F., Robinson, D. S., et al. (1993). How coping mediates the effect of optimism on distress: A study of women with early stage breast cancer. *Journal of Personality and Social Psychology, 65,* 375–390.

Carver, C. S., & Scheier, M. F. (1999). Stress, coping, and self-regulatory processes. In L. A. Pervin & O. P. John (Eds.), *Handbook of personality: Theory and research* (2nd ed) (pp. 553–575). New York: Guilford.

Carver, C. S., Scheier, M. F., & Weintraub, J. K. (1989). Assessing coping strategies: A theoretically based approach. *Journal of Personality and Social Psychology, 56,* 267–283.

Darwin, C. (1872/1965). *The expression of the emotions in man and animals.* Chicago: University of Chicago Press. (Original work published 1872)

DePaulo, B. M. (1992). Nonverbal behavior and self presentation. *Psychological Bulletin, 111,* 203–243.

DePaulo, B. M., & Friedman, H. S. (1998). Nonverbal communication. In D. T. Gilbert, S. T. Fiske, & G. Lindsey (Eds.), *The handbook of social psychology* (Vol. 2, pp. 3–40). Boston: McGraw-Hill.

DePaulo, B. M., & Kashy, D. A. (1998). Everyday lies in close and casual relationships. *Journal of personality and Social Psychology, 74,* 63–79.

DePaulo, B. M., Kashy, D. A., Kirkendol, S. E., Wyer, M. M., & Epstein, J. A. (1996). Lying in everyday life. *Journal of Personality and Social Psychology, 70,* 979–995.

Ekman, P. (1988). Self-deception and detection misinformation. In J. S. Lockard & D. L. Paulhus (Eds.), *Self-deception: An adaptive mechanism?* (pp. 229–250). Englewood Cliffs, NJ: Prentice Hall.

Ekman, P. (1992). Are there basic emotions? *Psychological Review, 99,* 550–553.

Ekman, P. (1993). Facial expression and emotion. *American Psychologist, 48,* 384–392.

Ekman, P. & Friesen, W. V. (1969). The repertoire of nonverbal behavior: Categories,origins, usage, and coding. *Semiotica, 1,* 49–98.

Ekman, P., & Friesen, W. (1975). *Unmasking the face.* Englewood Cliffs, NJ: Prentice Hall.

Feldman, R. S., Forrest, J. A., & Happ, B. R. (2002). Self-presentation and verbal deception: Do self-presenters lie more? *Basic and Applied Social Psychology, 24,* 163–170.

Feldman, R. S., Jenkins, L., & Popoola, O. (1979). Detection of deception in adults and children via facial expressions. *Child Development, 50,* 350–355.

Festinger, L., Schachter, S., & Back, K. (1950). *Social pressures in informal groups.* New York: Harper Collins.

Fiske, S. T., & Taylor. S. E.(1991) *Social cognition.* New York: McGraw-Hill.

Gilbert, D., & Cooper, J. (1985). Social psychological strategies in self-deception. In M. W. Martn (Ed.), *The denial of stress* (pp. 83–96). New York: International Universities Press.

Goffman, E. (1959). *The presentation of self in everyday life.* New York: Doubleday.

Graham, S., Weiner, B., & Benesh-Weiner, M. (1995). An attributional analysis of the development of excuse giving in aggressive and nonaggressive African American boys. *Developmental Psychology, 31*, 274–284.

Grandey, A. A. (2000). Emotion regulation in the workplace a new way to conceptualize emotional labor. *Journal of Occupational Health Psychology, 5*, 95–110.

Greenwald, A. G. (1988). Self-knowledge and self-deception. In J. S. Lockard & D. L. Paulhus (Eds.), *Self-Deception: An Adaptive Mechanism?* (pp. 113–131). Englewood Cliffs, NJ: Prentice Hall.

Gross, J. J. (1998). The emerging field of emotional regulation: An integrative review. *Review of General Psychology, 2*, 271–199.

Gross, J. J. (1999). Emotion regulation: Past, present, and future. *Cognition and Emotion, 13*, 551–573.

Hochschild, A. R. (1983). *The managed heart: Commercialization of human feeling.* Berkeley: University of California Press.

Hodgins, H. S., Liebeskind, E., & Schwartz, W. (1996). Getting out of hot water: Facework in social predicaments. *Journal of Personality and Social Psychology, 71*, 300–314.

Hrubes, D., & Feldman, R. S. (2001). *Emotion-focused deception.* Manuscript in preparation.

Izard, C. (1971). *The face of emotion.* New York: Appleton-Century-Crofts.

Kashy, D. A., & DePaulo, B. M. (1996). Who lies? *Journal of Personality and Social Psychology, 70*, 1037–1051.

Keoske, G. F., Kirk, S. A., & Keoske, R. D. (1993). Coping with job stress: Which strategies work best? *Journal of Occupational and Organizational Psychology, 66*, 319–335.

Lazarus, R. S. (1991). *Emotion and Adaptation.* New York: Oxford University Press.

Levine, J. M. (1980). Reaction to opinion deviance in small groups. In P. B. Paulus (Ed.), *Psychology of group influence* (pp. 375–429). Hillsdale, NJ: Lawrence Erlbaum Associates, Inc.

Lewis, M., & Saarni, C. (1993). Deceit and illusion in human affairs. In M. Lewis & C. Saarni (Eds.), *Lying and deception in everyday life.* (pp. 1–29). New York: Guilford.

Lippard, P. V. (1988). "Ask me no questions, I'll tell you no lies": Situational exigencies for interpersonal deception. *Western Journal of Speech Communication, 52*, 91–103.

Lockard, J. S., & Paulhus, D. L. (Eds.). (1988). *Self-deception: An adaptive mechanism?* Englewood Cliffs, NJ: Prentice Hall.

Mearns, J. (1991). Coping with a breakup: Negative mood regulation expectancies and depression following the end of a romantic relationship. *Journal or Personality and Social Psychology, 60*, 327–334.

Mehlman, R. C., & Snyder, C. R. (1985). Excuse theory: A test of the self-protective role of attributions. *Journal of Personality and Social Psychology, 49*, 994–1001.

Miller, D. T., & Ross, M. (1975). Self-serving biases in the attribution of causality: Fact or fiction? *Psychological Bulletin, 82*, 213–225.

Miller, G. R., & Stiff, J. B. (1996). *Deceptive communications.* Thousand Oaks, CA: Sage.

Morris, J. A., & Feldman, D. C. (1997). The dimensions, antecedents, and consequences of emotional labor. *Academy of Management Review, 21*, 986–1010.

Paulhus, D. L. (1998). Interpersonal and intrapsychic adaptiveness of trait self-enhancement: A mixed blessing? *Journal of Personality and Social Psychology, 74*, 1197–1208.

Peterson, S. (1996). Deception in intimate relationships. *International Journal of Psychology, 31*, 279–288.

Repetti, R. L. (1993). Short-term effects of occupational stressors on daily mood and health complaints. *Health Psychology, 12*, 125–131.

Saarni, C. (1993). Socialization of emotion. In M. Lewis & J. Haviland (Eds.), *Handbook of emotions* (pp. 435–446). New York: Guilford.

Sampson, E. E., & Brandon, A. C. (1964). The effects of role and opinion deviation on small group behavior. *Sociometry, 27*, 261–281.

Saxe, L. (1991). Lying: Thoughts of an applied social psychologist. *American Psychologist, 46*, 409–415.

Schachter, S. (1951). Deviation, rejection, and communication. J*ournal of Abnormal and Social Psychology, 46*, 190–207.

Scherer, K. R. (1988). Criteria for emotion-antecedent appraisal: A review. In V. Hamilton, G. H. Bower, & N. H. Frijda (Eds.), *Cognitive perspectives on emotion and motivation* (pp. 89–126). Dordrecht, Netherlands: Nijhoff.

Schlenker, B. R. (1980). *Impression management: The self-concept, social identity, and interpersonal relations*. Monterey, CA: Brooks/Cole.

Smith, C. A., & Ellsworth, P. C. (1985). Patterns of appraisal in emotion. *Journal of Personality and Social Psychology, 48*, 813–838.

Snyder, C. R. (1985). Collaborative companions: The relationship of self-deception and excuse making. In M. W. Martin (Ed.), *Self-deception and self-understanding* (pp. 35–51). Lawrence: University Press of Kansas.

Snyder, C. R., & Higgins, R. L. (1988). From making excuses to being the excuse: An analysis of deception and verbal/nonverbal issues. *Journal of Nonverbal Behavior, 12*, 237–252.

Taylor, S. E., & Brown, J. D. (1988). Illusion and well being: A social psychological perspective on mental health. *Psychological Bulletin, 103*, 193–210.

Tesser, A. (1988). Toawrd a self-evaluation maintenance model of social behavior. In L. Berkowitz (Ed.), *Advances in experimental social psychology*, (Vol. 21) (pp. 181–227). New York: Academic.

Tesser, A., & Collins, J. (1988). Emotion in social reflection and comparison situations: Intuitive, systematic, and exploratory approaches. *Journal of Personality and Social Psychology, 55*, 696–709.

Tomkins, S. S. (1962). *Affect, imagery, consciousness: Vol. 1. The positive affects*. New York: Springer-Verlag.

Tomkins, S. S. (1963). *Affect, imagery, consciousness: Vol, 2. The negative affects*. New York: Springer-Verlag.

Tooke, W., & Camire, L. (1991). Patterns of deception in intersexual and intrasexual mating strategies. *Ethology & Sociobiology, 12*, 345–364.

Tyler, J. M., & Feldman, R. S. (under review). *Deflecting threats to one's self-image: Dissembling personal information as a self-presentation strategy.*

Wayment, H., & Taylor, S. (1995). Self-evaluation processes: Motives, information use, and self-esteem. *Journal of Personality, 63*, 729–757.

Weiner, B., Amirkhan, J., Folkes, V. S., & Verette, J. A. (1987). An attributional analysis of excuse giving: Studies of a naïve theory of emotion. *Journal of Personality and Social Psychology, 52*, 316–324.

Weiner, B., Figueroa–Munoz, A., & Kakihara, C. (1991). The goals of excuses and communication strategies related to causal perceptions. *Personality and Social Psychology Bulletin, 17*, 4–13.

Weiner, B., & Handel, S. (1985). Anticipated emotional consequences of causal communications and reported communication strategy. *Developmental Psychology, 21*, 102–107.

Whisner, W. (1989). Self-deception, human emotion, and moral responsibility: Toward a pluralistic conceptual scheme. *Journal for the Theory of Social Behavior, 19*, 389–410.

Willaims, K. D., Cheung, C. K., & Choi, W. (2000). Cyberostracism: Effects of being ignored over the internet. *Journal of Personality and Social Psychology, 79*, 748–762.

Wills, T. A. (1981). Downward comparison principles in social comparison. *Psychological Bulletin, 90*, 245–271.

Zajonc, R. (1980). Felling and thinking: Preferences need no inferences. *American Psychologists, 35*, 151–175.

Zuckerman, M., Hall, J. A., DeFrank, R. S., & Rosenthal, R. (1976). Encoding and decoding of spontaneous and posed facial expressions. *Journal of Personality and Social Psychology, 34*, 966–977.

10

Collective and Personal Processes in Regulating Emotions: Emotion and Self in Japan and the United States

Shinobu Kitayama
University of Michigan

Mayumi Karasawa
Tokyo Woman's University

Batja Mesquita
Wake Forest University

According to a dual process model of emotion regulation, a network of practices and public meanings of culture render the experience of certain emotions far more likely than the experience of certain other emotions. Moreover, these practices and meanings reinforce, either positively or negatively, certain emotions more than certain others. These collective-level processes of emotion regulation give rise to a number of spontaneous emotions, which may in turn be deliberately and optionally controlled by personal regulatory strategies. Available evidence for the model was reviewed to show that whereas socially disengaging emotions such as pride and anger are strongly afforded and reinforced in North America, socially engaging emotions such as friendly feelings and shame are strongly afforded and reinforced in Japan. Implications for cultural psychological research on emotion are discussed.

In recent years, a number of researchers have emphasized social and intelligent aspects of emotion (e.g., Damasio, 1994; Frank, 1988; Frijda, 1986; Frijda & Mesquita, 1994; Kitayama, Mesquita, & Karasawa, 2002; Mesquita & Ellsworth, 2001; Nassbaum, 2001; Oatley, 1992; Salovey & Mayer, 1990). They argued that emotion may be best seen as nature's way to help the self navigate in uncertain terrains of daily social life in more or less adaptive ways. According to this view, emotions serve as indispensable "pathfinders" for the self (Damasio, 1994).

In this chapter, we discuss how this view of self and emotion may account for their cultural variations in general and the variations in emotion regulation in particular. By emotion regulation, we broadly mean all processes involved in the selection and implementation of emotion responses and emotion-related action strategies. We propose that emotion regulation occurs at two distinct levels. Whereas some regulatory processes operate at a collective or societal level, some others function at a personal or individual level. We then use this "dual process model" of emotion regulation to understand some pronounced variations in self and emotion between Western cultures and Eastern cultures. We specifically focus on the United States and Japan.

This analysis is grounded in a cultural psychological perspective (e.g., Benson, 2001; Bruner, 1990; Geertz, 1973; Kitayama, 2002; Markus & Kitayama, 1991; Miller, 1999; Shore, 1996; Shweder & Sullivan, 1993). This perspective holds that both self and emotion are interdependent with culture's practices and meanings. By now, this argument has been quite well accepted for the self (Heine, Lehman, Markus, & Kitayama, 1999; Kitayama & Markus, 1999; Markus & Kitayama, 1991; Triandis, 1989). For emotion, however, this view might initially seem counterintuitive insofar as emotion is perceived to be inside the body, and thus, fully shielded from culture. This perception might be bolstered by a widespread belief across cultures that emotional responses involve involuntary bodily sensations and feelings (Scherer & Wallbott, 1994). Furthermore, in emotion research the image of emotions as biologically hardwired has had a strong sway. In particular, this image promoted universalist theories of emotion. Following Darwin (1872/1965), these theories proposed that emotions are largely uniform across cultures. In this view, cultural influence is limited largely to the regulation of expressive behaviors. Thus, people are supposedly capable of either magnifying or suppressing emotional expressions in accordance with cultural rules of emotion display (Ekman, 1984); but emotions themselves, at their core, are held to be independent of sociocultural influence, and therefore, they are supposedly universal and cross-culturally invariant.

The perspective of cultural psychology suggests that what is perceived to be the biological core of the body might already be deeply cultural (Lutz, 1988). Indeed, as reviewed in later sections of this chapter, emotion may have already incorporated culture in such a way that spontaneous emotional responses, even if largely involuntary, are still closely attuned to the surrounding systems of practices and meanings. Without this attunement between emotion and the contingencies that are present in the sociocultural environment, emotion will never be able to function as a reliable pathfinder.

All in all, then, the emerging view of emotion that emphasizes its adaptive and rational aspects is quite consistent with the cultural psychological view of emotion. Both views assume that although solidly grounded in biology, emotion is likely to be both quite variable and malleable depending, in part, on the sociocultural backgrounds of each individual. The dual process model to be presented in this chapter represents our own effort to elaborate on this general theoretical framework.

SELF AND EMOTION IN JAPAN AND THE US

Independent and Interdependent Models of Self

In an attempt to understand cultural variation of self from a wide-angle perspective, Markus and Kitayama (1991, 1994) have proposed that very different models of self are culturally sanctioned in different parts of the world (see also Rothbaum, Pott, Azuma, Miyake, & Weisz, 2000; Shweder & Bourne, 1984; Triandis, 1989, 1990, 1995; Weisz, Rothbaum, & Blackburn, 1984). Particularly in North America, the self is assumed to be an independent, bounded entity. Its actions are organized by its own internal attributes such as motives, abilities, and personality traits. Social relations do matter in these cultures, of course. However, these relations are presumed to be contingent on the choices and preferences of individual selves. As a consequence, social relations emerge out of personal decisions to enter such relations (Rothbaum et al., 2000). In contrast, in East Asia, the self is assumed to be an interdependent, connected entity. Its actions are organized by its obligations, roles, and duties vis-à-vis others in a relationship. Personal attributes of the self such as abilities, motives, and personality traits do matter, of course. But they are thought to be contingent on and therefore to emerge out of the self's immersion into specific social relationships (Kitayama, Snibbe, Markus, & Suzuki, in press; Kitayama & Markus, 1999).

Along with a number of theorists (e.g., Guisinger, & Blatt, 1994), we assume that independence and interdependence are two fundamental tasks that are present in all human cultures. Furthermore, the two tasks are dialectically related. Thus, cultures have invented a variety of ways to resolve this dialectic. Some cultures have chosen to put a greater weight on interdependence, but some others have chosen to value independence more, with substantial consequences in terms of social practices, public meanings, and associated psychological processes and tendencies.

In analyzing the cultural shaping of emotion in independent and interdependent cultures, it is important to define one dimension of emotional experience that has so far received insufficient research attention in the extant literature. This dimension pertains to social orientation associated with different emotions (Kitayama, Markus, & Kurokawa, 2000; Kitayama, Markus, & Matsumoto, 1995; Kitayama et al., 2002). See Table 10.1 for the six types of emotions defined by their pleasantness and social orientation.

Specifically, some emotions arise from success or failure in achieving goals that express the independence of the self such as achieving the potential of the self and realizing its own values and worldviews. When the self achieved these goals and therefore distinguished itself as a competent, morally admirable, and autonomous entity, certain positive emotions (e.g., pride, feelings of self-esteem) would arise and, once they did, they would affirm, in a subjectively convincing fashion, the independence and social disengagement of the self. If, however, the pursuit of the independent goals were thwarted for some reasons, equally disengaging, but negative emotions (e.g., anger and frustration) would arise and, once they did, they would motivate the self to restore its own autonomy and independence. These emotions are therefore likely to promote the self's social disengagement and autonomy. These emotions may be called socially disengaging.

TABLE 10.1

Pleasantness and Social Orientation of Emotions. The Six Types of Emotions Defined by These Dimensions and Some Examples for Each Type

Social Orientation	*Pleasantness*	
	Positive	*Negative*
General	Positive General Emotions	Negative General Emotions
	Happy	Unhappy
	Elated	Depressed
Engaging	Positive Engaging Emotions	Negative Engaging Emotions
	Close feelings	Guilt
	Feelings of respect	Feelings of indebtedness
Disengaging	Positive Eisengaging Emotions	Negative Disengaging Emotions
	Pride	Anger
	Feelings of self-esteem	Frustration

In contrast, some other emotions arise from success or failure in meeting interdependent goals such as achieving the connectedness of the self with others in a relationship or in fitting-in to communally shared values and visions. When the self achieved these goals, positive engaging emotions (e.g., friendly feelings and respect) would arise and, once they did, they would provide subjectively convincing evidence for its interdependence and engagement in the pertinent social relationship. If, however, the self failed to achieve the interdependent goals, equally engaging, but negative emotions (e.g., guilt and feelings of indebtedness) would arise and, once they did, they would motivate the self to restore its harmonious interdependence and close connectedness with the pertinent others. Therefore, they are likely to promote social engagement and connectedness of the self with others. These emotions have been referred to as socially engaging.

Finally, some other emotions are more abstract and general in both antecedents and consequences. For example, happiness can arise from both disengaging and engaging experiences as long as they are positive. Likewise, unhappiness can also arise from both types of experiences as long as they are negative. These emotions are called general emotions.

Cultural Variation in Emotional Experience

The social orientation dimension of emotions closely corresponds to the independence versus interdependence dimension of self. When experienced, engaging emotions are indicative of the self's interdependence with others, whereas disengaging emotions are signaling the self's independence. Kitayama and colleagues (1995, 2000, 2002) have thus suggested that in cultural worlds that are organized in terms of independent models of self (e.g., North American middle class cultures), social disengagement is likely to provide a key theme in organizing emotional experience. In contrast, in the worlds that are organized in terms of interdependent models of self (e.g., Asian cultures), social engagement is likely to become the central theme that permeates the emotional experience. According to this analysis, Americans may be predicted to experience disengaging emotions both more frequently and strongly than engaging emotions. In contrast, Japanese may be predicted to experience engaging emotions more than disengaging emotions.

Recently, we tested these predictions. Both Japanese and American college students were presented with a number of mundane social situations (Kitayama et al., 2002). Some of the situations were pleasant (e.g., something good happened to a family member), whereas some others were unpleasant (e.g., getting ill or injured). The participants read each situation carefully and remembered the latest episode that fitted with each situational description. They then reported how strongly they experienced each of the emotions listed in Table 10.1. The rating scale ranged from 0 (*not at all*) to 4 (*very intensely*). We first examined frequency and intensity of emotional experience separately. The frequency of experience was coded in terms of whether any given type of emotion was experienced (receiving responses of 1 or higher), whereas the intensity of experience was based on how strongly emotions were reported to have been experienced when they were experienced (Diener, Larsen, Levine, & Emmons, 1985). Because the same pattern emerged in the two measures, we report the mean ratings from the original 5-point rating scale. Further, preliminary analysis indicated, not too surprisingly, that emotions that were matched in pleasantness with the attendant situations were more strongly experienced than those that were unmatched. Thus, this variable was included in all subsequent analyses.

The relevant data are summarized in Fig. 10.1. The predicted pattern was observed for the emotions that were matched in pleasantness with the attendant situa-

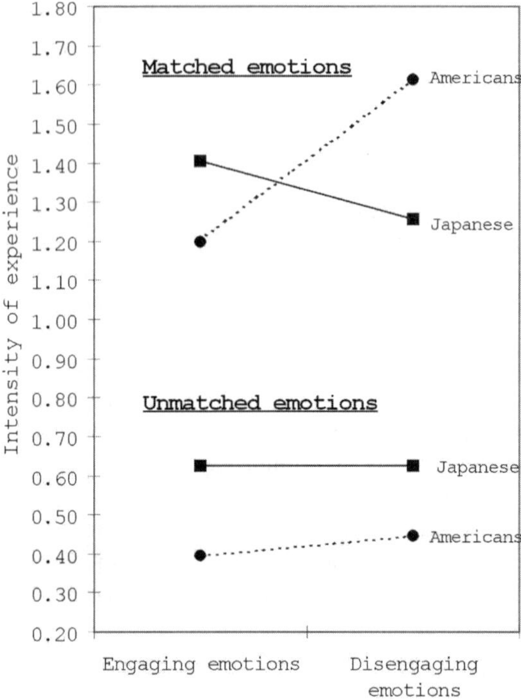

Fig 10.1. Intensity of experiencing engaging versus disengaging emotions for Americans and Japanese: When the emotions were matched in pleasantness with the attendant situations, Americans reportedly felt disengaging emotions more stongly than engaging emotions, but Japanese showd an opposite pattern. The reported intensity was very low regardless of social orientation when the emotions were unmatched in pleasantness with the attendant situations (drawn from the data reported in Kitayama, Mesquita, & Karasawa, 2002)

tions (called the matched emotions). Americans experienced disengaging emotions such as pride and anger significantly more strongly than engaging emotions such as friendly feelings and shame. In contrast, Japanese experienced the engaging emotions significantly more than the disengaging emotions. Importantly, very similar patterns were observed for both positive emotions and negative emotions. As can be seen in Fig. 10.1, the intensity of experience was very low for the emotions that were not matched in pleasantness with the attendant situations (called the unmatched emotions). As may be expected, there was little variation in the intensity of experience as a function of their social orientations.

A Dual Process Model of Cultural Regulation of Emotion

How might the cultural models of self as independent or as interdependent influence individual behaviors and psychological processes and eventually generate the cross-cultural variation in emotional experience such as the one illustrated in Fig. 10.1? In an attempt to answer this question, Kitayama, Markus, and colleagues have argued that these models of self are inscribed into daily practices, behavioral routines, and social institutions of the respective cultural worlds (e.g., Kitayama & Markus, 1999; Kitayama, Markus, Matsumoto, & Norasakkunkit, 1997; Markus, Mullaly, & Kitayama, 1997). Whereas in North America there are many more and a greater variety of practices, lay theories, and other cultural resources that are based on independent models of self, in Asian cultures, there are many more and a greater variety of practices, meanings, and other cultural resources that are based on interdependent models of self. When immersed and engaged in the divergent cultural worlds, individuals will eventually develop the correspondingly divergent repertoires of spontaneous emotions. They may also develop the correspondingly divergent sets of personal strategies for emotion regulation. These strategies modify the experience of the emotions.

The foregoing analysis is schematically illustrated in Fig. 10.2. According to this "duel process model" of emotion regulation, culture shapes emotional experience through two distinct levels of processes. One is collective and the other, personal.

Culture. In accordance with a number of contemporary theoretical analyses (Adams & Markus, 2001; Cole, 1996; Geertz, 1973; Shweder & Sullivan, 1993), the model defines culture as an entire set of ideas, lay theories, schemas, scripts, commonsense, and other symbolic resources that are often, if not always, embodied in daily practices, routines, customs, and social institutions of any given geographic regions or social groups (Kitayama, 2002). These defining features of culture may be called more simply practices and meanings of culture. These practices and meanings constitute the life space or the cultural world for those people who engage in and live with them. The cultural world is fundamentally semiotic, carrying the potential for meaning.

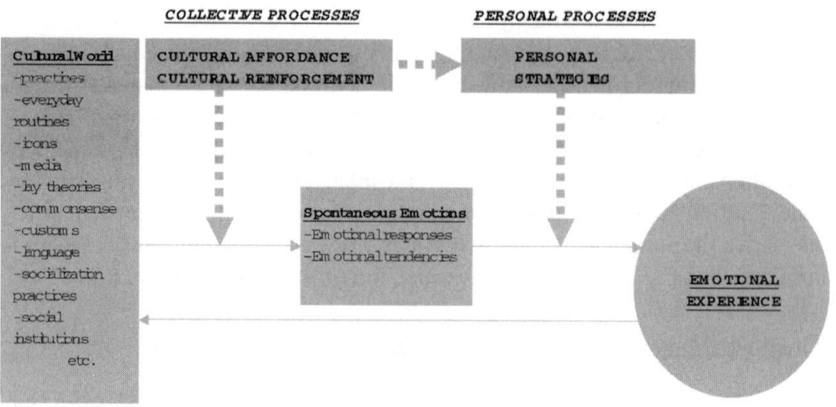

Fig 10.2. The dual process model of emotion regulation: Culture influences each person's emotional experience by collectively affording and reinforcing both certain emotions and personal strategies for managing the experience and expression of these emotions.

Humans are biologically equipped to orient themselves in the culturally constituted semiotic space (Taylor, 1989; Tomasello, 1999). However, the semiotic landscape of culture does vary across regions, times, and specific social groups or roles and, furthermore, under certain circumstances it can change quite rapidly. Accordingly, a continuous effort of each individual to orient himself or herself to a particular sociocultural context becomes the integral part of being a person and self. A number of cultural psychologists have proposed that many, if not most, of psychological processes and structures can best be seen as tools for cultural adaptation and, therefore, they are often culture-contingent (e.g., Fiske, Kitayama, Markus, & Nisbett, 1998; Markus & Kitayama, 1991; Nisbett, Peng, Choi, & Norenzayan, 2001).

The one set of ideational resources that are especially powerful in forming and organizing other such resources are the cultural models of self we discussed earlier in this chapter. Whereas North American cultures tend to be organized in terms of the models of the self as independent, Asian cultures tend to be organized in terms of the models of the self as interdependent.

Cultural Shaping of Emotions. The dual process model assumes that there are multiple, often highly redundant ways in which culture shapes and influences human behaviors. Specifically, it proposes that many divergent practices and meanings of culture can encourage and sanction different emotional responses and tendencies. Because cultural practices and meanings are recurrent, the responses and tendencies which they encourage will eventually be automatized. They become both spontaneous and involuntary. These emotional responses and tendencies will then be perceived to be derived from a hardwired mechanism that is shielded from culture. Indeed, this perception provides an important basis for the subjective quality of emotion as internally generated in response to an external event. Because of this perception, emotion is perceived as an "inner voice" of the self. It can therefore serve as a pathfinder for the self. It is important to keep in mind, however, that although importantly rooted in numerous biological processes, these spontaneous emotions themselves have already been culturally shaped and saturated. The processes that are responsible for this cultural shaping take place collectively as a function of socially shared ideational resources of culture.

Moreover, the practices and meanings of culture also give rise to personal strategies of emotion regulation. Once developed and established, these strategies are selectively deployed by each individual. The processes involved here are therefore personal. These personal strategies are likely to be deployed whenever the spontaneous emotions need to be controlled in ways that are more appropriate for a specific social circumstance.

In general, online emotional experience is constructed as a joint function of both the spontaneous emotions and the personal strategies. Whereas the spontaneous emotions are assumed to occur automatically whenever self-relevant events happen in the environment, the personal strategies are deliberate and optional. In many situations, especially in those that have no obvious social norms for emotion regulation, the involvement of personal strategies may be negligible. Under these circumstances, the emotional experience is largely a function of the collective regulation process alone. Yet, when certain personal regulation strategies are evoked in a given social situation, they may suppress or augment the external expressions of the spontaneously felt emotions and, furthermore, they may also transform the very experience of the emotions.

Mutual Constitution of Culture and Emotion. Importantly, the resulting emotional experience is likely to be embedded and integrated into the culture's practices and meanings and, therefore, this experience may be best understood as part of cultural complexes within which both psychological processes and cultural realities are closely interwoven. Although the emotional experience is fostered and reinforced by cultural practices and meanings, it is simultaneously instrumental in sustaining and transmitting the very practices and meanings from which it has been derived (Bourdieu, 1972; Giddens, 1984). For example, if some practices (e.g., debating) are to continue to take hold in a given cultural community, they may have to attract people who are capable of spontaneously experiencing appropriate emotions, say, certain aggressive feelings. These individuals become new "carriers" of the practices. But some other practices (e.g., consensus seeking) will require a spontaneous experience of more engaging feelings such as respect, appreciation, and other communal emotions.

Although the process by which emotion helps maintain culture (the process indicated in Fig. 10.2 by the arrow pointing to the left) is as important as the process by which culture shapes emotion (the process indicated by the arrows pointing to the left), our primary focus in this chapter is on the latter.

EMPIRICAL EVIDENCE FOR THE DUAL PROCESS MODEL

This model assumes that emotional experience of each individual is fostered and influenced both collectively by cultural practices and meanings and individually by personal regulatory strategies. However, because the personal strategies themselves are also derived from and have to be always reinforced by the cultural practices and meanings, the theoretical pillar of this analysis lies in the collective-level processes. We discuss available evidence for these processes in some detail, followed by a brief review of evidence for the personal-level processes.

Collective-Level Processes

Cultural Affordance. We distinguish between two theoretically distinct processes by which each culture's practices and meanings shape emotion-related psychological tendencies. To begin with, depending on the models of the self that organize the respective cultural worlds, very different kinds of covert and overt acts are made much easier in which to engage. For example, Japanese cultural practices tend to encourage harmonious social relationship to a greater extent than do American cultural practices. The potential of cultural practices to produce such specific psychological processes and experiences has been called *cultural affordances* (Kitayama, 2002; Kitayama & Markus, 1999). Notice cultural affordances encourage or foster certain actions and responses, making them more likely than the rest. Yet, they never determine individual actions and responses. Thus, there can be many different ways of acting on any given affordance. Moreover, for a variety of reasons, individuals can, and sometimes do, decide to engage in behaviors that are counter to any given affordances of a culture.

Is it really true that whereas disengagement is constantly encouraged in American cultures, engagement is constantly encouraged in Japanese culture? Anecdotal evidence abounds (Weisz et al., 1984). For example, in making personal decisions, American practices emphasize personal choices, but Japanese practices often emphasize either adjustment to or consideration of others' preferences and expectations. In engaging in interpersonal discussions, American practices are far more likely than Asian ones to allow individuals to be assertive and self-expressive.

Similar differences can be observed in psychotherapies. For example, whereas American therapies often encourage the patient to take control of one's own life circumstances and to influence the latter, Asian therapies put a far greater emphasis on the effort toward changing the self in accordance with the seemingly problematic life circumstances so as to be able to live with them (Ozawa-de Silva, 2002). It would seem likely that participating and getting involved in these cross-culturally divergent practices are likely to give rise to correspondingly divergent psychological experiences.

To more systematically test this analysis, we may formulate the problem in two steps. First, there is an issue of relative prevalence of certain types of cultural practices, situational construals, and scripts. We may hypothesize that there are more and a greater variety of situations and scripts that are based on independent models of self in the United States than in Japan. Likewise, there may be more and a greater variety of situations and scripts that are based on interdependent models of self in Japan than in the United States.

Morling, Kitayama, and Miyamoto (2002) examined the prevalence of cultural affordances for independence and interdependence in the U.S. culture and Japanese culture. Drawing on earlier work by Weisz and colleagues (1984), the researchers proposed that whereas independent models of self emphasize acts of influencing (called by Weisz et al., 1984, *primary control*), interdependent models of self emphasize acts of adjusting (called by them, *secondary control*). To assess the relative prevalence of the two types of situations, they asked Americans and Japanese to describe actual social situations in which "they influenced or changed the surrounding people, events, or objects according to their own wishes" or in which "they adjusted themselves to surrounding people, objects and events." Examples of influence situations included the following: "I have a lot of hair and it is difficult to wash. So I cut it short so it is easy to wash now" (from Japan) and "I talked my sister out of dating a guy who I knew was a jerk" (from the United States). Examples of adjustment situations included the following: "When I am out shopping with my friend, and she says something is cute, even when I don't think it is, I agree with her" (from Japan) and "I had to adjust last school year when one of my roommates' boyfriends moved into our house (from the United States)."

The participants were to report how many days ago each situation happened. As predicted, the median latency of the most recent influencing situations was 2 days ago in the United States, but it was 5 days ago in Japan, whereas the median latency of the most recent adjusting situations was 1 day ago in Japan, but 7 days ago in the United States. This indicates that influencing situations are more common and memorable in the United States, but adjusting situations are more common and memorable in Japan.

The second issue concerns psychological consequences of participating in different sorts of situations and practices. Specifically, situations based on independent models of self may be expected to be more conducive to perceived disengagement and independence of the self. Moreover, although these situations are likely to be commonly available in all cultures, we may expect that they are scripted, defined, and eventually constructed differently so that situations that are recurrent in the United States are more "effective" than their Japanese counterparts in producing the sense of disengagement and independence. This prediction is based on the hypothesis that American culture carries greater affordances for disengagement than does Japanese culture. Likewise, situations based on interdependent models of self may be expected to be more conducive to perceived engagement and interdependence of the self. However, in this regard, Japanese situations may be predicted to be more "effective" than their American counterparts.

One major component of social disengagement and independence of the self is self-esteem—a close correlate of socially disengaging emotions (e.g., pride). Although there are numerous social situations that implicate self-esteem in all cultures, there is evidence that these situations are constructed in cross-culturally very diverse fashion so that some cultures afford self-esteem and consequent disengagement of the self to a greater extent than do some other cultures.

Kitayama and colleagues (Kitayama et al., 1997) asked both Japanese and American college students to describe as many situations as possible in which their own self-esteem went up or went down. Examples of the situations that were generated are given in Table 10.2. To determine whether these situations are constructed differently between the two cultures, the researchers randomly sampled 100 situations in each of the four conditions defined by the direction of self-esteem change (increase—called the *success situations* or decrease—called the *failure situations*) and the cultural origins of the situations (Japanese-made vs. American-made). The resulting set of 400 situations were prepared in both Japanese and

TABLE 10.2

Examples of Success and Failure Situations That Were Sampled From the United States. and Japan (Based on Kitayama, Markus, Matsumoto, & Norasakkunkit, 1997)

Success Situations
Japanese-made
When bowling, I made a strike.
When I could solve a math problem precisely and accurately on the first try.
American-made
Seeing a physical change in my body working out with weights.
When I made a hard decision and know it was the best I could do.
Failure Situations
Japanese-made
When I failed in a university entrance examination.
When I thought I would really like to help the people around me that I belong to, and instead I always cause them trouble.
American-made
Thoughts of "I'm not who I should be."
When a boyfriend/girlfriend lies to me or cheats on me.

English and presented, one at a time, to new groups of both Japanese and American students in their native languages. All Japanese were native Japanese speakers, but approximately half were students at a Japanese university and the rest were students who were temporarily studying at a U.S. university. The participants were asked to imagine that they were in each situation and to indicate how much increase or decrease of self-esteem they would experience in the situation (–4 = *self-esteem would decrease very much*, +4 = *self-esteem would increase very much*).

The tendency toward social disengagement and independence may be captured by a strong propensity toward self-esteem. To obtain an overall index of the propensity toward self-esteem, three steps were taken. First, we computed how much self-esteem decrease each participant predicted in failure situations. Second, we also computed how much self-esteem increase he or she predicted in success situations. Third, the mean predicted self-esteem decrease in the failure situations was subtracted from the mean predicted self-esteem increase in the success situations to yield an index of the relative tendency toward self-esteem increase (as opposed to decrease). Whereas positive scores indicate greater propensities toward self-esteem increase (as opposed to decrease), negative scores indicate opposite propensities. This overall index was computed separately for the Japanese-made situations and the American-made situations.

The relative self-esteem change score is displayed in Fig. 10.3. As can be seen, Americans showed a quite strong tendency toward self-esteem increase. Replicating numerous findings on self-enhancement in North America (Taylor & Brown, 1988), this evidence indicates that Americans are quite strongly inclined toward social disengagement. Conversely, Japanese showed an equally strong tendency toward self-esteem decrease. The Japanese effect is consistent with the suggestion that self-criticism is valued in Japanese culture. Self-criticism is likely to serve several mutually related functions. First, it may lead to relational self-improvement whereby individuals correct their shortcomings vis-à-vis socially shared standards for excellence, thereby fitting-in (Heine et al., 2001). Second, it may allow one to maintain interpersonal harmony and, third, it may help the person to receive sympathetic responses from others in a relationship (Kitayama & Uchida, 2003). In all cases, self-criticism is likely to encourage social engagement.

As predicted by the notion of divergent cultural affordances for self-esteem and social disengagement, the aforementioned culture-specific psychological effects were most pronounced when the participants were responding to the situations that had been sampled from their own cultural contexts. Thus, the American tendency toward self-esteem increase was much more pronounced when the Americans were responding to the American-made situations than when they were responding to the Japanese-made situations. Indeed, nearly 90% of Americans showed a self-enhancing tendency when they responded to American-made situations. Conversely, the Japanese tendency toward self-criticism was equally more pronounced when the Japanese were responding to the Japanese-made situations than

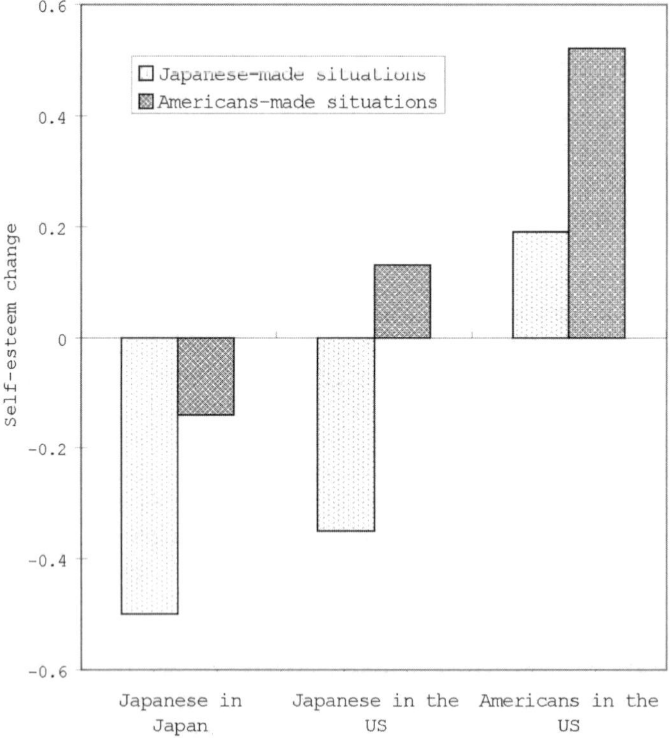

Fig 10.3. Self-esteem change reported by Japanese and American participants when they were exposed to self-esteem related situations that had been smapled from the two cultural contexts (drawn from the data reported in Kitayama, Markus, Matsumoto, & Norasakkunkit, 1997).

when they were responding to the American-made situations. Indeed, nearly 90% of Japanese in Japan showed a self-critical tendency when they responded to Japanese-made situations. Finally, the effect shown by the Japanese in the U.S. was an interesting composite of both the Japanese effect and the American effect. This finding may indicate that the psychological effects discussed here are potentially quite variable and malleable.

In sum, the evidence summarized here suggests that social disengagement and engagement are constantly afforded by mundane social situations. Strongest evidence for this possibility comes from cases where individuals are exposed to situations sampled from different cultures. In these circumstances, individuals are likely to show correspondingly different psychological characteristics. Thus, for example, although typically quite high in efficacy and self-esteem, Americans are likely to show a lowered esteem and efficacy when placed in interdependent, socially engaging social relations (Kitayama & Uchida, in press). Likewise, although usually low in efficacy and esteem, Japanese may show a quite high efficacy and esteem when placed in independent, socially disengaging social relations. The bottom line, then, is that cultural context is not psychologically inert. Subtly, but powerfully, cultural context can shape human behavior and experience. Cultural affordance as defined within our theoretical framework (Fig. 10.2) refers to this very capacity of cultural context.

Cultural Reinforcement. The second mechanism by which culture regulates emotion may be called cultural reinforcement. According to this mechanism, whereas some acts are praised, encouraged, and authenticated, some others are punished, discouraged, and disparaged. For example, social practices that give rise to a harmonious social relationship, say, interpersonally adjusting to others' demands or needs, are not only common, but also positively valued in Japan. But they are often strongly disparaged as de-individuating or ingratiating in the mainstream American culture (Markus & Kitayama, 1994). This process of positive and negative interpersonal and societal feedbacks is very similar to the behaviorist notions of conditioning and reinforcement. Although we do not wish to commit ourselves to the details of the behaviorist dogma, we still think it reasonable to use the term reinforcement to capture the culture-specific patterns of valuing and devaluing different sorts of covert and overt actions. These actions include, although by no means are they limited to, emotion-related actions and tendencies. Along with cultural affordance, cultural reinforcement powerfully regulates emotional responses and eventually shapes their repertoire.

Evidence for cultural reinforcement comes from studies that examine correlates of happiness and subjective well-being (Diener & Suh, 2000; Kitayama & Markus, 2000). From the hypothesis that disengagement (or engagement) is constantly reinforced in North America (or in Japan), it should follow that this behavioral characteristic would be closely associated with general happiness or subjective well-being.

Available evidence is consistent with the foregoing analysis. To begin with, Kitayama and colleagues (2000) have shown that the reported frequency of experiencing happiness is closely associated with the reported frequency of experiencing pride and other socially disengaging positive emotions in the United States, but it is closely associated instead with friendly feelings and other socially engaging positive emotions in Japan. This finding has since been replicated by Kitayama et al. (2002). Other studies have examined personality correlates of subjective well-being (which constitutes a cognitive correlate of happiness). Expanding on a pioneering study by Diener and Diener (1995), Kwan, Bond, and Singelis (1997) demonstrated that subjective well-being is best predicted by a trait measure of self-esteem (a correlate of socially disengaging emotions) for Americans. For Hong Kong Chinese, however, subjective well-being was equally well predicted by both trait self-esteem and a personality propensity toward social engagement (called *relationship harmony*).

A similar point has been made in a recent study by Uchida, Kitayama, Mesquita, and Reyes (2002; Study 2). In this study, the researchers administered scales designed to tap either independence and disengagement of the self (self-esteem) or interdependence and engagement of the self (perceived emotional support from close others). These measures were then used to predict the reported levels of happiness. As shown in Fig. 10.4, self-esteem was somewhat more powerful in predicting well-being for Americans than for Asians (i.e., Japanese and Filipinos). In contrast, emotional support was significantly more powerful in predicting happiness for Asians than for Americans (see also, e.g., Kitayama et al., 2002; Mesquita & Karasawa, 2002; Suh, Diener, Oishi, & Triandis, 1998).

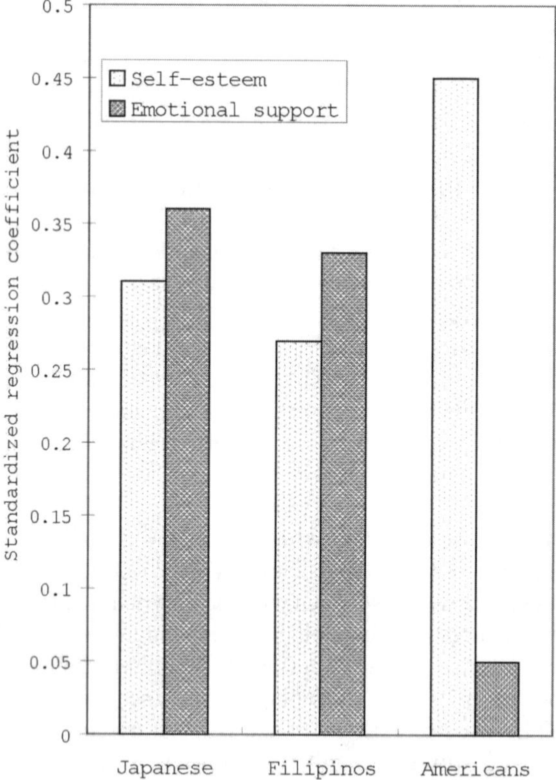

Fig 10.4. Standardized regression coefficients used to predict happiness as a function of self-esteem and emotional support from close others: The effect of self-esteem is greater for Americans than for Asians (Japanese and Filipinos combined); but the effect of emotional support is greater for Asians than for Americans (drawn from the data reported in Uchida, Kitayama, Mesquita, & Reyes, 2002).

Personal-Level Processes

By emphasizing the two collective processes of affordance and reinforcement, we do not wish to underplay the critical role of more psychological or more personalized processes that are implicated in emotion regulation. Specifically, once spontaneous emotional tendencies have been shaped and established as part of the self-system, the spontaneous emotions may become relatively oblivious to the expectations and rules of immediate sociocultural contexts. Although these immediate sociocultural contexts are also part of the general culture, they may sometimes diverge considerably from the cultural contexts in which the self has been socialized and his or her emotions have been nurtured and trained. As a consequence, there will likely arise many conflicts and rifts between spontaneous emotions of the self and the immediate sociocultural expectations and demands. In turn, these conflicts and rifts between the person and the situation are likely to encourage each individual to develop more personalized strategies in coping with them.

It is important to keep in mind that the ultimate origin of these personalized strategies lies in culture. Thus, these strategies are also sampled from the culture's resources and appropriated by each person for his or her own use. We thus hypothesize that individuals are likely to develop personalized strategies of regulating emotions such that either engagement or disengagement of the self are augmented in Japanese and American cultural contexts, respectively.

In a large interview study, Mesquita, Karasawa, Haire, and Izumi (2002) found support for this analysis. American and Japanese respondents, men and women, community and student samples, were asked to describe situations in which they had encountered an offense. The most frequent ways of coping in the American group were in fact consistent with an independent model of the self. A majority of Americans reported blaming the offender (69%)—a disengaging act. However, only a small minority of Japanese did so. Unlike strategies chosen by Americans, those preferred by Japanese were geared more toward adjustment, engagement, and interdependence. First, about half of the Japanese respondents, as opposed to only a small percentage of Americans, reported doing nothing. This nonaction, however, may be motivated by a concern for social harmony. Second, a quarter of the Japanese, as opposed to very few Americans, took responsibility for the offense. This may also serve the function of relationship maintenance. Finally, a quarter of the Japanese, as opposed to a much smaller percentage of Americans, responded to offense by seeking closeness to the offender, a behavior that precisely serves the maintenance or repair of relationships.

Future work should explore within culture variations in personal regulatory strategies. For example, even in the United States, where disengagement and independence of the self is generally highly valued, certain social contexts (entertainment of guests [as opposed to, e.g., business]) and social roles (women [as opposed to men]) require very different value priorities. For example, in a well-known study, Hochschild (1979) found that flight attendants in a major

American carrier strived for total agreeableness. They were trained to adopt several strategies to avoid anger, of which the first two had to do with their shifting of attention and their regulation of appraisal by using a strategy of, for example, focusing "on what the *other* person might be thinking and feeling: imagine a reason that excuses his or her behavior" (Hochschild, 1983, p. 113). Similar analyses have to be extended to a variety of different situations involving conflicts between spontaneous emotions fostered by culture at large and expectations associated with specific roles and social categories.

CONCLUSIONS

To sum up, in this chapter we have argued that emotions are regulated both at a cultural and collective level and at a personal and individual level. The collective regulation of emotion is effected by two functions that are inherent in practices and meanings of a culture—namely, affordance and reinforcement. That is to say, a network of practices and meanings that are prevalent in a given cultural context tend to make it easier to engage in certain emotional response tendencies while making it more difficult to engage in some others. Furthermore, they also tend to either positively or negatively sanction such emotional tendencies when they happen. In contrast, the personal regulation of emotion implies each person's more or less deliberate and effortful attempt to control and modify his or her own emotion-related actions. Notice that each person's specific strategies of emotion regulation are also likely to be constantly culturally afforded and positively sanctioned for them to be held in place within the person's psychological systems.

Drawing on this global theoretical framework, we examined cultural variation in emotion regulation by focusing specifically on Japan and the United States. In particular, we highlighted the dimension of social engagement and disengagement that permeates emotional experience. In independent cultural contexts (e.g., the United States), disengaging emotions provide the central theme for emotional experience. Conversely, in interdependent cultural contexts (e.g., Japan), engaging emotions provide the central organizing theme for emotional experience. Several lines of empirical work were reviewed to support different aspects of the proposed theoretical analysis.

Although our theoretical framework is quite promising and powerful enough to integrate a diverse array of empirical findings concerning cross-cultural differences of Japanese and Americans, several significant issues are left uninvestigated. Most important, the comparisons between Japanese and American samples should not be taken to indicate that cultural meaning systems are neatly divided by national boundaries. It should also not be assumed that cultures are internally homogenous. Furthermore, our work is focused mostly on Japan and the United States. More effort is required to examine regional variations within either

Asia or North America. Moreover, the same analysis needs to be extended to other areas and ethnic groups.

So far in the literature, cultural influence is often assumed to be mediated by subjective values and attitudes. According to this analysis, Japanese, for example, are assumed to endorse the values of interdependence. Moreover, the personal commitment to these values is believed to be causally responsible for the assortment of psychological consequences (Oyserman, Coon, & Kemmelmeier, 2002; Takano & Osaka, 1999). In contrast, the theoretical framework presented in this chapter emphasizes the pivotal role of collectively shared practices and meanings in mediating effects of cultural models of self on psychological processes. Our analysis indicates that the interface between culture and psychology is simultaneously much more dynamic (Chiu, Morris, Hong, & Menon, 2000) and tacit (Durkheim, 1953; Kitayama, 2002) than the existent cross-cultural literature on subjective values and beliefs suggests.

Further advance in our understanding of cultural variations in psychological processes will become possible by going beyond cross-cultural attitude and value surveys and by directly addressing the interface between culture and the self. This basic point applies not only to emotion, but also to all other areas of psychology including cognition (Kitayama, Duffy, Kawamura, & Larsen, in press; Nisbett et al., 2001), communication (Ambady, Koo, Lee, & Rosenthal, 1996; Ishii, Reyes, & Kitayama, 2003), and motivation (Heine et al., 2001; Iyengar & Lepper, 1999). We believe that further effort toward integrating the collective and the personal processes in all these areas of inquiry will be quite instrumental in furthering our understanding about the central role culture plays in the constitution of the psychological systems.

REFERENCES

Adams, G., & Markus, H. R. (2001). Culture as patterns: An alternative approach to the problem of reification. *Culture and Psychology, 7*, 283–296.

Ambady, N., Koo, J., Lee, F., & Rosenthal, R. (1996). More than words: Linguistic and nonlinguistic politeness in two cultures. *Journal of Personality and Social Psychology, 70*, 996–1011.

Benson, C. (2001). *The cultural psychology of self: Place, morality and art in human worlds.* New York: Routledge.

Bourdieu, P. (1972). *Outline of a theory of practice.* Cambridge, England: Cambridge University Press.

Bruner, J. (1990). *Acts of meaning.* Cambridge, MA: Harvard University Press.

Chiu, C., Morris, M. W., Hong, Y., & Menon, T. (2000). Motivated cultural cognition: The impact of implicit cultural theories on dispositional attribution varies as a function of need for closure. *Journal of Personality and Social Psychology, 78*, 247–259.

Cole, M. (1996). *Cultural psychology.* Cambridge, MA: Harvard University Press.

Darwin, C. (1965). *The expression of emotions in man and the animals.* Chicago: University of Chicago Press. (Original edition published 1872)

Damasio, A. R. (1994). *Descartes' error: Emotion, reason, and the human brain.* New York: Putnam.

Diener, E., & Diener, M. (1995). Cross cultural correlates of life satisfaction and self-esteem. *Journal of Personality and Social Psychology, 68*, 653–663.

Diener, E., Larsen, R. J., Levine, S., & Emmons, R. A. (1985). Intensity and frequency: Dimensions underlying positive and negative affect. *Journal of Personality and Social Psychology, 48*, 1253–1265.

Diener, E., & Suh, E. M. (2000). *Cultural and subjective well-being*, Cambridge, MA: MIT Press.

Durkheim, E. (1953). Individual representations and collective representations. In D. F. Pocock (Ed. And Trans.), *Sociology and philosophy* (pp. 1–38). New York: Free Press. (Reprinted from *Revue deMetaphysique, 6*, 274–302), 1898

Ekman, P. (1984). Expression and the nature of emotion. In K. Scherer & P. Ekman (Eds.), *Approaches to emotion* (pp. 319–343). Hillsdale, NJ: Lawrence Erlbaum Associates, Inc.

Fiske, A., Kitayama, S., Markus, H. R., & Nisbett, R. E. (1998). The cultural matrix of social psychology. In D. Gilbert, S. Fiske, & G. Lindzey (Eds.), *The handbook of social psychology* (4th ed., pp. 915–981). San Francisco: McGraw-Hill.

Frank, R. (1988). Passion within reason: *The strategic role of the emotions.* New York: Norton.

Frijda, N. H. (1986). *The emotions.* Cambridge, England: Cambridge University Press.

Frijda, N. H., & Mesquita, B. (1994). The social roles and functions of emotions. In S. Kitayama & H. R. Markus (Eds.), *Emotion and culture: Empirical studies of mutual influence* (pp. 51–88). Washington, DC: American Psychological Association.

Geertz, C. (1973). *Interpretation of culture.* New York: Basic.

Giddens, A. (1984). *The constitution of society.* Oxford, England: Polity.

Guisinger, S., & Blatt, S. J. (1994). Individuality and relatedness: Evolution of a fundamental dialect. *American Psychologist, 49*, 104–111.

Heine, S. J., Kitayama, S., Lehman, D. R., Takata, T., Ide, E., Leung, C., et al. (2001). Divergent consequences of success and failure in Japan and North America: An investigation of self-improving motivations and malleable selves. *Journal of Personality and Social Psychology, 81*, 559–615.

Heine, S. J., Lehman, D. R., Markus, H. R., & Kitayama, S. (1999). Is there a universal need for positive self-regard? *Psychological-Review, 106* (4), 766–794.

Hochschild, A. R. (1979). Emotion work, feeling rules, and social structure. *American Journal of Sociology, 85*, 551–575.

Ishii, K., Reyes, J. A., & Kitayama, S. (2003). Spontaneous attention to word content versus emotional tone: Differences among three cultures. *Psychological Science, 14*, 39–46.

Iyengar, S. S., & Lepper, M. R. (1999). Rethinking the value of choice: A cultural perspective on intrinsic motivation. *Journal of Personality and Social Psychology, 76*, 349–366.

Kitayama, S. (2002). Culture and basic psychological processes: Toward a system view of culture. *Psychological Bulletin, 128*, 189–196.

Kitayama, S., Duffy, S., Kawamura, T., & Larsen, J. T. (2003). A cultural look at New Look: Perceiving an object and its context in two cultures. *Psychological Science.*

Kitayama, S., & Markus, H. R. (1999). Yin and yang of the Japanese self: The cultural psychology of personality coherence. In D. Cervone & Y. Shoda (Eds.), *The coherence of personality: Social cognitive bases of personality consistency, variability, and organization* (pp. 242–302). New York: Guilford.

Kitayama, S., & Markus, H. R. (2000). The pursuit of happiness and the realization of sympathy: Cultural patterns of self, social relations, and well-being. In E. Diener & E. M. Suh (Eds.), *Cultural and subjective well-being* (pp. 113–161). Cambridge, MA: MIT Press.

Kitayama, S., Markus, H. R., & Kurokawa, M. (2000). Culture, emotion, and well-being: Good feelings in Japan and the United States. *Cognition and Emotion, 14*, 93–124.

Kitayama, S., Markus, H. R., & Matsumoto, H. (1995). Culture, self, and emotion: A cultural perspective on "self-conscious" emotions. In J. P. Tangney & K. W. Fisher (Eds.), *Self-conscious emotions: The psychology of shame, guilt, embarrassment, and pride* (pp. 439–464). New York: Guilford.

Kitayama, S., Markus, H. R., Matsumoto, H., & Norasakkunkit, V. (1997). Individual and collective processes in the construction of the self: Self-enhancement in the United States and self-criticism in Japan. *Journal of Personality and Social Psychology, 72*, 1245–1267.

Kitayama, S., Mesquita, B., & Karasawa, M. (2002). Emotional basis of independent and interdependent selves: Intensity of experiencing engaging and disengaging emotions in the US and Japan. Unpublished manuscript, University of Michigan, Ann Arbor.

Kitayama, S., Snibbe, A. C., Markus, H. R., & Suzuki, T. (In press). Is there any free choice? Self and dissonance in two cultures. *Psychological Science.*

Kitayama, S., & Uchida, Y. (in press). Explicit self-criticism and implicit self-regard: Evaluating self and friend in two cultures. *Journal of Experimental Social Psychology.*

Kwan, V. S. Y., Bond, M. H., & Singelis, T. M. (1997). Pancultural explanations for life satisfaction: Adding relationship harmony to self-esteem. *Journal of Personality and Social Psychology, 73*, 1038–1051.

Lutz, C. (1988). *Unnatural emotions: Everyday sentiments on a Micronesian atoll and their challenge to Western theory.* Chicago: University of Chicago Press.

Markus, H. R., & Kitayama, S. (1991). Culture and the self: Implications for cognition, emotion, and motivation. *Psychological Review, 98*, 224–253.

Markus, H. R., & Kitayama, S. (1994). A collective fear of the collective: Implications for selves and theories of selves. Personality and Social Psychology Bulletin, 20, 568–579.

Markus, H. R., Kitayama, S., & Heiman, R. (1996). Culture and "basic" psychological principles. In E. T. Higgins & A. W. Kruglanski (Eds.), *Social psychology: Handbook of basic principles* (pp. 857–913). New York: Guilford.

Markus, H. R., Mullally, P., & Kitayama, S. (1997). Selfways: Diversity in modes of cultural participation. In U. Neisser & D. Jopling (Eds.), *The conceptual self in context: Culture, experience, self-understanding* (pp. 13–61). Cambridge, England: Cambridge University Press.

Mesquita, B., & Ellsworth, P. (2001). The role of culture in appraisal. In K. R. Scherer & A. Schorr (Eds.), *Appraisal processes in emotion: Theory, methods, research* (pp. 233–248). New York: Oxford University Press.

Mesquita, B., & Karasawa, M. (2002). Different emotional lives. *Cognition and Emotion, 16*, 127–141.

Mesquita, B., Karasawa, M., Haire, A., & Izumi, S. (2002). The emotion process as a function of cultural models: A comparison between American, Mexican, and Japanese cultures. Manuscript in preparation.

Miller, J. G. (1999). Cultural psychology: Implications for basic psychological theory. *Psychological Science, 10*, 85–91.

Morling, B. A., Kitayama, S., & Miyamoto, Y. (2002). Cultural practices emphasize influence in the U. S. and adjustment in Japan. *Personality and Social Psychology Bulletin, 28*. 311–328.

Nassbaum, M. C. (2001). *Upheavals of thought: The intelligence of emotions.* Chicago: University of Chicago Press.

Nisbett, R. E., Peng, K., Choi, I., & Norenzayan, A. (2001). Culture and systems of thought: Holistic vs. analytic cognition. *Psychological Review, 108*, 291–310.

Oatley, K. (1992). *Best laid schemes: The psychology of emotions.* Cambridge, England: Cambridge University Press.

Oyserman, D., Coon, H. M, & Kemmelmeier, M. (2002). Rethinking individualism and collectivism: Evaluation of theoretical assumptions and meta–analyses. *Psychological Bulletin, 128*, 3–72.

Ozawa-de Silva, C. (2002). Beyond the body/mind: Japanese contemporary thinkers on alternate sociologies of the body. *Body and Society, 8*, 21–38.

Rothbaum, F., Pott, M., Azuma, H., Miyake, K., & Weisz, J. (2000). The development of close relationships in Japan and the US: Pathways of symbiotic harmony and generative tension. *Child Development, 71*, 1121–1142.

Salovey, P., & Mayer, J. D. (1990). Emotional intelligence: Imagination, Cognition, & Personality, 9, 185–211.

Scherer, K. R., & Wallbott, H. G. (1994). Evidence for universality and cultural variation of differential emotion response patterning. *Journal of Personality and Social Psychology, 66*, 310–328.

Shore, B. (1996). *Culture in mind: Cognition, culture and the problem of meaning.* New York: Oxford University Press.

Shweder, R. A., & Bourne, L. (1984). Does the concept of the person vary cross-culturally? In R. A. Shweder & R. A. LeVine (Eds.), *Culture theory: Essays on mind, self, and emotion* (pp. 158–199). New York: Cambridge University Press.

Shweder, R. A., & Sullivan, M. (1993). Cultural psychology: Who needs it? *Annual Review of Psychology, 44*, 497–523.

Suh, E., Diener, E., Oishi, S., & Triandis, H. C. (1998). The shifting basis of life satisfaction judgments across cultures: Emotions versus norms. *Journal of Personality and Social Psychology, 74*, 482–493.

Takano, Y., & Osaka, E. (1999). An unsupported common view: Comparing Japan and the U. S. on individualism/collectivism. *Asian Journal of Social Psychology, 2*, 311–341.

Taylor, C. (1989). *Sources of the self: The making of modern identity.* Cambridge, MA: Harvard University Press.

Taylor, S. E., & Brown, J. D. (1988). Illusion and well-being: A social psychological perspective on mental health. *Psychological Bulletin, 103*, 193–210.

Tomasello, M. (1999). *The cultural origins of human cognition.* Cambridge, MA: Harvard University Press.

Triandis, H. C. (1989). The self and social behavior in differing cultural contexts. *Psychological Review, 96*, 506–520.

Triandis, H. C. (1990). Cross-cultural studies of individualism and collectivism. In J. Berman (Ed.), *Nebraska Symposium on Motivation, 1989* (pp. 41–133). Lincoln: University of Nebraska Press.

Triandis, H. C. (1995). *Individualism and collectivism.* Boulder, CO: Westview.

Uchida, Y., Kitayama, S., Mesquita, B., & Reyes, J. A. (2002). *Cultural variation in happiness: Subjective judgment versus inter-subjective state.* Manuscript submitted for publication.

Weisz, J. R., Rothbaum, F. M., & Blackburn, T. C. (1984). Standing out and standing in: The psychology of control in America and Japan. American Psychologist, 39, 955–969.

IV

Individual Differences and the Development of Emotion Regulation

11

Emotion-Related Regulation: Its Conceptualization, Relations to Social Functioning, and Socialization

Nancy Eisenberg, Tracy L. Spinrad,
and Cynthia L. Smith
Arizona State University

The purpose of this chapter was threefold: (a) to consider important conceptual distinctions in regard to different types of emotion-related regulation and control, (b) to selectively review empirical research on the role of emotion-related regulation in children's socioemotional development and adjustment, and (c) to examine theory and research on the role of parents' emotion-related socialization in children's emotionality, regulation, and social functioning. We begin with a discussion of important conceptual distinctions, including between effortful and reactive control. Next, research on relations between regulation and control, and children's social functioning and adjustment, is reviewed; findings indicate that children with poor emotion-related regulation display more negative emotions, more behavior problems, and less social competence. Finally, research on the socialization of emotion and related behavior is discussed. In general, sensitive, supportive parenting behaviors, parental expression of positive (rather than negative) emotion, and the discussion of emotion have been associated with the development of regulation and well-regulated social behavior.

In the past decade, the topic of emotion-related regulation has been a topic of considerable interest to developmental scientists. This is partly due to the resurgence of interest in emotion among psychologists in the past two decades, and partly due to the purported role of emotion regulation in children's socioemotional development and adjustment. In this chapter, we first discuss conceptualizations of emotion-related regulation or control and their predicted relations with social competence and adjustment. Next, we selectively review research on the relation between emotion-related regulation or control and social functioning during infancy and toddlerhood, as well as childhood. Finally, the potential role of parental socialization in the development of regulation and regulated behavior (e.g., social competence and adjustment) is discussed, and illustrative research is reviewed. Throughout, research from the laboratories in which the authors have worked is emphasized, although other related work sometimes is reviewed.

CONCEPTUALIZATION OF EMOTION-RELATED REGULATION

In the last decade, a variety of definitions of emotion regulation have been proposed and these differ in their focus on the mechanisms involved, the domains of functioning affected, the timing of the regulatory activities, and the role of other people in the process. Given the complexity of the phenomena of interest and changes with regulation with age, it is not surprising that investigators do not always focus on the same variables. For example, Kopp and Neufeld (2003) suggested that "emotion regulation during the early years is a developmental process that represents the deployment of intrinsic and extrinsic processes—at whatever maturity level the young child is at—to (1) manage arousal states for effective biological and social adaptations, and (2) achieve individual goals" (p. 360). Thompson (1994) defined emotion regulation as the "extrinsic and intrinsic processes responsible for monitoring, evaluating, and modifying emotional reactions, especially their intensive and temporal features, to achieve one's goals" (pp. 27–28). Building on the work of Ross Thompson (1994), Pamela Cole and colleagues (Campos, Mumme, Kermoian, & Campos, 1994; Cole, Michel, & Teti, 1994), and others, we define *emotion-related regulation* rather broadly, as the process of initiating, avoiding, inhibiting, maintaining, or modulating the occurrence, form, intensity, or duration of internal feeling states, emotion-related physiological processes, emotion-related goals, and the behavioral concomitants of emotion, generally in the service of accomplishing one's goals.

We have found a variety of distinctions to be helpful when thinking about the nature of emotion-related regulation. Consistent with the thinking of Campos,

Mumme, Kermoian, and Campos (1994), it has proved useful to differentiate between the regulation of internal states and processes and the regulation of overt behaviors associated with emotion. Work with infants has focused primarily on the regulation of emotional arousal, whereas work with older children focuses as much or more on the regulation of behavior associated with the experience of emotion. The regulation of internal feeling and physiological states is believed to be accomplished with mechanisms such as orienting, self-comforting, avoidance, and communicative behaviors in infancy and the toddler years (e.g., Kopp & Neufeld, in press; Rothbart, Ziaie, & O'Boyle, 1992; Stifter & Braungart, 1995); voluntary control of attentional processes such as the abilities to shift and focus attention as needed are deemed more important with age (Derryberry & Rothbart, 1988; Windle & Lerner, 1986). Moreover, cognitive strategies such as cognitive distraction—thinking of something else to alleviate emotional arousal or distress—and positive cognitive restructuring—reframing the situation to highlight positive aspects of it, are believed to be important mechanisms for regulating emotion in childhood and adulthood (Lazarus & Folkman, 1984; Sandler, Tein, & West, 1994). In addition, the modification of one's goals or their relative valuation (e.g., by devaluing the importance of sports if one is a poor athlete) is another way to alter or prevent the experience of emotion (Heckhausen & Schulz, 1995; Skinner; 1999).

The regulation of the behavioral concomitants of emotions includes control or modulation of facial and gestural reactions and other overt behaviors or action patterns that stem from, or are associated with, internal emotion-related psychological or physiological states and goals (Eisenberg, Fabes, Guthrie, & Reiser, 2000). Such regulation often is assessed with measures of inhibitory or activational control, that is, the abilities to voluntarily inhibit or activate behavior as required by the situation (Derryberry & Rothbart, 1997; Kochanska, Murray, & Harlan, 2000; Rothbart & Bates, 1998).

In our view, emotion-related regulation is a process that can occur prior, during, or after the elicitation of emotion. Usually, investigators have studied regulation of emotion while it is being elicited or after it has occurred. Regulation prior to its elicitation has been called proactive coping or antecedent emotion regulation (Aspinwall & Taylor, 1997; Gross, 1999; Thompson, 1994). Unfortunately, little is known about how children actively avoid emotion-eliciting events or use attentional and cognitive strategies to inhibit, initial, or modulate emotional reactions prior to their occurrence.

In thinking about the relation of emotion-related regulation to developmental outcomes, it is especially important to differentiate between regulation and control, with the latter defined as inhibition or restraint. Successful regulation likely involves optimal levels of control, as well other capacities such as the ability to initiate action as needed. We, like Block and Block (1980) and Cole et al. (1994), believe that well-regulated individuals are not overly controlled or undercontrolled; they have the capacity to respond to the varying demands of experience with a range of responses that are socially acceptable and sufficiently flexible to allow for spontaneity in behavior as well as the inhibition of spontaneous reactions as required in the given context.

The notion of voluntary control is very similar to Rothbart's concept of effortful control, "the ability to inhibit a dominant response to perform a subdominant response" (Rothbart & Bates, 1998, p. 137). Effortful control is reflected in effortful attentional regulation—the abilities to voluntarily focus or shift attention as needed in a given situation—as well as in inhibitory and activational control—or the abilities to effortfully inhibit behavior or activate behavior as needed, even if the person doesn't really want to do it. Effortful control is believed to involve executive functioning in the prefrontal cortex (Mirsky, 1996) and associated areas—including the anterior cingulate gyrus—which appears to be directly related to awareness of one's planned behavior, correction of errors, and the control of thoughts and feelings (Posner & DiGirolamo, 2000; Posner & Rothbart, 1998).

In contrast to effortful regulation, there are aspects of control, or the lack thereof, that appear to be relatively involuntary, such as impulsivity and interested approach or rigidity and overcontrol as in children who are timid, constrained, and lack flexibility in novel or stressful situations (behaviorally inhibited children; Kagan, 1998; see also Derryberry and Rothbart, 1997; Nigg, 2000). Jeffrey Gray (Pickering & Gray, 1999) and others have argued that overly inhibited and impulsive (uncontrolled) behaviors are associated with subcortical systems such as Gray's (1975, 1987) Behavioral Inhibition System (BIS), which is activated in situations involving novelty and stimuli signaling punishment or frustrative nonreward, and the Behavioral Activation System or BAS, which involves sensitivity to cues of reward and cessation of punishment.

THE RELATION OF EMOTION-RELATED REGULATION TO QUALITY OF SOCIAL FUNCTIONING

It is logical to expect effortful control (or regulation) and less voluntary types of control to relate differently to children's social competence, adjustment, and resiliency. Such a notion is evident in current work in personality as well as in developmental psychology.

Theoretical Framework

Based on the ideas of Block and Block (1980), Pulkkinen (1982), and other early work on regulation-related constructs, Eisenberg and Fabes (1992) argued that individual differences in emotionality (especially negative emotionality; Eisenberg, Fabes, et al., 2000) and regulation jointly predict the quality of children's social functioning. They suggested that children who are high in negative emotionality and unable to modulate their arousal are prone to undercontrolled interactions with others and to behave in socially unconstructive ways. In contrast, children who can optimally and voluntarily modulate their level of emotional arousal and behavior through regulatory processes (e.g., the abilities to effortfully shift and focus attention and the abilities to inhibit or activate behavior when so required) are expected to behave in more socially constructive ways. Thus, they proposed that there are often additive and sometimes multiplicative effects of emotionality and regulation for predicting quality of people's social functioning.

Reminiscent of the work of Block and Block (1980), Eisenberg and colleagues (Eisenberg & Fabes, 1992; Eisenberg, Fabes, Guthrie, & Reiser, 2000) differentiated among three styles of regulation or control—highly inhibited, undercontrolled, and optimally regulated—and developed a heuristic model of how these types of dispositional control and emotionality jointly predict social behavior and adjustment. Highly inhibited individuals are viewed as high in involuntary inhibition of behavior (often labeled behavioral inhibition in the temperament literature, e.g., inhibition in novel and stressful contexts, rigidity of behavior; Derryberry & Rothbart, 1997), low to average in voluntary inhibitory control, low in activation control, and low to moderate in attentional regulation. Highly inhibited individuals are hypothesized to be overcontrolled behaviorally, but their inhibition is not due to voluntary inhibition of behavior. As already noted, behaviorally inhibited children fall into this group, and are believed to be prone to negative emotions such as fear and anxiety (as well as to involuntary inhibition). Some individuals may be overcontrolled but not especially prone to negative emotionality; they are predicted to be prone to internalizing problems such as social withdrawal but not anxiety or fearfulness.

Undercontrolled individuals are hypothesized to be low in effortful and involuntary modes of control, including inhibitory, attentional, and activational control, and high in BAS impulsive tendencies. Undercontrolled individuals are expected to be prone to externalizing problem behaviors and to be low in social competence.

Finally, *optimally regulated* individuals are hypothesized to be relatively high in various modes of effortful regulation, including inhibitory, activational, and attention control. However, because effortful modes of control can be used as appropriate, such children are expected to be flexible in their use of regulatory behavior. Moreover, they are viewed as moderate in the use of involuntary modes of control and approach, so they are not overly impulsive or inhibited. Thus, optimally regulated individuals are hypothesized to be well-adjusted, socially competent, and resilient.

The three styles of control bear a substantial resemblance to personality types recently found by several groups of researchers in different countries (Asendorpf & van Aken, 1999; Hart, Hofmann, Edelstein, & Keller, 1997; Newman, Caspi, Moffitt, & Silva. 1997; Robins, John, Caspi, Moffitt, & Stouthamer–Loeber, 1996). Moreover, the findings in these studies regarding the relations of children's over-controlled, under-controlled, and optimally controlled styles with their social functioning are consistent with Eisenberg and Fabes's hypotheses (see

Eisenberg, Fabes, et al., 2000). However, in these studies, the items used to classify children into the three groups included ratings of a wide variety of social behaviors, as well as some items pertaining to regulation and emotionality. Thus, these investigators did not really examine the relations of individual differences in regulation and emotionality to social functioning and adjustment.

Empirical Relations of Emotion-Related Regulation and Emotionality to Social Functioning

Investigators tend to study emotion-related regulation in either infants and toddlers or older children. Some of the measures of regulation differ across age groups, as might be expected given age-related differences in children's cognitive and behavioral capacities.

Infants and Toddlers

The importance of emotionality and regulation in infancy and toddlerhood is considered a pivotal achievement in socioemotional development (Thompson, 1994). In general, researchers studying infants and toddlers have focused on their emotionality and behavioral strategies for the regulation of emotion, as well as the relations of both to social functioning. Some, albeit a limited amount, of this work pertains to the development of effortful versus reactive and involuntary control and their relations to quality of social functioning.

Behavioral Strategies. A common approach to studying emotion regulation in infancy involves examining the actions or behavioral strategies that infants and toddlers use to reduce or modulate emotional responding, including gaze aversion, orienting behaviors, self-comforting, distraction, and social referencing. In particular, a good deal of work has been done on the development of these strategies over the course of infancy and toddlerhood. Kopp (1989) suggested that as infants mature, significant improvements in the ability to regulate emotions occur as a result of changes in cognitive and language capacities. In fact, there is evidence that children gain more sophisticated strategies to deal with their emotions over time (Grolnick, Bridges, & Connell, 1996; Mangelsdorf, Shapiro, & Marzolf, 1995; Parritz, 1996; Rothbart et al., 1992). For example, Mangelsdorf and colleagues (1995) found that toddlers use more self-distraction (redirecting attention) and self-soothing strategies than do younger infants and are more likely to attempt to direct potentially stressful interactions than are younger infants.

Moreover, researchers frequently have focused on the effectiveness of infants' and toddlers' regulatory strategies in reducing negative emotions (Calkins & Johnson, 1998; Grolnick et al., 1996; Stifter & Braungart, 1995). It is likely that some behaviors serve a regulatory function (i.e., reduce negative affect) whereas other strategies are linked with increased negative arousal. Stifter and Braungart (1995) examined the efficacy of certain regulatory behaviors in response to frustrating tasks at 5 and 10 months of age. They found that self-comforting behaviors were linked to the regulation of negative arousal at both ages; orienting behaviors also seemed to be helpful for reducing arousal during periods of low negative reactivity when infants were 10 months of age. On the other hand, avoidance and communicative behaviors were observed when infants exhibited increases in negative reactivity. These findings suggest that some of the behaviors thought to regulate distress are successful in that function whereas others may not be.

Another distinction that is useful when evaluating the effectiveness of regulatory strategies is the distinction among various emotions. Infants' behavioral strategies in response to anger, for example, may operate differently than their responses to fear. Buss and Goldsmith (1998) found some regulatory behaviors (i.e., distraction, approach) to be effective in regulating anger but not fear. Similarly, Diener and Mangelsdorf (1999) found that avoidance appeared to be an effective strategy for minimizing fear but not anger, and tension release (high intensity motor behavior) seemed to be successful in reducing anger but not fear. The results of these studies indicate that the specific emotion elicited is a significant consideration in determining the adaptiveness of certain behavioral strategies.

Researchers have been interested in understanding not only the effectiveness of behavioral strategies, but also the relation of emotionality and regulatory strategies to infants' and young children's social functioning. Some investigators have hypothesized that individuals who are low in negative emotionality or are able to regulate their emotions are well adjusted and relatively high in socially appropriate behavior. On the other hand, individuals who are prone to negative emotion or who are low in regulatory capacities are expected to be at risk for developing behavioral problems and be relatively low in social competence (e.g., Eisenberg & Fabes, 1992).

To test predictions of this sort, Stifter, Spinrad, and Braungart–Rieker (1999) examined the relations of infants' early emotionality and regulation to a precursor of children's problem behavior—defiant noncompliance. Because infants' responses to a request to comply involve behavioral control and may include negative emotion, it was expected that infants' early use of regulation strategies would predict their later ability to control their behavior. Consistent with expectations, infants who exhibited low levels of regulation (i.e., fewer behavioral strategies in response to challenging situations) were more noncompliant as toddlers. Moreover, there were several interactions between regulation and negative reactivity in predicting later noncompliance. For example, for infants who exhibited low levels of regulation, there was a positive relation between negative emotionality and defiance (i.e., refusal accompanied by negative affect). In addition, when infants were low in their levels of negative reactivity, they tended to be higher in passive noncompliance (ignoring), but only for children who exhibited low levels of regulation. These results suggest that the development of early regulatory skills is an important antecedent to the development of self-control in other contexts.

It is important to consider, however, the role of parental influences in the association between regulation and compliance. Although the aforementioned associations were concurrent, Braungart–Rieker, Garwood, and Stifter (1997) demonstrated that toddlers rated by their mothers as higher in negative reactivity were less compliant, but this finding was mediated by mothers' control. Specifically, toddlers who were rated as more negative by their mothers received greater maternal control during compliance tasks (e.g., mothers' statements such as, "don't touch that," spoken in a negative or neutral tone, or physically directing the child) and high levels of maternal control were linked with higher levels of toddlers' noncompliance. (We return to the issue of socialization shortly).

Emotionality and regulation in infancy and toddlerhood also have been linked to problem behaviors. There is a good deal of consensus that infants who exhibit high levels of negative affect in infancy and toddlerhood are at risk for the development of behavior problems (Bates, Maslin, & Fankel, 1985; Shaw, Keenan, Vondra, Delliquadri, & Giovannelli, 1997). In one recent investigation, for example, infants' affective responses to their mothers' still-face interaction predicted internalizing and externalizing behaviors at 18 months (Moore, Cohn, & Campbell, 2001). Moreover, a relation between emotion dysregulation and problem behaviors has been found. Calkins and Dedmon (2000; see also Calkins & Howse, this volume), for example, examined the differences between a group of 2-year-olds who were at risk for problem behaviors (a *t*-score of greater than 60 on the Child Behavior Checklist externalizing problems scale) and a group of toddlers who were at low risk (a *t*-score of less than 50). High-risk toddlers engaged in more dysregulated behavior (which included negative affect, venting, distraction, and low attention to challenging tasks) than did low-risk children. Findings such as these indicate that negative emotionality and specific behavioral strategies for regulating emotions are associated with behavior problems in very young children.

Another body of research concerns the associations between toddlers' behavioral strategies to regulate emotions and their social relationships. Specifically, behavioral strategies have been associated with attachment quality (Braungart & Stifter, 1991) and the quality of toddlers' play behaviors (Calkins, Gill, Johnson, & Smith, 1999). For example, Calkins et al. (1999) found that toddlers' negative emotionality (distress during a frustration task) was positively related to conflict with peers in a laboratory setting; moreover, toddlers who were both distressed and engaged in low levels of regulation (exhibited fewer total behavioral strategies, such as distraction or orienting toward their mother) were especially prone to conflict with peers.

To date, research with infants and toddlers illustrates the importance of studying individual differences in emotionality and the effectiveness of emotion-related regulation strategies, as well as their relations to social behavior. However, given current distinctions between effortful and reactive control and predictions regarding their differential relations to social behavior, it is worthwhile to compare findings for the two types of control. Unfortunately, one often does not know if the various measures used actually assess infants' effortful or involuntary control. Most likely, some tap both effortful and involuntary control, or tap effortful control for some individuals or in some situations and involuntary control for other people or in other contexts. We now consider the limited relevant research.

Effortful and Involuntary Control. As we discussed previously, we believe the distinction between effortful and reactive forms of control is key for understanding control and regulatory processes and their differing roles in socioemotional development. However, the majority of relevant studies has involved school children rather than young children (Eisenberg, Fabes, et al., 2000, Eisenberg, Cumberland, et al., 2001).

It is believed that effortful control begins to emerge in the 1st year of life and continues to develop and become more voluntary across the preschool years (Posner & Rothbart, 1998; Rothbart & Bates, 1998). For example, between 7 1/2 and 12 months of age, infants are able to resolve conflicts between reaching and the line of sight to retrieve an object (Diamond, 1990). This skill likely reflects both executive attention and inhibitory control; however, it is still a very immature form of executive control. Executive attention appears to become more developed by 18 months of age and undergoes considerable further refinement in the 3rd year of life (Posner & Rothbart, 1998). Moreover, there is evidence that effortful behavioral control (i.e., inhibitory control) improves considerably between 22 and 33 months (Kochanska et al., 2000; Reed, Pien, & Rothbart, 1984).

Attentional regulation is a key component of effortful control in the early years of life (Rothbart & Bates, 1998). Researchers have found that high levels of attentional control have been associated with lower distress in infancy, although they have used a variety of methods to assess attention. For example, 4-month-old infants who demonstrated high levels of refocusing attention away from one location to another were less distressed in laboratory situations (Rothbart et al, 1992). In addition, Matheny, Riese, and Wilson (1985) demonstrated that infants' focused attention to objects was concurrently related to better regulated negative affect and more positive affect at 9 months. In another investigation, children who were capable of longer focused attention during block play exhibited less discomfort and fewer anger reactions in response to aversive stimuli (Kochanska, Coy, Tjebkes, & Husarek, 1998). Although it is not clear how much of early attentional control is effortful, it is likely that part of the capacities assessed in these studies did tap early effortful processes.

Attentional control also has been linked with indexes of socially appropriate behaviors. For example, Kochanska et al. (1998) found that focused attention at 8 to 10 months was modestly associated with a higher rate of committed compliance during a clean-up period several months later. In addition, infants who were higher in focused attention were more restrained in response to maternal prohibitions. Attentional control in infancy also has been linked with long-term regulation. In a recent investigation, for example, toddlers' use of effective attentional strategies to cope with maternal separation (e.g., distraction) predicted the use of effective delay-of-gratification strategies at age 5 (Sethi, Mischel, Aber, Shoda, & Rodriguez, 2000).

As hypothesized by Eisenberg and Fabes (1992; Eisenberg, Fabes, et al., 2000), interactions between attentional regulation and emotionality have been found when predicting quality of social functioning. Belsky, Friedman, and Hsieh (2001) found that observed attentional persistence moderated the relation of negative emotionality to mothers' ratings of social competence. Specifically, high levels of negative emotionality at 15 months predicted lower social competence at age 3, but only for toddlers classified as low in attentional persistence.

As already noted, the abilities to inhibit or activate behavior as needed, like attentional regulation, are components of effortful regulation. Kochanska and colleagues conducted a line of research examining the relation of behavioral (inhibitory) control to children's social competence. In a number of studies, toddlers' behavioral control has been associated with better regulation of emotions (Kochanska et al., 1998; Kochanska et al., 2000), committed compliance (Kochanska, Coy, & Murray, 2001), and moral internalization (e.g., internalization of prohibitions without surveillance; Kochanska, Murray, Jacques, Koenig, & Vandegeest, 1996; Kochanska, Tjebas, & Forman, 1988). For instance, in one recent study, effortful control correlated positively with committed compliance in contexts in which children were requested to suppress a pleasant behavior ("don't" contexts) at 14, 22, 33, and 45 months of age (Kochanska et al., 2001).

In terms of involuntary regulation, the majority of work with infants and toddlers has focused on the development of behavioral inhibition and temperamental reactivity to novelty stressful stimuli. Kagan and colleagues have found that high reactivity (frequent and vigorous limb activity and distress to stimulation) at 4 months of age predicted fearfulness at 14 and 21 months of age (Kagan, 1998). Such reactivity generally is linked to behavioral inhibition, which we believe reflects reactive overcontrol. Researchers have demonstrated considerable stability in behavioral inhibition over time (Kagan, Reznick, & Snidman, 1988).

It is becoming clear that behavioral inhibition also is associated with children's social competence. Specifically, behaviorally inhibited toddlers are at risk for anxiety disorders. These children have been found to be socially withdrawn, fearful, and clingy (Kagan, 1989; Kagan, Reznick, & Snidman, 1987; Kagen et al. ,1988; Kagan, Snidman, & Arcus, 1998) and tend to develop internalizing problems over time (Biederman et al., 1990; Kagan, Snidman, Zentner, & Peterson, 1999). However, children's fearfulness also has been identified as a positive contributor to the development of children's compliance (Kochanska & Aksan, 1995; Kochanska et al., 2001) and maternal reports of conscience (i.e., reactions to wrongdoing that includes guilt, apology, and concern; Kochanska, 1995; Kochanska, DeVet,

Golman, Murray, & Putnam, 1994), particularly when mothers used reasoning in their socialization (Kochanska, 1993). Perhaps positive parenting moderates some of the potentially negative effects of fearfulness on development.

Preschoolers and School-Aged Children

The majority of research in our laboratory has been with children ages 4 or older. In this work, we have been able to (a) examine relations of effortful regulation and impulsivity (and emotionality) to quality of social functioning, concurrently and over time; and (b) test hypotheses regarding the differential relations of effortful and less voluntary aspects of control to children's social functioning. We have examined both adjustment and social competence as outcomes, with the latter including variables such as socially appropriate behavior, popularity, prosocial behavior, and sympathy. Due to space limitations, we summarize the general pattern of findings.

Relations of Effortful Regulation to Adjustment and Social Competence. We, like an increasing number of other investigators (e.g., Gilliom, Shaw, Beck, Schonberg, & Lukon, 2002; Kochanska, Murray, & Cox, 1997; Kochanska et al., 1996; Olson, Schilling, & Bates, 1999; Rothbart, Ahadi, & Hershey, 1994; for reviews, see Eisenberg, Fabes et al., 2000; Rothbart & Bates, 1998), have obtained clear evidence for the relation of effortful control with positive developmental outcomes for children. For example, we have found that teachers' or parents' reports of effortful attentional control relate positively with preschoolers' constructive rather than nonconstructive responding to real-life negative emotion in preschool or kindergarten (e.g., the use of nonabuse language to deal with anger with peers; Eisenberg, Fabes, Nyman, Bernzweig, and Pinuelas, 1994), popularity with peers, and adult-reported socially appropriate behavior (Eisenberg et al., 1993). It also related to sympathy and social competence 2 years later (Eisenberg, Fabes, Murphy, et al., 1996; Eisenberg, Fabes, Murphy, Maszk, et al., 1995; Eisenberg, Fabes, et al., 1997). In other samples of school-aged children, attentional control also has been linked to low levels of externalizing problems (Eisenberg, Fabes, Guthrie, et al., 1996; Eisenberg, Guthrie, et al., 2000), prosocial behavior (Eisenberg, Fabes, Karbon, et al., 1996) and social competence (socially appropriate behavior and popularity; Eisenberg, Fabes, Shepard, et al., 1997; Eisenberg, Fabes et al., 2000). Similarly, a measure of persistence on a puzzle task rather than cheating when working toward a reward predicted social competence and low problem behaviors, although more for younger than middle elementary school children (Eisenberg, Fabes, Guthrie, et al., 1996; Eisenberg, Fabes, et al., 2000; Eisenberg, Guthrie, et al., 1995). This behavioral measure may have tapped both effortful control and involuntary approach tendencies (i.e., BAS reward-related approach).

Associations also have been obtained across time. For example, Eisenberg, Guthrie, et al. (2000) found that attentional control predicted low externalizing problems across 2 years, even when controlling for externalizing problems 2 years prior (in a structural equation model [SEM]). Similarly, attentional control positively predicted social competence over 2 years and the path from earlier social competence to later social competence was unnecessary in the SEM model (indicating that controlling it would not change the findings; Eisenberg, Fabes, et al., 2000). The paths from attentional control to popularity and socially appropriate behavior were mediated by resiliency—a point that we return to shortly.

In our earliest longitudinal study, we combined effortful attentional control with inhibitory control and low impulsivity and examined the relation of this composite measure of regulation and control to externalizing problems (as reported by parents) and social competence (as reported by teachers and sometimes assessed with a measure in which children acted out their responses in conflict situations) over a 4-year period in elementary school. Although not all relations were significant, in general this composite was positively related to sympathy (Eisenberg, Fabes, Murphy et al, 1996; Eisenberg, Fabes, Shepard, et al., 1998; Murphy, Eisenberg, Fabes, Shepard, & Guthrie 1999), low externalizing problems, and high social competence concurrently and 2 and 4 years later (Eisenberg, Fabes, Shepard, et al., 1997; Murphy, Shepard, Eisenberg, & Fabes, 2001). In addition, in another sample, a measure of behavioral overcontrol versus undercontrol, based on items from the Block and Block Q-sort (1980), was related to socially appropriate behavior and low levels of externalizing problems over 2 years in early elementary school in another sample (Eisenberg, Fabes, et al., 2000; Eisenberg, Guthrie, et al., 1997, 2000). This measure of control likely reflected a combination of effortful control and involuntary control versus involuntary undercontrol.

Differential Relations of Effortful Control and Impulsivity to Quality of Social Functioning. In recent studies, we have examined the relations of measures of effortful control and impulsivity (with the latter viewed as an index of less voluntary approach [BAS] and low BIS tendencies; Pickering & Gray, 1999) with children's social functioning and resiliency. Based on our thinking about styles of regulation and control, we predicted that involuntary low control (i.e., impulsivity or even low levels of behavioral inhibition), like low effortful control, would predict externalizing problems and problems in regard to social competence. In contrast, internalizing problem behaviors (e.g., social withdrawal, anxiety and depression) were expected to relate to low attentional control, low to average inhibitory control, and high levels of behavioral inhibition and low impulsivity.

Initial support has been obtained for these predictions in our laboratory. Eisenberg, Cumberland, et al. (2001) obtained teachers' and parents' (usually mothers') reports of children's inhibitory control and abilities to shift and focus attention as needed (attention shifting and focusing), as well as impulsivity. Mothers, fathers, and teachers reported on children's externalizing and internalizing problem behaviors (using the Child Behavior Checklist or Teacher Report

Form; Achenbach, 1991). In addition, several behavioral measures of children's abilities to regulate themselves were obtained: (a) their ability to sit still when asked to do so while they were hooked to physiological equipment, (b) their facial reactions to a disappointing toy (Saarni, 1984), and (c) their persistence (rather than cheating or doing nothing) on a puzzle task. Their measures were viewed as reflecting primarily effortful control, although the persistence task could tap a combination of effortful control and BAS-related approach behavior (impulsivity) because a reward was offered for high performance on the puzzle task.

In general, and consistent with predictions, nondisordered children scored higher than externalizing children (classified with mothers', fathers', or teachers' reports as high in externalizing behavior only or high on both externalizing and internalizing behavior) on effortful control, including adult-reported attentional shifting and focusing and inhibitory control. Externalizing children also scored lower on inhibitory control when asked to sit still, were less persistent on the puzzle task, showed marginally more negative emotion in response to the gift, and were rated by adults as higher in impulsivity. In contrast, internalizing children did not differ much from nondisordered children in adult-reported inhibitory control or on the behavioral measures (see Eisenberg, Fabes, & Murphy, 1995, for similar results with adults); however, they were lower in attention shifting and focusing and in impulsivity. Externalizing children, in comparison to internalizing children (using pure rather than comorbid cases), were quite impulsive and somewhat lower on measures of attention shifting and focusing and inhibitory control. Thus, the distinctions among various types of effortful control, and between effortful and less voluntary control, proved useful when predicting problems in adjustment.

In addition, we have found differential relations between effortful control and impulsivity when predicting personality resiliency. Block and Block (1980) defined ego resiliency (labeled resiliency for convenience) as "the dynamic capacity of an individual to modify his/her modal level of ego-control, in either direction, as a function of the demand characteristics of the environmental context" (p. 48). High resilience involves resourceful adaptation to changing circumstances and flexible use of problem-solving strategies; low resilience involves little adaptive flexibility, an inability to respond to changing circumstances, the tendency to perseverate or become disorganized when dealing with change and stress, and difficulty recouping after stressful experiences. We hypothesized that resilient children would be expected to be able to effortfully regulate as much as necessary to adapt to situations, but would not be expected to be inflexible and overregulated. Consistent with our prediction, Block and Kremen (1996) asserted that, "When one is more undercontrolled than is adaptively effective or more overcontrolled than is adaptively required, one is not resilient" (p. 351). Indeed, some spontaneity, as reflected in what appears to be mild impulsivity (but probably could be effortfully controlled, if necessary), might contribute to resiliency. Consistent with this view, Block and Kremen (1996) argued that, "the human goal is to be as undercontrolled as possible and as overcontrolled as necessary" (p. 351).

We have examined the relation of effortful control or impulsivity to resiliency in several studies. In one longitudinal study, we found that attentional control (shifting and focusing) was positively related to resiliency both in early elementary school and 2 years later. A measure of ego control (Block & Block, 1980) used in this study generally was unrelated to resiliency, but the index of ego control likely reflected a combination of effortful and involuntary overcontrol (and there was some evidence of a quadratic relation between ego control and resiliency at the first assessment, but not the second assessment; Eisenberg, Guthrie, et al., 1997; Eisenberg, Fabes, Reiser, et al., 2000). In another study with preschoolers, we assessed resiliency with a subset of items from Block and Block's (1980) Q-sort that were rated by a panel of experts as most representative of ego resiliency (e.g., "Can the child bounce back or recover after a stressful or bad experience?"; Cumberland, Eisenberg, & Reiser, in press). Using correlations and SEM, we found that both impulsivity and effortful control were positively related to resiliency and provided some unique prediction of it. Similarly, in another sample including children with at least borderline levels of externalizing or internalizing problems (or well as nondisordered children), we examined the relations of effortful control and impulsivity to resiliency when the children were 4½ to nearly 8 years old and then 2 years later (Eisenberg, Spinrad, & Morris, 2002). At both assessments, measures of effortful regulation (attentional and inhibitory control) tended to be positively correlated with resiliency (within and sometimes across reporter), with the correlations being somewhat stronger at the older age. There also were modest significant positive correlations between impulsivity and resiliency at the youngest age for both teachers' and parents' reports of the constructs. These correlations were positive but generally nonsignificant 2 years later. However, at both ages, there was a quadratic relation between teachers' (but not parents') reports of impulsivity and resilience, such that children at the mean level of impulsivity were more resilient than children low in impulsivity, and children average and high in impulsivity were similar on resiliency. Thus, resiliency in children seems to be positively related to both effortful control and impulsivity (which we assume reflects low levels of involuntary control), although the latter relation is modest and may decrease with age. The fact that measures of effortful regulation and impulsivity are both positively related to resiliency is quite interesting in light of the fact that these two variables generally are moderately negatively related and relate differently to internalizing problems in children. Clearly, indexes of effortful control and low impulsivity are not assessing the same construct and it is important conceptually and empirically to differentiate between the two.

SOCIALIZATION OF EMOTION-RELATED REGULATION AND ASSOCIATED DEVELOPMENTAL OUTCOMES

Although the literature on the socialization of emotion and its regulation is limited in quantity, initial findings are consistent with the view that socializers' characteristics and behaviors are related to children's regulation of emotion and emotion-related behavior. Because most of this work is correlational, it is impossible to determine the degree to which socializers influence children rather than the reverse; it is highly probable that the socialization process is bidirectional in its effects. Moreover, obtained relations likely are partly genetically mediated. Hereditary characteristics of children likely evoke some parental reactions, and genetically-based similarities between parents and children in emotion-relevant characteristics probably account for some portion of the variance in associations between parental characteristics or behaviors and children's emotion-relevant regulation and its socioemotional correlates.

Investigators interested in emotion-relevant socialization typically have studied socializers' reactions to children's emotions, socializers' expression of emotion in the family or toward the child, and socializers' discussion of emotion. Work on these topics, especially that from our own laboratory, is summarized briefly (see Eisenberg, Cumberland, & Spinrad, 1998). In this summary, we sometimes draw on work concerning the relations of these emotion-related aspects of socialization to expressed emotion, regulation, and socioemotional functioning. It is our assumption that the quality of social functioning often reflects individuals' abilities to regulate emotion and emotion-related behavior; thus, consideration of the relation of the socialization of emotion to quality of socioemotional functioning is informative to thinking about the socialization of emotion regulation.

Socialization of Emotion-Related Regulation in Infancy and the Toddler Years

Studies of emotion socialization in infancy and the first few years of life often focus on one aspect of parenting—how parents respond to and deal with infants' expression of negative emotion—or on the sensitivity of parenting more generally. According to Kopp (1989), successful regulation of emotion and emotion-linked behavior in infants and young children can be indexed by how closely the child meets family and social conventions, including the expression of emotions in an appropriate manner. She further argued that infants and young children must have external support for regulating their emotions and that the development of their emotion-related regulation involves a give-and-take between the children's needs and caregivers' behaviors. In addition, elements of young children's emotion-related self-regulation are believed to be derived from social interactions with caregivers. Unfortunately, although caregivers likely play an important role in the development of children's emotion-related regulation, few researchers have examined how maternal strategies interact with child behaviors in the development of emotion-related regulation.

Like Kopp, Calkins (1994; Calkins & Howse, this volume) proposed a model where the development of emotion regulation involves an interaction between the infant and the caregiver. Over time, bidirectional influences between infants' own biologically-based reactivity and caregivers' strategies for regulating infants' emotional arousal can produce either optimal patterns of emotion regulation or dysfunctional patterns of regulation in children. The positive and negative outcomes discussed by Calkins (1994) are similar to the three types of regulation we outlined earlier: highly inhibited, undercontrolled, and optimally regulated. Children who display undercontrolled patterns of emotion regulation have a tendency to be easily frustrated in infancy. If parents are sensitive and nonintrusive, then optimal patterns of regulation will develop; however, if parents are controlling and coercive, then undercontrolled patterns of regulation will be more likely to develop. On the other hand, children who develop a highly inhibited style of control are believed to have parents who do not alleviate the infants' distress in response to novelty and who are overprotective and controlling. Infants prone to exhibit early arousal to novelty will be more likely to develop optimal patterns of regulation and less reactive inhibition when parents use responsive caregiving that is nonintrusive and supportive during situations where the infants feel distress.

Calkins and colleagues have tested their ideas in several studies. Toddlers who were more distressed than their peers during a frustrating situation had mothers who interfered in the toddlers' activities and did things for their toddlers instead of allowing themto complete the activities on their own (Calkins & Johnson, 1998). Calkins and Johnson (1998) also found links between infant regulation strategies and maternal behavior. Toddlers who were more likely to use distraction and constructive coping during frustrating situations had mothers who were more likely to use positive guiding behaviors. In a follow-up of this sample, Calkins, Smith, Gill, and Johnson (1998) found that maternal positive and negative caregiving strategies were not related to reactivity when the children were 24 months old but were related to the regulation strategies employed by the children at this age. Mothers with more negative caregiving styles had children who used less adaptive regulation strategies. When frustrated, these children were more likely to orient to and manipulate an object they were prevented from having and were less likely to show distraction away from the denied object. Consistent with Calkins's work, Gilliom et al. (2002) found that warm, supportive (versus hostile, punitive) parenting when children were 1½ years old predicted children's ability to shift attention from a source of frustration at age 3½.

Preliminary results from a sample of 6-month-old infants recruited based on maternal report and laboratory observations of frustration have also supported Calkins's (1994) idea that patterns of caregiver behavior are different for children showing early signs of problems with frustration than for children not displaying early frustration. The easily frustrated group of infants used less distraction, more scanning, and oriented to the mother more during frustration tasks and displayed less attention during attention tasks (Calkins, Dedmon, Gill, Lomax, & Johnson, in press). The mothers of these frustrated infants were observed to be less sensitive, more intrusive, and provided less physical stimulation to the infants than mothers of nonfrustrated infants (Calkins, Gill, Dedmon, Johnson, & Lomax, 2000). For the most part, these studies are consistent with the view that maternal behavior is related to children's ability to regulate their behavior. As suggested by Calkins et al. (1998), children's reactivity was not consistently related to maternal behavior; however, more consistent relations would be expected between maternal behavior and regulation than between maternal behavior and reactivity because reactivity likely is more biologically based. However, it is important to keep in mind that although infants and young children may be learning regulation strategies within the context of the caregiver relationship, these strategies may not be adaptive in other contexts, for example with peers (Cummings & Davies, 1996; Thompson & Calkins, 1996).

Socialization of Emotion-Related Regulation in Childhood

Similar to investigators studying socialization of emotion-related regulation in the early years, researchers examining socializers' emotion-related socialization sometimes have examined their reactions to children's expression of emotion, especially negative emotion. Investigators have suggested that these parental reactions affect the likelihood of children acknowledging and exhibiting negative emotions and whether situations involving these emotions become intrinsically distressing. For example, Ross Buck (1984) suggested that people who have a history of receiving sanctions for emotional expressiveness tend, as adults, to experience heightened physiological responding in situations involving negative emotion but tend not to exhibit external markers of emotional responding. This is because children who receive negative reactions to their displays of emotion gradually learn to hide their emotions but feel anxious when in emotionally evocative situations due to the prior repeated association between punishment or other sanctions and emotional expressivity. Analogously, Sylvan Tomkins (1963) suggested that children learn to express distress without shame and to respond sympathetically to others if their parents respond openly with sympathy and nurturance to children's feelings of distress and helplessness.

In support of Buck's (1994) reasoning, Eisenberg, Fabes, Schaller, Carlo, and Miller (1991) found mothers' reports of restrictiveness in response to elementary school boys' expression of their own negative emotions that were unlikely to harm another (e.g., sadness and anxiety) were associated with their sons' facial distress and physiological reactivity (skin conductance and heart rate) when viewing an empathy-inducing film, accompanied by boys' reports of low distress. These boys seemed prone to experience distress when confronted with others' distress—they exhibited considerable physiological arousal and somewhat higher facial distress than did other boys—but apparently they did not want others to know what they were feeling (or did not know themselves).

In other studies, parents' nonsupportive—that is, punitive or minimizing—reactions to children's negative emotions have been associated with mothers' or teachers' reports of children's avoidant coping and low levels of constructive coping, popularity, social skills, and understanding of emotion (Denham, Mitchell–Copeland, Strandberg, Auerbach, & Blair, 1997; Eisenberg, Fabes, & Murphy, 1996; McDowell & Parke, 2000), as well as low effortful regulation (Eisenberg et al., 1999). Findings in regard to supportive practices are more mixed (Eisenberg, Fabes, & Murphy, 1996; Jones, Eisenberg, Fabes, & MacKinnon, 2002). Gottman, Katz, and Hoovan (1996, 1997) found that parents who generally were aware and supportive of the expression of emotion had children who were physiologically well-regulated and therefore did not appear to require substantial parental intervention to regulate their emotional arousal in social contexts; moreover, this ability for self-regulation predicted children's competence with peers. In addition, parents with this supportive approach to dealing with emotions were less likely to derogate their children, which also predicted children's peer competence (i.e., derogation mediated the effects of parental philosophy on peer competence). However, in other studies, there is evidence that parents who typically comfort their children when distressed, especially if their children are prone to negative emotion, have children who are prone to exhibit negative emotion and are low in social competence (Denham, 1993; Jones et al., 2002). High levels of parental comforting after infancy may be a reaction to particularly vulnerable children or may be a style of parenting that does not promote the child's learning of autonomous means of coping.

Another type of parental reaction to children's stress and emotion involves an emphasis on taking care of or solving the problem rather than dealing directly with children's emotion. Parents can model a problem-focused approach or encourage the child to do so himself or herself. Parental modeling of instrumental problem-solving responses when their children are upset (e.g., putting a bandage on the child when he or she was hurt) has been positively related to children's social competence (Roberts & Strayer, 1987), whereas parental (usually maternal) encouragement of children's instrumental problem solving has been associated with high levels of sons' sympathy (Eisenberg et al. 1991) and comforting behavior (Eisenberg, Fabes, & Murphy, 1996), as well as girls' social skills, popularity, and constructive coping (Eisenberg, Fabes, & Murphy, 1996). However, in one study of school children, parental reactions promoting problem solving were positively related to social and emotional competence for boys but negatively related for girls (Jones et al., 2002), and in another study, there was a negative relation between fathers' (but not mothers') reports of encouraging children's problem-focused responses to dealing with negative emotion and girls' social skills and popularity (Eisenberg, Fabes, & Murphy, 1996). Thus, there is some evidence that parental modeling and encouragement of problem-focused coping may foster children's emotional and social competence, although it appears that findings sometimes differ by gender. Perhaps, due to the gender-typed nature of taking an instrumental approach to coping, parents sometimes encourage such an approach primarily for daughters who are having difficulties in regard to their social competence (Eisenberg, Fabes, & Murphy, 1996).

Parents' expression of emotion in the home more generally has also been associated with children's emotional expressivity and social competence, as well as their regulation. Parents' expression of emotion can be contagious; it teaches children about where and when to express emotion, and it can affect children's perceptions of, and feelings about, themselves and others. Amy Halberstadt and her colleagues found that when positive emotion is prevalent in the home, children tend to express positive emotion themselves; are socially skilled, able to understand others' emotions (at least in childhood), low in aggression, and well-adjusted; and tend to have high self-esteem (Halberstadt, Crisp, & Eaton, 1999). In contrast, predominant expression of negative emotion in the family, especially intense and hostile emotion, is likely to be associated with low levels of social competence and effortful control and high expression of negative emotion (Eisenberg, Gershoff, et al., 2001; Halberstadt et al., 1999). However, the relation of parental expressivity to children's socioemotional development likely differs across cultures. For example, in Indonesia, as in the United States, parental negative expressivity was negatively related to children's regulation and adjustment and social competence, but parental positive expressivity was unrelated to child outcomes. This may be because in Indonesia the strong overt expression of emotion, even positive emotion, is viewed as disrupting social relationships and emotional well-being (Eisenberg, Liew, & Pidada, 2001). The pattern of mediation was maintained two years later in the U.S. sample for positive, but not negative, emotion (Eisenberg et al., 2003).

In recent work, Eisenberg and colleagues have obtained evidence that the relations between parental expressivity and children's social competence and externalizing problems are mediated by children's effortful control. Parents who tend to express relatively high levels of positive emotion and low levels of abrasive negative emotion tend to have young school children who are relatively high in effortful control. In turn, their level of effortful control predicted their social competence and low levels of externalizing problems (and these relations were mediated; Eisenberg, Gershoff, et al., 2001). These data provide evidence of a direct relation between parental expressivity and children's effortful control. A similar pattern of mediated findings was obtained in Indonesia for parents' expression of negative emotions but not positive emotions (Eisenberg, Liew, & Pidada, 2001).

The third aspect of parental socialization that has been studied with some frequency is parental discussion of emotion. Parental discussion of emotion has been associated with the development of an awareness and understanding of others' emotional states (Denham, Cook, & Zoller, 1992; Denham, Zoller, & Couchoud, 1994). Parents who discuss emotions with their children likely teach them about the meanings of emotions, the circumstances in which they should and should not be expressed, and the consequences of expressing or not expressing them (Dunn & Brown, 1994; Gottman et al., 1997). As a result, their children tend to display better emotional understanding than do children whose parents do not discuss emotions with them. Judy Dunn and her colleagues have found, for example, that whether 2- to 3-year-olds are exposed to, and participate in, discussions of emotions with family members predicts their understanding of others' emotions months later and at age 6 (Brown & Dunn, 1996; Dunn, Brown, & Beardsall, 1991; Dunn, Brown, Slomkowski, Tesla, & Youngblade, 1991; see also Denham et al., 1997; Denham et al. 1994).

Parental discussion of emotion has been linked not only with children's understanding of emotion, but also with their competence in social interactions, such as their social status with peers and low levels of aggression (Gottman et al., 1997; Laird, Pettit, Mize, Brown, & Lindsey, 1994). However, the degree to which discussion of emotion is related to aspects of positive social functioning probably is moderated by the type of emotion typically expressed in the home and when discussion of emotions occurs. If the discussion of emotion is primarily during hostile exchanges or in response to problematic behavior by the child, it is not likely to foster children's understanding of emotion and their social competence (Dunn & Brown, 1994).

In general, correlations of measures of parental emotion-related practices to children's regulation and socioemotional functioning are modest. This is not surprising given that many aspects of socialization, many socializers, and many factors besides socialization can influence children's emotion-related regulation and related socioemotional functioning. Moreover, in thinking about the topic of emotion socialization, it is important to recognize that children can evoke certain parenting reactions and that the process of influence is likely bidirectional. For example, parents' reports of nonsupportive emotion-related practices in response to children's negative emotions, such as minimizing the child's emotion or punitive reactions, sometimes have been related to parents' perceptions that their children are emotionally intense, prone to negative emotion, or low in attentional control (e.g., Eisenberg, Fabes, & Murphy, 1996; cf. Jones et al., 2002). Moreover, mothers tend to discuss emotion differently with their children if they perceive them as easily dysregulated by negative emotion. In one study, mothers displayed more positive versus negative emotion when telling emotional stories to their kindergartners than second graders (kindergartners also were perceived as more emotionally vulnerable than second graders) and mothers were especially likely to do so if they perceived their kindergartner as relatively vulnerable to distress when exposed to others' negative emotion (Fabes et al., 1994).

Eisenberg et al. (1999) examined the issue of bidirectionality of effects by assessing relations between children's effortful control and mothers' reports of punitive reactions to children's emotions across time. Children's effortful regulation and parental punitive reactions to children's negative emotions were assessed at three times, when children were ages 6 to 8, 8 to 10, and 10 to12 years. In a SEM, problem behavior at ages 10 to 12 was significantly predicted by low regulation at that age and by problem behavior at ages 6 to 8, and was marginally, directly predicted by concurrent punitive parental reactions. Of the most interest, children's regulation at ages 6 to 8 predicted low levels of parental punitive reactions at ages 8 to 10, which in turn predicted children's regulation at ages 10 to 12. Thus, the pattern was consistent with the view that there was bidirectional causality between children's regulation and parental punitive reactions, and that the relation of punitive reactions to problem behavior was partially indirect through children's level of regulation (and perhaps, to a limited degree, vice versa). These findings are consistent with the view that socialization and characteristics of the child are interrelated and likely shape one another across over time.

Despite the correlational nature of the socialization literature, there is evidence in the prevention literature that experimental interventions designed to improve children's understanding and regulation of emotion—using procedures similar to those that occur during socialization in the home—do have effects. For example, procedures involving identification and discussion of emotions, as well as emotion management and self-control, are basic to the PATHS curricula being used as an intervention in numerous schools by Greenberg and his colleagues (Greenberg, 1996). Training has been related to range of children's vocabulary and fluency in discussing emotional experiences, efficacy beliefs regarding the management of emotion, and children's understanding of some aspects of emotion (Greenberg, Kusche, Cook, & Quamma, 1995), as well as improvements in the abilities to stop and calm down, to resolve peer conflicts, and to show empathy for others (Greenberg, 1996). In general, the intervention was most successful for children high in internalizing or externalizing behavior (Greenberg et al., 1995). Moreover, the results of intervention studies with parents of aggressive children suggest that modifying mothers' behaviors affects how children express their emotions behaviorally (Eddy & Chamberlain, 2000; Forgatch & DeGarmo, 1999).

SUMMARY

In thinking about emotion regulation, we have found it important to differentiate between voluntary control (i.e., effortful control) and involuntary control (e.g., impulsivity, behavioral inhibition). We have argued that voluntary and involuntary control relate differently to children's social competence. In particular, although most of the current literature has been conducted with older children, effortful control has been found to predict positive social functioning, whereas involuntary control often relates to less adaptive behavior (although involuntary approach tendencies also relate to resiliency).

Moreover, our review of the relevant literature is consistent with the view that from a very young age, children display differences in emotionality and regulation and these differences are related to individual differences in children's behavior, including their level of problem behavior and social competence. Moreover, initial research suggests that different aspects of effortful regulation and reactive control may differentially relate to various developmental outcomes (e.g., internalizing and externalizing problem behavior).

We have also shown that development of emotion regulation is related to socialization practices. Early in children's lives, parents who use more control and are more negative have infants who display more negativity, frustration, and noncompliance. In older children, parents' nonsupportive reactions to children's negative emotions have also been related to suboptimal outcomes for the children, including low social competence and relatively high levels of behavior problems. Parental expression of emotion and discussion of emotion were also found to relate to high levels of children's regulation, social competence, and adjustment.

There are a number of questions that still remain involving research on emotion regulation. First, although a good deal of work in this area is being done with older children, more work is needed with very young children. For example, there is a need for additional longitudinal research exploring the development of effortful control and the ways that infants' behavioral strategies function to regulate emotions. Key goals in such work might be to understand the antecedents of effortful control, specific socialization influences, and how changes (i.e., instability) in infants' abilities to regulate emotions can be explained. Moreover, research that differentiates between young children's reward-driven impulsivity and their lack of effortful control (and the correlates) is sorely needed, although it is difficult to distinguish between the two constructs. Further, data pertaining to the regulation of positive emotion is limited, including work on how young and older children amplify their positive emotion.

An issue in research on emotion-related regulation is differentiating coping strategies that are effective versus ineffective at reducing children's negative emotionality. If a given strategy co-occurs with high negative emotionality, it may reflect either an unsuccessful strategy or a consequence of the negative emotionality. Studies involving sequential analyses may be needed to better delineate causal sequences.

In addition, there is a need for more longitudinal data designed to test causal hypotheses regarding the consequences of early regulation. The use of statistical strategies such as structural equation models in which prior levels of regulation and social functioning are included when predicting outcomes over time allows investigators to make somewhat stronger causal inferences than simple correlational findings. Moreover, factors that might mediate or moderate the relation between children's effortful control (or their reactive control) and their social functioning (e.g., gender, other aspects of temperament, socialization) would contribute to our understanding of emotion regulation and control.

Finally, because differences in emotion regulation appear to have important developmental consequences, researchers could draw on this work when developing interventions to promote children's social competence. For example, prevention researchers could focus on teaching children ways to enhance their effortful control or could design programs to foster parenting practices associated with children's effortful control. Certainly some investigators have drawn on the emotion regulation literature in designing interventions (e.g., Greenberg et al., 1995), but such work is still limited.

In summary, emotion regulation, broadly defined, is influenced by the child's dispositional characteristics, environmental influences, and the combination of these factors. It is a process embedded in the ongoing flow and interface of internal psychological and physiological processes with the social world in which the child is immersed. The topic of emotion regulation is very exciting because it has implications for understanding many aspects of the child's social functioning, as well as for designing interventions to deal with social and emotional problems.

REFERENCES

Achenbach, T. M. (1991). *Manual for the Child Behavior Checklist/4–18 and 1991 profile.* Burlington, VT: University of Vermont, Department of Psychiatry.

Asendorpf, J. B., & van Aken, M. A. G. (1999). Resilient, overcontrolled, and undercontrolled, personality prototypes in childhood: Replicability, predictive power, and the trait-type issue. *Journal of Personality and Social Psychology, 77*, 815–832.

Aspinwall, L. G., & Taylor, S. E. (1997). A stitch in time: Self-regulation and proactive coping. *Psychological Bulletin, 121*, 417–436.

Bates, J., Maslin, C., & Fankel, K. (1985). Attachment security, mother-child interaction, and temperament and predictors of behavior problem ratings at age 3 years. *Monographs for the Society for Research in Child Development, 50*, (1–2, Serial No. 209).

Belsky, J., Friedman, S. L., & Hsieh, K. H. (2001). Testing a core emotion-regulation prediction: Does early attentional persistence moderate the effect of infant negative emotionality on later development? *Child Development, 72*, 123–133.

Biederman, J., Rosenbaum, J. F., Hirshfeld, D. R., Faraone, S. V., Bolduc, E. A., Gersten, M., et al. (1990). Psychiatric correlates of behavioral inhibition in young children of parents with and without psychiatric disorders. *Archives of General Psychiatry, 47*, 21–26

Block, J. H., & Block, J. (1980). The role of ego-control and ego-resiliency in the organization of behavior. In W. A. Collins (Ed.), Development of cognition, affect, and social relations. *The Minnesota Symposia on Child Psychology* (Vol. 13, pp. 39–101). Hillsdale, NJ: Lawrence Erlbaum Associates, Inc.

Block, J., & Kremen, A. M. (1996). IQ and ego-resiliency: Conceptual and empirical connections and separateness. *Journal of Personality and Social Psychology, 70*, 349–360.

Braungart, J. M., & Stifter, C. A. (1991). Regulation of negative reactivity during the strange situation: Temperament and attachment in 12-month-old infants. *Infant Behavior and Development, 14*, 349–364.

Braungart–Rieker, J., Garwood, M. M., & Stifter, C. A. (1997). Compliance and noncompliance: The roles of maternal control and child temperament. *Journal of Applied Developmental Psychology, 18*, 411–428.

Brown, J. R., & Dunn, J. (1996). Continuities in emotion understanding from 3–6 yrs. *Child Development, 67*, 789–802.

Buck, R. (1984). *The communication of emotion.* New York: Guilford.

Buss, K., & Goldsmith, H. H. (1998). Fear and anger regulation in infancy: Effects on the temporal dynamics of affective expression. Child Development, 69, 359–374.

Calkins, S. D. (1994). Origins and outcomes of individual differences in emotion regulation. In N. A. Fox (Ed.), Emotion regulation: Behavioral and biological considerations. *Monographs of the Society for Research in Child Development, 59*(2–3, Serial No. 240).

Calkins, S. D., & Dedmon, S. E. (2000). Physiological and behavioral regulation in two-year-old children with aggressive/destructive behavior problems. *Journal of Abnormal Child Psychology, 28*, 103–118.

Calkins, S. D., Dedmon, S. E., Gill, K. L., Lomax, L. E., & Johnson, L. M. (2002). Frustration in infancy: Implications for emotion regulation, physiological processes, and temperament. *Infancy, 3*, 175–197.

Calkins, S. D., Gill, K., Dedmon, S., Johnson, L., & Lomax, L. (April, 2000). *Mothers' interactions with temperamentally frustrated infants.* Poster session presented at the 12th Biennial International Conference on Infant Studies, Brighton, England.

Calkins, S. D., Gill, K. L., Johnson, M. C., & Smith, C. L. (1999). Emotional reactivity and emotional regulation strategies as predictors of social behavior with peers during toddlerhood. *Social Development, 8*, 310–334.

Calkins, S. D., & Johnson, M. J. (1998). Toddler regulation of distress to frustrating events: Temperamental and maternal correlates. *Infant Behavior and Development, 21, 379–395.*

Calkins, S. D., Smith, C. L., Gill, K. L., & Johnson, M. C. (1998). Maternal interactive style across contexts: Relations to emotional, behavioral, and physiological regulation during toddlerhood. *Social Development, 7*, 350–369.

Campos, J. J., Mumme, D. L., Kermoian, R., & Campos, R. G. (1994). A functionalist perspective on the nature of emotion. In N. A. Fox (Ed.), The development of emotion regulation: Biological and behavioral considerations. *Monographs of the Society for Research in Child Development, 59*(2–3, Serial No. 240).

Cole, P. M., Michel, M. K., & Teti, L. O. (1994). The development of emotion regulation and dysregulation: A clinical perspective. *Monographs of the Society for Research in Child Development, 59*(2–3, Serial No. 240).

Cumberland, A. J., Eisenberg, N., & Reiser, M. (in press). Relations of young children's agreeableness and resiliency to effortful control, impulsivity, and social competence. *Social Development.*

Cummings, E. M., & Davies, P. (1996). Emotional security as a regulatory process in normal development and the development of psychopathology. *Development and Psychopathology, 8*, 123–139.

Denham, S. A. (1993). Maternal emotional responsiveness and toddlers' social–emotional competence. *Journal of Child Psychology and Psychiatry, 34*, 715–728.

Denham, S. A., Cook, M., & Zoller, D. (1992). 'Baby looks very sad.' Implications of conversations about feelings between mother and preschooler. *British Journal of Developmental Psychology, 10*, 301–315.

Denham, S. A., Mitchell-Copeland, J., Strandberg, K., Auerbach, S., & Blair, K. (1997). Parental contributions to preschoolers' emotional competence: Direct and indirect effects. *Motivation and Emotion, 21*, 65–86.

Denham, S. A., Zoller, D., & Couchoud, E. A. (1994). Socialization of preschoolers' emotion understanding. *Developmental Psychology, 30*, 928–936.

Derryberry, D., & Rothbart, M. K. (1988). Arousal, affect, and attention as components of temperament. *Journal of Personality and Social Psychology, 55*, 958–966.

Derryberry, D., & Rothbart, M. K. (1997). Reactive and effortful processes in the organization of temperament. *Development and Psychopathology, 9*, 633–652.

Diamond, E. (1990). Developmental time course in human infants and infant monkeys, and the neural bases of inhibitory control in reaching. *Annals of the New York Academy of Sciences, 608*, 637–676.

Diener, M. L., & Mangelsdorf, S. C. (1999). Behavioral strategies for emotion regulation in toddlers: Associations with maternal involvement and emotional expressions. *Infant Behavior and Development, 22*, 569–583.

Dunn, J., & Brown, J. (1994). Affect expression in the family, children's understanding of emotions, and their interactions with others. *Merrill-Palmer Quarterly, 40*, 120–137.

Dunn, J., Brown, J., & Beardsall, L. (1991). Family talk about feeling states and children's later understanding of others' emotions. *Developmental Psychology, 27*, 448–455.

Dunn, J., Brown, J., Slomkowski, C., Tesla, C., & Youngblade, L. (1991). Young children's understanding of other people's feelings and beliefs: Individual differences and their antecedents. Child Development, 62, 1352–1366.

Eddy, J. M., & Chamberlain, P. (2000). Family management and deviant peer association as mediators of the impact of treatment condition on youth antisocial behavior. *Journal of Consulting and Clinical Psychology, 66*, 857–863.

Eisenberg, N., Cumberland, A., & Spinrad, T. L. (1998). Parental socialization of emotion. Psychological Inquiry, 9, 241–273.

Eisenberg, N., Cumberland, A., Spinrad, T. L., Fabes, R. A., Shepard, S. A., Reiser, M., et al. (2001). The relations of regulation and emotionality to children's externalizing and internalizing problem behavior. *Child Development, 72*, 1112–1134.

Eisenberg, N., & Fabes, R. A. (1992). Emotion, regulation, and the development of social competence. In M. S. Clark (Ed.), *Review of personality and social psychology, Vol. 14. Emotion and social behavior* (pp. 119–150). Newbury Park, CA: Sage.

Eisenberg, N., Fabes, R. A., Bernzweig, J., Karbon, M., Poulin, R., & Hanish, L. (1993). The relations of emotionality and regulation to preschoolers' social skills and sociometric status. *Child Development, 64*, 1418–1438.

Eisenberg, N., Fabes, R. A., Guthrie, I. K., Murphy, B. C., Maszk, P., Holmgren, R., et al. (1996). The relations of regulation and emotionality to problem behavior in elementary school children. *Development and Psychopathology, 8*, 141–162.

Eisenberg, N., Fabes, R. A., Guthrie, I. K., & Reiser, M. (2000). Dispositional emotionality and regulation: Their role in predicting quality of social functioning. *Journal of Personality and Social Psychology, 78*, 136–157.

Eisenberg, N., Fabes, R. A., Karbon, M., Murphy, B. C., Wosinski, M., Polazzi, L., et al. (1996). The relations of children's dispositional prosocial behavior to emotionality, regulation, and social functioning. *Child Development, 67*, 974–992.

Eisenberg, N., Fabes, R. A., & Murphy, B. C. (1996). Parents' reactions to children's negative emotions: Relations to children's social competence and comforting behavior. *Child Development, 67*, 2227–2247.

Eisenberg, N., Fabes, R. A., & Murphy, B. (1995). The relations of shyness and low sociability to regulation and emotionality. *Journal of Personality and Social Psychology, 68*, 505–517.

Eisenberg, N., Fabes, R. A., Murphy, M., Maszk, P., Smith, M., & Karbon, M. (1995). The role of emotionality and regulation in children's social functioning: A longitudinal study. *Child Development, 66*, 1239–1261.

Eisenberg, N., Fabes, R. A., Murphy, B., Karbon, M., Smith, M., & Maszk, P. (1996). The relations of children's dispositional empathy-related responding to their emotionality, regulation, and social functioning. *Developmental Psychology, 32,* 195–209.

Eisenberg, N., Fabes, R. A., Nyman, M., Bernzweig, J., & Pinuelas, A. (1994). The relations of emotionality and regulation to children's anger-related reactions. *Child Development, 65*, 109–128.

Eisenberg, N., Fabes, R. A., Schaller, M., Carlo, G., & Miller, P. A. (1991). The relations of parental characteristics and practices to children's vicarious emotional responding. *Child Development, 62*, 1393–1408.

Eisenberg, N., Faabes, R. A., Shepard, S. A., Guthrie, I. K., Murphy, B. C., & Reiser, M (1999). Parental reactions to children's negative emotions: Longitudinal relations to quality of children's social functioning. *Child Development, 70*, 513–534.

Eisenberg, N., Fabes, R. A., Shepard, S. A., Murphy, B. C., Guthrie, I. K., Jones, S., et al. (1997). Contemporaneous and longitudinal prediction of children's social functioning from regulation and emotionality. *Child Development, 68*, 642–664.

Eisenberg, N., Fabes, R. A., Shepard, S. A., Murphy, B. C., Jones, J., & Guthrie, I. K. (1998). Contemporaneous and longitudinal prediction of children's sympathy from dispositional regulation and emotionality. *Developmental Psychology, 34*, 910–924.

Eisenberg, N., Gershoff, E. T., Fabes, R. A., Shepard, S. A., Cumberland, A. J., Losoya, S. H., et al. (2001). Mothers' emotional expressivity and children's behavior problems and social competence: Mediation through children's regulation. *Developmental Psychology, 37*, 475–490.

Eisenberg, N., Guthrie, I. K., Fabes, R. A., Reiser, M., Murphy, B. C., Holmgren, R., et al. (1997). The relations of regulation and emotionality to resiliency and competent social functioning in elementary school children. *Child Development, 68*, 295–311.

Eisenberg, N., Guthrie, I. K., Fabes, R. A., Shepard, S., Losoya, S., Murphy, B., et al. (2000). Prediction of elementary school children's externalizing problem behaviors from attentional and behavioral regulation and negative emotionality. *Child Development, 71*, 1367–1382.

Eisenberg, N., Liew, J., & Pidada, S. (2001). The relations of parental emotional expressivity with the quality of Indonesian children's social functioning. *Emotion, 1*, 116–136.

Eisenberg, N., Spinrad, T. L., & Morris, A. S. (2002). Regulation, resiliency, and quality of social functioning. *Self and Identity.*

Eisenberg, N., Valiente, C., Morris, A. S., Fabes, R. A., Cumberland, A., Reiser, M., Gershoff, E. T., Shepard, S. A., & Losoya, S. (2003). Longitudinal relations among parental emotional expressivity, children's regulation, and quality of socioemotional functioning. *Developmental Psychology, 39*, 2–19.

Fabes, R. A., Eisenberg, N., Karbon, M., Bernzweig, J., Speer, A. L., & Carlo, G. (1994). Socialization of children's vicarious emotional responding and prosocial behavior: Relations with mothers' perceptions of children's emotional reactivity. *Developmental Psychology, 30*, 44–55.

Forgatch, M. S., & DeGarmo, D. S. (1999). Parenting through change: An effective prevention program for single mothers. *Journal of Consulting and Clinical Psychology, 67*, 711–724.

Gilliom, M., Shaw, D. S., Beck, J. E., Schonberg, M. A., & Lukon, J. L. (2002). Anger regulation in disadvantaged preschool boys: Strategies, antecedents, and the development of self-control. *Developmental Psychology, 38*, 222–235.

Gottman, J. M., Katz, L. F., & Hooven, C. (1996). Parental meta-emotion philosophy and the emotional life of families: Theoretical models and preliminary data. *Journal of Family Psychology, 10*, 243–268.

Gottman, J. M., Katz, L. F., Hooven, C. (1997). *Meta-emotion: How families communicate emotionally.* Mahwah, NJ: Lawrence Erlbaum Associates, Inc.

Gray, J. A. (1975). *Elements of a two-process theory of learning.* New York: Academic.

Gray, J. A. (1987). Perspectives and anxiety and impulsivity: A commentary. *Journal of Research in Personality, 21*, 493–509.

Greenberg, M. T. (1996). *Final report to NIMH. The PATHS Project: Preventive Intervention for Children* (Grant No. R01MH42131). University of Washington, Seattle.

Greenberg, M. T., Kusche, C. A., Cook, E. T., & Quamma, J. P. (1995). Promoting emotional competence in school-aged children: The effects of the PATHS curriculum. *Development and Psychopathology, 7*, 117–136.

Grolnick, W. S., Bridges, L. J., & Connell, J. P. (1996). Emotion regulation in two-year-olds: Strategies and emotional expression in four contexts. *Child Development, 67*, 928–941.

Gross, J. J. (1999). Emotion and emotion regulation. In L. A. Pervin & O. P. John (Eds.), *Handbook of personality: Theory and research* (2nd ed.; pp. 525–552). New York: Guilford.

Halberstadt, A. G., Crisp, V. W., & Eaton, K. L. (1999). Family expressiveness: A retrospective and new directions for research. In P. Philippot, R. S. Feldman, & E. Coats (Eds.), *The social context of nonverbal behavior* (pp. 109–155). New York: Cambridge University Press.

Hart, D., Hofmann, V., Edelstein, W., & Keller, M. (1997). The relation of childhood personality types to adolescent behavior and development: A longitudinal study of Icelandic children. *Developmental Psychology, 33*, 195–205.

Heckhausen, J., & Schulz, R. (1993). *A life-span theory of control. Psychological Review, 102*, 284–304.

Jones, S., Eisenberg, N., Fabes, R. A., & MacKinnon, D. (2002). Parents' reactions to elementary school children's negative emotions: Relations to social and emotional functioning at school. *Merrill-Palmer Quarterly, 48,* 133–159.

Kagan, J. (1989). The concept of behavioral inhibition to the unfamiliar. In J. S. Reznick (Ed.), *Perspectives on behavioral inhibition* (pp. 1–24). Chicago: University of Chicago Press.

Kagan, J. (1998). Biology and the child. In W. Damon (Series Ed.) and N. Eisenberg (Vol. Ed.), *Social, emotional and personality development. Vol. 3. Handbook of child psychology* (pp. 177–235). New York: Wiley.

Kagan, J., Reznick, J. S., & Snidman, N. (1987). The physiology and psychology of behavioral inhibition in children. Child Development, 58, 1459–1473.

Kagan, J., Reznick, J. S., & Snidman, N. (1988). Biological bases of childhood shyness. *Science, 240*, 167–171.

Kagan, J., Snidman, N., & Arcus, D. (1998). Childhood derivatives of high and low reactivity in infancy. *Child Development, 69*, 1483–1493.

Kagan, J., Snidman, N., Zentner, M., & Peterson, E. (1999). Infant temperament and anxious symptoms in school age children. *Development and Psychopathology, 11*, 209–224.

Kochanska, G. (1993). Toward a synthesis of parental socialization and child temperament in early development of conscience. *Child Development, 64*, 325–347.

Kochanska, G. (1995). Children's temperament, mothers' discipline, and security of attachment: Multiple pathways to emerging internalization. *Child Development, 66*, 597–615.

Kochanksa, G., & Aksan, N. (1995). Mother–child mutually positive affect, the quality of child compliance to requests and prohibitions, and maternal control as correlates of early internalization. *Child Development, 66*, 236–254.

Kochanska, G., Coy, K. C., & Murray, K. T. (2001). The development of self-regulation in the first four years of life. *Child Development, 72*, 1091–1111.

Kochanska, G., Coy, K. C., Tjebkes, T. L., & Husarek, S. J. (1998). Individual differences in emotionality in infancy. *Child Development, 64*, 375–390.

Kochanska, G., DeVet, K., Golman, M., Murray, K., & Putnam, S. P. (1994). Maternal reports of conscience development and temperament in young children. *Child Development, 65,* 852–868.

Kochanska, G., Murray, K., & Coy, K. (1997). Inhibitory control as a contributor to conscience in childhood: From toddler to early school age. *Child Development, 68*, 263–277.

Kochanska, G., Murray, K. T., & Harlan, E. T. (2000). Effortful control in early childhood: Continuity and change, antecedents, and implications for social development. *Developmental Psychology, 36*, 220–232.

Kochanska, G., Murray, K., Jacques, T. Y., Koenig, A. L., & Vandegeest, K. A. (1996). Inhibitory control in young children and its role in emerging internalization. *Child Development, 67*, 490–507.

Kochanska, G., Tjebkes, T. L., & Forman, D. R. (1998). Children's emerging regulation of conduct: Restraint, compliance, and internalization from infancy to the second year. *Child Development, 69*, 1378–1389.

Kopp, C. B. (1989). Regulation of distress and negative emotions: A developmental view. *Developmental Psychology, 25*, 343–354.

Kopp, C. B., & Neufeld, S. J. (2003). Emotional development during infancy. In R. Davidson & K. Scherer (Eds.) and H. H. Goldsmith (Section Ed.), *Handbook of affective sciences* (pp. 247–274). New York: Oxford University Press.

Laird, R. D., Pettit, G. S., Mize, J., Brown, E. G., & Lindsey, E. (1994). Mother–child conversations about peers: Contributions to competence. *Family Relations, 43*, 425–432.

Lazarus, R. S., & Folkman, S. (1984). *Stress, appraisal, and coping*. New York: Springer.

Mangelsdorf, S. C., Shapiro, J., R., & Marzolf, D. (1995). Developmental and temperamental differences in emotion regulation in infancy. *Child Development, 66*, 1817–1828.

Matheny, A. P., Riese, M. L., & Wilson, R. S. (1985). Rudiments of infants' temperament: Newborn to 9 months. *Developmental Psychology, 21*, 486–494.

McDowell, D. J., & Parke, R. D. (2000). Differential knowledge of display rules for positive and negative emotions: Influences from parents, influences on peers. *Social Development, 9*, 415–432.

Mirsky, A. F. (1996). Disorders of attention: A neuropsychological perspective. In G. R. Lyon & N. A. Krasnegor (Eds.), *Attention, memory, and executive function* (pp. 71–93). Baltimore: Brookes.

Moore, G. A., Cohn, J. F., & Campbell, S. B. (2001). Infant affective responses to mother's still face at 6 months differentially predict externalizing and internalizing behaviors at 18 months. *Developmental Psychology, 37*, 706–714.

Murphy, B. C., Eisenberg, N., Fabes, R. A., Shepard, S., & Guthrie, I. K. (1999). Consistency and change in children's emotionality and regulation: A longitudinal study. *Merrill-Palmer Quarterly, 46*, 413–444.

Murphy, B. C., Shepard, S. A., Eisenberg, N., & Fabes, R. A. (2001). *Concurrent and across time prediction of young adolescents' social functioning*. Manuscript submitted for publication.

Newman, D. L., Caspi, A., Moffitt, T. E., & Silva, P. A. (1997). Antecedents of adult interpersonal functioning: Effects of individual differences in age 3 temperament. *Developmental Psychology, 33*, 206–217.

Nigg, J. T. (2000). On inhibition/disinhibition in developmental psychopathology: Views from cognitive and personality psychology and a working inhibition taxonomy. *Psychological Bulletin, 126*, 220–246.

Olson, S. L., Schilling, E. M., & Bates, J. E. (1999). Measurement of impulsivity: Construct coherence, longitudinal stability, and relationship with externalizing problems in middle childhood and adolescence. *Journal of Abnormal Child Psychology, 27*, 151–165.

Parritz, R. H. (1996). A descriptive analysis of toddler coping in challenging circumstances. *Infant Behavior and Development, 19*, 171–180.

Pickering, A. D., & Gray, J. A. (1999). The neuroscience of personality. In L. Pervin & O. John (Eds.), *Handbook of personality* (pp. 277–299). San Francisco: Guilford.

Posner, M. I., & DiGirolamo, G. J. (2000). Cognitive neuroscience: Origins and promise. *Psychological Bulletin, 126*, 873–889.

Posner, M. I., & Rothbart, M. K. (1998). Attention, self-regulation, and consciousness. *Transactions of the Philosophical Society of London, B, 1915–1927.*

Pulkkinen, L. (1982). Self-control and continuity from childhood to late adolescence. In P. B. Baltes & O. G. Brim, Jr. (Eds.), *Life-span development and behavior* (Vol. 4., pp. 63–105). New York: Academic.

Reed, M., Pien, D. L., & Rothbart, M. K. (1984). Inhibitory self control in preschool children. *Merrill-Palmer Quarterly, 30*, 131–147.

Roberts, W., & Strayer, J. (1987). Parents' responses to the emotional distress of their children: Relations with children's competence. *Developmental Psychology, 23*, 415–432.

Robins, R. W., John, O. P., Caspi, A., Moffitt, T. E., & Stouthamer–Loeber, M. (1996). Resilient, overcontrolled, and undercontrolled boys: Three replicable personality types. *Journal of Personality and Social Psychology, 70*, 157–171.

Rothbart, M. K., Ahadi, S. A., & Hershey, K. L. (1994). Temperament and social behavior in childhood. *Merrill-Palmer Quarterly, 40*, 21–39.

Rothbart, M. K., & Bates, J. E. (1998). Temperament. In W. Damon (Series Ed.) and N. Eisenberg (Vol. Ed.), *Handbook of child psychology. Vol. 3. Social, emotional, personality development* (pp. 105–176). New York: Wiley.

Rothbart, M. K., Ziaie, H., & O'Boyle, C. G. (1992). Self regulation and emotion in infancy. *New Directions for Child Development, 55*, 7–23.

Saarni, C. (1984). An observational study of children's attempts to monitor their expressive behavior. Child Development, 55, 1504–1513.

Sandler, I. N., Tein, J., & West, S. G. (1994). Coping, stress and the psychological symptoms of children of divorce: A cross-sectional and longitudinal study. *Child Development, 65*, 1744–1763.

Sethi, A., Mischel, W., Aber, J. L., Shoda, Y., & Rodriguez, M. L. (2000). The role of strategic attention deployment in development of self-regulation: Predicting preschoolers' delay of gratification from mother–toddler interactions. *Developmental Psychology, 36*, 767–777.

Shaw, D. S., Keenan, K., Vondra, J. I., Delliquadri, E., & Giovannelli, J. (1997). Antecedents of preschool children's internalizing problems: A longitudinal study of low-income families. *Journal of the American Academy of Child and Adolescent Psychiatry, 36*, 1760–1767.

Skinner, E. A. (1999). *Action-regulation, coping, and development.* In J. B. Brandtstadter & R. M. Lerner (Eds.), *Action and self-development* (pp. 465–503). Thousand Oaks, CA: Sage.

Stifter, C. A., & Braungart, J. M. (1995). The regulation of negative reactivity in infancy: Function and development. *Developmental Psychology, 31*, 448–455.

Stifter, C. A., Spinrad, T. L., & Braungart–Rieker, J. M. (1999). Toward a developmental model of child compliance: The role of emotion regulation in infancy. *Child Development, 70*, 21–32.

Thompson, R. A. (1994). Emotional regulation: A theme in search of definition. *Monographs of the Society for Research in Child Development, 59* (2–3, Series No. 240).

Thompson, R. A., & Calkins, S. D. (1996). The double-edged sword: Emotional regulation for children at risk. *Development and Psychopathology, 8*, 163–182.

Tomkins, S. S. (1963). *Affect, imagery, consciousness. Vol. 2 Negative affects.* New York: Springer.

Windle, M., & Lerner, R. M. (1986). Reassessing the dimensions of temperamental individuality across the life span: The revised dimensions of temperament survey (DOTS–R). *Journal of Adolescent Research, 1*, 213–230.

12

Individual Differences in Self-Regulation: Implications for Childhood Adjustment

Susan D. Calkins and Robin B. Howse
University of North Carolina at Greensboro

In this chapter, we propose that emotion regulation is one dimension of a multileveled self-regulatory system that governs children's behavior. Moreover, self-regulatory processes are hypothesized to be critical to early personality and childhood behavioral adjustment. Such processes develop over the course of the first several years of life and can be observed in physiological, attentional, emotional, cognitive, and interpersonal domains of functioning. Deficits in these particular levels of self-regulation may underlie childhood internalizing and externalizing disorders. Data from longitudinal studies suggest that an empirical approach designed to capture these multiple dimensions of self-regulation may be most informative to our understanding of their etiology and consequences. However, significant gaps remain in our knowledge of the pathways to disordered behavior and the role that self-regulation plays in such pathways. Suggestions are made for the ways in which future longitudinal studies might address these gaps.

The topic of emotion regulation, and the broader construct of self-regulation, has received considerable attention in the developmental literature over the last 10 years (Calkins, 1994; Eisenberg, Murphy, Maszk, Smith, & Karbon, 1995, Eisenberg et al., 1996; Fox, 1994; Kochanska, Coy, & Murray, 2001; Posner & Rothbart, 2000; Thompson, 1990). In fact, recent approaches to the study of individual differences in personality during infancy and early childhood have conceptualized these differences in terms of variability in temperamental reactivity and self-regulation (Calkins & Johnson, 1998; Fox, Henderson, & Marshall, in press; Gunnar, Porter, Wolf, Rigatuso, & Larson, 1995; Posner & Rothbart, 2000; Rothbart & Derryberry, 1981; Stifter & Braungart, 1995). In defining self-regulation, Rothbart and colleagues (Posner & Rothbart, 2000; Rothbart & Derryberry, 1981; Rothbart & Posner; 1985) have focused on a general definition that encompasses multiple levels of analysis of regulation. In this approach, self-regulation is defined as the child's ability to modulate behavior according to the cognitive, emotional, and social demands of a particular situation (Posner & Rothbart, 2000).

Recently, Rothbart and Posner's conceptualization was examined with a specific emphasis on defining the levels of analysis that are encompassed by the term self-regulation (Calkins & Fox, 2002). From this perspective, self-regulation was defined as physiological, attentional, emotional, behavioral, and cognitive processes that underlie adaptive behavior. Moreover, it was argued that differences in such processes could be observed between children with different personality tendencies (Calkins & Fox, 2002). In particular, children who differed in terms of early temperamental tendencies were found to display different patterns of self-regulation across several different levels including physiological, attentional, emotional, and behavioral regulation.

An examination of the developmental literature suggests an even more important role for self-regulation in early social and emotional functioning. Clearly, the acquisition of regulatory skills is an important developmental achievement. By the time the child has reached the end of the toddler period, there is the expectation that he or she is capable of emotional, behavioral, and physiological regulation that support an emergent independent identity and self-sufficient behavior (Cicchetti, Ganiban, & Barnett, 1991; Kopp, 1982). However, although there is an identifiable developmental progression in the acquisition of self-regulatory skills and abilities within these domains, there are also individual differences in the extent to which a child demonstrates competent regulation. These individual differences have been shown to have important implications for psychosocial adaptation and the acquisition of important developmental achievements (Sroufe, 1996). Thus, their role in specific types of adjustment difficulties is worth consideration.

In this chapter, we examine the hypothesis that regulatory differences underlie not just personality differences, but early adjustment difficulties as well. We focus this examination on internalizing and externalizing spectrum disorders as seen in preschool and early childhood. We argue that the development of self-regulation proceeds through several hierarchically organized levels across the infancy, toddler, preschool, and early childhood periods. In this framework, early deficits are conceptualized as constraints on later self-regulatory achievements. Such a conceptualization has implications for the study of early adjustment difficulties, including an empirical approach that necessitates longitudinal research that examines different skill deficits as a function of the developmental level of the child. Such a process-oriented view of self-regulation and adjustment problems may enable us to develop a more differentiated picture of such difficulties, and may also suggest possible strategies for intervention.

This chapter is divided into several sections. First, we examine the development of self-regulation across the period of infancy and early childhood, with a special emphasis on the emergence of more sophisticated regulatory developments within particular developmental transitions. Next, we examine the evidence from existing research that finds support for the notion that self-regulatory deficits underlie adjustment difficulties, with a focus on internalizing and externalizing spectrum difficulties. In addition, we present data from our own longitudinal research that has systematically examined different types of regulatory deficits at different points in development and their relation to early disruptive behavior problems. Finally, we provide suggestions for future work that could illuminate further the relations between the development of self-regulation and competent versus incompetent social and emotional functioning in early childhood.

NORMATIVE DEVELOPMENTS IN SELF-REGULATION THROUGH EARLY CHILDHOOD

During infancy and early childhood, children gradually acquire the necessary self-regulation skills and strategies that enable them to cope with a variety of developmental challenges and that will support the successful transition to the school and peer environment (Cicchetti et al., 1991; Kopp, 1982, 1989; Tronick, 1989). Thus, one challenge that has faced researchers interested in self-regulation has been to specify the distinct regulatory processes that emerge and develop over this developmental period. For example, inherent in Posner and Rothbart's (2000) theory is the view that biological systems underlie the developments in behavioral regulation (Posner & Rothbart, 2000). And, Cole, Michel, and Teti (1994) have articulated a view that places emotional regulation at the heart of child development and adjustment. It has been noted, however, that self-regulation occurs on a number of different, and likely interrelated, levels (Calkins & Fox, 2002; Eisenberg et al., 2000). Thus, one way to conceptualize the self-regulatory system is to describe it as adaptive control that may be observed at the level of physiological, attentional, emotional, behavioral, cognitive, and interpersonal or social processes. And, control at these various levels emerges, at least in primitive form, across the prenatal, infancy, toddler, and early childhood periods of development. Importantly, however, the mastery of earlier regulatory tasks becomes an important component of later competencies, and by extension, the level of mastery of these early skills may constrain the development of later skills. Thus, understanding the development of specific regulatory processes becomes integral to understanding how regulatory deficits affect the emergence of childhood adjustment difficulties.

Regulatory processes begin to develop prenatally and evolve into more sophisticated and self-initiated processes over the course of the toddler, preschool, and school years (Posner & Rothbart, 2000; Rothbart & Jones, 1998). In infancy, the regulatory achievements include the control of physiological arousal (increases or decreases in heart rate to stimuli, such as something frightening), mastery of basic attentional processes (attention engagement or disengagement), and acquisition of primitive emotion regulation skills (self-soothing or help seeking during an upsetting or stressful event).

The initial responses of the infant are characterized by his or her physiological and behavioral reactions to sensory stimuli of different qualities and intensities. This reactivity is thought to be present at birth and reflects a relatively stable characteristic of the infant (Rothbart, Derryberry, & Hershey, 2000). So, for example, infants may differ initially in their threshold to respond to visual or auditory stimuli of a certain intensity (e.g., Calkins, Fox, & Marshall, 1996). Over the course of development, the child's increasing capacity to regulate her motoric and affective behavior, first as a result of a supportive caregiving context and later as a function of voluntary and effortful control, moderates these initial reactive responses. And, much of the development of self-regulation is a result of increasing control over physiological and attentional processes as well as enhanced inhibitory control over motor behavior (Fox, Henderson, Rubin, Calkins, & Schmidt, 2001; Ruff & Rothbart, 1996).

This description of the normative developments of infancy points to the central role played by control of physiological arousal, which is achieved during very early infancy, and underlies mastery of state regulation and control of sleep–wake cycles. So, for example, infants must control physiological arousal to calm themselves to transition to a sleep state. Current approaches to developmental psychophysiological work emphasize that certain underlying physiological processes and functioning may play an important role in the etiology of early regulatory behaviors (Fox, 1994; Fox & Card, 1999) and is believed to underlie functioning in many domains of infant and child behavior (Bornstein & Suess, 2000; Fox, 1994; Porges, 1991, 1996). Three primary types of measures have been used to study relations between physiology and self-regulatory behavior to a variety of elicitors: measures of heart rate, brain electrical activity, and adreno-cortical activity (Fox, Schmidt, & Henderson, 2000; Gunnar, 1990; Porges, 1991; Stansbury & Gunnar, 1994). Control of physiological arousal eventually becomes integrated into the processes of attention engagement and disengagement (Porges, 1996; Richards, 1985, 1987), emotional regulation, and behavioral regulation

(Belsky, Friedman, & Hsieh, 2001; Rothbart, Posner, & Boylan, 1990; Sethi, Mischel, Aber, Shoda, & Rodriquez, 2000).

The capacity for attentional self-regulation begins to emerge and mature toward the end of the 1st year and continues throughout the preschool and school years (Rothbart, 1989). Individual differences in the ability to voluntarily sustain focus, shift attention, and initiate and inhibit actions are believed to be early behavioral manifestations of an emerging system of behavioral control (Ahadi & Rothbart, 1994). For example, the ability to shift attention away from a negative event (such as something frightening) to a positive distracter may lead to decreases in the experience of negative affect. Importantly, there are clear individual differences in the ability to utilize attention to successfully control emotion and behavior. For example, Rothbart (1981, 1986) found increases in positive affect and decreases in distress from 3 to 6 months during episodes of focused attention, suggesting that attentional control is tied to affective experience. Moreover, negative affectivity is believed to interfere with the child's ability to explore and learn about the environment (Ruff & Rothbart, 1996).

During the second half of the 1st year of life there is good evidence that infants become capable of self-initiated emotion regulation behaviors. Emotion regulatory processes refer to processes that serve to manage arousal and support adaptive social and nonsocial responses (Calkins, 1994; Thompson, 1994). Emotion regulation strategies such as self-comforting, help-seeking, and distraction may assist the child in managing early temperament-driven frustration and fear responses in situations where the control of negative emotions may be necessary (Stifter & Braungart, 1995). A child who is confronted by a frustrating situation may be better able to control negative affect by thumbsucking or focusing on a toy or object. Emotion regulation skills may be useful in situations of positive affective arousal in that they allow the child to keep arousal within a manageable and pleasurable range (Grolnick, Cosgrove, & Bridges, 1996; Stifter & Moyer, 1991), for example, temporarily disengaging attention when positive affect (such as laughing) threatens to overarouse the child. Importantly, recent research on the self-regulation of emotion demonstrates quite convincingly that the displays of affect and affect regulation are powerful mediators of interpersonal relationships and socioemotional adjustment in the first few years of life (Calkins, 1994; Calkins & Fox, 1992; Cicchetti et al, 1991; Malatesta, Culver, Tesman, & Shephard, 1989; Rothbart, 1989; Thompson, 1994).

Toddlerhood marks another important transition period in the development of self-regulation. During toddlerhood, the ability to use self-regulating behaviors becomes critical as the child is gaining independence, control, and an identity separate from the caregiver (Kochanska et al., 2001). During the 2nd and 3rd years of life, children begin to gain control over impulses and actions that are mostly activated by the situation. During the preschool years, children become aware of the factors that affect their attention such as motivation and noise (Miller & Zalenski, 1982). Examples of behavioral management or control include compliance to maternal directives and the ability to control impulsive responses (Kopp, 1982; Kuczynski & Kochanska, 1995). Increasingly, these kinds of demands are placed on children during toddlerhood; the task for the toddler is to overcome impulsive reactions or to suspend desired activity to meet external demands. Self-control is demonstrated when a child is able to comply with demands, delay specific activities, and monitor his own behavior; for example, a child who tolerates having to wait for a present by talking to himself or a child who wants a toy being used by another child but resisting the impulse to take it. As the balance of control shifts from external regulation to internal regulation, the different dimensions of self-control begin to be exhibited more frequently and in situations when caregivers are not present (Kopp, 1982). Importantly, each of these skills will support the emergence of the kind of independent and adaptive behavioral functioning that is necessary for the child to transition successfully to the school and peer environment. It is important to note, however, that these normative developments do not preclude the possibility that both reactivity and regulation may be influenced by environmental events and alter the trajectory of a child's development (Cicchetti & Rogosch, 1996).

As children move through the preschool period into the early school years, the capacity for regulation moves into the cognitive domain and the ability for cognitive self-regulation increases. Paris and Newman (1990) defined this type of self-regulation as involving planfulness, control, reflection, competence, and independence. An example of this type of regulation is a preschooler who approaches building a lego house with a plan, works independently and monitors the building to examine if it is satisfactory. Self-regulation has also been defined as self-directedness and performance-control before, during, and after a task activity (Zimmerman, 1998). Importantly, this more sophisticated level of self-regulation is likely supported by earlier forms of self-regulation. In fact, Kuhl and Kraska (1993) argued that children's school performance is influenced not only by behavioral self-regulation, but also by attention control, motivation control, and emotion control or emotion regulation.

In sum, research on infant and childhood development suggests that there are important regulatory developments that are occurring on multiple levels and that these developments are likely to be hierarchically organized with basic physiological processes contributing to early developments in attention and emotional functioning. Individual differences in these processes are likely to be implicated in both personality and behavioral adjustment during the early childhood years when the self-regulation of emotion and behavior becomes core indexes of successful adaptation. These early-developing levels of regulation—physiological, attentional, and caregiver-supported emotional regulation—play a critical role in very early personality and social behavior, and these early emerging behaviors will be reciprocally involved in the development of more complex levels of regulation, such as those involved in behavioral control, interpersonal processes, and metacognitions (Cole, Michel, & Teti, 1994; Stifter, Spinrad, & Braungart–

Rieker, 1999). Moreover, failures of regulation may be observed on one or more of these levels and these failures may contribute to childhood behavioral difficulties.

SELF-REGULATION AND CHILDHOOD EXTERNALIZING BEHAVIOR

One dimension of early childhood behavioral problems, externalizing behavior, refers to problems characterized by acting-out types of behaviors including aggressive and destructive behaviors. Approximately 8% of toddlers exhibit a level of externalizing behavior requiring clinical intervention (Achenbach, 1991). In addition to aggressive behaviors, 3% to 5% of children have Attention Deficit Hyperactivity Disorder (ADHD; Barkley, Anastopoulos, Guevremont, & Fletcher, 1991), and many of these children may display early signs of problems before they are diagnosed, which often occurs in elementary school.

The significance of the early display of externalizing-type problems for later behavior has been well-established. Preschoolers displaying aggressive, noncompliant, destructive, and impulsive behaviors are likely to display such behaviors during school age (Cummings, Ianotti, & Zahn–Waxler, 1989; Rose, Rose, & Feldman, 1989) and are at risk for peer rejection and associated problems (i.e., dropping out of school; Parker & Asher, 1987). Aggressive behavior in childhood is predictive of aggression in early adulthood (Olweus, 1979). In characterizing the behavior of children with early externalizing behavior problems, there is often reference to a lack of control, undercontrol, or poor regulation (Campbell, 1995; Lewis & Miller, 1990). However, less focus has been given to the specific nature of the regulation problems displayed by children with externalizing problems.

There is mounting evidence that physiological measures of regulation are related to behavior problems in young children. Specifically, several measures of cardiac functioning show consistent relations to self-regulation and externalizing behavior. One dimension of cardiac activity that has been linked to regulation in young children is heart rate variability. Although there are multiple ways to measure this variability, Porges (1985, 1991, 1996) and colleagues have developed a method that measures the amplitude and period of the oscillations associated with inhalation and exhalation. Thus, this measure refers to the variability in heart rate that occurs at the frequency of breathing (respiratory sinus arrythmia; RSA) and is thought to reflect the parasympathetic influence on heart rate variability via the vagus nerve. Porges has termed this measure of heart rate variability vagal tone (Vna; Porges 1996; Porges, & Byrne, 1992). High resting RSA is one index of autonomic functioning that has been associated with appropriate emotional reactivity (Stifter & Fox, 1990) and good attentional ability (Richards, 1985, 1987; Suess, Porges, & Plude, 1994). Several studies have linked high RSA in newborns with good developmental outcomes, suggesting that it may be an important physiological component of appropriate engagement with the environment (Hofheimer, Wood, Porges, Pearson, & Lawson, 1995; Richards & Cameron, 1989).

This research suggests that children with low RSA may be at risk because they may have difficulty attending and reacting to environmental stimulation (Porges, 1991; Wilson & Gottman, 1996). However, there have been few studies examining the relations between RSA and aggressive behavior in young children. Heart rate variability has been found to be reduced in children with conduct disorder (Pine et al., 1996). Eisenberg et al. (1995) found that greater heart rate variability was also related to better social competence. Pine and colleagues (Pine et al., 1996) recently reported that 11-year-old boys with externalizing symptoms had lower heart period variability. Mezzacappa and colleagues (Mezzacappa et al., 1997) reported similar findings among adolescent males. These researchers concluded that such relations may occur because of parasympathetic links to regulatory abilities involving attentional and behavioral control.

A related measure of cardiac functioning that may be more directly related to the kinds of problems displayed by aggressive children is decrease (suppression) in RSA or heart rate variability during situations where coping or emotional and behavioral regulation is required. Suppression of RSA is thought to be a physiological strategy that permits sustained attention and behaviors indicative of active coping that are mediated by the parasympathetic nervous system (Porges, 1991, 1996; Wilson & Gottman, 1996). Recent research indicates that suppression of RSA during challenging situations is related to better state regulation, greater self-soothing and more attentional control in infancy (DeGangi, DiPietro, Greenspan, & Porges, 1991; Huffman et al., 1998), fewer behavior problems and more appropriate emotion regulation in preschool (Calkins, 1997; Porges, Doussard-Roosevelt, Portales, & Greenspan, 1996), and sustained attention in school-age children (Suess et al., 1994). A deficiency in this ability to decrease heart rate variability may be related to early behavior problems, particularly problems characterized by a lack of behavioral and emotional control (Porges, 1996; Wilson & Gottman, 1996).

Although there is mounting evidence suggesting that physiological regulatory processes may underlie young children's behavioral difficulties, considerable research has established that emotion regulation very early in life is predictive of later behavior and behavior problems (Cole, Zahn-Waxler, & Smith, 1994). Stifter et al. (1999) found that emotional regulation in response to frustration in infancy was related to compliance in toddlerhood. Eisenberg and her colleagues (Eisenberg et al., 1994, 1995, 1996) consistently found relations among emotion regulation and behavior problems and peer competence.

One example of how problematic emotion regulation may lead to deficiencies in social competence is in the relation between anger management and aggression. Eisenberg, Fabes, and colleagues (Eisenberg et al., 1993, 1994; Fabes & Eisenberg, 1992) have studied the role that anger, and the regulation of anger reactions, may play in the development of social competence. They found that individuals who are highly emotional in response to anger-inducing events and low in regulation are likely to display aggression. Eisenberg hypothesized that the intensity of anger is related to a loss of behavioral control. Strategies such as attentional control, avoidance, and instrumental coping, may be useful in dealing with anger (Eisenberg et al., 1993, 1994).

One context where the emotion regulation-psychopathology connection has been found is in a disappointment paradigm. Cole, Zahn–Waxler, and Smith (1994) used this paradigm to examine expressive control in children exhibiting high and low levels of behavior problems. Cole et al. (1994) found that high risk boys displayed more negative affect after disappointment when an experimenter was present than did low risk boys. In addition, boys' negative emotion, particularly anger, predicted their aggression and oppositionality during the disappointment. These findings are consistent with previous findings by Cole and Smith (1993) that in a disappointment paradigm, behavior-problem preschoolers show negative emotions more quickly and for longer periods than nonproblem children.

Although most of the research examining deficits in children with externalizing behavior problems has focused on the role of emotion regulation, more sophisticated types of regulation are also implicated in these disorders. For example, evidence exists for a negative relation between the child's success at behavioral regulation (compliance, control of impulsivity, and delay of gratification ability) and externalizing problem behavior. Eisenberg and colleagues (1997) have examined the relation between behavioral regulation and externalizing behaviors among older children. In one study, Eisenberg (1997) found that teacher and parent ratings of children's problem behavior were related to children's persistence on a behavioral regulation task. In addition, parent ratings of impulsivity, inhibition control, and global self-control predicted parent ratings of later problem behavior and teacher ratings of children's social competence (Eisenberg et al., 1997). In a separate sample of 214 children (ages 4½–8) Eisenberg et al. (2001) found a negative correlation between child persistence and mother report of externalizing behavior. There was also a negative correlation between both teacher and parent ratings of regulation and the other reporters' rating of externalizing behavior. Although there is clearly a direct link between behavioral regulation and externalizing behavior in young children, Eisenberg and colleagues (2001) have explored behavioral regulation as a mediator of these relations. They found that regulation mediated the relation between maternal positive and negative expressivity and children's internalizing and externalizing behaviors. These findings suggest that behavioral regulation plays an important role in how parenting behaviors affect child outcomes, both directly and indirectly.

In sum, data from a variety of studies suggest that deficits in regulation that may be observed on multiple levels underlie externalizing type behavior problems in young children. This work has largely been conducted with school-age children, however, and there is little evidence to suggest whether, in fact, early developing regulatory abilities actually constrain the development of more sophisticated abilities. Moreover, almost no research has been conducted that attempts to investigate these multiple levels of regulation across time.

SELF-REGULATION AND CHILDHOOD INTERNALIZING BEHAVIOR

Based on the evidence that self-regulation is related to externalizing behavior, it is not surprising that regulatory processes have also been investigated in relation to internalizing disorders in young children (Cicchetti & Toth, 1991; Fox & Calkins, 1993; Schultz, Izard, Ackerman, & Youngstrom, 2001). Internalizing spectrum behavior includes social withdrawal, inhibition, shyness, anxiety, and depression (Achenbach & Edelbrock, 1978, 1981; Hinshaw, 1987; Rubin & Asendorpf, 1991). Although these disorders may appear to be less common in younger children, this may be due to the fact that such disorders may be less obvious to parents and teachers. Externally-based reports used for the assessment of internalizing disorders are much less reliable than for externalizing behaviors, which are much more easily observed (Links, Boyle, & Offord, 1989).

Much research in this area involving infants and very young children has focused on the phenomena of behavioral inhibition. Behavioral inhibition refers to the child's initial response to novel events or unfamiliar adults. First described by Kagan and colleagues (Garcia Coll, Kagan, & Reznick, 1984; Kagan & Snidman, 1991), young children who are behaviorally inhibited display low approach tendencies, become and remain vigilant for the duration of exposure to the novel object, and often seek the proximity of a caregiver when exposed to novel events or situations. This behavioral pattern appears to have a distinct physiological profile. Beginning at infancy, inhibited children display significant differences from their uninhibited peers across a number of physiological measures. Kagan, Snidman, and Arcus (1993) reported that inhibited and uninhibited infants differ in the magnitude of cardiac acceleration and papillary dilation to mild stress. Moreover, Suomi (1987) found that a small group of rhesus monkeys who are fearful and timid to the unfamiliar also display physiological characteristics such as high heart rate, and resemble the profile of inhibited children. Inhibited children consistently display greater motor activity and frequent crying to novel stimuli when they are infants (Kagan et al.,1993; Lagasse, Gruber, & Lipsitt, 1989). Kagan argued that limbic system differences underlie the pattern of emotional and behavioral responding seen in inhibited children (Kagan, 1989). Calkins (1994) suggested that these emotional and behavioral differences are at the core of a regulatory style that limits inhibited children's exposure to novel events and stimuli that are beyond the regulatory abilities of these children.

Social withdrawal is a more mature form of inhibition and refers to the older child's social response to unfamiliar peers (Coplan, Rubin, Fox, Calkins, & Stewart, 1994). Children who exhibit social withdrawal when confronted with unfamiliar peers do not engage in social interaction, and they do not initiate or respond with social behaviors to social bids from unfamiliar peers. This pattern of social behavior is also believed to have a distinct underlying physiological profile. Fox and colleagues (Calkins et al., 1996; Fox et al., 1995; Fox, Schmidt, Calkins, Rubin, & Coplan, 1996) have examined the pattern of brain electrical activity that characterizes inhibition and social withdrawal and have postulated that individual differences in EEG activation are involved in regulation and are associated with approach or withdrawal behaviors. Fox speculated that a stable resting pattern of frontal EEG asymmetry may reflect an underlying "trait" disposition for the motivational states of approach or withdrawal and that such motivational states may facilitate adaptive regulatory behavior under conditions of emotional challenge (Fox, 1994; Fox et al., in press; Fox et al., 1996). Superimposed on this foundation of lateralized brain function are processes such as attention which function to provide competencies to the child for adaptive emotion regulation. It is the interaction of lateralization, which predisposes the child to engage in approach versus withdrawal behaviors (depending on whether left or right frontal region is more activated), and attention skills that enable the child to use specific strategies. A child with well-developed attention control skills who is predisposed to withdraw from a threatening stimulus may be better able to engage in self-distraction than a child with a similar predisposition, but without such skills.

It is important to distinguish between the notion of lateralized brain systems for basic underlying motivational behaviors and those brain systems involved in cognitive processes such as verbal mediation, analytic abilities, monitoring, and inhibition of prepotent responses, all of which may be directly tied to emerging regions of frontal cortex. So for example, orbito-frontal cortex appears to be important in decision-making processes involving emotion, whereas regions of anterior cingulate have been implicated in error detection and attention, and dorso lateral frontal cortex appears critical for working memory (Davidson, Putnam, & Larson, 2000). These competencies (decision making, error detection, working memory) are all involved in adaptive emotion regulation and are a function of the prefrontal cortex. Again, as with attention processes, emotional control processes are a consequence of the dynamic interaction of the frontal regions (Fox, 1994).

In a series of longitudinal studies, Fox and colleagues (1994) have demonstrated that the pattern of frontal EEG asymmetry may be integral to the ability to regulate emotion and behavior and that patterns of emotional and behavioral regulation may predict social withdrawal and internalizing disorders in children. For example, Calkins et al. (1996) found that infants with greater relative right frontal activation had higher amounts of negative affect and motor activity at 9 months than infants with greater relative left frontal activation. In addition, infants who were high on reactivity to visual auditory and olfactory stimuli were more likely to exhibit social withdrawal at 4 years of age compared to similarly reactive infants who exhibited left frontal reactivity. These findings suggest that prefrontal skills involved in regulation are predictive of internalizing in early childhood.

A dimension of regulation that has been linked consistently to internalizing spectrum behaviors is emotional regulation, or, more specifically, poor regulation of negative affect (Fox et al., 1995; Rubin, Coplan, Fox, & Calkins, 1995; Shaw, Keenan, Vondra, Delliquadri, & Giovannelli, (1997). Shaw et al. (1997) found that infants' difficulty (proneness to negative emotionality) predicted internalizing scores from the Child Behavior Checklist (Achenbach, 1992) at age 5. Specifically, 2-year infant difficulty predicted 5-year internalizing, withdrawal, and depression or anxiety. Interestingly, in this study, an interaction between infant difficulty and conflict exposure at 24 months predicted a unique amount of variance in both withdrawal and depression or anxiety, suggesting that regulatory difficulties interact with environmental stressors to predict problem behaviors. Fox (1994) argued that parents under stress and with psychopathology will themselves have dimensions of emotion dysregulation that promote those patterns in children. For example, children being treated for an anxiety disorder have a greater likelihood of having a parent with an anxiety disorder than children with other clinical problems (Bradley, 1990; Reeves, Werry, Elkind, & Zametkin, 1987). In this way, difficulty regulating distress and negative affect can be a function of child characteristics as well as caregiver traits and functioning.

Research suggests that there is some evidence for the stability of internalizing problems (Rubin & Hymel, 1987; Sacco & Graves, 1984) and their relation to difficulties in behavioral and interpersonal regulation. However, Rubin et al. (1995) found that the regulation-internalizing connection may differ for different groups of children. They examined five groups of children, based on children's amount of social interaction and level of emotion dysregulation. The groups were low social interaction-good emotion regulators; low social interaction-poor emotion regulators; high-social interaction-good emotion regulators; high social interaction-poor emotion regulators; and an average group of children who did not fall into these categories. Rubin et al. (1995) found that the low social interaction children who were poor regulators displayed more wary and anxious behaviors during free play and other episodes and more internalizing than the low social interaction children who were good regulators or the average group. These results suggest that children who are low on social interaction are not necessarily at risk for internalizing problems, and that the ability to regulate affect may serve as a protective factor displacing them from a potentially problematic trajectory.

Behavioral regulation may also predict internalizing in children from a very young age. Behaviorally inhibited toddlers have been found to be more socially wary and reticent than their noninhibited counterparts when interacting with peers at 4 years of age (Calkins & Fox, 1995). Vondra, Shaw, Swearingen, Cohen, and Owens (2001) found that 2-year old children who displayed greater behavioral regulation had fewer internalizing behavior problems at age 3½ . Brody and Flor (1998) found a strong correlation between behavioral regulation and teacher ratings of withdrawal, anxiety, and depression in a sample of African–American 6- to 9-year-olds living in single-parent households. Moreover, behavioral regulation mediated the connection between maternal measures (maternal parenting style, mother–child relationship, and maternal school involvement) and internalizing problems. This is consistent with findings by Eisenberg et al. (2001) that children's behavioral regulation mediated the relation between maternal positive and negative expressivity and children's internalizing problems in a sample of 4- to 6-year-olds. These findings suggest that behavioral regulation may not simply be a direct predictor of internalizing behavior, but may play a role in the link between parenting and internalizing for young children.

This review of the literature examining the relations between regulation and behavior problems reveals that such inquiries would benefit from longitudinal studies examining such processes over time and across multiple domains. In our program of research, we have attempted to conduct such a comprehensive study of regulation and adjustment across the infancy, toddler, and early childhood periods and with respect to acting-out, externalizing disorders.

INTEGRATIVE STUDY OF THE DEVELOPMENT OF SELF-REGULATION AND CHILDHOOD PSYCHOLOGICAL ADJUSTMENT

In recent research, we have applied a model of self-regulation development (Calkins, 1994; Calkins & Fox, 2002) to the study of early-emerging externalizing problems (Calkins & Dedmon, 2000; Calkins, Gill, & Williford; 1999; Calkins et al., 2002; Gill & Calkins, 2003; Howse, Calkins, Anastopolous, Keane, & Shelton, 2003; Keane, Calkins, & Howse, under review; Smith, Lomax, & Calkins, 1998). This model, which is depicted in Fig. 12.1, assumes that early disruptive behavior problems are a function of deficits in self-regulation that may be observed across multiple levels (physiological, attentional, emotional, behavioral, and cognitive). These regulatory deficits are influenced by both child characteristics and parenting, broadly construed. Child characteristics such as temperament and intelligence may directly constrain self-regulation, or affect self-regulation through their affects on parenting. Parenting, including parenting behavior and functioning, may moderate the relation between child characteristics and self-regulation. Importantly, however, the model allows for multiple pathways to externalizing-type problems. Understanding the nature and source of specific deficits in regulation will lead to a clear explication of the problems associated with the various types of externalizing problems.

In two longitudinal studies, we investigated the self-regulatory components of early social behavior by focusing on children with early-appearing problems managing frustration and aggressive behavior. In one study, for example, we recruited, using two separate administrations of the Child Behavior Checklist for 2- to

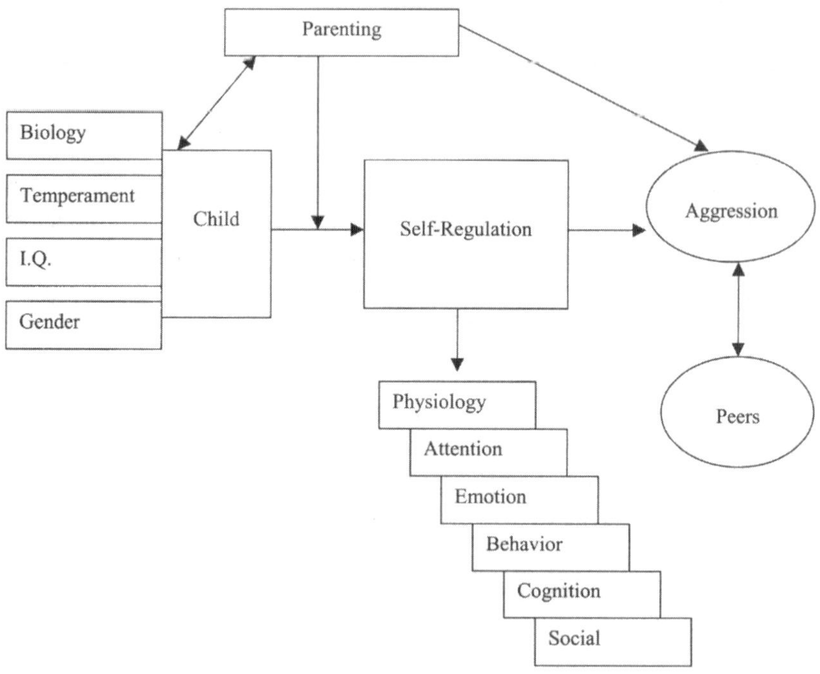

Fig. 12.1 A hypothetical model of self-regulatory functioning and aggression in childhood.

3-year-olds (CBCL–2/3), 50 2-year-old children with stable externalizing behavior problems (aggression and destruction) in the borderline clinical range (labeled "high risk") and 50 children without such problems (labeled "low risk"). The children were matched on age, gender, socioeconomic status, and race. We assessed these children in the laboratory in a series of procedures (emotion tasks, attention tasks, delay of gratification, and compliance tasks) designed to elicit regulation across multiple levels. Our physiological measures were resting and response measures of Heart Rate and Respiratory Sinus Arrythmia. Previous research with inhibited infants and children suggests that regulatory efforts may be in part a consequence of parasympathetic nervous system functioning (Porges, 1996; Stifter & Fox, 1990) as well as frontal brain activity. In addition, we examined maternal behaviors in the laboratory in a different set of tasks. Finally, and in a second assessment, we observed the children in a peer play situation and examined the degree to which the aggressive children displayed socially appropriate versus inappropriate behavior.

The findings from this study provided preliminary support for the idea that early developments in self-regulation support early adjustment, and that failures of self-regulation may be implicated in the display of acting-out, or externalizing, behavior problems. First, we observed that high risk 2-year-olds did not display the same pattern of vagal suppression as low risk children when challenged behaviorally and emotionally (Calkins & Dedmon, 2000). Indeed, across all of the challenging situations with which they were presented, aggressive children showed only modest decreases in RSA from baseline to challenge, unlike their control counterparts, who consistently displayed significant decreases. The behavior of the children mapped onto their physiological response as well. Aggressive children spent less time attending to the task, more time fretting or tantrumming, and they engaged in fewer putative regulatory behaviors than did the control children. These children also were having difficulty complying with maternal requests and displayed significantly more defiance as well (Calkins & Dedmon, 2000).

In a second assessment of these children at age 2, we found that children characterized as aggressive by parents were, in fact, more aggressive in play with an unfamiliar peer, even when the mothers of the children were present in the room. Moreover, the aggressive behavior became more frequent over the course of the play session. Thus, these children have difficulty controlling aggressive impulses under conditions of novelty and when their behavior is being closely monitored (Calkins, Gill, Johnson, & Smith, 1999). In sum, there is good evidence from this study that these children displayed deficits in regulation across several levels of functioning—physiological, emotional, attentional, behavioral, and social (Calkins & Dedmon, 2000; Calkins, Gill, Johnson, & Smith, 1999)—and that this pattern of deficits is evident during the 3rd year of life.

We have conducted follow-up assessments of these children at ages 4 and 5 with the aim of understanding whether these early deficits affected children's behavior in social and academic domains of functioning. Our preliminary data suggest, first, that there is a high degree of stability of these problems and, indeed, good evidence that early regulatory deficits are linked to ADHD. The correlation between CBCL externalizing behavior at age 2 and age 4 was $r = .67, p < .0001$, whereas the percentage of children in the high risk category who received a clinical diagnosis of ADHD at 4½ yeares was 40% versus 10% for the control children (Gerrard, Anastopoulos, Calkins, & Shelton, 2000). Moreover, early regulatory difficulties predicted peer liking in kindergarten, with both parents and teachers reporting that children displaying noncompliance, aggression, and poor emotion regulation were significantly less liked by their peers than children without these difficulties (Keane, Calkins, & Howse, under review). Finally, early emotional and behavioral regulation predicted academic achievement, above and beyond the effects of social class and IQ, two of the strongest predictors of academic achievement (Howse et al., 2003). These data suggest that early regulatory deficits constrain, at least to some degree, the child's functioning in the peer and school domains.

These data provide some evidence, then, that regulatory deficits are implicated in early externalizing-type behavior problems, but they do not necessarily provide support for a developmental model of self-regulatory contributors to behavior problems. Given that the self-regulation data were collected contemporaneously with the toddler behavior problem data, we do not know whether they are a cause or merely a symptom of early behavior problems. However, it is clear that emotional regulatory deficits and behavior problems early in development lead to other, more serious developmental difficulties in both the peer and school domains.

To address the role of very early developing self-regulation and the emergence of behavior problems, we are conducting a second longitudinal study in which we selected infants that might be predisposed to difficulty with aggression because of a susceptibility to be easily angered. Toward this end, we screened a cohort of 360 6-month-olds infants using a battery adapted from Goldsmith's LAB–TAB assessment of anger (Goldsmith & Rothbart, 1993). We selected infants who scored above the 50th percentile on the anger measure from the laboratory assessment and above the 50th percentile on the anger scale from the Infant Behavior Questionnaire, a maternal report measure of infant temperament. Of the larger sample, 77 infants met the criteria for the "low frustration" group and 85 met the criteria for the "high frustration" group. Preliminary analyses revealed that there was no relation between frustration group and sex of child (47 of the 85 infants in the high frustration group were girls, compared with 36 of the 77 infants in the low frustration group), marital status, and child birth order.

To examine the regulatory functioning of these infants, we observed them in a battery of emotion and attention tasks while collecting cardiac data. Our analysis of their regulatory functioning revealed that easily frustrated infants displayed less physiological regulation during a sustained attention task, they had difficulty sustaining attention, and they engaged in different sorts of regulatory behaviors during emotion-eliciting situations. They engaged in less visual distraction and more tantrumming than did less-easily frustrated infants (Calkins et al., in press). We propose that these infants are displaying potentially problematic self-regulatory functioning very early in development. Important to their developmental outcome is the extent to which they receive environmental support that may assist them in acquiring the regulatory skills that seem to be lacking due to their excessive temperamental reactivity.

In prior work, we found that there were significant links between environmental support (parenting behaviors) and child regulation at the levels of physiological, emotional, and behavioral regulation (Calkins, Smith, Gill, & Johnson, 1998). Toddlers of mothers who used more positive, reinforcing, and guiding behaviors were more physiologically well-regulated, engaged in more constructive emotion regulation behaviors, and were more compliant in adult-directed contexts than were toddler of mothers who were more controlling and negative. Our expectation with our infant sample is that, with sensitive and contingent caregiving, these regulatory achievements will not, in the long term, be compromised.

Our analysis of maternal behavior, however, suggests that the reciprocal processes that take place between infant and caregiver may be more challenging for these frustrated infants. We found that, across several different types of mother–infant interactions, mothers of frustrated infants were significantly more intrusive and less sensitive than were mothers of nonfrustrated infants. However, it was also the case that the frustrated infants were displaying more negative affect even in these low-stress interactions. Once this negative affect was controlled for statistically, the differences between the two groups of mothers no longer existed (Calkins et al., 2003). These findings suggest that the day-to-day interactions between mother and infant are being driven, at least to some extent, by the infant's frustrated temperament. Again, however, the long-term implications of such a dynamic are unclear.

Our longitudinal studies of regulatory precursors of externalizing difficulties suggest that a hierarchical model of such developments may best capture the trajectory of these problems over the course of very early development. Nevertheless, a number of issues remain to be addressed, the study of which would inform our understanding of both internalizing and externalizing disorders of childhood.

FUTURE DIRECTIONS

An examination of the empirical literature on early childhood adjustment disorders suggests that a core feature of both internalizing and externalizing is self-regulatory deficits that may be observed across multiple domains of functioning. In addition, our longitudinal studies of early adjustment that focus on multiple measures of regulation provide support for the proposition that these multiple levels of self-regulation are implicated in early personality development and the emergence of some types of behavioral problems. However, our attempts to integrate data that are collected across multiple domains of functioning create a number of unresolved questions and challenges.

First, it will be important to understand the differential trajectories of early internalizing and externalizing disorders. This issue is complicated somewhat by the observation that these two types of disorders often co-occur, leaving open the question of whether this represents a third pattern of early adjustment difficulties or merely a more severe form of early psychopathology. Nevertheless, despite this complication, it will be necessary to try to understand what specific sorts of regulatory deficits lead to these very different kinds of disorders.

Second, although many researchers and theorists posit a strong role for the environment in the development of self-regulation, the effects of these environmental factors on the multiple levels of regulation have yet to be explored. Many researchers hypothesize that caregiving behavior, for example, plays an important role in the development of different types of regulation (Calkins, 1994; Calkins & Fox, in press; Eisenberg, et al., 1996; Thompson, 1990), but the specific relations between caregiving and types of regulation, and the developmental periods during which these environmental factors exert their unique effects, have yet to be specified.

Third, although there are some clearly identifiable development progressions that have been identified at the physiological, attentional, emotional, and social regulatory levels, there has been less emphasis on how developments in each of these levels affect one another. So, for example, although much is known about the changes in emotional regulation that can be observed across the infancy and childhood period, less work has been conducted linking these changes to specific changes in other types of regulation. Moreover, the direction of effects of individual differences in specific levels of regulation on other levels of regulation is another largely unexplored area. Future investigations must be aimed at the more microlevel to address the issue of how individual differences in particular types of physiological regulation affect the development of specific emotion regulatory processes that are implicated in the development of childhood internalizing and externalizing disorders. These process-oriented questions are likely to be the key to our understanding of different developmental outcomes and to the nature of different types of adjustment problems in early childhood. Clearly, the answer to these questions lies in the conduct of carefully designed longitudinal studies that chronicle developments at different levels of regulation over time.

REFERENCES

Achenbach, T. M. (1991). *Manual for the Child Behavior Checklist/4–18 and 1991 Profiles.* Burlington: University of Vermont Department of Psychiatry.

Achenbach, T. M. (1991). *Manual for the Child Behavior Checklist/2–3 and 1992 Profiles.* Burlington: University of Vermont Department of Psychiatry.

Achenbach, T. M., & Edelbrock, C. S. (1978). The classification of child psychopathology: A review and analysis of empirical efforts. *Psychological Bulletin, 85,* 1275–1301.

Achenbach, T. M., & Edelbrock, C. S. (1981). Behavioral problems and competencies reported by parents of normal and disturbed children aged four through sixteen. *Monographs of the Society for Research in Child Development, 46* (1, Serial No. 82).

Ahadi, S. A., & Rothbart, M. K. (1994). Temperament, development, and the Big Five. In C. F. Halverson, Jr., & G. A. Kohnstamm (Eds.), *The developing structure of temperament and personality from infancy to adulthood.* (pp. 189–207). Hillsdale, NJ: Lawrence Erlbaum Associates, Inc.

Barkley, R. A., Anastopoulos, A. D., Guevremont, D. C., & Fletcher, K. E. (1991). Adolescents with ADHD: Patterns of behavioral adjustment, academic functioning, and treatment utilization. *Journal of American Academy of Child and Adolescent Psychiatry, 30,* 752–761.

Belsky, J., Friedman, S. L., & Hsieh, K. H. (2001). Testing a core emotion-regulation prediction: Does early attentional persistence moderate the effect of infant negative emotionality on later development? *Child Development. 72,* 123–133.

Bornstein, M., & Suess, P. (2000). Physiological self-regulation and information processing in infancy: Cardiac vagal tone and habituation. *Child Development, 71,* 273–287.

Bradley, S. J., (1990). Affect regulation and psychopathology: Bridging the mind–body gap. *Canadian Journal of Psychiatry, 35,* 540–547.

Brody, G. H., & Flor, D. L. (1998). Maternal resources, parenting practices, and child competence in rural, single-parent African American families. *Child Development, 69,* 803–816.

Calkins, S. D. (1994). Origins and outcomes of individual differences in emotional regulation. In N. A. Fox (Ed.), Emotion regulation: Behavioral and biological considerations, *Monographs of the Society for Research in Child Development*, 59(2-3, Serial No. 240).

Calkins, S. D. (1997). Cardiac vagal tone indices of temperamental reactivity and behavioral regulation in young children. *Developmental Psychobiology, 31,* 125–135.

Calkins, S. D. (in press). Temperament and emotional self-regulation: Multiple models of early development. Chapter to appear in M. Beauregard (Ed.), *Consciousness, emotional self-regulation and the brain.* New York: John Benjamins Publishing Company.

Calkins, S. D., & Dedmon, S. A. (2000). Physiological and behavioral regulation in two-year-old children with aggressive/destructive behavior problems. *Journal of Abnormal Child Psychology, 2,* 103–118.

Calkins, S. D., & Fox, N. A. (1992). The relations among infant temperament, security of attachment and behavioral inhibition at 24 months. *Child Development, 63*, 1456–1472.

Calkins, S. D., & Fox, N. A. (1995). *Longitudinal correlates of toddler inhibition.* Paper presented at the biennial meeting of the Society for Research in Child Development, Indianapolis, IN.

Calkins, S. D., & Fox, N. A. (2002). Self-regulatory processes in early personality development: A multilevel approach to the study of childhood social withdrawal and aggression. *Development and Psychopathology, 15*, 55–71.

Calkins, S. D., Fox, N. A., & Marshall, T. R. (1996). Behavioral and physiological antecedents of inhibition in infancy. *Child Development, 67,* 523–540.

Calkins, S. D., Gill, K. A., Johnson, M. C., & Smith, C. (1999). Emotional reactivity and emotion regulation strategies and predictors of social behavior with peers during toddlerhood. *Social Development, 8*, 310–341.

Calkins, S. D., & Johnson, M. C. (1998). Toddler regulation of distress to frustrating events: Temperamental and maternal correlates. *Infant Behavior and Development 21,* 379–395.

Calkins, S. D., Smith, C. L., Gill, K. L., & Johnson, M. C. (1998). Maternal interactive style across contexts: Relations to emotional, behavioral and physiological regulation during toddlerhood. *Social Development, 7,* 350–369.

Campbell, S. B. (1995). Behavior problems in preschool children: A review of recent research. *Journal of Child Psychology and Psychiatry, 36,* 113–149.

Cicchetti, D., Ganiban, J., & Barnett, D. (1991). Contributions from the study of high-risk populations to understanding the development of emotional regulation. In J. Garber & K. A. Dodge (Eds.). *The development of emotion regulation and dysregulation* (pp. 69–88). Cambridge, England: Cambridge University Press.

Cicchetti, D., & Rogosch, F. A. (1996). Equifinality and multifinality in developmental psychopathology. *Development & Psychopathology, 8,* 597–600.

Cicchetti, D., & Toth S. L. (1991). *Internalizing and externalizing expressions of dysfunction: Rochester Symposium on Developmental Psychopathology* (Vol. 2). Hillsdale, NJ: Larence Erlbaum Associates.

Cole, P., Michel, M. K., & Teti, L. (1994). The development of emotion regulation and dysregulation. In N. A. Fox (Ed.), Emotion regulation: Behavioral and biological considerations. *Monographs of the Society for Research in Child Development, 59*(2–3, Serial No. 240).

Cole, P. M., & Smith, K. D. (1993). *Preschoolers' behavioral difficulties and the self-regulation of negative emotion.* Paper presented at the meeting for the Society for Research in Child Development, New Orleans, LA.

Cole, P. M., Zahn–Waxler, C., & Smith, K. D. (1994). Expressive control during a disappointment: Variations related to preschoolers' behavior problems. *Developmental Psychology, 30,* 835–846.

Coplan, R. J., Rubin, K. H., Fox, N. A., Calkins, S. D & Stewart, S. (1994). Being alone, playing alone and acting alone: Distinguishing among reticence, and passive- and active-solitude in young children. *Child Development, 65*, 129–*137.*

Cummings, E. M., Ianotti, R. J., & Zahn–Waxler, C. (1989). Aggression between peers in early childhood: Individual continuity and developmental change. *Child Development, 60,* 887–895.

Davidson, R. J., Putnam, K. M., & Larson, C. L. (2000). Dysfunction in the neural circuitry of emotion regulation—A possible prelude to violence. *Science, 289,* 591–594.

Dawson, G., Hessl, D., & Frey, K. (1994). Social influences on early developing biological and behavioral systems related to affective disorder. *Development and Psychopathology, 6,* 759–779.

DeGangi, G., DiPietro, J.,Porges, S. W., & Greenspan, S., (1991). Psychophysiological characteristics of the regulatory disordered infant. *Infant Behavior and Development, 14,* 37–50.

Eisenberg, N, Cumberland, A., Spinrad, T. L., Fabes, R. A., Shepard, S. A., Reiser, M., et al., (2001). The relations of regulation and emotionality to children's externalizing and internalizing problem behavior. *Child Development, 72,* 1112–1134.

Eisenberg, N., Fabes, R. A., Bernzweig, J., Karbon, M., Poulin, R., & Hanish, L. (1993). The relations of emotionality and regulation to preschoolers' social skills and sociometric status. *Child Development, 64,* 1418–1438.

Eisenberg, N., Fabes, R., Guthrie, I, Murphy, B., Maszk, P., Holmgren, R., et al. (1996). The relations of regulation and emotionality to problem behavior in elementary school. *Development and Psychopathology, 8,* 141–162.

Eisenberg, N., Fabes, R. A., Nyman, M., Bernzweig, J., Bernzweig, J., & Pinuelas, A. (1994). The relations of emotionality and regulation to children's anger-related reactions. *Child Development, 65,* 109–128.

Eisenberg, N., Fabes, R. A., Shephard, S. A., Murphy, B. C., Gutherie, I. K., Jones, S., et al. (1997). Contemporaneous and longitudinal prediction of children's social functioning from regulation and emotionality. *Child Development, 68,* 642–664.

Eisenberg, N., Guthrie, I. K., Fabes, R. A., Shepard, S., Losoya, S., Murphy, B. C., et al., (2000). Prediction of elementary school children's externalizing problem behaviors from attention and behavioral regulation and negative emotionality. *Child Development, 71,* 1367–1382.

Eisenberg, N., Murphy, B. C., Maszk, P., Smith, M., & Karbon, M. (1995). The role of emotionality and regulation in children's social functioning: A longitudinal study. *Child Development, 66,* 1360–1384.

Fabes, R., & Eisenberg, N. (1992). Young children's coping with interpersonal anger. *Child Development, 63,* 116–128.

Fox, N. A. (1994). Dynamic cerebral process underlying emotion regulation. In N. A. Fox (Ed.) Emotion regulation: Behavioral and biological considerations., *Monographs of the Society for Research in Child Development, 59*(1–2, Serial No. 240).

Fox, N. A., & Calkins, S. D. (1993). Pathways to aggression and social withdrawal: Interactions among temperament, attachment, and regulation. In K. Rubin & J. Asendorpf (Eds.), *Social withdrawal, inhibition and shyness in children* (pp. 167–184). Hillsdale, NJ: Lawrence Erlbaum Associates, Inc.

Fox, N. A., & Calkins, S. D. (2003) The development of self-control of emotion: Intrinsic and extrinsic influences. *Motivation and Emotion, 27*, 7–26.

Fox, N. A., Calkins, S. D., Porges, S. W., Rubin, K., Coplan, R. J., Stewart, S., et al. (1995). Frontal activation asymmetry and social competence at four years of age. *Child Development, 66,* 1770–1784.

Fox, N. A., & Card, J. (1999). Psychophysiological measures in the study of attachment. In J. Cassidy & P. Shaver (Eds.), *The handbook of attachment* (pp. 226–244). New York: Guilford.

Fox, N. A., Henderson, H. A., & Marshall, P. J. (in press). The biology of temperament: An integrative approach. In C.A. Nelson & M. Luciana (Eds)., *The handbook of developmental cognitive neuroscience.* Cambridge, MA: MIT Press.

Fox, N. A., Henderson, H. A., Rubin, K. H., Calkins, S. D., & Schmidt, L. A. (2001). Continuity and discontinuity of behavioral inhibition and exuberance: Psychophysiological and behavioral influences across the first four years of life. *Child Development, 72,* 1–21.

Fox, N. A., Schmidt, L. A., Calkins, S. D., Rubin, K. H., & Coplan, R. J. (1996). The role of frontal activation in the regulation and dysregulation of social behavior during the preschool year. *Development and Psychopathology, 8,* 89–102.

Fox, N.A., Schmidt, L. A., & Henderson, H. (2000). Developmental psychophysiology: Conceptual and methodological perspective. In J. Cacioppo, L. Tassinary, & G. Bernsten (Eds.), *Handbook of psychophysiology,* (2nd ed., pp. 665–686). Cambridge, England: Cambridge University Press.

Garcia Coll, C., Kagan, J., & Reznick, J. (1984). Behavioral inhibition in young children, *Child Development, 55,* 505–529.

Gerrard, L., Anastopoulos, A. D., Calkins, S. D., & Shelton, T. L. (2000, August). *ADHD symptoms and attachment security in young children.* Poster session presented at the annual Conference of the American Psychological Association, Washington, DC.

Gill, K. A., & Calkins, S. D. (2003). Do aggressive toddlers lack concern for others? Behavioral and physiological indices of empathic responding in two-year old children. *Development and Psychopathology, 15*, 55–71.

Goldsmith, H. H., & Rothbart, M. K. (1993). The laboratory temperament assessment battery (LAB–TAB). University of Wisconsin, Madison, Wisconsin.

Grolnick, W., Cosgrove, T., & Bridges, L. (1996). Age-graded change in the initiation of positive affect. *Infant Behavior and Development, 19,* 153–157.

Gunnar, M. R. (1990). The psychobiology of infant temperament. In J. Colombo & J. Fagen (Eds.) *Individual differences in infancy: Reliability, stability, and prediction* (pp. 387–409). Hillsdale, NJ: Lawrence Erlbaum Associates, Inc.

Gunnar, M. R., Porter, F. L., Wolf, C. M., Rigatuso, J., & Larson, M. C. (1995). Neonatal stress reactivity: Predictors to later emotional temperament. *Child Development, 66,* 1–13.

Hayano, J., Sakakibara, Y., Yamada, A., Yamada, M., Mukai, S., Fujinami, T., et al. (1991). Accuracy of assessment of cardiac vagal tone by heart rate variability in normal subjects. *American Journal of Cardiology, 67,* 199–204.

Hinshaw, S. P. (1987). On the distinction between attentional deficit/hyperactivity and conduct problems/aggression in child psychopathology. *Psychological Bulletin,101,* 443–447.

Hofheimer, J. A., Wood, B. R., Porges, S. W., Pearson, E., & Lawson, E. (1995). Respiratory sinus arrhthymia and social interaction patterns in preterm newborns. *Infant Behavior and Development, 18,* 233–245.

Howse, R. B., Calkins, S. D., Anastopoulos, A. D., Keane, S. P., & Shelton, T. L. (2003). Regulatory contributors to children's kindergarten achievement. *Early Education and Development, 14,* 101–119.

Huffman, L. C., Bryan, Y. E., del–Carmen, R., Pedersen, F. A., Doussard–Roosevelt, J. A., & Porges, S. W. (1998). Infant temperament and cardiac vagal tone: Assessments at twelve weeks of age. *Child Development, 69,* 624–635.

Kagan, J. (1989). The concept of behavioral inhibition to the unfamiliar. In J. S. Reznick (Ed.), *Perspectives on behavioral inhibition. The John D. and Catherine T. MacArthur Foundation series on mental health and development* (pp. 1–23). Chicago: The University of Chicago Press.

Kagan, J., & Snidman, N. (1991). Temperamental factors in human development. *American Psychologist, 46,* 856–862.

Kagan, J., Snidman, N., & Arcus, D. (1993). On the temperamental categories of inhibited and uninhibited children. In K. H. Rubin & J. B. Asendorpf (Eds.), *Social withdrawal, inhibition, and shyness in childhood* (pp. 19–28). Hillsdale, NJ: Lawrence Erlbaum Associates, Inc.

Keane, S. P., Calkins, S. D., & Howse, R. B. Manuscript submitted for publication.

Kochanska, G., Coy, K. C., & Murray, K. Y. (2001). The development of self-regulation in the first four years of life. *Child Development, 72,* 1091–1111.

Kopp, C. (1982). Antecedents of self-regulation: A developmental perspective. *Developmental Psychology, 18,* 199–214.

Kopp, C. (1989). Regulation of distress and negative emotions: A developmental view. *Developmental Psychology, 25,* 243–254.

Kuczynski, L., & Kochanska, G. (1995). Function and content of maternal demands: Developmental significance of early demands for competent action. *Child Development, 66,* 616–628.

Kuhl, J., & Kraska, K. (1993). Self-regulation: Psychometric properties of a computer-aided instrument. *German Journal of Psychology, 17,* 11–24.

Lagasse, L. L., Gruber, C. P., & Lipsitt, L. P. (1989). The infantile expression of avidity in relation to later assessments of inhibition and attachment. In J. S. Reznick (Ed.). *Perspectives on behavioral inhibition. The John D. and Catherine T. MacArthur Foundation series on mental health and development* (pp. 159–176). Chicago: The University of Chicago Press.

Lee, C. L., & Bates, J. E. (1985). Mother-child interaction at age two years and perceived difficult temperament. *Child Development, 56,* 1314–1325.

Lewis, M., & Miller, S. (1990). *Handbook of developmental psychopathology*. New York: Plenum.

Links, P. S., Boyle, M. H., & Offord, D. R. (1989). The prevalence of emotional disorder in children. *Journal of Nervous and Mental Disease, 177,* 85–91.

Malatesta, C. Z., Culver, C., Tesman, J., & Shephard, B. (1989). The development of emotion expression during the first two years of life. *Monographs of the Society for Research in Child Development, 59* (1–2, Serial No. 219).

Mezzacappa, E., Tremblay, R. E., Kindlon, D., Saul, J. P., et al. (1997). *Journal of Child Psychology and Psychiatry and Allied Disciplines, 38.* 457–469.

Miller, P. H., & Zalenski, R. (1982). Preschoolers' strategies of attention on a same–different task. *Developmental Psychology, 18,* 871–857.

Olweus, D. (1979). Stability of aggressive reactive patterns in males: A review. *Psychological Bulletin, 86*, 852–875.

Paris, S. G., & Newman, R. S. (1990). Developmental aspects of self-regulated learning. *Educational Psychologist, 25,* 87–102.

Parker, J. G., & Asher, S. R. (1987). Peer relations and later personal adjustment: Are low accepted children at risk? *Psychological Bulletin, 102,* 357–389.

Pine, D. S., Wasserman, G., Coplan, J., Fried, J., Sloan, R., Myers, M., et al. (1996). Serotonergic and cardiac correlates of aggression in children. *Annals of New York Academy of Sciences, 794,* 391–393.

Porges, S. W. (1985). Illinois Classroom Assessment Profile: Development of the instrument. *Multivariate Behavioral Research, 20,* 141–159.

Porges, S. W. (1991). Vagal tone: An autonomic mediatory of affect. In J. A. Garber & K. A. Dodge (Eds.), *The development of affect regulation and dysregulation* (pp. 11–128). New York: Cambridge University Press.

Porges, S. W. (1996). Physiological regulation in high-risk infants: A model for assessment and potential intervention. *Development and Psychopathology, 8,* 29–42.

Porges, S. W., & Byrne, E. A. (1992). Research methods for measurement of heart rate and respiration. *Biological Psychology, 34,* 93–130

Porges, S. W., Doussard–Roosevelt, J. A., Portales, A. L., & Greenspan, S. I. (1996). Infant regulation of the vagal "brake" predicts child behavior problems: A psychobiological model of social behavior. *Developmental Psychobiology, 29,* 697–712.

Posner, M. I., & Rothbart, M. K. (2000). Developing mechanisms of self-regulation. *Development and Psychopathology, 12,* 427–441.

Reeves, J. C., Werry, J. S., Elkind, G. S., & Zametkin, A. (1987). Attention deficit, conduct, oppositional, and anxiety disorders in children: II. Clinical characteristics. *Journal of the American Academy of Child and Adolescent Psychiatry, 26,* 144–155.

Richards, J. E. (1985). Respiratory sinus arrhythmia predicts heart rate and visual responses during visual attention in 14- and 20-week-old infants. *Psychophysiology, 22,* 101–109.

Richards, J. E. (1987). Infant visual sustained attention and respiratory sinus arrhythmia. *Child Development, 58,* 488–496.

Richards, J. E., & Cameron, D. (1989). Infant heart rate variability and behavioral developmental status. *Infant Behavior and Development, 12,* 45–58.

Richters, J. E. (1997). The Hubble hypothesis and the developmentalist's dilemma. *Development and Psychopathology, 9,* 19–230.

Rose, S. L., Rose, S. A., & Feldman, J. (1989). Stability of behavior problems in very young children. *Development and Psychopathology, 1,* 5–19.

Rothbart, M. K. (1981). Measurement of temperament in infancy. *Child Development, 52,* 569–578.

Rothbart, M. K. (1986). Longitudinal observation of infant temperament. *Developmental Psychology, 22,* 356–365.

Rothbart, M. K. (1989). Temperament and development. In G. Kohnstamm, J. Bates, & M.K. Rothbart (Eds.), *Temperament in childhood* (pp. 187–248). Chichester, England: Wiley

Rothbart, M. K., & Derryberry, D. (1981). Development of individual differences in temperament. In M. E. Lamb & A. L. Brown (Eds.), *The neuropsychology of individual differences: A developmental perspective* (pp. 93–123). New York: Plenum.

Rothbart, M. K., Derryberry, D., & Hershey, K. (2000). Stability of temperamant in childhood: Laboratory infant assessment to parent report at seven years. In V. J. Molfese & D. L. Molfese. *Temperament and personality development across the life span* (pp. XXX–XXX). Mahwah, NJ: Lawrence Erlbaum Associa.tes

Rothbart, M. K., & Jones, L. (1998). Temperament, self-regulation and education. *School Psychology Review, 27,* 479–491.

Rothbart, M. K., & Posner, M. I. (1985). Temperament and the development of self-regulation. In L. C. Hartlage & C. F. Telzrow (Eds.), *The neuropsychology of individual differences: A developmental perspective* (pp. 93–123). New York: Plenum.

Rothbart, M. K., & Posner, M. I. (1990). Regulatory mechanisms in infant development. In J. T. Enns (Ed.), *The development of attention: Research and theory* (pp. 139–160). Amsterdam: Elsevier.

Rothbart, M. K., Posner, M. I., & Boylan, A. (1990). Regulatory mechanisms in infant development. In J. T. Enns (Ed.), *The development of attention: Research and theory. Advances in psychology,* (pp. 47–66). Amsterdam: University of British Columbia, Department of Psychology.

Rubin, K. (1998). Social and emotional development from a cultural perspective. *Developmental Psychology, 34,* 611–615.

Rubin, K. H., & Asendorpf, J. (1991). *Social withdrawal, inhibition, and shyness in childhood.* Hillsdale, NJ: Lawrence Erlbaum Associates, Inc.

Rubin, K. H., Coplan, R. J., Fox, N. A., & Calkins, S. D. (1995). Emotionality, emotion regulation and preschooler's social adaptation. *Development and Psychopathology 7,* 49–62.

Rubin, K. H., & Hymel, S. (1987, April). *Predicting depression in childhood: A longitudinal investigation,* Paper presented at the biennial meetings of the Society for Research in Child Development, Baltimore.

Ruff, H., & Rothbart, M. K. (1996). *Attention in early development.* New York: Oxford University Press.

Sacco, W. P., & Graves, D. J. (1984). Childhood depression, interpersonal problem-solving, and self-ratings of performance. *Journal of Clinical Psychology, 13,* 10–15.

Schultz, D., Izard, C. E., Ackerman, B. O., & Youngstrom, E. A. (2001). Emotion knowledge in economically disadvantaged children: Self-regulatory antecedents and relations to social difficulties and withdrawal. *Development and Psychopathology, 13,* 53–67.

Sethi, A., Mischel, W., Aber, J. L., Shoda, Y., & Rodriquez, L. (2000). The role of strategic attention deployment in development of self-regulation: Predicting preschoolers' delay of gratification from mother–toddler interactions. *Developmental Psychology, 36,* 767–777.

Shaw, D. S., Keenan, K., Vondra, J. I., Delliquadri, E., & Giovannelli, J. (1997). Antecedents of preschool children's internalizing problems: A longitudinal study of low-income families. *Journal of the American Academy of Child and Adolescent Psychiatry, 36,* 1760–1767.

Smith, C. L., Lomax, L. E., & Calkins, S. D. (1998, April). *Patterns of mother–child interaction in two-year-old children with externalizing behavior problems.* Paper presented at the biennial meeting of the International Society for Infant Studies, Atlanta, GA.

Sroufe, A. L. (1996). *Emotional development: The organization of emotional life in the early years.* New York: Cambridge University Press.

Stansbury, K., & Gunnar, M. (1994). Adrenocortical activity and emotion regulation. In N. A. Fox (Ed.) Emotion regulation: Behavioral and biological considerations. *Monographs of the Society for Research in Child Development*, 59(1–2, Serial No. 240).

Stifter, C. A., & Braungart, J. M. (1995). The regulation of negative reactivity in infancy: Function and development. *Developmental Psychology, 31,* 448–455.

Stifter, C. A., & Fox, N. A. (1990). Infant reactivity: Physiological correlates of newborn and 5-month temperament. *Developmental Psychology, 26,* 582–588.

Stifter, C. A., & Moyer, D. (1991). The regulation of positive affect: Gaze aversion activity during mother–nfant interaction. *Infant Behavior and Development, 14*, 111–123.

Stifter, C. A., Spinrad, T., & Braungart–Rieker, J. (1999). Toward a developmental model of child compliance: The role of emotion regulation. *Child Development, 70,* 21–32.

Suess, P. E., Porges, S. W., & Plude, D. J. (1994). Cardiac vagal tone and sustained attention in school-age children. *Psychophysiology, 31,* 17–22.

Suomi, S. (1987). Genetic and maternal contributions to individual differences in rhesus monkey biobehavioral development. In N. A. Krasnegor, E. M. Blass, & M. A. Hofer (Eds.), *Perinatal development: A psychobiological perspective* (pp. 397–419). San Diego, CA: Academic.

Thompson, R. A. (1990). Emotion and self-regulation. In R. A. Thompson (Ed.), *Nebraska Symposium on Motivation: Vol. 36. Socioemotional development.* Lincoln: University of Nebraska Press.

Thompson, R. A. (1994). Emotion regulation: A theme in search of definition. *Monographs of the Society for Research in Child Development, 59* (2–3 Serial No. 240).

Tronick, E. Z. (1989). Emotions and emotional communication in infants. *American Psychologist, 44,* 112–119.

Wilson, B., & Gottman, J. (1996). Attention—The shuttle between emotion and cognition: Risk, resiliency, and physiological bases. In E. Hetherington & E. Blechman (Eds.), *Stress, coping and resiliency in children and families* (pp. 3–22). Mahwah, NJ: Lawrence Erlbaum Associates, Inc.

Vondra, J. I., Shaw, D. S., Swearingen, L., Cohen, M., & Owens, E. B. (2001). Attachment stability and emotional and behavioral regulation from infancy to preschool age. *Development and Psychopathology, 13,* 13–33.

Zimmerman, B. J. (1998). Developing self-fulfilling cycles of academic regulation: An analysis of exemplary instructional models. In D. H. Schunk & B. J. Zimmerman (Eds.) *Self-regulated learning: From teaching to self-reflective practice* (pp. 1–19). New York: Guilford.

13

Physiological Consequences of Emotion Regulation: Taking into Account the Effects of Strategies, Personality and Situation

Cornelia Anna Pauls
University of Marburg

It is generally believed that the tight control of negative emotions either by repression or the inhibition of emotional expression adversely affects physical health. In the first part of this chapter, the actual physiological consequences of experimentally evoked emotion regulation strategies are reviewed. From this review, it is concluded that experimentally evoked emotion suppression seems to have rather negative consequences, whereas manipulated intrapsychic emotion regulation, such as positive reappraisal, intellectualization, distancing, and so forth, are rather effective in modulating one's physiological responses. In the second part, it is discussed whether some emotion regulation strategies are really better than others with respect to their physiological effects given the diversity of situations people are confronted with and the kind of emotion to be regulated. In the third part, the interplay between situational constraints, emotion, and personality is exemplified by reviewing the research on habitual anger and anxiety regulation. Finally, the ecological validity of laboratory findings concerning the long- and short-term physiological consequences of certain emotion regulation strategies is questioned.

A number of emotion researchers agree that emotions are biologically-based reactions that organize an individual's responses to important events (e.g., Arnold, 1960; Frijda, 1986; Levenson, 1988; Plutchik, 1980). Although these responses seem to be rather functional in a number of situations (e.g., Damasio, 1994; see the chapters of Bechara and of Stemmler in this volume), people are nevertheless frequently confronted with situations, in which unregulated and uncontrolled emotion responses would not be appropriate to attain individual short- or long-term goals. In addition, emotions are accompanied by feeling states, which signal the individual that something must be changed to attain a desired—mostly a more pleasant—feeling state. Thus, emotion regulation helps to achieve individual goals by modulating and manipulating the original emotion response.

These modulations may be automatic and unconscious, such as turning one's attention away from potentially upsetting material, or controlled and conscious, such as expressing one's anger to change the behavior of an opponent. Emotional feeling states may be regulated either by modulating the feeling state directly (emotion-focused regulation) or by modification of the emotion eliciting situation (problem-focused regulation; Lazarus, 1991).

Within these two broad classes of emotion regulation, more fine-grained distinctions may be made. For example, emotion-focused regulation includes strategies of (a) attentive allocation, in which one turns attention toward or away from something to influence one's feeling state (see the review of Philippot, Baeyens, Douilliez, & Francart, in this volume); (b) defense, such as repression, projection, and reaction formation; or (c) cognitive change, in which one reappraises the situation or one's capacity to manage the situation (e.g., Butler & Gross, this volume; Gross, 1998b). Apart from these intrapsychic strategies, there are also action-related strategies of emotion-focused regulation, such as avoiding a situation, drug consumption, or to go in for sports to calm down. As mentioned earlier, problem-focused regulation includes strategies, which should alter the emotional impact of a situation itself, such as acting out, expressing, or suppressing one's feeling state to impress an opponent, receive social support, or avoid social disapproval.

Which emotion regulation strategy is chosen in a particular situation depends on characteristics of the person, such as temperamental factors, individual motives, beliefs as well as emotion regulation competencies, and on characteristics of the situation, such as the situational appropriateness of certain emotion regulation strategies (Lazarus, 1991). These points are discussed in later sections.

THE PHYSIOLOGICAL CONSEQUENCES OF CONTROLLING ONE'S EMOTIONS

It is a widely held belief that different forms of emotion regulation have different consequences with respect to subjective distress reduction (e.g., Stanton & Snider, 1993), problem solving (e.g., McCrae & Costa, 1986), and physical health (e.g., Suls & Fletcher, 1985; Taylor, Kemeny, Reed, Bower, & Gruenewald, 2000). Most of these considerations are implicitly influenced by psychodynamic theory, which stipulates that certain forms of emotion regulation are unhealthy, such as repression and behavioral suppression of emotions, whereas actively acting out or disclosing one's emotion is seen as healthy. Whereas the original psychodynamic theory was focused on the somatic effects of unconscious defenses (e.g., Freud, 1936), later researchers investigated the health-endangering effects of emotion suppression that means the more or less intentional and conscious inhibition of emotion behavior (e.g., Alexander, 1950). One central theory in this respect is emotional discharge theory, which posits an inverse relation between the outward expression of an emotion and the inward autonomic response (e.g., Jones, 1935). According to this hydraulic model, emotion is viewed as a form of energy and as such must follow the basic dynamics of energy conservation. Emotional arousal must be discharged either directly through expression or indirectly through internal pathways.

The joint hallmark of these traditions is that emotion regulation results in discrepancies between the experiential, physiological, and expressive components that constitute an emotion, and that the tight control of negative emotions, either by repression or the inhibition of emotional expression, may adversely affect physical health.

Emotion Suppression

The first studies in which emotional expressivity was directly manipulated were conducted by Lanzetta and coworkers. Contrary to the expectations derived from discharge theory, Lanzetta and coworkers found that participants had smaller skin conductance responses and lower ratings of pain when asked to hide their reactions to electric shocks than when asked to exaggerate their reactions (Colby, Lanzetta, & Kleck, 1977; Lanzetta, Cartwright Smith, & Kleck, 1976). Compared to participants who responded spontaneously, Bush, Barr, McHugo, and Lanzetta (1989) found that participants instructed to inhibit their expressive behavior had similar heart rates but lower ratings of amusement during a film comedy. Zuckerman, Klorman, Larrance, and Spiegel (1981) found that participants instructed to respond with neutral facial expressions to pleasant and unpleasant films had lesser increases in physiological arousal than participants instructed to respond naturally or to exaggerate their responses.

Despite the evidence in some studies that emotional suppression does not heighten physiological responses, there are other studies which suggest the opposite. For example, Pennebaker and Chew (1985) instructed participants to deceive the experimenter in a guilty knowledge test paradigm while electrodermal activity was measured. Results indicated that deception was associated with increases in skin conductance level. In addition, several studies concerning expressive styles demonstrated that emotionally unexpressive adults and children are physiologically more reactive to a variety of emotional stimuli than are expressive participants (Buck, 1979; Field & Walden, 1982; Funkenstein, King, & Drolette, 1954; Notarius & Levenson, 1979). The evidence that emotional suppression is associated with strong physiological activation was supported by a range of studies conducted by Gross and coworkers (Gross, 1998a; Gross & Levenson, 1993, 1997). The aim of these studies was to test the effects of emotional suppression, defined as the conscious inhibition of emotional expressive behavior while emotionally aroused. In the study of Gross and Levenson (1993), participants watched a short disgust-eliciting film while their behavioral, physiological, and subjective responses were recorded. Participants were told to simply watch the film (no suppression condition) or watch the film while behaving in such a way that another person watching the participant would not know the participant were feeling anything (suppression condition). Suppression reduced expressive behavior and decreased heart rate reactivity. At the same time, sympathetic nervous system activation was increased, as reflected in increased skin conductance responses and eye blinking, decreased finger pulse amplitude, and shortened pulse transmission times to the finger. The results were explained by the enhanced effort associated by behavioral suppression, and it was assumed that the physiological activation associated with suppression reflects an additional metabolic demand. Because disgust is typically associated with lower levels of heart rate compared with other negative emotions such as anger, fear, or sadness (e.g., Ekman, Levenson, & Friesen, 1983; Levenson, Ekman, & Friesen, 1990), it was assumed that the suppression of disgust resulted in greater "disgust-like" physiological responding.

Gross and Levenson (1993) assumed that the inconsistencies concerning the physiological costs of emotional suppression can in part be ascribed to the fact that compared to the suppression of disgust, suppression of amusement, pain, or other emotions, may have different consequences. Therefore, Gross and Levenson (1997) conducted a study in which participants were instructed either to inhibit their expressive behavior or to simply watch sad, neutral, or amusing films. It could be shown that suppression had no physiological consequences in the neutral film, but clear effects in both negative and positive emotional films. Concretely, during the amusement film, suppression participants showed lower heart rates, but greater sympathetic activation in other cardiovascular parameters (derived by combining pulse transit time to the finger, finger pulse amplitude, pulse transit time to the ear, and finger temperature). During the sadness film, suppression participants showed greater skin conductance, greater sympathetic activation of the cardiovascular system, and greater respiratory activity (derived by combining respiratory period and respiratory depth) than no-suppression participants. These results show that despite some specificity to the emotion elicited, the behavioral inhibition of rather distinct emotions is actually accompanied by enhanced sympathetic activation. However, it should be mentioned that the inconsistencies to earlier studies concerning emotional suppression are not removed, and therefore it seems that further research is necessary concerning the boundary conditions for the physiological effects of emotion suppression.

Intrapsychic Strategies of Emotion Regulation

Typically, the general effects of intrapsychic strategies of emotion regulation are investigated by instructing participants to appraise a stressful situation in a more relieving or positive way. For example, Lazarus and Alfert (1964) presented students with a filmed circumcision ritual and manipulated the accompanying soundtrack. Some participants heard a soundtrack that had been designed to minimize the negative emotional impact of the film by denying the pain involved in the surgery and by emphasizing the joyful aspects of the procedure. Other participants heard no soundtrack at all. Compared with the no-soundtrack condition, participants who heard the soundtrack had lower heart rates, lower skin conductance levels, and higher pleasant mood ratings. These findings suggested that leading participants to view the film less negatively decreased the stressfulness of what otherwise would have been a quite distressing experience.

In a study by Holmes and Houston (1974), participants were either told that they would receive a series of painful electric shocks (threat condition), or they were not told so (no-threat condition). In addition, participants of the threat condition were either instructed to reduce stress by thinking of the shocks as interesting new physiological sensations (threat redefinition condition), or to reduce stress by remaining detached and uninvolved (threat isolation condition), or they received no special instruction (control condition). It could be demonstrated that participants using redefinition and isolation showed smaller increases in heart rate and skin conductance responses than control participants. Likewise, Dandoy and Goldstein (1990) found that an intellectualization instruction decreased galvanic skin response in comparison to a control condition with no instruction when participants watched a distressing film.

Although these results seem to be convincing, there are also findings that do not coincide with the view that cognitive regulation strategies are effective in decreasing one's physiological responses. For example, Steptoe and Vögele (1986) manipulated the cognitive appraisal of participants watching a distressing film by giving the instruction either to focus on physical sensations and experience, to appraise the film in a detached, analytic fashion (intellectualization), or to simply watch the film. Heart rate, skin conductance, and respiration rate were monitored continuously. Contrary to expectation, no significant differences were found in the subjective or physiological reactions of the intellectualization and control groups. Sensation focusing even led to a diminution of cardiac and electrodermal reactions.

Because of the inconsistencies in the research concerning the physiological effects of reappraisal and cognitive change, Gross (1998a) conducted a study in which participants were shown a disgusting amputation film while their experiential, behavioral, and physiological responses were recorded. Participants were told to either think about the film in such a way that they would feel nothing (reappraisal condition), behave in such a way that someone watching would not know they were feeling anything (suppression condition), or simply watch the film (control condition). Compared with the control condition, suppression increased sympathetic activation as in the former studies by Gross and Levenson (1993, 1997). Contrary to expectation, reappraisal participants did not show fewer physiological signs of emotion. Rather, their physiological responses were indistinguishable from those of the control participants. From this finding, Gross (1998a) concluded that reappraisal either simply does not affect the physiological component of an emotion response or that the potency of the amputation film gave reappraisal participants little chance to shut down its powerful autonomic effects.

Results of an older study conducted by Houston and Holmes (1974) offer an explanation of why studies concerning the general effects of certain emotion regulation strategies are not always successful in replicating earlier findings. These authors investigated the use of avoidant thinking as a means of coping with stress. The focus of the study was on stress under conditions of temporal uncertainty, where threat was manipulated by telling participants either that they would or would not receive electrical shocks sometime during the experimental period. During the experimental period, avoidant thinking was manipulated by instructing half of the threatened and half of the nonthreatened participants to read an interesting story that kept them cognitively occupied. No distraction was provided for the remaining participants. Contrary to predictions, physiological measures of stress indicated that threatened participants who used avoidant thinking showed stronger increases in heart rate and skin conductance responses than threatened participants who did not use avoidant thinking. Additional analyses revealed that threatened participants who were not instructed to use avoidant thinking took the opportunity to reappraise the threat less seriously and thereby reduced their level of stress. Participants who used avoidant thinking apparently were unable to effectively reappraise the threat of electric shock, and therefore their stress remained high. The results of this study imply that participants of control conditions may spontaneously use cognitive strategies to attenuate their overwhelming feelings, when watching amputation procedures or the like (see also, Suls & Fletcher, 1985). This may explain why in some studies participants of the treatment condition do not differ from participants in the control condition, such as in the studies of Gross (1998a) and Steptoe and Vögele (1986).

Concerning the physiological and somatic effects of avoidant versus attentive strategies of emotion regulation, Suls and Fletcher (1985) accomplished a meta-analysis of studies conducted between 1957 and 1983. Avoidant strategies were defined as strategies that focus attention away from either the source of the stress or away from one's psychological or somatic reactions to the stressor by means of denial, distraction, repression, and so forth. They divided the studies in those that investigated the short-term consequences and those that investigated the long-term consequences of avoidant and attentive strategies. Nearly all of the short-term studies had physiological responses or pain indicators as outcome measures. The overall results of the short-run studies suggested that avoidant strategies have some efficacy over attentive strategies, although the difference was rather small. However, supplementary analyses suggested an influence of boundary conditions that define the relative efficacy of a specific strategy. For example, attention was even superior to avoidance if the former involved a focus on sensory schemata that permitted a threatening or noxious stimulus to be codified in an unemotional way. Attention without explicit instruction as well as attention to emotional cues of the stimulus were both inferior to avoidance. Reappraisal, defined by the authors as a strategy somewhere in between attention and avoidance, was not different from avoidance. By comparing attention to unemotional cues of the threatening or noxious stimulus to uninstructed control groups, it was found that attentive strategies provided more relief than no instruction. In addition, avoidance was superior to no instruction in dealing with noxious or threatening stimulation. This means that both attention and avoidance are helpful relative to no systematic strategy. In terms of long-term outcomes, avoidance indicated better outcomes initially, but with time, attention was associated with more positive outcomes. Suls and Fletcher (1985) assumed that avoidance is a very useful coping strategy as long as a stressful life occurrence is relatively brief. More serious events, however, such as recovery from surgery, probably call for active coping and instrumental behavior. In this case, avoidant strategies will discourage action and do little to change the circumstances.

By and large, studies concerning the general effects of intrapsychic regulation strategies such as positive reappraisal, distancing, intellectualization, distraction, and attention to unemotional cues of the threatening stimulus, imply that these strategies are rather effective in reducing physiological activation compared to unregulated emotion

SITUATIONAL CONSTRAINTS OF EMOTION REGULATION

As mentioned earlier, characteristics of the situation in which the emotional encounter takes place may constrain the choice of a successful emotion regulation strategy. Situations differ with respect to familiarity, range of available behavioral choices, and options for interpretation. In addition, the behavioral options are typically bounded by cultural and social rules guiding emotional expressions (e.g., Matsumoto, 1993) and social roles (Underwood, Coie, & Herbsman, 1992).

Behavioral options are also constrained by the quality of the emotion that is generated in a particular situation. This means emotion regulation should vary according to whether the emotion being regulated is anger, disgust, sadness, or some other emotion. In line with these considerations, Scherer and Wallbott (1994) showed that some emotions are more controlled cross-culturally than others. For example, anger and disgust are relatively freely expressed, whereas shame and guilt are the most strongly controlled emotions. In addition, these authors showed that joy, anger, and sadness are most likely to be accompanied by many nonverbal expressions. One major factor behind these differences among emotions is probably the stronger need to communicate joy, anger, and sadness in comparison to fear and disgust, because fear and disgust often occur in nonsocial situations, elicited by natural, rather than social, stimuli. Inhibiting the expression of guilt and shame might protect self-esteem.

All in all, the notion that some emotion regulation strategies are better than others with respect to their physiological effects needs to be qualified by the situations people face day by day. One emotion regulation strategy may be good in some situations, but unproductive or even detrimental in others. For example, positively reappraising a situation may be functional in those situations where nothing else can be done, but may be dysfunctional, when active modification of the situation is necessary. Given the strong dependence of emotion regulation from situational characteristics, inconsistencies in the findings concerning the physiological consequences of certain emotion regulation strategies are not astonishing (Suls & Fletcher, 1985).

PERSONALITY

It is common knowledge that there are enormous individual differences in how people regulate their emotions. It is far from clear, however, who would respond how and when. Concerning the question "who would respond," the literature offers a broad range of personality characteristics that should be associated with certain emotion regulation styles. The most prominent emotion regulation styles are anger-in, anger-out (Spielberger et al., 1985), Type A-behavior (Friedman & Rosenman, 1974) or hostility (e.g., Williams et al., 1980), and the repression concept (e.g., Weinberger, 1990; Weinberger, Schwartz, & Davidson, 1979). Despite the rather long research tradition concerning emotion regulation styles, the evidence is rather weak that certain emotion regulation styles are associated with certain actual regulation strategies. There are, however, at least two points that are problematic in this research: First, there is no consistent procedure concerning the operationalization of actual emotion regulation strategies and second, it is often neglected that the emotion regulation strategy individuals choose is strongly influenced by the situational characteristics in which emotion regulation takes place, as well as by the emotion, which has to be regulated (discussed earlier).

Anger Regulation Styles

For the assessment of anger regulation styles, several questionnaires have been constructed. A particular prominent one has been the State-Trait Anger Expression Inventory (Spielberger et al., 1985). In this line of research, anger response is assumed to be a trait variable that can be assessed via self-report. Such habitual anger response styles have been studied as to their consequences for physiological reactivity and health variables. The findings have been rather inconsistent. Some studies concluded that anger-in or anger suppression would lead to higher blood pressure (Dimsdale et al., 1986; Feshbach, 1986; Goldstein, Edelberg, Meier, & Davis, 1989; Johnson, Schork, & Spielberger, 1987; Thomas, 1997). Such findings suggest that anger suppression could be a risk factor for the development of essential hypertension (Cottington, Matthews, Talbott, & Kuller, 1986; Diamond, 1982; Vögele & Steptoe, 1993). Some research suggested that anger-out is related to a lower risk of developing coronary heart disease (van Elderen, Maes, Komproe, & van der Kamp, 1997). Other studies, however, found an open expression of anger to have potentially detrimental consequences for health (Feshbach, 1986; Gentry, Chesney, Gary, Hall, & Harburg, 1982; Siegman, 1993; Siegman, Anderson, Herbst, Boyle, & Wilkinson, 1992; Tavris, 1984).

The concept of Type A behavior (or, more specifically, hostility) is another example for an individual differences variable that is supposed to influence anger regulation. Type A has been suggested to be a predictor for higher experimental blood pressure responses (Hokanson, 1960; Suarez & Williams, 1989; Weidner, Friend, Ficarrotto, & Mendell, 1989), for essential hypertension (Baer, Collins, Bourianoff, & Ketchel, 1979), or for coronary heart disease (Booth Kewley & Friedman, 1987; Dembroski, MacDougall, & Schmidt, 1985; Diamond, 1982; Williams et al., 1980). Similarly, trait anger led to higher resting blood pressure (e.g., Schneider, Egan, Johnson, Drobny, & Julius, 1986). Other studies, however, found no relation between hostility and blood pressure (Bages, Warwick Evans, & Falger, 1997; Smith & Houston, 1987), or it was argued that interpersonal factors should be followed up more closely (Feshbach, 1986; Tavris, 1984).

Concerning the relation between trait anger and actual anger responses in the separate components of anger experience, expression, and physiology, trait anger was associated with experiential anger but not with heart rate responses in anger-inducing situations (Deffenbacher, Demm, & Brandon, 1986). In a different study, trait anger was related to experienced anger and to higher physiological reactivity after provocation, and also to more suppression of anger (Deffenbacher, Oetting, Lynch, & Morris, 1996). Anger-in predicted negative mood, whereas anger-out was unrelated to anger experiences in daily life (Martin & Watson, 1997). Instead, anger-out was related to higher physiological reactivity during harassment (Faber & Burns, 1996). Finally, and not unexpectedly, anger control correlated negatively with physiological activity (Schäffel, 1993).

There may be at least two explanations for the inconsistent results in this research. First, the questionnaires used to assess habitual anger response have seldom been validated through observations of actual anger regulation responses. For example, the habitual anger-in scale may assess an accentuation of felt compared to expressed anger, but not necessarily the inhibition of expressed compared to felt anger. This consideration is in line with the finding that anger-in typically shows a moderate to high correlation with neuroticism (e.g., Martin & Watson, 1997). Neuroticism is strongly related to health complaints and self-reports of negative emotions, but unrelated to objective health symptoms (Brown & Moskowitz, 1997; Myrtek, 1998) and physiological reactivity (Clark, Hemsley, & Nason–Clark, 1987; Fahrenberg, 1987, 1992). Thus, habitual anger-in may be positively associated with felt anger, but may be unrelated to physiological reactivity. This objection also illustrates that anger regulation styles cannot be equated with any single component of anger. Therefore, an important validation strategy is to investigate the actual response pattern that means the discrepancies between the experiential, expressive, and physiological components of anger associated with different habitual anger regulation styles.

A rationally derived model for the construction of actual anger response style dimensions was presented in Stemmler, Schäfer, and Marwitz (1993) and in Böddecker and Stemmler (2000). The model assumes that the anger components of physiology, experience, and behavior can vary somewhat independently across participants. The independent variation between the components of an emotion response mainly results from differences in the social visibility and voluntary controllability of each anger response component. For example, physiological reactions are rather difficult to control; behavior and feeling states, on the other hand, rather easy. Such differences in controllability alone lead to the expectation that discrepancies among components are likely to occur. In this model, an actual anger response style is defined as a prototypical profile of reactivity in the three components. For ease of presentation, the responses of each component were divided into classes of "strong" or "weak" reactivity. The combination of the three response components with two classes each results in eight response style categories (see Fig. 13.1). These eight style categories are the endpoints of four continuous response style dimensions.

1. High versus low anger intensity—This style is characterized by high versus low reactivity in all three components, representing the overall intensity of the anger reaction.

2. High versus low anger suppression—High suppression is defined by high physiological and experiential reactivity but behaviorally concealed anger. Low suppression is characterized by the inverse pattern: an angry expression void of experiential and physiological signs of anger. With low suppression, anger expression is presumably used merely instrumentally.

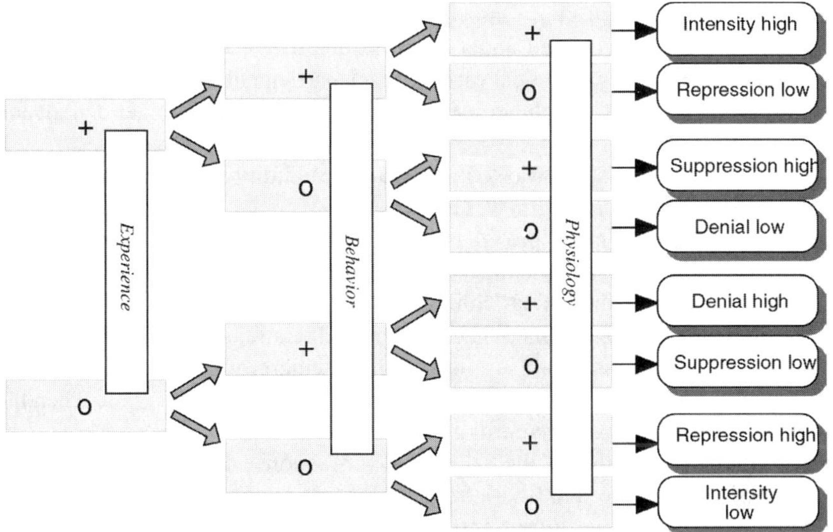

Fig. 13.1. Anger response style model of Stemmler, Schäfer, and Marwitz (1993) showing three components of an actual anger response (experience, behavior, physiology) with resulting actual anger response style categories.

3. High versus low anger denial—High anger denial is defined by physiological plus behavioral anger reactivity without an experiential equivalent, a concept that is similar to alexithymia. Low denial, however, is characterized by only an experiential reaction, which might occur in persons who pretend to be angry, for example, when they wish to conform to perceived experimental demands.

4. High versus low anger repression—Typical for high repression is reacting exclusively physiologically; low repression stands for anger expression in the experiential and behavioral component and might occur in sensitizers.

In the study of Böddecker and Stemmler (2000), a total of 80 female participants were randomly assigned to either a treatment or a control group. Anger was induced through real-life provocations. Participants of the control group received a complete disclosure before the anger induction. Otherwise, control group participants were treated exactly as the treatment participants. Participants completed a German version of the State-Trait Anger Expression Inventory (STAXI; Schwenkmezger, Hodapp, & Spielberger, 1993) and the Freiburg Personality Inventory–Revised (FPI–R; Fahrenberg, Hampel, & Selg, 1989). From the STAXI, the scales trait anger, anger-in, anger-out, and anger control were used; the more global traits extraversion and neuroticism were assessed with the FPI–R.

For each participant a score on each of the response style dimensions was calculated: baseline-adjusted scores for diastolic blood pressure, activity of the m.

extensor digitorum and skin temperature at the forehead, and raw scores for self-reported and video-rated anger, were standardized across all participants. Separately for each physiological variable, each participant obtained an actual anger response style score for anger intensity, anger suppression, anger denial, and anger repression.

The first aim of the study was to investigate the validity of habitual anger regulation styles, and the second aim was to investigate if actual anger regulation styles can be predicted by more global personality traits such as extraversion and neuroticism. Finally, it was assumed that the relation between actual emotion regulation styles and personality variables would be moderated by the situational context. Concretely, it was assumed that the expected relations between actual anger regulation styles and personality traits would only emerge when the emotion of anger is activated (treatment group), but they should not be demonstrable when the emotion of anger is absent (control group).

It could be shown that of the habitual anger response scales, only trait anger was significantly correlated with an actual anger style: anger repression was negatively associated with trait anger across both conditions. This means that participants with high trait anger reported and showed more anger than would be expected from their physiological reaction. Whereas evidence concerning habitual anger regulation styles was rather weak, a number of significant results were found for the more global traits extraversion and neuroticism. It could be shown that denial (calculated with skin temperature at the forehead) increased with extraversion in the treatment group, but decreased in the control group. These findings correspond to observations that even under adverse conditions, extraverts tend to experience positive emotionality (Chang, 1997; Larsen & Diener, 1987; Rusting & Larsen, 1997). However, this finding also implies that differences between positive and negative emotionality might preferably be found in the experiential component. In addition, the dissociation between the experiential response on the one side and the behavioral and physiological responses on the other side, points to the possibility that the high positive emotionality and the higher subjective well being of extraverts (Lu & Shih, 1997) might be due to a denial of negative experiences, which is "paid for" with higher physiological and behavioral reactivities.

Concerning neuroticism, the most important finding was that neuroticism was negatively related to anger denial (calculated with diastolic blood pressure) within the treatment group, but positively related to anger denial in the control group. Thus, in the control condition, higher neuroticism led to stronger physiological and behavioral than experiential emotion responses, whereas in the anger-provoking situation, physiological and behavioral responses were dampened and anger self-reports were elevated for participants with high compared to low scores in neuroticism, replicating results from Stemmler et al. (1993). This finding suggests that the larger negative emotional reactivity reported for highly emotional individuals (Chang, 1997; Larsen & Diener, 1987; McFatter, 1994; Rusting

& Larsen, 1997) might be applicable only to the experiential component, an effect opposite to the one described earlier for extraversion. In addition, this result coincides with studies already referred to earlier in which neuroticism was strongly related to health complaints and self-reports of negative emotions, but unrelated to objective health symptoms or physiological reactivity.

By and large, the most important findings of this study were, first, that habitual anger regulation styles assessed with the STAXI do not predict actual anger response styles, which, however, do the broad personality traits of extraversion and neuroticism. Second, it could be shown that the self-reported state is only half the truth as demonstrated for neuroticism and extraversion. Thus, although individuals claim to be angry or to be calm, objective indicators like physiological and spontaneous behavioral responses may tell another story.

Anxiety Regulation Styles

As mentioned earlier, one of the most prominent concepts in the research of anxiety regulation styles is repression. This concept evolved from the assumption that compared to true low-anxious individuals, repressors maladaptively avoid the perception or experience of negative affect. The separation of truly low-anxious individuals from repressors was accomplished by the combination of an anxiety scale with the Marlowe–Crowne (MC) Scale. Crowne and Marlowe collected considerable evidence that their scale was measuring affect inhibition, defensiveness (Crowne & Marlowe, 1964, pp. 150, 190), and the prevention of threat to self-esteem from anticipated social rejection (e.g., Asendorpf & Scherer, 1983; Crowne, 1979, p. 169; Weinberger, 1990). In addition, although the MC scale was originally constructed for the assessment of social desirable responding as a response style (Crowne & Marlowe, 1960), soon it emerged that the scale was primarily measuring a substantive individual difference dimension rather than a response style. Since that time, a formidable body of research has demonstrated that high MC scorers generally believe what they are reporting and attempt to behave accordingly (e.g., Derakshan & Eysenck, 1997; McCrae & Costa, 1983).

By combining the MC scale with an anxiety scale, four personality groups can be distinguished: the low-trait-anxiety scorers are separated into true low-anxious individuals with low MC scales scores, and repressors, with high MC scale scores. The high-trait-anxiety scorers are separated into high-anxious individuals with low MC scales scores, and defensive high-anxious individuals, with high MC scale scores.

From the very beginning in repressive coping research, the main aim was the demonstration that repressive copers are intrinsically anxious, despite their extremely low self-reported negative affect. It was assumed that their anxiety would be manifested especially in those components of the emotion response that are inaccessible to manipulation, such as spontaneously expressed behavioral anxiety and physiological responses.

Studies, which combine emotion self-reports with physiological and behavioral measures, could actually show that repressors compared to the other personality groups showed strong physiological activation and behavioral anxiety but only low scores in self-reported state anxiety, when their overly positive self-concept was threatened (e.g., Asendorpf & Scherer, 1983; Derakshan & Eysenck, 1997; Gudjonsson, 1981; Newton & Contrada, 1992; Weinberger et al., 1979).

However, psychophysiological studies could not always replicate these findings (e.g., Brody, Veit, & Rau, 1997). One important reason for the inconsistencies in repressive coping research may be the fact that situational contexts and tasks varied from study to study. Newton and Contrada (1992) speculated that verbal-autonomic response dissociation in repressive copers is potentiated by conditions that enhance social evaluative concerns. In the study of these authors, female participants had to give a speech about the most undesirable aspect of their personality, ostensibly observed by three researches (public condition) in comparison to a condition, where a single researcher allegedly observed the participants (private condition). It could be shown that female repressors exhibited heart rate elevations that were greater in magnitude than their self-reports of negative affect, but only in the public condition. Barger, Kircher, and Croyle (1997) tried to replicate these results but did not find that repressive coping was moderated by the social evaluative nature of the context.

In addition, in some studies, repressors were confronted with or had to talk about self-concept threatening topics, for example, they had to talk about the most undesirable characteristics of their personality or had to complete sentences with sexual and aggressive content (Asendorpf & Scherer, 1983; Weinberger et al., 1979). This confrontation with self-concept threatening topics may have been the critical aspect for the heightened physiological reactivity of repressive copers. However, other researchers found effects of repressive defensive coping even in fairly nonthreatening contexts (e.g., Brown et al., 1996; Gudjonsson, 1981; King, Taylor, Albright, & Haskell, 1990). Thus, the evidence concerning the key features in the situational context for the activation of repressive defensive coping is unclear.

Inconsistencies in the repressive defensive coping research may also be due to the physiological variable selection. In most studies, heart rate was registered and combined either with systolic and diastolic blood pressure or with measures of electrodermal activity, such as the number of spontaneous skin conductance responses. It is striking that in nearly all studies in which spontaneous skin conductance responses were recorded, repressors or defensive persons showed higher reactivity during or after threat (Barger et al., 1997; Gudjonsson, 1981; Tomaka, Blascovich, & Kelsey, 1992; Tremayne & Barry, 1994; Weinberger et al., 1979). There are also numerous studies that demonstrated repressive defensive coping effects for heart rate (e.g., Asendorpf & Scherer, 1983; Derakshan & Eysenck, 1997; Newton & Contrada, 1992; Weinberger et al., 1979), diastolic blood pressure (Jamner, Shapiro, Goldstein, & Hug, 1991; Kiecolt–Glaser & Greenberg, 1983;

Shapiro, Goldstein, & Jamner, 1995), and systolic blood pressure (Fishman, 1965; King et al., 1990). It is interesting that most of the studies demonstrating effects for blood pressure were designed to induce anger, frustration, or investigated assertive behavior, but not fear.

According to Weinberger (1990), repressors are characterized not only by low subjective experience of distress, but also by a high level of self-restraint or inhibition of egoistic impulses. In fact, most MC items have little to do with denying distress; rather, they primarily refer to an extreme inhibition of one's own needs when in conflict with the needs of others (Weinberger, 1990). This observation is in line with experiments, which show an inhibition of aggressive behavior in high MC scorers when angered and frustrated (e.g., Fishman, 1965; Taylor, 1970). In addition, when high MC scorers counteraggressed, they manifested a continued elevation in systolic blood pressure, whereas low MC scorers manifested a decline in blood pressure (Fishman, 1965). In addition, the MC scale shows its highest correlation with emotional stability, but also with agreeableness (e.g., McCrae & Costa, 1983). Other evidence that repressive defensive copers have considerable difficulty in expressing their needs originates from assertion research (Kiecolt & McGrath, 1979; Kiecolt–Glaser & Murray, 1980). Kiecolt–Glaser and Greenberg (1983) assessed participants' physiological reactions to scenes requiring assertiveness. When the participants were asked to imagine responding to the scenes, the repressors had significantly larger increases in diastolic blood pressure than high-anxious or low-anxious groups (defensive high-anxious persons were not investigated). When interacting with a confederate, repressors had greater heart rate changes than the truly low-anxious group.

Finally, there are also obscurities concerning the question of whether the effects found for repressors may be true for high defensive persons. According to Ritz and Dahme (1996) and Barger et al. (1997), the sample size of the defensive high-anxious group is often small because of the low to moderate negative relation between the MC scale and anxiety scales. Therefore, this group has often not been included in group comparisons (e.g., Kiecolt–Glaser & Greenberg, 1983; Newton & Contrada, 1992; Weinberger et al., 1979). As a consequence, any main effects of defensiveness might be attributed to the repressor group. In other studies that had the potential for a factorial analysis, coping categories were treated as levels of just one factor rather than distributed in a two-factor design (e.g., Asendorpf & Scherer, 1983; Derakshan & Eysenck, 1997; King et al., 1990). In fact there are several studies with psychophysiological parameters as dependent variables, which revealed main effects of defensiveness (e.g., Gudjonsson, 1981; Jamner et al., 1991; Shapiro et al., 1995; Tomaka et al., 1992; Warrenburg et al., 1989). Others found effects for repressors only, despite the fact that the defensive high-anxious group was included (Asendorpf & Scherer, 1983; Barger et al., 1997; Derakshan & Eysenck, 1997; Tremayne & Barry, 1994).

This short review makes clear that there are a lot of obscurities in the research concerning repressive defensive coping. What is clear, however, is that repressive defensive copers show different emotion regulation strategies and physiological responses depending on the situational context realized and the kind of emotion they regulate.

In one of our studies (Pauls & Stemmler, in press), we compared the coping responses of repressive defensive participants during two socially evaluative contexts, conceptualized to induce fear and anger. Fear was induced by the announcement to give a speech about the European Union in front of a "speech expert." Anger was induced by the direct confrontation with personal critic, frustration, and unfair accusations, while participants had to perform three cognitively demanding tasks. The main expectation was that emotion regulation of repressive defensive copers would be moderated by the situational context.

Concretely, in line with studies, in which fear of negative evaluation was induced (Barger et al., 1997; Newton & Contrada, 1992), we hypothesized that during fear, repressors (or defensive persons), compared to other personality groups, would exhibit increased heart rate reactivity and increases in the number of skin conductance responses. In addition, we predicted that repressors (or defensive persons) have lower scores in self-reports of fear, strain, displeasure, and the bodily sensation of a pounding heart than other participants, but at the same time show facial expressions of negative emotions reflected in an increased activity of the Corrugator Supercilii. This expectation was derived from the Asendorpf and Scherer study, where repressors compared to the low-anxious group showed more facial anxiety during a phrase-association task with affective content (Asendorpf & Scherer, 1983).

Concerning the anger induction condition, we expected that direct confrontation with social disapproval should be very threatening not only for repressors, but also for defensive high-anxious persons. In line with the results of those studies, in which responses to anger, frustration, or assertive behavior were investigated (e.g., Fishman, 1965; Kiecolt–Glaser & Greenberg, 1983), we expected a positive relation between defensiveness and blood pressure reactivity. Because there is some evidence that repressive defensive copers have difficulty with assertiveness and the open expression of anger (e.g., Fishman, 1965; Kiecolt–Glaser & Greenberg, 1983; Taylor, 1970), we hypothesized a negative relation between defensiveness and Corrugator Supercilii activity. Because defensive persons cannot bear social rejection, we hypothesized that they would try to regain the appreciation from the experimenter and to appease him with smiling (see Keltner & Buswell, 1997). Therefore, we expected a positive relation between defensiveness and the activity of the Zygomaticus Major.

A total of 78 female participants were randomly assigned to the fear and anger condition. Trait-anxiety was measured with a German version of the State-Trait-Anxiety-Inventory (STAI; Laux, Glanzmann, Schaffner, & Spielberger, 1981) and defensiveness was measured with a German version of the Marlowe–Crowne Social Desirability Scale (Lück & Timaeus, 1969).

Emotion responses were captured with seven emotion self-report scales including embarrassment, fear, sadness, anger, heartbeat, strain, and displeasure, and with nine physiological variables including heart rate, heart rate variability, preejection period, systolic blood pressure, diastolic blood pressure, total peripheral resistance, number of skin conductance responses, and activities of the Corrugator Supercilii and Zygomaticus Major. The physiological variables should capture a broad spectrum of autonomic activity reflecting cardiac (heart period, heart period variability, systolic blood pressure, preejection period), vascular (diastolic blood pressure, total peripheral resistance), general sympathetic activation (number of skin conductance responses), as well as facial activity.

Instead of dichotomizing the score distribution of the STAI and MC scales and comparing personality group means by analysis of variance, we calculated moderated regressions (Type I or sequential sum of squares regression analysis) with emotion conditions (fear, anger), anxiety (STAI), defensiveness (MC scale), and their cross products as predictors for physiological and self-report variables (baseline-adjusted scores).

Results obtained during fear partly confirmed our expectations. Defensiveness was marginally positively related to an increase in the number of skin conductance responses and Corrugator activity. In addition, repressors compared to all other participants showed the largest increase in Corrugator activity, indicating more behavioral negative affect for repressors compared to other personality groups. For heart rate reactivity, our hypothesis could not be confirmed. Concerning self-reports of emotion, defensiveness as expected was negatively correlated with self-reported fear, strain, and displeasure, and repressors compared to other personality groups had the lowest scores in self-reports of these negatively valenced feeling states.

As expected during anger, defensiveness was positively related to diastolic blood pressure reactivity. In addition, defensiveness was positively related to Zygomaticus activity, and there was a trend for a negative relation between defensiveness and Corrugator activity.

The emotion condition (fear, anger) × Anxiety (STAI) × Defensiveness (MC scale) moderated regression analyses should inform about differences in the relation between the dependent variables and personality during fear and anger. Indeed, emotional responses of defensive persons during anger differed considerably from those found during fear. The most important finding was that during fear, but not during anger, defensiveness was negatively related to heart rate variability indicating stronger vagal withdrawal for high compared to low defensive persons.

In sum, our results showed that the physiological, emotional, and behavioral response pattern of repressive defensive copers strongly depends on the situational context. Despite the quite distinct physiological responses of repressive defensive copers during fear and anger, the most striking result of the study seemed to be that during fear, repressive defensive copers compared to other personality groups showed high behavioral and low self-reported negative affect, whereas during anger, defensiveness was negatively related to behavioral and slightly positively or unrelated to self-reported negative affect. If the model of actual anger regulation styles (Stemmler et al., 1993) is transferred to the regulation of emotions in general, the actual emotion regulation style of repressive defensive copers during anger can be characterized as high suppression (if one assumes that it is rather atypical for repressive defensive copers to report negative affect at all), whereas during fear, the response pattern can be characterized as high denial.

Another striking result of the study was that main effects of defensiveness emerged not only during anger, but also during fear. Although during fear participants were not directly confronted with negative evaluation, there was nevertheless the impending danger to be negatively evaluated by the speech expert. Therefore, the main effects of defensiveness during fear may be explained by the fact that fear of negative evaluation and social rejection were threatening not only for repressors, but for defensive high-anxious participants as well.

By and large, results of this study showed (a) that it is worthwhile to investigate defensiveness alone, and in combination with trait anxiety; (b) that depending on the social context, repressive defensive copers adopt rather different emotion regulation strategies; and (c) that the emotion regulation strategies of repressive defensive copers do not seem to be very effective in modulating their physiological responses.

IMPLICATIONS, LIMITATIONS, AND FUTURE RESEARCH CONCERNING THE PHYSIOLOGICAL CONSEQUENCES OF EMOTION REGULATION

At the end of this review concerning the physiological effects of emotion regulation, two points are worth mentioning: First, although the boundary conditions concerning the physiological consequences of manipulated emotion regulation are not quite clear, it seems that manipulated emotion suppression has rather negative consequences, whereas manipulated intrapsychic emotion regulation, such as positive reappraisal, intellectualization, distancing, and so forth, are rather effective in modulating one's physiological responses. However, the picture may change when people use one of these strategies habitually (Gross, 1998a). For example, the strategy of repressive defensive copers to avoid negative affect by means of denial, repression, positive reappraisal, or whatever, does not prevent them from being physiologically activated. Second, even if some individuals habitually use emotion regulation strategies that are rather nonfunctional in laboratory settings, this does not necessarily mean that these individuals are at higher risk to develop somatic diseases; most of the time people are not passively confronted with certain situations as they are, for example, in laboratory settings; rather they actively select and create situations (e.g., Caspi & Bem, 1990) in which their preferred emotion regulation strategy will probably succeed. For example, it is likely that repressive defensive copers actively avoid situations in which they could be confronted with revilement and insult. In addition, it is also probable that their conforming and agreeable behavior prevents other people from acting annoyed and hostile.

If it is right that people select and create situations in which their preferred emotion regulation strategy will probably succeed, it may be the match or mismatch between situational demands and the individual's preferred or habitually used emotion regulation strategy that is the crucial factor concerning the physiological consequences of emotion regulation in laboratory settings. In the study of Engebretson, Matthews, and Scheier (1989), participants were randomly assigned to work on a task with either an annoying or a pleasant confederate and subsequently to write either a negative or a positive evaluation of the confederate. Participants' preferred anger expression strategy was assessed by calculating the difference of the anger-in and anger-out scales of the STAXI. The results showed that participants who habitually express their anger outwardly showed a decline in systolic blood pressure reactivity when instructed to write a negative evaluation about the annoying confederate, whereas when required to write a positive evaluation, they did not show this. Conversely, those participants who habitually held their anger in showed a decline in systolic blood pressure reactivity when instructed to write a positive evaluation about the annoying confederate, whereas when required to write a negative evaluation, they did not show a decline. Similarly, Hokanson, Willers, and Koropsak (1968) showed that participants who habitually exhibited friendly and nonaggressive responses when harassed produced rapid reductions in peripheral vasoconstriction levels only if they exhibited friendly or nonaggressive responses. The findings of these studies suggest that as long as situations allow the exertion of a broad spectrum of emotion regulation strategies, people will use those strategies that have previously been successful in establishing their subjective well-being (Engebretson et al., 1989). However, physiological stress responses are likely to occur when people are confronted with situations in which their preferred emotion regulation strategy is not applicable, or because the required emotion regulation strategy (for example, anger expression) contravenes with the individual's habits, goals, motives, needs, attitudes, and beliefs (for example, the motivation to avoid disapproval). These considerations imply that in the long run, those individuals should be physically healthier who have access to a broad spectrum of emotion regulation strategies, which can be flexibly adapted to the demands of the situation.

In sum, there are a lot of questions surrounding the field of emotion regulation strategies and their effectiveness in modulating physiological responses. These questions go far beyond those of whether emotion suppression or repression is healthier than acting out or to disclose one's emotion. Future research in the realm of emotion regulation should more strongly bear in mind that the specific emotion regulation response is the outcome of a rather complex interplay between the objective situation, situational appraisals, and personality (e.g., Lazarus, 1991).

REFERENCES

Alexander, F. (1950). *Psychosomatic medicine: Its principles and applications*. New York: Ronald Press.

Arnold, M. B. (1960). *Emotion and personality.* New York: Columbia University Press.

Asendorpf, J. B., & Scherer, K. R. (1983). The discrepant repressor: Differentiation between low anxiety, high anxiety, and repression of anxiety by autonomic-facial-verbal patterns of behavior. *Journal of Personality and Social Psychology, 45*, 1334–1346.

Baer, P. E., Collins, F. H., Bourianoff, G. C., & Ketchel, M. F. (1979). Assessing personality factors in essential hypertension with a brief self-report instrument. *Psychosomatic Medicine, 41*, 321–330.

Bages, N., Warwick Evans, L., & Falger, P. R. J. (1997). Differences between informants about Type A, anger, and social support and the relationship with blood pressure. *Psychology and Health, 12*, 453–465.

Barger, S. D., Kircher, J. C., & Croyle, R. T. (1997). The effects of social context and defensiveness on the physiological responses of repressive copers. *Journal of Personality and Social Psychology, 73*, 1118–1128.

Böddeker, I., & Stemmler, G. (2000). Who responds how and when to anger? The assessment of actual anger response styles and their relation to personality. *Cognition and Emotion, 14*, 737–762.

Booth Kewley, S., & Friedman, H. S. (1987). Psychological predictors of heart disease: A quantitative review. *Psychological Bulletin, 101*, 343–362.

Brody, S., Veit, R., & Rau, H. (1997). Lie scores are associated with less cardiovascular reactivity to baroreceptor stimulation and to mental arithmetic stress. *Personality and Individual Differences, 22*, 677–681.

Brown, K. W., & Moskowitz, D. S. (1997). Does unhappiness make you sick? The role of affect and neuroticism in the experience of common physical symptoms. *Journal of Personality and Social Psychology, 72*, 892–906.

Brown, L. L., Tomarken, A. J., Orth, D. N., Loosen, P. T., Kalin, N. H., & Davidson, R. J. (1996). Individual differences in repressive-defensiveness predict basal salivary cortisol levels. *Journal of Personality and Social Psychology, 70*, 362–371.

Buck, R. (1979). Individual differences in nonverbal sending accuracy and electrodermal responding: The externalizing–internalizing dimension. In R. Rosenthal (Ed.), *Skill in nonverbal communication* (pp. 140–170). Cambridge, MA: Oelgeschlager, Gunn & Hain.

Bush, L. K., Barr, C. L., McHugo, G. J., & Lanzetta, J. T. (1989). The effects of facial control and facial mimicry on subjective reactions to comedy routines. *Motivation and Emotion, 13*, 31–52.

Caspi, A., & Bem, D. J. (1990). Personality continuity and change across the life course. In L. A. Pervin (Ed.), *Handbook of personality: Theory and research* (pp. 549–575). New York: Guilford.

Chang, E. C. (1997). Positive and negative affectivity for academic and interpersonal domains: Relations to general affectivity, extraversion, and neuroticism. *Personality and Individual Differences, 22*, 929–932.

Clark, D. A., Hemsley, D. R., & Nason-Clark, N. (1987). Personality and sex differences in emotional responsiveness to positive and negative cognitive stimuli. *Personality and Individual Differences, 8*, 1–7.

Colby, C. Z., Lanzetta, J. T., & Kleck, R. E. (1977). Effects of the expression of pain on autonomic and pain tolerance responses to subject-controlled pain. *Psychophysiology, 14*, 537–540.

Cottington, E. M., Matthews, K. A., Talbott, E., & Kuller, L. H. (1986). Occupational stress, suppressed anger, and hypertension. *Psychosomatic Medicine, 48*, 249–260.

Crowne, D. P. (1979). *The experimental study of personality.* Hillsdale, NJ: Lawrence Erlbaum Associates, Inc..

Crowne, D. P., & Marlowe, D. (1960). A new scale of social desirability independent of psychopathology. *Journal of Consulting Psychology, 24*, 349–354.

Crowne, D. P., & Marlowe, D. (1964). *The approval motive.* New York: Wiley.

Damasio, A. R. (1994). *Descartes' error. Emotion, reason, and the human brain.* New York: Avon Books.

Dandoy, A. C., & Goldstein, A. G. (1990). The use of cognitive appraisal to reduce stress reactions: A replication. *Journal of Social Behavior and Personality, 5*, 275–285.

Deffenbacher, J. L., Demm, P. M., & Brandon, A. D. (1986). High general anger: Correlates and treatment. *Behaviour Research and Therapy, 24*, 481–489.

Deffenbacher, J. L., Oetting, E. R., Lynch, R. S., & Morris, C. D. (1996). The expression of anger and its consequences. *Behaviour Research and Therapy, 34*, 575–590.

Dembroski, T. M., MacDougall, J. M., & Schmidt, T. H. (1985). Effects of competitive challenge on cardiovascular reaction of pattern A and B subjects. In L. J. P. van Doornen (Ed.), *Psychophysiology of cardiovascular control. Models, methods, and data* (pp. 733–743). New York: Plenum.

Derakshan, N., & Eysenck, M. W. (1997). Interpretive biases for one's own behavior and physiology in high-trait-anxious individuals and repressors. *Journal of Personality and Social Psychology, 73*, 816–825.

Diamond, E. L. (1982). The role of anger and hostility in essential hypertension and coronary heart disease. *Psychological Bulletin, 92*, 410–433.

Dimsdale, J. E., Pierce, C., Schoenfeld, D., Brown, A., Zusman, R., & Graham, R. (1986). Suppressed anger and blood pressure: The effects of race, sex, social class, obesity, and age. *Psychosomatic Medicine, 48*, 430–436.

Ekman, P., Levenson, R. W., & Friesen, W. V. (1983). Autonomic nervous system activity distinguishes among emotions. *Science, 221*, 1208–1210.

Engebretson, T. O., Matthews, K. A., & Scheier, M. F. (1989). Relations between anger expression and cardiovascular reactivity: Reconciling inconsistent findings through a matching hypothesis. *Journal of Personality and Social Psychology, 57*, 513–521.

Faber, S. D., & Burns, J. W. (1996). Anger management style, degree of expressed anger, and gender influence cardiovascular recovery from interpersonal harassment. *Journal of Behavioral Medicine, 19*, 31–53.

Fahrenberg, J. (1987). Concepts of activation and arousal in the theory of emotionality (neuroticism). A multivariate conceptualization. In H. J. Eysenck (Ed.), *Personality dimensions and arousal* (pp. 99–120). New York: Plenum.

Fahrenberg, J. (1992). Psychophysiology of neuroticism and anxiety. In M. W. Eysenck (Ed.), *Handbook of individual differences: Biological perspectives* (pp. 179–226). Chichester, England: Wiley.

Fahrenberg, J., Hampel, R., & Selg, H. (1984). *Das Freiburger Persönlichkeitsinventar FPI* (4th ed.) [Manual of the Freiburg Personality Inventory, Revision]. Göttingen, Germany: Hogrefe.

Feshbach, S. (1986). Reconceptualizations of anger: Some research perspectives. *Journal of Social and Clinical Psychology, 4*, 123–132.

Field, T. M., & Walden, T. A. (1982). Production and discrimination of facial expressions by preschool children. *Child Development, 53*, 1299–1311.

Fishman, C. G. (1965). Need for approval and the expression of aggression under varying conditions of frustration. *Journal of Personality and Social Psychology, 2*, 809–816.

Freud, S. (1936). Inhibitions, symptoms, and anxiety. *Psychoanalytic Quarterly, 5*, 415–443.

Friedman, M., & Rosenman, R. H. (1974). *Type A behavior and your heart*. New York: Knopf.

Frijda, N. (1986). *The emotions*. Cambridge, England: Cambridge University Press.

Funkenstein, D. H., King, S. H., & Drolette, M. (1954). The direction of anger during a laboratory stress-inducing situation. *Psychosomatic Medicine, 16*, 404–413.

Gentry, W., Chesney, A. P., Gary, H. E., Hall, R. P., & Harburg, E. (1982). Habitual anger-coping styles: I. Effect on mean blood pressure and risk for essential hypertension. *Psychosomatic Medicine, 44*, 195–202.

Goldstein, H. S., Edelberg, R., Meier, C. F., & Davis, L. (1989). Relationship of expressed anger to forearm muscle vascular resistance. *Journal of Psychosomatic Research, 33*, 497–504.

Gross, J. J. (1998a). Antecedent- and response-focused emotion regulation: Divergent consequences for experience, expression, and physiology. *Journal of Personality and Social Psychology, 74*, 224–237.

Gross, J. J. (1998b). The emerging field of emotion regulation: An integrative review. *Review of General Psychology, 2*, 271–299.

Gross, J. J., & Levenson, R. W. (1993). Emotional suppression: Physiology, self-report, and expressive behavior. *Journal of Personality and Social Psychology, 64*, 970–986.

Gross, J. J., & Levenson, R. W. (1997). Hiding feelings: The acute effects of inhibiting negative and positive emotion. *Journal of Abnormal Psychology, 106*, 95–103.

Gudjonsson, G. H. (1981). Self-reported emotional disturbance and its relation to electrodermal reactivity, defensiveness and trait anxiety. *Personality and Individual Differences, 2*, 47–52.

Hokanson, J. E. (1960). Vascular and psychogalvanic effects of experimentally aroused anger. *Journal of Personality, 29*, 30–39.

Hokanson, J. E., Willers, K. R., & Koropsak, E. (1968). The modification of autonomic responses during aggressive interchange. *Journal of Personality, 36, 386–404.*

Holmes, D. S., & Houston, B. K. (1974). Effectiveness of situation redefinition and affective isolation in coping with stress. *Journal of Personality and Social Psychology, 29*, 212–218.

Houston, B. K., & Holmes, D. S. (1974). Effect of avoidant thinking and reappraisal for coping with threat involving temporal uncertainty. *Journal of Personality and Social Psychology, 30*, 382–388.

Jamner, L. D., Shapiro, D., Goldstein, I. B., & Hug, R. (1991). Ambulatory blood pressure and heart rate in paramedics: Effects of cynical hostility and defensiveness. *Psychosomatic Medicine, 53*, 393–406.

Johnson, E. H., Schork, N. J., & Spielberger, C. D. (1987). Emotional and familial determinants of elevated blood pressure in Black and White adolescent females. *Journal of Psychosomatic Research, 31*, 731–741.

Jones, H. E. (1935). The galvanic skin reflex as related to overt emotional expression. *American Journal of Psychology, 47*, 241–251.

Keltner, D., & Buswell, B. N. (1997). Embarrassment: Its distinct form and appeasement functions. *Psychological Bulletin, 122*, 250–270.

Kiecolt–Glaser, J. K., & Greenberg, B. (1983). On the use of physiological measures in assertion research. *Journal of Behavioral Assessment, 5*, 97–109.

Kiecolt–Glaser, J. K., & McGrath, E. (1979). Social desirability in the measurement of assertive behavior. *Journal of Consulting and Clinical Psychology, 47*, 640–642.

Kiecolt–Glaser, J. K., * Murray, J. A. (1980). Social desirability bias in self-monitoring data. *Journal of Behavioral Assessment, 2*, 239–247.

King, A. C., Taylor, C. B., Albright, C. A., & Haskell, W. L. (1990). The relationship between repressive and defensive coping styles and blood pressure responses in healthy, middle-aged men and women. *Journal of Psychosomatic Research, 34*, 461–471.

Lanzetta, J. T., Cartwright Smith, J., & Kleck, R. E. (1976). Effects of nonverbal dissimulation on emotional experience and autonomic arousal. *Journal of Personality and Social Psychology, 33*, 354–370.

Larsen, R. J., & Diener, E. (1987). Affect intensity as an individual difference characteristic: A review. *Journal of Research in Personality, 21*, 1–39.

Laux, L., Glanzmann, P., Schaffner, P., & Spielberger, C. D. (1981). *Das State-Trait-Angstinventar* [The State-Trait-Anxiety-Inventory]. Weinheim, Germany: Beltz.

Lazarus, R. S. (1991). *Emotion and adaptation*. New York: Oxford University Press.

Lazarus, R. S., & Alfert, E. (1964). Short-circuiting of threat by experimentally altering cognitive appraisal. *Journal of Abnormal and Social Psychology, 69*, 195–205.

Levenson, R. W. (1988). Emotion and the autonomic nervous system: A prospectus for research on autonomic specificity. In H. L. Wagner (Ed.), *Social psychophysiology and emotion: Theory and clinical applications* (pp. 17–42). Chichester, England: Wiley.

Levenson, R. W., Ekman, P., & Friesen, W. V. (1990). Voluntary facial action generates emotion-specific autonomic nervous system activity. *Psychophysiology, 27*, 363–384.

Lu, L., & Shih, J. B. (1997). Personality and happiness: Is mental health a mediator? *Personality and Individual Differences, 22*, 249–256.

Lück, H. E., & Timaeus, E. (1969). Skalen zur Messung manifester Angst (MAS) und sozialer Wünschbarkeit (SDS-E und SDS-CM) [Scales for the assessment of manifest anxiety and social desirability (SDS-E and SDS-CM)]. *Diagnostica, 15*, 134–137.

Martin, R., & Watson, D. (1997). Style of anger expression and its relation to daily experience. *Personality and Social Psychology Bulletin, 23*, 285–294.

Matsumoto, D. (1993). Ethnic differences in affect intensity, emotion judgments, display rule attitudes, and self-reported emotional expression in an American sample. *Motivation and Emotion, 17*, 107–123.

McCrae, R. R., & Costa, P. T. (1983). Social desirability scales: More substance than style. *Journal of Consulting and Clinical Psychology, 51*, 882–888.

McCrae, R. R., & Costa, P. T. (1986). Personality, coping, and coping effectiveness in an adult sample. *Journal of Personality, 54*, 385–405.

McFatter, R. M. (1994). Interactions in predicting mood from extraversion and neuroticism. *Journal of Personality and Social Psychology, 66*, 570–578.

Myrtek, M. (1998). *Gesunde Kranke—kranke Gesunde* [The healthy sick persons—the sick healthy persons]. Bern, Switzerland: Huber.

Newton, T. L., & Contrada, R. J. (1992). Repressive coping and verbal-autonomic response dissociation: The influence of social context. *Journal of Personality and Social Psychology, 62*, 159–167.

Notarius, C. I., & Levenson, R. W. (1979). Expressive tendencies and physiological response to stress. *Journal of Personality and Social Psychology, 37*, 1204–1210.

Pauls, C. A., & Stemmler, G. (in press). Repressive defensive coping during fear and anger. *Emotion*.

Pennebaker, J. W., & Chew, C. H. (1985). Behavioral inhibition and electrodermal activity during deception. *Journal of Personality and Social Psychology, 49*, 1427–1433.

Plutchik, R. (1980). A general psychoevolutionary theory of emotion. In R. Plutchik & H. Kellerman (Eds.), *Emotion: Theory, research, and experience* (Vol. 1, pp. 3–31). New York: Academic.

Ritz, T., & Dahme, B. (1996). Repression, self-concealment and rationality/emotional defensiveness: The corresponedence between three questionnaire measures of defensive coping. *Personality and Individual Differences, 20*, 95102.

Rusting, C. L., & Larsen, R. J. (1997). Extraversion, neuroticism, and susceptibility to positive and negative affect: A test of two theoretical models. *Personality and Individual Differences, 22*, 607–612.

Schäffel, U. (1993). *Ärgerintensität und Ärgerverarbeitung*. Unpublished doctoral dissertation. Albert-Ludwigs-Universität, Freiburg, Germany.

Scherer, K. R., & Wallbott, H. G. (1994). Evidence for universality and cultural variation of differential emotion response patterning. *Journal of Personality and Social Psychology, 66*, 310–328.

Schneider, R. H., Egan, B. M., Johnson, E. H., Drobny, H., & Julius, S. (1986). Anger and anxiety in borderline hypertension. *Psychosomatic Medicine, 48*, 242–248.

Schwenkmezger, P., Hodapp, V., & Spielberger, C. D. (1993). *Das State-Trait-Ärgerausdrucks-Inventar (STAXI)* [The State-Trait Anger Expression Inventory (STAXI)]. Göttingen, Germany: Hogrefe.

Shapiro, D., Goldstein, I. B., & Jamner, L. D. (1995). Effects of anger/hostility, defensiveness, gender, and family history of hypertension on cardiovascular reactivity. *Psychophysiology, 32*, 425–435.

Siegman, A. W. (1993). Cardiovascular consequences of expressing, experiencing, and repressing anger. *Journal of Behavioral Medicine, 16*, 539–569.

Siegman, A. W., Anderson, R., Herbst, J., Boyle, S., & Wilkinson, J. (1992). Dimensions of anger–hostility and cardiovascular reactivity in provoked and angered men. *Journal of Behavioral Medicine, 15*, 257–272.

Smith, M. A., & Houston, B. (1987). Hostility, anger expression, cardiovascular responsivity, and social support. *Biological Psychology, 24*, 39–48.

Spielberger, C. D., Johnson, E. H., Russell, S. F., Crane, R. J., Jacobs, G. A., & Worden, T. J. (1985). The experience and expression of anger: Construction and validation of an Anger Expression Scale. In R. H. Rosenman (Ed.), *Anger and hostility in cardiovascular and behavioral disorders* (pp. 5–30). Washington, DC: Hemisphere.

Stanton, A. L., & Snider, P. R. (1993). Coping with a breast cancer diagnosis: A prospective study. *Health Psychology, 12*, 16–23.

Stemmler, G., Schäfer, H., & Marwitz, M. (1993). Zum Konzept und zu den Operationalisierungen von Stilen der Ärgerverarbeitung [The concept and the operationalization of anger coping styles]. In P. Schwenkmezger (Ed.), *Ärger und Ärgerausdruck* (pp. 71–111). Bern, Switzerland: Huber.

Steptoe, A., & Vögele, C. (1986). Are stress responses influenced by cognitive appraisal? An experimental comparison of coping strategies. *British Journal of Psychology, 77*, 243–255.

Suarez, E. C., & Williams, R. B. (1989). Situational determinants of cardiovascular and emotional reactivity in high and low hostile men. *Psychosomatic Medicine, 51*, 404–418.

Suls, J., & Fletcher, B. (1985). The relative efficacy of avoidant and nonavoidant coping strategies: A meta-analysis. *Health Psychology, 4*, 249–288.

Tavris, C. (1984). On the wisdom of counting to ten: Personal and social dangers of anger expression. *Review of Personality and Social Psychology, 5*, 170–191.

Taylor, S. (1970). Aggressive behavior as a function of approval motivation and physical attack. *Psychnomic Science, 18*, 195–196.

Taylor, S. E., Kemeny, M. E., Reed, G. M., Bower, J. E., & Gruenewald, T. L. (2000). Psychological resources, positive illusions, and health. *American Psychologist, 55*, 99–109.

Thomas, S. P. (1997). Women's anger: Relationship of suppression to blood pressure. *Nursing Research, 46*, 324–330.

Tomaka, J., Blascovich, J., & Kelsey, R. M. (1992). Effects of self-deception, social desirability, and repressive coping on psychophysiological reactivity to stress. *Personality and Social Psychology Bulletin, 18*, 616–624.

Tremayne, P., & Barry, R. J. (1994). Repressive defensiveness and trait anxiety effects in an orienting task with a manipulation of embarrassment. *Anxiety, Stress and Coping, 7*, 35–52.

Underwood, M. K., Coie, J. D., & Herbsman, C. R. (1992). Display rules for anger and aggression in school-age children. *Child Development, 63*, 366–380.

van Elderen, T., Maes, S., Komproe, I., & van der Kamp, L. (1997). The development of an anger expression and control scale. *British Journal of Health Psychology, 2*, 269–281.

Vögele, C., & Steptoe, A. (1993). Ärger, Feindseligkeit und kardiovaskuläre Reaktivität: Implikationen für essentielle Hypertonie und koronare Herzkrankheit [Anger, hostility, and cardiovascular reactivity: Implications for essential hypertension and coronary diseaseXXXXXXXX]. In P. Schwenkmezger (Ed.), *Ärger und Ärgerausdruck* (pp. 169–191). Bern, Switzerland: Huber.

Warrenburg, S., Levine, J., Schwartz, G. E., Fontana, A. F., Kerns, R. D., Delaney, R., et al. (1989). Defensive coping and blood pressure reactivity in medical patients. *Journal of Behavioral Medicine, 12*, 407–424.

Weidner, G., Friend, R., Ficarrotto, T. J., & Mendell, N. R. (1989). Hostility and cardiovascular reactivity to stress in women and men. *Psychosomatic Medicine, 51*, 36–45.

Weinberger, D. A. (1990). The construct validity of the repressive coping style. In J. L. Singer (Ed.), *Repression and dissociation: Implications for personality theory, psychopathology, and health* (pp. 337–386). Chicago: University of Chicago Press.

Weinberger, D. A., Schwartz, G. E., & Davidson, R. J. (1979). Low-anxious, high-anxious, and repressive coping styles: Psychometric patterns and behavioral and physiological responses to stress. *Journal of Abnormal Psychology, 88*, 369–380.

Williams, R. B., Haney, T. L., Lee, K. L., Kong, Y. H., Blumenthal, J. A., & Whalen, R. E. (1980). Type A behavior, hostility, and coronary atherosclerosis. *Psychosomatic Medicine, 42*, 539–549.

Zuckerman, M., Klorman, R., Larrance, D. T., & Spiegel, N. H. (1981). Facial, autonomic, and subjective components of emotion: The facial feedback hypothesis versus the externalizer–internalizer distinction. *Journal of Personality and Social Psychology, 41*, 929–944.

14

Emotion Regulation and Psychopathology

Ann M. Kring and Kelly H. Werner
University of California, Berkeley

Emotion disturbances are very common in psychopathology, and research over the last several decades has more clearly specified the nature of these disturbances. However, the extent to which these emotion disturbances can be cast as emotion regulation problems remains less clear. One major impediment to clarifying this issue has been the definitional ambiguity surrounding the concept of emotion regulation, and this is an urgent need for the field to address. We argue that advances in basic research on emotion regulation nevertheless hold much promise toward uncovering how emotion regulation difficulties may (or may not) characterize different types of disorders. We adopt the process model of emotion regulation developed by Gross and colleagues (e.g., Gross, 1998, 2001) to examine how emotion regulatory processes may play a part in psychopathology, reviewing the evidence for emotion regulation difficulties in a number of disorders (major depression, bipolar disorder, schizophrenia, anxiety disorders, borderline personality disorders, and frontotemporal lobar dementia). We conclude with a discussion of the implications for assessment and treatment, and the limits and potential for emotion regulation research in psychopathology.

"The distraction of our mind is result of our blind surrender to our desires, our incapacity to control or moderate our passions.

—Sauvages, 1772, as quoted in Foucault, 1965, p. 77.

Emotions play a central role in human life. They help us to respond to problems and challenges in our environment; they help us to organize our thoughts and actions, both explicitly and implicitly; and they guide our behavior. Perhaps because our emotions exert such widespread influence, we spend a good deal of time trying to influence or regulate how we feel and how we present our emotions to others. Given their centrality, it is not surprising that emotion disturbances figure prominently in many different forms of psychopathology. By one analysis, as many as 85% of psychological disorders include disturbances in emotional processing of some kind (Thoits, 1985), whether they be "excesses" in emotion; "deficits" in emotion, or the lack of coherence among emotional components. Indeed, as illustrated in Table 14.1, many of the disorders found in the current *Diagnostic and Statistical Manual of Mental Disorders* (4th ed., text revision; DSM–IV–TR; American Psychiatric Association, 2000) include one or more symptoms reflecting an emotion disturbance. Research designed to uncover the nature of emotion disturbances in different psychological disorders has flourished in the last 15 years (for reviews, see Berenbaum, Raghavan, Le, Vernon, & Gomez, in press; Keltner & Kring, 1998; Kring, 2001). At the same time, research in the emerging field of emotion regulation has also burgeoned, with an emphasis on understanding the basic properties associated with the regulation of the experience and expression of emotion (e.g., Cicchetti, Ackerman, & Izard, 1995; Gross, 1998; Thompson, 1994). As the aforementioned quote illustrates, the notion that unregulated emotions lead to madness has a firm place in history. Moreover, contemporary writings on emotion and psychopathology often cast emotion disturbances as problems in regulation. Unfortunately, the framing of emotion disturbances in psychopathology as problems in emotion regulation has often been done with limited empirical support. The central goal of this chapter is to critically consider the extent to which the emotion disturbances in psychopathology can be construed as problems in emotion regulation. To do so, we first discuss current definitions of emotion and emotion regulation and the ways in which these two constructs may (or may not) be distinguishable. Second, we consider the concept of emotion dysregulation and the ways in which dysregulation can be distinguished from regulation. Next, we review the evidence for emotion regulation problems in different types of psychological disorders, focusing our attention primarily on disorders that affect adults (for consideration of emotion regulation problems and developmental psychopathology, see Calkins & Howse, this volume). Finally, we conclude with a consideration of the implications that emotion regulation problems in psychopathology have for assessment and treatment, with an eye toward future research.

TABLE 14.1

Emotion-Related Symptoms in *Diagnistic and Statistical Manual of Mental Disorders*, 4th ed., Text Revision Disorders of Adulthood

Disorder	*Emotion-Related Symptom*
Schizophrenia, Schizoaffective, Schizophrenisorm Disorder	Affective flattening, anhedonia
Major depressive episode	Depressed mood; anhedonia
Manic episode	Elevated, expansive, or irritable mood
Dysthymia	Depressed mood
Hypomanic episode	Elevated, expansive, or irritable mood
Panic Disorder	Intense fear or discomfort
Agoraphobia	Anxiety
Specific phobia	Marked and persistent fear, anxious anticipation
Social phobia	Marked and persistent fear, anxious anticipation
Obsessive–Compulsive Disorder	Marked anxiety or distress
Posttraumataic Stress Disorder	Irritability, anger, physiological reactivity, distress, anhedonia, restricted range of affect
Acute Stress Disorder	Symptoms of anxiety or increased arousal
Generalized Anxiety Disorder	Excessive anxiety and worry, irritability
Hypochondriasis	Preoccupation with fears of having disease
Anorexia Nervosa	Fear of gaining weight
Sleep Terror Disorder	Intense fear and signs of autonomic arousal
Pathological Gambling	Iritability, dysphoric mood
Adjustment Disorder	Marked distress
Poaranoid Personality Disorder	Quick to react angrily
Schizoid Personality Disorder	Emotional coldness, detachment, flattened affectivity
Schizotypal Personality Disorder	Inappropriate or constricted affect, excessive social anxiety
Antisocial Personality Disorder	Lack of remorse, irritability
Borderline Personality Disorder	Affective instability due to marked reactivity of mood, inappropriate intense anger, or difficulty controlling anger
Histrionic Personality Disorder	Rapidly shifting and shallow expressions of emotions
Narcissistic Personality Disorder	Lacks empathy
Avoidant Personality Disorder	Fear of criticism, disapproval, or rejection
Dependent Personality Disorder	Fear of being unable to care for self, being left alone
Alcohol intoxication	Mood lability
Alcohol withdrawal	Anxiety
Amphetamine intoxication	Euphoria or affective blunting; anxiety, tension, anger
Amphetamine withdrawal	Dysphoric mood
Caffeine intoxication	Nervousness, excitement
Cannabis intoxication	Euphoria, anxiety
Cocaine intoxication	Euphoria or affective blunting; anxiety, tension, anger
Cocaine withdrawal	Dysphoric mood
Hallucinogen intoxication	Anxiety or depression
Inhalant intoxication	Belligerence, euphoria

TABLE 14.1 (cont.)

Disorder	*Emotion-Related Symptom*
Nicotine withdrawal	Dysphoric or depressed mood; irritability, frustration, anger, anxiety
Opioid intoxication	Euphoria followed by dysphoria
Opioid withdrawal	Dysphoric mood
Phencyclidine intoxication	Belligerence
Sedative (etc.) intoxication	Mood lability
Sedative (etc.) withdrawal	Anxiety

DEFINING EMOTION

Drawing from over a century of theory and research, there is fairly good consensus that emotions are adaptive and serve important functions. We concur with a host of theorists who define emotions as complex systems that developed through the course of human evolutionary history to prepare an organism to act in response to environmental stimuli and challenges. Furthermore, emotions are comprised of a number of components, including (but not limited to) expressive, feeling or experiential, and physiological, that are typically coordinated within the individual. Indeed, the coordination of these components, under most circumstances, serves a number of important intrapersonal and interpersonal functions (e.g., Ekman, 1994; Frijda, 1986; Keltner & Kring, 1998; Lang, Bradley, & Cuthbert, 1990; Levenson, 1992).

In addition to the term *emotion*, a number of other terms are used in the emotion literature. Although the terms *affect* and *emotion* have been used interchangeably, a number of theorists and researchers have distinguished between the terms, both conceptually and empirically. Generally speaking, the term affect is most often used in reference to feeling states, whereas emotions comprise multiple components (only one of which is a feeling state) and are hypothesized to occur in response to some object, person, or situation, whether real or imagined (e.g, Feldman Barrett & Russell, 1999). Russell and Feldman Barrett (1999; see also, Feldman Barrett & Russell, 1999) argued that affect, or as they described, *core affect*, reflects feeling states that are ever-present and are just one of many constituents of what they refer to as *prototypical emotion episodes*. Prototypical emotion episodes are hypothesized to occur in response to some event, whether internal or external, and are comprised of cognitive, behavioral, feeling, and physiological components. In their analysis, moods are core affects that endure for a longer period of time. Using the framework of Russell and Feldman Barrett (1999), much of the research on emotion disturbance in psychopathology has been concerned with the various components of prototypical emotional episodes, one of which is (core) affect, although some research has been concerned with just one component, namely the experience of feeling states or core affects.

Although the theorizing of Feldman, Barrett, and Russell (1999) has contributed a good deal toward disambiguating various emotion constructs, not all studies and measures used in various studies follow this rubric. Thus, integrating findings about emotion disturbances in psychopathology is hindered by a lack of clarity in definition and use of terminology. Nevertheless, in our review, we explicitly note the component of emotion each measure refers to if it is not already obvious.

DEFINING EMOTION REGULATION

Although there is fairly good consensus in the field as to what constitutes emotion, there is less agreement on what constitutes emotion regulation. Perhaps owing to the relatively recent research emphasis on emotion regulation, a number of key definitional issues have yet to be fully resolved. Despite the definitional ambiguity surrounding the concept of emotion regulation, there is often an explicit assumption that different psychological disorders, particularly those affecting children, are rife with problems in emotion regulation. This assumption may come, in part, from historical notions that out-of-control emotions or passions led to madness, as illustrated by the quote by Sauvages (1772, as quoted in Foucault, 1965) presented at the beginning of the chapter. Furthermore, different types of psychotherapy emphasize gaining or regaining control over one's emotions as a pathway to mental health (e.g., Greenberg & Safran, 1987). Emphasizing emotion regulation in treatment implicitly suggests that loss of control over one's emotions may have contributed to the development of the problem, much the same way that pharmacotherapy targeted toward particular neurotransmitter systems implies that problems in these neurotransmitter systems contributed to the development of the disorder.

In our view, however, these assumptions are premature. Indeed, until greater conceptual clarity surrounding the concept of emotion regulation is achieved, progress toward understanding emotion regulation problems in psychopathology will be stalled. Here, we briefly outline some of the key definitional problems associated with the concept of emotion regulation.

The Scope of Emotion Regulation

Although a number of definitions of emotion regulation have been offered, they differ in a number of ways, including what types of regulatory processes are involved, what types and components of emotion are regulated, whether the regulatory processes are internal or external (or both), and whether regulatory processes are implicit or explicit (or both). One of the most recent and influential definitions of emotion regulation has been offered by Gross (1998), who defined the construct as " … the processes by which individuals influence which emotions they have, when they have them, and how they experience and express these emotions" (p. 275). This definition locates emotion regulation within the individual, and importantly, it emphasizes that multiple components of emotion (expression, experience) can be regulated. Gross argued that regulatory processes can be explicit or implicit, and his empirical work has demonstrated that regulatory processes can occur before an emotion is generated as well as after it comes "online." For example, taking a different route to the office to bypass a confrontational coworker is a means of regulating feelings of anger before they occur; suppressing laughter in church is a way of regulating ongoing feelings of amusement. Furthermore, Gross proposed that emotion regulatory processes vary on a continuum of conscious, effortful regulatory processes to those that are less effortful, outside of conscious awareness, or automatic. Contributing to the influence of Gross's conceptual work on emotion regulation is the program of empirical research that has been conducted in the past several years to support the processes outlined by his definition (see Gross, 2001, for a review).

Other definitions include the notion that external influences, particularly other people, also figure into the regulation of emotion (e.g., Calkins, 1994; Eisenberg & Fabes, 1992; Thompson, 1994). According to Thompson (1994), "Emotion regulation consists of the extrinsic and intrinsic processes responsible for monitoring, evaluating, and modifying emotional reactions, especially their intensive and temporal features, to accomplish one's goals" (pp. 27–28). According to Thompson, an important regulatory process is located with interactions with and influences from other people. For example, a wife's anger at her husband's behavior is soothed by her husband's attempts to offer reparations for his transgression. Parents often exert regulatory efforts toward their children's emotions, by, for example, reframing a particular situation ("the shirt from Grandma is not so bad; you can wear it for Halloween!"). Still other definitions emphasize that emotion regulatory processes also necessarily regulate other cognitive processes, such as attention (e.g., Cole, Michel, & Teti, 1994).

The role of context is differentially emphasized in definitions of emotion regulation. To be sure, situational and contextual demands on regulatory processes are great. Moreover, momentary changes in context may require different regulatory efforts. For example, when celebrating a victory among teammates, shouts of jubilation are context-appropriate; however, if the opposing team enters the room, thus altering the context, a more dampened display would be appropriate. The emphasis on context is more explicitly acknowledged in those definitions generated from the developmental tradition, emphasizing how children do and do not regulate their emotions (e.g., Cole et al., 1994; Thompson, 1994). Indeed, ineffective emotion regulation among children is often inferred on the basis of context-inappropriate nonverbal behavior. Among adults, contextual influences are still great, but they are difficult to ascertain and distinguish from regulatory processes that have likely become more automatic or effortless across time and multiple exposures to a particular context or situation. For example, children are notoriously bad at suppressing laughter in an inappropriate context (e.g., classroom, church), whereas adults, presumably with more practice, are much better able to squelch inappropriate giggles.

Distinguishing Emotion From Emotion Regulation

Perhaps one of the more vexing issues facing the field of emotion regulation is distinguishing emotion that is and is not regulated. Davidson (2000) offered, " ... regulatory processes are an intrinsic part of the landscape of emotion, and rarely does an emotion get generated in the absence of associated regulatory processes" (p. 372). Similarly, Cole et al. (1994) suggested, " ... emotion is inherently regulatory and regulated, two processes that are subsumed under the term emotion regulation" (p. 74). By these accounts, then, emotion does not need to be distinguished from emotion regulation because (nearly) all emotion is regulated (see also Frijda, 1986). Although the conceptual and empirical challenges associated with distinguishing emotion and emotion regulation are great, suggesting that all emotion is regulated emotion seems akin to saying that all behavior is unconsciously motivated—it is an assertion that is essentially untestable.

Furthermore, recasting problems of emotion as problems in emotion regulation has the potential to oversimplify the nature of emotion-related problems, minimize the role of individual differences in emotional experience and expression, and implicitly attribute a problem where none may actually exist. For example, if an individual experiences strong negative emotions, is this a problem in regulation insofar as the individual can't down-regulate these strong feelings? By contrast, might this be a person who simply feels things more strongly and thus does not have a regulatory problem at all? It is likely that both types of individuals exist in the world, and that the emotion-related outcomes associated with these two individuals would be quite different. To illustrate with a different example: If a child displays anger when a favorite toy is taken away, is this a problem in emotion regulation or is it a child who more readily displays his or her feelings when angry? In other words, is this a highly expressive child? A child who failed to express anger in this scenario could be viewed as an effective emotion regulator, to the extent that an anger display was considered inappropriate to the context. However, the child might be a relatively unexpressive child who does not readily show his or her feelings. Or, the child may not actually feel anger in this situation, and thus the lack of anger expression would match the feeling state.

Equating differences in amount or intensity of facial expression with an emotion regulatory process can minimize the important role of individual differences in emotional expression and experience (Gross, John, & Richards, 2000). Furthermore, regulation of an emotion assumes that the emotion has somehow changed course (Gross, 1998). Yet, this assumption requires knowing the trajectory of that emotion in its unregulated form, and this is unfortunately not often included in studies presuming to assess emotion regulation.

Distinguishing between emotion and emotion regulation has important implications for understanding emotion-related disturbances in psychopathology. For example, in mania, it would seem important to distinguish whether the abundance of positive emotion (and irritability) is a problem in down-regulating excess emotion, matching emotion to context, or simply an excess of emotion that is experienced with control processes intact. To further illustrate, children with Attention Deficit and Hyperactivity Disorder (ADHD) are often ascribed with deficits in emotion regulation. A common paradigm with these children is the disappointing prize scenario whereby children are shown a group of desirable (e.g., candy) and undesirable (e.g., baby toy) prizes. Children are then presented a desirable and undesirable prize in the presence of an experimenter, and their nonverbal behavior is recorded and later coded. In a study of children with ADHD, ineffective emotion regulation was inferred when children displayed negative nonverbal behavior in the disappointing condition (e.g., Maedgen & Carlson, 2000). Presumably, showing frustration or anger in the presence of an experimenter was considered inappropriate to context and therefore ineffective emotion regulation. However, it is not entirely clear how this nonverbal behavior can be construed as a problem in emotion regulation. Indeed, measuring only one component of emotion, nonverbal behavior, does not allow for unambiguous conclusions about emotion versus emotion regulation. Why is a child who displays frustration considered to have a problem in emotion regulation compared to a child who feels no frustration at all? The answer to this question cannot be ascertained without looking at the relationship between experience and expression.[1] To be sure, assessing emotional experience among children is not as straightforward as it is among adults. Nevertheless, inferences about emotion regulation are difficult to make when only one component of emotion is assessed.

Rather than inferring a problem in emotion regulation, findings from basic research on emotion regulation can be used to help clarify the nature of an observed emotion disturbance in different psychological disorders. For example, of the more replicable findings in schizophrenia is that patients are markedly less expressive than individuals without schizophrenia (e.g., Berenbaum & Oltmanns, 1992; Kring & Earnst, 1999; Kring, Kerr, Smith, & Neale, 1993; Kring & Neale, 1996). Recent research on emotion regulation provides important clues as to whether schizophrenia patients' diminished expressive behavior reflects a disturbance in emotion or an emotion regulation strategy that may be employed too often. Work by Gross and colleagues (e.g., Gross & Levenson, 1993, 1997) has demonstrated that one form of emotion regulation, suppressing the expression of an ongoing feeling, is linked to increases in autonomic nervous system (ANS) activity. In schizophrenia, finding that patients' diminished expressivity is associated with heightened ANS activity would suggest that patients are employing an emotion regulation strategy (suppression). By contrast, finding that their diminished expressive display is not linked to such an ANS increase would suggest a problem in emotion expression. The evidence to date favors the latter scenario: schizophrenia patients' diminished expressive behavior is not reliably associated with increases in ANS activity (Kring et al., 2003; Kring & Neale, 1996). These brief examples illustrate both the promise and difficulties associated with distinguishing emotion from emotion regulation. One further definitional issue to be considered is the distinction between emotion dysregulation and emotion regulation.

Defining Emotion Dysregulation

Trying to distinguish emotion regulation from dysregulation is a bit like trying to distinguish normal from abnormal or disorder from nondisorder. It seems likely that emotion dysregulation involves both a deficiency in regulatory processes as well as maladaptive implementation of otherwise intact processes.

Cicchetti et al. (1995) distinguished emotion dysregulation from problems in emotion regulation. According to these authors, emotion dysregulation involves the inappropriate or maladaptive application of emotion regulatory processes that are nevertheless present and available for appropriate use. By contrast, problems in emotion regulation reflect the absence of, or deficits in, regulatory processes. To illustrate with a simple example, an individual who is able to suppress an emotional display but does so toward maladaptive ends (e.g., to lie) would be considered to be exhibiting emotion dysregulation. An individual who has failed to learn to suppress an emotional display would be exhibiting a problem in emotion regulation. By this account, emotion dysregulation emphasizes functional impairments or maladaptive outcomes associated with the implementation of emotion regulatory processes; problems in emotion regulation reflect a more fundamental disturbance in the building blocks of emotion regulatory processes. Although this may not necessarily be the way nature has carved the emotion regulatory joints, it is nonetheless a useful rubric for considering emotion regulation in psychopathology. Furthermore, this approach suggests that basic emotion regulatory processes must be understood before either dysregulation or problems in emotion regulation can be fully understood. Thus, research from basic emotion that attempts to unpack the nature of emotion regulatory processes will be wholly informative with respect to understanding the role of emotion regulation (or dysregulation) in psychopathology. Moreover, distinguishing whether regulatory processes are deficient or employed during inopportune moments or situations has enormous implications for treatment. Working to develop a regulatory strategy would require a different intervention than would working to match situations with regulatory strategies already at one's disposal.

Adopting a somewhat different approach, Keenan (2000) articulated a number of important considerations for definitions of emotion dysregulation. First, she noted that many component behaviors used to define emotion regulation, particularly among children (e.g., crying, increases in heart rate), are typical behaviors. Emotion dysregulation, according to Keenan, reflects a repeated pattern of these behaviors across time and in extreme form. By this account, emotion regulation and dysregulation form a type of continuum, ranging from regulatory processes and behaviors implemented in appropriate contexts to these same processes used ineffectively and out of context. Indeed, context plays a central role in distinguishing regulation and dysregulation according to this view. Furthermore, outcomes associated with regulatory processes are also emphasized in Keenan's conceptualization, particularly the level of impairment associated with the implementation of any given regulatory process. Not surprisingly, impairments in functioning are central to several conceptualizations of emotion dysregulation (e.g., Cole et al., 1994; Gross & Munoz, 1995; Thompson, 1994), much the same way that impairment in functioning figures into definitions of mental disorder (e.g., DSM–IV–TR; Wakefield, 1992). Finally, Keenan emphasized the importance of considering multiple regulatory components (behavior, experience, physiology, social) and that emotion dysregulation likely involves disruptions to more than one component. Keenan's account consisted of three considerations: (a) Emotion dysregulation consists of behaviors and processes that are part of the "normal" spectrum, but they are exhibited frequently, out of context, or in extreme form; (b) emotion dysregulation is associated with an impairment in functioning; and (c) emotion dysregulation involves disturbances in multiple regulatory components. The first consideration again requires knowledge of basic emotion regulatory processes to help determine when they are out of context and when they are too frequent or extreme.

EMOTION REGULATION AND PSYCHOPATHOLOGY?

What type of evidence is available for examining whether emotion regulatory processes are disturbed or absent in different psychological disorders? There is a rich accumulation of clinical case descriptions of various disorders that provides hints at regulatory problems. Furthermore, some of the diagnostic criteria explicitly refer to emotion regulation difficulties. For example, the criteria "difficulty controlling anger" in Borderline Personality Disorder; "efforts to avoid feelings" in Posttraumatic Stress Disorder (PTSD); "difficulty controlling worry" in Generalized Anxiety Disorder; and "rapidly shifting expressions of emotion" in Histrionic Personality Disorder, all suggest difficulties in regulating emotions. Although this descriptive information sets the stage for further empirical investigation, these descriptions alone do not provide overwhelming evidence for emotion regulation problems in different psychological disorders.

Based on our earlier discussion of emotion dysregulation, it would seem that to establish whether emotion dysregulation is a part of various psychological disorders, we must (a) delineate some of the basic processes comprising emotion regulation, and (b) demonstrate that the use of (or failure to use) emotion regulatory processes is associated with an impairment in functioning. Although we know that most psychological disorders are associated with impaired functioning, empirical work that links these impairments to emotion regulatory problems as opposed to other deficits associated with a particular disorder remains to be conducted.

What are the basic processes associated with emotion regulation? At the broadest level, emotion regulation involves processes that not only serve to regulate emotion, but also serve other important self-regulatory functions. For example, psychological processes, such as attention, working memory, decision making, social skill, and emotion knowledge, to name but a few, all likely figure in the successful regulation of emotion (e.g., Cicchetti et al., 1995; Cole et al., 1994; Davidson, 2000; Derryberry & Reed, 1996; Feldman Barrett & Gross, 2001; Gross, 1998, 2001). Furthermore, neurobiological structures and pathways, including neurotransmitters, neuroendocrine systems, and cortical and subcortical structures, also figure prominently in emotion and emotion regulation (e.g., Davidson, 2000; Gross, 1998; LeDoux, 1996; Panksepp, 1998). To consider the role of these multiple levels is well beyond the scope of this chapter. Furthermore, that these different psychological processes and neurobiological systems are involved in emotion regulation as well as other important self-regulatory, emotional, behavioral, and cognitive functions makes uncovering their specific contribution to emotion regulation undeniably challenging.

Berenbaum et al. (2003) has proposed a taxonomy of emotional disturbances in psychopathology, which includes what they call *emotional intensity/regulation disturbances*. Emotional intensity/regulation disturbances are defined as excesses or deficits in both positive and negative emotions. For example, mania characterized by excesses in both positive (joy, euphoria) and negative (irritability) emotions would be construed as an emotional intensity/regulation disturbance. Unfortunately, this conceptualization does not articulate the regulatory processes that are either missing, gone awry, or linked to maladaptive outcomes. What is needed to more firmly establish a link between emotion regulatory problems and psychological disorders is an empirical strategy that articulates hypotheses specific to emotion regulatory processes.

To begin to examine how emotion regulatory processes may figure into different psychological disorders, we have adopted Gross's (1998) process model of emotion regulation. This model articulates a number of emotion regulatory processes or strategies which are situated along the temporal unfolding of an emotion. Gross has distinguished regulatory processes that occur before an emotion is generated (labeled *antecedent-focused*) from those processes that occur after an emotion is generated (labeled *response-focused*). Table 14.2 presents the antecedent-focused and response-focused processes or strategies outlined by Gross.

This model holds great promise for examining the role of emotion regulation in psychopathology in at least three ways. First, work by Gross and colleagues has begun to uncover the mechanisms and outcomes of two forms of emotion regulation, one antecedent-focused (reappraisal) and one response-focused (suppression; for a review, see Butler & Gross, this volume). To briefly summarize, reappraising, a form of cognitive change, is associated with decreases in expres-

TABLE 14.2

Antecedent- and Response-Focused Emotion Regulation Strategies

	Strategy	*Description*
Antecedent-Focused strategies (before an emotion is generated)	Situation Selection	Choosing among situations
	Situation Modification	Changing aspects of the situation, once in it
	Attention Deployment	Focusing attention on a particular aspect of a situation
	Cognitive Change	Altering the meaning associated with the aspect of the situation
Response-Focused strategies (after an emotion is generated)	Response Modulation	Altering the expression, experience, or physiology of an emotional response

Note. Adapted from Gross's (1998) process model of emotion regulation.

sive behavior, emotional experience, but no detrimental physiological consequences. By contrast, suppression is associated with decreases in expressive behavior, no changes in emotional experience, heightened physiological responding, impaired memory, and interference with social interactions. These findings can help to illuminate whether emotion disturbances in psychopathology may be construed as problems in emotion regulation. In addition, the laboratory work by Gross and colleagues has laid the methodological foundation for future studies that will illuminate the precursors and outcomes of different emotion regulatory processes in both disordered and nondisordered populations. Second, indirect evidence from other areas of psychopathology research can be used to support the possibility that emotion regulatory processes, such as situation selection or attention deployment, may be disrupted in various psychological disorders. For example, one of the more replicable findings in the anxiety literature is the finding that anxious individuals tend to focus their attention on anxiety or threat-related information (e.g., Mathews & MacLeod, 1994). Third, some of the observed emotion disturbances in psychopathology may be construed as an additional response-focused emotion regulation strategy not currently included in Gross's (1998) model. For example, the failure to inhibit an ongoing emotion has been hypothesized to be a central deficit in depression (e.g., Tomarken & Keener, 1998). The failure to stop or down-regulate an emotion is likely a response modulation problem. Of course, the empirical work needed to constrain hypotheses about other antecedent-focused and response modulation problems in psychopathology remains to be done.

In the next section, we draw on the promise of this model to examine how emotion regulation difficulties may characterize a number of different psychological disorders. Unfortunately, given the state of the field, most of the ideas about emotion regulation and psychopathology we outline have yet to be empirically verified. Thus, much of what we present is a framework for future research. However, we believe that adopting this process model approach has tremendous potential for testing hypotheses about how emotion regulation is (or is not) linked to different psychological disorders.

EMOTION REGULATION AND SPECIFIC PSYCHOLOGICAL DISORDERS

To consider the question of how emotion regulation (or dysregulation) figures into all of the DSM–IV–TR disorders with emotional symptoms (cf. Table 14.1) would be worthy of an entire book. Here, we focus on a subset of those disorders, particularly those that have accumulated evidence of specific emotion-related disturbances.

Major Depressive Disorder

Prolonged sad or depressed mood and loss of interest or pleasure (anhedonia) are two emotional features associated with major depressive disorder. Anxiety and guilt are also commonly part of the emotional landscape of this disorder (Mineka, Watson, & Clark, 1998). Moreover, depression has been broadly characterized by low levels of positive affect and heightened levels of negative affect (e.g., Watson, Clark, & Carey, 1988). Persons with low levels of positive affect are likely to experience emotions such as sadness and to be interpersonally disengaged. By contrast, persons with high levels of negative affect are likely to frequently experience emotions such as anxiety, guilt, and anger.

Recent empirical work has linked this pattern of heightened negative affect and low levels of positive affect to asymmetrical patterns of electrocortical activation in frontal cortex. Resting left frontal hypoactivation has been observed in both currently depressed (e.g., Henriques & Davidson, 1991) and previously but not currently depressed individuals (Henriques & Davidson, 1990). In contrast, greater relative left anterior hyperactivation has been observed in individuals reporting high levels of positive affectivity and thus presumably not prone to major depressive disorder (Tomarken, Davidson, Wheeler, & Doss, 1992). Researchers have proposed that stable, resting left frontal hypoactivation is a diathesis for depression that is linked to a number of emotion-related deficits (e.g., Davidson, 1992; Davidson & Tomarken, 1989; Henriques & Davidson, 1990; Tomarken & Keener, 1998). A number of these emotion-related deficits can be construed as antecedent- and response-focused emotion regulatory deficits, such as the relative incapacity to respond to positive emotional stimuli (antecedent-focused), the prolonged maintenance of negative affect (response-focused), and deficits in the capacity to use positive events to shift into positive emotional states (antecedent-focused). What is needed are investigations that examine emotional responding in depression as well as the capacity to implement antecedent- and response-focused emotion regulatory strategies. Findings from studies that have assessed multiple components of emotional response suggest that depressed patients exhibit dampened expressive behavior to positive stimuli, and in some cases, dampened experience to both positive and negative emotional stimuli (e.g., Berenbaum & Oltmanns, 1992; Rottenberg, Gross, Wilhelm, Najmi, & Gotlib, 2002; Rottenberg, Kasch, Gross, & Gotlib, 2002; Sloan, Strauss, & Wisner, 2001; Ulrich & Harms, 1985; Waxer, 1974). Extension of these findings into studies of specific emotion regulation processes is still needed.

Accumulated evidence indicates that depression is also linked with a number of cognitive biases in the processing of emotional stimuli, including a memory bias for mood-congruent information (e.g., Bradley, Mogg, & Williams, 1995), attentional biases toward mood-congruent information (e.g., MacLeod & Mathews, 1991), and self-focused rumination (e.g., Nolen–Hoeksema & Morrow, 1993), to name but a few. Furthermore, these cognitive and attentional biases and distortions have been hypothesized to contribute to the maintenance of depressed mood (e.g., Tomarken & Keener, 1998). To the extent that these processes are also antecedent-focused emotion regulatory strategies, it may be the case that individuals with depression have difficulty regulating negative emotions once they have already begun. Although the extant empirical work remains to be done, we can hypothesize that depressed individuals may have difficulties in situation selection, attention deployment, and cognitive change, all antecedent-focused regulatory strategies.

Bipolar Disorder

One of the features that distinguish bipolar disorder from major depressive disorder is the presence of at least one manic episode. Indeed, an episode of depression is not even required for the diagnosis, and as many as a third of bipolar patients report only manic episodes (e.g., Kessler et al., 1997). Although an episode of mania can involve high levels of positive emotions such as euphoria, it can also involve high levels of irritability. Furthermore, manic episodes can also include symptoms of depression (Johnson & Kizer, in press). Perhaps not surprisingly, bipolar patients appear to have more intense positive emotional experiences than unipolar patients (e.g., Bagby et al., 1996). However, bipolar patients who experience depression demonstrate increased levels of negative affect, similar to patients with unipolar depression (Lozano & Johnson, 2001).

Although research is beginning to characterize the nature of disturbances in emotional experience in Bipolar Disorder, there is still much to be learned about expressive behavior and physiological reactivity. Furthermore, there has yet to be a direct study of emotion regulation among bipolar patients. As discussed earlier, additional research is needed to ascertain whether the prolonged and intense positive and negative emotional experience of bipolar patients reflects an inability to down-regulate their emotional responses (i.e., a response-focused emotion regulation problem). A laboratory investigation that sought to test whether bipolar patients could influence their feelings, expressive behavior, and physiological arousal when presented with emotional stimuli, would go a long ways toward discovering potential emotion regulation problems.

Indirect evidence suggests that emotion regulatory processes may aid in recovery. In a prospective study of bipolar patients, Johnson and colleagues (Johnson, Winett, Meyer, Greenhouse, & Miller, 1999) found that social support predicted a more rapid recovery, as well as a decrease in depressive symptoms, but not manic symptoms. To the extent that social support serves as an external regulator of emotion, this finding suggests that social support may be an effective external emotion regulator that works toward decreasing the prolonged sad or depressed mood in depression episodes, whether part of Major Depressive Disorder or Bipolar Disorder.

Schizophrenia

As noted earlier, accumulated evidence indicates that schizophrenia patients are markedly less expressive than individuals without schizophrenia. This diminished expressive behavior is not accompanied, however, by a corresponding decrement in experienced emotion (e.g., Berenbaum & Oltmanns, 1992; Kring & Earnst, 1999; Kring et al., 1993; Kring & Neale, 1996). Moreover, although one study has found that schizophrenia patients exhibit heightened ANS reactivity in response to emotional stimuli, this increase is not specific to emotional stimuli (Kring & Neale, 1996), and this more generalized heightened reactivity is seen only among a subgroup of schizophrenia patients (Kring et al., 2003). As noted earlier, one form of response-focused emotion regulation, suppression of expressive behavior, is associated with greater ANS reactivity. Thus, the accumulated findings to date on diminished expressivity in schizophrenia do not suggest that schizophrenia patients are down-regulating (suppressing) their emotions. However, might it be the case that schizophrenia patients have a deficit in up-regulation? That is, might their diminished expressive behavior be a failure (or inability) to summon the expressive component of emotion in a manner commensurate with other emotion components? This possibility remains to be tested empirically. A study could be fashioned that asks patients to magnify their display of feelings in an effort to see if patients can indeed produce outwardly observable displays of experienced emotion. An inability to do so would suggest a problem in emotion regulation insofar as matching expression with experience is construed as a form of response-focused emotion regulation. To date, there is no evidence to suggest that schizophrenia patients have a deficit or lack of antecedent-focused regulatory strategies, however, this lack of evidence stems largely from a lack of research into this area. Additional studies that examined whether schizophrenia patients are able to reappraise, one form of cognitive-change proposed by Gross's (1998) model that has been investigated among nondisordered individuals, would be a good place to begin.

Feldman Barrett and Gross (2001) have argued that knowledge and awareness of one's emotions are a necessary prerequisite to effective emotion regulation. However, simply having knowledge about emotion is not sufficient. Rather, greater accessibility of that emotion knowledge is believed to promote effective emotion regulation. Individuals who describe their feelings in a more differentiated manner (e.g., sad, confused, elated) rather than more globally (e.g., good, bad) have greater accessibility to and awareness of emotion knowledge and use this knowledge in a more specific way. This ability to differentiate among emotional states is believed to provide individuals with information about when the regulation of emotion may be necessary. Feldman Barrett, Gross, and colleagues hypothesized and later empirically confirmed that greater emotion awareness and differentiation is linked with emotion regulation capability, particularly for negative emotions (Feldman Barrett, Gross, Christensen, & Benvenuto, 2001). In the schizophrenia literature, recent evidence indicates that schizophrenia patients do not appear to differ from individuals without schizophrenia in terms of their emotion knowledge. However, schizophrenia patients appear to differentiate less among emotional states, and thus may be less effective at emotion regulation (Kring et al., in press).

Anxiety Disorders

Although the anxiety disorders are a heterogeneous group of disorders, most, if not all of them involve heightened negative affect more generally and fear, anxiety, and disgust more specifically (e.g., Chorpita & Barlow, 1998; Clark & Watson, 1991; Watson et al., 1995; Zinbarg & Barlow, 1996). One common clinical feature that many of the anxiety disorders share is recognition that the anxiety, worry, or fear is excessive, as well as a relative inability to modify or stop these feelings. Furthermore, among individuals with anxiety disorders, the presence of negative emotions is not dysfunctional per se. For example, the fear response that characterizes a panic attack is an otherwise normal or functionally adaptive response that occurs at an inappropriate time (Barlow, 2001). That the clinical features common to a number of anxiety disorders indicate difficulties in the modification and timing of anxiety-related emotions suggests that a problem in emotion regulation may be centrally relevant.

Indirect evidence supports the proposition that individuals with anxiety disorders may have problems with antecedent-focused emotion regulation. For example, a number of studies have found that panic disorder patients misperceive harmless events or objects in the environment as threatening (Barlow, 2001; Clark,

1988; McNally, 1990). In addition, cumulative evidence suggests that anxious patients are more likely to attend to threatening stimuli and make biased judgments about the likelihood of negative outcomes as well as the covariation between these outcomes and feared stimuli (Mathews & MacLeod, 1994; Mineka & Sutton, 1992; Tomarken, Mineka, & Cook, 1989; Tomarken, Sutton, & Mineka, 1995). These findings suggest that anxious patients may have difficulties in situation selection, attention deployment, and cognitive change, although empirical work is needed to test out these notions.

One of the clinical characteristics associated with PTSD is emotional numbing, which refers to patients' general restriction of feelings, particularly when reminded of or reexposed to trauma.[2] Recent empirical work by Litz and colleagues has demonstrated that PTSD patients do not have an overall dampening of feelings when cued with prior trauma. Rather, PTSD patients exhibit a dampening of positive expressive behavior in response to positive stimuli (e.g., Litz, Orsillo, Kaloupek, & Weathers, 2000). Litz and colleagues have suggested that this dampening of positive facial expressions reflects automatic emotional suppression, perhaps as a means of coping with the trauma reexposure (Litz & Gray, 2002; Litz et al., 2000). Borrowing from the findings of Gross and Levenson (1997), suppression in response to positive stimuli would be expected to be accompanied by an increase in ANS reactivity. Findings from Litz et al. (2000) indicated that PTSD patients had greater heart rate reactivity to all stimuli, regardless of whether they were exposed to prior trauma. Thus, it remains unclear whether PTSD patients are actually suppressing in this context. Evidence from a self-report study suggests, however, that PTSD patients do indeed suppress their emotional reactions. Combat veterans with PTSD reported that they were more likely to deliberately keep their feelings hidden from others than combat veterans without PTSD (Roemer, Litz, Orsillo, & Wagner, 2001). Additional research that asks PTSD patients to suppress their outward expressions in response to emotional stimuli and assesses expressive behavior, experience, and ANS reactivity would be informative.

Importantly, these findings point to the importance of considering context when developing hypotheses about emotion regulation and psychopathology. Indeed, Litz and Gray (2002) have argued that exposing combat veterans to combat-related images differentially impacts emotional responding by heightening attention to threat and thereby raising the threshold required to emotionally respond to positive stimuli. Thus, emotion regulatory problems are likely to be apparent when cues to trauma are readily available.

Borderline Personality Disorder

Many of the clinical characteristics associated with Borderline Personality Disorder (BPD) can be viewed as quintessential emotion regulation problems. Clinically, these emotion regulation problems have been described in various ways, including an oversensitivity to emotional events, an instability in affective response, excessive fluctuations in mood and emotional response, and a failure to return to "baseline" following an emotional event (e.g., Farchaus–Stein, 1996; Levine, Marziali, & Hood, 1997; Linehan, 1987; Lumsden, 1993; Snyder & Pitt, 1985). As noted earlier and in Table 14.1, several of the DSM–IV–TR criteria for BPD involve emotion, and suggest difficulty with response-focused emotion regulation. Recent research has found that BPD patients report chronic and intense feelings of a number of negative emotions, including anger, hostility, depression, loneliness, and anxiety (e.g., Coid, 1993; Farchaus–Stein, 1996; Gunderson, Carpenter, & Strauss, 1975; Gunderson & Phillips, 1991; Kruedelbach, McCormick, Schultz, & Grueneich, 1993; Snyder & Pitt, 1985; Soloff, 1981; Soloff & Ulrich, 1981). Furthermore, a daily diary study found that not only do BPD patients report greater negative emotion than individuals without BPD, they also exhibit greater variability in their daily negative emotion (Farchaus–Stein, 1996). Thus, not only do patients with BPD report experiencing more negative emotion than controls, their negative emotions are also much more variable (see also Cowdry,Gardner, O'Leary, Liebenluft, & Rubinow, 1991). Theorists have suggested that BPD patients exhibit a number of emotion-related maladaptive behaviors, such as suicidal gestures, aggression, avoidance, overreacting, and other impulsive acts in an attempt to regulate these strong negative emotions (e.g., Linehan, 1987; Paris, 1992; Shearin & Linehan, 1994).

A recent and comprehensive study on emotion disturbances in BPD found that compared to nonpatients, BPD patients were less aware of their own and others' emotions, had fewer empathetic responses, reported more intense negative but not positive emotions, and performed more poorly on a test of facial emotion perception (Levine et al., 1997).That BPD patients are less aware of their own emotions suggests that they will regulate their emotions less often, because as noted earlier, emotional awareness is an important prerequisite for regulation of emotion (cf. Feldman Barrett et al., 2001). Interventions that aim to increase emotional awareness among BPD patients may therefore hold great promise toward increasing emotion regulation capabilities.

Frontotemporal Lobar Dementia

Frontotemporal lobar dementia (FTLD) is characterized by a decline in social conduct, impaired regulation of behavior, emotional blunting, low motivation, and loss of insight (Neary et al., 1998). The neuronal deterioration of FTLD occurs predominantly in the amygdala, anterior temporal lobes, and prefrontal cortex (Miller, Ikonte, Ponton, & Levy, 1997). In perhaps one of the most comprehensive examinations of emotion in FTLD, Levenson and colleagues have embarked on an ambitious program of research whereby they are testing emotional reactivity and emotion regulation capabilities in FTLD patients and a comparable sample of individuals without FTLD. Although preliminary, findings to date indicate that FTLD patients exhibit comparable facial expression, experience, and physiology in response to emotionally evocative material. However, when asked to suppress their outward reactions to these stimuli, FTLD patients have difficulty in doing so (Werner et al., 2003). Furthermore, when control participants are told that a loud "gun-shot like" noise will occur in 10 sec, they "brace" themselves both physiologically and psychologically. This bracing is manifested by a reduction in somatic activity and limited facial movement. These efforts could be construed as an antecedent-focused emotion regulatory process, insofar as these individuals are likely deploying their attention elsewhere and focusing inward to prepare for the impending loud noise. By contrast, FTLD patients do not appear to exhibit such antecedent-focused emotion regulation in the face of an unwarned noxious stimulus (Levenson, 2001). Thus, FTLD patients may have a deficit in both response-focused and antecedent-focused emotion regulation yet no deficit in emotional reactivity. These findings point to the importance of distinguishing emotion from emotion regulation.

IMPLICATIONS FOR ASSESSMENT AND TREATMENT

Although it might seem a bit premature to discuss implications because the empirical findings on emotion regulation difficulties in psychological disorders are so few in number, we chose to do so because we believe the implications are enormous. Broadly speaking, greater dissemination of laboratory-based findings on emotion and psychopathology to clinicians is needed. Empirical evidence has disconfirmed some commonly held clinical notions, thus changing the way assessment and treatment may be approached. For example, the term *flat affect* implies that all of emotion is dampened, and this was presumed by many to be the case in schizophrenia. However, laboratory findings that schizophrenia patients experience strong emotions despite their lack of outward display (see Kring, 1999, for a review), coupled with findings that schizophrenia patients do not have a marked deficit in the ways in which they represent their emotions (Kring, Feldman, Barrett, & Gard, 2003), suggest a shift in treatment and assessment goals is needed. In other words, interventions aimed at increasing patients' awareness of their emotions are likely misdirected. Rather, interventions targeted toward increasing expressive behavior, as is often done in psychosocial interventions emphasizing social skills, will likely be more fruitful. Indeed, an important component of social skills interventions for schizophrenic patients is the development of nonverbal and emotion-related behaviors (e.g., Liberman, DeRisi, & Mueser, 1989; Mueser & Sayers, 1992).

Similarly, the concept of emotional numbing in PTSD was associated with the belief that patients experienced widespread deficits in experienced emotion. Laboratory research suggests that emotional numbing is much more context and valence specific, such that PTSD patients exhibit a diminution of positive expressive behavior after being exposed to or primed with prior trauma cues (Litz et al., 2000). Thus, interventions targeted toward increasing positive expressive behavior will likely be more advantageous than interventions that seek to increase patients' feelings more generally.

Findings specific to emotion regulation in psychological disorders suggest a number of important assessment and treatment implications. First, creating assessment instruments to measure antecedent-focused and response-focused regulation strategies would be a tremendous asset for clinicians. For example, we have speculated that individuals with depression and anxiety may have difficulties with situation selection, attention deployment, and cognitive change. The development and validation of a self-report measure that assesses the use of these different processes across varied contexts would be an important tool that can be used to test these notions.

In the absence of a measure to tap emotion regulatory processes, simply asking patients about their regulatory efforts as part of a routine assessment can provide a tremendous amount of clinically useful information. Roemer et al. (2001) found that combat veterans with PTSD reported more frequent and intense bouts of withholding their emotional displays than combat veterans without PTSD. This finding indicates that PTSD patients are actively employing regulatory efforts, and that they are aware that they do so. Asking these questions of other patient populations may yield information indicating an inability or unawareness of emotion regulatory efforts.

More generally, including a weekly assessment of emotion experience or expression in the context of therapy, and then charting these reports, can also provide clinically useful information (e.g., Persons, Davidson, & Tompkins, 2001). This can provide a closer look at the variability of emotion so prominent in BPD. It could also serve to increase awareness of emotion and failed regulatory attempts during a given week. These weekly reports are not only useful with respect to assessment, but they could also serve as valuable points of intervention.

CONCLUSIONS AND DIRECTIONS

Emotion disturbances are very common in psychopathology, and research over the last several decades has more clearly specified the nature of these disturbances (for reviews, see Berenbaum et al., in press; Keltner & Kring, 1998; Kring, 2001; Kring & Bachorowski, 1999). However, the extent to which emotion regulation problems play a role in various disorders is less well understood. Advances in basic research on emotion regulation hold promise for illuminating how emotion regulation difficulties may or may not characterize different types of psychopathology. Yet, before this promise can be fully realized, we believe that a number of conceptual and empirical issues must first be addressed. For example, resolving the definitional ambiguity surrounding the concept of emotion regulation will help to constrain hypotheses and theories about how and when emotion regulatory processes may go awry.

We have suggested that adopting the process model of Gross (1998) is a fruitful way to begin to delineate emotion regulatory deficits in psychopathology. This model can guide interpretation of existing findings on emotion disturbance as well as suggest new directions and methods for addressing emotion regulation in psychopathology. Findings on emotion regulation disturbances in psychopathology can in turn contribute toward bolstering the model. Indeed, evidence of emotion disturbances in various disorders suggests a form of response-focused emotion regulation not currently captured in the model. For example, the prolonged maintenance of emotional states characterizes mood disorders and suggests a difficulty in "shutting off" a response once it has been initiated.

There are a number of important directions for future research. First, basic research to further delineate the mechanisms and outcomes of emotion regulatory processes among nondisordered individuals needs to be done. We are just beginning to understand the characteristics of two forms of emotion regulation: suppression and reappraisal (Gross, 2002). It will be important to investigate the consequences of other forms of antecedent- and response-focused emotion regulatory strategies. These findings can then aid our understanding of how emotion dysregulation may figure into various psychological disorders. It will also be important to further characterize the adaptive value of different emotion regulatory strategies. For example, under what conditions is it adaptive to suppress?

An additionally important direction is to consider contextual variables in emotion regulatory models. For example, the role of gender has not been fully investigated with respect to emotion regulation. Findings among adults suggest that men and women do not differ in their emotion regulation efforts (e.g., Gross & Levenson, 1993, 1997). However, gender differences are the rule more often than the exception within psychopathology. Might it be the case that some of the gender differences in psychopathology can be accounted for by differences in emotion regulation? In its current form, Gross's (1998) model does not account for emotion regulatory strategies being appropriate in some contexts, and not in others. Expanding the model across and within different contexts is a necessary next step for the study of emotion regulation among disordered and nondisordered individuals.

Indeed, although we believe that Gross's (1995) emotion regulation model represents a good place to begin to examine emotion regulation strategies in depression, the model is not without shortcomings. For example, the model does not account for the role of other people as emotion regulators. Yet, understanding the interaction between, for example, depressed and anxious persons with other people will undeniably be important for understanding emotion regulation in these disorders.

Recent studies on emotion and psychopathology have incorporated methods developed and validated in the basic emotion literature. For instance, findings from studies of depression, schizophrenia, and PTSD that have included measures of multiple emotion components have advanced our understanding of emotion disturbances in these disorders well beyond what studies incorporating only one component of emotion have done (e.g., Kring & Earnst, 1999; Litz et al., 2000; Rottenberg et al., 2002). In the same way, incorporating the methods for studying emotion regulation will be fruitful.

Moreover, a combination of both laboratory and naturalistic research will likely yield the most complete picture of emotion regulation disturbances in psychopathology. For example, laboratory findings of diminished positive expressive behavior among PTSD patients have been confirmed in studies assessing patients' use of regulatory strategies in daily life (e.g., Litz et al., 2000; Roemer et al., 2001). Combining these approaches with more traditional clinical interviews will undoubtedly illuminate a richer account of how emotion regulation does or does not play a role in various forms of psychopathology.

REFERENCES

American Psychiatric Association, (2000). *Diagnostic and statistical manual of mental disorders*, (4th ed., text revision). Washington, DC: Author.

Bagby, R. M., Young, L. T., Schuller, D. R., Bindseil, K. D., Cooke, R. G., Dickens, S. E., et al. (1996). Bipolar disorder, unipolar depression and the Five-Factor model of personality. *Journal of Affective Disorders, 41*, 25–32.

Barlow, D. H. (2001). *Anxiety and Its Disorders* (2nd ed.). New York: Guilford.

Berenbaum, H., & Oltmanns, T. F. (1992). Emotional experience and expression in schizophrenia and depression. *Journal of Abnormal Psychology, 101*, 37–44.

Berenbaum, H., Raghavan, G., Le, H-N., Vernon, L. L., & Gomez, J. J. (2003). A taxonomy of emotional disturbances. *Clinical Psychology: Science and Practice, 10*, 206–226.

Bradley, B. P., Mogg, K., & Williams, R. (1995). Implicit and explicit memory for emotion-congruent information in clinical depression and anxiety. *Behavior Research and Therapy, 33*, 755–770.

Calkins, S. D. (1994). Origins and outcomes of individual differences in emotion regulation. *Monographs of the Society for Research in Child Development, 59*(2, Serial No. 240).

Chorpita, B. F., & Barlow, D. H. (1998). The development of anxiety: The role of control in the early environment. *Psychological Bulletin, 124*, 3–21

Cicchetti, D., Ackerman, B. P., & Izard, C. E. (1995). Emotions and emotion regulation in developmental psychopathology. *Development and Psychopathology, 7*, 1–10.

Clark, D. M. (1988). A cognitive model of panic. In S. Rachman and J. Maser (Eds.) *Panic: Psychological perspectives* (pp. 71–89). Hillsdale, NJ: Lawrence Erlbaum Associates, Inc.

Clark, L. A., & Watson, D. (1991). Tripartite model of anxiety and depression: Psychometric evidence and taxonomic implications. *Journal of Abnormal Psychology, 100*, 316–336.

Coid, J. W. (1993). An affective syndrome in psychopaths with borderline personality disorder. *British Journal of Psychiatry, 162*, 641–650.

Cole, P. M., Michel, M. K., & Teti, L. O. (1994). The development of emotion regulation and dysregulation: A clinical perspective. *Monographs of the Society for Research in Child Development, 59*(2, Serial No. 240).

Cowdry, R., Gardner, D. L., O'Leary, K. M., Lieberluft, E., * Rubinow, D. R. (1991). Mood variability: A study of four groups. *American Journal of Psychiatry, 148*, 1505–1511.

Davidson, R. J. (1992). Prolegomenon to the structure of emotion: Gleanings from neuropschology. *Cognition and Emotion, 63*, 245–268.

Davidson, R. J. (2000). The functional neuroanatomy of affective style. In R. D. Lane & L. Nadel (Eds)., *Cognitive neuroscience of emotion* (pp. 371–388). New York: Oxford University Press.

Davidson, R. J., & Tomarken, A. J. (1989). Laterality and emotion: An electrophysiological approach. In F. Boller & J. Grafman (Eds.), *Handbook of neuropsychology* (Vol. 3, pp. 419–441). Amsterdam, The Netherlands: Elsevier.

Derryberry, D., & Reed, M. A. (1996). Regulatory processes and the development of cognitive representations. *Development and Psychopathology, 8*, 215–234.

Eisenberg, N., & Fabes, R. A. (1992). Emotion, regulation, and the development of social competence. In M. S. Clark (Ed.), *Emotion and social behavior: Vol. 14. Review of personality and social psychology* (pp. 119–150). Newbury Park, CA: Sage.

Ekman, P. (1994). Strong evidence for universals in facial expression: A reply to Russell's mistaken critique. *Psychological Bulletin, 115*, 268–287.

Farchaus–Stein, K. (1996). Affect instability in adults with a borderline personality disorder. *Archives of Psychiatric Nursing, 10*, 32–40.

Feldman Barrett, L., & Gross, J. J. (2001). Emotional intelligence: A process model of emotion representation and regulation. In T. J. Mayne & G. A. Bonanno (Eds.), *Emotions: Current issues and future directions* (pp. 286–310). New York: Guilford.

Feldman Barrett, L., Gross, J. J., Christensen, T. C., & Benvenuto, M. (2001). Knowing what you're feeling and knowing what to do about it: Mapping the relation between emotion differentiation and emotion regulation. *Cognition and Emotion, 15*, 713–724.

Feldman Barrett, L., & Russell, J. A. (1999). The structure of current affect: Controversies and emerging consensus. *Current Directions in Psychological Science, 8*, 10–14.

Foucault, M. (1965). *Madness and civilization: A history of insanity in the age of reason*. New York: Plume Books.

Frijda, N. (1986). *The emotions*. Cambridge, England: Cambridge University Press.

Greenberg, L. S., & Safran, J. D. (1987). *Emotions in psychotherapy*. New York: Guilford.

Gross, J. J. (1998). The emerging field of emotion regulation: An integrative review. *Review of General Psychology, 2*, 271–299.

Gross, J. J. (2001). Emotion regulation in adulthood: Timing is everything. *Current Directions in Psychological Science, 10*, 214–219.

Gross, J. J. (2002). Emotion regulation: Affective, cognitive, and social consequences. *Psychophysiology, 39*, 281–291

Gross, J. J., John, O. P., & Richards, J. M. (2000). The dissociation of emotion expression from emotion experience: A personality perspective. *Personality and Social Psychology Bulletin, 26*, 712–726.

Gross, J. J., & Levenson, R. L. (1993). Emotional suppression: Physiology, self-report, and expressive behavior. *Journal of Personality and Social Psychology, 64*, 970–986.

Gross, J. J., & Levenson, R. L. (1997). Hiding feelings: The acute effects of inhibiting positive and negative emotions. *Journal of Abnormal Psychology, 106*, 95–103.

Gross, J. J., & Munoz, R. F. (1995). Emotion regulation and mental health. *Clinical Psychology: Science and Practice, 2*, 151–164.

Gunderson, J. G., Carpenter, W. T., & Strauss, J. S. (1975). Borderline and schizophrenic patients: A comparative study. *American Journal of Psychiatry, 132*, 1259–1264.

Gunderson, J. G., & Phillips, K. A. (1991). A current view of the interface between borderline personality disorder and depression. *American Journal of Psychiatry, 148*, 967–975.

Henriques, J. B., & Davidson, R. J. (1990). Regional brain electrical asymmetries discriminate between previously depressed subjects and healthy controls. *Journal of Abnormal Psychology, 99*, 22–31.

Henriques, J. B., & Davidson , R. J. (1991). Left frontal hypoactivation in depression. *Journal of Abnormal Psychology, 100*, 535–545.

Johnson, S. L., Winett, C. A., Meyer, B., Greenhouse, W. J., & Miller, I. (1999). Social support and the course of bipolar disorder. *Journal of Abnormal Psychology, 108*, 558–566.

Keenan, K. (2000). Emotion dysregulation as a risk factor for child psychopathology. *Clinical Psychology: Science and Practice, 7*, 418–434.

Keltner, D. & Kring, A. M. (1998). Emotion, social function, and psychopathology. *Review of General Psychology, 2*, 320–342.

Kessler, R. C., Rubinow, D. R., Holmes, C., Abelson, J. M., & Zhao, S. (1997). The epidemiology of DSM-III-R bipolar I disorder in a general population survey. *Psychological Medicine, 27*, 1079–1089.

Kring, A. M. (1999). Emotion in schizophrenia: Old mystery, new understanding. *Current Directions in Psychological Science, 8*, 160–163.

Kring, A. M. (2001). Emotion and psychopathology. In T. J. Mayne & G. A. Bonanno (Eds.), *Emotions: Current issues and future directions* (pp. 337–360). New York: Guilford.

Kring, A. M., & Bachorowski, J.-.A. (1999). Emotion and psychopathology. *Cognition and Emotion, 13*, 575–599.

Kring, A. M., & Earnst, K. S. (1999). Stability of emotional responding in schizophrenia. *Behavior Therapy, 30*, 373–388.

Kring, A. M., Feldman Barrett, L., & Gard, D. E. (2003). On the broad applicability of the affective circumplex: Representations of affective knowledge among schizophrenia patients *Psychological Science, 14*, 207–214.

Kring, A. M., Kerr, S. L, Smith, D. A., & Neale, J. M. (1993). Flat affect in schizophrenia does not reflect diminished subjective experience of emotion. *Journal of Abnormal Psychology, 102*, 507–517.

Kring, A. M., & Neale, J. M. (1996). Do schizophrenics show a disjunctive relationship among expressive, experiential, and psychophysiological components of emotion? *Journal of Abnormal Psychology 105*, 249–257.

Kring, A. M., Triesch, S., Germans, M. K., & Putnam, K. M. (2003). Heightened electrodermal activity to emotional stimuli in schizophrenia: Boundaries and specificity. Manuscript submitted for publication.

Kruedelbach, N., McCormick, R.A., Schultz, S. C., & Grueneich, R. (1993). Impulsivity, coping styles, and triggers for craving in substance abusers with borderline personality disorder. *Journal of Personality Disorders, 7*, 214–222.

Lang, P. J., Bradley, M. M., & Cuthbert, B. N. (1990). Emotion, attention, and the startle reflex. *Psychological Review, 97*, 377–395.

LeDoux, J. E. (1996). *The emotional brain.* New York: Simon & Schuster.

Levenson, R. W. (1992). Autonomic nervous system differences among emotions. *Psychological Science, 3*, 23–27.

Levenson, R. W. (2001, October). *The architecture of emotion: Form, function, and dysfunction.* Presidential address given at the annual meeting of the Society for Psychophysiological Research, Montreal, Quebec, Canada.

Levine, D., Marziali, E., & Hood, J. (1997). Emotion processing in borderline personality disorders. *Journal of Nervous and Mental Disease, 185*, 240–246.

Liberman, R. P., DeRisi, W. J., & Mueser, K. T. (1989). *Social skills training for psychiatric patients.* New York: Pergamon.

Linehan, M. M. (1987). Dialectical behavior therapy for borderline personality disorder. *Bulletin of the Menninger Clinic, 51*, 261–276.

Litz, B. T., & Gray, M. J. (2002). Emotional numbing in posttraumatic stress disorder: Current and future research directions. Australian and New Zealand *Journal of Psychiatry, 36*, 198–204.

Litz, B.T., Orsillo, S.M., Kaloupek, D., & Weathers, F. (2000). Emotional-processing in posttraumatic stress disorder. *Journal of Abnormal Psychology, 109*, 26–39.

Lozano, B. L., & Johnson, S. L. (2001). Can personality traits predict increases in manic and depressive symptoms? *Journal of Affective Disorders, 63*, 103–111.

Lumsden, E. A. (1993). Borderline personality disorder: A consequence of experiencing affect within a truncated time frame? *Journal of Personality Disorders, 7*, 265–274.

MacLeod, C., & Mathews, A. (1991). Cognitive-experimental approaches to the emotional disorders. In P. Martin (Ed.), *Handbook of behavior therapy and psychological science: An integrative approach* (pp. 116–150). New York: Pergamon.

Maedgen, J. W., & Carlson, C. L. (2000). Social functioning and emotional regulation in the attention deficit hyperactivity subtypes. *Journal of Clinical Child Psychology, 29*, 30–42.

Mathews, A. M., & MacLeod, C. (1994). Cognitive approaches to emotion and the emotional disorders. *Annual Review of Psychology, 45*, 25–50.

McNally, R. J. (1990). Psychological approaches to panic disorder: A review. *Psychological Bulletin, 108*, 403–419.

Miller, B. L., Ikonte, C., Ponton, M., & Levy, M. (1997). A study of the Lund Manchester research criteria for frontotemporal dementia: Clinical and single-photon emission CT correlations. *Neurology, 48*, 937–942.

Mineka, S., & Sutton, S. K. (1992). Cognitive biases and the emotional disorders. *Psychological Science, 3*, 65–69.

Mineka, S., Watson, D., & Clark, L. A. (1998). Comorbidity of anxiety and unipolar mood disorders. *Annual Review of Psychology, 49*, 377–412.

Mueser, K. T., & Sayers, M. D. (1992). Social skills assessment. In D. J. Kavanagh (Ed.), *Schizophrenia: An overview and practical handbook* (pp. 182–204). London: Chapman & Hall.

Neary, D., Snowden, J. S., Gustafson, L., Passant, U., Stuss, D., Black, S., et al. (1998). Frontotemporal lobar degeneration: A consensus on clinical diagnostic criteria. *Neurology, 51*, 1546–1554.

Nolen–Hoeksema, S., & Morrow, J. (1993). Effects of rumination and distraction on naturally occurring depressed mood. *Cognition and Emotion, 7*, 561–570.

Panksepp, J. (1998). *Affective neuroscience: The foundations of human and animal emotions*. Oxford, England: Oxford University Press.

Paris, J. (1992). Social risk factors for borderline personality disorder: A review and hypothesis. *Canadian Journal of Psychiatry, 37*, 510–515.

Persons, J. B., Davidson, J., & Tompkins, M. A. (2001). *Essential components of cognitive-behavior therapy for depression.* Washington, DC: American Psychological Association.

Roemer, L., Litz, B. T., Orsillo, S. M., & Wagner, A. W. (2001). A preliminary investigation of the strategic withholding of emotions in PTSD. *Journal of Traumatic Stress, 14*, 149–156.

Rottenberg, J., Gross, J. J., Wilhelm, F. H., Najmi, S., & Gotlib, I. H. (2002). Crying threshold and intensity in major depressive disorder. *Journal of Abnormal Psychology, 111*, 302–312.

Rottenberg, J., Kasch, K. L., Gross, J. J., & Gotlib, I. H. (2002). Sadness and amusement reactivity differentially predict concurrent and prospective functioning in major depressive disorder. *Emotion, 2*, 135–146.

Russell, J. A., & Feldman Barrett, L. (1999). Core affect, prototypical emotion episodes, and other things called *emotion*: Dissecting the elephant. *Journal of Personality and Social Psychology, 76*, 805–819.

Shearin, E. N., & Linehan, M. M. (1994). Dialectical behavior therapy for borderline personality disorder: Theoretical and empirical foundations. *Acta Psychiatrica Scandinavica, Supplementum, 379*, 61–68.

Sloan, D. M., Strauss, M. E., & Wisner, K. L. (2001). Diminished response to pleasant stimuli by depressed women. *Journal of Abnormal Psychology, 110*, 488–493.

Snyder, S., & Pitt, W. M. (1985). Characterizing anger in the DSM–III borderline personality disorder. *Acta Psychiatrica Scandinavica, 72*, 464–469.

Soloff, P. H. (1981). A comparison of borderline with depressed and schizophrenic patients on a new diagnostic interview. *Comprehensive Psychiatry, 22*, 291–300.

Soloff, P. H., & Ulrich, R. F. (1981). Diagnostic interview for borderline patients: A replication study. *Archives of General Psychiatry, 38*, 686–692.

Thoits, P. A. (1985). Self-labeling processes in mental illness: The role of emotional deviance. *American Journal of Sociology, 92*, 221–249.

Thompson, R. A. (1994). Emotion regulation: A theme in search of definition. *Monographs of the Society for Research in Child Development, 59*(2, Serial No. 240).

Tomarken, A. J., Davidson, R. J., Wheeler, R. E., & Doss, R. C. (1992). Individual differences in anterior brain asymmetry and fundamental dimensions of emotion. *Journal of Personality and Social Psychology, 62*, 676–687.

Tomarken, A. J., & Keener, A. D. (1998). Frontal brain asymmetry and depression: A self-regulatory perspective. *Cognition and Emotion, 12*. 387–420.

Tomarken, A. J., Mineka, S., & Cook, M. (1989). Fear-relevant selective associations and covariation bias. *Journal of Abnormal Psychology, 98*, 381–394.

Tomarken, A. J., Sutton, S., & Mineka, S., (1995). Fear-relevant illusory correlations: What types of associations promote judgmental bias? *Journal of Abnormal Psychology, 104*, 312–326.

Ulrich, G., & Harms, K. (1985). A video analysis of the nonverbal behavior of depressed patients and their relation to anxiety and depressive disorders. *Journal of Affective Disorders, 9*, 63–67.

Wakefield, J. C. (1992). The concept of mental disorder: On the boundary between biological facts and social values. *American Psychologist, 47*, 373–388.

Watson, D., Clark, L. A., & Carey, G. (1988). Positive and negative affectivity and their relation to anxiety and depressive disorders. *Journal of Abnormal Psychology, 97*, 346–353.

Watson, D., Clark, L. A., Weber, K., Assenheimer, J. S., Strauss, M. E., & McCormick, R. A. (1995). Testing a tripartite model: II. Exploring the symptom structure of anxiety and depression in student, adult, and patient samples. *Journal of Abnormal Psychology, 104*, 15–25.

Waxer, P. H. (1974). Nonverbal cues for depression. *Journal of Abnormal Psychology, 83*, 319–322.

Werner, K. H., Smith, V. E., McCarthy, M. E., Rosen, H. J., Miller, B. L., & Levenson, R. W. (2003). *Emotional Processing among patients with Frontotemporal Lobar Dementia.* Manuscript in preparation.

Zinbarg, R. E., & Barlow, D. H. (1996). Structure of anxiety and the anxiety disorders: A hierarchical model. *Journal of Abnormal Psychology, 105*, 181–193.

ENDNOTES

[1]In the Maedgen & Carlson (2000) study, children were asked to report how they felt in the nondisappointing and disappointing conditions; however, these data were not included in the report.

[2]Emotional numbing suffers from a similar definitional ambiguity that plagues emotion regulation research. For a discussion of the issues associated with emotional numbing and PTSD, see Litz & Gray (2002).

Author Index

A

C

D

E

F

G

H

I

J

M

Q

R

S

T

U

V

W

Y

Z

Subject Index